STUDENT SOLUTIONS MANUAL

FOR

OXTOBY, GILLIS,
AND
NACHTRIEB'S

PRINCIPLES OF MODERN CHEMISTRY

FIFTH EDITION

Wade Freeman

THOMSON
BROOKS/COLE

Australia • Canada • Mexico • Singapore • Spain • United Kingdom • United States

Printed in the United States of America
1 2 3 4 5 6 7 06 05 04 03 02

Printer: Globus Printing Company, Inc.

ISBN: 0-534-40266-6

For more information about our products, contact us at:
Thomson Learning Academic Resource Center
1-800-423-0563

For permission to use material from this text, contact us by:
Phone: 1-800-730-2214
Fax: 1-800-731-2215
Web: http://www.thomsonrights.com

Asia
Thomson Learning
5 Shenton Way #01-01
UIC Building
Singapore 068808

Australia
Nelson Thomson Learning
102 Dodds Street
South Street
South Melbourne, Victoria 3205
Australia

Canada
Nelson Thomson Learning
1120 Birchmount Road
Toronto, Ontario M1K 5G4
Canada

Europe/Middle East/South Africa
Thomson Learning
High Holborn House
50/51 Bedford Row
London WC1R 4LR
United Kingdom

Latin America
Thomson Learning
Seneca, 53
Colonia Polanco
11560 Mexico D.F.
Mexico

Spain
Paraninfo Thomson Learning
Calle/Magallanes, 25
28015 Madrid, Spain

FOREWORD

The fifth edition of *Principles of Modern Chemistry,* by David W. Oxtoby, H. P. Gillis, and Norman H. Nachtrieb, presents a thorough introduction to University chemistry organized in seven major parts, or units:

1. The first three chapters cover macroscopic principles and the classical description of chemical bonding;

2. Chapters 4 through 6 cover kinetic molecular theory as it explains the existence and behavior of the different states of matter;

3. Chapters 7 through 12 treat chemical equilibrium and thermodynamics;

4. Chapters 13 and 14 concern the rates of chemical and physical processes;

5. Chapters 15-18 treat the current theory of atomic and molecular structure and modern spectroscopy;

6. Chapters 29 and 20 take up important and useful chemical processes;

7. The final three chapters explain the chemistry of both traditional and modern materials.

All 24 chapters include extensive problem sets. The first portion of each problem set is organized according to the topical sections of the chapter. The problems are paired—they treat the same or closely related material. The final portion of the problem sets consists of unpaired problems in two categories: "Additional Problems" and "Cumulative Problems".

• **Purpose of this Manual.** Students cannot expect to succeed in a serious chemistry course without solving problems, which are universally used to illustrate concepts and to test understanding. This book offers detailed solutions to all of the odd-numbered problems in the text to assist students in working through the problems.

• **How to Study Using this Manual.** Students should use an electronic calculator featuring scientific notation, logarithms and a y^x key. They should read over the chapter and then try some odd-numbered problems at the end, devoting five to ten minutes to an earnest attempt on each. They should write things down as they go back over the related passages in the text. If *no* progress is made, they should turn to the solutions in this Manual for help. Reading the solution is not enough. They should complete a *written* solution on their own. After working several odd-numbered problems, they should rest. Later, they should try the related even-numbered problems to see whether the freshly acquired knowledge has been retained. The solutions to all of the even-numbered problems are given in the "Instructor's Manual" available to instructors from the publisher.

What is a Detailed Solution? The "Detailed Solutions" give the answers, most of which are enclosed in $\boxed{\text{boxes}}$ to make them easier to spot, but are intended as illustrations of problem-solving techniques as well as a source of answers. They therefore show the set-up of all required calculations. Moreover, they give alternative methods of attack, point out common pitfalls, and offer additional insights. **Tip.** This heading identifies such additional material.

Extra Problems as a Source for Exam Questions. The large number of problems in the text makes it unlikely that any student will write out solutions to them all. Students should not however ignore unassigned or apparently duplicative problems, but instead study the solutions given here to confirm their understanding.

Queries. Send queries about solutions to the problems and report difficulties in using this Manual directly to the author via Internet. The address is WFreeman@uic.edu.

Wade A. Freeman

June, 2002

Contents

b) Because the Pu atom is electrically neutral, its extranuclear electrons contribute exactly enough negative charge to balance the positive charge of the 94 protons in the nucleus. The charges on the electron and proton are equal in magnitude, so the atom has $\boxed{\text{94 electrons}}$.

1.17 The atomic number of americium is 95; americium has $\boxed{\text{95 protons}}$ in its nucleus. In the neutral atom there are also exactly $\boxed{\text{95 electrons}}$ because the negative charge of the electrons balances the positive charge of the protons. Of the 241 nucleons, those that are not protons are neutrons. There are accordingly $\boxed{\text{146 neutrons}}$.

1.19 The atomic mass of naturally-occurring Si is the *weighted* mean (weighted average) of the atomic masses of the three isotopes listed. What does weighting an average imply? The *un*-weighted mean of the masses of the three isotopes would be:

$$\text{regular mean} = \bar{n} = \frac{1}{3}(27.97693) + \frac{1}{3}(28.97649) + \frac{1}{3}(29.97376)$$

Weighting corresponds to replacing the $\frac{1}{3}$'s in this expression with values telling each isotope's *true* contribution to the total. These values are the abundances. Fractional abundances (which add up to exactly 1.00) rather than percent abundances (which add up to 100.0) must be used:

$$\text{weighted mean} = 0.9221(27.97693) + 0.0470(28.97649) + 0.0309(29.97376) = \boxed{28.086}$$

1.21 The relative atomic mass of natural boron is the weighted mean of the relative masses of the two isotopes:

$$A_{\text{boron}} = A_{^{10}\text{B}}\,p_{^{10}\text{B}} + A_{^{11}\text{B}}\,p_{^{11}\text{B}}$$

where the A's represent relative atomic masses and the p's represent fractional abundances. With one exception, all of the quantities in this equation are known:

$$10.811 = (10.013)(0.1961) + A_{^{11}\text{B}}(0.8039) \qquad \text{hence} \qquad A_{^{11}\text{B}} = \boxed{11.01}$$

1.23 The mass of a single iodine atom is

$$m_{\text{I}} = \left(\frac{126.90447\text{ g}}{1\text{ mol I}}\right) \times \left(\frac{1\text{ mol I}}{6.022142 \times 10^{23}\text{ atom I}}\right) = \boxed{2.107298 \times 10^{-22}\,\frac{\text{g}}{\text{atom I}}}$$

1.25 Use the relative atomic masses from the inside back cover of the text.

a) P_4O_{10}: $4(30.974) + 10(15.999) = \boxed{283.886}$.

b) BrCl: $79.904 + 35.453 = \boxed{115.357}$.

c) $Ca(NO_3)_2$: $40.08 + 2\big(14.01 + 3(16.00)\big) = \boxed{164.09}$.

d) $KMnO_4$: $39.098 + 54.938 + 4(15.999) = \boxed{158.032}$.

e) $(NH_4)_2SO_4$: $2\big(14.007 + 4(1.0079)\big) + 32.06 + 4(15.999) = \boxed{132.13}$.

1.27 Set up the entire computation as a single string of unit-factors:

$$m_{\text{Au}} = 80\text{ yr} \times \left(\frac{365.25\text{ d}}{1\text{ yr}}\right) \times \left(\frac{24\text{ h}}{1\text{ d}}\right) \times \left(\frac{3600\text{ s}}{1\text{ h}}\right) \times \left(\frac{1\text{ atom Au}}{1\text{ s}}\right)$$
$$\times \left(\frac{1\text{ mol Au}}{6.022 \times 10^{23}\text{ atoms Au}}\right) \times \left(\frac{197\text{ g Au}}{1.00\text{ mol Au}}\right) = \boxed{8.3 \times 10^{-13}\text{ g Au}}$$

Advanced microbalances can detect down to about 10^{-10} g. Even after a lifetime of counting, the mass of the counted atoms is much too small to detect.

1.29 According to the formula, 51 atoms of all kinds are contained in a single molecule of vitamin A. Use this with a series of unit-factors to find out how many atoms there are in 1.000 mol of vitamin A:

$$N_{\text{atoms}} = 1.000 \text{ mol vit A} \times \left(\frac{N_0 \text{ molecule}}{1 \text{ mol vit A}}\right) \times \left(\frac{51 \text{ atoms}}{1 \text{ molecule}}\right) = 51.00 N_0 \text{ atoms}$$

Now compute the chemical amount of vitamin A_2 that contains this number of atoms:

$$n_{A_2} = 51.00 N_0 \text{ atoms} \times \left(\frac{1 \text{ molecule } A_2}{49 \text{ atoms}}\right) \times \left(\frac{1 \text{ mol } A_2}{N_0 \text{ molecule}}\right) = \boxed{1.041 \text{ mol } A_2}$$

Tip. The N_0's cancel out. The numerical value of Avogadro's number is not needed to complete the problem, just the concept that such a number exists.

1.31 The volume of a "flask" of mercury equals the volume per unit mass of mercury multiplied by the mass of mercury contained in a flask. The volume per unit mass is the reciprocal of the density (the density divided into one):

$$V_{\text{flask}} = 34.5 \times 10^3 \text{ g} \times \left(\frac{1 \text{ cm}^3 \text{ Hg}}{13.6 \text{ g Hg}}\right) \times \left(\frac{1 \text{ L}}{1000 \text{ cm}^3}\right) = \boxed{2.54 \text{ L}}$$

1.33 Use unit-factors to progress from volume of Al_2O_3 to the number of atoms of Al. The correct answer must be on the order of 10^{23} atoms because the amount of corundum is on the ordinary human scale:

$$N_{\text{Al}} = 15.0 \text{ cm}^3 \text{ Al}_2\text{O}_3 \times \left(\frac{3.97 \text{ g Al}_2\text{O}_3}{1 \text{ cm}^3 \text{ Al}_2\text{O}_3}\right) \times \left(\frac{1 \text{ mol Al}_2\text{O}_3}{101.96 \text{ g Al}_2\text{O}_3}\right)$$
$$\times \left(\frac{6.022 \times 10^{23} \text{ Al}_2\text{O}_3 \text{ units}}{1 \text{ mol Al}_2\text{O}_3}\right) \times \left(\frac{2 \text{ atom Al}}{1 \text{ Al}_2\text{O}_3 \text{ unit}}\right) = \boxed{7.03 \times 10^{23} \text{ atom Al}}$$

Tip. Unit-factors can be "flipped over" (numerator and denominator exchanged) at will. To make progress with a chain of unit-factors, arrange each one so the desired unit is in the top (numerator) and the unit to be canceled away is in the bottom (denominator). Note the rather creative last unit-factor in the preceding equation.

1.35 Substitute 0.270 kg and the estimated speed of the spiked ball into the formula for kinetic energy:

$$KE = 1/2\, mv^2 = 1/2\,(0.270 \text{ kg})(100 \text{ mi h}^{-1})^2 = 1350 \text{ kg mi}^2 \text{h}^{-2}$$

The arithmetic is correct, but the units are non-standard. Convert to joules, the SI units of energy. This requires knowing how many meters in a mile and how many seconds in an hour. Some memorize such numbers. Others use calculators that are programmed with conversion factors or look them conversion factors in tables. The conversion proceeds

$$KE = 1350 \frac{\text{kg mi}^2}{\text{h}^2} \times \left(\frac{1 \text{ h}}{3600 \text{ s}}\right)^2 \times \left(\frac{1609 \text{ m}}{1 \text{ mi}}\right)^2 = \boxed{3 \times 10^2 \text{ J}}$$

Tip. Confirm in Appendix B that a joule equals a kilogram meter squared per second squared.

1.37 a) Soft-wood chips: wood is a $\boxed{\text{mixture}}$ of many substances. Water: H_2O is a $\boxed{\text{pure compound}}$. Sodium hydroxide: NaOH is a $\boxed{\text{pure compound}}$.

b) Because the iron vessel was sealed, nothing was able to enter or escape, including gases. Therefore, all of the original mass is still contained in the vessel—no more, no less. The total mass is $17.2 + 150.1 + 22.43 =$ $\boxed{189.7 \text{ kg}}$.

1.39 The density of the nucleus of ^{127}I equals its mass divided by its volume. The problem gives the nuclear mass explicitly and provides a route to the nuclear volume. Start with the formula for the volume of a sphere in terms of its radius r and substitute with the formula for the radius of a nucleus in terms of the mass number A:

$$V_{^{127}\mathrm{I}} = \frac{4}{3}\pi r^3 = \frac{4}{3}\pi(kA^{\frac{1}{3}})^3 = \frac{4}{3}\pi k^3 A$$
$$= \frac{4}{3}\pi(1.3 \times 10^{-13}\ \mathrm{cm})^3(127) = 1.17 \times 10^{-36}\ \mathrm{cm}^3$$

The density of the iodine nucleus then equals:

$$\rho_{^{127}\mathrm{I}} = \frac{m_{^{127}\mathrm{I}}}{V_{^{127}\mathrm{I}}} = \frac{2.1 \times 10^{-22}\ \mathrm{g}}{1.17 \times 10^{-36}\ \mathrm{cm}^3} = \boxed{1.8 \times 10^{14}\ \mathrm{g\ cm^{-3}}}$$

This is billions of times more dense than solid iodine!

1.41 Dalton's postulates were:

1. *Matter consists of indivisible atoms.* We now know that atoms are not indivisible. Some elements (such as uranium and radium) are radioactive, and the atoms spontaneously decompose to different atoms and subatomic particles (see Chapter 12).
2. *All atoms of a given chemical element are identical in mass and in all other properties.* Dalton had no way of knowing about isotopes. Atoms of a given chemical element can have different masses. For example, the element hydrogen has three isotopes. Isotopes have virtually identical chemical properties.
3. *Different chemical elements have different kinds of atoms, and in particular, such atoms have different masses.* This statement (so far) needs no modification or extension.
4. *Atoms are indestructible and retain their identity in chemical reactions.* Atoms are not indestructible. They can be split to give new kinds of atoms in particle accelerators. No instances of atoms changing their identity in chemical reactions are known.
5. *The formation of a compound from its elements occurs through combining atoms of unlike elements in small whole-number ratios.* Certain solid compounds have compositions that vary within a range. They are non-stoichiometric compounds.[1] The law of definite proportions is strictly true for gaseous and liquid compounds but not for all solid compounds.

1.43 a) Assume that atoms of ^{32}S and atoms of P have the same mass in the distant galaxy that they have on Earth. Then, treat the problem of evaluating the exotic Ordagova's number (symbolized N_{or}) as an exercise in the conversion of units. An Earthly mole of ^{32}S contains N_0 (6.022142×10^{23}) atoms of ^{32}S. Therefore:

$$N_{\mathrm{or}} = \frac{N_0\ \mathrm{atom}\ ^{32}\mathrm{S}}{31.972\ \mathrm{g}\ ^{32}\mathrm{S}} \times \frac{4.8648\ \mathrm{g}\ ^{32}\mathrm{S}}{1\ \mathrm{marg}\ ^{32}\mathrm{S}} \times \frac{32.000\ \mathrm{marg}\ ^{32}\mathrm{S}}{1\ \mathrm{elom\ of}\ ^{32}\mathrm{S}} = N_0 \frac{(4.8648)(32.000)\ \mathrm{atom}}{31.972\ \mathrm{elom}}$$
$$= (6.022142 \times 10^{23}) \frac{(4.8648)(32.000)\ \mathrm{atom}}{31.972\ \mathrm{elom}} = \boxed{2.9322 \times 10^{24}\ \mathrm{atom\ elom^{-1}}}$$

b) On Earth, the molar mass of phosphorus is 30.9738 g mol^{-1}. String together unit-factors to convert this mass to marg elom^{-1}:

$$\mathcal{M}_{\mathrm{P}} = \frac{30.9738\ \mathrm{g\ P}}{1\ \mathrm{mol\ P}} \times \frac{1\ \mathrm{marg\ P}}{4.8648\ \mathrm{g\ P}} \times \frac{1\ \mathrm{mol\ P}}{N_0\ \mathrm{atom\ P}} \times \frac{N_{\mathrm{or}}\ \mathrm{atom\ P}}{1\ \mathrm{elom\ P}} = N_{\mathrm{or}}\left(\frac{1}{N_0}\right)\frac{30.9738}{4.8648}\ \mathrm{marg\ elom^{-1}}$$

From the previous part, it is true that:

$$N_{\mathrm{or}} = N_0 \frac{(4.8648)(32.000)\ \mathrm{atom}}{31.972\ \mathrm{elom}}$$

[1] See text Section 21.5.

Substituting this expression gives

$$\begin{aligned}\mathcal{M}_{\rm P} &= \left(N_0 \frac{(4.8648)(32.000)}{31.972}\right)\left(\frac{1}{N_0}\right)\frac{30.9738}{4.8648}\ \text{marg elom}^{-1}\\ &= (32.000)\frac{30.9738}{31.972} = \boxed{31.001\ \text{marg elom}^{-1}}\end{aligned}$$

Tip. N_0 and 4.8648 cancel away. This means that the answer does not depend on the definition of a "marg" in terms of a gram or an "elom" in terms of a mole. Such a result makes sense because aliens in a distant galaxy would hardly need our definitions to do their chemistry.

Chapter 2

Chemical Formulas, Chemical Equations, and Reaction Yields

2.1 The repetition of F in the formula implies that this compound contains F in at least two different settings. Such a distinction does not matter in obtaining mass percentages, so rewrite the formula as $PtClO_2F_8$. Exactly one mole of this substance has a mass of 414.52 g, a result obtained by multiplying the molar masses (in g mol^{-1}) of the various elements by their subscripts in the formula and adding the results (as in **1.25**). The mass percentage of each element is the mass that it contributes divided by the mass of the whole and multiplied by 100%:

$$\text{for Cl:}\quad \frac{1\ \text{mol}\,(35.453\ \text{g mol}^{-1})}{414.52\ \text{g}} \times 100\% = \boxed{8.553\%\ \text{Cl}}$$

$$\text{for F:}\quad \frac{8\ \text{mol}\,(18.998\ \text{g mol}^{-1})}{414.52\ \text{g}} \times 100\% = \boxed{36.67\%\ \text{F}}$$

$$\text{for O:}\quad \frac{2\ \text{mol}\,(15.999\ \text{g mol}^{-1})}{414.52\ \text{g}} \times 100\% = \boxed{7.720\%\ \text{O}}$$

$$\text{for Pt:}\quad \frac{1\ \text{mol}\,(195.08\ \text{g mol}^{-1})}{414.52\ \text{g}} \times 100\% = \boxed{47.06\%\ \text{Pt}}$$

Although Pt ties with Cl as the least prevalent element in the compound on the basis of number of atoms, it is by far the most prevalent on the basis of mass.

2.3 The mass percentage of H in each compound can be calculated,[1] and the resulting numbers used to get the required order. The results are 11.19% for H_2O, 15.35% for $C_{12}H_{26}$, 9.742% for N_4H_6, and 12.68% for LiH, Therefore:

$$\boxed{N_4H_6 < H_2O < LiH < C_{12}H_{26}}$$

Tip. A faster method is to settle for estimates of the H content. Get the estimates by adding up the masses of the non-H atoms and dividing by the number of H's. Exact arithmetic is not necessary. Thus: H_2O has $16/2 \approx 8$ units of non-H mass per hydrogen atom; $C_{12}H_{26}$ has $144/26 \approx 6$ such units; N_4H_6 has $56/6 \approx 9$ such units; LiH has 7.9 such units. The compound that is richest in H has the smallest amount of non-H mass per hydrogen atom.

2.5 Calculate the fraction (not percentage) by mass of hydrogen (H) in the compound C_4H_{10} (butane) by the method of **2.1** and multiply the result by 0.0130, the fraction of butane in "Q-gas". This fraction-of-a-fraction

[1] As in **2.1**.

method works because helium, the other component of Q-gas, contains no hydrogen:

$$\left(\frac{10 \times (1.008)\text{ g H}}{(4 \times 12.011) + (10 \times 1.008)\text{ g butane}}\right) \times \left(\frac{0.0130\text{ g butane}}{1\text{ g Q gas}}\right) = \frac{0.00225\text{ g H}}{1\text{ g Q-gas}}$$

Multiply by 100% to obtain the desired percentage: $\boxed{0.225\%\text{ H}}$ by mass.

2.7 The empirical formula of a compound is the smallest whole-number ratio of atoms of different kinds (or moles of atoms of different kinds) in the compound. First, calculate the chemical amount of each element from the given masses:

$$n_{\text{O}} = 16.58 \times 10^{-3}\text{ g O} \times \left(\frac{1\text{ mol O}}{15.999\text{ g O}}\right) = 1.036 \times 10^{-3}\text{ mol O}$$

$$n_{\text{P}} = 8.02 \times 10^{-3}\text{ g P} \times \left(\frac{1\text{ mol P}}{30.97\text{ g O}}\right) = 2.59 \times 10^{-4}\text{ mol P}$$

$$n_{\text{Zn}} = 25.40 \times 10^{-3}\text{ g Zn} \times \left(\frac{1\text{ mol Zn}}{65.38\text{ g Zn}}\right) = 3.885 \times 10^{-4}\text{ mol Zn}$$

Next, divide through by the smallest number of moles. This puts the quantities on a fair basis for comparison:

$$\frac{n_{\text{O}}}{n_{\text{P}}} = \frac{1.036 \times 10^{-3}\text{ mol}}{2.59 \times 10^{-4}\text{ mol}} = 4.00 \qquad \text{and} \qquad \frac{n_{\text{Zn}}}{n_{\text{P}}} = \frac{3.885 \times 10^{-4}\text{ mol}}{2.59 \times 10^{-4}\text{mol}} = 1.50$$

This gives the formula $Zn_{1.5}PO_4$. But the empirical formula is defined as the smallest whole-number ratio of moles of elements in a compound. Simply multiply all subscripts by two to get rid of the fractions. The result is $\boxed{Zn_3P_2O_8}$, which is often written $Zn_3(PO_4)_2$ to show how the atoms are organized in the compound.

2.9 The percentages of Fe and Si in the crystalline grain in the fulgurite apply to any arbitrary amount of the compound. For example, a 100.0 g sample would contain 46.01 g Fe and 53.99 g Si. Compute the chemical amounts of Fe and Si in a 100.0 g sample:

$$n_{\text{Fe}} = 46.01\text{ g Fe} \times \left(\frac{1\text{ mol Fe}}{55.847\text{ g Fe}}\right) = 0.8239\text{ mol Fe}$$

$$n_{\text{Si}} = 53.99\text{ g Si} \times \left(\frac{1\text{ mol Si}}{28.086\text{ g Si}}\right) = 1.922\text{ mol Si}$$

The two chemical amounts have the ratio 2.333 mol of Si to 1.000 mol of Fe. This is expressed by the formula $FeSi_{2.333}$. Multiplying through by 3 to eliminate fractions gives the empirical formula $\boxed{Fe_3Si_7}$.
Tip. The wrong answer $FeSi_2$ is fairly common. It comes from reckless rounding off: 2.333 differs a *lot* from 2.00.

2.11 Consider the two cases separately. 100.000 g of the first compound contains 90.745 g of Ba and, by subtraction, 9.255 g of N. The chemical amounts of the two elements are

$$n_{\text{Ba}} = 90.745\text{ g Ba} \times \left(\frac{1\text{ mol Ba}}{137.33\text{ g Ba}}\right) = 0.66078\text{ mol Ba}$$

$$n_{\text{N}} = 9.255\text{ g N} \times \left(\frac{1\text{ mol N}}{14.007\text{ g N}}\right) = 0.6607\text{ mol N}$$

The Ba and N are present in equal chemical amounts, that is, in a 1-to-1 molar ratio. Thus, the empirical formula is $\boxed{\text{BaN}}$. For the second compound: 100.000 g of it contains 93.634 g of Ba and, by subtraction,

6.366 g of N. Hence:

$$n_{\text{Ba}} = 93.634 \text{ g Ba} \times \left(\frac{1 \text{ mol Ba}}{137.33 \text{ g Ba}}\right) = 0.68182 \text{ mol Ba}$$

$$n_{\text{N}} = 6.366 \text{ g N} \times \left(\frac{1 \text{ mol N}}{14.007 \text{ g N}}\right) = 0.4545 \text{ mol N}$$

Dividing both these chemical amounts by the smaller establishes that the Ba and N are present in a 1.500-to-1 molar ratio. The empirical formula is accordingly $\boxed{Ba_3N_2}$.

2.13 a) Burning the compound in oxygen gives 0.692 g of H_2O and 3.381 g of CO_2. Determine the masses of elemental H and C in these amounts of H_2O and CO_2:

$$m_{\text{H}} = 0.692 \text{ g H}_2\text{O} \times \left(\frac{2.016 \text{ g H}}{18.015 \text{ g H}_2\text{O}}\right) = \boxed{0.0774 \text{ g of H}}$$

$$m_{\text{C}} = 3.381 \text{ g CO}_2 \times \left(\frac{12.01 \text{ g C}}{44.01 \text{ g CO}_2}\right) = \boxed{0.9226 \text{ g of C}}$$

b) The masses of C and H in the CO_2 and H_2O add up to 1.000 g. The compound therefore contains $\boxed{\text{no other elements}}$.

c) The compound is $\boxed{7.74\% \text{ H}}$ and $\boxed{92.26\% \text{ C}}$ by mass.

d) To determine the empirical formula of the compound, convert the masses of C and H in the sample to chemical amounts (in moles) and determine their ratio:

$$n_{\text{H}} = 0.0774 \text{ g H} \times \left(\frac{1 \text{ mol H}}{1.008 \text{ g H}}\right) = 0.0767 \text{ mol H}$$

$$n_{\text{C}} = 0.9226 \text{ g C} \times \left(\frac{1 \text{ mol}}{12.0107 \text{ g C}}\right) = 0.0768 \text{ mol C}$$

The C and H are present in a 0.0768/0.0767 molar ratio, which is a 1.00-to-1.00 molar ratio. The empirical formula is therefore $\boxed{CH}$.

2.15 a) Imagine that some fluorine and some of the fluorocarbon are confined side-by-side in identical vessels that hold exactly 1 L. The vessels hold the same number of molecules because equal volumes of gases under the same conditions contain the same number of molecules (Avogadro's hypothesis). The sample of fluorocarbon has a mass of 8.93 g whereas the sample of fluorine has a mass of only 1.70 g. It follows that the molecules of the fluorocarbon are 8.93/1.70 times more massive than those of fluorine (F_2). The relative mass of F_2 equals 38.0. Therefore:

$$\text{Relative mass of fluorocarbon} = 38.0 \times \left(\frac{8.93}{1.70}\right) = 200$$

A relative mass of 200 requires four CF_2 units (each of which contributes a relative mass of $12 + 2 \cdot 19 = 50$. Hence the molecular formula of the fluorocarbon is $(CF_2)_4$, or $\boxed{C_4F_8}$.

2.17 a) The unknown binary compound is gaseous. Although it is 1.94 times more dense than gaseous O_2, the unknown has the same number of molecules per liter (Avogadro's hypothesis). Therefore, the mass of its molecules is 1.94 times larger than the mass of O_2 molecules. An O_2 molecule has a relative molecular mass of 32.0. This makes the relative molecular mass of the unknown $1.94 \times 32.0 = \boxed{62.1}$.

b) The unknown compound contains hydrogen (H) and one other element. Burning 1.39 g of it in oxygen gives 1.21 g of water. This amount of water contains all of the H present in the unknown. Compute the chemical amount of this H:

$$n_H = 1.21 \text{ g } H_2O \times \left(\frac{1 \text{ mol } H_2O}{18.0153 \text{ g } H_2O}\right) \times \left(\frac{2 \text{ mol}}{1 \text{ mol } H_2O}\right) = 0.1343 \text{ mol H}$$

Compare this to the chemical amount of the unknown compound. First obtain the number of moles of the unknown:

$$n_{\text{unknown}} = 1.39 \text{ g unknown} \times \left(\frac{1 \text{ mol unknown}}{62.08 \text{ g unknown}}\right) = 0.0224 \text{ mol}$$

Then do the comparison by dividing the chemical amount of H by the chemical amount of unknown:

$$\frac{n_H}{n_{\text{unknown}}} = \frac{0.1343 \text{ mol H}}{0.0224 \text{ mol unknown}} = \frac{6.00 \text{ mol H}}{1 \text{ mol unknown}}$$

There are 6 mol of H per mole of the unknown, and therefore $\boxed{6}$ atoms of H per molecule of unknown.

c) The unknown contains H and one other element, call it Z. Its molecular mass is 62.1. The maximum possible atomic mass of Z is $62.1 - 6(1.00794) = \boxed{56.0}$. This is the atomic mass of Z if exactly one atom of Z is present per molecule of unknown, that is, if the molecular formula of the unknown is ZH_6.
d) The molecule may contain more than one atom of Z. Two atoms of Z implies a relative atomic mass for Z of 28.0; Three atoms of Z implies a relative atomic mass for Z of 18.7. As the subscript of Z gets larger, the atomic mass of Z gets smaller:

Formula	Atomic Mass of Z	Formula	Atomic Mass of Z
Z_1H_6	56.0	Z_2H_6	28.0
Z_3H_6	18.7	Z_4H_6	14.
Z_5H_6	11.21	Z_6H_6	9.33
Z_9H_6	6.23	$Z_{14}H_6$	4.00
$Z_{56}H_6$	1.00		

Compare the atomic masses in this list with the established relative atomic masses of the elements. If the subscript of Z equals 2 or 4, values quite close to the atomic masses of $\boxed{\text{Si}}$ and $\boxed{\text{N}}$ come out. Most other subscripts give atomic masses not corresponding to atomic masses of authentic elements. A subscript of 56 gives an atomic mass of 1.00, which is close to the atomic mass of H, but the unknown would then be H_{62}, which is not a binary compound. A subscript of 14 gives an atomic mass of 4.00, but helium (atomic mass 4.00) forms no compounds.
e) The compound is either Si_2H_6 (silane, molecular mass 62.2186) or N_4H_6 (tetrazane, molecular mass 62.0746). Both substances exist, but $\boxed{Si_2H_6}$ is more stable.

2.19 Balance the equations by inspection. For example, in part a, assign 1 as the coefficient of NH_3. This obliges a coefficient on $\frac{1}{2}$ for the N_2 because $\frac{1}{2}$ mol of N_2 furnishes the whole 1 mol of N that is signified in "1 NH_3." Similarly, it obliges a coefficient of $\frac{3}{2}$ for the H_2 because $\frac{3}{2}$ mol of H_2 contains exactly the same number of atoms of H as 1 mol of NH_3. The answer to part a in the following table clears the fractions from this set of coefficients by multiplying them all by 2.

a) $3\ H_2 + N_2 \rightarrow 2\ NH_3$
b) $2\ K + O_2 \rightarrow K_2O_2$
c) $PbO_2 + Pb + 2\,H_2SO_4 \rightarrow 2\ PbSO_4 + 2\ H_2O$
d) $2\ BF_3 + 3\,H_2O \rightarrow B_2O_3 + 6\ HF$
e) $2\ KClO_3 \rightarrow 2\ KCl + 3\ O_2$
f) $CH_3COOH + 2\ O_2 \rightarrow 2\ CO_2 + 2\ H_2O$
g) $2\ K_2O_2 + 2\ H_2O \rightarrow 4\ KOH + O_2$
h) $3\ PCl_5 + 5\ AsF_3 \rightarrow 3\ PF_5 + 5\ AsCl_3$

2.21 a) According to the balanced equation $Mg + 2\,HCl \rightarrow H_2 + MgCl_2$, the reaction produces 1 mol of H_2 for every 1 mol of Mg consumed. Diatomic hydrogen has a relative molecular mass of $2 \times 1.00794 = 2.01588$, and Mg has a relative atomic mass of 24.305. Therefore, "1 mol Mg $\rightarrow$ 1 mol H_2" implies "24.305 g Mg $\rightarrow$ 2.01594 g H_2". This fact provides a unit-factor to compute the mass of Mg that yields 1.000 g of H_2:

$$m_{\mathrm{Mg}} = 1.000\ \mathrm{g\ H_2} \times \left(\frac{24.305\ \mathrm{g\ Mg}}{2.01594\ \mathrm{g\ H_2}}\right) = \boxed{12.06\ \mathrm{g\ Mg}}$$

b) The equation states that 1 mol of I_2 arises from every 2 mol of $CuSO_4$:

$$2\,\mathrm{CuSO_4} + 4\,\mathrm{KI} \rightarrow 2\,\mathrm{CuI} + \mathrm{I_2} + 2\,\mathrm{K_2SO_4}$$

Write down unit-factors to create a train of conversions, starting from the 1.000 g of I_2:

$$m_{\mathrm{CuSO_4}} = 1.000\ \mathrm{g\ I_2} \times \left(\frac{1\ \mathrm{mol\ I_2}}{253.809\ \mathrm{g\ I_2}}\right)\left(\frac{2\ \mathrm{mol\ CuSO_4}}{1\ \mathrm{mol\ I_2}}\right)\left(\frac{159.608\ \mathrm{g\ CuSO_4}}{1\ \mathrm{mol\ CuSO_4}}\right) = \boxed{1.258\ \mathrm{g\ CuSO_4}}$$

c) According to the balanced equation, 1 mol of $NaBH_4$ yields 4 mol of H_2. Some might argue that such a reaction is not possible, reasoning that no chemical reaction can transform the 4 H atoms of $NaBH_4$ into the 8 H atoms of 4 H_2. In fact, the extra H comes from the other reactant, water. Write a series of unit-factors:

$$m_{\mathrm{NaBH_4}} = 1.000\ \mathrm{g\ H_2} \times \left(\frac{1\ \mathrm{mol\ H_2}}{2.0158\ \mathrm{g\ H_2}}\right)\left(\frac{1\ \mathrm{mol\ NaBH_4}}{4\ \mathrm{mol\ H_2}}\right)\left(\frac{37.833\ \mathrm{g\ NaBH_4}}{1\ \mathrm{mol\ NaBH_4}}\right) = \boxed{4.692\ \mathrm{g\ NaBH_4}}$$

2.23 An examination of the formula establishes that one mole of $K_2Zn_3[Fe(CN)_6]_2$ contains 12 moles of C. Since carbon has no other place to go, 12 mol of K_2CO_3 must form per mole of $K_2Zn_3[Fe(CN)_6]_2$. This fact provides the second unit-factor in the following. The other factors are routine:

$$m = 18.6\ \mathrm{g\ K_2CO_3} \times \left(\frac{1\ \mathrm{mol\ K_2CO_3}}{138.2\ \mathrm{g\ K_2CO_3}}\right) \times \left(\frac{1\ \mathrm{mol\ K_2Zn_3[Fe(CN)_6]_2}}{12\ \mathrm{mol\ K_2CO_3}}\right)$$
$$\times \left(\frac{698.2\ \mathrm{g\ K_2Zn_3[Fe(CN)_6]_2}}{1\ \mathrm{mol\ K_2Zn_3[Fe(CN)_6]_2}}\right) = \boxed{7.83\ \mathrm{g\ K_2Zn_3[Fe(CN)_6]_2}}$$

2.25 Balance a chemical equation to learn the relationship between the chemical amount of Si_2H_6 consumed and the chemical amount of SiO_2 formed. By inspection:

$$2\ \mathrm{Si_2H_6} + 7\ \mathrm{O_2} \rightarrow 4\ \mathrm{SiO_2} + 6\ \mathrm{H_2O}$$

Next, use the density and volume of the gaseous Si_2H_6 to obtain its chemical amount. Then obtain the number of moles of the SiO_2 product and finally the mass of the SiO_2. The following does this all in a single series of unit-factors:

$$m_{\mathrm{SiO_2}} = 25.0\ \mathrm{cm^3} \times \left(\frac{2.78 \times 10^{-3}\ \mathrm{g}}{1.00\ \mathrm{cm^3}}\right) \times \left(\frac{1\ \mathrm{mol\ Si_2H_6}}{62.2186\ \mathrm{g\ Si_2H_6}}\right) \times \left(\frac{4\ \mathrm{mol\ SiO_2}}{2\ \mathrm{mol\ Si_2H_6}}\right)$$
$$\times \left(\frac{60.084\ \mathrm{g\ SiO_2}}{1\ \mathrm{mol\ SiO_2}}\right) = \boxed{0.134\ \mathrm{g\ SiO_2}}$$

2.27 Use a series of unit-factors to pass from grams of Al_2O_3 to grams of cryolite:

$$m_{\mathrm{Na_3AlF_6}} = 287\ \mathrm{g\ Al_2O_3} \times \left(\frac{1\ \mathrm{mol\ Al_2O_3}}{101.962\ \mathrm{kg\ Al_2O_3}}\right) \times \left(\frac{2\ \mathrm{mol\ Na_3AlF_6}}{1\ \mathrm{mol\ Al_2O_3}}\right) \times \left(\frac{209.94\ \mathrm{g\ Na_3AlF_6}}{1\ \mathrm{mol\ Na_3AlF_6}}\right)$$
$$= \boxed{1.18 \times 10^3\ \mathrm{g\ Na_3AlF_6}}$$

2.29 It does not matter whether the substance in question is a product or reactant. The form of the unit-factors is similar:

$$m_{\text{KCl}} = 567 \text{ g KNO}_3 \times \frac{1 \text{ mol KNO}_3}{101.103 \text{ g KNO}_3} \times \frac{1 \text{ mol KCl}}{1 \text{ mol KNO}_3} \times \frac{74.551 \text{ g KCl}}{1 \text{ mol KCl}} = \boxed{418 \text{ g}}$$

For the mass of the by-product switch direction after the first unit-factor:

$$m_{\text{Cl}_2} = 567 \text{ g KNO}_3 \times \frac{1 \text{ mol KNO}_3}{101.103 \text{ g KNO}_3} \times \frac{2 \text{ mol Cl}_2}{4 \text{ mol KNO}_3} \times \frac{70.906 \text{ g Cl}_2}{1 \text{ mol Cl}_2} = \boxed{199 \text{ g}}$$

2.31 a) The small whole-number ratios in chemical formulas and balanced chemical equations refer to chemical amount, never to mass. The balanced equation given in this problem assures that the chemical amounts of XCl_2 and XBr_2 are equal. To use this fact, convert the mass of XBr_2 to a chemical amount of XBr_2. Also, convert the mass of XCl_2 to a chemical amount of XCl_2. The conversions require the molar masses of the two compounds, which require the unknown molar mass of X. Call this quantity x:

$$\text{molar mass XBr}_2 = 2(79.909) + x \text{ g mol}^{-1}$$
$$\text{molar mass XCl}_2 = 2(35.453) + x \text{ g mol}^{-1}$$

The chemical amounts of the two compounds are:

$$n_{\text{XBr}_2} = 1.500 \text{ g XBr}_2 \times \left(\frac{1 \text{ mol XBr}_2}{(159.808 + x) \text{ g XBr}_2}\right) = \frac{1.500}{159.808 + x} \text{ mol XBr}_2$$
$$n_{\text{XCl}_2} = 0.890 \text{ g XCl}_2 \times \left(\frac{1 \text{ mol XCl}_2}{(70.906 + x) \text{ g XCl}_2}\right) = \frac{0.890}{70.906 + x} \text{ mol XCl}_2$$

But the chemical amounts of the XBr_2 and XCl_2 are equal: Hence:

$$\frac{1.500}{159.808 + x} = \frac{0.890}{70.906 + x}$$

This equation is easily solved for x, the molar mass of the unknown element. It equals 58.8 g mol^{-1}; the relative atomic mass of the element is $\boxed{58.8}$.

b) A check of atomic masses in the periodic table shows that the unknown element is most likely $\boxed{\text{nickel}}$.

2.33 There seems to be insufficient information. What is overlooked is that both NaCl and KCl furnish only a set, definite fraction of their mass to the total mass of chlorine. These two fractions are readily available from the formulas KCl and NaCl and a table of relative atomic masses. Thus, in addition to the obvious relationship: $m_{\text{NaCl}} + m_{\text{KCl}} = 1.0000$ g we can write:

$$\text{mass of Cl from NaCl} + \text{mass of Cl from KCl} = \text{mass of Cl in AgCl}$$

Compute the molecular masses of NaCl, KCl and AgCl and use them to get the fraction of each compound that is Cl:

$$\left(\frac{35.4527}{58.4425}\right) m_{\text{NaCl}} + \left(\frac{35.4527}{74.5510}\right) m_{\text{KCl}} = \left(\frac{35.4527}{143.3209}\right) 2.1476 \text{ g}$$

Dividing both sides of this equation by 35.4527 gives

$$\frac{m_{\text{NaCl}}}{58.4425} + \frac{m_{\text{KCl}}}{74.5510} = \left(\frac{1}{143.3209}\right) 2.1476 \text{ g}$$

Combining this equation with $m_{NaCl} + m_{KCl} = 1.0000$ and solving gives

$$m_{NaCl} = 0.4249 \text{ g} \qquad \text{and} \qquad m_{KCl} = 0.5751 \text{ g}$$

The mass percentages of NaCl and KCl in the original mixture of NaCl and KCl are then $\boxed{42.49\%}$ and $\boxed{57.51\%}$ respectively.

2.35 Write the balanced chemical equation for the reaction:

$$HCl(g) + NH_3(g) \rightarrow NH_4Cl(s)$$

One mole of HCl gas weighs 36.46 g, and one mole of NH_3 weighs only 17.03 g. It takes fewer heavy molecules than light molecules to make up a specific mass. Therefore, equal masses of HCl and NH_3 contain more molecules of NH_3. When the two react in a 1-to-1 molar ratio, the HCl is used up first. This means HCl is the limiting reactant. When the HCl is used up, the reaction stops, leaving excess NH_3. The mass of NH_4Cl is

$$m_{NH_4Cl} = 2.00 \text{ g HCl} \times \left(\frac{1 \text{ mol HCl}}{36.46 \text{ g HCl}}\right) \times \left(\frac{1 \text{ mol NH}_4\text{Cl}}{1 \text{ mol HCl}}\right) \times \left(\frac{53.49 \text{ g NH}_4\text{Cl}}{1 \text{ mol NH}_4\text{Cl}}\right) = \boxed{14.7 \text{ g NH}_4\text{Cl}}$$

Since 20.0 g of matter was present originally, the mass of left-over NH_3 is $(20.0 - 14.7) = \boxed{5.3 \text{ g NH}_3}$. The preceding is a conceptual method to identify the limiting reactant. The recommended method is to compute that 10.0 g of NH_3 and unlimited HCl would give 31.4 g of NH_4Cl, whereas 10.0 g of HCl and unlimited NH_3 would give only 14.7 g of NH_4Cl.

Tip. A quick way to identify the limiting reactant is to divide the chemical amount of each reactant by the coefficient that the reactant has in the balanced chemical equation. The smallest answer identifies the limiting reactant.

2.37 Compute the maximum possible yield (the theoretical yield) of Fe as follows:

$$433.2 \text{ g Fe}_2\text{O}_3 \times \left(\frac{1 \text{ mol Fe}_2\text{O}_3}{159.69 \text{ g Fe}_2\text{O}_3}\right) \times \left(\frac{2 \text{ mol Fe}}{1 \text{ mol Fe}_2\text{O}_3}\right) \times \frac{55.87 \text{ g Fe}}{1 \text{ mol Fe}} = \boxed{303.0 \text{ g Fe}}$$

The percent yield, a ratio, is

$$\text{Percent Yield} = \frac{\text{Actual Yield}}{\text{Theoretical Yield}} \times 100\% = \frac{254.3 \text{ g Fe actual}}{303.0 \text{ g Fe theoretical}} \times 100\% = \boxed{83.93\%}$$

2.39 a) The problem requires more significant figures than the computations in **1.25** but follows the same principles. The relative molecular mass of the human parathormone is 13, 932.24. The mass percentages are: C, 59.571%; H, 6.4967%; N, 12.5668%; O, 18.833%; S, 2.532%.

2.41 a) "Binary" means that the only elements in the three compounds are oxygen and the metal (label it M). The first compound contains 13.38 g of O for every 86.62 g of M, which, by division, is $\boxed{0.15457 \text{ g}}$ of O per 1 g of M. The second and third compounds have $\boxed{0.1029 \text{ g}}$ of O and $\boxed{0.07721 \text{ g}}$ of O per 1 g of M, respectively.
b) If the first compound is MO_2, then the second is $MO_{4/3}$ because the second compound has 2/3 as much oxygen per given quantity of M as the first. This formula is improved by multiplying both subscripts by 3 to clear the fraction. The answer is $\boxed{M_3O_4}$. The third compound is $\boxed{MO}$ if the first is MO_2 because it has almost exactly 1/2 as much oxygen per quantity of M.
c) Continue the assumption that the first compound is MO_2. Compute the amount of metal that combines with 2 mol of O (2×15.9994 g of O) in each of the first compounds. It is 207.2 g. Because the formula

tells us that there is 1 mol of M per 2 mol of O, the relative atomic mass of M equals 207.2. Consulting the periodic table establishes that M is $\boxed{\text{lead}}$.

2.43 Imagine 1.000 g of the first oxide. It contains 0.6960 g of Mn and 0.3040 g of O. Dividing these masses by the relative atomic masses of Mn and O gives the relative numbers of moles of the two elements. The smallest whole-number ratio of these chemical amounts gives the subscripts in the compound's empirical formula:

$$\text{Mn}_{\frac{0.6960}{54.94}}\text{O}_{\frac{0.3040}{16.00}} \Longrightarrow \text{Mn}_{0.01267}\text{O}_{0.01900} \Longrightarrow \text{Mn}_{1.000}\text{O}_{1.500} \Longrightarrow \boxed{\text{Mn}_2\text{O}_3}$$

Repeat the procedure for the second oxide:

$$\text{Mn}_{\frac{0.6319}{54.94}}\text{O}_{\frac{0.3681}{16.00}} \Longrightarrow \text{Mn}_{0.01150}\text{O}_{0.02301} \Longrightarrow \text{Mn}_{1.000}\text{O}_{2.000} \Longrightarrow \boxed{\text{MnO}_2}$$

Tip. Getting from the second to the third formula in the preceding requires dividing each subscript by the smallest of the subscripts.

2.45 a) The balanced equations for the conversion of cyanuric acid to isocyanuric acid and the reaction of isocyanuric acid with nitrogen dioxide are:

$$\boxed{\text{C}_3\text{N}_3(\text{OH})_3 \rightarrow 3\,\text{HNCO}} \quad \text{and} \quad \boxed{8\,\text{HNCO} + 6\,\text{NO}_2 \rightarrow 7\,\text{N}_2 + 8\,\text{CO}_2 + 4\,\text{H}_2\text{O}}$$

Balancing by inspection in the second equation works requires some care. Assign 1 as the coefficient of HNCO. Then, focus on C and O because these elements occur in only one compound on each side of the equation. If HNCO on the left has a coefficient of 1, CO_2 on the right must have a coefficient of 1 and H_2O on the right must have a coefficient of 1/2 to achieve balance in C and H. These two coefficients on the right imply a total of $2\frac{1}{2}$ mol of O on the right. The "1 HNCO" on the left supplies only 1 mol of O, and its coefficient must not be changed. The NO_2 must supply the other 3/2 mol of O. To do this, its coefficient must be 3/4. The left side now has 7/4 mol of N. The coefficient of N_2 on the right must therefore equal 7/8 because $7/8 \times 2 = 7/4$ (the 2 comes from the subscript in N_2). Multiplying all five coefficients by 8 eliminates fractional coefficients.

b) Use a series of unit-factors constructed from the molar masses of the compounds and the coefficients of the two balanced equations:

$$m_{\text{C}_3\text{N}_3(\text{OH})_3} = 1.70 \times 10^{10}\ \text{kg NO}_2 \times \left(\frac{1\ \text{mol NO}_2}{0.046\ \text{kg NO}_2}\right) \times \left(\frac{8\ \text{mol HNCO}}{6\ \text{mol NO}_2}\right)$$
$$\times \left(\frac{1\ \text{mol C}_3\text{N}_3(\text{OH})_3}{3\ \text{mol HNCO}}\right) \times \left(\frac{0.129\ \text{kg C}_3\text{N}_3(\text{OH})_3}{1\ \text{mol C}_3\text{N}_3(\text{OH})_3}\right) = \boxed{2.1 \times 10^{10}\ \text{kg C}_3\text{N}_3(\text{OH})_3}$$

2.47 The only product of the reaction that contains nitrogen is *m*-toluidine; the only reactant that contains nitrogen is 3′-methylphthalanilic acid. It follows that the mass of nitrogen in the 3′-methylphthalanilic acid must equal the mass of nitrogen in the *m*-toluidine. The *m*-toluidine (empirical formula C_7H_9N) is 13.1% nitrogen by mass (calculated as in **2.1**). The 5.23 g of *m*-toluidine therefore contains 0.685 g of nitrogen. The 3′-methylphthalanilic acid contains 5.49% nitrogen by mass (as given in the problem). The issue thus becomes finding the mass of 3′-methylphthalanilic acid that contains 0.685 g of nitrogen. Let this mass equal x. Then $0.0549x = 0.685$ g. Solving gives x equal to 12.5 g. This analysis is equivalent to the following:

$$5.23\ \text{g toluidine} \times \left(\frac{13.1\ \text{g N}}{100\ \text{g toluidine}}\right) \times \left(\frac{100\ \text{g 3}'\text{-methyl}}{5.49\ \text{g N}}\right) = \boxed{12.5\ \text{g 3}'\text{-methyl}}$$

2.49 a) Write an unbalanced equation to represent what the problem tells about the process:

$$C_{12}H_{22}O_{11} + O_2 \rightarrow C_6H_8O_7 + H_2O$$

Balance this equation as to carbon by inserting the coefficient 2 in front of the citric acid. Then balance the hydrogens by putting a 3 in front of the water (of the 22 H's on the left, 16 appear in the citric acid, and the rest appear in the water). Next, consider the oxygen. The right side has $(2 \times 7) + (3 \times 1) = 17$ O's. On the left side, the sucrose furnishes 11 O's so the remaining 6 must come from 3 molecules of oxygen. The balanced equation is

$$\boxed{C_{12}H_{22}O_{11} + 3\,O_2 \rightarrow 2\,C_6H_8O_7 + 3\,H_2O}$$

b) The balanced equation provides the information to write the second unit-factor in the following:

$$m_{C_6H_8O_7} = 15.0 \text{ kg sucrose} \times \left(\frac{1 \text{ kmol sucrose}}{342.3 \text{ kg sucrose}}\right) \times \left(\frac{2 \text{ kmol citric acid}}{1 \text{ kmol sucrose}}\right) \times \left(\frac{192.13 \text{ kg citric acid}}{1 \text{ kmol citric acid}}\right) = \boxed{16.8 \text{ kg citric acid}}$$

Tip. Save time by creating factors such as "1 kilomole sucrose / 342.3 kg sucrose." Also, only *part* of the balanced equation is needed, namely the 2 : 1 molar ratio of citric acid from sucrose. The O_2 and H_2O could have been left unbalanced.

2.51 a) Compute the chemical amount of XBr_2 that is present and recognize that two moles of AgBr appear for every one mole of XBr_2 present in the 5.00 g sample. This fact appears in the second unit-factor in the following:

$$1.0198 \text{ g AgBr} \times \left(\frac{1 \text{ mol AgBr}}{187.77 \text{ g AgBr}}\right) \times \left(\frac{1 \text{ mol XBr}_2}{2 \text{ mol AgBr}}\right) = 0.002716 \text{ mol XBr}_2$$

The molar mass $\mathcal{M}$ of any substance equals its mass divided by its chemical amount:

$$\mathcal{M}_{XBr_2} = \frac{m_{XBr_2}}{n_{XBr_2}} = \frac{0.500 \text{ g}}{0.002716 \text{ mol}} = \boxed{184.1 \text{ g mol}^{-1}}$$

b) The atomic mass of X equals the molecular mass of the compound minus the contribution of the bromine:

$$\text{atomic mass of X} = 184.1 - 2(79.9) = \boxed{24.3}$$

Checking the atomic masses in the periodic table shows that X is magnesium, $\boxed{\text{Mg}}$.

2.53 In the Solvay process, one mole of NH_3 takes up one mole of CO_2, holds it for NaCl to attack, and departs as NH_4Cl. Each mole of the $NaHCO_3$ that results then goes on to give 1/2 mol of Na_2CO_3. Thus, for each mole of NH_3 1/2 mol of Na_2CO_3 forms. In the following equation the prefix "M" in a unit stands for mega:[2]

$$m_{Na_2CO_3} = 1 \text{ metric ton NH}_3 \times \left(\frac{1 \text{ Mmol NH}_3}{17.03 \text{ metric ton NH}_3}\right) \times \left(\frac{1 \text{ Mmol Na}_2\text{CO}_3}{2 \text{ Mmol NH}_3}\right) \times \left(\frac{105.98 \text{ Mg Na}_2\text{CO}_3}{1 \text{ Mmol Na}_2\text{CO}_3}\right) = 6.22 \text{ Mg Na}_2\text{CO}_3$$

A metric ton equals a megagram, so $\boxed{6.22 \text{ metric tons}}$ of sodium carbonate is produced per metric ton of ammonia.

---

[2] See text Table B.3, text page A.10.

2.55 Assume that the limestone raw material is pure calcium carbonate. Then compute the theoretical yield of ethylene in the three-step process. An essential unit-factor comes from viewing the equations as a group: it takes 1 mol of $CaCO_3$ to produce 1 mol of C_2H_2. It is *not* necessary to compute the theoretical yield of the lime (CaO) and calcium carbide (CaC_2) produced and later consumed on the way to the final product. The following conversions use an additional short-cut—just as a metric ton (1000 kg) is a million times bigger than a gram, a megamole (Mmol) is a million time bigger than a mole:

$$m_{C_2H_2} = 10.0 \text{ metric ton } CaCO_3 \times \left(\frac{1 \text{ Mmol } CaCO_3}{100.1 \text{ metric ton } CaCO_3}\right) \times \left(\frac{1 \text{ Mmol } C_2H_2}{1 \text{ Mmol } CaCO_3}\right)$$
$$\times \left(\frac{26.03 \text{ metric ton } C_2H_2}{1 \text{ Mmol } C_2H_2}\right) = 2.60 \text{ metric ton } C_2H_2$$

The percent yield equals the actual yield divided by the theoretical yield and multiplied by 100%:

$$\text{percent yield } C_2H_2 = \frac{2.32 \text{ metric ton } C_2H_2}{2.60 \text{ metric ton } C_2H_2} \times 100\% = \boxed{89.2\%}$$

Chapter 3

Chemical Bonding: The Classical Description

3.1 According to the periodic law, the properties of scandium should be intermediate between those of calcium and titanium. Simply average the numerical data:

Property	Predicted	Observed
Melting point	1250°C	1541°C
Boiling point	2386°C	2831°C
Density	3.02 g cm^{-3}	2.99 g cm^{-3}

The numbers in the "observed" column come from text Appendix F.

3.3 Antimony is in Group V: $\boxed{SbH_3}$; bromine is in Group VII: $\boxed{HBr}$; tin is in Group IV: $\boxed{SnH_4}$; selenium is in Group VI: $\boxed{H_2Se}$.

3.5 Use the periodic trends in ionization energy discussed on text pages 51-54.

a) $\boxed{\text{Sr}}$ has a higher first ionization energy than Rb.

b) $\boxed{\text{Rn}}$ has a higher IE_1 than Po.

c) $\boxed{\text{Xe}}$ has a higher IE_1 than Cs.

d) $\boxed{\text{Sr}}$ has a higher IE_1 than Ba.

3.7 Table 3.1 quotes the successive ionization energies of elements 1 through 21. Beryllium, element 4, has four ionization energies. Compute $\ln I_n$ (or $\log I_n$) for n equal 1 through 4. Dividing I_n by the unit MJ mol^{-1} amounts to simply disregarding the unit. This is necessary because it is not possible to take the logarithm of a quantity that has units. The large increase between I_2 and I_3 confirms the presence of two relatively easily removed electrons outside of a core of two tightly held electrons. The graph follows:

Logarithm of Successive Ionization Energies of Be

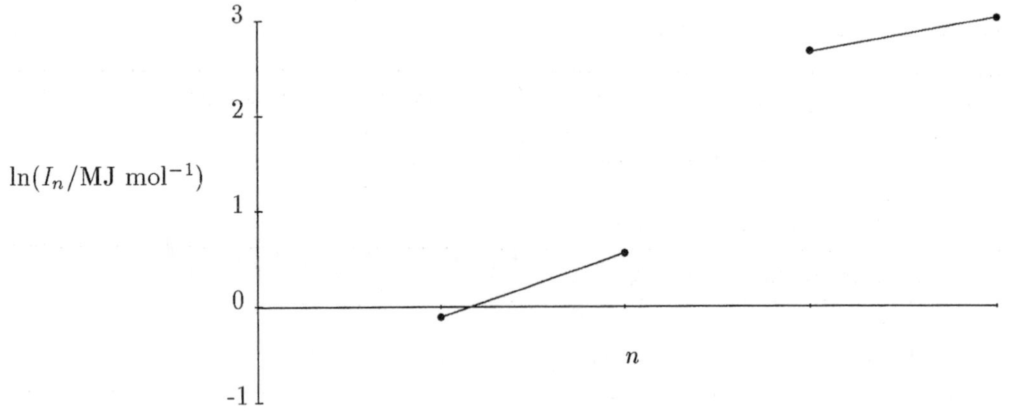

3.9 Use the periodic trends in electron affinity discussed on text page 55-56.

a) $\boxed{\text{Cs}}$ has a larger EA than Xe.

b) $\boxed{\text{F}}$ has a larger EA than Pm.

c) $\boxed{\text{K}}$ has a larger EA than Ca.

d) $\boxed{\text{At}}$ has a larger EA than Po.

3.11 $\boxed{\text{K} < \text{Si} < \text{S} < \text{O} < \text{F}}$. Electronegativity tends to increase moving up a group (column) in the periodic table and from left to right across the groups (rows) from I to VIII. Thus, electronegativity generally increases in a diagonal direction from lower left to upper right in the periodic table

---

3.13 a) An atom of radon has 86 electrons. Of these, 78 are core electrons, and 8 are valence electrons. The Lewis diagram is $:\ddot{\underset{..}{\text{Rn}}}:$

b) The monopositive strontium ion has a total of 37 electrons. Of these, 36 are core electrons and 1 is a valence electron. The diagram is $(\cdot\text{Sr})^+$

c) The selenide(2−) ion has a total of 36 electrons. Of these 28 are core electrons and 8 are valence electrons. The Lewis diagram is $(:\ddot{\underset{..}{\text{Se}}}:)^{2-}$

d) The antimonide(1−) ion has a total of 52 electrons. Of these 46 are core electrons and 6 are valence electrons. The Lewis diagram is $(\cdot\ddot{\underset{..}{\text{Sb}}}\cdot)^-$

3.15 The theme here is how simple rules on the transfer of valence electrons govern the formation of ionic compounds.

a) Cesium chloride (CsCl) is a compound between chlorine and cesium. The Lewis symbols for the elements before and after reaction are $\text{Cs}\cdot + :\ddot{\underset{..}{\text{Cl}}}\cdot \rightarrow (\text{Cs})^+ (:\ddot{\underset{..}{\text{Cl}}}:)^-$.

b) Calcium and astatine form $CaAt_2$, calcium astatide. Each At atom gains an electron and the Ca atom loses two: $\cdot\text{Ca}\cdot + 2\,(:\ddot{\underset{..}{\text{At}}}\cdot) \rightarrow (:\ddot{\underset{..}{\text{At}}}:)^- (\text{Ca})^{2+} (:\ddot{\underset{..}{\text{At}}}:)^-$.

c) Aluminum and sulfur form Al_2S_3, aluminum sulfide. Each S atom gains two electrons and each Al atom loses three: $2\,\cdot\ddot{\mathrm{Al}}\cdot + 3\,(\cdot\ddot{\underset{..}{\mathrm{S}}}\cdot) \rightarrow (\mathrm{Al}^{3+})_2\,(:\ddot{\underset{..}{\mathrm{S}}}:{}^{2-})_3$.

d) Potassium and tellurium form K_2Te, potassium telluride. Each Te atom gains two electrons and each K atom loses one: $2\,\mathrm{K}\cdot + (\cdot\ddot{\underset{..}{\mathrm{Te}}}\cdot) \rightarrow (\mathrm{K}^+)(:\ddot{\underset{..}{\mathrm{Te}}}:{}^{2-})(\mathrm{K}^+)$.

3.17 It is best just to memorize the patterns of the nomenclature of simple inorganic compounds.

a) Al_2O_3	aluminum oxide	**b)** Rb_2Se	rubidium selenide
c) $(NH_4)_2S$	ammonium sulfide	**d)** $Ca(NO_3)_2$	calcium nitrate
e) Cs_2SO_4	cesium sulfate	**f)** $KHCO_3$	potassium hydrogen carbonate

Another name for the last item is potassium bicarbonate.

3.19 The formulas of the anions come from text Table 3.2.

a) Silver cyanide	$AgCN$	**b)** Calcium hypochlorite	$Ca(OCl)_2$
c) Potassium chromate	K_2CrO_4	**d)** Gallium oxide	Ga_2O_3
e) Potassium superoxide	KO_2	**f)** Barium hydrogen carbonate	$Ba(HCO_3)_2$

3.21 The phosphate ion has the formula PO_4^{3-} (text Table 3.2). The systematic name for this ionic compound is $\boxed{\text{sodium phosphate}}$. Trisodium phosphate is therefore $\boxed{Na_3PO_4}$.

3.23 The problem is similar to text Example 3.2.[1] The gaseous KCl molecule is treated as two point charges separated by 2.67 Å. The energy of dissociation equals the negative of the change in energy arising from the Coulomb (electrostatic) attraction between the potassium and chloride ions minus the change in energy consumed in forming the ions by transferring an electron from a chlorine atom to the potassium ion:

$$\Delta E_{\mathrm{d}} = -\Delta E_{\mathrm{Coulomb}} - \Delta E_{\infty}$$

The Coulomb potential energy of a pair of charges separated by distance R_e is

$$\Delta E_{\mathrm{Coulomb}} = \frac{Q_1 Q_2}{4\pi\epsilon_0 R_e}$$

In the case of KCl(g), Q_1 and Q_2 equal $+1.602 \times 10^{-19}$ C (K^+ ion) and -1.602×10^{-19} C (Cl^- ion), and R_e equals 2.67×10^{-10} m. Substituting these values (and ϵ_0 and π) gives:

$$\Delta E_{\mathrm{coulomb}} = \frac{(+1.602 \times 10^{-19}\ \mathrm{C})(-1.602 \times 10^{-19}\ \mathrm{C})}{4(3.1416)(8.854 \times 10^{-12}\ \mathrm{C^2\,J^{-1}m^{-1}}(2.67 \times 10^{-10}\ \mathrm{m})} = -8.64 \times 10^{-19}\ \mathrm{J}$$

This is the Coulomb potential energy change in a *single* K^+ to Cl^- attraction. For a mole of such pair-wise attractions, multiply by Avogadro's number:

$$\Delta E_{\mathrm{Coulomb}} = -8.64 \times 10^{-19}\ \mathrm{J\ pair^{-1}} \times 6.022 \times 10^{23}\ \mathrm{pair\ mol^{-1}} = -520\ \mathrm{kJ\ mol^{-1}}$$

It requires +520 kJ to dissociate one mole of the KCl molecules to ions, that is, to move all the Cl^- ions an infinite distance away from the K^+ ions to which they are bonded and give a collection of $K^+(g)$ ions all infinitely distant one from another and a second collection of $Cl^-(g)$ ions, also infinitely distant one from another. Removing the electrons from the $Cl^-(g)$ ions would *consume* 349 kJ mol^{-1} (based on the electron affinity of Cl(g) compiled in text Appendix F). Feeding the electrons into the $K^+(g)$ ions would release 419 kJ mol^{-1} (based on the ionization energy of potassium). The energy change for the electron transfer accordingly is

$$\Delta E_{\infty} = 419 - 349 = 70\ \mathrm{kJ\ mol^{-1}}$$

---

[1] Text page 64.

Substituting in the original formula gives:

$$\Delta E_{\mathrm{d}} = -\Delta E_{\mathrm{Coulomb}} - \Delta E_{\infty}$$
$$= -(-520 \text{ kJ mol}^{-1}) - 70 \text{ kJ mol}^{-1} = \boxed{450 \text{ kJ mol}^{-1}}$$

3.25 The As—H bond length should lie between the 1.42 Å of P—H and the 1.71 Å of Sb—H. A length of 1.56 Å, (the average) is a reasonable guess. The experimental bond length is 1.519 Å. The X—H bond will be weakest in SbH_3, which has the longest bonds.

3.27 a) SO_4^{2-} In this structure the four O atoms have formal charges (f.c.'s) of −1, and the central S has f.c. +2.

Tip. Oxygen atoms with a single bond always have f.c. −1.

b) $S_2O_3^{2-}$ In this structure for the thiosulfate ion, the central sulfur has f.c. +2. The three oxygen atoms and the peripheral sulfur have f.c. −1.

c) SbF_3 All atoms have f.c. zero in this structure.

d) SCN^- The sulfur atom in this structure has f.c. −1; the C and N have f.c. zero.

Tip. Whenever C has four covalent bonds and no lone pairs in a Lewis structure, its formal charge is zero; whenever N has three covalent bonds and one lone pair, its formal charge is zero.

3.29 The structure $\mathrm{H{-}\ddot{N}{=}\ddot{O}:}$ has f.c. zero on all atoms. The isomeric structure $\mathrm{H{-}\ddot{O}{=}\ddot{N}:}$ has f.c.'s of zero on the H, +1 on the O and −1 on the N. The first of the isomers is favored because no formal charge builds up on any of the atoms.

Tip. The structures for HNO and HON are *not* resonance structures because they use different skeletons.

3.31 a) In this structure of "ZO_2" the oxygen atoms both possess a formal charge of 0. Since there is no net charge on the molecule, Z must also have an f.c. of 0. Therefore, it has 4 valence electrons and belongs to Group IV. CO_2 is an example.

b) In this Lewis structure of "Z_2O_7" each of the six peripheral O atoms has f.c. −1, but the bridging O atom has f.c. zero. Since the molecule has no net charge and is symmetrical, the f.c. on each Z is +3. Therefore, Z has 7 valence electrons and is in Group VII. An example is Cl_2O_7 (dichlorine heptaoxide).

c) In "ZO_2^-" one of the oxygen atoms has f.c. zero, but the other has f.c. −1. Since the species has a −1 net charge, Z must have f.c. zero. Therefore, it comes from Group V (5 valence electrons). An example is NO_2^- (nitrite ion).

d) In "$HOZO_3^-$" three of the O atoms have f.c. −1, and the other O atom and the H atom have f.c. zero. Since the ion has a −1 net charge, Z must have f.c. +2. Therefore Z has 6 valence electrons and comes from Group VI. An example is $HOSO_3^-$ (hydrogen sulfate ion).

3.33 The octet rule is satisfied for all atoms in these structures. Non-zero formal charges are indicated near the atom, and the non-zero overall charges of molecular ions are shown outside of enclosing brackets:

a) 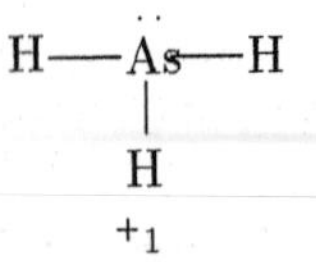

b) 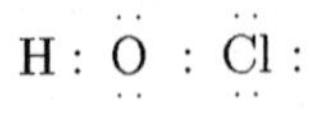

c) 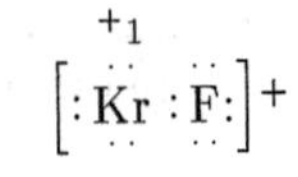

d) 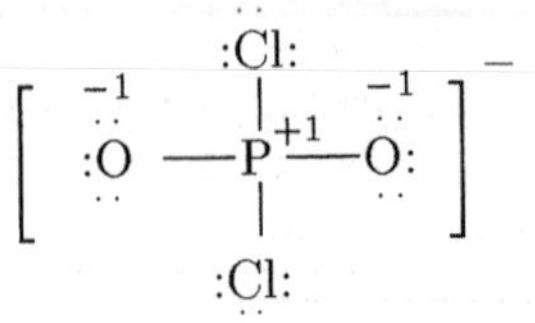

Tip. In Lewis structures, a line equals a pair of dots, but lines are rarely used for lone pairs.

3.35 Referring to text Table 3.6,[2] the bond lengths should be: N—H, 1.01×10^{-10} m; N—C, 1.47×10^{-10} m; C=O, 1.20×10^{-10} m. The following Lewis structure for urea has f.c. zero on all atoms:

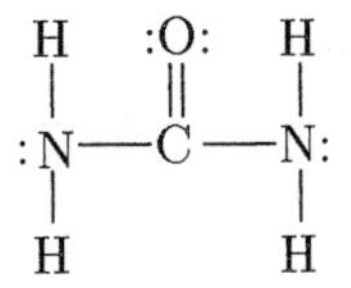

3.37 A Lewis structure for S_8:

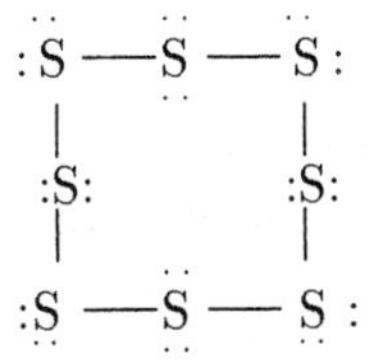

Each sulfur obeys the octet rule and has f.c. zero.

3.39 a) The nitrogen and boron atoms would both get 4 valence electrons if all bonds were broken and the two electrons from each pair parcelled out evenly between the two atoms that share them. The nitrogen atom is supposed to have 5 valence electrons, so its formal charge is [+1]. The f.c. is [−1] on the boron atom, and [zero] on the rest of the atoms:

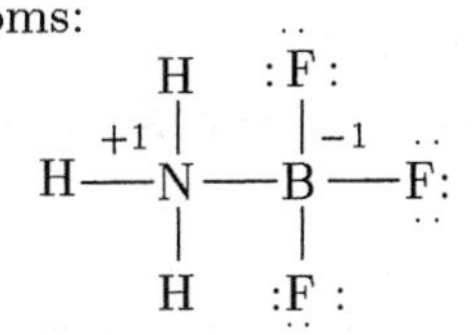

b) The single-bonded O atom has [f.c. −1]. All other f.c.'s are [zero]. A double-headed arrow indicates resonance structures:

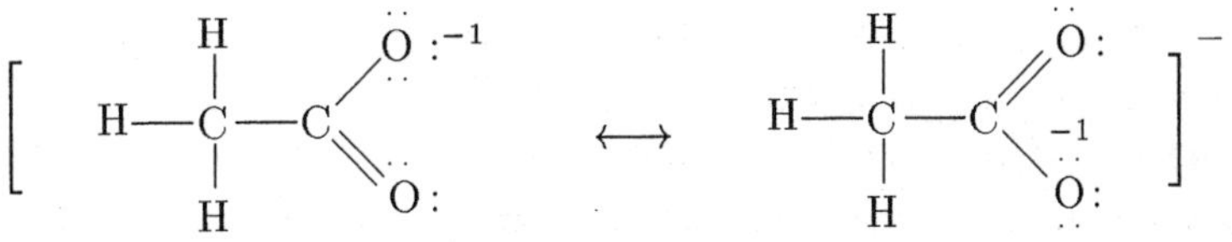

c) The hydrogen carbonate ion has 24 valence electrons. The C atom contributes 4, the H atom contributes 1, and the 3 O atoms contribute 6 each; a final electron comes from outside to make the overall charge −1. The resonance Lewis structures are:

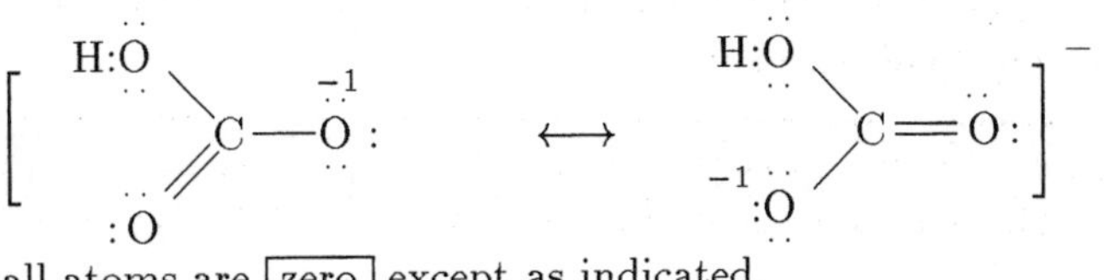

Formal charges on all atoms are [zero] except as indicated.

Tip. Resonance structures differ only in the positions of the electrons. A common error is to include a third structure in which the oxygen atom on the upper left shares two pairs of electrons with the central carbon atom and the H atom is moved to avoid putting a +1 formal charge onto that oxygen atom. Such a structure is *not* a resonance structure, because an atom as well as electrons has moved. Resonance structures always use the same atomic skeleton.

---

[2] Text page 66.

3.41 The main resonance structures (others break the octet rule) for NO_2^- ion are

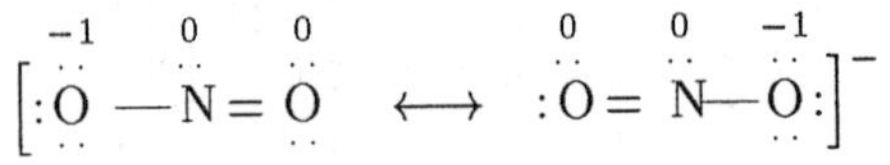

The two N-to-O bonds in this ion should be equivalent and intermediate in length between 1.43 Å (single bond) and 1.10 Å (double bond), that is, about $\boxed{1.27\ \text{Å}}$.

3.43 Resonance structures of methyl isocyanate include:

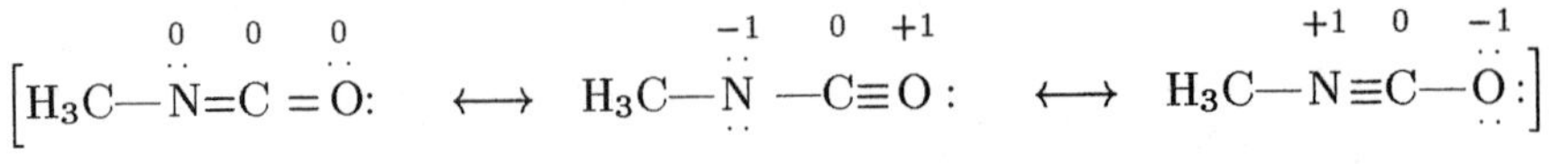

The left structure has f.c. zero on all atoms. The center structure has f.c. −1 on the N, f.c. +1 on the O and f.c. zero on the other atoms. The right structure has f.c. +1 on the N, −1 on the O and zero on all of the other atoms. The predominant resonance contributor is the left structure, which has f.c. zero on all atoms. **Tip.** The "iso" in methyl isocyanate suggests that the compound is an isomer of something. Here are Lewis structures for methyl cyanate, which contains the same atoms arranged differently. These Lewis structures are not resonance structures of the preceding three:

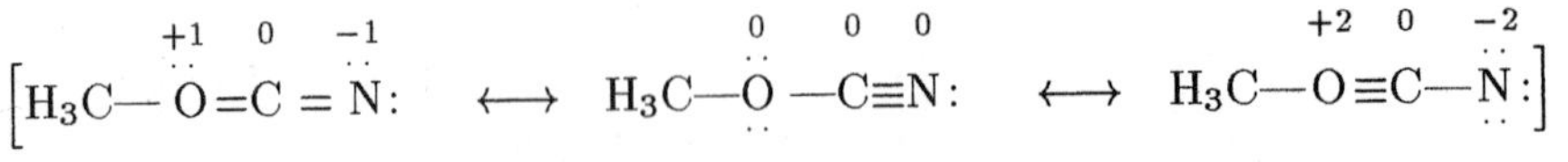

3.45 a) In the structure for PF_5, each atom has f.c. zero. Bonding on the F atoms obeys the octet rule but the P atom has an expanded octet (10 electrons).

b) In the structure for SF_4, bonding on all F atoms obeys the octet rule. The S has an expanded octet (10 electrons). All f.c.'s equal 0.

c) In the structure of XeO_2F_2, the F atoms and the O atoms obey the octet rule. The Xe has an expanded octet. All atoms have f.c. zero.

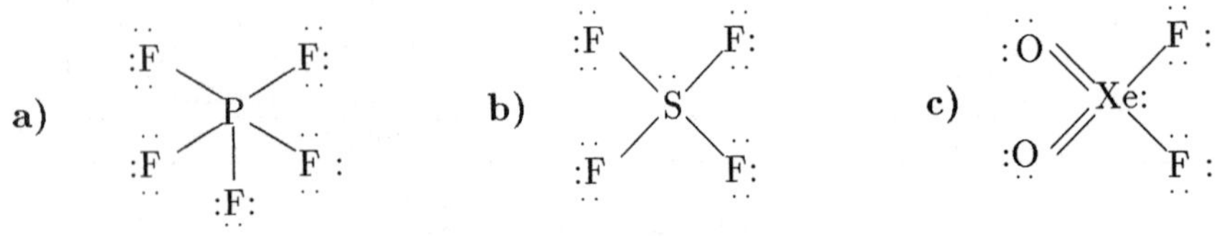

3.47 Binary ionic compounds have large differences in electronegativity between their elements whereas binary covalent compounds have small differences. High vapor pressure is associated with relatively weak intermolecular attractions and therefore with molecular (covalent) compounds. The correct choice in each case is the compound with the smaller difference in electronegativity:

a) $\boxed{CI_4}$ **b)** $\boxed{OF_2}$ **c)** $\boxed{SiH_4}$

3.49 In diatomic molecules, the fractional ionic character δ is

$$\delta = (0.2082\ \text{Å}\ \text{D}^{-1})\left(\frac{\mu}{R}\right)$$

when the dipole moment μ is in Debye and the bond distance R is in Ångstroms. The percent ionic character is just 100 times the fractional ionic character. Substitute in the formula to obtain:

Compound	Bond Length	Dipole Moment	(δ)	% Ionic Character
ClO	1.573 Å	1.239 D	0.16	16
KI	3.051	10.82	0.74	74
TlCl	2.488	4.543	0.38	38
InCl	2.404	3.79	0.33	33

3.51 The Δ in the expression $16\Delta + 3.5\Delta^2$ in this problem is *not* the Δ in the Pauling definition of electronegativity on text page 74. Rather it is $\chi_A - \chi_B$, the difference in electronegativity. Substitute in the formula to obtain:

Compound	$\lvert\chi_A - \chi_B\rvert$	Calc. % Ionic	Dipole % Ionic
HF	1.78	40	41
HCl	0.96	19	18
HBr	0.76	14	12
HI	0.46	8	6
CsF	3.19	87	70

Tip. The point of the problem is the generally good agreement between the ionic character calculated from differences in electronegativity and that based on dipole moment.

3.53 Construct the following table based on text Tables 3.12 and 3.14

SN of A	Molecular Type X is a bonded atom; E is a lone pair	Predicted Shape
2	AX_2	linear
3	AX_3	trigonal planar
	AX_2E	bent
4	AX_4	tetrahedral
	AX_3E	trigonal pyramidal
	AX_2E_2	bent
5	AX_5	trigonal bipyramidal
	AX_4E	distorted see-saw
	AX_3E_2	distorted T
	AX_2E_3	linear
6	AX_6	octahedral
	AX_5E	square pyramidal
	AX_4E_2	square planar

a)
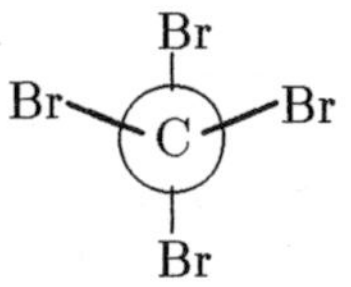

tetrahedral

b)
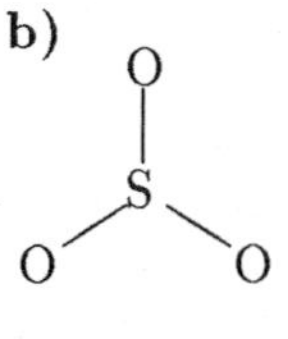

trigonal planar

c)
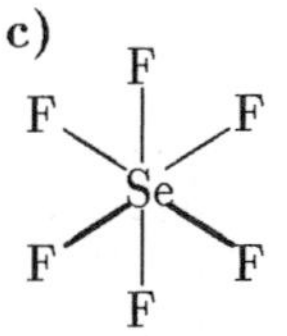

octahedral

d)
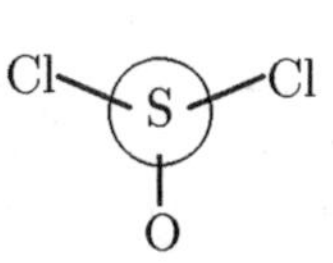

pyramidal

e)
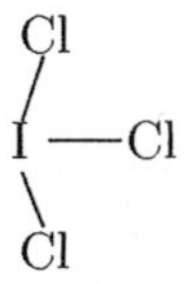

distorted T

In CBr_4, the central C atom has *SN* 4. There are no lone pairs on the central carbon atom so this is an AX_4 case, as shown in the table.

In SO_3, the central S atom has *SN* 3 and no lone pairs. The fact that one or more of the S-to-O bonds can be shown in a Lewis structure as a double bond does *not* affect the steric number.

In SeF_6, the central Se atom has $SN\ \boxed{6}$. There are no lone pairs on the central Se atom.

In $SOCl_2$, the central S has $SN\ \boxed{4}$ and one lone pair. It is a AX_3E case (see the preceding table). The disposition of the electron pairs about the S is approximately tetrahedral.

In ICl_3, the central I atom has $SN\ \boxed{5}$. It is surrounded by 3 Cl atoms and 2 lone pairs. The disposition of the electron pairs is trigonal bipyramidal. The true molecular geometry however considers only atoms.

3.55 a) The molecular ion ICl_4^- is square planar. The central I atom has $SN\ \boxed{6}$, which means the geometry of the electron pairs about the central I is octahedral. The 2 lone pairs lie opposite each other on the octahedral pattern, minimizing lone-pair to lone-pair interactions. The 4 Cl atoms surround the central I atom in a $\boxed{\text{planar square}}$.

b) In OF_2, the central O atom has $SN\ \boxed{4}$. The molecule is of the type AX_2E_2.[3] The molecule is $\boxed{\text{bent}}$ to accommodate the two lone pairs on the O atom. The F—O—F angle is less than 109.5°.

c) In BrO_3^-, the central Br atom has $SN\ \boxed{4}$ making the molecular type of the molecular ion AX_3E. The single lone pair on the central Br atom occupies one corner of a tetrahedron about the Br atom. The resulting molecule is $\boxed{\text{pyramidal}}$. The presence of the lone pair forces the O atoms together slightly, so that the O—Br—O angle is less than 109.5°.

d) In CS_2, the central C atom has $SN\ \boxed{2}$. Both of the C-to-S bonds are double bonds, but this plays no part in figuring the *SN* of the C atom. The molecule, which is of the type AX_2, is $\boxed{\text{linear}}$.

3.57 a) Planar AB_3: BF_3, BH_3, SO_3. **b)** Pyramidal AB_3: NH_3, NF_3. **c)** Bent AB_2^-: ClO_2^-, NO_2^-. **d)** Planar AB_3^{2-}: CO_3^{2-}.

3.59 A molecule or molecular ion has a dipole moment when the center of its spatial distribution of positive charge does not coincide with the center of its distribution of negative charge. The *bonds* in the listed compounds are all polar. The symmetry of certain molecular shapes however causes the vector sum of the individual bond dipoles to equal zero. Thus, SeF_6 (octahedral), CBr_4 (tetrahedral), and SO_3 (trigonal planar) have $\boxed{\text{non-polar molecules}}$.
The molecules, ICl_3 (distorted T) and $SOCl_2$ (pyramidal), are less symmetrical, and the vector sums of their bond dipoles are not zero. They are $\boxed{\text{polar}}$.

3.61 The fact that the molecule is bent is unhelpful in deciding between the formulations:

$$\overset{-1}{:\ddot{\text{N}}} = \overset{+1}{\ddot{\text{O}}} - \overset{0}{\ddot{\underset{..}{\text{F}}}}: \qquad \text{and} \qquad \overset{0}{:\ddot{\text{O}}} = \overset{0}{\ddot{\text{N}}} - \overset{0}{\ddot{\underset{..}{\text{F}}}}:$$

because both structures feature a central atom having *SN* 3 with 2 bonds and 1 lone pair. VSEPR theory predicts a bent molecule in both cases.

Tip. The above structures include the formal charges. Considerations of formal charge (as in **3.81**) favor the isomer on the right. Both isomers exist. The one on the right (nitrosyl fluoride) is a colorless gas of reasonable stability, but the one on the left is highly unstable and has been characterized only spectroscopically (by methods described in Chapter 16).

3.63 a) The resonance structures

$$\left[\ \overset{-1}{:\ddot{\text{N}}} = \overset{+1}{\text{N}} = \overset{0}{\ddot{\text{O}}}: \quad \longleftrightarrow \quad \overset{0}{:\text{N}} \equiv \overset{+1}{\text{N}} - \overset{-1}{:\ddot{\underset{..}{\text{O}}}}:\ \right]$$

---

[3] See page 23 of this Manual.

can be written for the NNO molecule. When either is considered, the *SN* of the central nitrogen atom equals two. The predicted molecular geometry is linear.

b) The linear geometry in NNO would cause the N=O and N=N bond dipoles to add vectorially to zero if they were equal in magnitude. The observed net dipole moment means that the two bond dipoles differ in magnitude. The N=O bond should be more polar than the N=N bond because O is more electronegative than N. The N end of the molecule is therefore expected to have the positive partial charge.

3.65 The oxidation numbers are determined by the standard rules:

$SrBr_2$	Sr +2	Br −1	$Zn(OH)_4^{2-}$	Zn +2	O −2	H +1		
SiH_4	Si −4	H +1	$CaSiO_3$	Ca +2	Si +4	O −2		
$Cr_2O_7^{2-}$	Cr +6	O −2	KO_2	K +1	O −1/2			
CsH	Cs +1	H −1	$Ca_5(PO_4)_3F$	Ca +2	P +5	O −2	F −1	

3.67 **a)** SiO_2 **b)** $(NH_4)_2CO_3$ **c)** PbO_2 **d)** P_2O_5 **e)** CaI_2 **f)** $Fe(NO_3)_3$.

3.69
a) Copper(I) sulfide and copper(II) sulfide **b)** Sodium sulfate
c) Tetraarsenic hexaoxide[4] or arsenic(III) oxide **d)** Zirconium(IV) chloride
e) Dichlorine heptaoxide or chlorine(VII) oxide **f)** Gallium(I) oxide

3.71 The difference in electronegativities of the atoms in HF is 1.78; the difference in LiCl is 2.18. The two compounds differ greatly in their bonding according to the evidence of their physical properties. Lithium chloride is an ionic compound (high boiling, high melting); hydrogen fluoride is a covalent compound (low melting, low boiling).

3.73 **a)** The energy ΔE_∞[5] equals the difference between the *IE* of M(g) and the *EA* of X(g). It equals the energy required to extract an electron from an isolated M(g) and place it on an isolated X(g). At the critical distance R_c, the decrease in energy from the Coulomb attraction between the $M^+(g)$ and $X^-(g)$ ions just compensates for ΔE_∞:[6]

$$\Delta E_\infty = IE - EA = -\Delta E_{\text{Coulomb}} = -\frac{Q_1 Q_2}{4\pi\epsilon_0 R_c}$$

The constant ϵ_0 is 8.854×10^{-12} C^2 J^{-1}m^{-1}, and, in alkali halides, Q_1 and Q_2 are $+1.60218 \times 10^{-19}$ C and -1.60218×10^{-19} C. Solve the preceding for R_c and substitute the various values:

$$R_c = -\frac{Q_1 Q_2}{4\pi\epsilon_0 \Delta_\infty} = \frac{(2.3071 \times 10^{-28}\ \text{J m})}{(IE - EA)\ \text{J}}$$

Text Appendix F and other sources give *IE*'s and *EA*'s on a per mole basis. Revise the preceding equation, which applies to a single pair of particles, to allow the use of *IE*'s and *EA*'s in joule per mole. Do this by multiplying the numerator by N_0:

$$R_c = \frac{(6.0221 \times 10^{23}\ \text{mol}^{-1})(2.3071 \times 10^{-28}\ \text{J m})}{(IE - EA)\ \text{J mol}^{-1}} = \frac{1.3894 \times 10^{-4}\ \text{J m mol}^{-1}}{(IE - EA)\ \text{J mol}^{-1}}$$

b) From Appendix F for LiF, $(IE - EA)$ is $520.2 - 328.0 = 192.2 \times 10^3$ J mol^{-1}. Substitution in the preceding expression gives R_c equal to 7.229×10^{-10} m.

For KBr, $(IE - EA)$ equals 94.1×10^3 J mol^{-1} giving R_c equal to 14.8×10^{-10} m.

For NaCl, $(IE - EA)$ equals 149.8 kJ mol^{-1}, making R_c equal to 9.275×10^{-10} m.

[5] See text Figure 3.5, text page 62.
[6] Obviously at this same distance ΔE_d equals zero.

3.75 From text Table 3.6[7], the order of the bond in C_2 should be 2, the same as that in ethylene, C_2H_4. The bond length should be close to 1.34 Å. The observed value (1.31 Å) is consistent with this prediction, being only slightly smaller.

3.77 a) A Lewis structure for OPCl in which the octet rule is obeyed for all atoms and in which all atoms have a formal charge of zero is $:\ddot{O}=\ddot{P}-\ddot{Cl}:$

Tip. In this compound, the oxidation number of O is −2, of Cl −1, and of P +3. Oxidation numbers are *not* the same as formal charge.

b) Three resonance Lewis structure for O_2PCl are given below. In the structure on the left, all atoms have f.c. zero, but the octet rule is violated on the P atom, which sees 10 electrons. In the two structures to the right, the octet rule is obeyed for every atom, but formal charges build up as shown. All three contribute to the "true" bonding:

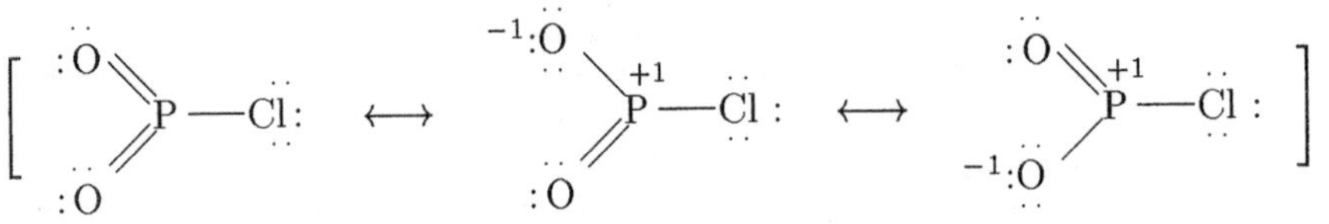

3.79 The following resonance structures of nitryl chloride together imply equivalent N-to-O bonds:

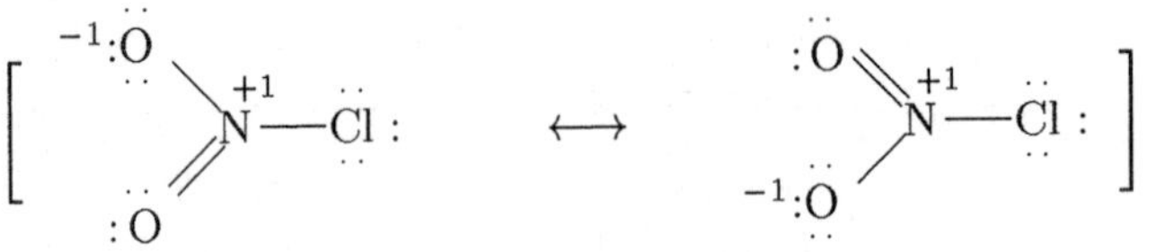

Tip. Nitryl chloride is a reactive gas that decomposes readily to nitrogen dioxide (see **3.81**) and chlorine. Despite this, it is named as a salt: nitryl ion, a +1 cation, in combination with chloride ion, a −1 anion. The following Lewis structure takes up the suggestion of this name by showing ionic bonding to the Cl. Note that the two N-to-O bonds are still equivalent, but the pair of electrons previously between N and Cl now belongs entirely to the Cl. The octet rule is satisfied for all atoms:

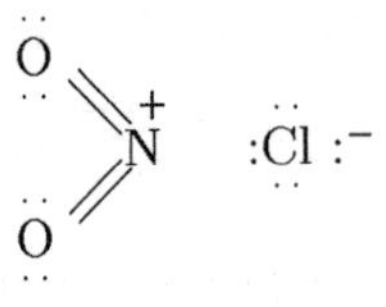

3.81 a) The molecule of nitrogen dioxide has 17 valence electrons. At least one atom cannot achieve an octet. The following four resonance structures are the candidates for best single Lewis structure:

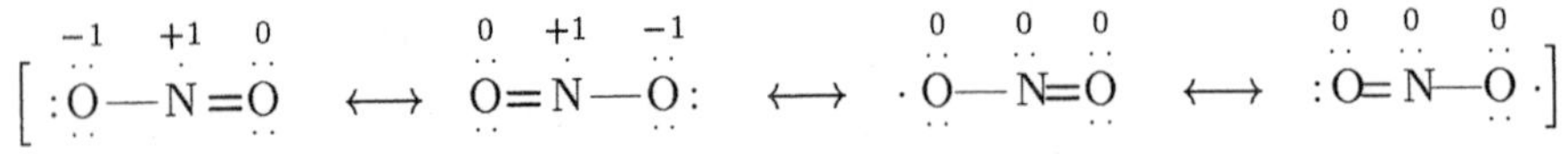

Other candidate structures break the octet rule on more than one atom or use octet expansion rather than octet deficiency. If the N atom is octet-deficient (left two structures), then formal charges build up as shown. If an O is octet-deficient (right two structures), all atoms have f.c. zero. The best structure puts the odd electron on the **O atoms**.

b) Four resonance structure can be drawn varying the relative positions of the double and single bonds:

---

[7] Text page 66.

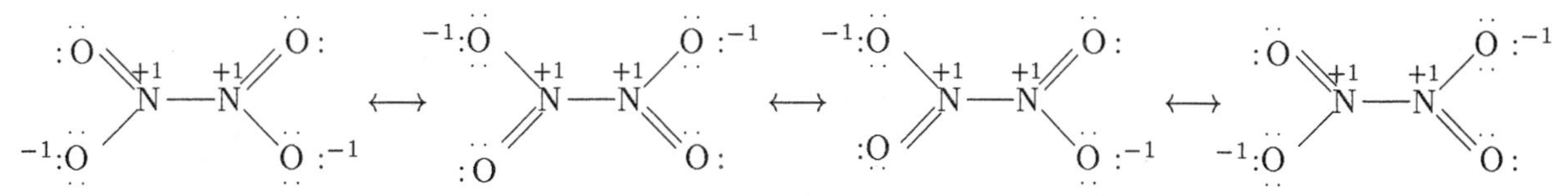

3.83 Xenon compounds always have an expanded octet:

a) $\left(:\overset{+1}{\ddot{\underset{\cdot\cdot}{Xe}}} - \ddot{\underset{\cdot\cdot}{F}}:\right)^{+}$ b) $:\ddot{\underset{\cdot\cdot}{F}} - \ddot{\underset{\cdot\cdot}{Xe}} - \ddot{\underset{\cdot\cdot}{F}}:$

3.85 a) The Lewis structures are $:\ddot{N}=\ddot{S}-\ddot{\underset{\cdot\cdot}{F}}:$ and $:\ddot{S}=\ddot{N}-\ddot{\underset{\cdot\cdot}{F}}:$ and $:\ddot{N}=\ddot{F}-\ddot{\underset{\cdot\cdot}{S}}:$

In the first, the formal charges are (from left to right) −1, +1, and 0. In the second, all three atoms have zero formal charge. In the third, the formal charges are −1, +2, and −1.
b) The structure with the least separation of formal charge has a central N. This is not consistent with the observation of a central S atom.
c) The electronegativity of N exceeds that of S; that is, N has a greater tendency than S to accept electrons in a chemical bond. This helps explain why the observed structure corresponds to a formal build-up of negative charge on the N and formal build-up of positive charge on the S. Also, the two most electronegative atoms (N and F) are separated, reducing electron-electron repulsions.

3.87 a) In $SbCl_5^{2-}$ ion, the central Sb atom has *SN* 6. It is surrounded by five bonding pairs (single bonds to the five fluorine atoms) and one lone pair. As an AX_5E case,[8] the molecular ion is square pyramidal.

b The central Sb atom in $SbCl_6^{3-}$ ion has *SN* 7. This steric number is rare. The required extension of VSEPR theory is inclusion of *SN* 7 and other higher *SN*'s. In fact, three geometries have been observed for *SN* 7: pentagonal bipyramidal, capped octahedral (in which the seventh atom occupies one face of an octahedron surrounding the central atom) and capped trigonal prism (in which the seventh atom occupies one rectangular face of a trigonal prism about the central atom).

3.89 The central S atom in F_4SO has *SN* 5 and falls into the class AX_5. The geometry of the molecule is therefore based on the trigonal bipyramid. The real question is whether the oxygen atom is equatorial or axial. Putting the double-bonded oxygen atom at an equatorial position minimizes 90° interactions with the four fluorine atoms and should be preferred, according to VSEPR theory. Also, the F—S—F angles will be slightly less than 90° and 120°.

3.91 Set up a coordinate system and position the oxygen atom at its origin. Let the y-axis bisect the angle θ defined by H—O—H:

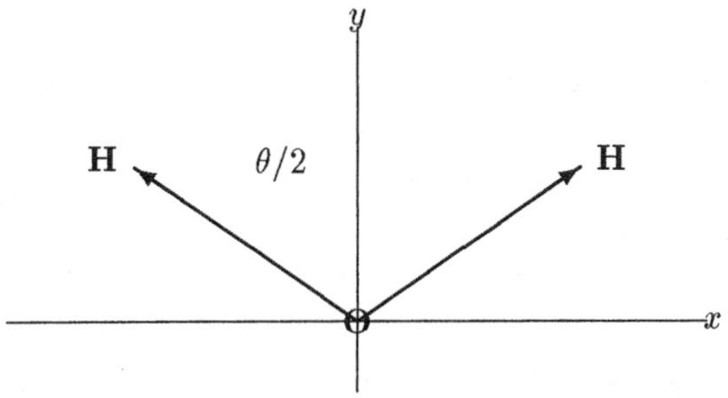

[8] See the table on page 23 of this Manual.

The dipole moments of the two O—H bonds are symbolized μ_{OH}. They parallel the two bonds. The x-components of these two vectors oppose each other and cancel. The y-components point in the same direction and add. The magnitude of the y-components is $\mu_{OH}\cos(\theta/2)$, and the sum of the two y-components equals the dipole moment of the molecule as a whole. Therefore:

$$\mu(H_2O) = 1.86 \text{ D} = 2\mu_{OH}\cos\left(\frac{\theta}{2}\right) = 2\mu_{OH}\cos\left(\frac{104.5^\circ}{2}\right)$$

Solving for μ_{OH} gives $\boxed{1.52 \text{ D}}$.

3.93 From the formula Bi_5^{3+} we must conclude that the oxidation number (or at least the average oxidation number) of the bismuth is $\boxed{+3/5}$. Because the oxidation number of F is -1 by convention, the oxidation number of the As is $\boxed{+5}$. The elevated dot in the formula means that SO_2 is loosely associated with this salt in its solid state. The oxidation number of S in SO_2 is $\boxed{+4}$; the oxidation number of O is $\boxed{-2}$.

3.95 a) The oxidation number of lead in PbO is +2; in PbO_2 it is +4; in Pb_2O_3 it is +3; in Pb_3O_4 it is +8/3.

b) Note that the formula "Pb_2O_3" is the sum of PbO and PbO_2. Perhaps in Pb_2O_3 half of the lead is Pb(II) and half is Pb(IV), as in "(PbO)(PbO_2)." Similarly, the lead in Pb_3O_4 may be 2/3 Pb(II) and 1/3 Pb(IV) as in "$(PbO)_2(PbO_2)$."

3.97 a) The element M loses two electrons in forming compounds, since it forms compounds MCl_2 and MO. It belongs to $\boxed{\text{group II}}$, the alkaline-earth metals.

b) The relative molecular mass of MCl_2 equals the sum of the relative masses of the three constituent atoms: $x + 2(35.453) = x + 70.906$ where x stands for the relative atomic mass of the element M. The fraction of mass that is chlorine is 0.447. So:

$$0.447 = \frac{70.906}{(x + 70.906)}$$

Solving gives $x = 87.7$. Reference to a list of relative atomic masses identifies the element M as $\boxed{\text{strontium}}$.

3.99 a) The elemental analysis reveals that the compound contains F, Cl, O, and no other elements Divide the respective mass percentages by the molar masses of the elements to obtain the relative number of moles of each (as in (**2.7**). The ratios correspond to the empirical formula $\boxed{ClO_3F}$.

b) The central atom in the molecule ClO_3F is certainly the Cl. One good Lewis structure is

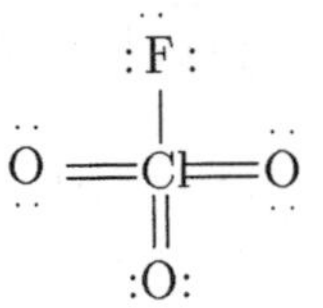

This structure shows an expanded octet on the central Cl, but the formal charges equal zero on all atoms. Resonance structures in which electrons are shifted from the double bonds to reside completely on the O's can also be written.[9]

c) The central Cl has a steric number of four. VSEPR theory predicts a structure based on the tetrahedron. Because F is more electronegative than O, it tends to attract electrons away from the central Cl, reducing the electron-pair repulsion and causing the F—Cl—O angles to become smaller than tetrahedral while the O—Cl—O angles become larger than tetrahedral.

---

[9] See **3.77b** on page 26 of this Manual.

Chapter 4

The Gaseous State

4.1 The decomposition of ammonium hydrosulfide produces ammonia NH_3 and hydrogen sulfide H_2S:

$$\boxed{NH_4HS(s) \rightarrow NH_3(g) + H_2S(g)}$$

Tip. To predict the course of chemical reactions, look for the formulas of stable gaseous compounds embedded in more complicated formulas. Heating often drives out such compounds. Look for water (H_2O), carbon dioxide (CO_2), carbon monoxide (CO), ammonia (NH_3), hydrogen chloride and the other hydrogen halides (HCl, HBr, HI, HF), oxygen (O_2), nitrogen (N_2), and hydrogen sulfide (H_2S).

4.3 Generate ammonia from ammonium bromide by dissolving the ammonium bromide in a small amount of water and adding a strong base, such as aqueous sodium hydroxide. NH_4Br dissolves in water to form ammonium ion $NH_4^+(aq)$ and bromide ion $Br^-(aq)$. The $NH_4^+(aq)$ ion donates a hydrogen ion to $OH^-(aq)$ to form gaseous ammonia $NH_3(g)$:

$$\boxed{NH_4^+(aq) + OH^-(aq) \rightarrow NH_3(g) + H_2O(l)}$$

Tip. Heating helps to liberate the ammonia (gases are usually less soluble in hot water than in cold).

4.5 Because water is less dense than mercury, a higher column of water is required to balance the pressure of the atmosphere. A pressure of 1.00 atm is balanced in a barometer by a column of mercury 76.0 cm high. The density of mercury is 13.6 g cm^{-3}, whereas the density of water is only 1.00 g cm^{-3}. The column of water must be longer in inverse proportion to the ratio of the densities:

$$h = 76.0 \text{ cm} \times \left(\frac{13.6 \text{ g cm}^{-3}}{1.00 \text{ g cm}^{-3}}\right) = 1.03 \times 10^3 \text{ cm} = \boxed{10.3 \text{ m}}$$

This is nearly 34 feet. Still, water barometers have been built.

Tip. The problem can also be solved by substitution into the equation $P = \rho g h$:

$$h = \frac{P}{\rho g} = \frac{101\,325 \text{ Pa}}{(1.00 \times 10^3 \text{ kg m}^3)(9.807 \text{ m s}^{-2})} = \boxed{10.3 \text{ m}}$$

Note the conversion of the pressure to pascals, the SI unit, and the conversion of the density of water to kilograms per cubic meter, a combination of SI base units. These conversions guarantee an answer in meters, the SI base unit of length.

4.7 Convert the 414 atm pressure to pascals (Pa), and then use the formula $P = \rho g h$ to compute the depth (h) of sea-water that exerts the same pressure. In this computation, g is the acceleration of the earth's gravity ($9.807\ \text{m s}^{-2}$) and ρ is the density of water. Take the density of sea-water as a constant $1.00 \times 10^3\ \text{kg m}^{-3}$ throughout the oceans.[1] The pressure is

$$P = 414\ \text{atm} \times \left(\frac{1.01325 \times 10^5\ \text{Pa}}{1\ \text{atm}}\right) = 4.19 \times 10^7\ \text{Pa}$$

The depth of water that exerts this pressure is

$$h = \frac{P}{\rho g} = \frac{4.19 \times 10^7\ \text{kg m}^{-1}\text{s}^{-2}}{(1.0 \times 10^3\ \text{kg m}^{-3})\ 9.807\ \text{m s}^{-2}} = 4.3 \times 10^3\ \text{m}$$

Text Table B.2[2] confirms that a pascal equals a $\text{kg m}^{-1}\text{s}^{-2}$. One meter equals 3.28 feet; a depth of 4300 m equals $\boxed{14\,000}$ feet.

4.9 The pascal (Pa) is a newton per square meter (N m^{-2}). One standard atmosphere is defined as 1.01325×10^5 Pa. Convert using unit factors as follows:

$$P = 172.00\ \text{MPa} \times \left(\frac{10^6\ \text{Pa}}{\text{MPa}}\right) \times \left(\frac{1\ \text{atm}}{1.01325 \times 10^5\ \text{Pa}}\right) = \boxed{1.6975 \times 10^3\ \text{atm}}$$

Convert the pressure from pascals to bars by multiplying by the proper unit factor:

$$P = (1.7200 \times 10^8\ \text{Pa}) \times \left(\frac{1\ \text{bar}}{10^5\ \text{Pa}}\right) = \boxed{1.7200 \times 10^3\ \text{bar}}$$

All of the unit factors in the preceding conversions come from definitions and therefore have an unlimited number of significant digits.

4.11 Assume that the N_2 in the tank behaves ideally. Since neither the temperature nor the amount of the N_2 changes during the expansion, use Boyle's law in the form $P_1V_1 = P_2V_2$. The initial pressure P_1 is 3.00 atm, the initial volume V_1 is 2.00 L, P_2 is the final pressure (this is the desired answer), and V_2 is the final volume. If the volumes of the valve and associated plumbing are negligibly small, $V_2 = 2.00 + 5.00 = 7.00$ L. Then:

$$P_2 = \frac{P_1V_1}{V_2} = (3.00\ \text{atm})\left(\frac{2.00\ \text{L}}{7.00\ \text{L}}\right) = \boxed{0.857\ \text{atm}}$$

4.13 Apply Charles's law in the form $V_1T_2 = V_2T_1$. The V_1 is given (4.00 L), and the absolute temperature is doubled, that is, $T_2 = 2T_1$. Accordingly, $V_2 = \boxed{8.00\ \text{L}}$.

4.15 Use Charles's Law. In this problem, $V_1 = 17.4$ gill and V_2 is required. The temperatures are given on the Fahrenheit scale and must be converted to an absolute scale for use with Charles's law. The following shows these as unit conversions:

$$T_1 = (100°\text{F} - 32°\text{F})\left(\frac{5°\text{C}}{9°\text{F}}\right)\left(\frac{1\ \text{K}}{1°\text{C}}\right) + 273.15\ \text{K} = 310.9\ \text{K}$$

$$T_2 = (0°\text{F} - 32°\text{F})\left(\frac{5°\text{C}}{9°\text{F}}\right)\left(\frac{1\ \text{K}}{1°\text{C}}\right) + 273.15\ \text{K} = 255.4\ \text{K}$$

Insert these T's into the equation for Charles's law:

$$V_2 = \left(\frac{T_2}{T_1}\right) V_1 = \left(\frac{255.4\ \text{K}}{310.9\ \text{K}}\right) 17.4\ \text{gill} = \boxed{14.3\ \text{gill}}$$

---

[1] The density of the deep sea is however somewhat affected by dissolved salts and the compression of overlying layers.

[2] Text page A.10.

Tip. Do not worry about converting gills to more familiar units.

4.17 The complete reaction of a set mass of CaC_2 produces a set mass of $C_2H_2(g)$ regardless of T and P. Since the pressure is the same (1 atm) in both cases, this is a Charles's law problem with $V_1 = 64.5$ L, $t_1 = 50°$C, $t_2 = 400°$C, and V_2 unknown. Convert the temperatures to kelvins. Then:

$$V_2 = \left(\frac{T_2}{T_1}\right) V_1 = \left(\frac{(400 + 273.15)\text{ K}}{(50 + 273.15)\text{ K}}\right) 64.5\text{ L} = \boxed{134\text{ L}}$$

4.19 The true pressure inside the bicycle tire is 14.7 psi (1 atm) more than the gauge pressure since the gauge reads zero when the pressure is 1 atm.[3] P is 30.0 + 14.7 = 44.7 psi. Assuming that the air in the tire behaves ideally:

$$\frac{P_1 V_1}{n_1 T_1} = \frac{P_2 V_2}{n_2 T_2}$$

where the subscripts refer to the variables before and after warming from 0°C to 32°C. Because the tire does not expand, V_1 equals V_2. Also, heating does not change the quantity of air inside the tire, so n_1 equals n_2. Converting the temperatures to the Kelvin scale gives $T_1 = 273$ K and $T_2 = 305$ K, and $P_1 = 44.7$ psi, as just established. Canceling the V's and n's, rearranging and substituting gives:

$$P_2 = \left(P_1 \frac{T_2}{T_1}\right) = P_1 \left(\frac{305\text{ K}}{273\text{ K}}\right) = 44.7\text{ psi}\left(\frac{305}{273}\right) = 49.9\text{ psi}$$

Gauge pressure is always 1 atm (14.7 psi) less than the actual pressure. The gauge pressure of the tire at 32°C is thus $49.9 - 14.7 = \boxed{35.2\text{ psi}}$.

Tip. The conversion to absolute temperature was necessary. Using temperatures in degrees Celsius leads to division by zero in this problem.

4.21 a) Let state 1 be the original state of the air, and let state 2 be the state of the air after the compression. Assume that the ideal-gas law applies. Neither the chemical amount of air nor its temperature changes between state 1 and state 2. Hence Boyle's law applies:

$$P_2 = \frac{P_1 V_1}{V_2} = \frac{(1.01\text{ atm})(20.6\text{ L})}{1.05\text{ L}} = \boxed{19.8\text{ atm}}$$

b) Let state 3 be the state of the bottled air in the European laboratory. The pressure in the bottle is bigger because T_3 (294 K) exceeds T_2 (253 K). Note the conversion of the temperatures to an absolute scale. Solve the ideal-gas equation for n/V and write it for states 2 and 3:

$$\frac{P_2}{RT_2} = \frac{n_2}{V_2} \quad \text{and} \quad \frac{P_3}{RT_3} = \frac{n_3}{V_3}$$

Neither the volume of the bottle nor the chemical amount of the air it contains changes during the trip to Europe. This means

$$\frac{n_2}{V_2} = \frac{n_3}{V_3} \quad \text{from which} \quad \frac{P_2}{T_2} = \frac{P_3}{T_3}$$

Solve this last equation for P_3, and substitute the known values of the other quantities:

$$P_3 = P_2\left(\frac{T_3}{T_2}\right) = (19.8\text{ atm})\left(\frac{294\text{ K}}{253\text{ K}}\right) = \boxed{23.0\text{ atm}}$$

---

[3] A flat tire still has 1 atm of air pressure inside it.

4.23 The information about the density of the gas is nearly worthless because gas densities depend strongly on P and T, but neither is specified. One might assume room P and T; but other assumptions are also plausible.
Using the fact that $n = m/\mathcal{M}$, the ideal-gas equation can be rewritten as:

$$PV = \frac{m}{\mathcal{M}}RT \quad \text{which gives} \quad \frac{m}{V} = \frac{P\mathcal{M}}{RT} \quad \text{which becomes} \quad \rho = \frac{P\mathcal{M}}{RT}$$

because the density ρ equals mass divided by volume. Solve the last equation for T and insert the stated density and the molar mass of the H_2Te, which are 6.234 g L^{-1} and 129.615 g mol^{-1} respectively:

$$T = \frac{P\mathcal{M}}{R\rho} = \frac{(1.00 \text{ atm})(129.615 \text{ g mol}^{-1})}{(0.08206 \text{ L atm mol}^{-1}\text{K}^{-1})(6.234 \text{ g L}^{-1})} = 253.4 \text{ K} = \boxed{-19.8°\text{C}}$$

4.25 a) The other product of the reaction is sodium chloride:

$$\boxed{2\,\text{Na}(s) + 2\,\text{HCl}(g) \rightarrow \text{H}_2(g) + 2\,\text{NaCl}(s)}$$

b) First, calculate the chemical amount of $H_2(g)$ produced by the complete reaction of 6.24 g of Na(s):

$$n_{\text{H}_2} = 6.24 \text{ g Na} \times \left(\frac{1 \text{ mol Na}}{22.99 \text{ g Na}}\right) \times \left(\frac{1 \text{ mol H}_2}{2 \text{ mol Na}}\right) = 0.1357 \text{ mol H}_2$$

Next, convert the temperature into kelvins (323 K), rearrange the ideal-gas equation to give V explicitly, and substitute the known values:

$$V_{\text{H}_2} = \frac{n_{\text{H}_2}RT}{P} = \frac{(0.1357 \text{ mol})(0.08206 \text{ L atm mol}^{-1}\text{K}^{-1})(323 \text{ K})}{0.850 \text{ atm}} = \boxed{4.23 \text{ L}}$$

4.27 Calculate the chemical amount of NaCl being reacted:

$$2.5 \times 10^6 \text{ g NaCl} \times \left(\frac{1 \text{ mol NaCl}}{58.44 \text{ g NaCl}}\right) = 4.28 \times 10^4 \text{ mol NaCl}$$

According to the balanced equation, 1 mol of HCl forms per 1 mol of NaCl consumed. Therefore, 4.28×10^4 mol NaCl in theory produces 4.28×10^4 mol HCl. Use the ideal-gas equation to compute the volume of this amount of gaseous HCl under the specified conditions. Note the conversion of the temperature from Celsius to absolute:

$$V_{\text{HCl}} = \frac{n_{\text{HCl}}RT}{P} = \frac{(4.28 \times 10^4 \text{ mol})(0.08206 \text{ L atm mol}^{-1}\text{K}^{-1})(823 \text{ K})}{0.970 \text{ atm}} = \boxed{3.0 \times 10^6 \text{ L}}$$

4.29 According to the balanced chemical equation, a 3-to-2 molar ratio exists between the O_2 formed and $KClO_3$ consumed. This fact furnishes a crucial unit factor in the following series:

$$n_{\text{O}_2} = 87.6 \text{ g KClO}_3 \times \left(\frac{1 \text{ mol KClO}_3}{122.54 \text{ g KClO}_3}\right) \times \left(\frac{3 \text{ mol O}_2}{2 \text{ mol KClO}_3}\right) = 1.072 \text{ mol O}_2$$

Now, use the ideal-gas equation to compute the volume, not forgetting to convert the temperature from Celsius to absolute:

$$V_{\text{O}_2} = \frac{n_{\text{O}_2}RT}{P} = \frac{(1.072 \text{ mol})(0.08206 \text{ L atm mol}^{-1}\text{K}^{-1})(13.2 + 273.15 \text{ K})}{1.04 \text{ atm}} = \boxed{24.2 \text{ L}}$$

4.31 a) The problem is similar to text Example 4.5[4] and to **4.25**. Calculate the theoretical amount of H_2S needed in this reaction to give 2.00 kg of S:

$$n_{H_2S} = (2.00 \times 10^3 \text{ g S}) \times \left(\frac{1 \text{ mol S}}{32.065 \text{ g S}}\right) \times \left(\frac{2 \text{ mol } H_2S}{3 \text{ mol S}}\right) = 41.58 \text{ mol } H_2S$$

Use the ideal-gas equation to compute the volume the gaseous H_2S occupies under the stated conditions:

$$V_{H_2S} = \frac{n_{H_2S}RT}{P} = \frac{(41.58 \text{ mol})(0.08206 \text{ L atm mol}^{-1}\text{K}^{-1})(273.15 \text{ K})}{1.00 \text{ atm}} = \boxed{932 \text{ L}}$$

Note the conversion of the temperature into kelvins. The final answer has three significant figures because the mass of sulfur was given to only three significant figures.
b) Copy the approach that worked in the preceding part:

$$n_{SO_2} = (2.00 \times 10^3 \text{ g S}) \times \left(\frac{1 \text{ mol S}}{32.066 \text{ g S}}\right) \times \left(\frac{1 \text{ mol } SO_2}{3 \text{ mol S}}\right) = 20.79 \text{ mol } SO_2$$

The mass of this chemical amount of sulfur dioxide is

$$m_{SO_2} = 20.79 \text{ mol } SO_2 \times \left(\frac{64.06 \text{ g } SO_2}{1 \text{ mol } SO_2}\right) = \boxed{1.33 \times 10^3 \text{ g } SO_2}$$

Obtain the volume occupied by the SO_2 by substituting n_{SO_2}, P, and T into the ideal-gas equation:

$$V_{SO_2} = \frac{n_{SO_2}RT}{P} = \frac{(20.79 \text{ mol})(0.08206 \text{ L atm mol}^{-1}\text{K}^{-1})(273.15 \text{ K})}{1.00 \text{ atm}} = \boxed{466 \text{ L}}$$

Another way to get V_{SO_2} is to use Avogadro's principle,[5] which requires that V_{SO_2} equal half of V_{H_2S}.

4.33 Apply the definition of mole fraction to the SO_3:

$$X_{SO_3} = \frac{n_{SO_3}}{n_{tot}} = \frac{17.0 \text{ mol}}{26.0 \text{ mol} + 83.0 \text{ mol} + 17.0 \text{ mol}} = \frac{17.0 \text{ mol}}{126.0 \text{ mol}} = \boxed{0.135}$$

The partial pressure of the SO_3 equals its mole fraction times the total pressure:

$$P_{SO_3} = X_{SO_3}P_{tot} = (0.135)(0.950 \text{ atm}) = \boxed{0.128 \text{ atm}}$$

4.35 Ideal gases under a given set of conditions take up volume in direct proportion to the number of molecules that comprise them. Hence the mole percentage (or fraction) of N_2 in Martian air equals its volume percentage (or fraction): $X_{N_2} = \boxed{0.027}$. The partial pressure of N_2 equals the total pressure multiplied by the mole fraction of N_2:

$$P_{N_2} = X_{N_2}P_{tot} = (0.027)(5.92 \times 10^{-3} \text{ atm}) = \boxed{1.6 \times 10^{-4} \text{ atm}}$$

4.37 a) The mole fraction of CO in the mixture equals:

$$X_{CO} = \frac{n_{CO}}{n_{tot}} = \frac{10.0 \text{ mol}}{10.0 \text{ mol} + 12.5 \text{ mol}} = \frac{10.0 \text{ mol}}{22.5 \text{ mol}} = \boxed{0.444}$$

b) The balanced chemical equation shows that formation of 3.0 mol of CO_2 requires consumption of 3.0 moles of CO. Therefore, the chemical amount of CO in the mixture at this point in the reaction is 7.0 mol.

---

[4] Text page 107.
[5] Text page 14.

The chemical amount of O_2 at this point equals 12.5 mol − (3.0 mol/2) = 11.0 mol where the factor 2 arises from the 2-to-1 stoichiometry between the CO_2 and O_2. The mixture of gases consists of 7.0 mol of CO, 11.0 mol of O_2, and 3.0 mol of CO_2. The mole fraction of CO is therefore:

$$X_{CO} = \frac{n_{CO}}{n_{tot}} = \frac{7.0 \text{ mol}}{7.0 \text{ mol} + 11.0 \text{ mol} + 3.0 \text{ mol}} = \frac{7.0 \text{ mol}}{21.0 \text{ mol}} = \boxed{0.33}$$

4.39 a) Treat the saturated air as a mixture of ideal gases that contribute to the total pressure according to Dalton's law. The volume of the mixture is 1.0 cm^3, its temperature is (20 + 273.15) K, and the partial pressure of water vapor equals 0.0230 atm. Solve the ideal-gas equation for n and applying it to the water vapor:

$$n_{H_2O} = \frac{P_{H_2O}V}{RT} = \frac{(0.0230 \text{ atm})(1.0 \text{ cm}^3)}{(82.057 \text{ cm}^3 \text{ atm K}^{-1}\text{mol}^{-1})(20 + 273.15) \text{ K}} = 9.56 \times 10^{-7} \text{ mol}$$

A mole of H_2O contains N_0 molecules. Consequently, the 1.00 cm^3 of saturated air contains:

$$\frac{9.56 \times 10^{-7} \text{ mol H}_2\text{O}}{1.0 \text{ cm}^3 \text{ air}} \times \left(\frac{6.022 \times 10^{23} \text{ molecules}}{1 \text{ mol}}\right) = \boxed{\frac{5.8 \times 10^{17} \text{ molecules H}_2\text{O}}{1.00 \text{ cm}^3 \text{ air}}}$$

b) 1.00 cm^3 of air holds only about 10^{-6} mol of water. Hence it requires more than 1.00 cm^3 to hold 0.500 mol of water. Use unit factors as follows:

$$0.500 \text{ mol H}_2\text{O} \times \left(\frac{1.00 \text{ cm}^3 \text{ sat. air}}{9.56 \times 10^{-7} \text{ mol H}_2\text{O}}\right) \times \left(\frac{1 \text{ L}}{1000 \text{ cm}^3}\right) = \boxed{520 \text{ L sat. air}}$$

4.41 a) The root-mean-square speed of the molecules in a gas is given by:

$$u_{rms} = \sqrt{\frac{3k_BT}{m}} = \sqrt{\frac{3RT}{\mathcal{M}}}$$

where k_B is the Boltzmann constant, T is the absolute temperature, m is the molecular mass, R is the gas constant, and $\mathcal{M}$ is the molar mass of the gas. For H_2 at 300 K

$$u_{rms} = \sqrt{\frac{3RT}{\mathcal{M}}} = \sqrt{\frac{3(8.3145 \text{ J K}^{-1}\text{mol}^{-1})(300 \text{ K})}{0.002016 \text{ kg mol}^{-1}}} = \boxed{1.93 \times 10^3 \text{ m s}^{-1}}$$

b) For sulfur hexafluoride SF_6 at 300 K:

$$u_{rms} = \sqrt{\frac{3RT}{\mathcal{M}}} = \sqrt{\frac{3(8.3145 \text{ J K}^{-1}\text{mol}^{-1})(300 \text{ K})}{0.14607 \text{ kg mol}^{-1}}} = \boxed{226 \text{ m s}^{-1}}$$

The heavier SF_6 molecules have a root-mean-square speed about 8.5 times slower than the lighter H_2 molecule at the same temperature. The ratio of the speeds equals the square root of the reciprocal of the ratio of the molar masses.

Tip. The analysis of the units is worth separate study:

$$\sqrt{\frac{\text{J K}^{-1}\text{mol}^{-1} \text{ K}}{\text{kg mol}^{-1}}} = \sqrt{\frac{\text{kg m}^2 \text{ s}^{-2} \text{ K}^{-1} \text{ mol}^{-1} \text{ K}}{\text{kg mol}^{-1}}} = \sqrt{\text{m}^2 \text{ s}^{-2}} = \text{m s}^{-1}$$

4.43 The rms speed of helium atoms at the surface of the sun (6000 K) is

$$u_{\rm rms} = \sqrt{\frac{3RT}{\mathcal{M}}} = \sqrt{\frac{3(8.31r5\ \text{J K}^{-1}\text{mol}^{-1})(6000\ \text{K})}{0.004003\ \text{kg mol}^{-1}}} = \boxed{6100\ \text{m s}^{-1}}$$

In an interstellar cloud at 100 K:

$$u_{\rm rms} = \sqrt{\frac{3RT}{\mathcal{M}}} = \sqrt{\frac{3(8.3145\ \text{J K}^{-1}\text{mol}^{-1})(100\ \text{K})}{0.004003\ \text{kg mol}^{-1}}} = \boxed{790\ \text{m s}^{-1}}$$

"Comparison" may mean to take the ratio of the two rms speeds rather than to calculate the actual speeds. Getting the ratio is simpler that the previous calculation because $3R$ and $\mathcal{M}$ cancel out:

$$\frac{u_{\rm rms}\ \text{(near sun)}}{u_{\rm rms}\ \text{(interstellar)}} = \sqrt{\frac{6000\ \text{K}}{100\ \text{K}}} = 7.7$$

The rms speed of the molecules of a gas goes up by a factor of only about eight between 100 K and 6000 K.

4.45 The molecular speeds in ClO_2 follow the Maxwell-Boltzmann distribution because the gas is at thermal equilibrium. If 35.0% of the molecules have speeds exceeding 400 m s^{-1}, then obviously 65.0% have speeds between 0 and 400 m s^{-1}. Since over half of the molecules have speeds less than 400 m s^{-1}, that speed lies well on the high side of the hump in the Maxwell-Boltzmann distribution.[6] An increase in temperature shifts the hump toward higher speeds and also flattens it out. Because the temperature increase is slight, the first effect predominates. The percentage of molecules having speeds in excess of 400 m s^{-1} will $\boxed{\text{increase}}$.
Tip. This answer can be confirmed numerically, but not very easily. The area under this Maxwell-Boltzmann curve from $u = 0$ to $u = 400$ m s^{-1} equals 0.65 of the total area under the curve. Integrate the Maxwell-Boltzmann function from $u = 0$ to $u = 400$, set the integral equal to 0.65, and determine the T that makes the integral equal to 0.65. The answer is 397 K. If the temperature is raised slightly, the area under the curve between 0 and 400 m s^{-1} changes as the hump in the distribution shifts to the right. Suppose the slightly higher new temperature is 407 K. The integral of the $T = 407$ Boltzmann-Maxwell function from 0 to 400 m s^{-1} is only 0.64. Hence, the percentage of molecules having speeds exceeding 400 m s^{-1} rises from 35% to about 36% when ClO_2 is heated from 397 to 407 K.

4.47 Compute the chemical amount of air that leaked into the 500 cm^3 bulb during the one-hour period immediately after it is sealed by inserting the pressure observed at the one-hour time and the known volume and temperature into the ideal-gas equation:

$$n_{\rm air} = \frac{PV}{RT} = \frac{(1.00 \times 10^{-7}\ \text{atm})(0.500\ \text{L})}{(0.082057\ \text{L atm mol}^{-1}\text{K}^{-1})(300\ \text{K})} = 2.03 \times 10^{-9}\ \text{mol}$$

The rate of the leak was:

$$\frac{2.03 \times 10^{-9}\ \text{mol}}{1\ \text{h}} \times \left(\frac{6.022 \times 10^{23}\ \text{molecule}}{\text{mol}}\right) \times \left(\frac{1\ \text{h}}{3600\ \text{s}}\right) = \frac{3.4 \times 10^{11}\ \text{molecule}}{\text{s}}$$

Outside air entered the vessel when its molecules "collided" with the area of the tiny hole. Therefore, work with the formula for the rate of wall collisions by a gas.[7] The rate at which molecules exit the bulb through the hole is surely negligible, so the observed rate of the leak equals Z_w in this formula. Compute the density of the outside air using the ideal-gas equation and its known temperature and pressure:

$$\left(\frac{n}{V}\right)_{\rm air} = \left(\frac{P}{RT}\right)_{\rm air} = \left(\frac{1.00\ \text{atm}}{(0.082057\ \text{L atm mol}^{-1}\text{K}^{-1})(300\ \text{K})}\right) = 4.062 \times 10^{-2}\ \text{mol L}^{-1}$$

[6] See graph on text page 114.
[7] Equation 4-13, text page 113.

Multiplying this result by N_0 converts it to a number density:

$$\frac{4.062\times10^{-2}\text{ mol}}{1\text{ L}}\times\left(\frac{6.022\times10^{23}\text{ molec.}}{\text{mol}}\right)\times\left(\frac{1000\text{ L}}{1\text{ m}^3}\right)=2.46\times10^{25}\text{ molecule m}^{-3}$$

Solve text equation 4-13 for A, the area of the wall:

$$A=4\frac{1}{N/V}\sqrt{\frac{\pi\mathcal{M}}{8RT}}Z_w$$

Insert numbers for the several quantities on the right, taking care with units:

$$A=4\left(\frac{1}{2.46\times10^{25}\text{ m}^{-3}}\right)\sqrt{\frac{3.1416(0.0288\text{ kg mol}^{-1})}{8(8.3145\text{ J K}^{-1}\text{mol}^{-1})(300\text{ K})}}(3.4\times10^{11}\text{ s}^{-1})=1.18\times10^{-16}\text{ m}^2$$

Because the hole is circular, its radius is

$$r=\sqrt{\frac{A}{\pi}}=\sqrt{\frac{1.18\times10^{-16}\text{ m}^2}{3.1416}}=\boxed{6.1\times10^{-9}\text{ m}}$$

4.49 The ratio of the rates of effusion of two gases is given by Graham's Law:[8]

$$\frac{\text{rate of effusion of A}}{\text{rate of effusion of B}}=\frac{N_\text{A}/V}{N_\text{B}/V}\sqrt{\frac{\mathcal{M}_\text{B}}{\mathcal{M}_\text{A}}}$$

Let the methane be A and the unknown be B. The ratio of N_A/V to N_B/V equals 1 because the gases in the two effusion experiments are held under identical conditions in the same container, and Avogadro's principle therefore applies. Insert the molar mass of methane and the observed rates of effusion of methane (gas A) and the unknown (gas B):

$$\frac{1.30\times10^{-8}\text{ mol s}^{-1}}{5.41\times10^{-9}\text{ mol s}^{-1}}=\sqrt{\frac{\mathcal{M}_\text{B}}{16.04\text{ g mol}^{-1}}}\qquad\text{from which}\qquad\mathcal{M}_\text{B}=\boxed{92.6\text{ g mol}^{-1}}$$

4.51 One pass of a mixture of $^{235}UF_6$ and $^{238}UF_6$ through a diffusion apparatus enriches the product mixture by a factor of $\sqrt{352.038/349.028}$ or 1.0043 in the lighter gas, $^{235}UF_6$. This is computed in text Examples 4-9 and 4-10.[9] This problem calls for enrichment from 0.72 percent $^{235}UF_6$ to 95 percent $^{235}UF_6$. It is understood that these percentages are number percentages, not mass percentages. Let (n_{235}/n_{238}) equal the ratio of the number of molecules of the lighter gas $^{235}UF_6$ to the number of molecules of the heavier gas $^{238}UF_6$ after any number of diffusion passes. Then:

$$\left(\frac{n_{235}}{n_{238}}\right)_\text{before}=\frac{0.72}{99.27}=0.0007253\qquad\left(\frac{n_{235}}{n_{238}}\right)_\text{after}=\frac{95}{5}=19$$

Each pass multiplies the light-heavy ratio from the previous pass by 1.0043. Let x equal the number of passes. Then:

$$(0.007253)(1.0043)^x=19$$

Dividing through by 0.007253 and taking the logarithm of both sides[10] gives:

$$x\log(1.0043)=\log\left(\frac{19}{0.007253}\right)\qquad\text{from which}\quad x=\boxed{1830}$$

---

[8] Equation 4.14, text page 116.
[9] Text page 114-115.
[10] See text Appendix C.

4.53 The key is to recognize that the pressure of the krypton is directly proportional to its number density. This follows from the ideal gas law:

$$P = \left(\frac{n}{V}\right) RT \qquad \text{from which} \qquad P = \frac{1}{N_0}\left(\frac{N}{V}\right) RT$$

because N, the number of molecules, divided by N_0, Avogadro's number, equals the number of moles of any substance. The mean free path (λ) of the molecules is

$$\lambda = \frac{1}{\sqrt{2}\pi d^2 (N/V)} \qquad \text{from which} \qquad \frac{N}{V} = \frac{1}{\sqrt{2}\pi d^2 \lambda}$$

where d is the molecular diameter. Substituting this equation into the preceding gives:

$$P = \frac{1}{N_0}\left(\frac{1}{\sqrt{2}\pi d^2 \lambda}\right) RT$$

Next, obtain the diameter of the spherical vessel. The volume equals 1.00 L (1.00×10^{-3} m^3). For a sphere, $V = (4/3)\pi r^3$. Solving for r gives the radius as 0.0620 m. Its diameter is therefore 0.124 m.

Set λ equal to 0.124 m, because the mean free path must be comparable to the diameter of the vessel. From the statement of the problem, T is 300 K and d is 3.16×10^{-10} m. The gas constant equals 8.206×10^{-5} m^3 atm mol^{-1}K^{-1} (note the carefully chosen units of R). Substitution gives:

$$P = \frac{1}{6.022 \times 10^{23}\ \text{mol}^{-1}}\left(\frac{1}{\sqrt{2}\pi(3.16 \times 10^{-10}\ \text{m})^2(0.124\ \text{m})}\right) \times (8.206 \times 10^{-5}\ \text{m}^3\,\text{atm mol}^{-1}\ \text{K}^{-1})(300\ \text{K})$$

$$= \boxed{7.4 \times 10^{-7}\ \text{atm}}$$

The number density (N/V) of the krypton is needed to calculate the diffusion constant. At this P and T, the ordinary density of krypton is

$$\rho_{\text{Kr}} = \frac{n}{V} = \frac{P}{RT} = \frac{7.4 \times 10^{-7}\ \text{atm}}{(0.08206\ \text{L atm mol}^{-1}\text{K}^{-1})(300\ \text{K})} = 3.00 \times 10^{-8}\ \text{mol L}^{-1}$$

Convert this to a number density:

$$\frac{3.00 \times 10^{-8}\ \text{mol}}{\text{L}} \times \left(\frac{6.022 \times 10^{23}\ \text{molecule}}{\text{mol}}\right) \times \left(\frac{1000\ \text{L}}{1\ \text{m}^3}\right) = \frac{1.81 \times 10^{19}\ \text{molecule}}{\text{m}^3}$$

Substitute into the formula for the diffusion constant of a gas:

$$D = \frac{3}{8}\sqrt{\frac{RT}{\pi\mathcal{M}}}\left(\frac{1}{d^2 N/V}\right)$$

$$= \frac{3}{8}\sqrt{\frac{8.3145\ \text{J K}^{-1}\text{mol}^{-1}(300\ \text{K})}{\pi(0.08380\ \text{kg mol}^{-1})}}\left(\frac{1}{(3.16 \times 10^{-10}\ \text{m})^2(1.81 \times 10^{19}\ \text{m}^{-3})}\right) = \boxed{20\ \text{m}^2\ \text{s}^{-1}}$$

Tip. Check the units separately:

$$\sqrt{\frac{\text{J K}^{-1}\text{mol}^{-1}\ \text{K}}{\text{kg mol}^{-1}}}\left(\frac{1}{\text{m}^2\ \text{m}^{-3}}\right) = \sqrt{\frac{\text{kg m}^2\ \text{s}^{-2}\ \text{K}^{-1}\ \text{mol}^{-1}\ \text{K}}{\text{kg mol}^{-1}}}\left(\frac{1}{\text{m}^{-1}}\right) = \text{m}^2\ \text{s}^{-1}$$

4.55 The problem is to use the van der Waals equation to estimate the pressure of 6.80 kg of gaseous oxygen in a 28.0 L container at 20°C. First, solve the van der Waals equation for P. Then substitute for n, V, P a and b and complete the arithmetic. The values $a = 1.360$ atm L^{2}mol^{-2} and $b = 0.031834$ L mol^{-1} come from text Table 4.3.[11] The chemical amount of O_2 equals 212.5 mol, which is its mass divided by its molar mass. The details of the substitution follow:

$$\begin{aligned} P &= \frac{nRT}{V - nb} - a\frac{n^2}{V^2} \\ &= \frac{(212.5 \text{ mol})(0.08206 \text{ L atm mol}^{-1}\text{K}^{-1})(273.15 + 20 \text{ K})}{28.0 \text{ L} - (212.5 \text{ mol})(0.031834 \text{ L mol}^{-1})} - a\frac{n^2}{V^2} \\ &= 240.6 \text{ atm} - (1.360 \text{ atm L}^2\text{mol}^{-2})\frac{(212.5)^2 \text{ mol}^2}{(28.0)^2 \text{ L}^2} \\ &= 240.6 \text{ atm} - 78.33 \text{ atm} = \boxed{162 \text{ atm}} \end{aligned}$$

This pressure is equivalent to $\boxed{2380 \text{ psi}}$, since 14.696 psi equals 1 atm.

4.57 The problem provides a comparison between the ideal-gas pressure and the van der Waals pressure of a typical gas under ordinary conditions. The data for this sample of CO_2 are:

$$n = 50.0 \text{ g}/44.0 \text{ g mol}^{-1} = 1.136 \text{ mol} \qquad \text{T} = 298.15 \text{ K} \qquad \text{V} = 1.00 \text{ L}$$

a) Solve the ideal-gas equation for P and substitute:

$$P = \frac{(1.136 \text{ mol})(0.08206 \text{ L atm mol}^{-1}\text{K}^{-1})(298.15 \text{ K})}{1.00 \text{ L}} = \boxed{27.8 \text{ atm}}$$

b) The van der Waals equation includes terms (a and b) that depend on the identity of the gas. For CO_2, a is 3.592 atm L^{2}mol^{-2} and b is 0.04267 L mol^{-1}. Solving the van der Waals equation for P and substitution give:

$$\begin{aligned} P &= \frac{nRT}{V - nb} - a\frac{n^2}{V^2} \\ &= \frac{(1.136 \text{ mol})(0.08206 \text{ L atm mol}^{-1}\text{K}^{-1})(298.15 \text{ K})}{1.00 \text{ L} - (1.136 \text{ mol})(0.04267 \text{ L mol}^{-1})} - a\frac{n^2}{V^2} \\ &= 29.2 \text{ atm} - (3.592 \text{ atm L}^2\text{mol}^{-2})\frac{(1.136)^2 \text{ mol}^2}{(1.00)^2 \text{ L}^2} \\ &= 29.2 \text{ atm} - 4.64 \text{ atm} = \boxed{24.6 \text{ atm}} \end{aligned}$$

Thus the van der Waals P is less than the ideal-gas P. The effect of the b term in the van der Waals equation was to increase P from 27.8 to 29.2 atm; the effect of a was to decrease P by 4.64 atm. The a term in this case is larger than the b term. That is, $\boxed{\text{attractive forces dominate}}$.

Tip. The corrections oppose each other. Consequently the ideal-gas equation gives fair approximations for P over a larger range of conditions that it would otherwise.

4.59 The solid earth is surrounded by an ocean of air that exerts an average pressure of 730 mm Hg all over its surface. Imagine the air replaced by an ocean of liquid mercury. To exert an equal pressure the mercury would need to be only 730 mm deep. The volume of the mercury would equal, to a close approximation, the surface area of the earth times its depth d. Insert $r = 6.370 \times 10^6$ m (converted from km) and $d = 730 \times 10^{-3}$ m into the formula for this area:

$$V_{\text{Hg}} = 4\pi r^2 d = 4(3.14159)(6.370 \times 10^6 \text{ m})^2(730 \times 10^{-3} \text{ m}) = 3.72 \times 10^{14} \text{ m}^3$$

[11] Text page 120.

Compute the mass of the ocean of mercury by multiplying its volume by its density, which is the density of mercury at ordinary temperatures:

$$m_{\rm Hg} = 3.72 \times 10^{14}\ \text{m}^3 \times \left(\frac{10^6\ \text{cm}^3}{1\ \text{m}^3}\right) \times \left(\frac{13.6\ \text{g}}{\text{cm}^3}\right) \times \left(\frac{1\ \text{kg}}{1000\ \text{g}}\right) = \boxed{5.06 \times 10^{18}\ \text{kg}}$$

This mass equals the mass of the atmosphere because the atmosphere exerts the same pressure at the surface of the earth as the hypothetical ocean of mercury.

4.61 From the equation $P = \rho g h$ the height h of the column of liquid in a barometer is inversely proportional at a given pressure P to the density of the liquid that is in it. Hence, the height that the column of Hg would have at 0.0°C is

$$h_{0.0^\circ\text{C}} = h_{35^\circ\text{C}} \times \left(\frac{13.5094\ \text{g cm}^{-3}}{13.5955\ \text{g cm}^{-3}}\right) = 760.0\ \text{mm} \times 0.993667 = 755.19\ \text{mm}$$

This height in a mercury barometer at 0.0°C means a pressure of 755.19 torr, which equals $\boxed{0.9937\ \text{atm}}$.
Tip. Substitution into the formula $P = \rho g h$ gives the same answer.

4.63 Reasoning by analogy to the textbook statements of Charles's law and Boyle's law, we conclude that Amontons's law must state that at constant volume, the pressure of a sample of a gas is directly proportional to its absolute temperature.

4.65 a) 1005 mol of helium displaces 1005 mol of air since the pressure and temperature of the gases inside and outside of the balloon are the same.[12] The masses of these gases are:

$$m_{\rm He} = 1005\ \text{mol He} \times \left(\frac{4.003\ \text{g He}}{1\ \text{mol He}}\right) = 4.023 \times 10^3\ \text{g He}$$

$$m_{\rm air} = 1005\ \text{mol air} \times \left(\frac{29.0\ \text{g air}}{1\ \text{mol air}}\right) = 2.91 \times 10^4\ \text{g air}$$

The answer is the difference between these two masses, which equals $\boxed{2.51 \times 10^4\ \text{g}}$.
b) The balloon still contains 1005 mol of He after the ascent, and the T and P inside the balloon still equal the T and P outside of it. Therefore the balloon, which has increased greatly in volume, still displaces 1005 mol of air. Therefore, the answer is again $\boxed{2.51 \times 10^4\ \text{g}}$.

4.67 One way to solve this problem is to think in terms of proportions. The ideal-gas law states that a given volume contains moles of gas in *inverse* proportion to their absolute temperature, as long as the pressure is constant. This means the higher the temperature, the lower the amount of gas. Also, the amount of products of a chemical reaction is in *direct* proportion to the amount of reactants. Raising the temperature at which HCl is collected from 323.15 to 773.15 K (from 50 to 500°C) multiplies T by 2.392. The number of moles of HCl produced in the high-temperature experiment therefore equals the number produced in the low-temperature experiment divided by this factor. Since the number of moles of HCl(g) equals the number of moles of NaCl reacted, the amount of NaCl used in the high-temperature experiment is less in the same proportion. The answer is simply 10.0 kg divided by 2.392. It equals $\boxed{4.18\ \text{kg NaCl}}$.
Another approach is to compute the "certain volume" and then find the chemical amount (number of moles) of gas it contains at both 323.15 K and 773.15 K. First, find the theoretical yield of HCl from 10.0 kg of NaCl:

$$n_{\rm HCl} = 10.0 \times 10^3\ \text{g NaCl} \times \left(\frac{1\ \text{mol NaCl}}{58.44\ \text{g NaCl}}\right) \times \left(\frac{1\ \text{mol HCl}}{1\ \text{mol NaCl}}\right) = 171.1\ \text{mol HCl}$$

[12] This follows from Avogadro's principle, text page 12.

The "certain volume" occupied by this HCl at 50°C (323.15 K) is

$$V_{\text{HCl}} = \frac{nRT}{P} = \frac{171.1\text{ mol}(0.08206\text{ L atm mol}^{-1}\text{K}^{-1})(323.15\text{ K})}{1\text{ atm}} = 4537\text{ L}$$

At 500°C (773.15 K) this volume contains fewer moles:

$$n_{500°\text{C}} = \frac{PV}{RT} = \frac{(1\text{ atm})(4537\text{ L})}{(0.08206\text{ L atm mol}^{-1}\text{K}^{-1})(773.15\text{ K})} = 71.51\text{ mol HCl}$$

Finally, compute the mass of NaCl required to produce this amount of HCl:

$$m_{\text{NaCl}} = 71.51\text{ mol HCl} \times \left(\frac{1\text{ mol NaCl}}{1\text{ mol HCl}}\right) \times \left(\frac{58.44\text{ g NaCl}}{1\text{ mol NaCl}}\right) \times \left(\frac{1\text{ kg NaCl}}{1000\text{ g NaCl}}\right) = \boxed{4.18\text{ kg NaCl}}$$

Tip. The second calculation is slower, but attractive in its concreteness. But suppose that the problem had simply stated that the pressure was the same in the two experiments (not telling what it was). None of the intermediate numbers in the second method could be computed, but the first method would work the same.

4.69 a) Balance the equations for the two reactions:

$$\text{CaCO}_3(s) \rightarrow \text{CaO}(s) + \text{CO}_2(g)$$
$$\text{CaO}(s) + \text{H}_2\text{O}(l) \rightarrow \text{Ca(OH)}_2(s)$$

Determine the chemical amount of CO_2 to produce 8.47 kg of $Ca(OH)_2$:

$$n_{\text{CO}_2} = 8.47\text{ kg Ca(OH)}_2 \times \left(\frac{1\text{ mol Ca(OH)}_2}{0.074093\text{ kg Ca(OH)}_2}\right) \times \left(\frac{1\text{ mol CO}_2}{1\text{ mol Ca(OH)}_2}\right) = 114.32\text{ mol CO}_2$$

Then, use the ideal-gas law to find the volume of the gaseous CO_2:

$$V_{\text{CO}_2} = \frac{nRT}{P} = \frac{(114.32\text{ mol})(0.08206\text{ L atm mol}^{-1}\text{K}^{-1})(1223\text{ K})}{0.976\text{ atm}} = \boxed{1.18 \times 10^4\text{ L}}$$

The final answer is rounded to three significant figures because the mass of $Ca(OH)_2$ was given to only three significant figures.

4.71 The total volume of the system is 12.00 L, the sum of the volumes of the three containers (neglecting the volume of the connecting tube). If the three gases behave ideally in their containers, their chemical amounts are:

$$n_{\text{O}_2} = \frac{2.51 \times 5.00\text{ L atm}}{RT} \qquad n_{\text{N}_2} = \frac{0.792 \times 4.00\text{ L atm}}{RT} \qquad n_{\text{Ar}} = \frac{1.23 \times 3.00\text{ L atm}}{RT}$$

The total pressure after the gases mix is also given by the ideal-gas equation, assuming Dalton's law holds. In the expression for P_{tot}, the total chemical amount of the mixed gas equals the sum of the chemical amounts of the three components:

$$\begin{aligned} P_{\text{tot}} = n_{\text{tot}}\frac{RT}{V} &= (n_{\text{O}_2} + n_{\text{N}_2} + n_{\text{Ar}})\frac{RT}{V} \\ &= \left(\frac{12.7\text{ L atm}}{RT} + \frac{3.168\text{ L atm}}{RT} + \frac{3.69\text{ L atm}}{RT}\right)\left(\frac{RT}{12.00\text{ L}}\right) = \boxed{1.63\text{ atm}} \end{aligned}$$

4.73 Assume the gases behave ideally before the catalyst is introduced and after the reaction is finished. The reaction itself is profoundly non-ideal behavior. Imagine that the temperature and volume of the system are such that the total chemical amount of gases equals 1.00 mol at the start. The reaction

$$C_2H_2(g) + 2\,H_2(g) \rightarrow C_2H_6(g)$$

then must decrease the total chemical amount of gas to 0.42 mol. This is true because chemical amount is directly proportional to pressure if T and V do not change. Let x represent the original chemical amount of $C_2H_2(g)$ and y the original chemical amount of $H_2(g)$. Before the reaction starts, there is no $C_2H_6(g)$ so:

$$x + y = 1.00 \text{ mol}$$

The reaction produces x mol of $C_2H_6(g)$ as it consumes $2x$ mol of $H_2(g)$ and x mol of $C_2H_2(g)$. Since $C_2H_2(g)$ is the limiting reagent, the reaction stops when the x mol of C_2H_2 gas is gone. At the end of the reaction, the vessel contains x mol of $C_2H_6(g)$, the product, and $(y - 2x)$ mol of left-over $H_2(g)$. Hence:

$$x + (y - 2x) = 0.42 \text{ mol}$$

Solving the two simultaneous equations gives $x = 0.029$. The original amount of $C_2H_2(g)$ is 0.29 mol; the original mole fraction of $C_2H_2(g)$ is $0.29/1.00 = \boxed{0.29}$.
Tip. Had we assumed the system to be big enough to hold, say, 100 mol of gases, all of the numbers in this computation, except the answer, would have been 100 times bigger.

4.75 a) The average kinetic energy of the atoms of deuterium, which is given in the problem, depends only on the absolute temperature (assuming ideal-gas behavior): $KE_{\text{avg}} = 3/2k_BT$. Solve for T and substitute:

$$T = \frac{2KE_{\text{avg}}}{3k_B} = \frac{2(8 \times 10^{-16} \text{ J})}{3(1.38 \times 10^{-23} \text{ J K}^{-1})} = \boxed{4 \times 10^7 \text{ K}}$$

The atomic mass of ^{2}H is not needed in this part of the problem.
b) The average kinetic energy of the particles in a gas equals $1/2m\overline{u^2}$. Write this relationship for ^{1}H and divide it by a similar relationship for ^{2}D:

$$\frac{1/2m_H\overline{u_H^2}}{1/2m_D\overline{u_D^2}} = \frac{32 \times 10^{-16} \text{ J}}{8 \times 10^{-16} \text{ J}}$$

Solve for the ratio of the rms speeds:

$$\frac{u_{\text{rms,H}}}{u_{\text{rms,D}}} = \sqrt{\frac{\overline{u_H^2}}{\overline{u_D^2}}} = \sqrt{\frac{32}{8}}\sqrt{\frac{2.015}{1.0078}} = \boxed{2.8}$$

4.77 For a Maxwell-Boltzmann speed distribution, the quantity $f(u)\Delta u$ equals the fraction of the molecules in a gas having speeds between u and $u + \Delta u$.[13] This fraction equals the desired probability and is

$$\frac{\Delta N}{N} = f(u)\Delta u = 4\pi\left(\frac{\mathcal{M}}{2\pi RT}\right)^{3/2} u^2\exp(-\mathcal{M}u^2/2RT)\Delta u$$

The gas in this case is O_2, for which $\mathcal{M} = 0.0320$ kg mol^{-1}. The temperature equals 300 K, and Δu equals 10 m s^{-1} (from 500 to 510 m s^{-1}). Evaluate $f(u)$ at $u = 500$ m s^{-1}:

$$f(u) = 4\pi\left(\frac{0.0320 \text{ kg mol}^{-1}}{2\pi(8.3145 \text{ J K}^{-1}\text{mol}^{-1})(300 \text{ K})}\right)^{3/2} \times (500 \text{ m s}^{-1})^2$$
$$\times \exp\left(\frac{-0.032 \text{ kg mol}^{-1}(500 \text{ m s}^{-1})^2}{2(8.3145 \text{ J K}^{-1}\text{mol}^{-1})(300 \text{ K})}\right) = 1.843 \times 10^{-3} \text{ s m}^{-1}$$

[13]Text page 113.

The value of $f(u)$ changes over the range of u. The hint proposes a way to deal with this change, which amounts to a 2.5 percent decrease as u rises from 500 to 510 meters per second. This decrease is shown in the following table:

u (m s^{-1})	$f(u)$ (s m^{-1})	u (m s^{-1})	$f(u)$ (s m^{-1})
500	1.843×10^{-3}	506	1.816×10^{-3}
501	1.839×10^{-3}	507	1.812×10^{-3}
502	1.834×10^{-3}	508	1.807×10^{-3}
503	1.830×10^{-3}	509	1.802×10^{-3}
504	1.825×10^{-3}	510	1.797×10^{-3}
505	1.821×10^{-3}	—	—

The desired probability $f(u)\Delta u$ equals the area under the distribution curve between 500 and 510 m s^{-1}.[14] This area has a width of 10 m s^{-1} and a smoothly changing height. Approximate it by 10 narrow columns of width 1 m s^{-1} and heights in s m^{-1} given by the first ten values of $f(u)$ in the table. The sum of these ten areas is 1.823×10^{-2} (no units). The desired probability is thus $\boxed{1.82 \text{ percent}}$.

4.79 Call the unknown gas Z. Convert the rates of effusion of the oxygen and Z from g min^{-1} to mol min^{-1} so that Graham's law can be applied. Use 32.0 g mol^{-1} as the molar mass of $O_2(g)$ and $\mathcal{M}_Z$ as the molar mass of Z. The two rates equal:

$$\text{rate}_{O_2} = \frac{3.25 \text{ g min}^{-1}}{32.0 \text{ g mol}^{-1}} = 0.1016 \text{ mol min}^{-1} \quad \text{rate}_Z = \frac{1.96 \text{ g min}^{-1}}{\mathcal{M}_Z \text{ g mol}^{-1}} = \frac{1.96}{\mathcal{M}_Z} \text{ mol min}^{-1}$$

Write Graham's law as a comparison of the two gases, as in text equation 4.14:[15]

$$\frac{\text{rate of effusion of } O_2}{\text{rate of effusion of Z}} = \frac{N_{O_2}}{N_Z}\sqrt{\frac{\mathcal{M}_Z}{\mathcal{M}_{O_2}}}$$

The numbers of molecules in the vessel are the same in the two experiments because the experiments are carried out as the same temperature and pressure. Hence N_{O_2} and N_Z cancel out of the preceding equation. Inserting the two rates gives:

$$\frac{0.1016 \text{ mol min}^{-1}}{(1.96/\mathcal{M}_Z) \text{ mol min}^{-1}} = \frac{0.1016\mathcal{M}_Z}{1.96} = \sqrt{\frac{\mathcal{M}_Z}{32.0 \text{ g mol}^{-1}}}$$

Solution of the last equation gives $\mathcal{M}_Z$ equal to $\boxed{11.6 \text{ g mol}^{-1}}$.

Tip. It is not necessary to know T and P as long as they were the same in the two experiments. A smaller mass of the unknown gas than of oxygen effuses in the given time. Despite this, the molar mass of the unknown is less than the molar mass of oxygen. The result is easier to accept when it is noted that 0.169 mol of the unknown effuses, but only 0.102 mol of oxygen effuses.

4.81 The mean free path is given by:

$$\lambda = \frac{1}{\sqrt{2}\pi d^2 (N/V)}$$

Substituting the ideal-gas law in the form $N/V = N_0 P/RT$[16] gives:

$$\lambda = \frac{1}{\sqrt{2}\pi d^2}\frac{(R/N_0)T}{P} = \frac{1}{\sqrt{2}\pi d^2}\frac{k_B T}{P}$$

---

[14] See text Appendix C, text page A-26.

[15] Text page 116.

[16] See the solution to **4.53**.

And solving for P gives:

$$P = \frac{k_B T}{\sqrt{2}\pi d^2 \lambda}$$

All the quantities on the right side of this equation are known. Substitute them:

$$P = \frac{(1.38 \times 10^{-23}\ \text{J K}^{-1})\,(300\ \text{K})}{\sqrt{2}\pi(3.1 \times 10^{-10}\ \text{m})^2(0.1\ \text{m})} = 0.097\ \text{J m}^{-3} = 0.097\ \text{Pa} = \boxed{9.7 \times 10^{-7}\ \text{atm}}$$

4.83 Molecules of UF_6 are much heavier than those of H_2, but the rms speed of UF_6 molecules is much slower than those of H_2 molecules. The pressure of a gas comes from the force exerted by its molecules hitting the walls of the container. This force depends not only on the mass of the molecules, but also on their speed, that is, upon their momenta.

4.85 Assume that the 2.00-mol sample of argon behaves ideally. This is reasonable because the pressure is low and the temperature range is well above the boiling point of argon. Equations in text Sections 4-5 and 4-6 give the dependence of the pressure P, the average energy per atom KE_{avg}, the root-mean-square speed u_{rms}, the rate of collisions per area of wall Z_{wall}, the frequency of Ar-Ar collisions Z_1, and the mean free path λ) upon T, V and n. The following table states the effects of the proposed changes as multiplying factors. Thus, the entry 1 means no change. It is assumed that T, V and n change singly.

Change	P	KE_{avg}	u_{rms}	Z_{wall}	Z_1	λ
a) T from 50 to −50°C	223/323	223/323	$\sqrt{223/323}$	$\sqrt{223/323}$	$\sqrt{223/323}$	1
b) V doubled	1/2	1	1	1/2	1/2	2
c) n_{Ar} from 2 to 3 mol	3/2	1	1	3/2	3/2	2/3

4.87 Data for both plots are in the following table:

Gas	b (L mol^{-1})	$N_0\sigma^3$ (L mol^{-1})	a (J m^3 mol^{-2})	$\epsilon\sigma^3 N_0^2$ (J m^3 mol^{-2})
Ar	0.03219	0.0237	0.13628	0.0236
H_2	0.02661	0.0151	0.02476	0.00466
CH_4	0.04278	0.0336	0.22829	0.0414
N_2	0.03913	0.0305	0.14084	0.0241
O_2	0.03183	0.0273	0.13780	0.0270

a) This part is concerned with b versus $N_0\sigma^3$, which are in the second and third columns of the table. The b's are copied directly from text Table 4.3.[17] The values of $N_0\sigma^3$ are computed from the Lennard-Jones σ's in text Table 4.4.[18] For example, for argon:

$$\left(N_0\sigma^3\right)_{\text{Ar}} = (6.022 \times 10^{23}\ \text{mol}^{-1})(3.40 \times 10^{-10}\ \text{m})^3 \times \left(\frac{10^3\ \text{L}}{\text{m}^3}\right) = 0.0237\ \text{L mol}^{-1}$$

Having $N_0\sigma^3$ in the same units as b allows easy comparison of the two. The table shows a strong correlation; the ratio of b to $N_0\sigma^3$ lies mostly in a range centered at 1.25.

b) The units of a in text Table 4.3 are atm L^2 mol^{-2}. Convert to the SI units J m^3 mol^{-2}. For example, for argon:

$$a_{\text{Ar}} = \frac{1.345\ \text{atm L}^2}{\text{mol}^2} \times \left(\frac{101.325\ \text{J}}{\text{L atm}}\right) \times \left(\frac{10^{-3}\ \text{m}^3}{\text{L}}\right) = 0.1363\ \text{J m}^3\ \text{mol}^{-2}$$

[17] text page 118.
[18] Text page 120.

The rest of the results are in the fourth column of the table. Next, combine the Lennard-Jones constants of each gas with Avogadro's number to obtain $\epsilon\sigma^3 N_0^2$. The motivation is that the units of this particular combination are J m^3 mol^{-2}, which are the same units that a has. For example, for argon:

$$(\epsilon\sigma^3 N_0^2)_{\text{Ar}} = (1.654 \times 10^{-21}\ \text{J})(3.40 \times 10^{-10}\ \text{m})^3(6.022 \times 10^{23}\ \text{mol}^{-1})^2 = 0.0236\ \text{J m}^3\ \text{mol}^{-2}$$

The rest of the results are in the fifth column in the table. The a's and $\epsilon\sigma^3 N_0^2$'s correlate strongly. The ratio of the two stays within the range from 5.1 to 5.8 for the five gases.

4.89 A sample of a gaseous hydrocarbon burns in excess oxygen to give 47.4 g of H_2O and 231.6 g of CO_2. Assume that these are the *only* compounds resulting from the combustion. Compute the chemical amount of the hydrocarbon from the *P-V-T* data:

$$n_{\text{hydrocarbon}} = \frac{PV}{RT} = \frac{(3.40\ \text{atm})(25.4\ \text{L})}{(0.08206\ \text{L atm mol}^{-1}\text{K}^{-1})(400\ \text{K})} = 2.63\ \text{mol}$$

Compute the chemical amounts of the carbon dioxide and water:

$$n_{CO_2} = 231.6\ \text{g}\ CO_2 \times \left(\frac{1\ \text{mol}\ CO_2}{44.01\ \text{g}\ CO_2}\right) = 5.262\ \text{mol}\ CO_2$$

$$n_{H_2O} = 47.4\ \text{g}\ H_2O \times \left(\frac{1\ \text{mol}\ H_2O}{18.015\ \text{g}\ H_2O}\right) = 2.63\ \text{mol}\ H_2O$$

2.63 mol of the hydrocarbon reacts to give 5.26 mol of C (tied up in the form of carbon dioxide) and 5.26 mol of H (tied up in the form of water). This can happen only if there is 2 mol of C per mole of the hydrocarbon and 2 mol of H per mole of the hydrocarbon. The molecular formula of the hydrocarbon is therefore $\boxed{C_2H_2}$.

4.91 Let x equal the mass of barium carbonate and y equal the mass of calcium carbonate in the mixture. The chemical amounts of $BaCO_3$ and $CaCO_3$ in the mixture equal:

$$n_{BaCO_3} = \frac{x\ \text{g}}{181.34\ \text{g mol}^{-1}} = \frac{x}{181.34}\ \text{mol} \qquad n_{CaCO_3} = \frac{y\ \text{g}}{100.08\ \text{g mol}^{-1}} = \frac{y}{100.08}\ \text{mol}$$

One mole of $BaCO_3$ generates one mole of CO_2 in reaction with the hydrochloric acid; one mole of $CaCO_3$ generates one mole of CO_2. Accordingly:

$$n_{CO_2} = \left(\frac{x}{181.34} + \frac{y}{100.08}\right)\ \text{mol}$$

Compute n_{CO_2} by substitution of the given *V-P-T* data into the ideal-gas equation:

$$n_{CO_2} = \frac{PV}{RT} = \frac{(0.904\ \text{atm})(1.39\ \text{L})}{(0.08206\ \text{L atm mol}^{-1}\text{K}^{-1})(323.15\ \text{K})} = 0.04738\ \text{mol}$$

Combining the two preceding equations gives:

$$0.04738 = \frac{x}{181.34} + \frac{y}{100.08}$$

Also, $x + y = 5.40$. Solving the two simultaneous equations gives:

$$x = 1.47\ \text{g} \qquad \text{and} \qquad y = 3.93\ \text{g}$$

This means that the $CaCO_3$ comprises $\boxed{72.8\%}$ of the mixture and the $BaCO_3$ comprises $\boxed{27.2\%}$.

Chapter 5

Solids, Liquids, and Phase Transitions

5.1 The substance is most likely to be a $\boxed{\text{gas}}$. Its large compressibility and large coefficient of thermal expansion are typical of gaseous materials.

5.3 a) Compute the density of the material

$$d = \left(\frac{2.71\text{ kg}}{258\text{ cm}^3}\right) \times \left(\frac{1000\text{ g}}{1\text{ kg}}\right) = 10.5\text{ g cm}^{-3}$$

The material is $\boxed{\text{condensed}}$, and not a gas because of its high density, which exceeds the density of water considerably.

b)

$$\text{molar volume} = V_\text{m} = \left(\frac{1\text{ cm}^3}{10.5\text{ g}}\right) \times \left(\frac{108\text{ g}}{1\text{ mol}}\right) = \boxed{10.3\text{ cm}^3\text{ mol}^{-1}}$$

5.5 The volume increase amounts to only 0.3%. Warming a gas from 293 K to 313 K would, according to Charles's law, cause an expansion of:

$$\frac{(313 - 293)\text{ K}}{293\text{ K}} \times 100\% = 6.8\%$$

A non-ideal gas would also expand by several percent during this change in temperature. The substance is accordingly $\boxed{\text{condensed}}$.

5.7 The huge increase in volume is due to the transition of water from a condensed phase (liquid water) to a gaseous phase (steam) at 100°C.

5.9 Non-directional ion-ion interactions maintain the structure of solid sodium chloride. Weaker dispersion forces maintain carbon tetrachloride as a solid. Indentation requires breaking bonds in the solid. Solid NaCl is $\boxed{\text{harder}}$ than solid CCl_4 because the ion-ion interactions in NaCl are stronger than the dispersion interactions in CCl_4.

5.11 In all three phases, the diffusion constant should $\boxed{\text{decrease}}$ as the density of the phase is increased. At higher densities molecules are closer to each other. In gases they will collide more often and travel shorter distances between collisions. In liquids and solids, there will be less space for molecules to move around each other.

5.13 Ion-dipole forces arise from molecular or ionic properties that are always present, as in the interaction of the permanent charge of the potassium ion and the permanent dipole of a water molecule. Ion-induced dipole forces arise when the charge on an ion induces a temporary separation of charge in another species. An induced dipole does not exist in the absence of the ion that induces it. An example is the attraction between an Fe^{3+} ion and the temporary dipole that it induces in a molecule of oxygen.

5.15 a) Potassium and fluorine differ considerably in electronegativity. As explained in text Section 3.3, the bonding in the compound potassium fluoride is therefore expected to be ionic. These $\boxed{\text{ion-ion}}$ attractions predominate in this compound; dispersion forces are also present.

b) $\boxed{\text{Dipole-dipole}}$ attractions predominate in the interactions between molecules in hydrogen iodide. The positive (H) end of one molecule is attracted by the negative (I) end of another, but repelled by its positive (H) end. Dispersion forces are also present.

c) $\boxed{\text{Dispersion forces}}$ are the only forces operating among the atoms in a sample of radon. Single Rn atoms have completely symmetrical (spherically symmetrical) distributions of charge. Two neighboring Rn atoms induce temporary dipoles in each other that cause them to attract each other.

d) $\boxed{\text{Dispersion forces}}$ are the only intermolecular forces possible between molecules of N_2.

5.17 A sodium ion should be most strongly attracted to a $\boxed{\text{bromide ion}}$. The attraction between ions of unlike charge such as these is stronger than the ion-dipole attraction between Na^+ and HBr and the ion-induced dipole attraction between Na^+ and Kr.

5.19 a) Read along the horizontal axis in Figure 5.9[1] to find the locations of the minima in the potential energy curves. These locations give the bond distances. In Cl_2 the bond is about $\boxed{2.0 \times 10^{-10}\ \text{m}}$ long; in molecular KCl, the bond is about $\boxed{2.5 \times 10^{-10}\ \text{m}}$ long.

b) The bond in Cl_2 is shorter than the bond in KCl, but is distinctly weaker, as shown by the depth of the minimum in the potential energy curve for Cl—Cl (about -225 kJ mol^{-1}) compared to the depth for K—Cl (about -490 kJ mol^{-1}).

Tip. Potential energy curves such as the ones in Figure 5.9 are much more informative than the type of over-general statement quoted in the problem.

5.21 The boiling point and melting point of a substance depend on the strength of the attractive forces operating among the particles that comprise the liquid or solid substance. These forces tend to increase with increasing molar mass in a group of related substances. The halogens are certainly closely related chemically. Therefore their boiling and melting points tend to rise with increasing molar mass.

Tip. The observed melting points and boiling points of the halogens are:

Substance	$\mathcal{M}$ (g mol^{-1})	m.p. (°C)	b.p. (°C)
F_2	38	−219.6	−187.9
Cl_2	71	−101	−34.05
Br_2	160	−7.2	58.2
I_2	254	113.6	184.5

5.23 Substances with the strongest intermolecular forces require the highest temperature to make them boil. Liquid RbCl has strong Coulomb (electrostatic) forces holding its ions together. It has the highest boiling point. Liquid NH_3 has dipole-dipole attractions, as does liquid NO. In liquid NH_3, these are particularly strong. They are hydrogen bonds. In liquid NO, the dipole-dipole attractions are weaker. Liquid NH_3 boils at a higher temperature than liquid NO. Induced dipole-induced dipole forces are the only intermolecular attractions in liquid neon. Consequently, it has the lowest boiling point of all: $\boxed{\text{Ne} < \text{NO} < \text{NH}_3 < \text{RbCl}}$.

---

[1] Text page 139.

5.25 The facts suggest the $(CH_3OH)_4$ molecule has a $\boxed{\text{cyclic}}$ structure. Why would a straight chain of molecules stop at exactly four links? The ring is probably maintained by hydrogen bonding between the —OH hydrogen atom and the O of a neighboring molecule. the ring would be puckered and consist of a total of eight atoms—four H's and 4 O's in alternation

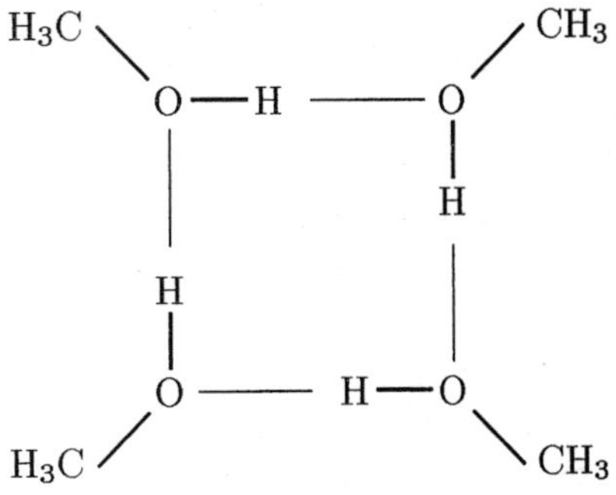

5.27 Although the two substances have comparable molar masses, the boiling point of hydrazine N_2H_4 should $\boxed{\text{exceed}}$ the boiling point of ethylene C_2H_4 because N—H···N hydrogen bonds are present in hydrazine but no hydrogen bonds occur in ethylene.

5.29 Compute the number of molecules of water present in the sample:

$$N_{H_2O} = 1.0 \text{ kg } H_2O \times \left(\frac{1 \text{ mol } H_2O}{0.018 \text{ kg } H_2O}\right) \times \left(\frac{6.022 \times 10^{23} \text{ molecules}}{1 \text{ mol } H_2O}\right) = 3.35 \times 10^{25} \text{ molecules}$$

Each water molecule is involved in a maximum of 4 hydrogen bonds. Also, each bond has 1 water at each end. Therefore the maximum number of H-bonds in the sample is twice the number of molecules: $\boxed{6.7 \times 10^{25}}$.

5.31 Rearrange the ideal-gas equation and use it as follows

$$V_{H_2} = \frac{n_{H_2}RT}{P} = \frac{(1.00 \text{ mol})(0.08206 \text{ L atm mol}^{-1}\text{K}^{-1})(16.0 \text{ K})}{0.213 \text{ atm}} = \boxed{6.16 \text{ L}}$$

This volume is 27% of the volume of one mole of gaseous hydrogen at STP.

5.33 First compute the number of moles of Hg per unit volume in the space above the surface of the mercury.

$$\frac{n}{V} = \frac{P}{RT} = \frac{2.87 \times 10^{-6} \text{ atm}}{(0.08206 \text{ L atm mol}^{-1}\text{K}^{-1})(300.15 \text{ K})} = 1.165 \times 10^{-7} \text{ mol L}^{-1}$$

Multiply by Avogadro's number to find the number of Hg atoms per unit volume:

$$N_{Hg} = 1.165 \times 10^{-7} \text{ mol L}^{-1} \times \left(\frac{6.022 \times 10^{23} \text{ molecules}}{1 \text{ mol}}\right) \times \left(\frac{1 \text{ L}}{1000 \text{ cm}^3}\right) = \boxed{7.02 \times 10^{13} \text{ atom cm}^{-3}}$$

5.35 The pressure on the interior walls of the vessel containing the collected acetylene comes from collisions by molecules of H_2O molecules as well as C_2H_2. Therefore, subtract the partial pressure of the water vapor from the total pressure inside the container. This gives the pressure that the acetylene would exert if it were present by itself. The partial pressure of water vapor depends on solely on the temperature. The required value is given, so:

$$P_{C_2H_2} = P_{\text{total}} - P_{\text{water}} = 0.9950 - 0.0728 = 0.9222 \text{ atm}$$

Use the ideal gas law to compute the chemical amount of acetylene per unit volume of collected gases that exerts a pressure of 0.9222 atm at a T of 40°C (313.15 K):

$$\frac{n_{C_2H_2}}{V} = \frac{P_{C_2H_2}}{RT} = \frac{0.9222 \text{ atm}}{(0.08206 \text{ L atm mol}^{-1}\text{K}^{-1})(313.15 \text{ K})} = 0.03589 \text{ mol L}^{-1}$$

The molar mass of acetylene equals 26.038 g mol^{-1}. Multiplying the chemical amount by this molar mass gives $\boxed{0.9345 \text{ g L}^{-1}}$ as the mass of acetylene present per unit volume of gas.

5.37 Determine the partial pressure of the CO_2, and then use the ideal gas law to obtain the chemical amount of CO_2. From the balanced equation, the number of moles of $CaCO_3$ that reacts equals the number of moles of CO_2 that forms. Convert this amount of $CaCO_3$ to a mass.

$$P_{CO_2} = P_{\text{total}} - P_{\text{water}} = 0.9963 \text{ atm} - 0.0231 \text{ atm} = 0.9732 \text{ atm}$$

$$n_{CO_2} = \frac{P_{CO_2} V_{\text{gases}}}{RT} = \frac{(0.9732 \text{ atm})(0.722 \text{ L})}{(0.08206 \text{ L atm mol}^{-1}\text{K}^{-1})(293.15 \text{ K})} = 0.0292 \text{ mol } CO_2$$

$$m_{CaCO_3} = 0.0292 \text{ mol } CO_2 \times \left(\frac{1 \text{ mol } CaCO_3}{1 \text{ mol } CO_2}\right) \times \left(\frac{100.09 \text{ g } CaCO_3}{1 \text{ mol } CaCO_3}\right) = \boxed{2.92 \text{ g } CaCO_3}$$

5.39 Reading from text Figure 5.15,[2] the vapor pressure of water at 90°C is approximately $\boxed{0.70 \text{ atm}}$. Because the whole of the earth's atmosphere exerts a pressure of 1 atm, this means that 70% of the earth's is above the level of the explorer's camp; $\boxed{30\%}$ of the atmosphere is below the level of the camp.

5.41 The trends in boiling and melting points indicate that the interatomic attractions are much stronger in iridium than in sodium. The surface tension of molten $\boxed{\text{iridium}}$ should therefore be higher than that of molten sodium.

5.43 Compression favors the denser phase, but the denser phase (the liquid) is already present. The sample of Pu $\boxed{\text{stays liquid}}$.

5.45

Phase Diagram for NH_3 (not to scale)

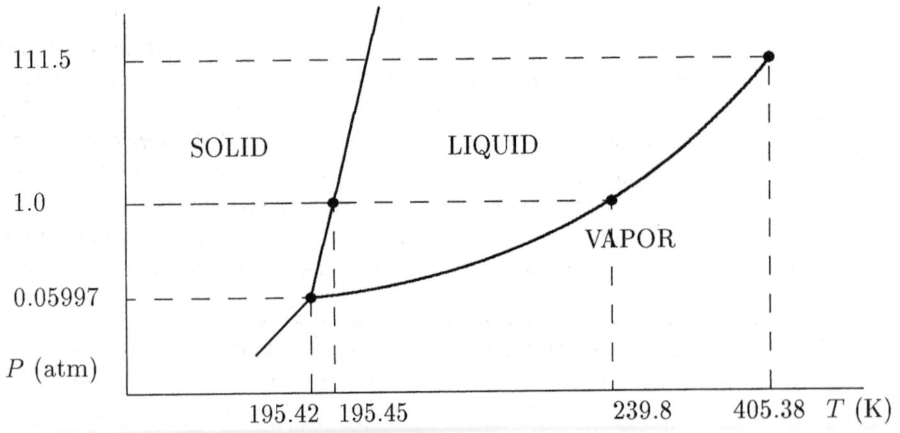

5.47 Check whether the specified point is within the boundaries of the solid, liquid, or gas region on the phase diagram of argon that appears in text Figure 5.21.[3]

[2] Text page 142.
[3] Text page 149.

a) liquid **b)** gas **c)** solid **d)** gas.

5.49 a) The temperature of the triple point of acetylene lies above −84.0°C. For a pure substance, T's at which liquid and gas are in equilibrium equal or exceed T's at which liquid and solid are in equilibrium.

b) Note that 0.8 atm is *less* than 760 torr, which is the vapor pressure of solid acetylene at −84°C. If solid acetylene is heated at $P = 0.8$ atm, it therefore passes directly into the vaporous (gaseous) state without ever existing as a liquid. It sublimes at some temperature below −84.0°C.

5.51 The nitrogen confined in the glass tube becomes supercritical as it is heated past the critical temperature. This is assured because the size of the container and the amount of nitrogen that it contains assure that the critical density of nitrogen is exceeded. Originally, a meniscus separates the liquid from gaseous nitrogen within the tube. The meniscus disappears at 126.19 K as the two phases merge into a single fluid phase of uniform density; the distinction between liquid and gas ceases to exist.

5.53 Candle wax at room temperature is a solid, although a low-melting one. Natural rubber, a polymer of an organic compound called isoprene (C_8H_8), is a solid at room conditions. Both are incompressible compared to a gas. Neither flows readily, compared to ordinary liquids and gases.

5.55 The HCl molecule is polar. When liquid hydrogen chloride dissolves an ionic compound, its molecules tend to line up with their positive ends (the H ends) closest to negatively charged ions and with their negative ends (the Cl atoms) closest to positively charged ions.

$$\overset{\delta-}{\text{Cl}}—\overset{\delta+}{\text{H}} \quad \ominus \quad \overset{\delta+}{\text{H}}—\overset{\delta-}{\text{Cl}} \qquad\qquad \overset{\delta+}{\text{H}}—\overset{\delta-}{\text{Cl}} \quad \oplus \quad \overset{\delta-}{\text{Cl}}—\overset{\delta+}{\text{H}}$$

Tip. The diagram shows two H—Cl molecules interacting with each ion, but the actual number is generally more, depending on the size and charge of the ion.

5.57 Water at $T = 10$ K (−263°C) and $P = 1$ atm exists at equilibrium as a solid (ice). As the temperature of this very cold ice is raised, the average internal kinetic energy, which is the energy associated with the movement of its molecules, rises in (approximately) direct proportion. Its average internal potential energy, which is the energy that its molecules have by virtue of their relative positions with respect to the attractions that link them, increases slightly (as the ice expands against the constant outside pressure of 1 atm).
At 273.15 K (and $P = 1$ atm), the ice starts to melt. During this phase change the temperature stays constant and so does the average kinetic energy of the molecules despite the continuing addition of energy in the form of heat. The energy goes to overcome some of the attractions among the molecules. It increases the average internal potential energy. Once the sample is entirely liquefied, more added energy goes mostly to raising the internal kinetic energy. The internal potential energy increases only slightly as the liquid is heated. At 373.15 K the liquid water starts to boil. During boiling, the average internal kinetic energy of the molecules stays constant. The average internal potential energy of the molecules increases as the molecules, which attract each other, are repositioned from being fairly close neighbors to locations remote from each other.

5.59 "Saturation" means that the vapor pressure of the water in the room has reached its maximum—the humidity is 100% and drops of water are condensing on the walls. The partial pressure of water vapor in the room is very close to the vapor pressure of pure water at the given temperature.[4] This vapor pressure equals 0.03126 atm. The rest of the pressure in the room comes from oxygen, nitrogen, and the other components of the air. Compute the volume of the room

$$V_{\text{room}} = 110 \text{ m}^3 \times \left(\frac{10^3 \text{ L}}{\text{m}^3}\right) = 1.10 \times 10^3 \text{ L}$$

---

[4] The difference derives from the interaction of the water with the air.

Combine this with the known partial pressure of water to obtain the chemical amount and the mass of the water vapor in the air in the room:

$$n_{H_2O} = \frac{PV}{RT} = \frac{0.03126 \text{ atm}(1.10 \times 10^3 \text{ L})}{(0.08206 \text{ L atm mol}^{-1}\text{K}^{-1})(298.15 \text{ K})} = 140.5 \text{ mol}$$

$$m_{H_2O} = 140.5 \text{ mol H}_2\text{O} \times \left(\frac{18.02 \text{ g H}_2\text{O}}{1 \text{ mol H}_2\text{O}}\right) = \boxed{2530 \text{ g H}_2\text{O}}$$

This is roughly 2.5 L of liquid water.

Tip. Converting R to m^3 atm mol^{-1} K^{-1} (to fit the units of volume as given) leads to the same answer. See **4.53**. A standard reference[5] gives the measured mass of water in one cubic meter of saturated air at 1 atm and 298.15 K as 23.14 g m^{-3}. This corresponds to 2545 g of water in 110 m^3 of air, which is quite close to the above answer.

5.61 The only substance within the sealed can is water. If liquid water and water vapor coexist at 60°C, the pressure of the water vapor[6] must equal $\boxed{0.20 \text{ atm}}$.

5.63 Why don't spacecraft just boil away in the vacuum of space? The term "boiling" implies an active or even violent event. Spacecraft do tend to lose individual atoms from their hulls into the vacuum of space. This process is however so very slow that no change is apparent.

5.65 When chunks of solid CO_2 are added to room-temperature ethanol in an open beaker, portions of the solid sublime off as gaseous CO_2. Much bubbling and roiling accompany the escape of this gas. The process will in theory chill the ethanol to $\boxed{-78.5°\text{C}}$, the sublimation temperature of the solid CO_2, but no lower. Since ethanol at $P = 1$ atm requires a temperature below −114.5°C to freeze, it stays liquid in this experiment. Once the ethanol is good and cold, small amounts of further sublimation take place to counteract heat flowing in from the surroundings; the mixture will always fizz a little.

5.67 Substitution of the appropriate "VDW" (van der Waals) a's and b's in the three equations quoted in the problem gives the results that appear in columns four through six of the following table. Because the different VDW constants are in atm L^2 mol^{-2} and L mol^{-1} respectively, a value of 0.082057 L atm $mol^{-1}K^{-1}$ should be used for R. The answer columns include the observed values (in parentheses) for comparison.

Gas	a (atm L^2mol^{-2})	b (L mol^{-1})	T_c (K)	P_c (atm)	$(V/n)_c$ (L mol^{-1})
O_2	1.360	0.03183	154.3 (154.6)	49.72 (49.8)	0.09549 (0.0734)
CO_2	3.592	0.04267	303.9 (304.2)	73.07 (72.9)	0.1280 (0.0940)
H_2O	5.464	0.03049	647.1 (647.1)	217.7 (217.6)	0.09147 (0.0567)

Tip. The observed values T_c and P_c for the gases are taken from experimental reports and are more precise than can be obtained by reading the scale in text Figure 5.21. Molar volumes cannot be read from P-T phase diagrams at all.

---

[5] Kaye and Laby, *Tables of Physical and Chemical Constants*, 16th edition, page 38.

[6] See text Figure 5.15, text page 142.

5.69 a)

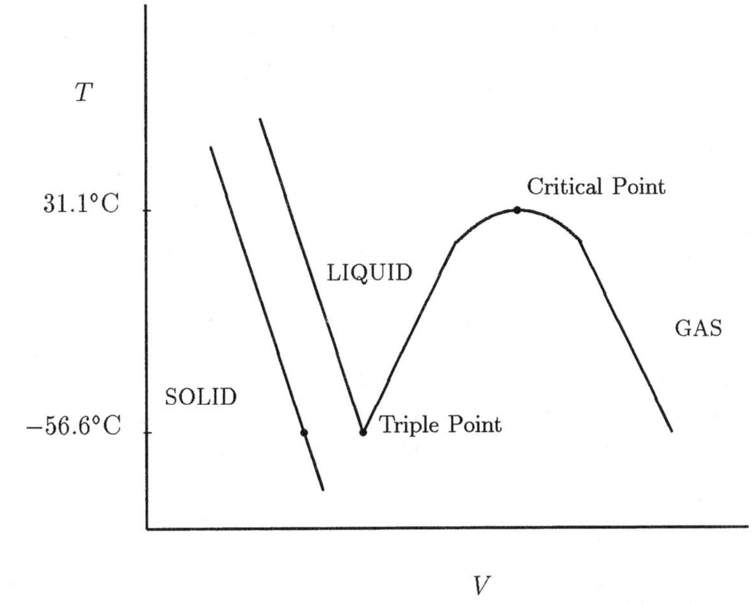

b) Such a diagram cannot be drawn because two different phases (liquid and solid) can have the same temperature and molar volume.

5.71 The problem gives the boiling points of fluorides of elements in the second row of the periodic table. The high boiling points of LiF and BeF_2 result from the strong ion-ion attractions in the liquids. The large decrease in boiling point going from BeF_2 to BF_3 suggests a changeover from ion-ion forces to much weaker dipole-dipole or induced-dipole forces. The continued decrease in boiling point of the chlorides across the rest of the second period corresponds to decreasing ionic character in the bonds and a parallel decrease in the strength of the intermolecular attractions.

5.73 The bonds in SbF_5 have less ionic character than in SbF_3. Ionic character tends to decrease with increasing oxidation number of the metal. The bonds in AsF_5 should have less ionic character than those in SbF_5 because Sb lies below As in the periodic table. The bond in F_2 has the least ionic character of all, since it is a covalent bond. Therefore the trend in ionic character is

$$\text{least} \quad F_2 < AsF_5 < SbF_5 < SbF_3 \quad \text{most}$$

If the boiling points increase with increasing ionic character, then:

$$\boxed{F_2 < AsF_5 < SbF_5 < SbF_3}$$

Tip. The experimental boiling points of the first three substances equal: −188.14, −53, and 149.5°C. SbF_3 sublimes at a temperature exceeding 319°C.

Chapter 6

Solutions

6.1 a) The molar mass of cholesterol is 386.64 g mol^{-1}; one liter (L) equals 10 deciliters (dL); one gram (g) equals 1000 milligrams (mg). Use unit factors written from these equivalencies as follows:

$$c_{\text{cholesterol}} = \frac{214\text{ mg}}{1\text{ dL}} \times \left(\frac{1\text{ g}}{1000\text{ mg}}\right) \times \left(\frac{10\text{ dL}}{1\text{ L}}\right) \times \left(\frac{1\text{ mol}}{386.64\text{ g}}\right) = \boxed{0.00553\text{ mol L}^{-1}}$$

b) Assume that blood, like water, has a density of 1.0 g mL^{-1}. One liter (1000 mL) of blood then has a mass of 1.0 kg, of which 2.14 g (0.00214 kg) is cholesterol. Assume that the remaining 0.998 kg is solvent water. Insert these numbers into the definition of molality:

$$m_{\text{cholesterol}} = \frac{\text{moles of cholesterol}}{\text{kilograms of solvent}} = 2.14\text{ g} \times \left(\frac{1\text{ mol}}{386.64\text{ g}}\right) \times \frac{1}{0.998\text{ kg}} = \boxed{0.0055\text{ mol kg}^{-1}}$$

c) If there is 2.14 g of cholesterol per liter of blood, then one liter of blood contains 2.14 g of cholesterol. This simple turn-about gives the unit factor in the following:

$$V_{\text{blood}} = 8.10\text{ g cholesterol} \times \left(\frac{1\text{ L blood}}{2.14\text{ g cholesterol}}\right) = \boxed{3.79\text{ L blood}}$$

Tip. The second answer has only two significant figures because the assumption about the density of blood is weak. Whole blood in fact has a density of 1.06 g mL^{-1}. This means that 1000 mL of blood weighs 1.06 kg. Taking this into account alters the calculation of the molality of the cholesterol

$$m = \frac{0.00553\text{ mol cholesterol}}{1.0578\text{ kg solvent}} = 0.0052\text{ mol kg}^{-1}$$

Clearly, the subtraction of the 2.14 g is superfluous in both calculations.

6.3 To compute the various quantities, obtain the masses and chemical amounts of HCl and H_2O in some set quantity of solution. Then use the definitions. Exactly 100.0 g of solution contains 38.00 g of HCl and 62.00 g of H_2O. Its volume is

$$V_{\text{solution}} = 100\text{ g solution} \times \left(\frac{1\text{ mL solution}}{1.1886\text{ g solution}}\right) = 84.133\text{ mL}$$

Use the molar masses of HCl and H_2O to convert their masses to chemical amounts:

$$n_{\text{HCl}} = \frac{38.00\text{ g HCl}}{36.4606\text{ g mol}^{-1}} = 1.0422\text{ mol HCl} \qquad n_{\text{H}_2\text{O}} = \frac{62.00\text{ g H}_2\text{O}}{18.0153\text{ g mol}^{-1}} = 3.4415\text{ mol H}_2\text{O}$$

The molarity of the HCl equals the number of moles of HCl divided by the number of liters of solution. The 84.133 mL (0.084133 L) sample of solution contains 1.0422 mol of HCl, for a molarity of $\boxed{12.39 \text{ mol L}^{-1}}$.

The molality of the HCl equals the number of moles of HCl divided by the mass of solvent in kilograms. 1.0422 mol of HCl is dissolved in 62.00 g (0.06200 kg) of water. The molality of the HCl is therefore $\boxed{16.81 \text{ mol kg}^{-1}}$.

The mole fraction of water is the number of moles of water divided by the total number of moles of all components of the solution:

$$X_{H_2O} = \frac{3.4415 \text{ mol}}{1.0422 + 3.4415 \text{ mol}} = 0.7676$$

Only two components are present; X_{HCl} is simply $1 - 0.7676 = \boxed{0.2324}$.

6.5 Compute the mass of acetic acid in 1 kg of the 6.0835 M solution. To do this, use the molarity of the acetic acid and the density of the solution in unit factors:

$$1 \text{ kg sol'n} \times \left(\frac{1 \text{ L sol'n}}{1.0438 \text{ kg sol'n}}\right) \times \left(\frac{6.0835 \text{ mol } C_2H_4O_2}{1 \text{ L sol'n}}\right) \times \left(\frac{60.052 \text{ g } C_2H_4O_2}{\text{mol } C_2H_4O_2}\right) = 350.00 \text{ g } C_2H_4O_2$$

By subtraction, 1 kg of solution contains 650.00 g (0.65000 kg) of water. The 350.00 g of acetic acid equals 5.8282 mol of acetic acid. The molality of the acetic acid equals the number of moles of acetic acid divided by the mass of the solvent in kilograms:

$$m_{C_2H_4O_2} = \frac{5.8282 \text{ mol } C_2H_3O_2}{0.65000 \text{ kg}} = \boxed{8.9665 \text{ mol kg}^{-1}}$$

6.7 Water is the solute, and liquid nitrogen is the solvent, but the definition of mole fraction works the same. Use it to write the equation

$$X_{H_2O} = 1.00 \times 10^{-5} = \frac{n_{H_2O}}{n_{N_2} + n_{H_2O}} = \frac{n_{H_2O}}{35.6972 + n_{H_2O}}$$

where 35.6972 is the number of moles of N_2 in 1.00 kg of N_2 (non-significant figures are carried along deliberately). Solving the equation for n_{H_2O} becomes simpler when it is realized that n_{H_2O} can be neglected in the denominator. Thus, the 1.00 kg of N_2 contains 3.5697×10^{-4} mol of H_2O. This amounts to $\boxed{0.00643 \text{ g}}$ of H_2O.

6.9 **a)** According to the problem, 100.00 g of commercial $H_3PO_4(aq)$ contains 90.00 g of pure H_3PO_4 and 10.00 g of H_2O. This much H_3PO_4 is 0.9184 mol of H_3PO_4 ($\mathcal{M} = 97.995 \text{ g mol}^{-1}$). Then:

$$\rho = \frac{100.00 \text{ g solution}}{0.9184 \text{ mol } H_3PO_4} \times \left(\frac{12.2 \text{ mol } H_3PO_4}{1 \text{ L solution}}\right) = \frac{1.33 \times 10^3 \text{ g solution}}{1 \text{ L solution}}$$

This is a correct answer, but densities are usually given in gram per milliliter. In those units, the answer is $\boxed{1.33 \text{ g mL}^{-1}}$.

b) The 2.00 L of 1.00 M $H_3PO_4(aq)$ must contain 2.00 mol of H_3PO_4. The volume of the 12.2 M $H_3PO_4(aq)$ solution that provides 2.00 mol of H_3PO_4 is

$$V_{\text{solution}} = 2.00 \text{ mol } H_3PO_4 \times \left(\frac{1 \text{ L solution}}{12.2 \text{ mol } H_3PO_4}\right) = \boxed{0.164 \text{ L solution}}$$

To make 2.00 L of a 1.00 M $H_3PO_4(aq)$ solution, put 0.164 L (164 mL) of 12.2 M H_3PO_4 in a 2-liter volumetric flask and then add water to bring the total volume up the 2.00 L mark.

6.11 First calculate how many moles of NaOH were in the solution before any solid NaOH was added:

$$n_{\text{NaOH}} = 1.50 \text{ L solution} \times \left(\frac{2.40 \text{ mol NaOH}}{1 \text{ L solution}}\right) = 3.60 \text{ mol NaOH}$$

The molar mass of NaOH is 40.00 g mol^{-1}, so the added 25.0 g of NaOH equals 0.625 mol. After the addition, the total amount of NaOH in the container equals $3.60 + 0.625 = 4.23$ mol. Meanwhile, the final volume of the solution is 4.00 L. The final concentration of NaOH is therefore:

$$c_{\text{NaOH}} = \frac{4.23 \text{ mol NaOH}}{4.00 \text{ L}} = \boxed{1.06 \text{ mol L}^{-1}}$$

6.13 Break up each soluble reactant and product into its component ions; cancel out the spectator ions appearing on both sides of the equation:

a) $Ag^+(aq) + Cl^-(aq) \rightarrow AgCl(s)$

b) $K_2CO_3(s) + 2\ H^+(aq) \rightarrow 2\ K^+(aq) + CO_2(g) + H_2O(l)$

c) $2\ Cs(s) + 2\ H_2O(l) \rightarrow 2\ Cs^+(aq) + 2\ OH^-(aq) + H_2(g)$

d) $2\ MnO_4^-(aq) + 16\ H^+(aq) + 10\ Cl^-(aq) \rightarrow 5\ Cl_2(g) + 2\ Mn^{2+}(aq) + 8\ H_2O(l)$

6.15 The balanced chemical equation given in the problem indicates a 4-to-2 molar relationship between HNO_3 and PbO_2 in the reaction. Use this fact to construct a unit factor. The given molarity also gives a unit factor, and the molar mass of PbO_2 (239.2 g mol^{-1}) furnishes another. The computation using these three factors goes as follows:

$$V_{\text{sol'n}} = 15.9 \text{ g PbO}_2 \times \left(\frac{1 \text{ mol PbO}_2}{239.2 \text{ g PbO}_2}\right) \times \left(\frac{4 \text{ mol HNO}_3}{2 \text{ mol PbO}_2}\right) \times \left(\frac{1 \text{ L sol'n}}{7.91 \text{ mol HNO}_3}\right) = \boxed{0.0168 \text{ L sol'n}}$$

6.17 The carbon dioxide in this problem is a gas (with volume measured in liters), and the potassium carbonate is in aqueous solution (with volume measured in liters).[1] According to the balanced equation, the $CO_2(g)$ and $K_2CO_3(aq)$ react in a 1-to-1 molar ratio. The following uses this fact together with the concentration of the $K_2CO_3(aq)$ to determine the chemical amount of $CO_2(g)$ that reacts:

$$n_{\text{CO}_2} = 187 \text{ L solution} \times \left(\frac{1.36 \text{ mol K}_2\text{CO}_3}{1 \text{ L solution}}\right) \times \left(\frac{1 \text{ mol CO}_2}{1 \text{ mol K}_2\text{CO}_3}\right) = 254.3 \text{ mol CO}_2$$

The volume occupied by this much $CO_2(g)$ depends on T and P. Insert the given T and P in the ideal-gas equation:

$$V_{\text{CO}_2} = \frac{nRT}{P} = \frac{(254.3 \text{ mol})(0.08206 \text{ L atm mol}^{-1}\text{K}^{-1})(323.15 \text{ K})}{1.00 \text{ atm}} = \boxed{6.74 \times 10^3 \text{ L}}$$

6.19 When a salt forms in an acid-base reaction, the cation derives from the base, and the anion from the acid:

a) $Ca(OH)_2(aq) + 2\,HF(aq) \rightarrow CaF_2(s) + 2\,H_2O(l)$
calcium hydroxide + hydrofluoric acid → calcium fluoride + water

b) $2\,RbOH(aq) + H_2SO_4(aq) \rightarrow Rb_2SO_4(aq) + 2\,H_2O(l)$
rubidium hydroxide + sulfuric acid → rubidium sulfate + water

c) $Zn(OH)_2(aq) + 2\,HNO_3(aq) \rightarrow Zn(NO_3)_2(aq) + 2\,H_2O(l)$
zinc hydroxide + nitric acid → zinc nitrate + water

d) $KOH(aq) + HCH_3COO(aq) \rightarrow KCH_3COO(aq) + H_2O(l)$
potassium hydroxide + acetic acid → potassium acetate + water

---

[1] The use of the same unit can cause confusion between the two.

6.21 The reaction is $H_2S + 2\,NaOH \rightarrow Na_2S + 2\,H_2O$. $\boxed{\text{Sodium sulfide}}$ is the salt produced by this neutralization reaction.

Tip. Without the hint, NaHS (sodium hydrogen sulfide) is a possible answer.

6.23 a) Phosphorus trifluoride is PF_3; phosphorous acid is H_3PO_3, and hydrofluoric acid is HF. The equation is easily balanced by inspection. Assign 1 as the coefficient for PF_3. All of the fluorine ends up in HF. This means the coefficient for HF is 3. All of the oxygen ends up in H_3PO_3, making 3 the coefficient for the H_2O:

$$\boxed{PF_3 + 3\ H_2O \rightarrow H_3PO_3 + 3\ HF}$$

b) First determine the chemical amount of $PF_3(g)$ in 1.94 L of gaseous PF_3 at 25° C (298 K) and 0.970 atm:

$$n_{PF_3} = \frac{PV}{RT} = \frac{(0.970 \text{ atm})(1.94 \text{ L})}{(0.08206 \text{ L atm mol}^{-1}\text{K}^{-1})(298 \text{ K})} = 0.07695 \text{ mol}$$

According to the equation, 1 mol of PF_3 reacts to give 1 mol of H_3PO_3 and 3 mol of HF. This means 0.07695 mol of H_3PO_3 and 0.2309 mol of HF are produced from 0.07695 mol of PF_3. Both acids dissolve as they are formed. Enough water is present to give a final volume of 872 mL (0.872 L). The acids are mixed with each other, but their respective concentrations are computed by *separately* dividing chemical amount by the final volume:

$$[H_3PO_3] = \frac{0.07695 \text{ mol}}{0.872 \text{ L}} = \boxed{0.0882 \text{ M}} \qquad [HF] = \frac{0.2309 \text{ mol}}{0.872 \text{ L}} = \boxed{0.265 \text{ M}}$$

6.25 The problem is very similar to text Example 6.6.[2] Each mole of KOH dissolves in water to give one mole of $K^+(aq)$ ion and one mole of $OH^-(aq)$ ion. Therefore, the chemical amount of $OH^-(aq)$ in 37.85 mL of 0.1279 M aqueous KOH is

$$n_{OH^-} = 37.85 \text{ mL} \times \left(\frac{0.1279 \text{ mmol}}{1 \text{ mL}}\right) = 4.841 \text{ mmol}$$

Nitric acid furnishes one mole of $H^+(aq)$ ion per mole dissolved. Also, the stoichiometric ratio in the acid-base reaction between HNO_3 and KOH is 1-to-1. Thus, the chemical amount of HNO_3 in the 100.0 mL sample before the reaction was also 4.841 mmol. The concentration of HNO_3 in the original solution was:

$$[HNO_3] = \frac{4.841 \text{ mmol}}{100.0 \text{ mL}} = \frac{0.04841 \text{ mmol}}{1 \text{ mL}} = \boxed{0.04841 \text{ mol L}^{-1}}$$

Tip. Note the use of the convenient unit, the millimole (mmol). The concentration of a solution in mmol mL^{-1} is numerically equal to its concentration in mol L^{-1}.

6.27 a) $2\ \overset{+3}{P}F_2I(l) + 2\ \overset{0}{Hg}\ (l) \rightarrow \overset{+2}{P_2}F_4(g) + \overset{+1}{Hg_2}I_2(s)$

b) $2\ K\overset{+5}{Cl}\overset{-2}{O_3}(s) \rightarrow 2\ K\overset{-1}{Cl}(s) + 3\ \overset{0}{O_2}(g)$

c) $4\ \overset{-3}{N}H_3(g) + 5\ \overset{0}{O_2}(g) \rightarrow 4\ \overset{+2}{N}\overset{-2}{O}\ (g) + 6\,H_2\overset{-2}{O}\ (g)$

d) $2\ \overset{0}{As}(s) + 6\ NaO\overset{+1}{H}\ (l) \rightarrow 2\ Na_3\overset{+3}{As}O_3(s) + 3\ \overset{0}{H_2}\ (g)$

6.29 Refer to the rules on oxidation numbers. Neither hydrogen (oxidation state +1) nor oxygen (oxidation state −2) changes oxidation state in this reaction. The gold loses $3\,e^-$ per atom, passing from the zero to the +3 oxidation state; $\boxed{\text{Au}}$ is oxidized. The Se atom in H_2SeO_4 passes from the +6 to the +4 oxidation state; it gains $2\,e^-$, and so $\boxed{H_2SeO_4}$ is reduced. Note that only half of the H_2SeO_4 reacting is actually reduced.

---

[2] Text page 165.

6.31 The problem requires *completion* as well as balancing. This means the insertion of H_2O, OH^- ion and H_3O^+ ion on one or both sides of the equation. Follow the six-step procedure outlined in text Section 6.4.[3]

a) The following gives the results of each step. Indications of state such as (aq) or (s) are omitted until the end.

1.	$VO_2^+ \rightarrow VO^{2+}$	$SO_2 \rightarrow SO_4^{2-}$
2.	$VO_2^+ \rightarrow VO^{2+}$	$SO_2 \rightarrow SO_4^{2-}$
3.	$VO_2^+ \rightarrow VO^{2+} + H_2O$	$2\,H_2O + SO_2 \rightarrow SO_4^{2-}$
4.	$2\,H_3O^+ + VO_2^+ \rightarrow VO^{2+} + 3\,H_2O$	$6\,H_2O + SO_2 \rightarrow SO_4^{2-} + 4\,H_3O^+$
5.	$e^- + 2\,H_3O^+ + VO_2^+ \rightarrow VO^{2+} + 3\,H_2O$	$6\,H_2O + SO_2 \rightarrow SO_4^{2-} + 4\,H_3O^+ + 2\,e^-$
6.	$2\,e^- + 4\,H_3O^+ + 2\,VO_2^+ \rightarrow 2\,VO^{2+} + 6\,H_2O$	$6\,H_2O + SO_2 \rightarrow SO_4^{2-} + 4\,H_3O^+ + 2\,e^-$

$$\boxed{2\,VO_2^+(aq) + SO_2(g) \rightarrow 2\,VO^{2+}(aq) + SO_4^{2-}(aq)}$$

Step 5 shows that VO_2^+ is reduced (electrons must be put in on the left side of the half-equation to balance charge) and that SO_2 is oxidized (electrons must be put in on the right). In the final line, addition of the oxidation half-equation to the reduction half-equation has led, as planned, to the removal of e^-'s. The algebraic combining of terms removes six H_2O's and four H_3O^+'s.

Use the same method in the other parts of the problem.

b) $Br_2(l) + SO_2(g) + 6\ H_2O(l) \rightarrow 2\ Br^-(aq) + SO_4^{2-}(aq) + 4\ H_3O^+(aq)$

c) $Cr_2O_7^{2-}(aq) + 3\ Np^{4+}(aq) + 2\ H_3O^+ \rightarrow 2\ Cr^{3+}(aq) + 3\ NpO_2^{2+}(aq) + 3\ H_2O(aq)$

d) $5\ HCOOH(aq) + 2\ MnO_4^-(aq) + 6\ H_3O^+(aq) \rightarrow 5\ CO_2(g) + 2\ Mn^{2+}(aq) + 14\ H_2O(l)$

e) $3\ Hg_2HPO_4(s) + 2\ Au(s) + 8\ Cl^-(aq) + 3\ H_3O^+(aq) \rightarrow 6\,Hg(l) + 3\ H_2PO_4^-(aq) + 2\ AuCl_4^-(aq) + 3\ H_2O(l)$

Tip. The determination of oxidation numbers[4] is *not* necessary in balancing redox equations. However, oxidation numbers can come in handy in checking results. For example, in part a), vanadium is reduced from the +5 to the +4 state and sulfur is oxidized from the +4 to the +6 state. This requires a gain of one electron per vanadium atom and a loss of two electrons per sulfur atom, confirming the results of step 5.

6.33 Follow the six-step method given in the text. The steps are the same as those used in **6.31** except that now OH^- and H_2O are used to balance hydrogen in step 4.

a) The following lists the results of each step. Indications of state such as (aq) or (s) are omitted until the end.

1.	$Cr(OH)_3 \rightarrow CrO_4^{2-}$	$Br_2 \rightarrow Br^-$
2.	$Cr(OH)_3 \rightarrow CrO_4^{2-}$	$Br_2 \rightarrow 2\,Br^-$
3.	$H_2O + Cr(OH)_3 \rightarrow CrO_4^{2-}$	$Br_2 \rightarrow 2\,Br^-$
4.	$5\,OH^- + H_2O + Cr(OH)_3 \rightarrow CrO_4^{2-} + 5\,H_2O$	$Br_2 \rightarrow 2\,Br^-$
5.	$5\,OH^- + H_2O + Cr(OH)_3 \rightarrow CrO_4^{2-} + 5\,H_2O + 3\,e^-$	$2\,e^- + Br_2 \rightarrow 2\,Br^-$
6.	$10\,OH^- + 2\,H_2O + 2\,Cr(OH)_3 \rightarrow 2\,CrO_4^{2-} + 10\,H_2O + 6\,e^-$	$6\,e^- + 3\,Br_2 \rightarrow 6\,Br^-$

$$\boxed{10\,OH^-(aq) + 2\,Cr(OH)_3(s) + 3\,Br_2(aq) \rightarrow 2\,CrO_4^{2-}(aq) + 6\,Br^-(aq) + 8\,H_2O(l)}$$

In the final line, addition of the oxidation half-equation to the reduction half-equation has led, as planned, to the removal of e^-'s. Combining like terms then removes two H_2O's.

Use the same method in the other parts of the problem.

b) $ZrO(OH)_2(s) + 2\,SO_3^{2-}(aq) \rightarrow Zr(s) + 2\,SO_4^{2-}(aq) + H_2O(l)$

---

[3] Text page 167-168.

[4] Oxidation numbers are discussed text pages 82-84.

c) $7\,HPbO_2^-(aq) + 2\,Re(s) \rightarrow 7\,Pb(s) + 2\,ReO_4^-(aq) + H_2O(l) + 5\,OH^-(aq)$
d) $4\,HXeO_4^-(aq) + 8\,OH^-(aq) \rightarrow 3\,XeO_6^{4-}(aq) + Xe(g) + 6\,H_2O(l)$
e) $N_2H_4(aq) + 2\,CO_3^{2-}(aq) \rightarrow N_2(g) + 2\,CO(g) + 4\,OH^-(aq)$

6.35 The problem requires a reversal of the steps given for the completion and balancing of redox equations.

a) $$Fe^{2+}(aq) \rightarrow Fe^{3+}(aq) + e^- \quad \text{(oxidation)}$$
$$H_2O_2(aq) + 2\,H_3O^+(aq) + 2e^- \rightarrow 4\,H_2O(l) \quad \text{(reduction)}$$

b) $$5\,H_2O(l) + SO_2(aq) \rightarrow HSO_4^-(aq) + 3\,H_3O^+(aq) + 2\,e^- \quad \text{(oxidation)}$$
$$MnO_4^-(aq) + 8\,H_3O^+(aq) + 5\,e^- \rightarrow Mn^{2+}(aq) + 4\,H_2O(l) \quad \text{(reduction)}$$

c) $$ClO_2^-(aq) \rightarrow ClO_2(g) + e^- \quad \text{(oxidation)}$$
$$ClO_2^-(aq) + 4\,H_3O^+(aq) + 4\,e^- \rightarrow Cl^-(aq) + 6\,H_2O(l) \quad \text{(reduction)}$$

Tip. The last reaction is a disproportionation.

6.37 The oxidation state of nitrogen both increases and decreases in this reaction, which is a disproportionation. The two half-reactions are

$$HNO_2(aq) + 4\ H_2O(l) \rightarrow NO_3^-(aq) + 3\ H_3O^+(aq) + 3\ e^- \quad \text{(oxidation)}$$
$$HNO_2(aq) + H_3O^+(aq) \rightarrow NO(g) + 2\ H_2O(l) \quad \text{(reduction)}$$

Combining the two half-equations gives the overall equation:

$$\boxed{3\ HNO_2(aq) \rightarrow NO_3^-(aq) + 2\ NO(g) + H_3O^+(aq)}$$

6.39 The potassium dichromate solution contains 5.134 g of the solute per 1000 mL of solution. 34.26 mL of it brings the titration to the endpoint. The chemical amount of $K_2Cr_2O_7$ that reacts is

$$n_{K_2Cr_2O_7} = 34.26\ \text{mL sol'n} \times \left(\frac{5.134\ \text{g}\ K_2Cr_2O_7}{1000\ \text{mL sol'n}}\right) \times \left(\frac{1\ \text{mol}\ K_2Cr_2O_7}{294.18\ \text{g}\ K_2Cr_2O_7}\right) = 5.979 \times 10^{-4}\ \text{mol}$$

In aqueous solution, 1 mol of $Cr_2O_7^{2-}(aq)$ forms for every 1 mol of $K_2Cr_2O_7$ that dissolves. Also, according to the balanced equation (which is a net ionic equation), 1 mol of $Cr_2O_7^{2-}(aq)$ reacts with 6 mol of $Fe^{2+}(aq)$. Cast these facts as unit factors to compute the chemical amount of Fe^{2+}:

$$n_{Fe^{2+}} = 5.979 \times 10^{-4}\ \text{mol}\ K_2Cr_2O_7 \times \left(\frac{1\ \text{mol}\ Cr_2O_7^{2-}}{1\ \text{mol}\ K_2Cr_2O_7}\right) \times \left(\frac{6\ \text{mol}\ Fe^{2+}}{1\ \text{mol}\ Cr_2O_7^{2-}}\right) = 0.003587\ \text{mol}$$

This is the amount of Fe^{2+} in 500.0 mL of solution. The amount per liter (1000.0 mL) is twice as much. The concentration of Fe^{2+} in the sample is $\boxed{0.007175\ \text{mol L}^{-1}}$.

6.41 Add up the molar masses of acetone and benzophenone, and use them to compute the chemical amounts of the two in the solution:

$$n_{C_3H_6O} = 15.0\ \text{g}\ C_3H_6O \times \frac{1\ \text{mol}\ C_3H_6O}{58.08\ \text{g}\ C_3H_6O} = 0.86087\ \text{mol}\ C_3H_6O$$
$$n_{C_{13}H_{10}O} = 15.0\ \text{g}\ C_{13}H_{10}O \times \frac{1\ \text{mol}\ C_{13}H_{10}O}{182.22\ \text{g}\ C_{13}H_{10}O} = 0.0823\ \text{mol}\ C_{13}H_{10}O$$

The mole fraction of benzophenone in the solution equals:

$$X_{C_{13}H_{10}O} = \frac{0.0823}{0.0823 + 0.86087} = 0.08727$$

The change in vapor pressure of the acetone due to the presence of the benzophenone is

$$\Delta P_{C_3H_6O} = -X_{C_{13}H_{10}O} P^{\circ}_{C_3H_6O} = -0.08727(0.3270 \text{ atm}) = -0.02853 \text{ atm}$$

The final vapor pressure of the acetone equals its P° plus the change. This is 0.3270 atm minus 0.02853 atm or $\boxed{0.2985 \text{ atm}}$.

6.43 The boiling-point elevation of a solvent caused by a single nonvolatile solute is proportional to the molality of the solute:

$$\Delta T_b = K_b m \qquad \text{hence} \qquad K_b = \frac{\Delta T_b}{m}$$

To obtain m, use the definition of molality. The chemical amount of anthracene equals its mass divided by its molar mass, which is 178.2 g mol^{-1}:

$$n_{\text{anthracene}} = \frac{7.80 \text{ g}}{178.2 \text{ g mol}^{-1}} = 0.04376 \text{ mol}$$

The molality of the anthracene in the toluene is this number of moles divided by the mass of the toluene in kilograms:

$$m_{\text{anthracene}} = \frac{0.4376 \text{ mol}}{0.1000 \text{ kg}} = 0.4376 \text{ mol kg}^{-1}$$

The change in the boiling temperature is clearly $112.06 - 110.60 = 1.46°\text{C}$. Then:

$$K_b = \frac{\Delta T_b}{m} = \frac{1.46°\text{C}}{0.4376 \text{ mol kg}^{-1}} = 3.34°\text{C mol kg}^{-1}$$

This can also be expressed as $\boxed{3.34 \text{ K mol kg}^{-1}}$.

Tip. Convert both temperatures from Celsius to absolute, and subtract T_1 from T_2 to check this last statement.

6.45 Compute the molality of the aqueous solution of the nonvolatile, non-dissociating solute sugar using the formula for boiling-point elevation and taking K_b for water from text Table 6.2:[5]

$$m_{\text{sugar}} = \frac{\Delta T_b}{K_b} = \frac{0.30 \text{ K}}{0.512 \text{ K kg mol}^{-1}} = \frac{0.5859 \text{ mol}}{\text{kg}}$$

This means that 200.0 g of water contains 0.1172 mol of sugar. The mass of the sugar is given as 39.8 g. Its molar mass equals 39.8 mol/0.1172 mol = $\boxed{340 \text{ g mol}^{-1}}$.

6.47 Assume that the unknown is nonvolatile. The molality of the unknown then is related to the change in the freezing point of the camphor as follows:

$$m_{\text{unknown}} = -\frac{\Delta T_f}{K_f} = -\frac{(170.8 - 178.4)°\text{C}}{37.7°\text{C kg mol}^{-1}} = 0.20 \text{ mol kg}^{-1}$$

Note the switch in the temperature units in the freezing-point depression constant from K to °C.[6] There is 0.20 mol of unknown per kilogram of camphor, but the problem deals with 25.0 g (0.0250 kg) of camphor. Compute the amount of unknown in the 25.0 g of camphor:

$$n_{\text{unknown}} = 0.20 \text{ mol kg}^{-1} \times 0.0250 \text{ kg} = 0.0050 \text{ mol}$$

[5] Text page 174.

[6] The switch is legitimate since the problem concerns a *change* in temperature. See **6.43**.

The molar mass of a substance equals its mass divided by its chemical amount: 0.840 g/0.0050 mol = $\boxed{1.7 \times 10^2 \text{ g mol}^{-1}}$.

6.49 The ice-cream mixture contains 34 g of sucrose for every 66 g of water. Use this fact in a unit-factor to figure out how much sucrose is present in 1000 g (1 kilogram) of water:

$$m_{\text{sucrose}} = 1000 \text{ g water} \times \left(\frac{340 \text{ g sucrose}}{660 \text{ g water}}\right) = 515 \text{ g sucrose}$$

Divide this mass by 342.3 g mol^{-1}, the molar mass of sucrose, to convert to moles. The result is 1.50 mol. Since there is 1.50 mol of sucrose per 1000 g of water, the molality of the aqueous sucrose is 1.50 mol kg^{-1}. The change in the freezing point is

$$\Delta T = -K_f m = (-1.86 \text{ K mol kg}^{-1})(1.50 \text{ kg mol}^{-1}) = -2.8 \text{ K}$$

The freezing point of the mixture equals this change added to the freezing point of the pure solvent (0°C). It is $\boxed{-2.8°\text{C}}$.

Tip. As pure ice freezes out, the remaining solution becomes more concentrated in sucrose, and the freezing point is depressed further.

6.51 Calculate the effective molality from the change in the freezing point:

$$m = -\frac{\Delta T}{K_f} = -\frac{(-4.218 \text{ K})}{1.86 \text{ K kg mol}^{-1}} = 2.268 \text{ mol kg}^{-1}$$

The ratio of the effective molality to the actual molality is 2.268/0.8402 = 2.70. Thus each Na_2SO_4 unit dissociates effectively into $\boxed{2.70 \text{ particles}}$.

Tip. This is somewhat less than the theoretical value of 3.00 (corresponding to two Na^+ and one SO_4^{2-} per formula unit) because the positive and negative ions in this rather concentrated solution tend to associate, reducing the effective number of free ions.

6.53 The osmotic pressure π of this solution is related to the concentration of the unknown solute by the equation:

$$\pi = cRT$$

Measurements of osmotic pressure therefore give the concentration:

$$c_{\text{unknown}} = \frac{\pi}{RT} = \frac{0.0105 \text{ atm}}{(0.08206 \text{ L atm mol}^{-1}\text{K}^{-1})(300 \text{ K})} = 4.265 \times 10^{-4} \text{ mol L}^{-1}$$

This solution was obtained by dissolving 200 mg (0.200 g) of the solute in 25.0 mL of solution, a procedure that gives the same concentration as dissolving 8.00 g solute in 1.00 L of water. Thus 8.00 g of solute equals 4.265×10^{-4} mol of solute. Accordingly, the molar mass is

$$\mathcal{M}_{\text{unknown}} = \frac{8.00 \text{ g}}{4.265 \times 10^{-4} \text{ mol}} = \boxed{1.88 \times 10^4 \text{ g mol}^{-1}}$$

6.55 Text Figure 6.14[7] shows the experimental set-up. The difference h between the level of the solution in the tube and the level outside the tube is proportional to the osmotic pressure of the solution. The problem gives h as 15.2 cm (0.152 m) of solution. To get the osmotic pressure, substitute the density ρ of the solution

[7] Text page 179.

and the acceleration g of gravity in the formula $\pi = \rho g h$.[8] The density of the solution is 1.00 g cm^{-3}, which is equivalent to 1.00×10^3 kg m^{-3}. Then:

$$\pi = \rho g h = (1.00 \times 10^3 \text{ kg m}^{-3})(9.807 \text{ m s}^{-2})(0.152 \text{ m}) = 1.49 \times 10^3 \text{ kg m}^{-1}\text{s}^{-2}$$

This equals 1.49×10^3 Pa.[9] Converting to atm:

$$\pi = 1.49 \times 10^3 \text{ Pa} \times \left(\frac{1\text{atm}}{101\,325 \text{ Pa}}\right) = 0.0147 \text{ atm}$$

Now, calculate the concentration of the polymer in the solution:

$$c = \frac{\pi}{RT} = \frac{0.0147 \text{ atm}}{(0.08206 \text{ L atm mol}^{-1}\text{K}^{-1})(288.15 \text{ K})} = 6.22 \times 10^{-4} \text{ mol L}^{-1}$$

The solution holds 6.22×10^{-4} mol of polymer per liter. There are also 4.64 g of polymer per liter. Therefore:

$$\mathcal{M} = \frac{4.64 \text{ g}}{6.22 \times 10^{-4} \text{ mol}} = \boxed{7.46 \times 10^3 \text{ g mol}^{-1}}$$

Tip. It is possible to compute the concentration of the polymer without changing the pressure to atmospheres. Use SI units as follows:

$$c = \frac{\pi}{RT} = \frac{1.49 \times 10^3 \text{ Pa}}{(8.3145 \text{ J K}^{-1}\text{mol}^{-1})(288.15 \text{ K})} = 0.622 \text{ mol m}^{-3}$$

This answer is the same because there are 1000 L in a cubic meter. Confirm the cancellation of units as in **6.41**, using the equivalencies in text Appendix B.

6.57 a) The partial pressure of gaseous CO_2 above the aqueous solution of CO_2 is 5.0 atm. Henry's law relates the mole fraction the dissolved CO_2 to this partial pressure:

$$P_{CO_2} = k_{CO_2} X_{CO_2} \qquad \text{from which} \qquad X_{CO_2} = \frac{P_{CO_2}}{k_{CO_2}} = \frac{5.00 \text{ atm}}{(1.65 \times 10^3 \text{ atm})} = 0.0030$$

This fraction means that there is 0.0030 mol of CO_2 in solution for every 0.9970 mol of water. But there is 55.5 mol of water per liter of solution if the solution (which is dilute) has the same density as water. Hence:

$$c_{CO_2} = \frac{0.0030 \text{ mol CO}_2}{0.9970 \text{ mol H}_2\text{O}} \times \left(\frac{55.5 \text{ mol H}_2\text{O}}{1.00 \text{ L solution}}\right) = 0.17 \text{ mol L}^{-1}$$

The amount of CO_2 dissolved in a liter of water held under a pressure of 5.00 atm of gaseous CO_2 is therefore $\boxed{0.17 \text{ mol}}$.

b) Before the cap is removed, gaseous CO_2 in the small space above the liquid is in equilibrium with the dissolved CO_2. This means that CO_2 molecules are constantly moving from the gas phase to the dissolved phase and back. The rate of movement of CO_2 out of solution equals the rate of movement into solution. When the cap is removed, gaseous CO_2 escapes from the bottle because the partial pressure of CO_2 in the atmosphere is far less than 1 atm. Equilibrium is re-established with a far smaller concentration of CO_2 in the solution.

---

[8] Text page 179. Compare this formula to the formula for the "regular" pressure exerted by a gas that appears on text page 100.

[9] Text Table B.2 in text Appendix B.

6.59 Determine the chemical amount of the methane that was dissolved in the 1.00 kg of solution before the boiling. Assume that all the methane was expelled and that the expelled gas behaves ideally:

$$n_{CH_4} = \frac{PV}{RT} = \frac{(1.00 \text{ atm})(3.01 \text{ L})}{(0.08206 \text{ L atm mol}^{-1}\text{K}^{-1})(273.15 \text{ K})} = 0.1343 \text{ mol}$$

The molar mass of CH_4 is 16.04 g mol^{-1}, so the expelled methane has a mass of 2.154 g. The 1.00 kg of solution contained only water and methane. The mass of the water left after removal of methane is therefore 0.9978 kg. This mass of H_2O equals 55.39 mol of water.[10] Calculate the mole fraction of CH_4:

$$X_{CH_4} = \frac{0.1343 \text{ mol}}{0.1343 + 55.39 \text{ mol}} = 0.002419$$

This fraction of CH_4 was present with 1.00 atm of CH_4 above the solution. Henry's law applies, and the Henry's law k equals

$$k_{CH_4} = \frac{P_{CH_4}}{X_{CH_4}} = \frac{1.00 \text{ atm}}{0.002419} = \boxed{413 \text{ atm}}$$

6.61 Write Raoult's law for both the benzene and toluene:

$$P_{\text{benz}} = X_{\text{benz}} P^\circ_{\text{benz}} \qquad \text{and} \qquad P_{\text{tol}} = X_{\text{tol}} P^\circ_{\text{tol}}$$

Since equal numbers of moles of benzene and toluene were mixed, $X_{\text{benz}} = X_{\text{tol}} = 0.500$. Use these mole fractions and the vapor pressures of the pure substances to compute the partial pressure of each substance above the mixture:

$$P_{\text{benz}} = 0.500(0.0987 \text{ atm}) = 0.04935 \text{ atm}$$
$$P_{\text{tol}} = 0.500(0.0289 \text{ atm}) = 0.01445 \text{ atm}$$

The number of moles of a particular gas in a gaseous mixture at constant temperature is directly proportional to its partial pressure:

$$n_{\text{benz}} = P_{\text{benz}} \frac{V}{RT} \qquad \text{and} \qquad n_{\text{tol}} = P_{\text{tol}} \frac{V}{RT}$$

The mole fraction of benzene in the vapor is

$$X_{\text{benz,vap}} = \frac{n_{\text{benz}}}{n_{\text{benz}} + n_{\text{tol}}} = \frac{P_{\text{benz}}(V/RT)}{P_{\text{benz}}(V/RT) + P_{\text{tol}}(V/RT)} = \frac{P_{\text{benz}}}{P_{\text{benz}} + P_{\text{tol}}}$$
$$= \frac{0.04935 \text{ atm}}{(0.04935 + 0.01445) \text{ atm}} = \boxed{0.774}$$

Tip. Half of the molecules in the liquid are benzene, but over three quarters of the molecules in the vapors above the liquid are benzene. Such enrichment in the more volatile component is the basis for separation by distillation.

6.63 a) Convert the masses of CCl_4 and $C_2H_4Cl_2$ to chemical amount by dividing by their respective molar masses:

$$n_{CCl_4} = 30.0 \text{ g} \left(\frac{1 \text{ mol}}{153.82 \text{ g}}\right) = 0.1950 \text{ mol} \qquad n_{C_2H_4Cl_2} = 20.0 \text{ g} \left(\frac{1 \text{ mol}}{98.96 \text{ g}}\right) = 0.2021 \text{ mol}$$

Compute the mole fraction of CCl_4 in the solution from these values:

$$X_{CCl_4} = \frac{0.1950 \text{ mol}}{0.1950 + 0.2021 \text{ mol}} = \boxed{0.491}$$

[10] Using $\mathcal{M} = 18.0153$ g mol^{-1} for water.

b) The total vapor pressure above the solution equals the sum of the partial pressures of the two components in the vapors above the solution. Raoult's law gives these partial pressures. Therefore:

$$P_{\text{tot}} = P_{\text{CCl}_4} + P_{\text{C}_2\text{H}_4\text{Cl}_2} = X_{\text{CCl}_4} P^{\circ}_{\text{CCl}_4} + X_{\text{C}_2\text{H}_4\text{Cl}_2} P^{\circ}_{\text{C}_2\text{H}_4\text{Cl}_2}$$
$$= (0.491)(0.293 \text{ atm}) + (1 - 0.491)(0.209 \text{ atm}) = \boxed{0.250 \text{ atm}}$$

where the mole fraction of CCl_4 comes from the preceding part, and the vapor pressures of the pure components are given in the problem. The two mole fractions add up to one because there are only two components in the solution.

c) The mole fraction of a component in a gaseous mixture equals its partial pressure divided by the total pressure:

$$X_{\text{CCl}_4,\text{vap}} = \frac{P_{\text{CCl}_4}}{P_{\text{tot}}}$$

According to Raoult's law, the partial pressure of $CCl_4(g)$ in the vapor above the solution equals its mole fraction in the solution times its vapor pressure when pure:

$$X_{\text{CCl}_4,\text{vap}} = \frac{P_{\text{CCl}_4}}{P_{\text{tot}}} = \frac{X_{\text{CCl}_4} P^{\circ}_{\text{CCl}_4}}{P_{\text{tot}}}$$

But $P^{\circ}_{\text{CCl}_4}$ is given in the problem and X_{CCl_4} was found in part a). Substitution gives:

$$X_{\text{CCl}_4,\text{vap}} = \frac{0.491(0.293 \text{ atm})}{0.250 \text{ atm}} = \boxed{0.575}$$

Tip. The mole fraction of CCl_4 is 0.491 in the solution but 0.575 in the vapors above the solution. As in **6.61**, the vapors are enriched in the more volatile component.

6.65 a) The element iodine exists in the Donovan's solution in different chemical forms. However, the total amount of this element in the solution, which is prepared by mixing pure compounds that dissolve completely, depends only on the amounts of the compounds and the fraction of each comprised by iodine. The total mass of iodine in 100 mL of Donovan's solution is thus the fraction by mass of elemental iodine in AsI_3 ($\mathcal{M} = 455.6$ g mol^{-1}) multiplied by the 1.00 g of AsI_3 plus the fraction by mass of iodine in HgI_2 ($\mathcal{M} = 454.4$ g mol^{-1}) multiplied by the 1.00 g of HgI_2:

$$m_{\text{I}} = \left(\frac{(3)(126.9) \text{ g I}}{455.6 \text{ g AsI}_3}\right) 1.00 \text{ g AsI}_3 + \left(\frac{(2)(126.9 \text{ g I})}{454.4 \text{ g HgI}_2}\right) 1.00 \text{ g HgI}_2 = 1.39 \text{ g}$$

where 126.9 is the atomic mass of iodine. The mass of iodine per liter (which is 10 times 100 mL) of solution is 10 times this answer or $\boxed{13.9 \text{ g L}^{-1}}$.

b) The 0.100 M AsI_3 solution contains 45.56 g of AsI_3 per liter and therefore furnishes 4.556 g of AsI_3 per 100 mL. To make 3.50 L of Donovan's solution, 35.0 g of AsI_3 is needed. Measure out $(35.0/4.556) \times 100$ mL = 768 mL of the AsI_3 solution. Add to it 35.0 g of $HgI_2(s)$ and 31.5 g of $NaHCO_3(s)$. Then add enough water to bring the total volume to 3.50 L.

6.67 a) Bubbling a mixture of gases that contains the base ammonia through aqueous acetic acid causes the following reaction

$$\boxed{\text{NH}_3(g) + \text{HOAc}(aq) \rightarrow \text{NH}_4^+(aq) + \text{OAc}^-(aq)}$$

The original solution contains the weak electrolyte acetic acid and no other electrolytes and is a poor conductor of electricity. The final solution contains a good concentration of ions and is a good conductor of electricity. The electrical conductivity $\boxed{\text{increases significantly}}$ as the gas is absorbed.

The concentrations of the ions in the final solution equal their chemical amounts divided by the volume of the solution. The acetic acid is "just neutralized" by the ammonia, so the chemical amounts of the two product ions equal each other

$$n_{NH_4^+} = (1.50\text{ L})(0.200\text{ mol L}^{-1}) = 0.300\text{ mol} \qquad n_{OAc^-} = 0.300\text{ mol}$$

The concentrations of the two in the final solution are also equal

$$c_{NH_4^+} = \frac{0.300\text{ mol}}{1.50\text{ L}} = \boxed{0.200\text{ mol L}^{-1}} \qquad c_{OAc^-} = \boxed{0.200\text{ mol L}^{-1}}$$

b) Compute the initial chemical amount of gases in the mixture in the flask

$$n_{\text{gas,initial}} = \frac{PV}{RT} = \frac{5.0\text{ atm} \times 3.00\text{ L}}{(0.08206\text{ L atm mol}^{-1}\text{K}^{-1})300.2\text{ K}} = 0.609\text{ mol}$$

The pressure of gas in the flask falls from 3.00 atm to 1.00 atm when some escapes. The amount that remains is (1.00/3.00)(0.609) mol because n in the ideal gas law is directly proportional to P and neither the T nor V of the flask changes. Therefore (2.00/3.00)(0.609) mol of mixed gas escapes. The chemical amount of ammonia in the gas that escapes is readily computed because the ammonia neutralizes 0.300 mol of acetic acid

$$n_{NH_3} = (1.50\text{ L})(0.200\text{ mol HOAc L}^{-1}) \times \left(\frac{1\text{ mol NH}_3}{1\text{ mol HOAc}}\right) = 0.300\text{ mol NH}_3$$

The escaped gas contained 0.300 mol of NH_3. The rest was nitrogen

$$n_{N_2} = n_{\text{gas}} - n_{NH_3} = \left(\frac{2.00}{3.00}\right)(0.609\text{ mol}) - 0.300\text{ mol} = 0.106\text{ mol}$$

The mass fraction of NH_3 in the escaped gas is

$$w_{NH_3} = \frac{0.300\text{ mol}(17.0\text{ g mol}^{-1})}{0.300\text{ mol}(17.0\text{ g mol}^{-1}) + 0.106\text{ mol}(28.0\text{ g mol}^{-1})} = 0.63$$

The mass percentage of NH_3 in the gas is therefore $\boxed{63\%}$.

6.69 The vanadic sulfate, a good reducing agent, is oxidized according to the balanced half-equation

$$V_2(SO_4)_3(aq) + 8\ OH^-(aq) \rightarrow 2\ V(OH)_4^+(aq) + 3\ SO_4^{2-}(aq) + 4\ e^-$$

Compute the chemical amount of X from the titration data

$$n_X = 15.0\text{ mL} \times \left(\frac{0.200\text{ mmol V}_2(\text{SO}_4)_3}{1\text{ mL}}\right) \times \left(\frac{4\text{ mmol }e^-}{1\text{ mmol V}_2(\text{SO}_4)_3}\right) \times \left(\frac{1\text{ mmol X}}{\text{mmol }e^-}\right) = 12.0\text{ mmol X}$$

The balanced half-equation provides the second factor in parentheses in this equation. The statement of the problem provides the first and the third. The molar mass of X is

$$\mathcal{M}_X = \frac{540\text{ mg X}}{12.0\text{ mmol}} = 45.0\text{ mg mmol}^{-1} = \boxed{45.0\text{ g mol}^{-1}}$$

If each molecule of X accepted three electrons, then the third factor in parentheses in the preceding would have a 3 in the denominator instead of a 1. This would reduce the chemical amount of X by a factor of 3 (from 12.0 mmol to 4.00 mmol) and would increase the molar mass of X by a factor of 3, to $\boxed{135\text{ g mol}^{-1}}$.

6.71 The careful wording of the problem assures the reader that no Cl is lost at any point during the transformation $NaCl \rightarrow Cl_2 \rightarrow HCl$. For every mole of Cl present in the original 150 mL of 10.00% aqueous NaCl, one mole of Cl is formed in the 250 mL of $HCl(aq)$. Compute this number of moles:

$$n_{NaCl} = 150 \text{ mL sol'n} \times \left(\frac{1.0726 \text{ g sol'n}}{1 \text{ mL sol'n}}\right) \times \left(\frac{10.0 \text{ g NaCl}}{100 \text{ g sol'n}}\right) \times \left(\frac{1 \text{ mol NaCl}}{58.44 \text{ g NaCl}}\right) = 0.2753 \text{ mol}$$

Note the third term, in which the mass percentage of NaCl in the solution is used as a unit factor. The 0.2753 mol of NaCl implies 0.2753 mol of Cl, because each mole of NaCl contains one mole of Cl. All of the Cl ends up in the form of HCl, so 0.2753 mol of HCl is present in the 250 mL of solution that is formed. The concentration of the HCl is

$$c_{HCl} = \frac{0.2753 \text{ mol}}{0.250 \text{ L}} = \boxed{1.10 \text{ mol L}^{-1}}$$

6.73 The change in the vapor pressure ΔP is $0.3868 - 0.3914 = -0.0046$ atm. The mole fraction of the sulfur present in the sulfur-CS_2 system is therefore:

$$X_{sulfur} = -\frac{\Delta P}{P^{\circ}_{CS_2}} = -\frac{-0.0046 \text{ atm}}{0.3914 \text{ atm}} = 0.0117$$

The solution contains 1.00 kg of CS_2 which is 13.13 mol of CS_2.[11] Hence:

$$X_{sulfur} = 0.0117 = \frac{n_{sulfur}}{n_{sulfur} + n_{CS_2}} = \frac{n_{sulfur}}{n_{sulfur} + 13.13}$$

Solving for the chemical amount of sulfur gives 0.155 mol. Because this amount of sulfur is simultaneously 40.0 g of sulfur, the molar mass of sulfur as it exists in this solution is 40.0 g/0.155 mol = $\boxed{257 \text{ g mol}^{-1}}$. This is almost exactly eight times larger than 32 g mol^{-1}, the molar mass of S. The molecular formula of the sulfur in the solution must be $\boxed{S_8}$.

6.75 The soft drink is a solution of CO_2 (and other solutes) in water. When the cap is on, gaseous CO_2 in the space above the fluid is held at a pressure exceeding 1 atm. Henry's law requires a higher concentration of dissolved CO_2 than if the pressure of CO_2 were only 1 atm. The dissolved CO_2 depresses the freezing point of the solution. When the cap is popped, the partial pressure of CO_2 over the solution suddenly drops to far less than 1 atm. Gaseous CO_2 bubbles out of solution. The freezing point of the soft drink rises. If the temperature of the soft drink is colder than the elevated freezing point caused by loss of the gaseous solute, the solution will freeze.

6.77 Raoult's law allows calculation of the effective mole fraction of $CaCl_2$ in the solution at 25°C using the vapor-pressure lowering:

$$X_2 = -\frac{P_1 - P_1^0}{P_1^0} = -\frac{(0.02970 - 0.03126) \text{ atm}}{0.03126 \text{ atm}} = 0.0499$$

$CaCl_2$ dissociates in water to form one mole of $Ca^{2+}(aq)$ cations and two moles of $Cl^-(aq)$ anions per mole dissolved. The X_2 just calculated is therefore not the true mole fraction of the solute, but is an *effective* mole fraction that is larger that the true mole fraction because of the dissociation of $CaCl_2$ into ions. Now, calculate the effective molality of the $CaCl_2$:

$$\frac{0.0499 \text{ mol solute}}{(1.000 - 0.0499) \text{ mol } H_2O} \times \left(\frac{1 \text{ mol } H_2O}{0.018015 \text{ kg } H_2O}\right) = 2.92 \text{ mol kg}^{-1}$$

[11] $\mathcal{M} = 76.14$ g mol^{-1}

Put this effective molality into the standard formula for freezing-point depression:

$$\Delta T = -K_\text{f} m = -(1.86\ \text{K kg mol}^{-1})(2.92\ \text{mol kg}^{-1}) = -5.43\ \text{K} = -5.43°\text{C}$$

Recall that the kelvin and the degree Celsius are equal in size. The freezing point of the solution is the original freezing point plus the change:

$$0.00°\text{C} + (-5.43°\text{C}) = \boxed{-5.43°\text{C}}$$

Tip. It is assumed that the effective number of particles of solute is unchanged by cooling from 25°C, where the vapor pressure was recorded, to −5.43°C.

6.79 The salt $GaCl_2$ would be expected to dissociate in water according to:

$$\text{GaCl}_2(aq) \rightarrow \text{Ga}^{2+}(aq) + 2\,\text{Cl}^-(aq)$$

If the "$GaCl_2$" were actually $Ga[GaCl_4]$,[12] then the dissociation would be:

$$\text{Ga[GaCl}_4](aq) \rightarrow \text{Ga}^+(aq) + [\text{GaCl}_4]^-(aq)$$

In the first case, dissociation gives three ions; in the second case, it gives only two ions. We can therefore measure a colligative property to distinguish between the two cases. For example, imagine that enough compound is dissolved in water to make a solution that is 0.0100 mol kg^{-1} in $GaCl_2$. This solution would have a freezing point of −0.056°C if the formula $GaCl_2$ were correct. This freezing point is predicted using an effective molality of 0.0300 mol kg^{-1} in the formula for freezing-point depression. The effective molality is triple m_{GaCl_2} because three moles of ions are formed by dissociation of one mole of $GaCl_2$. Now try the formula $Ga[GaCl_4]$. The identical aqueous solution has a $m_{\text{Ga[GaCl}_4]}$ of 0.00500 mol kg^{-1}, because the new formula for the solute corresponds to a molar mass that is twice as large, and an effective molality of 0.0100 mol kg^{-1}, because two ions are formed upon dissociation. The predicted freezing point of −0.0186°C is measurably different.

6.81 Determine the effective molality of the NaCl solution that freezes at −0.406°C:

$$m_\text{NaCl} = -\frac{\Delta T_\text{f}}{K_\text{f}} = -\frac{-0.406\ \text{K}}{1.86\ \text{K kg mol}^{-1}} = 0.218\ \text{mol kg}^{-1}$$

This is also the effective molality of the contents of the red blood cell. It is assumed in the problem that the molality inside the cell equals the molarity. Then, 0.218 M can be used to calculate the osmotic pressure:

$$\pi = cRT = (0.218\ \text{mol L}^{-1})(0.08206\ \text{L atm mol}^{-1}\text{K}^{-1})(298.15\ \text{K}) = \boxed{5.33\ \text{atm}}$$

6.83 Write Henry's law for a solution of benzene in water:

$$P_\text{benz} = k_\text{benz} X_\text{benz} = (301\ \text{atm}) X_\text{benz}$$

The chemical amount of benzene in the solution described in the problem is 0.0256 mol, obtained by dividing 2.0 g by 78.11 g mol^{-1}, the molar mass of benzene. The mole fraction of benzene is

$$X_\text{benz} = \frac{0.0256\ \text{mol}}{0.0256 + (55.5 \times 10^3)\ \text{mol}} = 4.6 \times 10^{-7}$$

The large amount of water completely drowns out the contribution of the benzene to the denominator of this fraction. Insert the mole fraction of benzene and the given Henry's law constant into the equation for Henry's law:

$$P_\text{benz} = k_\text{benz} X_\text{benz} = (301\ \text{atm})(4.6 \times 10^{-7}) = \boxed{1.4 \times 10^{-4}\ \text{atm}}$$

[12] The bracketed group is a complex ion. See text Chapter 18.

Then substitute this pressure and the temperature in kelvins into the rearranged ideal-gas equation:

$$c_{\text{benz}} = \frac{n_{\text{benz}}}{V} = \frac{P_{\text{benz}}}{RT} = \frac{1.4 \times 10^{-4}\ \text{atm}}{(0.082057\ \text{L atm K}^{-1}\text{mol}^{-1})(298.15\ \text{K})} = 5.7 \times 10^{-6}\ \text{mol L}^{-1}$$

This result is the concentration of the benzene in the vapor above the solution. Convert to molecules per cubic centimeter (which is a *number density*) as follows

$$C_{\text{benz}} = \frac{5.7 \times 10^{-6}\ \text{mol}}{1\ \text{L}} \times \left(\frac{1\ \text{L}}{1000\ \text{cm}^3}\right) \times \left(\frac{6.022 \times 10^{23}\ \text{molecule}}{1\ \text{mol}}\right) = \boxed{3.4 \times 10^{15}\,\frac{\text{molecule}}{\text{cm}^3}}$$

6.85 The difference between a solution and a colloidal suspension lies with the size of the dispersed particles. In a solution, the solute is dispersed at the molecular (or ionic) level. Each particle is surrounded by a cage of several solvent molecules. Examples are solutions of NaCl or alcohol in water. In a colloidal suspension, the dispersed particles are aggregates of hundreds to thousands of solute molecules. The aggregates are frequently surrounded by interacting solvent molecules that prevent them from sticking together to form a visible precipitate. The particles do not settle on the bottom of the container because the agitation caused by collisions of neighboring molecules is strong enough to keep them up. An example of a colloid is homogenized milk. The white opacity of milk is caused by tiny particles of fat that are too small to be filtered. In some cases, it is difficult to classify a mixture definitively as solution or suspension. If the particles are aggregates of only small numbers of molecules, the properties of the mixture will be similar to those of a solution, but deviate somewhat toward those of a colloid.

6.87 First obtain the empirical formula of the compound. Compute the chemical amounts of C and H in the sample:

$$n_{\text{C}} = 5.46\ \text{g CO}_2 \times \left(\frac{1\ \text{mol CO}_2}{44.0\ \text{g CO}_2}\right) \times \left(\frac{1\ \text{mol C}}{1\ \text{mol CO}_2}\right) = 0.1241\ \text{mol}$$

$$n_{\text{H}} = 2.23\ \text{g H}_2\text{O} \times \left(\frac{1\ \text{mol H}_2\text{O}}{18.015\ \text{g H}_2\text{O}}\right) \times \left(\frac{2\ \text{mol H}}{1\ \text{mol H}_2\text{O}}\right) = 0.2476\ \text{mol}$$

These amounts correspond to 0.2495 g of H and 1.490 g of C, so the mass of oxygen in the combustion sample equals:

$$m_{\text{O}} = m_{\text{tot}} - m_{\text{H}} - m_{\text{C}} = 2.40 - 0.2495 - 1.490 = 0.6605\ \text{g}$$

The chemical amount of O is

$$n_{\text{O}} = 0.6611\ \text{g O} \times \left(\frac{1\ \text{mol O}}{15.9994\ \text{g O}}\right) = 0.0413\ \text{mol}$$

The three elements are present in the molar ratio $C_{0.124}H_{0.248}O_{0.0413}$, which gives the empirical formula C_3H_6O.

The observed depression of the freezing point gives the molality of the solution:

$$m = -\frac{\Delta T_{\text{f}}}{K_{\text{f}}} = -\frac{-0.97\ \text{K}}{1.86\ \text{K kg mol}^{-1}} = 0.522\ \text{mol kg}^{-1}$$

The 0.281 kg of solvent therefore contains 0.146 mol of the compound. The mass of this 0.146 mol of compound equals 8.69 g. Hence the molar mass of the compound is approximately 59 g mol^{-1}. The molecular formula is clearly $\boxed{C_3H_6O}$, which has a molar mass of 58.08 g mol^{-1}.

Chapter 7

Thermodynamic Processes and Thermochemistry

7.1 The work done *on* a gas in a change of volume at constant pressure is given by $w = -P_{\text{ext}}\Delta V$.[1] The problem states values for the external pressure and for the final and initial volumes. Substituting gives:

$$w = -P_{\text{ext}}\Delta V = -(50.0 \text{ atm})(974 \text{ L} - 542 \text{ L}) = -2.16 \times 10^4 \text{ L atm}$$

where, as ever, the change in a quantity (in this case the volume) is the final value minus the initial. To convert to joules, multiply by the proper unit factor:[2]

$$w = -2.16 \times 10^4 \text{ L atm} \times \left(\frac{101.325 \text{ J}}{1 \text{ L atm}}\right) = \boxed{-2.19 \times 10^6 \text{ J}}$$

Tip. Negative work is performed on the nitrogen; the nitrogen does positive work on its surroundings. The difference is a matter of point of view. Do we put ourselves with the gas looking at the surroundings, or in the surroundings looking at the gas?

7.3 A ball of mass M falls a distance Δh under the influence of gravity. It experiences a change in potential energy equal to $Mg\Delta h$, where Δh is the change in height and g is the acceleration of gravity. The (non-bouncing) ball stops dead when it hits the ground. According to the problem, the total energy of the ball does not change at impact. All of the potential energy instead is converted in internal energy that goes to heat up the ball. This is expressed mathematically:

$$Mc_{\text{s}}\Delta T + Mg\Delta h = 0$$

where c_{s} is the specific heat capacity of the ball. Cancel out the M's and solve for Δh:

$$\Delta h = -\frac{c_{\text{s}}\Delta T}{g}$$

In this problem, ΔT equals 1.00°C (which equals 1.00 K) and c_{s} equals $0.850 \times 10^3 \text{ J K}^{-1}\text{kg}^{-1}$. Note that c_{s} is put on a per-kilogram basis to aid the cancellation of units. Also, g is 9.81 m s^{-2}. Substituting gives:

$$\Delta h = -\frac{(0.850 \times 10^3 \text{ J K}^{-1}\text{kg}^{-1})(1.00 \text{ K})}{9.81 \text{ m s}^{-2}} = -86.6 \text{ J kg}^{-1}\text{m}^{-1}\text{s}^2$$

[1] This is text equation 7.1.

[2] From text page 202.

By its definition a joule equals a kg m^2s^{-2}. Therefore, in the above cluster of units all but the meter cancel out: Δh is -86.6 m. The negative sign simply means that the final height of the ball is less than the initial height. The ball falls a distance of $\boxed{86.6 \text{ m}}$ down.

7.5 The molar heat capacity of a substance equals its specific heat capacity multiplied by its molar mass. Here is a sample calculation for lithium:

$$c_\text{p} = c_\text{s}\mathcal{M} = 3.57 \text{ J K}^{-1}\text{g}^{-1}(6.94 \text{ g mol}^{-1}) = 24.8 \text{ J K}^{-1}\text{mol}^{-1}$$

The full set of values in the group:

Li(s)	Na(s)	K(s)	Rb(s)	Cs(s)	
24.8	28.3	29.6	31.0	32.2	J $\text{K}^{-1}\text{mol}^{-1}$

Beyond sodium there is a steady increase of about 1.3 J $\text{K}^{-1}\text{mol}^{-1}$ for every element. Extrapolation of the trend assigns francium a molar heat capacity of about $\boxed{33.5 \text{ J K}^{-1}\text{mol}^{-1}}$. Although the trend is small, it is distinct. Indeed, the molar heat capacities of the metallic elements are remarkably constant. This constancy is the law of Dulong and Petit (see **7.7**).

7.7 Again, the molar heat capacity of a substance equals its specific heat capacity multiplied by its molar mass. The calculations proceed as in **7.5** with the results:

Ni(s)	Zn(s)	Rh(s)	W(s)	Au(s)	U(s)	
26.1	25.4	25.0	24.3	25.4	27.6	J $\text{K}^{-1}\text{mol}^{-1}$

7.9 **a)** During the heating process, heat flows from the surroundings to the system. Therefore, $\boxed{q \text{ is positive}}$. Since the container is rigid, it neither expands nor contracts. Hence ΔV is zero. Consequently, no pressure-volume work is performed on the system. No other type of work is possible, so $\boxed{w = 0}$. Then, by the first law, $\boxed{\Delta E \text{ is positive}}$.

b) During the cooling process, the heat absorbed by the system is negative $\boxed{q < 0}$. No work can be done on the system $\boxed{w = 0}$. The energy of the system is therefore lowered $\boxed{\Delta E < 0}$.

c) Since no work was done in either step 1 or step 2, $\boxed{w_1 + w_2 = 0}$. Nothing in the problem suggests that the system is in the same thermodynamic state after it is cooled back to its original temperature. All that is stated is that the temperature is the same. Other variables, such as the internal energy, might be greatly affected by the heating-cooling cycle. Hence $\Delta E_1 + \Delta E_2$ is *not* necessarily zero.
Tip. A trap in this problem is to assume, without justification, that the system in the container is ideal gas (for which the internal energy depends only on the temperature). A related trap is to assume that any changes brought on by the heating are exactly reversed by the cooling. This is not the case when an egg is boiled so why should it be true here? All that can be said is $\boxed{\Delta E_1 + \Delta E_2 = q_1 + q_2}$. The two sides of this equation could be positive, negative, or zero.

7.11 Let the system under consideration consist of two sub-systems: the metal and the water. If the mixing of hot metal and cool water takes place in a well-insulated container (which prevents leaks of heat), then the heat absorbed by the system equals zero. The system is the sum of the two sub-systems. Therefore:

$$q_\text{sys} = 0 = q_\text{m} + q_\text{w}$$

For both sub-systems, the amount of heat gained equals the specific heat capacity times the mass times the temperature change:

$$q_\text{m} + q_\text{w} = M_\text{w}c_{s,\text{w}}\Delta T_\text{w} + M_\text{m}c_{s,\text{m}}\Delta T_\text{m} = 0$$

Solving for the specific heat capacity of the metal:

$$c_{s,\text{m}} = \frac{-M_\text{w} c_{s,\text{w}} \Delta T_\text{w}}{M_\text{m} \Delta T_\text{m}} = -\frac{(100.0 \text{ g})\, 4.18 \text{ J K}^{-1}\text{g}^{-1}(6.39°\text{C})}{(61.0 \text{ g})(-93.61°\text{C})} = \boxed{0.468 \text{ J K}^{-1}\text{g}^{-1}}$$

Tip. We do not bother to convert °C to K. A change of one degree Celsius is identical to a change of one kelvin. The Kelvin and Celsius scales have the same size increments and differ only in the location of their zeros.

7.13 Body 1 and body 2 are originally at different temperatures. They are brought into thermal contact with each other and held in thermal isolation from other objects. Then:

$$q_1 + q_2 = M_1 c_{s1} \Delta T_1 + M_2 c_{s2} \Delta T_2 = 0$$

If the masses of the two bodies are equal, then $M_1 = M_2$, and:

$$c_{s1} \Delta T_1 = -c_{s2} \Delta T_2 \qquad \text{from which} \qquad \boxed{\frac{c_{s1}}{c_{s2}} = -\frac{\Delta T_2}{\Delta T_1}}$$

The last equation shows that the specific heat capacities of the two bodies are inversely proportional to the temperature changes they undergo in this experiment.
Tip. The minus sign in the answer reflects the fact that the ΔT's of body 1 and body 2 are always of opposite signs; one warms up while the other cools down.

7.15 The difference in temperature ΔT between water at its boiling point and melting point is 100°C. The heat needed to bring 1.00 g of water at 0°C to 100°C equals:

$$q = M c_s \Delta T = (1.00 \text{ g})\left(4.18 \text{ J } (°\text{C})^{-1} \text{ g}^{-1}\right)(100°\text{C}) = 418 \text{ J}$$

The amount of heat needed to melt 1.00 g of ice is, according to the statement of Lavoisier and Laplace, 3/4 of this amount or $\boxed{314 \text{ J}}$. More recent experiments set the amount of heat to melt 1.00 g of ice at 333 J.

7.17 The 0.500 mol of neon expands against a constant pressure of 0.100 atm. Define the system as the neon. Before the expansion, the volume of the system is 11.20 L (calculated using the ideal-gas equation with n equal 0.500 mol at 1.00 atm and 273 K). The expanded volume is 43.08 L (calculated from the ideal-gas equation with $P = 0.200$ atm, $n = 0.500$ mol, and $T = 210$ K). The gas expands against a constant pressure (of 0.100 atm). The work done on the system is

$$w = -P_\text{ext} \Delta V = -0.100 \text{ atm}(43.08 - 11.20) \text{ L} = \boxed{-3.19 \text{ L atm}}$$

The gas cools from 273 to 210 K. Since it is an ideal monatomic gas, the change in its internal energy is directly proportional to the change in its temperature; the constant of proportionality is $n(\frac{3}{2})R$, the heat capacity at constant volume:

$$\Delta E = n c_\text{V} \Delta T = n\left(\frac{3}{2}R\right)\Delta T$$

Substituting gives:

$$\Delta E = 0.500 \text{ mol}\left(\frac{3}{2} 0.08206 \text{ L atm mol}^{-1}\text{K}^{-1}\right)(-63 \text{ K}) = \boxed{-3.88 \text{ L atm}}$$

By the first law:

$$q = \Delta E - w = -3.88 \text{ L atm} - (-3.19 \text{ L atm}) = \boxed{-0.69 \text{ L atm}}$$

The three answers can also be given in joules (1 L atm = 101.325 J):

$$w = -323 \text{ J} \qquad \Delta E = -393 \text{ J} \qquad q = -70 \text{ J}$$

7.19 a) The statement of the problem gives the initial quantity (2.00 mol), pressure (3.00 atm), and temperature (350 K) of the ideal monatomic gas. The initial volume of the gas is $V = nRT/P = 19.15$ L. The final volume is *twice* this original volume or $\boxed{38.3 \text{ L}}$. The change in volume ΔV equals $38.30 - 19.15 = 19.15$ L.

b) The adiabatic expansion occurs against a *constant* pressure of 1.00 atm. Under that circumstance, the work done on the gas is

$$w = -P\Delta V = -1.00(19.15) \text{ L atm} \times \left(\frac{101.325 \text{ J}}{1 \text{ L atm}}\right) = \boxed{-1.94 \times 10^3 \text{ J}}$$

The expansion is adiabatic so $\boxed{q = 0}$ by definition, and:

$$\Delta E = q + w = 0 - 1.94 \times 10^3 \text{ J} = \boxed{-1.94 \times 10^3 \text{ J}}$$

c) Any change in the internal energy of an ideal gas causes a change in temperature in direct proportion:

$$\Delta E = nc_V\Delta T$$

Solving for ΔT and substituting the various values:

$$\Delta T = \frac{\Delta E}{nc_V} = \frac{-1.94 \times 10^3 \text{ J}}{2.00 \text{ mol}(3/2)8.3145 \text{ J K}^{-1}\text{mol}^{-1}} = -77.8 \text{ K}$$

Thus, T_2, the final temperature, is $T_1 + \Delta T = 350 + (-77.8) = \boxed{272 \text{ K}}$.

7.21 The system consists of the 6.00 mol of argon. The change in internal energy of this monatomic gas (assuming ideality) is

$$\Delta E = nc_V\Delta T = (6.00 \text{ mol})\left(\frac{3}{2}8.3145 \text{ J K}^{-1}\text{mol}^{-1}\right)(150 \text{ K}) = 11.2 \times 10^3 \text{ J}$$

The change is adiabatic which means that $\boxed{q = 0}$. From the first law:

$$w = \Delta E - q = 11.2 \times 10^3 \text{ J} - 0 = \boxed{+11.2 \times 10^3 \text{ J}}$$

The work done on the argon is $\boxed{11.2 \times 10^3 \text{ J}}$, *all* of which goes to increase its internal energy.

7.23 The balanced equation tells the enthalpy change taking place during the production or consumption of a specific number of moles of product or reactant. All that is necessary is to put these enthalpy changes on a basis of mass.

a) $$\Delta H = \frac{-828 \text{ kJ}}{2 \text{ mol Na}_2\text{O}} \times \left(\frac{1.00 \text{ mol Na}_2\text{O}}{62.0 \text{ g Na}_2\text{O}}\right) = \boxed{-6.68 \text{ kJ g}^{-1}}$$

b) $$\Delta H = \frac{302 \text{ kJ}}{1 \text{ mol MgO}} \times \left(\frac{1.00 \text{ mol MgO}}{40.31 \text{ g MgO}}\right) = \boxed{7.49 \text{ kJ g}^{-1}}$$

c) $$\Delta H = \frac{33.3 \text{ kJ}}{2 \text{ mol CO}} \times \left(\frac{1.00 \text{ mol CO}}{28.01 \text{ g CO}}\right) = \boxed{0.594 \text{ kJ g}^{-1}}$$

7.25 Only 119.0 J of the measured 121.3 J of heat comes from the reaction of the 0.00288 mol of $Br_2(l)$. The rest of the heat (2.34 J) is added mechanically[3] by breaking the capsule and stirring the liquid. The amount of heat evolved from 1.00 mol of $Br_2(l)$ is

$$1.00 \text{ mol} \times \left(\frac{119.0 \text{ J}}{2.88 \times 10^{-3} \text{ mol}}\right) = \boxed{41.3 \times 10^3 \text{ J}}$$

---

[3]See text Figure 7.7, text page 204.

7.27 The vaporization is $CO(l) \rightarrow CO(g)$. For this change, ΔH_{vap} is 6.04 kJ mol^{-1}. The following series of conversions provides the answer:

$$\Delta H = 2.38\ \text{g CO} \times \left(\frac{1\ \text{mol CO}}{28.01\ \text{g CO}}\right) \times \left(\frac{6.04\ \text{kJ}}{1\ \text{mol CO}}\right) = \boxed{0.513\ \text{kJ}}$$

7.29 The 36.0 g ice cube contains 2.00 mol of H_2O because 1.00 mol of water equals 18.0 g of water. The cube is put in contact with 360 g of 20°C water. At −10°C, the ice is well below its melting point. It must heat up before it can start to melt. Warming the ice from −10°C to 0°C absorbs:

$$q = nc_p\Delta T = (2.00\ \text{mol})(38\ \text{J K}^{-1}\text{mol}^{-1})(10\ \text{K}) = 760\ \text{J}$$

Melting the ice at 0°C gives water at 0°C and absorbs:

$$q = n\Delta H_{\text{fus}} = (2.00\ \text{mol})(6007\ \text{J mol}^{-1}) = 12\,014\ \text{J}$$

On the other hand, cooling 360 g (20.0 mol) of water from 20°C to 0°C would absorb:

$$q = nc_p(T_f - T_i) = (20.0\ \text{mol})(75\ \text{J K}^{-1}\text{mol}^{-1})(-20\ \text{K}) = -3.0 \times 10^4\ \text{J}$$

This result can be rephrased: cooling 20.0 mol of water from 20°C to 0°C requires *removal* of $+3.0 \times 10^4$ J. Since the ice cube absorbs only 12774 J by warming up and then melting to liquid water at 0°C, T_f, the final temperature of the mixture, must be above 0°C.

No heat is lost to the surroundings. The heat absorbed in warming and melting the ice, and then warming the melt-water to the actual T_f can therefore be added with the heat absorbed in cooling the 20.0° water to T_f to equal zero:

$$\underbrace{12\,774\ \text{J}}_{q\ \text{for ice}} + \underbrace{(2.00\ \text{mol})(75\ \text{J K}^{-1}\text{mol}^{-1})(T_f - 0)}_{q\ \text{for meltwater}} + \underbrace{(20.0\ \text{mol})(75\ \text{J K}^{-1}\text{mol}^{-1})(T_f - 20.0)}_{q\ \text{for warm water}} = 0$$

Solving gives $T_f = \boxed{10.4°\text{C}}$.

Tip. A source of difficulty in this problem is the wrong concept that ice is always at 0°C. Like any other material, ice comes to the temperature of its surroundings.

7.31 Multiply the equation and ΔH for the combustion of methane by 2. Reverse the equation for the combustion of ketene and multiply its ΔH by −1:

$$2\,CH_4(g) + 4\,O_2(g) \rightarrow 2\,CO_2(g) + 4\,H_2O(g) \qquad \Delta H = -1604.6\ \text{kJ}$$
$$2\,CO_2(g) + H_2O(g) \rightarrow CH_2CO(g) + 2\,O_2(g) \qquad \Delta H = 981.1\ \text{kJ}$$

Adding these two equations gives the desired equation:

$$2\,CH_4(g) + 2\,O_2(g) \rightarrow CH_2CO(g) + 3\,H_2O(g) \qquad \Delta H = \boxed{-623.5\ \text{kJ}}$$

By Hess's law, the enthalpy of the total reaction equals the sum of the enthalpies of the two reactions that are added.

Tip. How does one know which equations to reverse or double in problems like this? Manipulate to put the correct number of moles of each substance on the correct side of the final equation. Thus, the ketene equation had to be reversed because ketene is among the products in the target equation.

7.33 The conversion C(*gr*) → C(*dia*) is endothermic (positive ΔH). Therefore, one pound of diamonds contains more enthalpy than one pound of graphite. Both diamond and graphite give the same product (carbon dioxide) when burned. When burned, the pound of $\boxed{\text{diamonds}}$ will give off more heat.

7.35 A reaction enthalpy is calculated by summing the enthalpies of formation of the products and subtracting the enthalpies of formation of the reactants:

$$N_2H_4(l) + 3\,O_2(g) \rightarrow 2\,NO_2(g) + 2\,H_2O(l)$$

$$\Delta H^\circ = 2\underbrace{(33.18)}_{NO_2(g)} + 2\underbrace{(-285.83)}_{H_2O(l)} - 1\underbrace{(50.63)}_{N_2H_4(l)} - 3\underbrace{(0)}_{O_2(g)} = \boxed{-555.93\text{ kJ}}$$

In the preceding equation, all of the ΔH_f°'s are in kJ mol^{-1}. All are multiplied by the number of moles of the substance represented in the balanced equation.

7.37 a) As in the preceding:

$$2\,ZnS(s) + 3\,O_2(g) \rightarrow 2\,ZnO(s) + 2\,SO_2(g)$$

$$\Delta H^\circ = 2\underbrace{(-348.28)}_{ZnO(s)} + 2\underbrace{(-296.83)}_{SO_2(g)} - 2\underbrace{(-205.98)}_{ZnS(s)} - 3\underbrace{(0)}_{O_2(g)} = \boxed{-878.26\text{ kJ}}$$

b) Compute the chemical amount of ZnS (in moles) and multiply it by the molar ΔH° to get the amount of heat absorbed in the roasting of the 3.00 metric tons of ZnS. It is known that 2 mol of ZnS(*s*) has a ΔH° of −878.26 kJ. Hence:

$$q_p = \Delta H^\circ = 3.0\text{ metric ton ZnS} \times \left(\frac{10^6\text{ g}}{\text{metric ton}}\right) \times \left(\frac{1\text{ mol}}{97.456\text{ g}}\right) \times \left(\frac{-878.26\text{ kJ}}{2\text{ mol ZnS}}\right) = \boxed{-1.35 \times 10^7\text{ kJ}}$$

7.39 a) The balanced equation is $CaCl_2(s) \rightarrow Ca^{2+}(aq) + 2\,Cl^-(aq)$. Combine the enthalpies of formation as follows:

$$\Delta H^\circ = 2\underbrace{(-167.16)}_{Cl^-(aq)} - 1\underbrace{(542.83)}_{Ca^{2+}(aq)} - 1\underbrace{(-795.8)}_{CaCl_2(s)} = \boxed{-81.4\text{ kJ}}$$

b) Compute ΔH° for the dissolution of 20.0 g of $CaCl_2(s)$:

$$\Delta H^\circ = 20.0\text{ g } CaCl_2 \times \left(\frac{1\text{ mol } CaCl_2}{110.98\text{ g } CaCl_2}\right) \times \left(\frac{-81.35\text{ kJ}}{1\text{ mol } CaCl_2}\right) = -14.66\text{ kJ}$$

The process of dissolution absorbs −14.66 kJ. The immediate surroundings of the dissolution (the water) therefore must absorb +14.66 kJ. The temperature change of the water equals the heat it absorbs divided by its heat capacity:

$$\Delta T = \frac{q}{c_p M} = \frac{14.66 \times 10^3\text{ J}}{418\text{ J K}^{-1}} = 35.1\text{ K} = 35.1^\circ\text{C}$$

The final temperature is $T_f = 20.0^\circ\text{C} + 35.1^\circ\text{C} = \boxed{55.1^\circ\text{C}}$.

7.41 The balanced equation is $C_6H_{12}(l) + 9\,O_2(g) \rightarrow 6\,CO_2(g) + 6\,H_2O(l)$. Set up a calculation of a standard enthalpy of this combustion reaction in terms of standard enthalpies of formation of the products and reactants. The standard enthalpy of combustion is known, but one of the ΔH_f°'s is not known:

$$\Delta H^\circ = -3923.7\text{ kJ} = 6\underbrace{(-393.51)}_{CO_2(g)} + 6\underbrace{(-285.83)}_{H_2O(g)} - 1\,\Delta H_f^\circ\,(C_6H_{12}(l)) - 9\underbrace{(0)}_{O_2(g)}$$

The standard enthalpies of formation are all in kJ mol^{-1}. All are therefore multiplied by the number of moles of each substance appearing in the balanced equation. Solving gives the ΔH_f° of liquid cyclohexane as $\boxed{-152.3 \text{ kJ mol}^{-1}}$.

7.43 a) The equation is $\boxed{C_{10}H_8(s) + 12\,O_2(g) \rightarrow 10\,CO_2(g) + 4\,H_2O(l)}$.

b) The amount of heat evolved ($-q$) in the combustion of 0.6410 g of naphthalene was observed to equal 25.79 kJ. Since the combustion was performed at constant volume, no work was done on the system ($w = 0$). Therefore, $\Delta E = q + w = -25.79 \text{ kJ} + 0 = -25.79$ kJ. Put ΔE on a molar basis

$$\Delta E = \left(\frac{-25.79 \text{ kJ}}{0.6410 \text{ g } C_{10}H_8}\right) \times \left(\frac{128.17 \text{ g } C_{10}H_8}{1 \text{ mol } C_{10}H_8}\right) = -5157 \text{ kJ mol}^{-1}$$

The temperature is essentially 25°C both before and after the reaction. Hence, the ΔE° in the combustion of 1.000 mol of naphthalene is $\boxed{-5157 \text{ kJ}}$.

c) To calculate ΔH° use the definition

$$\Delta H^\circ = \Delta E^\circ + \Delta(PV)$$

As discussed on text page 215, this leads to

$$= \Delta E^\circ + (\Delta n_g)RT$$

for cases like this one. The Δn_g is the change in the number of moles of gases during the reaction. The combustion of 1.000 mol of naphthalene produces 10.00 mol of gases, while consuming 12.00 mol. Hence:

$$\begin{aligned}(\Delta n_g)RT &= (-2.00 \text{ mol})(8.3145 \text{ J K}^{-1}\text{mol}^{-1})(298.15 \text{ K}) = -4.96 \text{ kJ}\\ \Delta H^\circ &= \Delta E^\circ + (\Delta n_g)RT\\ &= -5157 - 4.96 = \boxed{-5162 \text{ kJ}}\end{aligned}$$

d) Use $\Delta H^\circ = \sum \Delta H_f^\circ(\text{products}) - \sum \Delta H_f^\circ(\text{reactants})$ to write:

$$\Delta H^\circ = -5162 \text{ kJ} = 10\underbrace{(-393.51)}_{CO_2(g)} + 4\underbrace{(-285.83)}_{H_2O(l)} - 12\underbrace{(\ 0\ )}_{O_2(g)} - 1\,\Delta H_f^\circ(\text{naphthalene}(s))$$

where each term on the right consists of a ΔH_f° in kJ mol^{-1} multiplied by the number of moles in the balanced equation. Solving gives the ΔH_f° of solid naphthalene as $\boxed{+84 \text{ kJ mol}^{-1}}$ at 25°C.

7.45 Write an equation for the formation of $CCl_3F(g)$ from the "naked atoms":

$$C(g) + 3\,Cl(g) + F(g) \rightarrow CCl_3F(g)$$

From the average bond enthalpies[4] estimate the ΔH° for this reaction as:

$$\Delta H^\circ = 1\underbrace{(-441)}_{C-F} + 3\underbrace{(-328)}_{C-Cl} = -1425 \text{ kJ}$$

Next, write equations that show the preparation of the naked atoms from the elements in their standard states. Each of these atomization processes has an associated enthalpy derived from the data in the text:[5]

$$\begin{aligned}C(s) &\rightarrow C(g) & \Delta H^\circ &= 716.7 \text{ kJ}\\ 3/2\,Cl_2(g) &\rightarrow 3\,Cl(g) & \Delta H^\circ &= 365.1 \text{ kJ}\\ 1/2\,F_2(g) &\rightarrow F(g) & \Delta H^\circ &= 79.0 \text{ kJ}\end{aligned}$$

[4] Text Table 7.3, text page 219.

[5] The atomization enthalpies in Table 7.3 are per mole of atom formed. Accordingly, each is multiplied by the number of moles of the atom involved.

Combine the four reactions to arrive at the formation reaction of $CCl_3F(g)$ from the elements in their standard states:

$$\begin{aligned}
C(g) + 3\,Cl(g) + F(g) &\rightarrow CCl_3F(g) & \Delta H^\circ &= -1425 \text{ kJ}\\
C(s) &\rightarrow C(g) & \Delta H^\circ &= 716.7 \text{ kJ}\\
3/2\,Cl_2(g) &\rightarrow 3\,Cl(g) & \Delta H^\circ &= 365.1 \text{ kJ}\\
1/2\,F_2(g) &\rightarrow F(g) & \Delta H^\circ &= 79.0 \text{ kJ}\\
C(s) + 3/2\,Cl_2(g) + 1/2\,F_2(g) &\rightarrow CCl_3F(g) & \Delta H^\circ &= -264 \text{ kJ}
\end{aligned}$$

The ΔH_f° is $\boxed{-264 \text{ kJ mol}^{-1}}$ because the reaction involves 1 mol of $CCl_3F(g)$.

7.47 The reaction is the combustion of propane in oxygen:

$$C_3H_8(g) + 5\,O_2(g) \rightarrow 3\,CO_2(g) + 4\,H_2O(g)$$

As this reaction proceeds, bonds are both broken and formed. Broken are 2 mol of C—C bonds, 8 mol of C—H bonds, and 5 mol of O=O double bonds. Formed are 6 mol of C=O double bonds and 8 mol of O—H bonds. The net enthalpy of the reaction approximately equals:

$$\Delta H \approx 6\underbrace{(728)}_{\text{C=O}} + 8\underbrace{(463)}_{\text{O-H}} - 5\underbrace{(498)}_{\text{O=O}} - 8\underbrace{(413)}_{\text{C-H}} - 2\underbrace{(348)}_{\text{C-C}} = \boxed{-1.58 \times 10^3 \text{ kJ}}$$

Tip. The answer -1.582×10^3 kJ is correct according to the rules for significant digits.[6] In view of the fact that bond enthalpies are only approximately constant[7] -1.58×10^3 kJ is a more sensible answer.

7.49 The Lewis structures are:

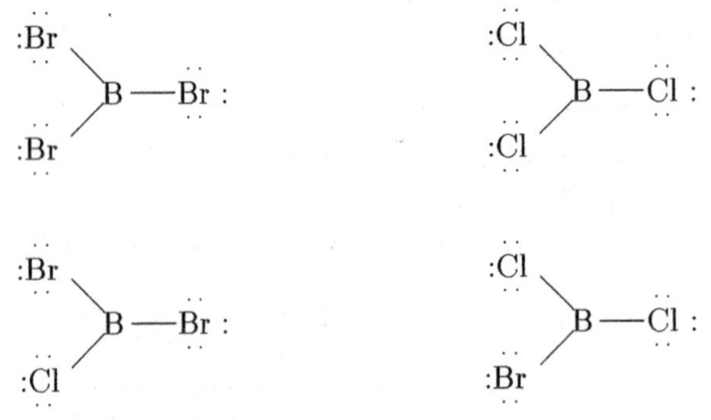

The reaction breaks but then reforms a mole of boron-bromine bonds and a mole of boron-chlorine bonds. Therefore, the sum of the average bond enthalpies in the products equals the sum of the average bond enthalpies in the reactants.

Tip. Boron tribromide and boron trichloride are octet-deficient molecules.

7.51 The system is the 2.00 mol of ideal gas. In an isothermal change, no change of temperature occurs. $(\Delta T = 0)$. The internal energy of an ideal gas depends only on its temperature which means that $\boxed{\Delta E = 0}$. As for the enthalpy:

$$\Delta H = \Delta E + \Delta(PV) = 0 + \Delta(nRT) = 0 + nR\Delta T = \boxed{0}$$

[6] Text page A.6.

[7] Text page 220.

The expansion is reversible. Hence:

$$w = -nRT \ln\left(\frac{V_2}{V_1}\right) = -(2.00 \text{ mol})\left(\frac{8.3145 \text{ J}}{\text{mol K}}\right)(298 \text{ K}) \ln\left(\frac{36.00}{9.00}\right) = \boxed{-6.87 \text{ kJ}}$$

The first law requires that $\Delta E = q + w$. Hence q equals $\boxed{+6.87 \text{ kJ}}$.

7.53 During any adiabatic process $q = 0$. During this *reversible* adiabatic expansion of an ideal gas:

$$T_1 V_1^{\gamma-1} = T_2 V_2^{\gamma-1}$$

where γ is c_p/c_v and the subscripts refer the initial and final states of the gas. In this problem, V_1 is 20.0 L, V_2 is 60.0 L, γ is 5/3, and T_1 is 300 K. Solving for T_2 and substituting gives:

$$T_2 = T_1\left(\frac{V_1}{V_2}\right)^{\gamma-1} = (300 \text{ K})\left(\frac{20.0 \text{ L}}{60.0 \text{ L}}\right)^{2/3} = 144.22 \text{ K} = \boxed{144 \text{ K}}$$

Meanwhile, the ΔE of the ideal gas depends solely on its change in temperature:

$$\Delta E = nc_v\Delta T = (2.00 \text{ mol})\left(\frac{3}{2}\ 8.3145 \text{ J K}^{-1}\text{mol}^{-1}\right)(-155.78 \text{ K}) = \boxed{-3.89 \text{ kJ}}$$

This number also equals w, the work done on the gas, because $\Delta E = q + w$ and q is zero in this process. Finally, ΔH of an ideal gas also depends entirely on ΔT:

$$\Delta H = nc_p\Delta T = (2.00 \text{ mol})\left(\frac{5}{2}\ 8.3145 \text{ J K}^{-1}\text{mol}^{-1}\right)(-155.78 \text{ K}) = \boxed{-6.48 \text{ kJ}}$$

Tip. Notice that $\Delta H = \gamma\Delta E$ for this reversible adiabatic process.

7.55 The law of Dulong and Petit states that all metals have a molar heat capacity of approximately 25 J $\text{K}^{-1}\text{mol}^{-1}$. The molar heat capacity equals the specific heat capacity of a substance multiplied by its molar mass. Hence:

$$c = c_s\mathcal{M} \approx 25 \text{ J K}^{-1}\text{mol}^{-1}$$

The experimental specific heat capacity of indium is 0.233 J $\text{K}^{-1}\text{g}^{-1}$. A molar mass of 76 g mol^{-1} combines with this number to give a molar heat capacity for indium of only 17.7 J $\text{K}^{-1}\text{mol}^{-1}$. This violates the law of Dulong and Petit badly. The modern value of $\mathcal{M}$ for indium (114.8 g mol^{-1}) gives a c that is consistent with the law of Dulong and Petit.

Tip. For solids and liquids the distinction between c_p and c_v is unimportant, especially in an approximate relationship. For this reason there is no p or v subscript on c in this problem.

7.57 a) The system is the 2.00 mol of argon gas. The work done *on* the system is $-P\Delta V$. Since the gas is ideal and P is constant, $P\Delta V = nR\Delta T$ for the system. In this case ΔT is given as -100 K. Then:

$$w = -nR\Delta T = -(2.00 \text{ mol})(8.3145 \text{ J K}^{-1}\text{mol}^{-1})(-100 \text{ K}) = \boxed{+1.66 \times 10^3 \text{ J}}$$

b) The process goes on at constant pressure so the heat absorbed is q_p:

$$q_p = nc_p\Delta T = (2.00 \text{ mol})\left(\frac{5}{2}\ 8.3145 \text{ J K}^{-1}\text{mol}^{-1}\right)(-100 \text{ K}) = \boxed{-4.16 \times 10^3 \text{ J}}$$

c) Use the first law of thermodynamics: $\Delta E = q + w = -4157 + 1663 = -2494$ J. This rounds off to $\boxed{-2.49 \times 10^3 \text{ kJ}}$. Note the use of un-rounded answers from parts a and b in the addition.

d) The ΔH of a system always equals q_p. Hence, ΔH is $\boxed{-4.16 \text{ kJ}}$.

7.59 Because frictional losses and leaks do not occur, the amount of work done by the gas on the paddle mechanism equals the negative of the work absorbed by the gas:

$$w = -(-P\Delta V) = (1.00 \text{ atm})(13.00 - 5.00) \text{ L} = 8.00 \text{ L atm}$$

This work amounts to 811 J because 1 L atm is 101.325 J. All of this work is converted to heat in the 1.00 L of water. Hence the heat absorbed by the water is +811 J. At the given density, the 1.00 L of water weighs 1.00×10^3 g. Therefore:

$$\Delta T = \frac{q}{c_s M} = \frac{811 \text{ J}}{(4.18 \text{ J K}^{-1}\text{g}^{-1})(1.00 \times 10^3 \text{ g})} = \boxed{0.194 \text{ K}}$$

7.61 Use the molar mass of glucose ($C_6H_{12}O_6$) as a unit-factor to obtain the chemical amount of glucose in the candy bar. Then use the molar enthalpy of combustion of glucose as a unit-factor to obtain the heat absorbed:

$$q = 14.3 \text{ g } C_6H_{12}O_6 \times \left(\frac{1 \text{ mol } C_6H_{12}O_6}{180.16 \text{ g } C_6H_{12}O_6}\right) \times \left(\frac{-2820 \text{ kJ}}{1 \text{ mol } C_6H_{12}O_6}\right) = -223.8 \text{ kJ}$$

The heat absorbed by the surroundings of the reaction (which are the person's body) therefore equals +223.8 kJ. When this amount of heat is absorbed by 50 kg of water:

$$\Delta T = \frac{q}{c_s M} = \frac{223.8 \times 10^3 \text{ J}}{(4.18 \text{ J K}^{-1}\text{g}^{-1})(50 \times 10^3 \text{ g})} = \boxed{1.1 \text{ K}}$$

7.63 Determine which liquid is a better coolant near the boiling point by comparing their specific heat capacities. He(l) absorbs 4.25 J of heat per gram as it heats up by 1 K. $N_2(l)$ absorbs only 1.95 J of heat per gram as it warms by the same amount. Therefore, $\boxed{\text{He}(l)}$ is a better coolant near the boiling point.

At their boiling point, the two liquids cool by vaporization; $\boxed{N_2(l)}$ is better because it absorbs much more heat per gram in vaporization than He(l).

7.65 a) The combustion of isooctane is represented:

$$\boxed{C_8H_{18}(l) + \tfrac{25}{2}\, O_2(g) \rightarrow 8\, CO_2(g) + 9\, H_2O(l)}$$

b) The combustion of 0.542 g of isooctane is exothermic (isooctane is a fuel) and takes place at constant volume in a bomb calorimeter. This closed system consists of three sub-systems: the combustion reaction, the calorimeter body, and the water inside the calorimeter. As a whole, the system neither gains nor loses heat because the bomb calorimeter is well-insulated. The amounts of heat gained by the three sub-systems add up to zero:

$$q_{\text{sys}} = q_{H_2O} + q_{\text{calorimeter}} + q_{\text{combustion}} = 0 \qquad \text{constant } V$$

The heat absorbed by a system (or sub-system) in a change at constant volume equals:

$$q_V = c_V \Delta T \qquad \text{or} \qquad q_V = M c_s \Delta T$$

depending on whether a heat capacity or specific heat capacity is available. The problem gives the heat capacity c_V of the calorimeter (48 J K^{-1}) and the specific heat capacity of water (4.184 J $K^{-1}g^{-1}$). The ΔT of the calorimeter equals $28.670 - 20.450 = 8.220$°C, which also equals 8.220 K. The ΔT of the 750 g of water also equals 8.220 K, because the water and calorimeter are in thermal contact. Insert these numbers for the q's of the water and calorimeter:

$$\underbrace{(48 \text{ J K}^{-1})(8.22 \text{ K})}_{\text{calorimeter}} + \underbrace{(750 \text{ g})(4.184 \text{ J K}^{-1}\text{g}^{-1})(8.22 \text{ K})}_{\text{water}} + q_{\text{combustion}} = 0$$

Solving for the last q gives -2.62×10^4 J. This equals the heat absorbed by this combustion reaction at constant volume. At constant volume, zero work is done by or upon the combustion reaction. Hence:

$$\Delta E_{\text{combustion}} = q + w = q_{\text{v}} + 0 = \boxed{-2.62 \times 10^4 \text{ J}}$$

c) The molar mass of C_8H_{18} is 114.23 g mol^{-1}. The combustion of an entire mole of isooctane absorbs more heat than the combustion of 0.542 g:

$$\Delta E = \frac{-2.62 \times 10^4 \text{ J}}{0.542 \text{ g}} \times 114.23 \text{ g mol}^{-1} = -5.52 \times 10^6 \text{ J mol}^{-1} = \boxed{-5520 \text{ kJ mol}^{-1}}$$

d) By definition, $\Delta H = \Delta E + \Delta(PV)$. If the gases in the combustion reaction are ideal and the liquids have negligible volume, then $\Delta(PV) = (\Delta n_{\text{g}})RT$, where Δn_{g} is the change in the number of moles of gas. The balanced equation for the combustion of 1 mol of isooctane shows that $\Delta n_{\text{g}} = 8 - 12.5 = -4.5$ mol. Therefore:

$$(\Delta n_{\text{g}})RT = (-4.5 \text{ mol})(0.008315 \text{ kJ mol}^{-1}\text{K}^{-1})(298 \text{ K}) = -11.15 \text{ kJ}$$

Although the temperature rises from 20.450° to 28.670°C, taking it as a constant 25°C (298 K) causes little error. Complete the calculation as follows:

$$\Delta H = \Delta E + \Delta(PV) = -5520 + (-11.15) = \boxed{-5530 \text{ kJ}}$$

e) The standard enthalpy of the combustion reaction written above is given by the equation

$$\Delta H^\circ = 8\ \Delta H_f^\circ(CO_2(g)) + 9\ \Delta H_f^\circ(H_2O(l)) - \Delta H_f^\circ(\text{isooctane})$$

The ΔH obtained from the bomb calorimetry experiment does not equal the ΔH° of this reaction at 298.15 K, but should approximate it closely. Insert the ΔH on the left in the preceding, substitute ΔH_f°'s from text Appendix D on the right, and solve for ΔH_f°(isooctane)

$$-5530 \text{ kJ} = 8\ \underbrace{(-393.51)}_{CO_2(g)} + 9\ \underbrace{(-285.83)}_{H_2O(l)} - \Delta H_f^\circ(\text{isooctane}) - \frac{25}{2}\ \underbrace{(0.00)}_{O_2(g)}$$

$$\Delta H_f^\circ(\text{isooctane}) = \boxed{-190 \text{ kJ mol}^{-1}}$$

7.67 a) To get ΔH° in the combustion of 1 mol of acetylene, combine ΔH_f°'s as follows:

$$\Delta H^\circ = 2\ \underbrace{(-393.51)}_{CO_2(g)} + 1\ \underbrace{(-241.82)}_{H_2O(g)} - 1\ \underbrace{(226.73)}_{C_2H_2(g)} - \frac{5}{2}\ \underbrace{(0.00)}_{O_2(g)} = \boxed{-1255.57 \text{ kJ}}$$

b) The total heat capacity of the mixture of the two gases equals the molar heat capacity of the first multiplied by the number of moles of the first plus the molar heat capacity of the second multiplied by the number of moles of the second:

$$nc_{\text{p}} = (2.00 \text{ mol})\ \underbrace{(37 \text{ J K}^{-1}\text{mol}^{-1})}_{CO_2} + (1.00 \text{ mol})\ \underbrace{(36 \text{ J K}^{-1}\text{mol}^{-1})}_{H_2O} = \boxed{110 \text{ J K}^{-1}}$$

c) Assume for convenience that 1.00 mol of $C_2H_2(g)$ is burned. Then the product gases, which are 2.00 mol of $CO_2(g)$ and 1.00 mol of $H_2O(g)$, absorb 1255.57 kJ of heat. For these gases, which comprise the flame:

$$\Delta T = \frac{q}{nc_{\text{p}}} = \frac{1.25557 \times 10^6 \text{ J}}{110 \text{ J K}^{-1}} = 1.14 \times 10^4 \text{ K} = 11400°\text{C}$$

If the temperature before combustion is 25°C, the maximum flame temperature is $\boxed{11400°\text{C}}$.

7.69 Define the system as the contents of the engine cylinder. Before the explosive combustion of the octane, the temperature is 600 K, the volume is 0.150 L, and the pressure is 12.0 atm. Apply the ideal-gas equation to the mixed contents of the cylinder before the combustion:

$$n_{\text{before}} = n_{\text{octane}} + n_{\text{air}} = \frac{PV}{RT} = \frac{(12.0\text{ atm})(0.150\text{ L})}{(0.08206\text{ L atm mol}^{-1}\text{K}^{-1})(600\text{ K})} = 0.03656\text{ mol} = 36.56\text{ mmol}$$

Also, the cylinder holds octane and air in a 1-to-80 molar ratio:

$$80 n_{\text{octane}} = n_{\text{air}}$$

Solving these simultaneous equations gives:

$$n_{\text{octane}} = 0.4514\text{ mmol} \quad \text{and} \quad n_{\text{air}} = 36.11\text{ mmol}$$

According to the problem, the system does not change its volume during the actual combustion of the fuel, so w is zero. Furthermore, q is zero (the combustion happens so fast that there is no time for heat to be lost or gained). Since w and q both equal zero, ΔE of the system equals zero. Imagine the combustion to occur in two stages: a: the reaction goes at a constant temperature of 600 K; b: the product gases heat up at constant volume. The sum of these two changes is the overall change within the cylinder. Therefore:

$$\Delta E_{\text{sys}} = 0 = \Delta E_a + \Delta E_b \quad \text{which means} \quad \Delta E_a = -\Delta E_b$$

The problem offers data pertaining to enthalpy changes, not energy changes, in the two steps. Deal with this by substituting for the ΔE_a and ΔE_b in terms of ΔH's:

$$\Delta H_a - \Delta(PV)_a = -\Big(\Delta H_b - \Delta(PV)_b\Big)$$

Step a involves ideal gases, takes place at a constant temperature, and involves change in the chemical amount of gas. Therefore $\Delta(PV)_a$ equals $\Delta n_g RT$, where Δn_g is the change in the chemical amount of gases during the reaction. Step b is the heating of the ideal gases inside the cylinder. The term $\Delta(PV)_b$ therefore equals $n_{\text{after}} R\Delta T$ where "after" refers to the chemical amount of gases present *after* the reaction. Also, for the change in temperature that comprises step b, ΔH_b is equal to $n_{\text{after}} c_{\text{p}} \Delta T$, as long as the molar heat capacity c_{p} is independent of temperature. Substitution of these relations gives:

$$\Delta H_a - \Delta n_g RT = -(n_{\text{after}} c_{\text{p}} \Delta T - n_{\text{after}} R\Delta T)$$

In this equation T is 600 K, and ΔT is the temperature change during the heating. The plan is to compute all the other quantities and then substitute in this equation to get ΔT and, from it, the final temperature.

The cylinder contains 36.11 mmol of air and 0.4514 mmol of octane before the reaction. Air is 80% N_2 and 20% O_2 on a molar basis. Therefore

$$n_{N_2} = 0.80(36.11)\text{ mmol} \quad n_{O_2} = 0.20(36.11)\text{ mmol} \quad n_{\text{octane}} = 0.4514\text{ mmol}$$

before the reaction. The octane burns according to

$$C_8H_{18}(g) + 12\tfrac{1}{2}\ O_2(g) \rightarrow 8\ CO_2(g) + 9\ H_2O(g)$$

so that after the reaction the amounts of the different gases are:

$$n_{N_2} = 0.80(36.11)\text{ mmol} \quad n_{O_2} = 0.20(36.11) - 12.5(0.4514)\text{ mmol}$$
$$n_{CO_2} = 8(0.4514)\text{ mmol} \quad n_{H_2O} = 9(0.4514)\text{ mmol}$$

Note that N_2 does not react, and that the octane, the limiting reactant, is all used up. Addition and subtraction confirm that

$$n_{\text{before}} = 36.56 \text{ mmol} \qquad n_{\text{after}} = 38.14 \text{ mmol} \qquad \text{and} \qquad \Delta n_{\text{g}} = +0.158 \text{ mmol}$$

The molar enthalpy of combustion of gaseous octane at 600 K can be approximately using the $\Delta H_{\text{f}}^{\circ}$'s of the products and reactants at 298.15 K as follows:

$$\Delta H = 9\underbrace{(-241.8)}_{\text{H}_2\text{O}(g)} + 8\underbrace{(-393.5)}_{\text{CO}_2(g)} - 1\underbrace{(-57.4)}_{\text{octane}(g)} - 12.5\underbrace{(0.00)}_{\text{O}_2(g)} = -5266.8 \text{ kJ}$$

This is *not* ΔH_a, the enthalpy of the combustion reaction in the cylinder. Only 0.4514 mmol of octane burns, so

$$\Delta H_a = -5266.8 \text{ kJ mol}^{-1} \times (0.4514 \times 10^{-3} \text{ mol}) = -2.377 \text{ kJ} = -2377 \text{ J}$$

The composite heat capacity of the contents of the cylinder after the reaction is the sum of the nc_{p} values for the four product gases, as in **7.67b**:

$$n_{\text{after}}c_{\text{p}} = (0.00158 \text{ mol})\underbrace{(35.2 \text{ J K}^{-1}\text{mol}^{-1})}_{\text{O}_2} + (0.0289 \text{ mol})\underbrace{(29.8 \text{ J K}^{-1}\text{mol}^{-1})}_{\text{N}_2}$$
$$+ (0.00406 \text{ mol})\underbrace{(38.9 \text{ J K}^{-1}\text{mol}^{-1})}_{\text{H}_2\text{O}} + (0.00361 \text{ mol})\underbrace{(45.5 \text{ J K}^{-1}\text{mol}^{-1})}_{\text{CO}_2} = 1.24 \text{ J K}^{-1}$$

Now, solve the equation derived previously for ΔT and make the various substitutions:

$$\Delta T = \frac{\Delta H_a - \Delta n_{\text{g}}RT}{n_{\text{after}}R - n_{\text{after}}c_{\text{p}}} = \frac{-2377 \text{ J} - (0.00158 \text{ mol})(8.3145 \text{ J K}^{-1}\text{mol}^{-1})(600 \text{ K})}{(0.03814 \text{ mol})(8.3145 \text{ J K}^{-1}\text{mol}^{-1}) - 1.24 \text{ J K}^{-1}} = 2580 \text{ K}$$

The maximum temperature inside the cylinder is $600 + 2580 = 3180$ K. This equals $\boxed{2910°\text{C}}$.

7.71 a) The gases trapped inside the cylinder of the "one-lung" engine have volume V_1 when the piston is fully withdrawn but a smaller volume V_2 when the piston is thrust home. The compression ratio is 8 : 1 so $V_1 = 8V_2$. The area of the base of the engine's cylinder is πr^2, where r is the radius of the base. The volume of a cylinder is the area of its base times its height h:

$$V_1 = Ah \quad \text{and} \quad V_2 = A(h - 12.00 \text{ cm})$$

which employs the (given) fact that full compression shortens h by 12.00 cm. Because r is 5.00 cm, the area A is 78.54 cm^2. Substituting for V_1 and V_2 in terms of A and h gives:

$$Ah = 8A(h - 12.00 \text{ cm})$$

The A's cancel, allowing solution for h. The result is 13.714 cm. With h known it is easy to compute V_1 and V_2, which equal 1.077 L and 0.1347 L respectively.

The temperature and pressure of the fuel mixture are 353 K (80°C) and 1.00 atm when the mixture enters the cylinder with fully withdrawn piston (V_1). Assuming the fuel mixture is an ideal gas:

$$n_{\text{mixture}} = \frac{(1.00 \text{ atm})(1.077 \text{ L})}{(0.08206 \text{ L atm mol}^{-1}\text{K}^{-1})(353 \text{ K})} = 0.0372 \text{ mol}$$

The molar ratio of air to fuel (C_8H_{18}) is 62.5 to 1. Then:

$$n_{\text{fuel}} + n_{\text{air}} = 0.0372 \text{ mol} \quad \text{and} \quad n_{\text{air}} = 62.5n_{\text{fuel}}$$

Solving these simultaneous equations establishes that at the start the cylinder contains 0.0366 mol of air and 5.86×10^{-4} mol of octane fuel.

During the compression stroke, the system undergoes an irreversible adiabatic compression to one-eighth of its initial volume. None of the relationships that govern *reversible* adiabatic processes apply. Assume however, as advised in the problem, that the compression is near to reversible. If it is, then:

$$T_1 V_1^{\gamma-1} \approx T_2 V_2^{\gamma-1} \quad \text{where } \gamma = \frac{35 \text{ J K}^{-1}\text{mol}^{-1}}{26.7 \text{ J K}^{-1}\text{mol}^{-1}} = 1.31$$

The temperature after the compression stroke is

$$T_2 \approx T_1 \left(\frac{V_1}{V_2}\right)^{\gamma-1} = (353 \text{ K}) \left(\frac{1.077 \text{ L}}{0.1347 \text{ L}}\right)^{0.31} = (353 \text{ K})(8)^{0.31} = \boxed{673 \text{ K}}$$

b) The compressed gases occupy a volume of $\boxed{0.135 \text{ L}}$ just before they are ignited, as calculated above.

c) The pressure of the compressed fuel mixture just before ignition is P_2. Compute it by applying the ideal-gas equation to the system with $T_2 = 673$ K, $V_2 = 0.1347$ L, and $n = 0.0372$ mol. It equals 15.3 atm. Alternatively, estimate P_2 using the formula for a reversible adiabatic change:

$$P_2 = P_1 \left(\frac{V_1}{V_2}\right)^{\gamma} = 1.00 \text{ atm} \left(\frac{1.077}{0.1347}\right)^{1.31} = \boxed{15.3 \text{ atm}}$$

d) ΔH for the combustion of gaseous octane at 600 K is -5266.8 kJ mol^{-1}, as estimated in **7.69**. This number is preferable to $\Delta H° = -5530$ kJ mol^{-1} for the combustion of liquid isooctane that was obtained in **7.65**. The latter is for combustion of a different compound (isooctane) in a different form (liquid, not gaseous) at a different temperature (298 K not 600 K) to give a different product (liquid water, not water vapor). The combustion mixture inside the cylinder contains 5.86×10^{-4} mol of octane. Consequently, the ΔH of combustion in this system equals:

$$\Delta H = \left(\frac{-5266.8 \text{ kJ}}{1 \text{ mol}}\right) \times (5.86 \times 10^{-4} \text{ mol}) = -3.09 \text{ kJ}$$

After the combustion, the cylinder contains CO_2, H_2O and unreacted O_2 and N_2, all gases. The balanced chemical equation shows that the combustion consumes 5.86×10^{-4} mol of octane and $12.5 \times (5.86 \times 10^{-4})$ mol of O_2 to produce $8 \times (5.86 \times 10^{-4})$ mol of CO_2 and $9 \times (5.86 \times 10^{-4})$ mol of H_2O. The effect of the reaction is to increase the chemical amount of gases in the cylinder by $3.5 \times (5.86 \times 10^{-4})$ mol. This is Δn_g for the reaction. The original quantity of gases is 0.0372 mol. After the combustion there is 0.0393 mol of gases. The *energy* (not enthalpy) released from the reaction all goes to heat up the gaseous contents of the cylinder as long as no heat escapes to the cylinder walls and no work is done until the power stroke starts. Therefore:

$$\Delta T = \frac{\Delta H_{\text{react}} - \Delta n_g RT}{nR - nc_p}$$

In this equation, which is derived in **7.69**, every quantity but ΔT is known:

$$\Delta T = \frac{-3090 \text{ J} - (0.002051 \text{ mol})(8.3145 \text{ J K}^{-1}\text{mol}^{-1})(673 \text{ K})}{(0.0393 \text{ mol})(8.3145 \text{ J K}^{-1}\text{mol}^{-1}) - (0.0393 \text{ mol})(35 \text{ J K}^{-1}\text{mol}^{-1})} = 2960 \text{ K}$$

The temperature inside the cylinder rises by 2960 K to a maximum of $\boxed{3630 \text{ K}}$.

e) Assume that the expansion stroke is not only adiabatic but reversible. Then the formula:

$$T_2 = T_1 \left(\frac{V_1}{V_2}\right)^{\gamma-1}$$

applies. In this case, T_1 is 3630 K. The ratio V_1 / V_2 is 1 to 8 because now the initial state is the *small* volume state just before the expansion stroke of the piston. The exponent $\gamma - 1$ is still 0.31, as previously established. Substituting gives:

$$T_2 = (3630\text{ K})\left(\frac{1}{8}\right)^{0.31} = \boxed{1900\text{ K}}$$

This is the temperature of the exhaust gases.

7.73 This oxidation of the $CO(g)$ can be represented

$$CO(g) + 1/2\ O_2(g) \rightarrow CO_2(g)$$

The standard enthalpy of this reaction at 25° is

$$\begin{aligned}\Delta H^\circ &= \Delta H_f^\circ(CO_2(g)) - 1/2\ \Delta H_f^\circ(O_2(g)) - \Delta H_f^\circ(CO(g))\\ &= -393.5\text{ kJ} - 1/2\ (0\text{ kJ}) - (-110.5\text{ kJ}) = -283.0\text{ kJ}\end{aligned}$$

Suppose that 1 g of air passes over the catalyst in the tube and that no heat is lost from the system when the CO in this air burns. Assume also that the actual ΔH for the reaction equals ΔH°. Then

$$\begin{aligned}q_{sys} &= q_{reaction} + q_{air}\\ 0 &= n_{CO}\left(\frac{-283.0\times 10^3\text{ J}}{1\text{ mol CO}}\right) + m_{air}c_{air}\Delta T\\ &= \frac{m_{CO}}{\mathcal{M}_{CO}}\left(\frac{-283.0\times 10^3\text{ J}}{1\text{ mol CO}}\right) + m_{air}c_s\Delta T\\ &= \frac{m_{CO}}{28.0\text{ g mol}^{-1}}\left(\frac{-283.0\times 10^3\text{ J}}{1\text{ mol CO}}\right) + 1\text{ g}(1.01\text{ J g}^{-1}\text{K}^{-1})\,3.2\text{ K}\end{aligned}$$

Solving the last equation for the only unknown, which is m_{CO}, the mass of the carbon monoxide, gives 3.2×10^{-4} g. The mass percentage of CO in the air is

$$\frac{3.2\times 10^{-4}\text{ g CO}}{1\text{ g air}}\times 100\% = \boxed{0.0032\%}$$

7.75 Solid $Ca(OH)_2$ dissolves in aqueous HCl according to

$$Ca(OH)_2(s) + 2\ H_3O^+(aq) \rightarrow Ca^{2+}(aq) + 4\ H_2O(l)$$

This event can be viewed as the dissolution of the solid followed by the neutralization of the OH^- ion. Use ΔH_f° values from text Appendix D to compute its ΔH°

$$\begin{aligned}\Delta H^\circ &= 1\ \Delta H_f^\circ(Ca^{2+}(aq)) + 4\ \Delta H_f^\circ(H_2O(l)) - 1\ \Delta H_f^\circ(Ca(OH)_2(s)) - 2\ \Delta H_f^\circ(H_3O^+(aq))\\ &= -542.83 + 4(-285.83) - (-986.98) - 2(-285.83) = -127.51\text{ kJ}\end{aligned}$$

in which the standard units of mol and kJ mol^{-1} are omitted for compactness. The greatest change in temperature occurs when the system is thermally insulated from its surroundings. Under that condition, the system as a whole absorbs zero heat as the subsystems "reaction" and "solution" exchange heat

$$0 = q_{sys} = q_{reaction} + q_{solution} = \Delta H + mc_s\Delta T$$

The q of the reaction should be quite close to ΔH° because the reactants and products are in standard states. The rise in temperature does affect ΔH°, but the effect is surely slight. The mass of the solution can be computed from its volume and its density. Approximate the density as 1.0 g mL^{-}1, which is the density of pure water at 25°C. Then

$$0 = 0.5\text{ mol Ca(OH)}_2\left(\frac{-127.51\times10^3\text{ J}}{1\text{ mol Ca(OH)}_2}\right) + 1\text{ L}\left(\frac{1.0\times10^3\text{ g}}{\text{L}}\right)(4.184\text{ J g}^{-1}\text{K}^{-1})\Delta T$$
$$0 = -63.7\times10^3\text{ J} + (4184\text{ J K}^{-1})\Delta T$$

Solving gives $\Delta T = 15$ K. The maximum temperature is $25° + 15° = \boxed{40°}$.

7.77 The chemical amount of the silane at the T and P stated in the problem equals:

$$n_{\text{SiH}_4} = \frac{PV}{RT} = \frac{(0.658\text{ atm})(0.250\text{ L})}{(0.08206\text{ L atm mol}^{-1}\text{K}^{-1})(298\text{ K})} = 6.727\times10^{-3}\text{ mol}$$

The combustion of this much silane at constant volume (in a bomb calorimeter) absorbs -9.757 kJ of heat at 25°C (which is the same as evolving $+9.575$ kJ). That is, $\Delta E = q_v = -9.757$ kJ. This is a standard ΔE (a $\Delta E°$) if the reactants and products are in standard states. Assume that they are. The standard molar energy of combustion of silane is then

$$\Delta E° = \frac{-9.757\text{ kJ}}{6.727\times10^{-3}\text{ mol}} = -1450\text{ kJ mol}^{-1}$$

Next, compute the $\Delta H°$ of the combustion of silane. The balanced equation given in the problem shows that 3 mol of gaseous reactants gives 0 mol of gaseous products:

$$\Delta H° = \Delta E° + RT\Delta n_g = -1450.4\text{ kJ} + (0.0083145\text{ kJ K}^{-1}\text{mol}^{-1})(298.15\text{ K})(-3\text{ mol}) = -1458\text{ kJ}$$

$\Delta H°$ for the combustion of silane equals the sum of the standard enthalpies of formation of the products minus the sum of the standard enthalpies of formation of the reactants. Taking values from Appendix D:

$$\Delta H° = -1458\text{ kJ} = 1\underbrace{(-910.94)}_{\text{SiO}_2\text{ quartz}} + 2\underbrace{(-285.83)}_{\text{H}_2\text{O}(l)} - 1\underbrace{(\Delta H_f°)}_{\text{SiH}_4(g)}$$

$$\underbrace{(\Delta H_f°)}_{\text{SiH}_4(g)} = \boxed{-25\text{ kJ mol}^{-1}}$$

Compute $\Delta E_f°$ of silane from $\Delta H_f°$ and the known Δn_g in the formation of 1 mol of silane from its elements:

$$\Delta E_f° = \Delta H_f° - RT\Delta n_g$$
$$= -25\text{ kJ} - (0.008315\text{ kJ K}^{-1}\text{mol}^{-1})(298.15\text{ K})(-1\text{ mol}) = \boxed{-23\text{ kJ}}$$

7.79 Substances with the strongest intermolecular forces have the highest enthalpies of vaporization. Liquid KBr has strong ion-ion forces holding its ions together. It has the highest ΔH_{vap}. NH_3 has dipole-dipole attractions, which are stronger than the weak dispersion (van der Waals) forces that maintain the liquid in Ar and He. The dispersion forces should be stronger in Ar than in He because Ar has a larger molar mass. Therefore: $\boxed{\text{He} < \text{Ar} < \text{NH}_3 < \text{KCl}}$.

7.81 a) Lewis structures for carbonic acid show two O—H single bonds, two C—O single bonds and one C=O double bond:

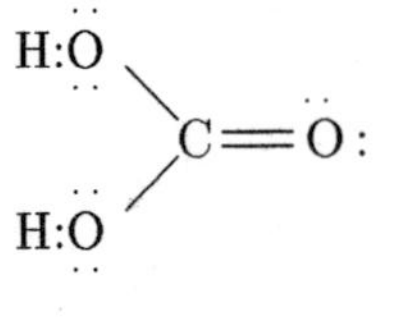

b) Imagine the reaction to proceed by the breaking of the five bonds in H_2CO_3 followed by the making of the four bonds in H—O—H plus O=C=O. The enthalpy of bond breaking is positive; the enthalpy of bond making is negative. Take bond enthalpies from text Table 7.3,[8] and combine them accordingly:

$$\Delta H = -2\underbrace{(463)}_{\text{O—H}} - 2\underbrace{(728)}_{\text{C=O}} + 2\underbrace{(463)}_{\text{O—H}} + 2\underbrace{(351)}_{\text{O—C}} + 1\underbrace{(728)}_{\text{C=O}} = \boxed{-26\text{ kJ}}$$

[8] Text page 219.

Chapter 8

Spontaneous Processes and Thermodynamic Equilibrium

8.1 The definition of a thermodynamical system is arbitrary. Once a system is defined, the surroundings are then automatically "the rest of the universe." Nevertheless, a wise choice of the system can greatly simplify the analysis of a thermodynamic problem. It also often pays explicitly to recognize the nature of a chosen system's *immediate* surroundings. The following are typical useful choices of system and surroundings.

a) The system is the reaction $NH_4NO_3(s) \rightarrow NH_4^+(aq) + NO_3^-(aq)$. This means that the system includes solid ammonium nitrate, the water in which it dissolves and the aquated ions that are the products of the dissolution process. The inclusion of water in the system is indicated only rather subtly (by the (aq)'s on the formulas of the product ions). The surroundings include the flask or beaker in which the system is held, the air above the system, and other neighboring materials. The dissolution of ammonium nitrate is $\boxed{\text{spontaneous}}$. Before the process can proceed, any physical barrier (such as a glass wall or a space of air) between the water and the ammonium nitrate must be removed. The parts (sub-systems) of a system need not be physically contiguous.

b) The system is the reaction $H_2(g) + O_2(g) \rightarrow$ products. Its surroundings are the walls of the bomb and other portions of its environment that might deliver heat or work to or else absorb heat or work. The reaction of hydrogen with oxygen is $\boxed{\text{spontaneous}}$. Once hydrogen and oxygen are mixed in a closed bomb, $\boxed{\text{no constraint}}$ exists to prevent their reaction. That is, the system just defined is thermodynamically unstable with respect to the explosion. It is found experimentally that this system gives products quite slowly at room temperature (no immediate explosion). It explodes instantly at higher temperatures.

c) The system is the rubber band. The surroundings consist of the weight (visualized as attached to the lower end of the rubber band), a hangar at the top of the rubber band, and the air in contact with the rubber band. The change is $\boxed{\text{spontaneous}}$ once a constraint such as a stand or support underneath the weight is removed.

d) The system is the gas contained in the chamber. The surroundings are the walls of the chamber and the moveable piston head. The process is spontaneous if the force exerted by the weight on the piston exceeds the force exerted by the collisions of the molecules of the gas on the bottom of the piston.[1] Because slow compression of the gas is observed, the change is $\boxed{\text{spontaneous}}$.

---

[1] The forces due to the mass of the piston itself and friction between the piston and the walls within which it slides are neglected.

e) The system is the drinking glass in the change glass → fragments. The surroundings are the floor, the air, and the other materials in the room. The change is $\boxed{\text{spontaneous}}$. It occurs when the constraint, which is whatever portion of the surroundings holds the glass above the floor, is removed.

8.3 a) The number of available microstates equals the number of possible ways for a number to come up on one die times the number of possible ways for a number to come up on the other die. Each die has six faces and therefore 6 available microstates. The total number of available microstates is $\boxed{36}$.

b) The probability that one die will show a six is 1/6. The same is true for the other die. It follows that the probability that two sixes show up at the same time is $(1/6)(1/6) = \boxed{1/36}$.

8.5 The driving force for

$$H_2O(l) + D_2O(l) \rightarrow 2\,HOD(l)$$

is the $\boxed{\text{tendency for the entropy to increase}}$. Two moles of HOD have a larger entropy than a mixture of one mol of H_2O and one mol of D_2O because there is a much larger number of ways for the available H's, D's and O's to be assembled into a collection of HOD molecules than into a collection of H_2O's and D_2O's. The change occurs spontaneously, once the reactants are mixed, even if the system is completely separated from its surroundings.

Tip. A mixture of HOD, H_2O, and D_2O will have an even larger entropy than either pure products or pure reactants. The reaction comes to equilibrium in an intermediate state consisting of just such a mixture.

8.7 Before the stopcock is opened, the number of microstates available to a single H_2 (or He) is proportional to the volume of the glass bulb: $\Omega = cV$ where c is a constant. There are N_0 molecules of H_2 and N_0 atoms of He. The number of possible microstates for each gas is

$$\Omega_{H_2} = (cV)^{N_0} \quad \text{and} \quad \Omega_{He} = (cV)^{N_0}$$

The number of microstates of the entire system, still before the valve is opened, is the product of the Ω's:

$$\Omega_{sys} = \Omega_{H_2}\Omega_{He} = (cV)^{2N_0}$$

This is the number of microstates that have all of the H_2 in the first bulb and all of the He in the second. By symmetry it is also the number of microstates that have all of the H_2 in the *second* bulb and all the He in the first. *After* the stopcock is opened, $2N_0$ molecules occupy a volume of $2V$ and:

$$\Omega_{sys} = (c\,2V)^{2N_0}$$

The probability p of the "cross-diffused" result, the state in which the H_2 and He trade places, is the number of ways in which it can be constituted divided by the number of ways in which the mixed system can be constituted:

$$p = \frac{(cV)^{2N_0}}{(c2V)^{2N_0}} = 2^{-2N_0}$$

Take the logarithm of both sides of this equation:

$$\log p = -2N_0 \log 2 = -2N_0(0.301) = -3.62 \times 10^{23}; \qquad \text{hence}: \quad p = \boxed{10^{-3.62\times 10^{23}}}$$

8.9 If the amount of disorder in a system increases when a process occurs, then the change in entropy ΔS of that system is positive.

a) When NaCl melts it goes from a highly ordered solid to a relatively disordered liquid state. This means an increase in disorder: $\boxed{\Delta S > 0}$.

b) When a building is demolished it goes from a ordered state to a highly disordered state: $\boxed{\Delta S > 0}$.

c) In this case a highly disordered system (air) has order imposed on it by the separation into three distinct subsystems. An increase in order means $\boxed{\Delta S < 0}$.

8.11 a) The maximum theoretical efficiency ϵ of an engine operating between two temperatures is attained when the engine operates reversibly. This maximum efficiency is, according to text equation 8.4:[2]

$$\epsilon = \frac{T_h - T_\ell}{T_h} = 1 - \frac{T_\ell}{T_h}$$

In this problem, T_ℓ is 300 K and T_h is 450 K so ϵ is $\boxed{0.333}$.

b) The efficiency of the engine is the ratio of the net work it *performs* to the heat that it *absorbs:*

$$\epsilon = \frac{-w_{net}}{q}$$

The minus sign is necessary to adhere to the convention that $+w$ is work absorbed. If 1500 J of heat is absorbed per cycle from the 400 K reservoir and ϵ is 0.333, then w_{net} is -500 J in each turn of the cycle. It follows from the first law that the engine discards 1000 J of heat $\boxed{q = -1000 \text{ J}}$ into the low-temperature reservoir during each cycle.

c) The engine has absorbed 1500 J of heat during one portion of the cycle of operation. It must lose this amount of energy by the time it completes the cycle (for which ΔE is zero). Of the 1500 J, 1000 J goes to the 300 K reservoir as heat. Accordingly, 500 J appears as work done by the engine. That is, $\boxed{w = -500 \text{ J}}$.

8.13 Consider a system consisting of solid tungsten at its melting point of 3410°C (3683 K). Imagine supplying 35.4 kJ of heat infinitely slowly and in such a way that the temperature stays constant but 1 mol of tungsten melts. 35.4 kJ then equals q_{rev} for the melting. Substitute this value and T in the definition of entropy. Since the change is at a constant temperature, T can be taken outside the integral sign:

$$\Delta S = \int \frac{dq_{rev}}{T} = \frac{1}{T} q_{rev} = \frac{35.4 \times 10^3 \text{ J mol}^{-1}}{3683 \text{ K}} = \boxed{9.61 \text{ J K}^{-1}\text{mol}^{-1}}$$

Tip. The temperature must be an absolute temperature (in kelvins, for example).

8.15 Trouton's rule states that ΔS_{vap}, the entropy of vaporization, equals 88±5 J mol^{-1}K^{-1} for most liquids Use the rule to estimate the molar enthalpy of vaporization of acetone as follows:

$$\Delta H_{vap} \approx (329.35 \text{ K})(88 \text{ J K}^{-1}\text{mol}^{-1}) = \boxed{29 \times 10^3 \text{ J mol}^{-1}}$$

The experimental ΔH_{vap} of acetone equals 30.2×10^3 J mol^{-1}.

8.17 Assume that the 4.00 mol of hydrogen behaves ideally. The internal energy of an ideal gas depends solely on its absolute temperature T. In an isothermal process, T does not change. Hence, ΔE equals $\boxed{\text{zero}}$.

To evaluate ΔH, use its definition:

$$\Delta H = \Delta E + \Delta(PV) \qquad \text{which implies:} \qquad \Delta H = \Delta E + nR\Delta T$$

since $PV = nRT$. But ΔT and ΔE equal zero. Hence, ΔH equals $\boxed{\text{zero}}$.

The work done *on* the gas during the reversible isothermal expansion from 12.0 L to 30.0 L is

$$w = -nRT \ln\left(\frac{V_2}{V_1}\right) = -4.00 \text{ mol}\left(\frac{8.3145 \text{ J}}{\text{mol K}}\right)(400 \text{ K}) \ln\left(\frac{30.0}{12.0}\right) = \boxed{-12.2 \text{ kJ}}$$

---

[2] Text page 244.

The first law requires that if $\Delta E = 0$, then $q = -w$. This means the gas absorbs 12.2 kJ of heat during its expansion, just enough to balance off the 12.2 kJ of work that it performs: $q = \boxed{+12.2 \text{ kJ}}$.

Finally, $\Delta S = q_{\text{rev}}/T$ for an isothermal process, and q_{rev} is the q just computed:

$$\Delta S = \frac{q_{\text{rev}}}{T} = \frac{+12.2 \times 10^3 \text{ J}}{400 \text{ K}} = \boxed{+30.5 \text{ J K}^{-1}}$$

8.19 Break down the overall process to the three steps described in the problem and calculate ΔS_{sys} for each. Then add up the three contributions. The steps are: I, warming of ice; II, melting of ice; III, warming of melted ice. As the text shows,[3] ΔS for any temperature change at constant pressure is given by the equation:

$$\Delta S = nc_{\text{p}} \ln\left(\frac{T_2}{T_1}\right) \qquad (\text{constant}P)$$

Use this formula to obtain ΔS of the system for the first and third steps:

$$\Delta S_{\text{I}} = (1.00 \text{ mol})(38 \text{ J K}^{-1}\text{mol}^{-1}) \ln(273.15/253.15) = 2.9 \text{ J K}^{-1}$$
$$\Delta S_{\text{III}} = (1.00 \text{ mol})(75 \text{ J K}^{-1}\text{mol}^{-1}) \ln(293.15/273.15) = 5.3 \text{ J K}^{-1}$$

In the second step, T stays at 273.15 K, and ΔS equals the quantity of heat absorbed reversibly by the system (q_{rev}) divided by this temperature:

$$\Delta S_{\text{II}} = \frac{6007 \text{ J}}{273.15 \text{ K}} = 21.99 \text{ J K}^{-1}$$

The *total* ΔS of the system equals:

$$\Delta S_{\text{sys}} = \Delta S_{\text{I}} + \Delta S_{\text{II}} + \Delta S_{\text{III}} = \boxed{+30.2 \text{ J K}^{-1}}$$

The entire process is reversible. Consequently, the entropy of the universe remains constant: $\Delta S_{\text{univ}} = \Delta S_{\text{sys}} + \Delta S_{\text{surr}} = \boxed{0}$, which means $\Delta S_{\text{surr}} = \boxed{-30.2 \text{ J K}^{-1}}$.

8.21 Hot iron is plunged into cool water. The final temperature is 16.5°C (289.65 K). This process is far from reversible. Nevertheless, the ΔS of the iron and the ΔS of the water may be computed using the equation

$$\Delta S = nc_{\text{p}} \ln\left(\frac{T_2}{T_1}\right)$$

This approach succeeds because entropy is a state function. Its change depends only on the original and final states of the system, not on the path by which the change occurs.

As computed in text Example 7.3[4], the iron cools from 373.15 K to 289.65 K. A 72.4 g mass of iron amounts to 1.296 mol, which equals 72.4 g divided by 55.847 g mol^{-1}, the molar mass of iron. Hence:

$$\Delta S_{\text{Fe}} = nc_{\text{p}} \ln\left(\frac{T_2}{T_1}\right) = (1.296 \text{ mol})(25.1 \text{ J K}^{-1}\text{mol}^{-1}) \ln\left(\frac{289.65 \text{ K}}{373.15 \text{ K}}\right) = \boxed{-8.24 \text{ J K}^{-1}}$$

The 100.0 g of water equals 5.55 mol. The c_{p} of water is 75.3 J K^{-1}mol^{-1}, and the water is warmed from 283.15 K to 289.65 K. Substituting as before:

$$\Delta S_{\text{H}_2\text{O}} = nc_{\text{p}} \ln\left(\frac{T_2}{T_1}\right) = 5.55 \text{ mol}(75.3 \text{ J K}^{-1}\text{mol}^{-1}) \ln\left(\frac{289.65}{283.15}\right) = \boxed{+9.49 \text{ J K}^{-1}}$$

The ΔS of the whole system is $\boxed{+1.25 \text{ J K}^{-1}}$, which is the sum of the ΔS's of the water and the iron.

---

[3] Text page 248.

[4] Text page 207.

8.23 a) The $\Delta S°$ of the reaction as written equals the standard molar entropies (the $S°$'s) of the products, each multiplied by its chemical amount in the balanced equation, minus the $S°$'s of the reactants, each multiplied by its chemical amount in the balanced equation:

$$\Delta S° = 2\underbrace{(239.95)}_{NO_2(g)} + 2\underbrace{(69.91)}_{H_2O(l)} - 1\underbrace{(121.21)}_{N_2H_4(l)} - 3\underbrace{(205.03)}_{O_2(g)} = \boxed{-116.58 \text{ J K}^{-1}}$$

where the numbers in parenthesis are standard molar entropies (in J $K^{-1}mol^{-1}$) from text Appendix D and the coefficients are the numbers of moles from the balanced chemical equation.

b) In the process $N_2H_4(l) \rightarrow N_2H_4(g)$, the disorder in the N_2H_4 increases, and therefore its ΔS exceeds 0. In other words, $S°$ for $N_2H_4(g)$ is more positive than $S°$ for $N_2H_4(l)$. This will cause $\Delta S°$ of the reaction of gaseous N_2H_4 with oxygen to be $\boxed{\text{algebraically smaller}}$ than when liquid N_2H_4 reacts.

8.25 The computations use the method of **8.23**.

$$\text{For LiCl:}\quad \Delta S° = 2\underbrace{(59.33)}_{LiCl(s)} - 2\underbrace{(29.12)}_{Li(s)} - 1\underbrace{(222.96)}_{Cl_2(g)} = \boxed{-162.54 \text{ J K}^{-1}}$$

$$\text{For NaCl:}\quad \Delta S° = 2\underbrace{(72.13)}_{NaCl(s)} - 2\underbrace{(51.21)}_{Na(s)} - 1\underbrace{(222.96)}_{Cl_2(g)} = \boxed{-181.12 \text{ J K}^{-1}}$$

$$\text{For KCl:}\quad \Delta S° = 2\underbrace{(82.59)}_{KCl(s)} - 2\underbrace{(64.18)}_{K(s)} - 1\underbrace{(222.96)}_{Cl_2(g)} = \boxed{-186.14 \text{ J K}^{-1}}$$

$$\text{For RbCl:}\quad \Delta S° = 2\underbrace{(95.90)}_{RbCl(s)} - 2\underbrace{(76.78)}_{Rb(s)} - 1\underbrace{(222.96)}_{Cl_2(g)} = \boxed{-184.72 \text{ J K}^{-1}}$$

$$\text{For CsCl:}\quad \Delta S° = 2\underbrace{(101.17)}_{CsCl(s)} - 2\underbrace{(85.23)}_{CsCl(s)} - 1\underbrace{(222.96)}_{Cl_2(g)} = \boxed{-191.08 \text{ J K}^{-1}}$$

The $\Delta S°$'s grow increasingly negative moving down the group, but RbCl is an exception.

8.27 By the second law of thermodynamics, $\Delta S_{univ} = \Delta S_{sys} + \Delta S_{surr} > 0$. In this example, $\Delta S_{sys} = -44.7$ J K^{-1}. Thus, $\boxed{\Delta S_{surr} > +44.7 \text{ J K}^{-1}}$.

8.29 The change is the breakdown of $SiO_2(s)$ to solid silicon and gaseous oxygen. The products consist of a mole of solid and a mole of gas, but the reactant is simply a mole of solid. The products have many more possible microstates both because there are more particles and because the particles are less well-organized.

8.31 a) Solid ammonia is held at a constant temperature of 170 K. It is implied that the pressure is a constant 1 atm. The molar Gibbs energy of fusion is

$$\Delta G_{fus} = \Delta H_{fus} - T\Delta S_{fus} = 5.65 \text{ kJ mol}^{-1} - (170 \text{ K})(0.0289 \text{ kJ K}^{-1}\text{mol}^{-1}) = 0.74 \text{ kJ mol}^{-1}$$

The change in the Gibbs energy of 1.00 mol of ammonia when ite melts is therefore $\boxed{+0.74 \text{ kJ}}$.

b) This case differs from previous only in the amount of ammonia. Multiply the molar Gibbs energy of fusion by 3.60 mol, the amount of NH_3 that is melted. The result is $\boxed{2.65 \text{ kJ}}$.

c) At 170 K, $\Delta G > 0$. Hence the melting of ammonia is $\boxed{\text{not spontaneous}}$ at 170 K (and 1 atm pressure).

d) If solid and liquid NH_3 are in equilibrium, then ΔG equals zero for the process solid $\rightleftharpoons$ liquid. Calculate the T that makes this true using the molar enthalpy and the molar entropy changes quoted in the problem:

$$\Delta G = \Delta H - T\Delta S = 0 \qquad \text{hence:} \quad T = \frac{\Delta H}{\Delta S} = \frac{5.65 \times 10^3 \text{ J mol}^{-1}}{28.9 \text{ J K}^{-1}\text{mol}^{-1}} = \boxed{196 \text{ K}}$$

8.33 When 1.00 mol of ethanol is vaporized at its normal boiling point, ΔH equals 38.7 kJ. The vaporization goes on at constant pressure, so $q_{\text{p}} = \Delta H$ and q is $\boxed{38.7 \text{ kJ}}$. The vaporization is isothermal and reversible, so q is also q_{rev}. Hence:

$$\Delta S = \frac{q_{\text{rev}}}{T} = \frac{38.7 \text{ kJ}}{351.1 \text{ K}} = 0.110 \text{ kJ K}^{-1} = \boxed{110 \text{ J K}^{-1}}$$

Now for the calculation of ΔE. From the definition of enthalpy:

$$\Delta E = \Delta H - \Delta(PV)$$

At constant pressure $\Delta(PV) = P\Delta V = P(V_2 - V_1)$. In this case, V_2 is the volume of one mole of vaporous ethanol at 351.1 K and V_1 is the volume of one mole of liquid ethanol, also at 351.1 K. The vapor behaves ideally:

$$V_2 = \frac{nRT}{P} = \frac{1.00 \text{ mol}(0.08206 \text{ L atm mol}^{-1}\text{K}^{-1})(351.15 \text{ K})}{1.00 \text{ atm}} = 28.8 \text{ L}$$

The volume of one mole of liquid ethanol (V_1) is less than 0.1 L, which makes it negligibly small compared to 28.8 L. Therefore:

$$P\Delta V = P(V_2 - V_1) = (1.00 \text{ atm})(28.8 \text{ L}) = 28.8 \text{ L atm} \times \left(\frac{0.101325 \text{ kJ}}{1 \text{ L atm}}\right) = 2.92 \text{ kJ}$$

Substitute these values into the expression for ΔE:

$$\Delta E = \Delta H - \Delta(PV) = 38.7 \text{ kJ} - 2.92 \text{ kJ} = \boxed{35.8 \text{ kJ}}$$

By expanding against a constant pressure, the system performs +2.92 kJ of pressure-volume work on its surroundings. This is the only kind of work possible. The total work done on the system is $\boxed{-2.92 \text{ kJ}}$.

For any reversible processes at constant T and P, $\Delta G = 0$. This can be verified in this case:

$$\Delta G = \Delta H - T\Delta S = 38.7 \text{ kJ} - (351.15 \text{ K})(0.110 \text{ kJ K}^{-1}) = \boxed{0.0 \text{ kJ}}$$

8.35 Add the two reactions given in the problem and their ΔG's:

$$\begin{aligned} 2\ Fe_2O_3(s) &\rightarrow 4\ Fe(s) + 3\ O_2(g) & \Delta G &= +840 \text{ kJ} \\ 3\ C(s) + 3\ O_2(g) &\rightarrow 3\ CO_2(g) & \Delta G &= -1200 \text{ kJ} \\ 2\ Fe_2O_3(s) + 3\ C(s) &\rightarrow 4\ Fe(s) + 3\ O_2(g) & \Delta G &= -360 \text{ kJ} \end{aligned}$$

The last reaction is spontaneous because it has a negative ΔG. The removal of O_2 by reaction with C drives the decomposition of the Fe_2O_3.

8.37 a) Calculate $\Delta H^\circ_{298.15}$ and $\Delta S^\circ_{298.15}$ from the data in Appendix D:

$$\Delta H^\circ_{298.15} = 2\underbrace{(-824.2)}_{Fe_2O_3(s)} - 4\underbrace{(0.00)}_{Fe(s)} - 3\underbrace{(0.00)}_{O_2(g)} = -1648.4 \text{ kJ}$$

$$\Delta S^\circ_{298.15} = 2\underbrace{(87.40)}_{Fe_2O_3(s)} - 4\underbrace{(27.28)}_{Fe(s)} - 3\underbrace{(205.03)}_{O_2(g)} = -549.41 \text{ J K}^{-1}$$

The problem asks for the temperature range in which the reaction is spontaneous. The changeover from spontaneity to non-spontaneity occurs at $\Delta G^\circ = 0$. Use the relationship $\Delta G^\circ = \Delta H^\circ - T\Delta S^\circ$ to obtain the temperature T that makes ΔG° equal zero. Take $\Delta H^\circ_{298.15}$ and $\Delta S^\circ_{298.15}$ as good approximations of the actual values of ΔH° and ΔS° at whatever turns out to be. Remember to convert $\Delta S^\circ_{298.15}$ to kJ K^{-1} or $\Delta H^\circ_{298.15}$ to J. The units must cancel:

$$T \approx \frac{\Delta H^\circ_{298.15}}{\Delta S^\circ_{298.15}} = \frac{-1648.1 \text{ kJ}}{-0.54941 \text{ kJ K}^{-1}} = 3000 \text{ K}$$

Because ΔH° and ΔS° are both negative, the reaction is spontaneous below 3000 K. Above 3000 K the ever-growing $-T\Delta S^\circ$ term finally makes ΔG° positive.

b) Perform similar calculations:

$$\Delta H^\circ_{298.15} = \underbrace{(-395.72)}_{SO_3(g)} - \underbrace{(-296.83)}_{SO_2(g)} - 0.5\underbrace{(0.00)}_{O_2(g)} = -98.89 \text{ kJ}$$

$$\Delta S^\circ_{298.15} = \underbrace{(256.65)}_{SO_3(g)} - \underbrace{(248.11)}_{SO_2(g)} - 0.5\underbrace{(205.03)}_{O_2(g)} = -93.98 \text{ J K}^{-1}$$

$$T \approx \frac{\Delta H^\circ_{298.15}}{\Delta S^\circ_{298.15}} = \frac{-98.89 \text{ kJ}}{-0.09398 \text{ kJ K}^{-1}} = 1052 \text{ K}$$

Since ΔH° and ΔS° are both negative, the reaction is spontaneous below 1050 K.

c)

$$\Delta H^\circ_{298.15} = \underbrace{(82.05)}_{N_2O)(g)} + 2\underbrace{(-241.82)}_{H_2O(g)} - \underbrace{(-365.56)}_{NH_4NO_3(s)} = -36.03 \text{ kJ}$$

$$\Delta S^\circ_{298.15} = \underbrace{(219.74)}_{N_2O)(g)} + 2\underbrace{(188.72)}_{H_2O(g)} - \underbrace{(151.08)}_{NH_4NO_3(s)} = 446.10 \text{ J K}^{-1}$$

$$T \approx \frac{\Delta H^\circ_{298.15}}{\Delta S^\circ_{298.15}} = \frac{-36.03 \text{ kJ}}{0.44610 \text{ kJ K}^{-1}} = -80.7 \text{ K}$$

A negative absolute temperature is physically meaningless. In this calculation it signals that the reaction is either never spontaneous (ΔS° positive and ΔH° negative) or always spontaneous (ΔS° negative and ΔH° positive).[5] Since ΔS° is positive, this reaction is spontaneous at all temperatures.

8.39 The reduction reaction is $WO_3(s) + 3\,H_2(g) \rightarrow W(s) + 3\,H_2O(g)$.
Calculate ΔH° and ΔS° for this process using the data in Appendix D. The method is the same as in **8.37**:

$$\Delta H^\circ_{298.15} = 1\underbrace{(0.00)}_{W(s)} + 3\underbrace{(-241.82)}_{H_2O(g)} - 1\underbrace{(-842.87)}_{WO_3(s)} - 3\underbrace{(0.00)}_{H_2(g)} = +117.41 \text{ kJ}$$

$$\Delta S^\circ_{298.15} = 1\underbrace{(32.64)}_{W(s)} + 3\underbrace{(188.72)}_{H_2O(g)} - 1\underbrace{(75.90)}_{WO_3(s)} - 3\underbrace{(130.57)}_{H_2(g)} = +131.19 \text{ J K}^{-1}$$

Because ΔH° and ΔS° are both positive, the reaction becomes spontaneous at high enough temperature. The changeover temperature is

$$T = \frac{\Delta H^\circ}{\Delta S^\circ} = \frac{117.41 \times 10^3 \text{ J}}{131.19 \text{ J K}^{-1}} = 895 \text{ K}$$

Tip. The reaction *does* proceed to some extent at temperatures below 895 K, but reactants predominate.

---

[5] See the discussion on text page 260.

8.41 The liquid and gaseous forms of a substance are in equilibrium at its normal boiling point. "Normal" means that the pressure equals 1.000 atm. It follows that ΔG for boiling equals zero as long as both liquid and vapor are present at 1 atm.

$$\text{If} \quad \Delta G = \Delta H_{\text{vap}} - T\Delta S_{\text{vap}} = 0 \quad \text{then} \quad \Delta S_{\text{vap}} = \frac{\Delta H_{\text{vap}}}{T}$$

Substitution of the values from the problem gives:

$$\Delta S_{\text{vap}} = \frac{38.74 \times 10^3 \text{ J}}{351.6 \text{ K}} = \boxed{110.2 \text{ J K}^{-1}\text{mol}^{-1}}$$

The computation is identical to **8.33** except that an additional significant figure is available.

Trouton's rule states that ΔS_{vap} is close to 88 J K^{-1}mol^{-1} for all liquids. The ΔS_{vap} for ethanol is 25% higher than predicted by Trouton's rule.

Tip. The ΔS_{vap} and ΔH_{vap} in the preceding computation are *not* the same as $\Delta H^\circ_{298.15}$ and $\Delta S^\circ_{298.15}$ for the vaporization of ethanol. Computing these two values from the 298.15 K data on $C_2H_5OH(l)$ and $C_2H_5OH(g)$ in Appendix D confirms this

$$\text{For } C_2H_5OH(l) \rightarrow C_2H_5OH(g) \qquad \Delta H^\circ_{298.15} = 42.59 \text{ kJ} \quad \Delta S^\circ_{298.15} = 121.89 \text{ J K}^{-1}$$

The reason for the difference is that boiling takes place at the boiling point and not at 25°C. This distinction is the point of problem **8.62.** Using the 298.15 K data gives 76.3°C as the boiling point of ethanol, which is more than 2°C low.

8.43 a) The compression of the oxygen is reversible and adiabatic. This means $q_{\text{rev}} = 0$. Therefore, ΔS_{sys} equals $\boxed{\text{zero}}$.

b) When an ideal gas is compressed reversibly and adiabatically from an initial (P_1, V_1) to a final state (P_2, V_2) then:

$$\frac{P_1}{P_2} = \left(\frac{V_2}{V_1}\right)^\gamma$$

where γ is the ratio of c_{p} to c_{v} of the gas. For oxygen γ equals 29.4 J K^{-1}mol^{-1} divided by 21.09 J K^{-1}mol^{-1} or 1.394. The original volume (V_1) of the 2.60 mol of oxygen in this problem is 64.0 L, as computed using the ideal-gas equation with $T_1 = 300$ K. Substitute this V_1, P_2 (8.00 atm), P_1 (1.00 atm) and γ into the preceding:

$$\frac{1.00 \text{ atm}}{8.00 \text{ atm}} = \left(\frac{V_2}{64.0 \text{ L}}\right)^{1.394} \qquad \text{so that} \qquad V_2 = 14.4 \text{ L}$$

Inserting P_2 and V_2 in the ideal-gas equation gives T_2. In summary, states 1 and 2 of the 2.60 mol of O_2 are:

$$P_1 = 1.00 \text{ atm} \qquad V_1 = 64.0 \text{ L} \qquad T_1 = 300 \text{ K}$$
$$P_2 = 8.00 \text{ atm} \qquad V_2 = 14.4 \text{ L} \qquad T_2 = 540 \text{ K}$$

The problem traces an alternative path from state 1 to state 2. The oxygen is first heated to T_2 at constant pressure and then compressed reversibly and isothermally to P_2. Compute all of the state variables in the *intermediate* state (subscripted i), after the isochoric heating but before the isothermal compression:

$$P_i = 1.00 \text{ atm} \qquad T_i = 540 \text{ K} \qquad V_i = 115.2 \text{ L}$$

The volume comes from the ideal-gas law, with $n = 2.60$ mol. The entropy change during the constant-pressure heating is

$$\Delta S_{1\rightarrow i} = nc_{\text{p}} \ln\left(\frac{T_i}{T_1}\right) = (2.60 \text{ mol})(29.4 \text{ J K}^{-1}\text{mol}^{-1}) \ln\left(\frac{540}{300}\right) = 44.9 \text{ J K}^{-1}$$

The entropy change during the constant-temperature compression is

$$\Delta S_{i\to 2} = nR\ln\left(\frac{V_2}{V_i}\right) = (2.60\text{ mol})(8.3145\text{ J K}^{-1}\text{mol}^{-1})\ln\left(\frac{14.40}{115.2}\right) = -45.0\text{ J K}^{-1}$$

The ΔS for the overall process is the sum of these two values. It equals $\boxed{\text{zero}}$, allowing for round-off errors.

8.45 a) If the motion of air masses through the atmosphere is adiabatic and reversible, then q_{rev} equals zero, and ΔS equals $\boxed{\text{zero}}$.

b) Upward displacement of an air mass causes its temperature and pressure to drop concurrently. Break down this overall process into two parts: a temperature change at constant pressure (step I) and a pressure change at constant temperature (step II). The initial values of temperature and pressure are T_0 and P_0 and the final values are T and P. For the two steps:

$$\Delta S_{\text{I}} = nc_{\text{P}}\left(\frac{T}{T_0}\right) \qquad \Delta S_{\text{II}} = nR\ln\left(\frac{P_0}{P}\right)$$

In the first step, ΔS is *less* than zero because cooling a system reduces its entropy. In the second step, ΔS is *greater* than zero. This step is the expansion of the air mass. The sum of the ΔS's must be zero because the overall process, the sum of the two steps, is isentropic:

$$\boxed{c_{\text{P}}\ln\left(\frac{T}{T_0}\right) + R\ln\left(\frac{P_0}{P}\right) = 0}$$

c) If $\ln(P/P_0)$ is approximately equal to $-\mathcal{M}gh/RT$, then:

$$-\ln\left(\frac{P}{P_0}\right) = \ln\left(\frac{P_0}{P}\right) \approx \frac{+\mathcal{M}gh}{RT}$$

Substitute this result into the final expression in part b and rearrange to obtain

$$T\ln\left(\frac{T}{T_0}\right) \approx \frac{-\mathcal{M}gh}{c_{\text{P}}}$$

All of the quantities on the right side are given in the problem:

$$T\ln\left(\frac{T}{T_0}\right) \approx \frac{-(0.029\text{ kg mol}^{-1})(9.8\text{ m s}^{-2})(5.9\times 10^3\text{ m})}{29\text{ J K}^{-1}\text{mol}^{-1}} = -57.8\text{ K}$$

This means that T, the temperature on top of the mountain, fulfills the equation:

$$T\ln\left(\frac{T}{311\text{ K}}\right) \approx -57.8\text{ K}$$

where the sea-level temperature (311 K) has replaced T_0. Obtain T by guessing a few trial values and using a calculator: $T = 246$ K or $\boxed{-27°\text{C}}$.

8.47 In **8.22**, a 1.000 mol piece of iron at 100°C is plunged into a large reservoir of water at 0°C. It loses 2510 J to the water as its temperature falls from 373 K to 273 K. Its entropy decreases. The change is

$$\Delta S_{\text{Fe}} = nc_{\text{P}}\ln\frac{T_2}{T_1} = (1.00\text{ mol})(25.1\text{ J K}^{-1}\text{mol}^{-1})\ln\left(\frac{373.15}{273.15}\right) = \boxed{-7.83\text{ J K}^{-1}}$$

a) The piece of iron is first cooled from 100 to 50°C and then from 50 to 0°C using two water reservoirs. It loses 1255 J of heat to the first reservoir and 1255 J of heat to the second. The entropy change of the first reservoir, which *absorbs* 1255 J of heat and which is so big it stays at 323.15 K, is

$$\Delta S_{\mathrm{I}} = \frac{q}{T} = \frac{1255\ \mathrm{J}}{323.15\ \mathrm{K}} = 3.88\ \mathrm{J\ K^{-1}}$$

The entropy change of the second reservoir, which also absorbs 1255 J of heat but at 273.15 K, is larger:

$$\Delta S_{\mathrm{II}} = \frac{q}{T} = \frac{1255\ \mathrm{J}}{273.15\ \mathrm{K}} = 4.60\ \mathrm{J\ K^{-1}}$$

These two reservoirs comprise the surroundings of the iron:

$$\Delta S_{\mathrm{surr}} = \Delta S_{\mathrm{I}} + \Delta S_{\mathrm{II}} = 3.88 + 4.60 = 8.48\ \mathrm{J\ K^{-1}}$$

The ΔS of the iron is still -7.83 J K^{-1} because only the path by which it cooled has changed. It still ends up in the same final state. Therefore:

$$\Delta S_{\mathrm{univ}} = \Delta S_{\mathrm{surr}} + \Delta S_{\mathrm{Fe}} = 8.48\ \mathrm{J\ K^{-1}} - 7.83\ \mathrm{J\ K^{-1}} = 0.65\ \mathrm{J\ K^{-1}}$$

b) Each of the four reservoirs absorbs 627.5 J, one-fourth of the total given up by the iron. The entropy changes of the four reservoirs are:

$$\Delta S_{\mathrm{I}} = \frac{627.5\ \mathrm{J}}{348.15\ \mathrm{K}} = 1.80\ \mathrm{J\ K^{-1}} \qquad \Delta S_{\mathrm{II}} = \frac{627.5\ \mathrm{J}}{323.15\ \mathrm{K}} = 1.94\ \mathrm{J\ K^{-1}}$$
$$\Delta S_{\mathrm{III}} = \frac{627.5\ \mathrm{J}}{298.15\ \mathrm{K}} = 2.11\ \mathrm{J\ K^{-1}} \qquad \Delta S_{\mathrm{IV}} = \frac{627.5\ \mathrm{J}}{273.15\ \mathrm{K}} = 2.30\ \mathrm{J\ K^{-1}}$$

ΔS_{surr} is the sum of the ΔS's of the four reservoirs. It is 8.15 J K^{-1}. The ΔS of the iron is still -7.83 J K^{-1}. Therefore:

$$\Delta S_{\mathrm{univ}} = \Delta S_{\mathrm{surr}} + \Delta S_{\mathrm{Fe}} = 8.15 - 7.83\ \mathrm{J\ K^{-1}} = \boxed{0.32\ \mathrm{J\ K^{-1}}}$$

c) Using four reservoirs makes the process more nearly reversible as shown by the smaller ΔS_{univ}. Making the process exactly reversible would require an infinite series of reservoirs each one absorbing an infinitesimal quantity of heat from the iron at a temperature infinitesimally less than the previous reservoir. The ΔS's of all the reservoirs would add up to $+7.83$ J K^{-1}, and ΔS_{univ} would be zero.

8.49 a) Several different ideal gases each occupy their own original volumes and all at the same temperature and pressure. Constraints are removed (for example, valves between the containers are opened) and the gases mix. Clearly ΔS is positive for the mixing. To get an expression for ΔS compute ΔS for each of the gases *separately*, and then add up the several contributions. Work with the i-th gas. This gas starts at V_1 and expands to V_2. In both state 1 and state 2, the entropy of the gases depends on its number of microstates Ω:

$$S_1 = k_{\mathrm{B}} \ln \Omega_1 \qquad S_2 = k_{\mathrm{B}} \ln \Omega_2$$

The *change* in entropy of the i-th gas is

$$\Delta S_i = S_2 - S_1 = k_{\mathrm{B}} \ln \Omega_2 - k_{\mathrm{B}} \ln \Omega_1 = k_{\mathrm{B}} \ln \left(\frac{\Omega_2}{\Omega_1}\right)$$

In both state 1 and state 2, the number of microstates available to one molecule of the gas is proportional to the volume ($\Omega = cV$). The number of microstates available to *all* the molecules of this gas is proportional to the volume raised to the power $n_i N_0$, the total number of molecules of the i-th gas (N_0 is Avogadro's number and n_i is the number of moles). The change in entropy for the i-th gas now equals:

$$\Delta S_i = k_{\mathrm{B}} \ln \left(\frac{\Omega_2}{\Omega_1}\right) = k_{\mathrm{B}} \ln \left(\frac{(cV_2)^{n_i N_0}}{(cV_1)^{n_i N_0}}\right) = n_i N_0 k_{\mathrm{B}} \ln \left(\frac{V_2}{V_1}\right)$$

Now, focus on the term (V_2/V_1). By Boyle's law, it equals (P_1/P_2), the ratio of the original pressure of the i-th gas to the final partial pressure of the i-th gas in the mixture. This latter pressure is, by Dalton's law:

$$P_2 = X_i P_{\text{tot}}$$

where X_i is the mole fraction of the i-th gas. But P_1, the original pressure of the i-th gas, *equals* P_{tot}, because all of the gases started at the same pressure.[6] Therefore:

$$\frac{V_2}{V_1} = \frac{P_1}{P_2} = \frac{P_{\text{tot}}}{X_i P_{\text{tot}}} = \frac{1}{X_i}$$

Substituting this result into the expression for ΔS_i gives

$$\Delta S_i = n_i N_0 k_{\text{B}} \ln\left(\frac{1}{X_i}\right) = -n_i N_0 k_{\text{B}} \ln X_i$$

Next, substitute R for $N_0 k_{\text{B}}$ and insert $X_i n$, where n is the total number of moles of gas, for n_i:

$$\Delta S_i = -(X_i n)\,(N_0 k_{\text{B}})\,\ln X_i = -nRX_i \ln X_i$$

Finally, add up the contributions of all of the gases to get the overall ΔS:

$$\boxed{\Delta S = \sum_i \Delta S_i = -nR\sum_i X_i \ln X_i}$$

b) Calculate the mole fractions of O_2, N_2, and Ar in the mixture and substitute into the preceding formula. Divide 50 g by the respective molar masses of the three gases to obtain the chemical amount of each. The mole fraction of each is its chemical amount divided by the total chemical amount in the mixture. The results of these calculations are:

Gas	Chemical Amount	X (Mole Fraction)	$X \ln X$
O_2	1.563 mol	0.3399	−0.3668
N_2	1.784	0.3879	−0.3673
Ar	1.252	0.2722	−0.3542
	4.596	1.0000	−1.0883

The last row in the table contains the sums of the columns. Then:

$$\Delta S = -nR\sum_i X_i \ln X_i = -4.596 \text{ mol}(8.3145 \text{ J K}^{-1}\text{mol}^{-1})(-1.0883) = \boxed{42 \text{ J K}^{-1}}$$

This is the entropy change of mixing at any temperature and pressure as long as the assumption of ideal-gas behavior holds.

c) Separating the components of air is the reverse of mixing them. The entropy change of separation is therefore the negative of the entropy change of mixing, assuming ideal-gas behavior. To solve the problem, compute ΔS_{sys} for the process of mixing and then change its sign. Table 4.1[7] gives the volume percentages of the various gases in the air. The mole fractions (X's) of the gases equal these numbers divided by 100. The following table give these mole fractions, and the quantity $X \ln X$ for each gas:

[6] Opening a valve between a container of gas 1 at 2.0 atm and a container of gas 2 also at 2.0 atm gives a mixture at 2.0 atm. Pressure is an intensive property.

[7] Text page 97.

Gas	X (Mole Fraction)	$X \ln X$
N_2	0.78110	-0.19297
O_2	0.20953	-0.32747
Ar	0.00934	-0.04365
Ne	0.00001818	-0.0001976

Continuing the table to include more trace gases does not provide $X \ln X$ values significantly different from zero. The sum of the numbers in the last column equals -0.56429. Hence:

$$\Delta S = -nR\sum_i X_i \ln X_i = -(4.09 \text{ mol})(8.3145 \text{ J K}^{-1}\text{mol}^{-1})(-0.56429) = 19.2 \text{ J mol}^{-1}$$

where n was obtained using the ideal-gas law with V equal to 100 L, T equal to 298.15 K, and P equal to 1 atm. The entropy change of separation of the components *of the system* is $\boxed{-19.2 \text{ J K}^{-1}}$.

Tip. The problem asks simply for the "entropy change." The entropy change of the universe cannot be calculated because there is no information about the surroundings of the system. It is of course certain that ΔS_{univ} exceeds zero.

8.51 The absolute entropy is proportional to the area under such a curve. Gold has the $\boxed{\text{higher}}$ absolute entropy at 200 K.

8-53 a) Higher temperature makes the conversion of rhombic to monoclinic sulfur a spontaneous process. From the discussion on text page 260, both $\Delta H°$ and $\Delta S°$ must then both be positive: if the two had unlike signs, then the changeover temperature would be negative (meaning no changeover). If both were negative, then the conversion would be favored by lower temperature.

b) Equilibrium between rhombic and monoclinic sulfur at constant temperature and pressure means $\Delta G° = \Delta H° - T\Delta S° = 0$. Rearranging and substituting the values from the problem gives:

$$\Delta S° = \frac{\Delta H°}{T} = \frac{400 \text{ J}}{368.5 \text{ K}} = \boxed{1.09 \text{ J K}^{-1}}$$

8.55 One mole of H_2O is undercooled (supercooled) to $-10°$C and thermally insulated from its surroundings. When freezing occurs in this system, the temperature of the system increases from -10 to $0°$C. The final state is a mixture of solid and liquid H_2O at $0°$C.

a) Assume that the freezing takes place at constant pressure. Then, the change in enthalpy of the system, ΔH_{sys}, equals q_{sys}, which is known to equal zero (because of the insulation). Imagine the change to take part in two steps. In step 1, the H_2O remains liquid but changes temperature from -10 to $0°$C. In step 2, some of the H_2O freezes. The enthalpy is a state function, so

$$\begin{aligned}\Delta H_{\text{sys}} &= \Delta H_1 + \Delta H_2\\ 0 &= n_{\text{liq}} c_{P\,(\text{liq})} \Delta T + n_{\text{ice}}(-\Delta H_{\text{fus}})\\ &= 1 \text{ mol}(75.3 \text{ J K}^{-1}\text{ mol}^{-1})(273 - 263) \text{ K} + n_{\text{ice}}(-6020 \text{ J mol}^{-1})\end{aligned}$$

where it has been assumed that the heat capacity of the undercooled liquid is constant between -10 and $0°$C. Solving the final equation gives $n_{\text{ice}} = 0.125$ mol. This is $\boxed{1/8}$ of the 1 mol system.

b) The determination of ΔS requires imagining a reversible path for the change. The obvious path consists of two steps that are similar to the steps just used: heating the 1 mol of undercooled water reversibly from

-10 to $0°$; then letting 0.125 mol of the water reversibly freeze. For this path

$$\begin{aligned}\Delta S_{sys} &= \Delta S_1 + \Delta S_2 \\ &= n_{liq} c_{P\,(liq)} \ln \frac{T_2}{T_1} + n_{ice} \frac{-\Delta H}{T} \\ &= 1 \text{ mol}(75.3 \text{ J K}^{-1} \text{ mol}^{-1}) \ln \frac{273 \text{ K}}{263 \text{ K}} + 0.125 \text{ mol} \frac{-6020 \text{ J mol}^{-1}}{273 \text{ K}} \\ &= 2.81 \text{ J K}^{-1} - 2.76 \text{ J K}^{-1} = \boxed{0.05 \text{ J K}^{-1}}\end{aligned}$$

Tip. The answer to part a) is good only to about 10% because of the temperature difference is known only to 1°C in 10.

8.57 The $\Delta H°$ and $\Delta G°$ of the reaction

$$3\ Fe_2O_3(s) \rightarrow 2\ Fe_3O_4(s) + 1/2\ O_2(g)$$

are computed similarly

$$\Delta H° = 2 \text{ mol } \Delta H_f°(Fe_3O_4(s)) + 1/2 \text{ mol } \Delta H_f°(O_2(g)) - 3 \text{ mol } \Delta H_f°(Fe_2O_3(s))$$
$$\Delta G° = 2 \text{ mol } \Delta G_f°(Fe_3O_4(s)) + 1/2 \text{ mol } \Delta G_f°(O_2(g)) - 3 \text{ mol } \Delta G_f°(Fe_2O_3(s))$$

Substitution of standard 25°C values from text Appendix D gives

$$\Delta H° = 2(-1118.4) + 1/2(0) - 3\,(-824.2) = \boxed{235.8 \text{ kJ}}$$
$$\Delta G° = 2(-1015.5) + 1/2(0) - 3\,(-742.2) = \boxed{195.6 \text{ kJ}}$$

The $\Delta G°$ of the reaction as it is written is positive. This means that the reverse reaction is favored when the products and reactants are in standard states at 25°. Therefore $\boxed{Fe_2O_3(s)}$ is favored under the stated conditions.

8.59 The reaction is $3\,CO_2(g) + Si_3N_4(s) \rightarrow 3\,SiO_2(s) + 2\,N_2(g) + 3\,C(s)$. The problem and text Appendix D supply the necessary $\Delta G_f°$ data:

$$\Delta G° = 3\underbrace{(-856.67)}_{SiO_2(s)} + 2\underbrace{(0)}_{N_2(g)} + 3\underbrace{(0)}_{C(s)} - 3\underbrace{(-394.36)}_{CO_2(g)} - 1\underbrace{(-642.6)}_{Si_3N_4(s)} = \boxed{-744.3 \text{ kJ}}$$

8.61 a) The reaction of interest is $2\,CuCl_2(s) \rightarrow 2\,CuCl(s) + Cl_2(g)$. Text Appendix D supplies $\Delta H_f°$ and $S°$ values for the computation of $\Delta H°$ and $\Delta S°$ of this reaction:

$$\Delta H°_{298.15} = 2\underbrace{(-137.2)}_{CuCl(s)} + 1\underbrace{(0)}_{Cl_2(g)} - 2\underbrace{(-220.1)}_{CuCl_2(s)} = 165.8 \text{ kJ}$$
$$\Delta S°_{298.15} = 2\underbrace{(86.2)}_{CuCl(s)} + 1\underbrace{(222.96)}_{Cl_2(g)} - 2\underbrace{(108.07)}_{CuCl_2(s)} = 179.2 \text{ J K}^{-1}$$

b) $\Delta G°_{590} \approx \Delta H°_{298.15} - T\Delta S°_{298.15} = 165.8 \text{ kJ} - (590 \text{ K})(0.1792 \text{ kJ K}^{-1}) = \boxed{60.1 \text{ kJ}}$

c) Use the experimental values at 590 K instead of the values at 298.15 K:

$$\Delta G°_{590} = \Delta H°_{590} - T\Delta S°_{590} = 158.36 \text{ kJ} - (590 \text{ K})(0.17774 \text{ kJ K}^{-1}) = \boxed{53.5 \text{ kJ}}$$

The answer using $\Delta H°_{298.15}$ and $\Delta S°_{298.15}$ is about 12% larger than the actual $\Delta G°_{590}$.

8.63 a) Potassium ions tend to transfer so as to equalize the K^+ concentrations on the two sides of the cell wall. Thus K^+ ions will $\boxed{\text{leave the muscle cells}}$ and pass into the surrounding fluids.

b) The problem is to compute ΔG for transporting 1.00 mol of K^+ ions from a concentration c_1 of 0.0050 M to a concentration c_2 of 0.15 M. The answer must be positive because the separation of a uniform concentration of K^+ ions into two regions of differing concentration is clearly non-spontaneous. Assume that the two solutions are ideal solutions and that T is the normal human body temperature of 37°C (310 K). Consult Section 9.3[8] where the text states the following equation for the change in the Gibbs free energy of the system as an ideal solution goes from c_1 to c_2:

$$\Delta G = nRT \ln\left(\frac{c_2}{c_1}\right)$$

Substitute the appropriate values:

$$\Delta G = (1.00 \text{ mol})(8.3145 \text{ J K}^{-1}\text{mol}^{-1})(310 \text{ K}) \ln\left(\frac{0.15}{0.0050}\right) = \boxed{8770 \text{ J}}$$

8.65 The problem deals with the vaporization

$$2.00 \text{ NH}_3(l,\ 1 \text{ atm},\ 240 \text{ K}) \rightarrow 2.00 \text{ NH}_3(g,\ 1 \text{ atm},\ 298 \text{ K})$$

a) The ΔH for the change equals the sum of the ΔH's of two steps: vaporization of NH_3 at 240 K and heating of the vapor from 240 K to 273 K. It is

$$\begin{aligned}\Delta H &= \Delta H_1 + \Delta H_2 = n\Delta H_{\text{vap}} + nC_P\Delta T \\ &= 2.00 \text{ mol}(23.4 \times 10^3 \text{ J mol}^{-1}) + 2.00 \text{ mol}\left(\frac{38 \text{ J}}{\text{K mol}}\right)(298 - 240) \text{ K} \\ &= 51.2 \times 10^3 \text{ J}\end{aligned}$$

The q for the two-stage change, like all others, depends on the path. Fortunately, this q is a q_P because both changes occur at constant pressure. The q therefore equals the preceding ΔH, that is, $q = \boxed{51.2 \times 10^3 \text{ J}}$. The change absorbs some pressure-volume work. Use text equation 7.1[9] to compute this work

$$w = -P\Delta V = -P(V_2 - V_1) = P(V_{\text{gas}} - V_{\text{liq}})$$

The V_{liq} in this equation is the volume of 2.00 mol of liquid ammonia at the starting temperature. According to the problem, this volume can be neglected in comparison to V_{gas}, which is the volume of the gas at the ending temperature. Therefore

$$w = -PV_{\text{gas}} = -P\frac{nRT}{P} = -(2.00 \text{ mol})8.3145 \text{ J K}^{-1}\text{mol}^{-1}(298 \text{ K}) = \boxed{-4.95 \times 10^3 \text{ J}}$$

By the first law of thermodynamics

$$\Delta E = q + w = 51.2 \times 10^3 \text{ J} + (-4.95 \times 10^3 \text{ J}) = \boxed{46.3 \text{ J}}$$

b) The molar entropy of vaporization is computed as shown on text page 247

$$\Delta S = \frac{\Delta H_{\text{vap}}}{T} = \frac{23.4 \times 10^3 \text{ J mol}^{-1}}{240 \text{ K}} = \boxed{97.5 \text{ J K}^{-1}\text{mol}^{-1}}$$

[8] Specifically, see Text page 281.
[9] text page 200

This is also the standard molar entropy of the transition at 240 K.

c) If $\Delta H°$ and $\Delta S°$ are independent of temperature, then their values at 273.15 K equal the values used in part a) and computed in part b) respectively. They can be used to obtain $\Delta G°$ at 273.15 K

$$\Delta G°_{273.15} = \Delta H° - T\Delta S° = 23.4 \times 10^3 \text{ J mol}^{-1} - 273.15 \text{ K}(97.5 \text{ J K}^{-1}\text{mol}^{-1}) = -3.23 \times 10^3 \text{ J mol}^{-1}$$

This allows computation of $\ln K$ and K for the vaporization at 273.15 K

$$\ln K = \frac{-\Delta G°}{RT} = \frac{+3.23 \times 10^3 \text{ J mol}^{-1}}{(8.3145 \text{ J K}^{-1}\text{mol}^{-1})(273.15 \text{ K})} = 1.42 \quad \text{and} \quad K = e^{1.42} = 4.1$$

This K equals P_{NH_3}, as can be confirmed by writing the equilibrium-constant expression for the vaporization. Therefore $P_{NH_3} = \boxed{4.1 \text{ atm}}$.

Chapter 9

Chemical Equilibrium

9.1 An equilibrium expression is only written with reference to a specific balanced equation. For these equations:

a) $\dfrac{(P_{H_2O})^2_{eq}}{(P_{H_2})^2_{eq}(P_{O_2})_{eq}}$ b) $\dfrac{(P_{XeF_6})_{eq}}{(P_{Xe})_{eq}(P_{F_2})^3_{eq}}$ c) $\dfrac{(P_{CO_2})^{12}_{eq}(P_{H_2O})^6_{eq}}{(P_{C_6H_6})^2_{eq}(P_{O_2})^{15}_{eq}}$

Tip. If equilibrium partial pressures are inserted directly into these expressions, the result in each case is a K_P. If all P_{eq}'s are divided first by a reference pressure (1 atm, for example), the result is a thermodynamic K.

9.3 One balanced equation and its associated mass-action expression are:

$$P_4(g) + 2\,O_2(g) + 6\,Cl_2(g) \rightleftharpoons 4\,POCl_3(g) \qquad \frac{P^4_{POCl_3}}{P_{P_4}P^2_{O_2}P^6_{Cl_2}}$$

The answer omits the subscript eq's, a common practice.

Tip. Other answers are possible. For example, if the coefficients in the balanced equation are doubled, then the exponents in the mass-action expression are doubled, and the overall expression is squared:

$$2\,P_4(g) + 4\,O_2(g) + 12\,Cl_2(g) \rightleftharpoons 8\,POCl_3(g) \qquad \frac{P^8_{POCl_3}}{P^2_{P_4}P^4_{O_2}P^{12}_{Cl_2}}$$

9.5 a) The law of mass action applied to the reaction

$$CO_2(g) + H_2(g) \rightleftharpoons CO(g) + H_2O(g)$$

states that the following equation, in which K is a constant, holds at equilibrium:

$$\boxed{\frac{(P_{CO_2}/P_{ref})(P_{H_2}/P_{ref})}{(P_{CO}/P_{ref})(P_{H_2O}/P_{ref})} = K}$$

b) The problem gives K and three of the four equilibrium partial pressures. Substitute in the mass-action expression

$$\frac{(0.70)(P_{H_2}/P_{ref})}{(0.10)(0.10)} = 3.9$$

In this equation, each numerical partial pressure has already been divided by the reference pressure of 1 atm. Solving for P_{H_2} gives $\boxed{0.056\text{ atm}}$.

9.7 a) The graph consists of the values in the second column of the following table plotted (on the y-axis) versus the values in the first column (on the x-axis). The values in the third column are those of the second divided by those of the first:

$[N_2O_4]$	$[NO_2]^2$	$[NO_2]^2/[N_2O_4]$
0.190×10^{-3} mol L^{-1}	0.784×10^{-5} mol^2 L^{-2}	4.12×10^{-2} mol L^{-1}
0.686	2.70	3.94
1.54	5.27	3.42
2.55	10.8	4.23
3.75	13.7	3.65
7.86	29.9	3.80
11.9	44.1	3.71

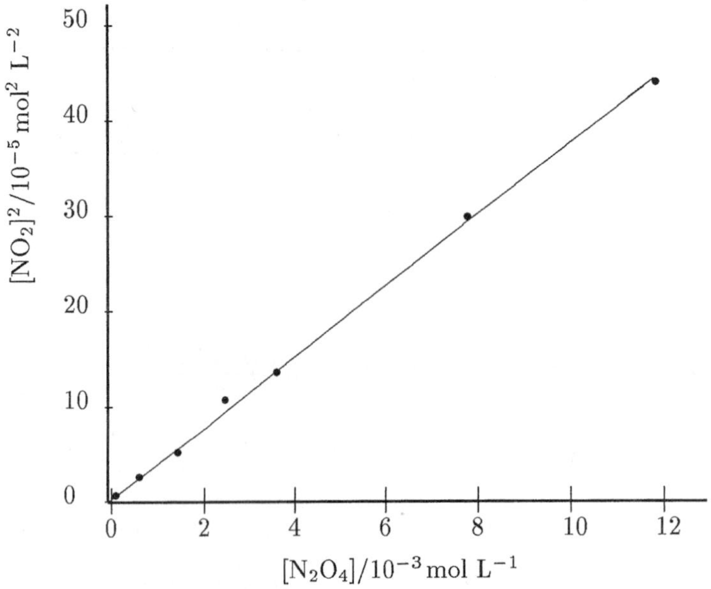

From the mass-action expression for this reaction it follows that:

$$[NO_2]^2 = K[N_2O_4]$$

The equation has the form of the equation for a straight line $y = mx + b$, with $y = [NO_2]^2$, $m = K$, $x = [N_2O_4]$ and $b = 0$. Thus, K equals the slope of the line just plotted.[1]

b) The mean of the values in the last column of the table in the preceding part is the mean experimental K. It is $\boxed{3.83 \times 10^{-2}}$.

9.9 The activities of pure solids and liquids equal 1 and may be omitted from the mass-action expressions:

a) $\dfrac{a^8_{H_2S}}{a^8_{H_2}} = K$ b) $\dfrac{a_{COCl_2}a_{H_2}}{a_{Cl_2}} = K$ c) $a_{CO_2} = K$ d) $\dfrac{1}{a^3_{C_2H_2}} = K$

In all three parts, the partial pressures of the gases divided by the standard-state pressure (1 atm) approximates the activity of the gas. This allows rewriting the answers as follows:

a) $\dfrac{P^8_{H_2S}}{P^8_{H_2}} = K$ b) $\dfrac{P_{COCl_2}P_{H_2}}{P_{Cl_2}} = K$ c) $P_{CO_2} = K$ d) $\dfrac{1}{P^3_{C_2H_2}} = K$

---

[1] See text page A.18 for a discussion of the determination of the slope of a straight-line graph.

9.11 Pure solids and liquids are omitted from the expressions because their activities equal 1.

a) $\dfrac{a_{Zn^{2+}}}{a^2_{Ag^+}} = K$ b) $\dfrac{a_{VO_3(OH)^{2-}}\,a_{OH^-}}{a_{VO_4^{3-}}} = K$ c) $\dfrac{a^6_{HCO_3^-}}{a^2_{As(OH)_6^{3-}}\,a^6_{CO_2}} = K$

In all three parts, the concentrations of the solutes divided by the standard state concentration (1 M) approximates the activity of the solute. Also, the activities of gases can be treated just as in **9.9**. This allows rewriting the answers as:

a) $\boxed{\dfrac{[Zn^{2+}]}{[Ag^+]^2} = K}$ b) $\boxed{\dfrac{[VO_3(OH)^{2-}][OH^-]}{[VO_4^{3-}]} = K}$ c) $\boxed{\dfrac{[HCO_3^-]^6}{[As(OH)_6^{3-}]^2 P^6_{CO_2}} = K}$

9.13 Insert data from text Appendix D into the usual form:

$$\Delta G^\circ_{298.15} = 2\underbrace{(51.29)}_{NO_2(g)} + 3\underbrace{(-228.59)}_{H_2O(g)} - 2\underbrace{(-16.48)}_{NH_3(g)} - 7/2\underbrace{(0)}_{O_2(g)} = \boxed{-550.23\ \text{kJ}}$$

Substitute this answer in the equation:

$$\ln K_{298.15} = \frac{-\Delta G^\circ_{298.15}}{RT} = \frac{-(-550.23 \times 10^3\ \text{J mol}^{-1})}{8.3145\ \text{J K}^{-1}\text{mol}^{-1}(298.15\ \text{K})} = 221.95$$

Hence, $K = e^{221.95} = \boxed{2.5 \times 10^{96}}$.

Tip. The $\Delta G^\circ_{298.15}$ is properly reported in kJ, but the value used in the calculation of K is in J mol^{-1}. The extra per mole refers to "per mole of the reaction as it is written." If the equation were rewritten with all the coefficients doubled, then ΔG° would double, and the equilibrium constant K would be squared.

9.15 a) Calculate the standard free energy change at 25° ($\Delta G^\circ_{298.15}$) for the reaction of 1 mol of SO_2 with $\frac{1}{2}$ mol of O_2 to give 1 mol of SO_3. This requires a table of molar free energies of formation (Appendix D). Then compute the equilibrium constant K using the relationship $\Delta G^\circ = -RT \ln K$:

$$\Delta G^\circ_{298.15} = 1\underbrace{(-371.08)}_{SO_3(g)} - 1\underbrace{(-300.19)}_{SO_2(g)} - 1\underbrace{(0.00)}_{O_2(g)} = -70.89\ \text{kJ}$$

$$\ln K_{298.15} = \frac{-\Delta G^\circ_{298.15}}{RT} = \frac{-(-70.89 \times 10^3\ \text{J mol}^{-1})}{8.3145\ \text{J K}^{-1}\text{mol}^{-1}(298.15\ \text{K})} = 28.6$$

$$K = e^{28.6} = \boxed{2.6 \times 10^{12} = \frac{P_{SO_3}}{P_{SO_2} P^{1/2}_{O_2}}}$$

It is understood that the partial pressures in the boxed equation must be divided by a reference pressure of 1 atm because the standard-state pressure for the ΔG° was 1 atm.

b)

$$\Delta G^\circ = 2\underbrace{(-1015.5)}_{Fe_3O_4(s)} + 1/2\underbrace{(0.00)}_{O_2(g)} - 3\underbrace{(-742.2)}_{Fe_2O_3(s)} = +195.6\ \text{kJ}$$

$$\ln K = \frac{195.6 \times 10^3\ \text{J mol}^{-1}}{-8.3145\ \text{J K}^{-1}\text{mol}^{-1}(298.15\ \text{K})} = -78.90$$

$$K = e^{-78.90} = \boxed{5.4 \times 10^{-35} = P^{1/2}_{O_2}}$$

c)

$$\Delta G^\circ = 1\underbrace{(65.49)}_{Cu^{2+}(aq)} + 2\underbrace{(-131.23)}_{Cl^-(aq)} - 1\underbrace{(-175.7)}_{CuCl_2(s)} = -21.27 \text{ kJ}$$

$$\ln K = \frac{-21.27 \times 10^3 \text{ J mol}^{-1}}{-8.3145 \text{ J K}^{-1}\text{mol}^{-1}(298.15 \text{ K})} = 8.58$$

$$K = e^{8.58} = \boxed{5.3 \times 10^3 = [Cu^{2+}][Cl^-]^2}$$

Tip. The form of the equilibrium expression derives from the set of coefficients that is used in the computation of the ΔG°. In the above, the set was "$1 + 1/2 \rightarrow 1$" and not "$2 + 1 \rightarrow 2$" or any of the other sets that balance the equation.

9.17 The reaction is the combustion of carbon disulfide to give carbon dioxide and sulfur dioxide. Equation 2 represents this as meaningfully as equation 1 but has all of the coefficients divided by three. The mass-action expression for equation 2 (K_2) therefore equals that for equation 1 (K_1) except with all of the exponents divided by 3. Dividing exponents by 3 corresponds to taking the cube root: $\boxed{K_2 = \sqrt[3]{K_1}}$.

9.19 When chemical equations 1 and 2 are added to obtain equation 3, the equilibrium constant associated with equation 3 equals the product of the equilibrium constants associated with equations 1 and 2. Also if a equation is reversed, the new equilibrium constant is the reciprocal of the original. Writing the first equation in this problem in reverse and adding the second equation gives the equation of interest. Thus, K for the reaction of interest equals $K_2 \times (1/K_1)$ or $\boxed{K_2/K_1}$.

9.21 Write the mass-action expression that corresponds to the equation given in the problem. Then substitute the equilibrium partial pressures and calculate K:

$$3\,Al_2Cl_6(g) \rightleftharpoons 2\,Al_3Cl_9(g) \qquad \frac{P^2_{Al_3Cl_9}}{P^3_{Al_2Cl_6}} = K = \frac{(1.02 \times 10^{-2})^2}{(1.00)^3} = \boxed{1.04 \times 10^{-4}}$$

9.23 The 1,3-di-*t*-butylcyclohexane is a gas at 580 K. In a collection of, say, 10,000 molecules, 642 would be in the chair form and 9358 would be in the boat form at equilibrium. The partial pressures of gases are proportional to the number of molecules present, assuming ideality. That is, $P_{gas} = kN$ where k is a constant of proportionality that depends on the temperature and volume only. Therefore:

$$K = \frac{P_{boat}}{P_{chair}} = \frac{kN_{boat}}{kN_{chair}} = \frac{9358}{642} = \boxed{14.6}$$

9.25 a) Calculate the chemical amount of SO_2Cl_2 from the mass of of SO_2Cl_2 that was put into the flask:

$$n_{SO_2Cl_2} = 3.174 \text{ g } SO_2Cl_2 \times \left(\frac{1 \text{ mol } SO_2Cl_2}{135.0 \text{ g } SO_2Cl_2}\right) = 0.02351 \text{ mol } SO_2Cl_2$$

Imagine that the SO_2Cl_2 vaporizes in one step and then reacts in a second distinct step. Use the ideal-gas law to compute the partial pressure of the $SO_2Cl_2(g)$ after it fills the flask at 100°C but before it has a chance to react:

$$P_{SO_2Cl_2} = n_{SO_2Cl_2}\left(\frac{RT}{V}\right) = 0.02351\left(\frac{(0.08206 \text{ L atm mol}^{-1}\text{K}^{-1})(373.15 \text{ K})}{1.000 \text{ L}}\right) = 0.7199 \text{ atm}$$

The partial pressures of both products equal zero at this point. As the reaction advances toward equilibrium, the three partial pressures change. The SO_2Cl_2 decomposes to generate SO_2 and Cl_2 in equal chemical amounts:

	$SO_2Cl_2(g) \rightleftharpoons$	$SO_2(g)$ +	$Cl_2(g)$
Init. pressure (atm)	0.7199	0	0
Change in pressure (atm)	$-x$	$+x$	$+x$
Equil. pressure (atm)	$0.7199 - x$	x	x

The total pressure in the flask at equilibrium is the sum of the three equilibrium partial pressures:

$$P_{\text{tot}} = 1.30 \text{ atm} = P_{SO_2Cl_2} + P_{Cl_2} + P_{SO_2} = (0.7199 - x) + x + x$$

Solving gives x equal to 0.5801 atm. The equilibrium partial pressures of the two products are accordingly both $\boxed{0.58 \text{ atm}}$, and the equilibrium partial pressure of the reactant is $\boxed{0.14 \text{ atm}}$.

b) K is computed by substituting equilibrium partial pressures into the appropriate mass-action expression:

$$K = \frac{(P_{SO_2}/1 \text{ atm})(P_{Cl_2}/1 \text{ atm})}{(P_{SO_2Cl_2}/1 \text{ atm})} = \frac{(0.58)(0.58)}{(0.14)} = \boxed{2.4}$$

9.27 a) Calculate the chemical amount n of the gaseous $C_6H_5CH_2OH$. Then use the ideal-gas law to calculate its initial partial pressure: Call this compound "BzOH."

$$n_{\text{BzOH}} = 1.20 \text{ g BzOH} \times \left(\frac{1 \text{ mol BzOH}}{108 \text{ g BzOH}}\right) = 0.0111 \text{ mol BzOH}$$

$$P_{\text{BzOH}} = \frac{n_{\text{BzOH}}RT}{V} = \frac{(0.0111 \text{ mol})(0.08206 \text{ L atm mol}^{-1}\text{K}^{-1})(523 \text{ K})}{2.00 \text{ L}} = 0.238 \text{ atm}$$

The following three-line table shows how the partial pressures of benzyl alcohol and its products change as equilibrium is approached:

	$C_6H_5CH_2OH(g) \rightleftharpoons$	$C_6H_5CHO(g)$ +	$H_2(g)$
Init. pressure (atm)	0.238	0	0
Change in pressure (atm)	$-x$	$+x$	$+x$
Equil. pressure (atm)	$0.238 - x$	x	x

Substitute the final pressures in the mass-action expression:

$$\frac{P_{C_6H_5CHO}P_{H_2}}{P_{\text{BzOH}}} = 0.558 = \frac{(x)(x)}{(0.238 - x)} \qquad \text{from which} \qquad x^2 + 0.558x - 0.133 = 0$$

Use the quadratic formula[2] to solve for x:

$$x = \frac{-(0.558) \pm \sqrt{(0.558)^2 - 4(1)(0.133)}}{2(1)} = \frac{-0.558 \pm 0.918}{2}$$

$$x = 0.180 \quad \text{and} \quad x = -0.738$$

Disregard the solution $x = -0.738$ because it leads to negative partial pressures for all three gases. The answer is $P_{C_6H_5CHO} = \boxed{0.180 \text{ atm}}$.

b) The fraction of the benzyl alcohol dissociated at equilibrium equals the amount dissociated divided by the initial amount. These amounts are respectively proportional to the decrease in partial pressure of the benzyl alcohol and the initial partial pressure of the benzyl alcohol. Hence:

$$f = \frac{\text{amount of BzOH dissociated}}{\text{original amount of BzOH}} = \frac{0.180 \text{ atm}}{0.238 \text{ atm}} = \boxed{0.756}$$

---

[2] Text page A.19.

9.29 At equilibrium, the bulb contains a mixture of $PCl_3(g)$ and $Cl_2(g)$, the two products, and whatever $PCl_5(g)$, the sole reactant, remains. The total pressure of this mixture is given as 0.895 atm. If this gaseous mixture follows Dalton's law, then its final total pressure is equal to the sum of the partial pressures of the components:

$$P_{\text{tot}} = P_{\text{PCl}_3} + P_{\text{Cl}_2} + P_{\text{PCl}_5} = 0.895 \text{ atm}$$

Assume that the reaction

$$\text{PCl}_5(g) \rightleftharpoons \text{Cl}_2(g) + \text{PCl}_5(g)$$

is the only reaction taking place. Then the partial pressure of PCl_3 and the partial pressure of Cl_2 always remain equal. Let these two pressures equal x atm. Then the partial pressure of PCl_5 equals $(0.895 - 2x)$ atm. At equilibrium, the partial pressures satisfy the equation:

$$K = 2.15 = \frac{P_{\text{Cl}_2} P_{\text{PCl}_3}}{P_{\text{PCl}_5}} = \frac{(x)(x)}{0.895 - 2x}$$

Solving (using the quadratic formula) gives $x = 0.40866$ and a physically meaningless root ($x = -4.7087$). The equilibrium partial pressures of the Cl_2 and the PCl_3 are both $\boxed{0.409 \text{ atm}}$, and the equilibrium partial pressure of the PCl_5 is $\boxed{0.078 \text{ atm}}$.

9.31 Write the equation for the reaction, and insert the given data in the usual table:

	$\text{Br}_2(g)$	$+\ \text{I}_2(g)$ $\rightleftharpoons$	$2\,\text{IBr}(g)$
Init. pressure (atm)	0.0500	0.0400	0
Change in pressure (atm)	$-x$	$-x$	$+2x$
Equil. pressure (atm)	$0.0500 - x$	$0.0400 - x$	$2x$

$$\frac{P_{\text{IBr}}^2}{P_{\text{Br}_2} P_{\text{I}_2}} = 322 = \frac{(2x)^2}{(0.0500 - x)(0.0400 - x)}$$

Rearrangement leads to the quadratic equation: $x^2 - 0.09113x + 2.025 \times 10^{-3} = 0$. Solving (using the quadratic formula) gives $x = 0.0384$ and $x = 0.0527$. The second root is "unphysical" because there was only 0.0400 atm of I_2 at the start. Going down by 0.0527 atm is impossible. The correct partial pressures come from the first root:

$$P_{\text{IBr}} = \boxed{0.0768 \text{ atm}} \qquad P_{\text{I}_2} = \boxed{0.0016 \text{ atm}} \qquad P_{\text{Br}_2} = \boxed{0.0116 \text{ atm}}$$

9.33 Write the equation, the initial partial pressures, the change in the pressures required to reach equilibrium, and the final partial pressures:

	$\text{N}_2(g)\ +$	$\text{O}_2(g)$ $\rightleftharpoons$	$2\,\text{NO}(g)$
Init. pressure (atm)	0.41	0.59	0.21
Change in pressure (atm)	$+x$	$+x$	$-2x$
Equil. pressure (atm)	$0.41 + x$	$0.59 + x$	$0.21 - 2x$

Note the sign of x. A positive x in this set-up corresponds to the loss of product and the formation of reactants as the reaction comes to equilibrium. The mass-action expression relates the equilibrium partial pressures to K:

$$K = 4.2 \times 10^{-31} = \frac{P_{\text{NO}}^2}{P_{\text{N}_2} P_{\text{O}_2}} = \frac{(0.21 - 2x)^2}{(0.41 + x)(0.59 + x)}$$

Before attempting to solve for x, consider the relative sizes of the numbers. This saves getting bogged down with algebra. The equilibrium constant is very small. Hence, the numerator of the equilibrium expression must be very small—almost all of the NO(g) is consumed at equilibrium. Suppose therefore that *all* of the

$NO(g)$ reacts. Then, $2x = 0.21$ and $x = 0.105$. Using this value of x gives an equilibrium pressure of N_2 of $0.41 + 0.105$ or $\boxed{0.52 \text{ atm}}$. The equilibrium pressure of O_2 is, by a similar computation, $\boxed{0.70 \text{ atm}}$. To get the true (non-zero) equilibrium partial pressure of NO, substitute these two pressures back into the original expression:

$$4.2 \times 10^{-31} = \frac{P^2_{NO}}{P_{N_2}P_{O_2}} = \frac{(P_{NO})^2}{(0.52)(0.70)}$$

Solving for P_{NO} gives $\boxed{3.9 \times 10^{-16} \text{ atm}}$. The reaction lies *quite* far toward the reactants at equilibrium.

9.35 The equation for the synthesis of ammonia that is given in the problem and the corresponding equilibrium expression are:

$$N_2(g) + 3\,H_2(g) \rightleftharpoons 2\,NH_3(g) \qquad \frac{P^2_{NH_3}}{P^3_{H_2}P_{N_2}} = K = 6.78 \times 10^5$$

This can be written almost effortlessly. The difficulty starts with translating the other statements in the problem into mathematical terms. If the H to N atom ratio is 3 to 1 then:

$$P_{H_2} = 3P_{N_2}$$

because the third component, NH_3, maintains, within itself, the required 3 to 1 ratio of atoms. The fact that the total pressure is 1.00 atm means:

$$P_{N_2} + P_{H_2} + P_{NH_3} = 1.00 \text{ atm}$$

Let x equal the equilibrium partial pressure of N_2. Then $P_{N_2} = 3x$ and $P_{NH_3} = 1.00 - 4x$ at equilibrium. Substitute in the mass-action expression:

$$6.78 \times 10^5 = \frac{(1.00 - 4x)^2}{(3x)^3 x} = \frac{(1.00 - 4x)^2}{27x^4}$$

This equation is not too hard to solve analytically (see below), but is it necessary even to try? The x is expected to be small because at equilibrium the mixture is mostly NH_3 (K is big). Using this idea simplifies the algebra. Suppose $4x << 1.00$. Then:

$$6.78 \times 10^5 \approx \frac{1.00}{27x^4} \quad \text{from which} \quad x \approx 0.0153$$

Improve this answer by doing successive approximations.[3] The idea is to guess values of x and compute the right-hand side of the equation for each. Improve each new guess based on the results of the previous computation. Soon, the computed value becomes sufficiently close to 6.78×10^5. The following table maps such a process. It starts with the x from the rough solution:

x	$(1.00 - 4x)^2$	$27x^4$	$(1.00 - 4x)^2/27x^4$
0.0153	0.8813	1.480×10^{-6}	5.96×10^5
0.0145	0.8874	1.194×10^{-6}	7.43×10^5
0.0149	0.8843	1.331×10^{-6}	6.64×10^5
0.0147	0.8859	1.261×10^{-6}	7.03×10^5
0.0148	0.8851	1.295×10^{-6}	6.83×10^5
0.01483	0.8849	1.306×10^{-6}	6.776×10^5

Therefore x equals 0.01483 to four significant digits. Then:

$$P_{N_2} = \boxed{0.0148 \text{ atm}} \quad P_{H_2} = \boxed{0.0445 \text{ atm}} \quad P_{NH_3} = \boxed{0.941 \text{ atm}}$$

---

[3] See text Appendix C, text page A.20.

Tip. Analytical solution of the equation:

$$6.78 \times 10^5 = \frac{(1.00 - 4x)^2}{27x^4}$$

proceeds by multiplying both sides of the equation by 27 and then taking the square root of both sides. This gives:

$$4.278 \times 10^3 = \frac{1.00 - 4x}{x^2} \qquad \text{from which comes} \qquad (4.278 \times 10^3)x^2 + 4x - 1.00 = 0$$

Substitution in the quadratic formula affords two roots:

$$x = \frac{-b \pm \sqrt{b^2 - 4ac}}{2a} = \frac{-4 \pm \sqrt{16 + 17122}}{8556} = +0.0148 \text{ and } -0.0158$$

The positive root is the same answer obtained by approximation. The negative root is physically meaningless.

9.37 The reaction and corresponding mass-action expression in terms of pressures are:

$$CO(g) + Cl_2(g) \rightleftharpoons COCl_2(g) \qquad \frac{P_{COCl_2}}{P_{CO}P_{Cl_2}} = K = 0.20$$

where the 0.20 comes from **9.6**. Write the mass-action expression in terms of concentrations. This expression is related to the above K as follows:[4]

$$\frac{[COCl_2]}{[CO][Cl_2]} = 0.20 \left(\frac{RT}{P_{ref}}\right)^{-\Delta n_g}$$

where Δn_g equals the change in the number of moles of gas from left to right in the reaction (-1 in this case because there is 1 mol of gas on the right and 2 mol on the left of the equation), and P_{ref} is the reference pressure used in obtaining the given K (1.00 atm in this case). Insert these values along with the gas constant R and the absolute temperature T:

$$\frac{[COCl_2]}{[CO][Cl_2]} = 0.20 \left(\frac{(0.08206 \text{ L atm mol}^{-1}\text{K}^{-1})(873.15 \text{ K})}{1 \text{ atm}}\right)^{-(-1)} = 14.3$$

Finally, substitute the equilibrium concentrations of the CO and Cl_2:

$$\frac{[COCl_2]}{[2.3 \times 10^{-4}][1.7 \times 10^{-2}]} = 14.3$$

and solve for $[COCl_2]$. The answer is $\boxed{5.6 \times 10^{-5} \text{ mol L}^{-1}}$.

9.39 Write equilibrium expressions for the reduction of iron(III) oxide with hydrogen and the reduction of carbon dioxide with hydrogen. Write expressions that correspond to the form of the equation given in the problem:

$$\frac{1}{P^3_{H_2}} = K_1 = 4.0 \times 10^{-6} \qquad \text{and} \qquad \frac{P_{CO}}{P_{CO_2}P_{H_2}} = K_2 = 3.2 \times 10^{-4}$$

If both reactions are simultaneously at equilibrium in the same container, then both equations must be satisfied simultaneously. Compute the partial pressure of the hydrogen from the first equation:

$$P_{H_2} = \sqrt[3]{\frac{1}{K_1}} = \sqrt[3]{\frac{1}{4.0 \times 10^{-6}}} = 63 \text{ atm}$$

---

[4] Text page 294.

Insert this partial pressure into the (slightly rearranged) second equation:

$$\frac{P_{CO}}{P_{CO_2}} = K_2 P_{H_2} = (3.2 \times 10^{-4})63 = \boxed{0.020}$$

9.41 a) The reaction and mass-action expression are:

$$NH_3(g) + HCl(g) \rightleftharpoons NH_4Cl(s) \qquad \frac{1}{P_{NH_3} P_{HCl}} = K = 4.0 \quad \text{at } 340°C$$

If P_{NH_3} is 0.80 atm at equilibrium, then, by substitution, the equilibrium partial pressure of $HCl(g)$ is $\boxed{0.31 \text{ atm}}$.

b) Obviously, the equilibrium cannot occur before addition of $NH_4Cl(s)$ to the container filled with $NH_3(g)$—the $NH_4Cl(s)$ is the only source of $HCl(g)$. For every mole of $HCl(g)$ that is produced, one mole of $NH_3(g)$ joins the quantity of $NH_3(g)$ that was responsible for the original 1.50 atm. The partial pressures of the $NH_3(g)$ and of $HCl(g)$ are directly proportional to their respective chemical amounts (assuming ideal-gas behavior). This means that for every atmosphere of $HCl(g)$ produced one additional atmosphere of $NH_3(g)$ is also produced. Let x equal the equilibrium partial pressure of HCl. Then the equilibrium partial pressure of NH_3 is $1.50 + x$ and:

$$P_{NH_3} P_{HCl} = (1.50 + x)x = 0.25 \qquad \text{which gives} \qquad x^2 + 1.50x - 0.25 = 0$$

Solving the quadratic equation gives x equal to 0.151 (the negative root is rejected). Therefore $P_{HCl} = \boxed{0.15 \text{ atm}}$, and $P_{NH_3} = 1.50 + 0.15 = \boxed{1.65 \text{ atm}}$.

9.43 a) The container holds no gas until some of the $NH_4HSe(s)$ decomposes. Breakdown of the solid is the only source of the two gases than eventually fill the container at equilibrium. The stoichiometry of the decomposition reaction requires that the partial pressure of the H_2Se equal the partial pressure of the NH_3 (assuming ideality). The total pressure equals the sum of the partial pressures of the two gases. In equation form:

$$P_{H_2Se} = P_{NH_3} \qquad \text{and} \qquad P_{H_2Se} + P_{NH_3} = 0.0184 \text{ atm}$$

Clearly both partial pressures equal 0.00920 atm at equilibrium. The equilibrium constant is

$$K = (P_{H_2Se})_{eq}(P_{NH_3})_{eq} = (0.00920)^2 = \boxed{8.46 \times 10^{-5}}$$

b) The size of the container has no effect on the K. The two partial pressures can differ, but their product must equal K at equilibrium:

$$8.46 \times 10^{-5} = P_{H_2Se} P_{NH_3} = P_{H_2Se}(0.0252) \quad \text{hence:} \quad P_{H_2Se} = \boxed{0.00336 \text{ atm}}$$

9.45 a) The reaction quotient Q has the form of a mass-action expression. A K is computed only by substitution of *equilibrium* partial pressures into this mathematical form. Computations of Q on the other hand may employ whatever partial pressures might temporarily prevail. In the following, the subscript zero means initial P's were used:

$$Q_0 = \frac{(P_{Al_3Cl_9})_0^2}{(P_{Al_2Cl_6})_0^3} = \frac{(1.02 \times 10^{-2})^2}{(0.473)^3} = \boxed{9.83 \times 10^{-4}}$$

b) From **9.21**, $K_{454} = 1.04 \times 10^{-4}$. The initial reaction quotient Q_0 exceeds this K so that the reaction approaches equilibrium by "shifting" from the right to the left (generating reactants at the expense of problems). The process $\boxed{\text{consumes } Al_3Cl_9}$ and produces Al_2Cl_6.

9.47 The fading of color means that the reaction consumes $Br_2(g)$ as it goes toward equilibrium: change goes from left to right in the reaction:

$$H_2(g) + Br_2(g) \rightleftharpoons 2\,HBr(g)$$

The initial reaction quotient Q_0 is accordingly less than K. The data given in the problem allow computation of Q_0:

$$Q_0 = \frac{(P_{HBr})_0^2}{(P_{H_2})_0(P_{Br_2})_0} = \frac{(0.90\text{ atm})^2}{(0.40\text{ atm})(0.40\text{ atm})} = 5.1$$

Thus $\boxed{K \text{ must exceed } 5.1}$.

9.49 The "water gas" reaction[5] and its associated mass-action expression:

$$C(s) + H_2O(g) \rightleftharpoons CO(g) + H_2(g) \qquad \frac{P_{CO}P_{H_2}}{P_{H_2O}}$$

If the reaction quotient Q is less than K, the reaction tends to proceed ("shifts") from left to right; if Q is greater than K, the reaction tends to proceed from right to left.

a) A Q is computed by substitution of in the mass-action expression:

$$Q = \frac{P_{CO}P_{H_2}}{P_{H_2O}} = \frac{(1.525)(0.805)}{0.600} = \boxed{2.05}$$

This Q is less than K (which is 2.6) so the reaction shifts from $\boxed{\text{left to right}}$.

b) All three partial pressures are higher than in the previous part. Use them in the mass-action expression:

$$Q = \frac{P_{CO}P_{H_2}}{P_{H_2O}} = \frac{(1.714)(1.383)}{0.724} = \boxed{3.27}$$

Since Q now exceeds K, the reaction shifts from $\boxed{\text{right to left}}$ to reach equilibrium.

9.51 a) Let P_{di} stand for the partial pressure of gaseous diphosphorus $P_2(g)$ and P_{tet} for the partial pressure of gaseous tetraphosphorus $P_4(g)$. For the process:

$$\frac{P_{di}^2}{P_{tet}} = Q$$

Initially, $P_{di} = 2.00$ atm and $P_{tet} = 5.00$ atm making $Q_0 = \boxed{0.800}$. Because $Q_0 > K$ the equilibrium shifts to the $\boxed{\text{left}}$ (reducing the numerator and increasing the denominator in the above fraction) until Q equals K.

b) Let x equal the increase in the pressure of $P_4(g)$ during the change. Then:

$$K = \frac{(2.00 - 2x)^2}{(5.00 + x)} = 0.612$$

The equation can be solved with the quadratic formula. It is instructive however to get x numerically.[6] Construct a table:

x	$(2.00 - 2x)^2$	$5.00 + x$	Q
0.00	4.00	5.00	0.800
0.100	3.24	5.10	0.635
0.120	3.10	5.12	0.605
0.115	3.13	5.115	0.612

[5] This reaction is a possible source of industrial hydrogen. See text page 676.
[6] See text Appendix C.

As x increases Q decreases from 0.800. As the table shows, progress to a good answer is quick. Electronic calculators make it painless. At $x = 0.120$, Q is only slightly less than K. If $x = 0.115$:

$$P_{\text{di}} = 2.00 - 2(0.115) = \boxed{1.77 \text{ atm}} \quad \text{and} \quad P_{\text{tet}} = 5.00 + 0.115 = \boxed{5.12 \text{ atm}}$$

c) If the volume of the system is increased, then, by LeChâtelier's principle, there will be net [dissociation] of P_4. The system responds to its forced rarefaction by producing more molecules to fill the larger volume.

9.53 Chemical systems always tend toward equilibrium. If a stress is applied to a system at equilibrium, the system reacts to minimize the stress.

a) The stress is the addition of $N_2O(g)$. The system reacts to decrease the concentration of N_2O. It does this by proceeding from [right to left] until a new equilibrium is reached.

b) The stress is the reduction in volume. The partial pressures of all the compounds will momentarily rise. The equilibrium will then shift in such a way as to reduce the number of molecules of gas (chemical amount of gas) in the container and reduce the total pressure. There are three moles of gas on the reactant side of the equation and two moles of gas on the product side. The equilibrium will thus shift from [left to right].

c) The reaction is exothermic. Cooling the mixture therefore shifts the equilibrium from [left to right] (to favor the products).

d) In order to maintain a constant pressure, the volume of the system must have increased. Thus, the reaction will shift from [right to left].

e) The partial pressures of the gases are unchanged by the addition of an inert gas, and the equilibrium law is independent of total pressure. There is [no effect] on the position of the equilibrium.

9.55 a) The equilibrium constant increases with decreasing temperature. This means that decreasing the temperature favors the products. Because removing heat shifts the reaction to the right, heat must be generated on the right. The reaction is [exothermic].

b) Reducing the volume shifts this particular equilibrium to the right. Shrinking favors the side of the reaction with fewer moles of gas. Hence, there is a net [decrease] in the number of gas molecules from left to right in the reaction.

9.57 Good design would provide for transferring the heat generated in the chlorination of the ethylene (the first reaction) into the dehydrochlorination of the dichloroethane (the second reaction). Removal of the product heat from the first reaction would tend to drive the first reaction toward the right; input of this heat to the second reaction would drive it toward its products. Good design would also arrange for the continuous removal of the gaseous products of both reactions. This would shift them in the desired direction.

9.59 The ΔH of the reaction is clearly less than zero. The hydration of ethylene to give ethanol is thus exothermic. Think of the heat as a reaction product:

$$C_2H_4(g) + H_2O(g) \rightarrow C_2H_5OH(g) + \text{ heat}$$

By LeChâtelier's principle, the equilibrium production of ethanol is maximized by running the reaction at [low temperature] (which allows the product heat to escape better). There are two moles of gas on the reactant side and only one mol of gas of the product side; [high pressure] will force the equilibrium from left to right, increasing the yield of ethanol.

9.61 Use the van't Hoff equation to calculate $\Delta H°$ for the reaction from the two K's and the temperatures at which the K's were measured:

$$\ln\frac{K(T_2)}{K(T_1)} = \frac{-\Delta H°}{R}\left(\frac{1}{T_2} - \frac{1}{T_1}\right)$$

$$\ln\left(\frac{0.00121}{6.8}\right) = -8.634 = \frac{-\Delta H°}{8.3145 \text{ J K}^{-1}\text{mol}^{-1}}\left(\frac{1}{473.15 \text{ K}} - \frac{1}{298.15 \text{ K}}\right)$$

$$\Delta H° = \boxed{-5.8 \times 10^4 \text{ J mol}^{-1}}$$

This is a close approximation of ΔH.
Tip. The "mol^{-1}" in the answer means per 1 mol of the reaction as it is written in the problem.

9.63 a) Use the equation $\Delta G° = -RT\ln K$:

$$\Delta G°_{298.15} = -RT\ln K = (-8.3145 \text{ J K}^{-1}\text{mol}^{-1})(298 \text{ K})\ln(9.3 \times 10^9) = -56.9 \times 10^3 \text{ J mol}^{-1}$$

For one mole of the reaction as written,the $\Delta G°_{298.15}$ is $\boxed{-56.9 \text{ kJ}}$.
b) Use the van't Hoff equation and the two values of K to obtain $\Delta H°$. Then $\Delta S°$ can be calculated from $\Delta G°_{298.15}$ (above) and the equation $\Delta G° = \Delta H° - T\Delta S°$. The van't Hoff equation gives:

$$\ln\left(\frac{3.3 \times 10^7}{9.3 \times 10^9}\right) = \frac{-\Delta H°}{8.3145 \text{ J K}^{-1}\text{mol}^{-1}}\left(\frac{1}{398 \text{ K}} - \frac{1}{298 \text{ K}}\right)$$

Completion of the arithmetic reveals that $\Delta H°$ equals -55.6 kJ mol^{-1}. This means that $\Delta H°$ in the reaction of 1/2 mol of Cl_2 and 1/2 mol of F_2 to give 1 mol of ClF is $\boxed{-55.6 \text{ kJ}}$. Finally:

$$\Delta S° = \frac{\Delta H° - \Delta G°}{T} = \frac{-55.63 \times 10^3 \text{ J} - (-56.88 \times 10^3 \text{ J})}{298 \text{ K}} = \boxed{4.2 \text{ J K}^{-1}}$$

9.65 Use the van't Hoff equation to calculate the equilibrium constant at 600 K (K_{600}) from the equilibrium constant at 298 K (K_{298}) and the standard enthalpy of the reaction$\Delta H°$, both of which are given:

$$\ln\left(\frac{K_{600}}{K_{298}}\right) = \frac{-\Delta H°}{R}\left(\frac{1}{T_2} - \frac{1}{T_1}\right)$$

$$\ln\left(\frac{K_{600}}{5.9 \times 10^5}\right) = \frac{-(-92.2 \times 10^3 \text{ J mol}^{-1})}{8.3145 \text{ J K}^{-1}\text{mol}^{-1}}\left(\frac{1}{600 \text{ K}} - \frac{1}{298 \text{ K}}\right)$$

$$K_{600} = \boxed{4.3 \times 10^{-3}}$$

9.67 a) Use the van't Hoff equation to calculate ΔH_{vap}. The equilibrium constants at T_1 and T_2 equal the vapor pressure of the liquid at T_1 and T_2:

$$\ln\left(\frac{P_2}{P_1}\right) = -\frac{\Delta H_{\text{vap}}}{R}\left(\frac{1}{T_2} - \frac{1}{T_1}\right)$$

$$\ln\left(\frac{4.2380 \text{ atm}}{0.4034 \text{ atm}}\right) = \frac{-\Delta H_{\text{vap}}}{8.3145 \text{ J K}^{-1}\text{mol}^{-1}}\left(\frac{1}{273.15 \text{ K}} - \frac{1}{223.15 \text{ K}}\right)$$

$$\Delta H_{\text{vap}} = \boxed{23.8 \text{ kJ mol}^{-1}}$$

b) The normal boiling point T_b of a liquid is defined as the temperature at which the vapor pressure of the liquid equals 1 atm exactly. Therefore, set P_1 equal to 1.000 atm and T_1 equal to T_b in the previous equation. Set $T_2 = 273.15$ K and $P_2 = 4.2380$ atm because 4.2380 atm is the vapor pressure at 273.15 K:

$$\ln\left(\frac{4.2380\ \text{atm}}{1.000\ \text{atm}}\right) = \frac{-2.38 \times 10^3\ \text{J}}{8.3145\ \text{J K}^{-1}\text{mol}^{-1}}\left(\frac{1}{273.15} - \frac{1}{T_\text{b}}\right)$$

$$T_\text{b} = \boxed{240\ \text{K}}$$

Using 0.4034 atm for P_2 along with 223.15 K for T_2 gives the same answer.

9.69 a) The numbers to plot are the second-to-last and last rows of the following table. Put $\ln K$ on the vertical axis and $1/T$ on the horizontal axis.

Temp. (K)	276.8	288.3	298	308	323.2
Equil. Constant K	1160	841	689	533	409
$1/T$ (K^{-1})	0.00361	0.00347	0.00336	0.00325	0.00309
$\ln K$	7.06	6.73	6.54	6.28	6.01

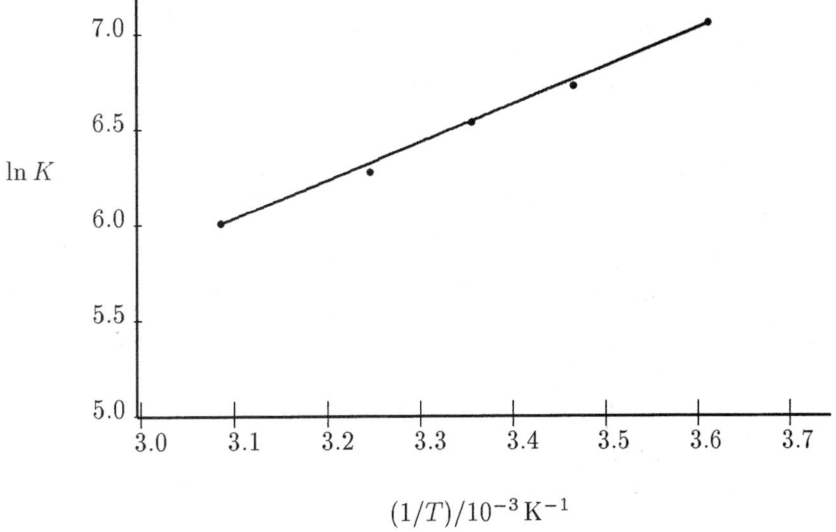

b) A form of the van't Hoff equation is

$$\ln K = \frac{-\Delta H^\circ}{R}\left(\frac{1}{T}\right) + \frac{\Delta S^\circ}{R}$$

Comparing this equation to the equation of a straight line ($y = mx + b$) reveals that the slope m of the straight line that results from plotting $\ln K$ versus $1/T$ equals $-\Delta H^\circ/R$. The slope m of the best straight line in the preceding graph comes out to 2020.3 K. Therefore:

$$\Delta H^\circ = -mR = -(2020.3\ \text{K})(8.3145\ \text{J K}^{-1}\text{mol}^{-1}) = \boxed{-16.8 \times 10^3\ \text{J mol}^{-1}}$$

9.71 Assume exactly 1 L each of H_2O and CCl_4. Then at equilibrium the water holds 1.30×10^{-4} mol of I_2, and the remaining I_2 must be in the CCl_4 layer:

$$n_{I_2\,(CCl_4)} = 1.00 \times 10^{-2} - 1.30 \times 10^{-4} = 9.9 \times 10^{-3}\ \text{mol}$$

The concentration of I_2 in the CCl_4 layer is this amount divided by the volume:

$$[I_2]_{(CCl_4)} = \frac{9.9 \times 10^{-3}\ \text{mol}}{1\ \text{L}} = 9.9 \times 10^{-3}\ \text{mol L}^{-1}$$

The equilibrium constant equals the ratio of the two concentrations:

$$K = \frac{[\mathrm{I_2}]_{(\mathrm{CCl_4})}}{[\mathrm{I_2}]_{(\mathrm{aq})}} = \frac{9.9 \times 10^{-3}}{1.30 \times 10^{-4}} = \boxed{76}$$

9.73 a) The mass-action expressions for the dissolution of benzoic acid in water (K_1) and the dissolution of benzoic acid in either(K_2) are quite simple:

$$K_1 = [\mathrm{C_6H_5COOH}]_{(\mathrm{aq})} \text{ and } K_2 = [\mathrm{C_6H_5COOH}]_{(\mathrm{ether})}$$

The concentrations of C_6H_5COOH at saturation (equilibrium) in water and in ether are:

$$c_{\mathrm{water}} = \frac{2.00\ \mathrm{g\ C_6H_5COOH}}{1\ \mathrm{L\ water\ solution}} \times \left(\frac{1\ \mathrm{mol\ C_6H_5COOH}}{122\ \mathrm{g\ C_6H_5COOH}}\right) = 0.0164\ \mathrm{mol\ L^{-1}}$$

$$c_{\mathrm{ether}} = \frac{660\ \mathrm{g\ C_6H_5COOH}}{1\ \mathrm{L\ ether\ solution}} \times \left(\frac{1\ \mathrm{mol\ C_6H_5COOH}}{122\ \mathrm{g\ C_6H_5COOH}}\right) = 5.4\ \mathrm{mol\ L^{-1}}$$

Hence K_1 is $\boxed{0.0164}$, and K_2 is $\boxed{5.4}$.

b) The partition reaction equals reaction 1 in the previous part subtracted from reaction 2. Subtracting a reaction is the same as reversing it and adding it. The equilibrium constant for the partition reaction (reaction 3) is accordingly:

$$K_3 = K_2\left(\frac{1}{K_1}\right) = \frac{5.4}{0.0164} = \boxed{330}$$

9.75 a) The partial pressures of the gases are in direct proportion to their chemical amounts (assuming that Dalton's law and the ideal-gas law apply):

$$P_{\mathrm{gas}} = n_{\mathrm{gas}}\left(\frac{RT}{V}\right)$$

Suppose that the volume of the container is such that the actual chemical amounts of the four gases are 90, 470, 200, and 45 mol. Then, the partial pressure of the $BCl_3(g)$ is $P_{\mathrm{BCl_3}} = 90(RT/V)$. Expressions for the partial pressures of the other three gases are similar. The equilibrium expression for reaction 1 is

$$\frac{P^3_{\mathrm{BFCl_2}}}{P^2_{\mathrm{BCl_3}} P_{\mathrm{BF_3}}} = K_1$$

Substituting the three partial pressures gives:

$$\frac{(45RT/V)^3}{(90RT/V)^2(470RT/V)} = K_1 = \frac{(45)^3}{(90)^2(470)} = \boxed{0.024}$$

The RT/V's canceled out! The cancellation means the volume of the container has no effect on the position of this particular equilibrium. We were therefore justified in making any assumption we wanted about the volume. A similar procedure with the equilibrium expression for reaction 2 gives $K_2 = \boxed{0.40}$.

b) The given equation (equation 3) equals the sum of equations 1 and 2 divided by three. Obtain the required equilibrium constant by taking the cube root of the product of K_1 and K_2. This gives $\boxed{0.21}$.

Tip. The same answer is obtained by substituting the original partial pressures into the mass-action expression for reaction 3, but the preceding emphasizes how K_3 derives entirely from K_1 and K_2; K_3 is a new number but adds no new information.

9.77 a) If we assume that 1.000 mol of the *cis* form is initially present, then the equilibrium chemical amounts of each species are:

	cis	$\rightleftharpoons$	*trans*
Initial amount mol	1.000		0
Change mol	$-x$		$+x$
Equilibrium amount mol	$1.000 - x$		x

At equilibrium, 73.6% of the *cis* has been converted to the *trans* form. Therefore x is 0.736 mol. The equilibrium chemical amounts are:

$$n_{cis} = 1.000 - x = 1.000 - 0.736 = 0.264 \text{ mol} \quad \text{and} \quad n_{trans} = x = 0.736 \text{ mol}$$

Assuming ideal-gas behavior, the equilibrium partial pressures of the two forms are:

$$P_{cis} = \frac{n_{cis}RT}{V} = \frac{(0.264)RT}{V} \qquad \text{and} \qquad P_{trans} = \frac{n_{trans}RT}{V} = \frac{(0.736)RT}{V}$$

Substitution in the mass-action expression gives K:

$$K = \frac{P_{trans}}{P_{cis}} = \frac{(0.736)RT/V}{(0.264)RT/V} = \boxed{2.79}$$

b) From the preceding it is clear that at equilibrium:

$$P_{trans} = 2.788(P_{cis}) \qquad \text{implying:} \qquad n_{trans} = 2.788(n_{cis})$$

Also, the combined chemical amount of the two forms of the compound is 0.525 mol because 1 mol of the *cis* is consumed for 1 mol of the *trans* created:

$$n_{trans} + n_{cis} = 0.525$$

Solving the two equations in two unknowns gives n_{trans} equal to 0.386 mol. The partial pressure of the *trans* form is

$$P_{trans} = n_{trans}\left(\frac{RT}{V}\right) = 0.386 \text{ mol}\left(\frac{(0.08206 \text{ L atm mol}^{-1}\text{K}^{-1})(698.75 \text{ K})}{15.00 \text{ L}}\right) = \boxed{1.48 \text{ atm}}$$

9.79 Imagine for simplicity that the SO_3/SO_2 equilibrium is established in a 1.000 L container. The contents of the container have a mass of 0.925 g. The chemical amount of the gas mixture in the container is

$$n_{\text{gas}} = \frac{PV}{RT} = \frac{(1 \text{ atm})(1.000 \text{ L})}{0.08257 \text{ L atm mol}^{-1}\text{K}^{-1}(627 + 273.15) \text{ K}} = 0.01354 \text{ mol}$$

A gas of the same mass that consists of undecomposed SO_3 contains somewhat fewer moles

$$n_{SO_3} = 0.925 \text{ g} \times \left(\frac{1 \text{ mol}}{80.06 \text{ g}}\right) = 0.01155 \text{ mol}$$

The partial decomposition of SO_3

$$SO_3(g) \rightleftharpoons SO_2(g) + 1/2\,O_2(g)$$

causes the increase from 0.01155 to 0.01354 mol. If x mol of SO_2 has formed when the reaction reaches equilibrium, then $x/2$ mole of O_2 has also formed and $0.1155 - x$ mol of SO_3 has been consumed. The unknown x is readily computed

$$n_{\text{tot}} = n_{SO_3} + n_{SO_2} + n_{O_2} = (0.01155 - x) \text{ mol} + x \text{ mol} + x/2 \text{ mol}$$
$$0.01354 \text{ mol} = (0.01155 + x/2) \text{ mol}$$
$$x = 0.00398 \text{ mol}$$

The degree of dissociation α of the SO_3 equals the amount converted to products divided by the original amount

$$\alpha = \frac{(0.00398)\text{ mol}}{0.01155\text{ mol}} = \boxed{0.345}$$

9.81 The set-up of the problem is exactly as given for **9.35** but now K is different, and the total pressure is 100 atm. The set-up yields the equation:

$$3.19 \times 10^{-4} = \frac{(100 - 4x)^2}{(3x)^3 x}$$

where x is the equilibrium partial pressure of nitrogen. Factor the numerator and multiply out the denominator to obtain:

$$3.19 \times 10^{-4} = \frac{16(25.0 - x)^2}{27x^4} \quad \text{which gives} \quad 5.383 \times 10^{-4} = \frac{(25.0 - x)^2}{x^4}$$

Taking the square root of both sides of this equation leads to a quadratic equation in x that can be solved routinely. It is also quite quick to solve by successive approximations. First, observe that x must be less than 25. If P_{N_2} exceeded 25 atm, the combined pressure of just two (the nitrogen and hydrogen) out of the three gases would exceed the total pressure in the container. Now, guess an x between 0 and 25 and compute the right-hand side of the equation. Revise the guess based on experience until the computed value becomes sufficiently close to 5.383×10^{-4}. The following table shows the process. The first guess is near the middle of the range:

x	$(25.0 - 4x)^2/x^4$	Comment
15	1.97×10^{-3}	x is too small
20	1.56×10^{-4}	x is too large
18	4.67×10^{-4}	x is too large
17.5	6.00×10^{-4}	x is too small
17.7	5.43×10^{-4}	x is a bit too small
17.72	5.375×10^{-4}	x acceptable

The answer is $x = 17.72$. If $x = 17.72$ then:

$$P_{N_2} = \boxed{17.7\text{ atm}} \qquad P_{H_2} = \boxed{53.2\text{ atm}} \qquad P_{NH_3} = \boxed{29.1\text{ atm}}$$

Tip. Check the answers by confirming that the sum of the three partial pressures is 100 atm and that:

$$\frac{P_{NH_3}^2}{P_{H_2}^3 P_{N_2}} = \frac{(29.1)^2}{(53.2)^3(17.7)} = 3.18 \times 10^{-4} = K$$

9.83 The first reaction and its mass-action expression are:

$$Cl_2(g) \rightleftharpoons Cl_2(aq) \qquad \frac{[Cl_2]}{P_{Cl_2}} = K$$

Note that the solvent does not appear in the mass-action expression. Both the equilibrium concentration of the dissolved chlorine and the partial pressure of the gaseous chlorine are given in the problem. Hence:

$$K_1 = \frac{[Cl_2]}{P_{Cl_2}} = \frac{0.061}{1.00} = 0.061$$

The second reaction and its mass-action expression are:

$$Cl_2(aq) + H_2O(l) \rightleftharpoons H^+(aq) + Cl^-(aq) + HOCl(aq) \qquad \frac{[HOCl][H^+][Cl^-]}{[Cl_2]} = K_2$$

K_2 is readily calculated because $[H^+]$ must be equal to $[Cl^-]$ and to [HOCl], based on the 1-to-1-to-1 stoichiometry of the reaction:

$$K_2 = \frac{[HOCl][H^+][Cl^-]}{[Cl_2]} = \frac{(0.030)(0.030)(0.030)}{(0.061)} = \boxed{4.4 \times 10^{-4}}$$

9.85 a) The decomposition reaction is $NH_4HS(s) \rightleftharpoons NH_3(g) + H_2S(g)$. One mole of gaseous ammonia forms per mole of gaseous hydrogen sulfide. Assuming that the product mixture follows Dalton's law, then the equilibrium partial pressure of each gas equals half the total pressure at equilibrium:

$$P_{NH_3} = P_{H_2S} = \frac{0.659 \text{ atm}}{2}$$

Insert these values into the mass-action expression and compute K:

$$K = P_{NH_3}P_{H_2S} = \left(\frac{0.659}{2}\right)^2 = \boxed{0.109}$$

b) Bringing the equilibrium partial pressure of $NH_3(g)$ to 0.750 atm will, by LeChâtelier's principle, reduce the partial pressure of $H_2S(g)$. It will not change the equilibrium constant. Hence:

$$P_{H_2S} = \frac{K}{P_{NH_3}} = \frac{0.109}{0.750} = \boxed{0.145 \text{ atm}}$$

Tip. In the first part, the 2 is used twice: once as a divisor and once as an exponent. This is all right.

9.87 The K for this reduction of nickel oxide to nickel relates the partial pressures of $CO(g)$ and $CO_2(g)$. The nickel and nickel(II) oxide are pure solids and do not enter the mass-action expression:

$$\frac{P_{CO_2}}{P_{CO}} = K = 255.4$$

The total pressure equals the sum of the two partial pressures:

$$P_{CO_2} + P_{CO} = 2.50 \text{ atm}$$

Once the system is at equilibrium, the two equations relating the two partial pressures must be satisfied simultaneously. Therefore:

$$\frac{P_{CO_2}}{(2.50 - P_{CO_2})} = 255.4$$

Solving gives P_{CO_2} equal to $\boxed{2.49 \text{ atm}}$. Substitution back into the mass-action equation gives P_{CO} equal to $\boxed{9.75 \times 10^{-3} \text{ atm}}$.

9.89 a) The reaction and reaction-quotient expression are:

$$PCl_5(g) \rightleftharpoons PCl_3(g) + Cl_2(g) \qquad \frac{P_{Cl_2}P_{PCl_3}}{P_{PCl_5}} = Q$$

The problem gives three initial partial pressures. Substitution gives an initial reaction quotient Q_0 of $\boxed{120}$. Since Q_0 exceeds K, the reaction proceeds to the $\boxed{\text{left}}$.

b) As originally mixed, the system has $Q = 120$ and $K = 11.5$. Let y equal the partial pressure of $Cl_2(g)$ consumed by the right-to-left reaction. An equal pressure of $PCl_3(g)$ is also consumed, and an equal pressure of $PCl_5(g)$ is created. This follows from the stoichiometry of the equation. Therefore:

$$K = 11.5 = \frac{(6.0 - y)(2.0 - y)}{(0.10 + y)} \qquad \text{from which} \quad y^2 - 19.5y + 10.85 = 0$$

The roots of the quadratic equation are 0.573 and 18.93. Only the first makes physical sense. The second corresponds to negative partial pressures. Complete the computation by finding the various partial pressures:

$$P_{PCl_3} = 2.0 - 0.573 = \boxed{1.4 \text{ atm}} \qquad P_{PCl_2} = 6.0 - 0.573 = \boxed{5.4 \text{ atm}}$$

$$P_{PCl_5} = 0.10 + 0.573 = \boxed{0.67 \text{ atm}}$$

c) By LeChâtelier's principle, an increase in volume causes the reaction to shift to the side having *more* moles of gas. The amount of $PCl_5(g)$ will $\boxed{\text{decrease}}$.

9.91 Equilibrium constants depend strongly on temperature. The equation in the problem gives the experimentally determined T-dependence of the K of the hydrogenation reaction:

$$C_5H_5N(g) + 3\,H_2(g) \rightleftharpoons C_5H_{11}N(g)$$

a) Substitute $T = 500$ K into the expression:

$$\log_{10} K = -20.281 + \frac{10560}{T} = -20.281 + \frac{10560}{500} = 0.839$$

Taking the antilog of both sides gives $K = 10^{0.839} = \boxed{6.90}$.

b) Assume that the hydrogenation reaction is at equilibrium. The fraction f of nitrogen in the form of C_5H_5N (pyridine or "py") equals the chemical amount of pyridine divided by the sum of the chemical amounts of pyridine and $C_5H_{11}N$ (piperidine or "pip"). If Dalton's law holds, these chemical amounts are directly proportional to the partial pressures of the two compounds. Hence:

$$f = \frac{n_{py}}{n_{py} + n_{pip}} = \frac{P_{py}}{P_{py} + P_{pip}}$$

Also, the partial pressures must satisfy the law of mass action:

$$\frac{P_{pip}}{P_{py} P_{H_2}^3} = K \qquad \text{which gives} \qquad \frac{P_{pip}}{P_{py}} = 6.90(1.00)^3$$

when $K = 6.90$ and $P_{H_2} = 1.00$ atm are put in. Let the partial pressure of the pyridine be y atm. The partial pressure of the piperidine is then, by the preceding equation, $6.90y$ atm. Insert the P's into the equation for f:

$$f = \frac{P_{py}}{P_{py} + P_{pip}} = \frac{y}{y + 6.90y} = \frac{1}{1 + 6.90} = \boxed{0.127}$$

9.93 Equal chemical amounts of PCB-2 and PCB-11 exist in solution in some volume V of water. Then, the same volume V of octanol is added. The treatment with octanol does nothing to alter the total chemical amount of either PCB but redistributes both. Once the redistribution comes to equilibrium:

$$n_{\text{PCB-2}} = [2]_{(aq)}\,V + [2]_{(oct)}\,V \qquad \text{and} \qquad n_{\text{PCB-11}} = [11]_{(aq)}\,V + [11]_{(oct)}\,V$$

where the bracketed numbers stand for the concentrations of the PCB-2 and PCB-11 and the "(aq)" and "(oct)" refer to water and octanol solutions. Setting the two chemical amounts equal to each other and dividing through by V gives:

$$[2]_{(aq)} + [2]_{(oct)} = [11]_{(aq)} + [11]_{(oct)}$$

The mass-action expressions for the partition of the PCB's between the solvents are:

$$K_2 = \frac{[2]_{(oct)}}{[2]_{(aq)}} \quad \text{and} \quad K_{11} = \frac{[11]_{(oct)}}{[11]_{(aq)}}$$

from which it follows that:

$$[2]_{(\text{oct})} = K_2[2]_{(\text{aq})} \quad \text{and} \quad [11]_{(\text{oct})} = K_{11}[11]_{(\text{aq})}$$

Substitution of these expressions into the first equation yields:

$$[2]_{(\text{aq})} + K_2[2]_{(\text{aq})} = [11]_{(\text{aq})} + K_{11}[11]_{(\text{aq})}$$

Solve this equation for the ratio of the concentration of the two PCB's in the water phase:

$$\frac{[2]_{(\text{aq})}}{[11]_{(\text{aq})}} = \frac{1+K_{11}}{1+K_2} = \frac{1+1.26\times10^5}{1+3.98\times10^4} = \boxed{3.17}$$

Tip. Try finding the ratio of the amounts of the two PCB's in the octanol. To start, divide the equation for $[2]_{(\text{oct})}$ in terms of K_2 by the similar expression for $[11]_{(\text{oct})}$ in terms of K_{11}:

$$\frac{[2]_{(\text{oct})}}{[11]_{(\text{oct})}} = \frac{K_2[2]_{(\text{aq})}}{K_{11}[11]_{(\text{aq})}} = \frac{K_2}{K_{11}}\left(\frac{[2]_{(\text{aq})}}{[11]_{(\text{aq})}}\right)$$

The quantity in parentheses was just determined. Substitute for it and insert the K's:

$$\frac{[2]_{(\text{oct})}}{[11]_{(\text{oct})}} = \frac{K_2}{K_{11}}\left(\frac{1+K_{11}}{1+K_2}\right) = \frac{3.98\times10^4}{1.26\times10^5}\left(\frac{1+1.26\times10^5}{1+3.98\times10^4}\right) = 1.00$$

Although the amount of PCB-2 entering the water is triple the amount of PCB-11, so little of either leaves the octanol that the relative amounts of the two in the octanol remain essentially unchanged.

9.95 a) The chemical amount of I_2 initially in the 0.100 L of aqueous solution is

$$0.100\text{ L}\times\left(\frac{2\times10^{-3}\text{ mol I}_2}{1\text{ L}}\right) = 2\times10^{-4}\text{ mol I}_2$$

Shaking the solution with 0.025 L of CCl_4 allows the I_2 to distribute itself between the two phases. Assume that this distribution comes to equilibrium. If y is the amount of I_2 that dissolves into the CCl_4, then the amount of I_2 left in the aqueous phase is $(2\times10^{-4} - y)$ mol. At equilibrium:

$$[\text{I}_2]_{(\text{aq})} = \left(\frac{2\times10^{-4}-y}{0.100}\right)\text{ mol L}^{-1} \quad \text{and} \quad [\text{I}_2]_{(\text{CCl}_4)} = \left(\frac{y}{0.025}\right)\text{ mol L}^{-1}$$

The mass-action expression for this system is

$$\frac{[\text{I}_2]_{(\text{CCl}_4)}}{[\text{I}_2]_{(\text{aq})}} = K = 85 \qquad \text{from which:} \qquad \frac{(2\times10^{-4}-y)/0.100}{y/0.025} = 85$$

The last equation is easily solved for y, which equals 1.91×10^{-4} mol. Remember that y is the amount of I_2 that transfers to the CCl_4. and not a concentration. By subtraction, the amount remaining in the water is 0.09×10^{-4} mol. The fraction remaining equals the amount remaining divided by the original amount:

$$f = \frac{0.09\times10^{-4}}{2\times10^{-4}} = 0.045 = \boxed{0.04}$$

b) The first extraction with 0.025 L of CCl_4 leaves only 0.045 (4.5%) of the I_2 in the water. Another extraction with a fresh 0.025 L of CCl_4 will leave only 0.045 of that 0.045. The fraction remaining after these successive treatments is

$$f = 0.045\times0.045 = \boxed{0.002}$$

c) From text Example 9.18,[7] the fraction of I_2 remaining in the water after a single 0.050 L extraction is 0.023, which is substantially larger than 0.0020.

Tip. It is about 11 times more efficient to extract the iodine with two half-sized portions of CCl_4 rather than one large portion. In general, it is more efficient to use several small portions of solvent, rather than one or two big ones in performing separations by extraction.

9.97 The reaction is the splitting of tetraphosphorus (P_4) into diphosphorus (P_2).[8]

a) The pressure of a sample of $P_4(g)$ will always exceed the pressure predicted by the ideal-gas law, because the reaction to give $P_2(g)$ furnishes extra molecules to strike the sides of the container. Consider a *P*-*V* experiment performed on a sample of $P_4(g)$ at constant temperature. In the experiment, the pressure is tracked as the volume of the sample is changed, and the results are plotted with P on the vertical axis and $1/V$ on the horizontal axis. Boyle's law predicts a straight-line plot: P rising in direct proportion as $1/V$ rises. The actual experimental plot will be a line that curves toward $\boxed{\text{higher}}$ pressure at low values of $1/V$.

b) Consider a *V*-*T* experiment in which the volume of a sample is $P_4(g)$ is tracked as the temperature is changed and the pressure is kept constant. Charles's law predicts that the volume should rise linearly with the temperature. But increasing the temperature shifts the endothermic equilibrium $P_4 \rightleftharpoons 2\,P_2$ toward the right, generating more molecules in the sample. The "extra" molecules cause the sample to expand an extra amount with temperature. Thus, a plot of the volume of the P_4 sample as a function of T curves toward $\boxed{\text{higher}}$ volumes than predicted by Charles's law as T increases.

9.99 Let the partial pressure of $N_2(g)$ before any of its molecules break down equal P_0. Let the fraction that has broken down at equilibrium equal α. The value of α is 0.0065 at 5000 K but rises to 0.116 at 6000 K. Represent the approach to equilibrium at either temperature in the usual way:

	$N_2(g)$	$\rightleftharpoons$	$2\,N(g))$
Init. Pressure (atm)	P_0		0
Change in Pressure (atm)	$-\alpha P_0$		$+2\alpha P_0$
Equil. Pressure (atm)	$P_0 - \alpha P_0$		$2\alpha P_0$

The total pressure of the equilibrium mixture equals 1.000 atm at both T's:

$$P_{N_2} + P_N = (P_0 - \alpha P_0) + 2\alpha P_0 = P_0(1+\alpha) = 1.000 \text{ atm}$$

Since α is given at both temperatures, the original pressure of N_2 at both temperatures is readily computed from the preceding equation: P_0 was 0.9935 atm at 5000 K and 0.8961 atm at 6000 K. Combine these original pressures with α as indicated above to get the equilibrium partial pressures of N and N_2 at the two temperatures:

Temperature	5000 K	6000 K
Equil. P_{N_2} (atm)	$P_0(1-\alpha) = 0.9871$	$P_0(1-\alpha) = 0.7921$
Equil. P_N (atm)	$2\alpha P_0 = 0.0129$	$2\alpha P_0 = 0.2079$

It is easy to verify that the partial pressures add up to 1.000 atm at both temperatures. Substitute these equilibrium partial pressures in the mass-action expression to obtain K's at the two temperatures:

$$K_{5000} = \frac{P_N^2}{P_{N_2}} = \frac{(0.0129)^2}{0.9871} = 1.69 \times 10^{-4} \qquad K_{6000} = \frac{P_N^2}{P_{N_2}} = \frac{(0.2079)^2}{0.7921} = 5.46 \times 10^{-2}$$

Next, use the van't Hoff equation to estimate $\Delta H°$ for the reaction from the two K's and their temperatures:

$$\ln \frac{K_{6000}}{K_{5000}} = \frac{-\Delta H°}{R}\left(\frac{1}{6000 \text{ K}} - \frac{1}{5000 \text{ K}}\right)$$

[7] Text page 305.
[8] The effect of a change in volume on this reaction is shown in text Figure 9.8, text page 299.

Substitute:

$$\ln\left(\frac{5.46\times10^{-2}}{1.69\times10^{-4}}\right)=5.78=\frac{-\Delta H^\circ}{8.3145\text{ J K}^{-1}\text{mol}^{-1}}\left(\frac{1}{6000\text{ K}}-\frac{1}{5000\text{ K}}\right)$$

Solving for ΔH° gives 1440 kJ mol^{-1}. Hence the standard enthalpy of the reaction as written is $\boxed{1440\text{ kJ}}$.

Tip. The answer is only an estimate because ΔH° and ΔS° are not constant over the 1000 K range. The answer exceeds the N≡N bond enthalpy[9] of 945 kJ mol^{-1}, which is a $\Delta H^\circ_{298.15}$, by over 50%.

9.101 Use ΔG°_f's from text Appendix D to calculate ΔG° for the reaction; obtain the equilibrium constant from ΔG°

$$\Delta G^\circ_{298.15}=1\underbrace{(0.00)}_{\text{Ni}(s)}+1/2\underbrace{(0.00)}_{\text{O}_2(g)}-1\underbrace{(-211.7)}_{\text{NiO}(s)}=211.7\text{ kJ}$$

$$\ln K_{298.15}=\frac{-\Delta G^\circ_{298.15}}{RT}=\frac{-(211.7\times10^3\text{ J mol}^{-1})}{(8.3145\text{ J K}^{-1}\text{mol}^{-1})(298.15\text{ K})}=-85.44$$

$$K=7.8\times10^{-38}$$

The partial pressure of oxygen is related to K through the mass-action expression for this reaction. Because two of the three substances involved in the reaction are pure solids, this expression is very simple: $\sqrt{P_{O_2}}=K$. It follows that the equilibrium pressure of oxygen is the square of the equilibrium constant. It equals $\boxed{6.1\times10^{-75}\text{ atm}}$. The decomposition of NiO(s) to its elements is *very* slight at room temperature!

9.103 The reaction is the sublimation of water, $H_2O(s)\rightleftharpoons H_2O(g)$. The K_{273} for this reaction equals the vapor pressure of ice at 273.15 K, which is 0.0060 atm. Ice at its freezing point sublimes spontaneously whenever the pressure of $H_2O(g)$ is less than 0.0060 atm. Cold ice sublimes less easily. Use the van't Hoff equation to calculate K for sublimation at −15°C (258.15 K)

$$\ln\left(\frac{K_{258}}{K_{273}}\right)=\frac{-\Delta H_{\text{sub}}}{R}\left(\frac{1}{258.15\text{ K}}-\frac{1}{273.15\text{ K}}\right)$$

$$\ln\left(\frac{K_2}{0.0060}\right)=\frac{-50.0\times10^3\text{ J mol}^{-1}}{8.3145\text{ J K}^{-1}\text{mol}^{-1}}\left(\frac{1}{258.15\text{ K}}-\frac{1}{273.15\text{ K}}\right)$$

$$K_{258}=0.0017$$

Therefore ice at 258.15 K sublimes if the partial pressure of $H_2O(g)$ is $\boxed{\text{less than 0.0017 atm}}$.

9.105 Water is a better solvent for more covalent and ionic substances, and carbon tetrachloride (CCl_4) is a better solvent for covalent compounds. On this basis

a) The polar covalent compound methanol (CH_3OH) has a larger concentration in $\boxed{H_2O}$.

b) The covalent compound hexachloroethane (C_2Cl_6) has a larger concentration in $\boxed{CCl_4}$.

c) Bromine (Br_2), which has a covalent bond, has a larger concentration in $\boxed{CCl_4}$.

d) The ionic compound sodium chloride (NaCl) has a larger concentration in $\boxed{H_2O}$.

9.107 a) Represent the dimerization reaction as

$$2\text{ NO}_2(g)\rightleftharpoons \text{N}_2\text{O}_4(g)$$

Text Appendix D furnishes the ΔG°_f's of the reactant and product

$$\Delta G^\circ=\Delta G^\circ_f(\text{N}_2\text{O}_4)-2\,\Delta G^\circ_f(\text{NO}_2)=97.82\text{ kJ mol}^{-1}-2\,(51.29\text{ kJ mol}^{-1})=-4.76\text{ kJ mol}^{-1}$$

[9] See text Table 7.3, text page 219.

The $\Delta G°$ for the reaction as written above is accordingly $\boxed{-4.76\text{ kJ}}$.

The logarithm of the equilibrium constant depends directly on $\Delta G°$

$$\ln K = \frac{\Delta G°}{-RT} = \frac{-4.76 \times 10^3 \text{ J mol}^{-1}}{-(8.3145 \text{ J K}^{-1}\text{mol}^{-1})(298.15 \text{ K})} = 1.92$$

$$K = \exp(1.92) = \boxed{6.8}$$

b) The ΔG of a reaction at a given temperature depends on both its standard Gibbs energy $\Delta G°$ at that temperature and the relative amounts of the various reactants and products. The reaction quotient Q gives the second effect

$$\Delta G = \Delta G° + RT \ln Q = \Delta G° + RT \ln\left(\frac{P_{N_2O_4}}{(P_{NO_2})^2}\right)$$

$$= -4.76 \times 10^3 \text{ J mol}^{-1} + (8.3145 \text{ J K}^{-1}\text{mol}^{-1})(298.15 \text{ K}) \ln\left(\frac{0.01}{0.01^2}\right)$$

$$= -4.76 \times 10^3 \text{ J mol}^{-1} + 11.4 \times 10^3 \text{ J mol}^{-1} = 6.65 \times 10^3 \text{ J mol}^{-1}$$

Hence the ΔG of this reaction is $\boxed{6.65\text{ kJ}}$. A positive ΔG means that the forward reaction is non-spontaneous, but that the reverse reaction is; the reaction tends to proceed from $\boxed{\text{right to left}}$.

9.109 The reaction is

$$CO_2(g) + H_2(g) \rightleftharpoons CO(g) + H_2O(g) \qquad K_{3500} = 8.28$$

Use the fundamental relationship between K and $\Delta G°$

$$\Delta G°_{3500} = -RT \ln K = -(8.3145 \text{ J K}^{-1}\text{mol}^{-1})(3500 \text{ K}) \ln 8.28 = -61.5 \times 10^3 \text{ J mol}^{-1}$$

This means that $\Delta G°_{3000}$ for 1 mol of reaction is $\boxed{-61.5\text{ kJ}}$.

The standard Gibbs energy is an exact measure of the driving force of a reaction only in the very special case that all reactants and products are present in standard states. When this is not the case, it is necessary to compute ΔG (without the naught), which is the non-standard (actual) Gibbs energy

$$\Delta G_{3500} = \Delta G°_{3500} + RT \ln Q = \Delta G°_{3500} + RT \ln\left(\frac{P_{CO}P_{H_2O}}{P_{CO_2}P_{H_2}}\right)$$

$$= -6.15 \times 10^4 \text{ J mol}^{-1} + (8.3145 \text{ J K}^{-1}\text{mol}^{-1})(3500 \text{ K}) \ln\left(\frac{(2)(2)}{(0.1)(0.1)}\right)$$

$$= -61.5 \times 10^3 \text{ J mol}^{-1} + 174.4 \times 10^3 \text{ J mol}^{-1} = 112.8 \times 10^3 \text{ J mol}^{-1}$$

The answer is accordingly $\boxed{112.8\text{ kJ}}$ for the amounts of substances specified in the statement of the problem. The reaction runs spontaneously from $\boxed{\text{left to right}}$, which is the reverse of the spontaneous direction when the reactants and products are in standard states at 3500 K.

9.111 a)

$$AgCl{\cdot}NH_3(s) \rightleftharpoons AgCl(s) + NH_3(g) \qquad \boxed{K = P_{NH_3}}$$

b) Addition of $AgCl(s)$ has $\boxed{\text{no effect}}$ on the equilibrium partial pressure of NH_3. The addition of a pure solid does not change its activity in an equilibrium system.

c) Pumping in NH_3 has $\boxed{\text{no effect}}$ on the equilibrium partial pressure of NH_3 as long as some $AgCl(s)$ remains. The added NH_3 simply reacts with $AgCl(s)$ until P_{NH_3} again equals K.

d) Lowering the temperature of an endothermic reaction decreases its equilibrium constant. The P_{NH_3} therefore $\boxed{\text{decreases}}$ because it stays equal to K.

Chapter 10

Acid-Base Equilibria

10.1 a) The chloride ion Cl^- cannot act as a Brønsted-Lowry acid because it has no hydrogen.

b) The hydrogen sulfate ion HSO_4^- can act as a Brønsted-Lowry acid; its conjugate base is $\boxed{SO_4^{2-}}$ (the sulfate ion).

c) The ammonium ion NH_4^+ can act as a Brønsted-Lowry acid; its conjugate base is $\boxed{NH_3}$ (ammonia).

d) Ammonia NH_3 can act as a Brønsted-Lowry acid; its conjugate base is $\boxed{NH_2^-}$ (the amide ion).

e) Water H_2O can act as a Brønsted-Lowry acid; its conjugate base is $\boxed{OH^-}$ (the hydroxide ion).

10.3 Citric acid donates hydrogen ion to the hydrogen carbonate ion, $\boxed{HCO_3^-(aq)}$, which serves as a base:

$$H_3C_5H_5O_7(aq) + HCO_3^-(aq) \rightleftharpoons H_2C_5O_7^-(aq) + H_2CO_3(aq)$$

The H_2CO_3 that is produced quickly decomposes to water and gaseous carbon dioxide, which causes the cookies to rise. A preliminary step is the dissolution of the solid sodium hydrogen carbonate in the lemon juice.

10.5 a) The slaking of lime: $\boxed{CaO(s) + H_2O(l) \rightarrow Ca(OH)_2(s)}$.

b) The reaction can be seen as a Lewis acid-base reaction. The $\boxed{CaO}$ is the Lewis base. It donates a pair of electrons (located on the oxide ion) to a hydrogen atom in the H_2O molecule. The result is a new O—H bond.

10.7 a) The fluoride ion (F^-) has a negative charge. In the Brønsted-Lowry system, an acid is a donor of a positive entity (the H^+ ion). By plus-minus symmetry then, an acid in this scheme is a $\boxed{\text{fluoride acceptor}}$.

b) In $ClF_3O_2 + BF_3 \rightarrow ClF_2O_2{\cdot}BF_4$, BF_3 accepts a F^- ion from ClF_3O_2, so BF_3 is the acid, and ClF_3O_2 is the base.
In $TiF_4 + 2\,KF \rightarrow K_2[TiF_6]$, TiF_4 accepts an F^- ion from KF, so TiF_4 is the acid, and KF is the base.

10.9 Oxides of metals are base anhydrides; oxides of nonmetals are acid anhydrides.

a) MgO is the base anhydride of magnesium hydroxide $Mg(OH)_2$.
b) Cl_2O is the acid anhydride of hypochlorous acid HOCl.
c) SO_3 is the acid anhydride of sulfuric acid H_2SO_4.
d) Cs_2O is the base anhydride of cesium hydroxide CsOH.

10.11 The equations illustrating the amphoteric behavior of $SnO(s)$ are:

$$\overset{\text{base}}{SnO}\ (s) + 2\,HCl(aq) \rightarrow Sn^{2+}(aq) + 2\,Cl^-(aq) + H_2O(l)$$

$$\overset{\text{acid}}{SnO}\ (s) + NaOH(aq) + H_2O(l) \rightarrow Sn(OH)_3^-(aq) + Na^+(aq)$$

10.13 The pH of an aqueous solution equals the negative logarithm of the hydronium-ion concentration: $pH = -\log[H_3O^+] = -\log(2.0 \times 10^{-4}) = \boxed{3.70}$.

10.15 The extremes of the pH range for urine each give a H_3O^+ concentration:

$$[H_3O^+]_{\text{high}} = 10^{-5.5} = \boxed{3 \times 10^{-6}\ \text{M}} \qquad [H_3O^+]_{\text{low}} = 10^{-6.5} = \boxed{3 \times 10^{-7}\ \text{M}}$$

The pOH comes from the pH using the relation $pOH = pK_w - pH$.

$$pOH = 14.0 - 5.5 = 8.5 \qquad pOH = 14.0 - 6.5 = 7.5$$

where the use of $pK_w = 14.0$ assumes a temperature of 25°C. Then:

$$[OH^-]_{\text{low}} = 10^{-8.5} = \boxed{3 \times 10^{-9}\ \text{M}} \qquad [OH^-]_{\text{high}} = 10^{-7.5} = \boxed{3 \times 10^{-8}\ \text{M}}$$

10.17 The pH of the seawater equals 8.00. Using the definition of pH:

$$[H_3O^+] = 10^{-8.00} = \boxed{1.0 \times 10^{-8}\ \text{M}}$$

Use 13.776 instead of 14.00 as pK_w when calculating pOH:

$$pOH = pK_w - pH = 13.776 - 8.00 = 5.78 \qquad [OH^-] = 10^{-5.78} = \boxed{1.7 \times 10^{-6}\ \text{M}}$$

10.19 The equation $\boxed{2\,K(s) + 2\,H_2O(l) \rightarrow 2\,KOH(aq) + H_2(g)}$ is the better representation of what really happens. The reaction starts fast and continues with great vigor. If the equation involving H_3O^+ applied, one would expect a slow process since H_3O^+ is only 10^{-7} M in pure water. Even if the reaction were vigorous at low concentrations of H_3O^+, the reaction generates $OH^-(aq)$, which lowers the concentration of H_3O^+. Loss of H_3O^+ would quickly cause progress to flag. The other equation represents a direct interaction between $K(s)$ and $H_2O(l)$. The concentration of H_2O remains relatively constant and high (about 56 M).

10.21 a) A base (Brønsted-Lowry) is a hydrogen-ion acceptor. In ephedrine and many other organic bases the site of attachment of the hydrogen ion is a nitrogen atom:

$$\boxed{C_{10}H_{15}ON(aq) + H_2O(l) \rightleftharpoons C_{10}H_{15}ONH^+(aq) + OH^-(aq)}$$

b) Use the equation $K_aK_b = K_w$, which relates the strength of an aqueous acid and its conjugate base. Substitution gives:

$$K_a = \frac{K_w}{K_b} = \frac{1.0 \times 10^{-14}}{1.4 \times 10^{-4}} = \boxed{7.1 \times 10^{-11}}$$

c) According to text Table 10.2,[1] the K_a for ammonium ion NH_4^+ equals 5.6×10^{-10}. The K_b for ammonia NH_3 is

$$K_b = \frac{K_w}{K_a} = \frac{1.0 \times 10^{-14}}{5.6 \times 10^{-10}} = 1.8 \times 10^{-5}$$

[1] Text page 328.

The larger the K_b the stronger the base. Because K_b for ephedrine (1.4×10^{-4}) exceeds K_b for ammonia (1.8×10^{-5}), ephedrine is $\boxed{\text{stronger}}$ as a base than ammonia.

10.23 The equation given in the problem can be obtained by combining two equations referenced in text Table 10.2:

$$H_2O(l) + HClO_2(aq) \rightleftharpoons H_3O^+(aq) + ClO_2^-(aq) \qquad K_a = 1.1 \times 10^{-2}$$
$$H_2O(l) + HNO_2(aq) \rightleftharpoons H_3O^+(aq) + NO_2^-(aq) \qquad K_a = 4.6 \times 10^{-4}$$

If the second is subtracted from the first, the equilibrium constant of the first is divided by the equilibrium constant of the second:

$$HClO_2(aq) + NO_2^-(aq) \rightleftharpoons HNO_2(aq) + ClO_2^-(aq) \qquad K = \frac{1.1 \times 10{-}2}{4.6 \times 10^{-4}} = \boxed{24}$$

In this case the constant exceeds 1, which means that equilibrium favors the products. The relatively small concentration of $HClO_2$ at equilibrium means that $\boxed{HClO_2}$ is a $\boxed{\text{stronger acid}}$ than HNO_2; the comparatively large concentration of HNO_2 at equilibrium means $\boxed{NO_2^-}$ is a $\boxed{\text{stronger base}}$ than ClO_2^-.

10.25 a) The color changes of indicators occur over ranges of 1 to 1.9 pH units.[2] Assume that the center of the range is roughly equal to the pK_a of the indicator. Then:

bromocresol green	$pK_a = 4.6$	$K_a = 2.51 \times 10^{-5}$
methyl orange	$pK_a = 3.8$	$K_a = 1.58 \times 10^{-4}$

The acid form of $\boxed{\text{methyl orange}}$ is the stronger acid because it has the larger K_a (smaller pK_a).

b) Text Figure 10.8 shows that both of these indicators are in their transition ranges. This means that the pH of the solution must simultaneously lie between pH 3.8 and pH 5.4 (bromocresol green) and 3.2 and 4.4 (methyl orange). Therefore, the pH of the solution lies in the range $\boxed{3.8\text{–}4.4}$.

10.27 Abbreviate $HC_9H_7O_4$ (aspirin) and its conjugate base as aspH and asp$^-$ respectively. Compute the concentration of aspH when 0.65 g of it dissolves in 50.0 mL of water:

$$n_{\text{aspH}} = 0.65 \text{ g aspH} \times \left(\frac{1 \text{ mol aspH}}{180.16 \text{ g aspH}}\right) = 0.00361 \text{ mol}$$

$$[\text{aspH}] = \frac{0.00361 \text{ mol}}{0.0500 \text{ L}} = 0.0722 \text{ mol L}^{-1} = 0.0722 \text{ M}$$

This result equals the "initial" concentration of aspH (*after* dissolution but *before* reaction with water). Next, consider the reaction between the aspirin and water

$$\text{aspH}(aq) + H_2O(l) \rightleftharpoons \text{asp}^-(aq) + H_3O^+(aq) \qquad \frac{[H_3O^+][\text{asp}^-]}{[\text{aspH}]} = K_a = 3.0 \times 10^{-4}$$

Call the concentration of H_3O^+ at equilibrium x:

	aspH(aq)	$+H_2O(aq) \rightleftharpoons$	asp$^-$(aq) +	$H_3O^+(aq)$
Init. Conc. (M)	0.0722	—	0	small
Change in Conc. (M)	$-x$	—	$+x$	$+x$
Equil. Conc. (M)	$0.0722 - x$	—	x	x

[2] See text Figure 10.9, text page 332.

Substitute the equilibrium concentrations into the mass-action expression:

$$\frac{[\text{asp}^-][\text{H}_3\text{O}^+]}{[\text{aspH}]} = K_a = \frac{x^2}{0.0722 - x} = 3.0 \times 10^{-4}$$

Solve for x using the quadratic formula or by successive approximation. The answer is $x = 4.5 \times 10^{-3}$. A hydrogen-ion concentration of 4.5×10^{-3} M translates to a pH of $\boxed{2.35}$.

Tip. Neglecting x compared to 0.0722 gives a hydrogen-ion concentration that is over 3% too high and an answer of 2.33, which is close, but incorrect.

10.29 a) Benzoic acid is C_6H_5COOH.[3] Represent it as HOBz. As the 0.20 M HOBz reacts with water, it generates H_3O^+:

	$\text{HOBz}(aq)$	$+\text{H}_2\text{O}(l) \rightleftharpoons$	$\text{OBz}^-(aq)$ +	$\text{H}_3\text{O}^+(aq)$
Init. Conc. (M)	0.20	–	0	small
Change in Conc. (M)	$-x$	–	$+x$	$+x$
Equil. Conc. (M)	$0.20 - x$	–	x	x

The concentration of H_3O^+ arising from the autoionization of water is very small compared to the concentration from the reaction of benzoic acid, so x equals the concentration of H_3O^+ at equilibrium. Insert x in the mass-action expression:

$$K_a = 6.46 \times 10^{-5} = \frac{[\text{OBz}^-][\text{H}_3\text{O}^+]}{[\text{HOBz}]} = \frac{x^2}{0.20 - x}$$

Rearrange to obtain: $x^2 + 6.46 \times 10^{-5}x - 1.29 \times 10^{-5} = 0$. Apply the quadratic formula:

$$x = \frac{-6.46 \times 10^{-5} \pm \sqrt{4.17 \times 10^{-9} + 5.16 \times 10^{-5}}}{2}$$

$$x = \frac{-6.46 \times 10^{-5} \pm 7.18 \times 10^{-3}}{2} = -0.00352 \text{ and } 0.00356$$

The negative root has no physical meaning. Using the positive root gives $[H_3O^+] = 0.00356$ M. The pH is $-\log[H_3O^+] = \boxed{2.45}$.

Tip. If x is neglected in comparison to 0.020 in the mass-action equation, then the very simple equation $x = \sqrt{(0.20)(6.46 \times 10^{-5})}$ results. The positive root of this equation is $x = 0.0036$. This equals, to two significant figures, the answer obtained using the quadratic equation. To get a feel for how approximation works, carry out a few computations both exactly and approximately, and compare the results.

b) The equilibrium concentration of $[H_3O^+]$ must equal 3.56×10^{-3} M. Start as in the preceding part, but now x is known and $[\text{HOAc}]_0$, the initial concentration of acetic acid is the goal:

$$K_a = \frac{x^2}{[\text{HOAc}]_0 - x} \quad \text{hence} \quad 1.76 \times 10^{-5} = \frac{(3.54 \times 10^{-3})^2}{[\text{HOAc}]_0 - 3.56 \times 10^{-3}}$$

Solving gives $[\text{HOAc}]_0 = 0.72$ M. This means $\boxed{0.72 \text{ mol}}$ of acetic acid must be dissolved per liter of solution.

10.31 Use the approach of **10.29a**:

	$\text{HIO}_3(aq)$	$+ \text{H}_2\text{O}(aq) \rightleftharpoons$	$\text{IO}_3^-(aq)$ +	$\text{H}_3\text{O}^+(aq)$
Init. Conc. (M)	0.100	–	0	small
Change in Conc. (M)	$-x$	–	$+x$	$+x$
Equil. Conc. (M)	$0.100 - x$	–	x	x

[3] Again, the single H segregated in the formula is an acidic hydrogen.

$$\frac{[IO_3^-][H_3O^+]}{[HIO_3]} = K_a \quad \text{hence} \quad \frac{x^2}{0.100 - x} = 0.16$$

This rearranges to: $x^2 + 0.16x - 0.016 = 0$. The quadratic formula gives:

$$x = \frac{-0.16 \pm \sqrt{0.0256 - 4(-0.016)}}{2} = 0.0697 \text{ and } -0.230$$

If $[H_3O^+] = 0.0697$ M, then pH = $\boxed{1.16}$. The pH is well on the acid side because HIO_3 is a rather strong weak acid.

Tip. The short-cut of neglecting x in comparison to 0.100 gives an H_3O^+ concentration of 0.126 M and a pH of 0.90, which is seriously wrong.

10.33 The $papH^+Cl^-$, a salt, dissolves completely in water to give $papH^+$ ion and Cl^- ion. The Cl^- ion does not react significantly with the water, but the $papH^+$ ion reacts as a weak acid:

$$papH^+(aq) + H_2O(l) \rightleftharpoons pap(aq) + H_3O^+(aq)$$

Assume that this reaction is the sole source of H_3O^+. The concentration of H_3O^+ is 4.90×10^{-4} M (calculated from the pH of 3.31), and the concentration of the conjugate base pap is also 4.90×10^{-4} M. The concentration of $papH^+$ equals its original concentration minus the portion converted into pap. This is $(0.205 - 4.90 \times 10^{-4})$ M. Substitute these equilibrium values into the K_a expression to compute K_a:

$$K_a = \frac{(4.90 \times 10^{-4})(4.90 \times 10^{-4})}{(0.205 - 4.90 \times 10^{-4})} = \boxed{1.2 \times 10^{-6}}$$

Tip. "Forgetting" to subtract in the denominator has a negligible effect.

10.35 The K_b applies to the reaction:

$$morph(aq) + H_2O(l) \rightleftharpoons morphH^+(aq) + OH^-(aq)$$

where "morph" stands for morphine. The initial concentration of morphine (*after* dissolution but *before* reaction with water) is

$$[morph]_0 = \frac{0.0400 \text{ mol}}{0.600 \text{ L}} = 0.0667 \text{ mol L}^{-1} = 0.0667 \text{ M}$$

Let x equal the loss in the concentration of morph in coming to equilibrium:

	morph(aq)	$+H_2O(aq) \rightleftharpoons$	morphH^+(aq) +	OH^-(aq)
Init. Conc. (M)	0.0667	–	0	small
Change in Conc. (M)	$-x$	–	$+x$	$+x$
Equil. Conc. (M)	$0.0667 - x$	–	x	x

Substitute the equilibrium concentrations into the mass-action expression:

$$\frac{[morphH^+][OH^-]}{[morph]} = K_b = \frac{x^2}{0.0667 - x} = 8 \times 10^{-7}$$

This equation can be solved using the quadratic formula. But, observe that x must be quite small compared to 0.0667. Neglecting the x in the denominator allows the quick conclusion that $x = 2.301 \times 10^{-4}$. This makes the equilibrium concentration of OH^- equal 2.3×10^{-4} M. The pOH is $-\log[OH^-] = 3.64$, and the pH is this number subtracted from 14.0, which is $\boxed{10.4}$. Use of one significant figure (the 4) in the final answer reflects the fact that K_b has only one significant figure.

10.37 Hydrofluoric acid is a weak acid in water:

$$HF(aq) + H_2O(l) \rightleftharpoons F^-(aq) + H_3O^+(aq) \qquad K_a = 6.6 \times 10^{-4}$$

Because the pH of the HF solution at 25°C is 2.13:

$$[H_3O^+] = \text{antilog}(-2.13) = 10^{-2.13} = 7.41 \times 10^{-3}\ \text{M}$$

Since the dissociation of hydrofluoric acid is the only important source of H_3O^+ in the solution, $[F^-]$ is also 7.41×10^{-3} M. The existence of the equilibrium guarantees that:

$$\frac{[H_3O^+][F^-]}{[HF]} = K_a = 6.6 \times 10^{-4}$$

All of the concentrations expect [HF] are known. Solve for [HF]:

$$[HF] = \frac{[H_3O^+][F^-]}{K_a} = \frac{(7.41 \times 10^{-3})^2}{6.6 \times 10^{-4}} = \boxed{0.083\ \text{M}}$$

10.39 Aqueous NaOH contains Na^+ ions and OH^- ions. The latter react with acetic acid to produce water and acetate ions. Acetate ion is a weak base in its own right. Its reaction (as a base) with water causes the solution of sodium acetate that results from treating acetic acid with an equal chemical amount of NaOH (a procedure called neutralization) to be basic, and have $\boxed{\text{pH greater than 7}}$.

Tip. One might think that "neutralization" gives solutions that are neutral. Not so. Chemical neutralization of an acid by a base does *not* in most cases give a neutral (pH 7) solution. When a weak acid is reacted with a strong base, the pH at the equivalence point exceeds 7. When a weak base is reacted with a strong acid, the pH at the equivalence point is less than 7. Exact neutralization of a strong acid by a strong base does give a solution of pH 7.

10.41 The ammonium bromide dissolves to give $NH_4^+(aq)$, a weak acid, and $Br^-(aq)$, which is not active as a base. The $NH_4^+(aq)$ ion reacts weakly with water to generate $H_3O^+(aq)$. The NH_4Br solution is therefore somewhat acidic. The hydrogen chloride reacts completely with water to give $Cl^-(aq)$ and $H_3O^+(aq)$, thereby creating a strongly acidic solution. The sodium hydroxide, a strong base, dissolves to $Na^+(aq)$ and $OH^-(aq)$; the latter makes the solution highly basic. The $NaCH_3COO$ gives $Na^+(aq)$ and $CH_3COO^-(aq)$, which reacts weakly as a base. The KI dissolves to $K^+(aq)$ and $I^-(aq)$, neither of which reacts as either acid or base. The order of increasing pH is therefore:

$$\boxed{HCl < NH_4Br < KI < NaCH_3COO < NaOH}$$

10.43 Compute the pK_a of the conjugate acid of "tris" from the pK_b of tris itself:

$$pK_a = 14.00 - pK_b = 14.00 - 5.92 = 8.08$$

The addition of HCl converts some tris to its conjugate acid:

$$\text{tris}(aq) + HCl(aq) \rightleftharpoons \text{trisH}^+(aq) + Cl^-(aq)$$

The resulting solution is a mixture of a weak acid (trisH^+) and its conjugate base (tris). It is a buffer by virtue of the reaction:

$$\text{trisH}^+(aq) + H_2O(l) \rightleftharpoons \text{tris}(aq) + H_3O^+(aq) \qquad K_a = \frac{[\text{tris}][H_3O^+]}{[\text{trisH}^+]}$$

Compute the concentrations of the tris and $trisH^+$ after complete reaction with the HCl but before the preceding equilibrium is established:

$$[\text{tris}]_0 = \frac{(0.050 - 0.025\text{ mol})}{2.00\text{ L}} = 0.0125\text{ M} \quad \text{and}quad[\text{trisH}^+]_0 = \frac{0.025\text{ mol}}{2.00\text{ L}} = 0.0125\text{ M}$$

The equilibrium now reduces the concentration of the $trisH^+$ as it forms H_3O^+ and tris in equal amounts. If x is the equilibrium concentration of $H_3O^+(aq)$ ion, then:

	$\text{trisH}^+(aq)$	$+H_2O(aq) \rightleftharpoons$	$\text{tris}(aq)$ +	$H_3O^+(aq)$
Init. Conc. (M)	0.0125	–	0.0125	small
Change in Conc. (M)	$-x$	–	$+x$	$+x$
Equil. Conc. (M)	$0.0125 - x$	–	$0.0125 + x$	x

$$K_a = \frac{[\text{tris}][H_3O^+]}{[\text{trisH}^+]} = \frac{(0.0125 + x)x}{(0.0125 - x)}$$

Assume that x is small compared to 0.0125. Then the 0.0125's cancel out and:

$$[H_3O^+] = K_a \quad \text{so that pH} = \text{p}K_a = \boxed{8.08}$$

Clearly x is less than 10^{-7}, so the assumption was justified.

Tip. The pH equals the pK_a of the weak acid. This is a general result in buffer solutions in which the acid and conjugate base concentrations are equal (and not extremely low).

10.45 a) The problem is exactly like Example 10-7.[4] After mixing and dissolution but before any other chemical change, the solution is 0.10 M in acetic acid and 0.040 M in acetate ion (from the sodium acetate). Then the weak-acid equilibrium comes into play. Let x equal the equilibrium concentration of H_3O^+:

	$\text{HOAc}(aq)$	$+H_2O(aq) \rightleftharpoons$	$\text{OAc}^-(aq)$ +	$H_3O^+(aq)$
Init. Conc.(M)	0.10	–	0.040	small
Change in Conc.(M)	$-x$	–	$+x$	$+x$
Equil. Conc.(M)	$0.10 - x$	–	$0.040 + x$	x

$$K_a = 1.76 \times 10^{-5} = \frac{[\text{OAc}^-][H_3O^+]}{[\text{HOAc}]} = \frac{(0.040 + x)x}{(0.10 - x)}$$

Assume that x is small compared to 0.10. If so, the x's that are added and subtracted can be neglected in the above expression to give:

$$x = 1.76 \times 10^{-5}\left(\frac{0.10}{0.040}\right) = 4.4 \times 10^{-5}$$

The result clearly justifies the assumption. The pH is $-\log(4.4 \times 10^{-5})$ or $\boxed{4.36}$.

b) The addition of 0.010 mol of $OH^-(aq)$ ion (in the form of NaOH) very quickly converts 0.010 mol of acetic acid (HOAc) to 0.010 mol of acetate ion (OAc^-). The concentrations of HOAc and OAc^- right after the conversion but before the reaction of HOAc as a weak acid are:

$$[\text{HOAc}] = \frac{0.050 - 0.010\text{ mol}}{0.500\text{ L}} = 0.080\text{ M} \quad \text{and} \quad [\text{OAc}^-] = \frac{0.020 - 0.010\text{ mol}}{0.500\text{ L}} = 0.060\text{ M}$$

Now consider the K_a equilibrium. Let y equal the equilibrium concentration of H_3O^+:

	$\text{HOAc}(aq)$	$+H_2O(aq) \rightleftharpoons$	$\text{OAc}^-(aq)$ +	$H_3O^+(aq)$
Init. Conc. (M)	0.080	–	0.060	small
Change in Conc. (M)	$-y$	–	$+y$	$+y$
Equil. Conc. (M)	$0.080 - y$	–	$0.060 + y$	y

[4] Text page 339.

$$K_a = \frac{[OAc^-][H_3O^+]}{[HOAc]} = 1.76 \times 10^{-5} = \frac{(0.060 + y)y}{(0.080 - y)}$$

Assume that y is small compared to 0.060 and 0.080. Then:

$$y = 1.76 \times 10^{-5} \left(\frac{0.080}{0.060}\right) = 2.34 \times 10^{-5}$$

The assumption is clearly justified. The pH is the negative logarithm of 2.34×10^{-5} or $\boxed{4.63}$.

Tip. The pH rises from 4.36 to only 4.63 despite addition of a very substantial (20% of the amount of weak acid present) portion of strong base. Resistance to changes in pH characterizes buffered solutions.

10.47 Buffer solutions are most efficient at resisting changes in pH at their **buffer points.** At the buffer point, the concentrations of the conjugate pair are equal, and the pH of the buffer equals the pK_a of the weak acid. The physician should therefore select a weak acid having a pK_a as close as possible to the desired pH. The best choice on the list is $\boxed{m\text{-chlorobenzoic acid}}$, $pK_a = 3.98$.

10.49 The answer is certainly less than 1000 mL, because adding that much NaOH solution to 500 mL of 0.100 M aqueous formic acid would neutralize all of the acid by the reaction

$$HCOOH(aq) + NaOH(aq) \rightarrow Na^+(aq) + HCOO^-(aq) + H_2O(l)$$

and create a dilute solution of sodium formate. Such solutions are known to have pH's exceeding 7 (see **10.39**). Before any NaOH is added, the solution contains mostly un-ionized formic acid, $HCOOH(aq)$ and also a small amount of the formate ion, $HCOO^-(aq)$. Adding the NaOH solution converts $HCOOH(aq)$ to $HCOO^-(aq)$ according to the preceding chemical equation. The addition raises the pH and also dilutes the whole system. It does *not* alter the total amount of formate-containing species, which keeps its original value:

$$n_{HCOOH} + n_{HCOO^-} = \left(\frac{0.100 \text{ mmol}}{\text{mL}}\right)(500 \text{ mL}) = 50.0 \text{ mmol}$$

The concentrations of formic acid and formate ion are related by the acid ionization equilibrium

$$HCOOH(aq) + H_2O(l) \rightleftharpoons HCOO^-(aq) + H_3O^+(aq) \qquad \frac{[H_3O^+][HCOO^-]}{[HCOOH]} = K = 1.77 \times 10^{-4}$$

At pH = 4.00, $[H_3O^+] = 1.0 \times 10^{-4}$ M. Inserting this value into the K_a expression gives:

$$1.77 \times 10^{-4} = \frac{(1.0 \times 10^{-4})[HCOO^-]}{[HCOOH]} \quad \text{which gives} \quad 1.77 = \frac{[HCOO^-]}{[HCOOH]}$$

Let the volume of 0.0500 M NaOH that is needed to raise the pH to 4.00 equal V mL. The final volume of the mixture at pH 4.00 then equals $(500 + V)$ mL. Each millimole of NaOH that is added converts one millimole of $HCOOH(aq)$ to $HCOO^-(aq)$. Assume that this acid-base reaction is the only source of $HCOO^-(aq)$. After $0.0500V$ mmol of NaOH has been added we have:

$$[HCOO^-] = \frac{0.0500V \text{ mmol}}{(500 + V) \text{ mL}}$$

in which the numerator is the chemical amount of $HCOO^-(aq)$ produced by the reaction and the denominator is the final volume of the solution. We also have

$$[HCOO^-] + [HCOOH] = \frac{50.0 \text{ mmol}}{(500 + V) \text{ mL}}$$

Solve for [HCOOH] and insert the expression for [$HCOO^-$]

$$[\text{HCOOH}] = \frac{50.0}{500+V} - [\text{HCOO}^-]$$
$$= \frac{50.0}{500+V} - \frac{0.0500V}{500+V} = \frac{50.0-0.0500V}{500+V}\ \text{M}$$

Substitute the expressions for [HCOOH] and [$HCOO^-$] into the equation for their ratio:

$$1.77 = \frac{[\text{HCOO}^-]}{[\text{HCOOH}]}$$
$$= \frac{0.0500V/(500+V)}{50.0-0.0500V/(500+V)}$$
$$= \frac{0.0500V}{50.0-0.0500V}$$
$$= 0.0500\left(\frac{V}{1000-V}\right)$$

It is easy to solve for V, which equals $\boxed{639\ \text{mL}}$. The final volume of the solution is 1139 mL and the concentrations of HCOOH(aq) and $HCOO^-$(aq) are 0.0158 and 0.0280 M respectively. Both are large in comparison to the final H_3O^+ concentration, 1.0×10^{-4} M. This means that the ionization equilibrium affects this two concentrations only negligibly.

10.51 The substance $Ba(OH)_2$ is a strong base. It ionizes completely in solution to give one mole of Ba^{2+} ion and two moles of OH^- ion per mole dissolved. Before any acid is added, $[\text{OH}^-] = 2\times 0.3750 = 0.7500$ M. The pOH, which equals the negative logarithm of this number, is 0.1249; pH= 14.000− pOH $= 14.00 - 0.1249 = \boxed{13.88}$.

The chemical amount of OH^- ion in the original 100.0 mL of $Ba(OH)_2$ equals its molarity multiplied by its volume (in liters). It is 0.07500 mol. This means that to reach the equivalence point requires 0.07500 mol of $HClO_4$. The volume of 0.4540 M $HClO_4$ that provides this much $HClO_4$ is

$$V = \frac{1\ \text{L}}{0.4540\ \text{mol HClO}_4} \times 0.0750\ \text{mol HClO}_4 = 0.1652\ \text{L} = 165.2\ \text{mL}$$

When the titration is 1.00 mL short of the equivalence point, only 164.2 mL of 0.4540 M $HClO_4$ has been added for a total of 0.07455 mol of $HClO_4$. Some OH^- ion remains unreacted. Its amount equals the difference between the amount of OH^- originally present and the amount reacted. The concentration of OH^- equals this same amount divided by the volume of the solution:

$$[\text{OH}^-] = \frac{(0.07500-0.07455)\ \text{mol}}{(0.1000+0.1642)\ \text{L}} = 0.0017\ \text{M}$$

Note the (correct) use of two significant figures in the answer. The pOH is 2.77, and the pH is therefore $\boxed{11.24}$.

The pH reaches $\boxed{7.00}$ at the equivalence point; this is a titration of a strong base with a strong acid.

When the titration is 1.00 mL past the equivalence point, all of the OH^- from $Ba(OH)_2$ has been reacted away, and excess $HClO_4$ is present. The amount of excess is

$$\left(\frac{0.4540\ \text{mol}}{1\ \text{L}} \times 0.1662\ \text{L}\right) - 0.07500\ \text{mol} = 4.5 \times 10^{-4}\ \text{mol HClO}_4$$

The excess $HClO_4$, a strong acid, is completely ionized to produce 4.5×10^{-4} mol of H_3O^+ (and, of course, an equal amount of ClO_4^- ion). The concentration of this H_3O^+ is

$$[H_3O^+] = \frac{4.5 \times 10^{-4} \text{ mol}}{(0.1000 + 0.1662) \text{ L}} = 0.0017 \text{ M}$$

Hence, $pH = -\log(0.0017) = \boxed{2.77}$. Throughout this analysis, the autoionization of water is ignored. Even very small amounts of strong acid or base completely overshadow water as a source of H_3O^+ or OH^- ion.

Tip. The pH plummets dramatically (from 11.24 to 2.77) upon addition of only 2 mL of acid in the range of the equivalence point.

10.53 Hydrazoic acid, a weak acid, reacts with water:

$$HN_3(aq) + H_2O(l) \rightleftharpoons N_3^-(aq) + H_3O^+(aq) \qquad \frac{[N_3^-][H_3O^+]}{[HN_3]} = K_a$$

• *Before Addition of Base.* The initial concentration of the HN_3 is 0.1000 M. Let x equal the concentration of H_3O^+ present at equilibrium in the solution. Then:

$$\frac{[N_3^-][H_3O^+]}{[HN_3]} = K_a = 1.9 \times 10^{-5} = \frac{x^2}{0.1000 - x}$$

where it has been assumed that hydrazoic acid is the only significant source of H_3O^+. Rearranging gives the quadratic equation:

$$x^2 + (1.9 \times 10^{-5})x - 1.9 \times 10^{-6} = 0$$

The positive root of this equation is 1.37×10^{-3}. Therefore:

$$[H_3O^+] = 1.37 \times 10^{-3} \text{ M} \quad \text{and} \quad pH = \boxed{2.86}$$

• *After Addition of 25.00 mL of Base.* Sodium hydroxide is a strong base. Each added mole of NaOH converts one mole of $HN_3(aq)$ to one mole of $N_3^-(aq)$. The 25.00 mL of 0.1000 M NaOH furnishes:

$$\frac{0.100 \text{ mol OH}^-}{1 \text{ L}} \times 0.250 \text{ L} = 2.500 \times 10^{-3} \text{ mol OH}^-$$

Assume that the added OH^- reacts completely with the HN_3. The reaction produces 2.500×10^{-3} mol of N_3^- and leaves 2.500×10^{-3} mol of HN_3. Exactly half of the hydrazoic acid is reacted—this is the **half-equivalence point** of the titration. The total volume of the solution is 0.0750 L, so the "original" concentrations of the weak acid and its conjugate base are both 0.0333 M. "Original" is in quotation marks because these concentrations are for the state after the mixing of the solutions but before the acid-base equilibrium gets established. As it becomes established, the equilibrium generates H_3O^+ and changes both concentrations slightly. The changes are so slight that the approximate equation:

$$pH \approx pK_a - \log \frac{[HN_3]_0}{[N_3^-]_0}$$

holds at this point in the titration.[5] Also, the calculation of the pH at this stage of a titration is just like the calculation shown in Example 10.10.[6] Substitution gives:

$$pH = 4.72 - \log \frac{0.0333}{0.0333} = \boxed{4.72}$$

[5] The equation is derived on text page 342.
[6] Text page 342.

The pH equals the pK_a of the weak acid being titrated. This is generally true at half-equivalence in the titration of a weak acid. A titration at half-equivalence is also a buffer at its buffer point. See **10.45.**

• *At the Equivalence Point.* The addition of 50.00 mL of the NaOH solution brings the titration to its equivalence point—the number of moles of OH^- added equals the number of moles of HN_3 originally present. If no hydrazoic acid at all is left, then the concentration of N_3^- ion equals

$$[N_3^-] = \frac{0.00500 \text{ mol}}{0.100 \text{ L}} = 0.0500 \text{ M}$$

In fact, N_3^- ion reacts with water because N_3^- is a weak base:

	$N_3^-(aq)$	$+ H_2O(aq) \rightleftharpoons$	$HN_3(aq) +$	$OH^-(aq)$
Init. Conc. (M)	0.0500	–	0	small
Change in Conc. (M)	$-x$	–	$+x$	$+x$
Equil. Conc. (M)	$0.0500 - x$	–	x	x

The K_b for this reaction is 5.26×10^{-10}, obtained by dividing K_w by the K_a of hydrazoic acid. Use the mass-action expression for the preceding to obtain:

$$\frac{[OH^-][HN_3]}{[N_3^-]} = K_b = 5.26 \times 10^{-10} = \frac{x^2}{0.0500 - x}$$

Solving for x gives $[OH^-] = 5.13 \times 10^{-6}$ M. This corresponds to a pOH of 5.29 and therefore a pH of $\boxed{8.71}$.

• *Beyond the Equivalence Point.* A total of 51.00 mL of NaOH(aq) has been added. All of the HN_3 has been reacted, and some OH^- remains in excess. The concentration of leftover OH^- equals the amount of OH^- added minus the amount reacted divided by the total volume of the solution:

$$[OH^-] = \frac{(0.05100 \text{ L} \times 0.100 \text{ M}) - 5.000 \times 10^{-3} \text{ mol}}{(0.05000 + 0.05100) \text{ L}} = 9.910 \times 10^{-4} \text{ M}$$

With this much "other" OH^- in solution, the reaction of N_3^- to HN_3 plus OH^- adds just a pittance to the concentration of OH^-. Hence:

$$\text{pOH} = -\log(9.901 \times 10^{-4}) = 3.00 \quad \text{hence pH} = \boxed{11.00}$$

10.55 The titration of the weak base ethylamine with the strong acid HCl falls into four ranges: *before* the addition of acid; *between* the first addition of acid and the equivalence point; *at* the equivalence point; *beyond* the equivalence point. The pH of the original 40.00 mL of 0.1000 M ethylamine exceeds 7 because ethylamine is a base. As 0.1000 M HCl is added, the pH falls. Abbreviate ethylamine and its conjugate acid as $EtNH_2$ and $EtNH_3^+$ respectively.

• *Before Addition of Acid.* Ethylamine raises the pH of pure water by the reaction:

$$EtNH_2(aq) + H_2O(l) \rightleftharpoons EtNH_3^+(aq) + OH^-(aq) \qquad \frac{[EtNH_3^+][OH^-]}{[EtNH_2]} = 6.41 \times 10^{-4}$$

Let $[OH^-] = y$, and assume that the concentration of hydroxide ion from the autoionization of water is small. Because no HCl has been added:

$$[OH^-] = [EtNH_3^+] = y \quad \text{and} \quad [EtNH_2] = 0.100 - y$$

$$6.41 \times 10^{-4} = \frac{y^2}{0.1000 - y}$$

This last has the same form as the equation developed in the text for the titration of acetic acid with NaOH. The difference is that y is now $[OH^-]$. Solving gives $y = [OH^-] = 0.00769$ M. The pOH is 2.11, and the pH is $14.00 - 2.114 = \boxed{11.89}$.

Tip. Formulas very similar to the ones developed in the text for the titration of a weak acid with a strong base work to compute the pH along this titration curve. The only difference is that the natural choice for an unknown is $[OH^-]$ rather than $[H_3O^+]$.

- *After First Addition of Acid, Before Equivalence Point.* In this range of the titration:

$$[EtNH_3{}^+] = \frac{c_t V}{V_0 + V} + y$$

where c_t is the concentration of the titrant, V_0 is the original volume of ethylamine solution, V is the volume of titrant added and y is the concentration of OH^-. The numerator c_tV equals the chemical amount of $EtNH_3^+$ generated by the 1-to-1 reaction between the titrant and the $EtNH_2(aq)$, the denominator $(V_0 + V)$ equals the total volume of the solution, and their quotient $c_tV/(V_0 + V)$ equals the concentration of $EtNH_3^+(aq)$ from the neutralization reaction alone. The reaction of $EtNH_2$ to produce $OH^-(aq)$ gives additional $EtNH_3^+(aq)$ and is responsible for the y on the right-hand side of the above equation. Similarly:

$$[EtNH_2] = \frac{c_0 V_0 - c_t V}{V_0 + V} - y$$

where c_0 stands for the original ethylamine concentration. In this titration, c_0 equals 0.1000 M, c_t equals 0.1000 M, and V_0 equals 0.0400 L. If 5.00 mL of HCl has been added, $V = 0.00500$ L. Substitution in the two preceding equations gives:

$$[EtNH_3^+] = 0.01111 + y \qquad \text{and} \qquad [EtNH_2] = 0.07777 - y$$

Put the concentrations into the K_b expression:

$$6.41 \times 10^{-4} = \frac{y(0.01111 + y)}{(0.07777 - y)}$$

In this equation, y is not negligible compared to 0.01111 or 0.07777. Omitting it from the two terms on the right-hand side gives a trial y of 0.00487, which is 43% of 0.01111! Solve the equation by rearranging it and using the quadratic formula. The answer is $[OH^-] = 0.00331$ M; $\boxed{\text{pH} = 11.52}$.

At 20.00 mL, the same formulas give $[OH^-] = 6.18 \times 10^{-4}$ M, and a pH of $\boxed{10.79}$; at 39.90 mL, the same formulas give pH $\boxed{8.20}$.

- *At the Equivalence Point.* At equivalence, the reaction mixture consists of 80.00 mL of 0.05000 M ethylammonium chloride, $EtNH_3^+Cl^-$. The cation of this salt reacts as a weak acid:

$$EtNH_3^+(aq) + H_2O(l) \rightleftharpoons EtNH_2(aq) + H_3O^+(aq)$$

The equilibrium constant for this reaction is $K_a = K_w/K_b$. Let $x = [H_3O^+]$. Then:

$$K_a = 1.56 \times 10^{-11} = \frac{x^2}{(0.05000 - x)}$$

Solving gives $x = 8.83 \times 10^{-7}$ so the pH $= -\log(8.83 \times 10^{-7}) = \boxed{6.05}$

Tip. Using the formulas that work in the range before the equivalence point gives a deceptive result at this point:

$$[EtNH_2] = 0 - [OH^-] \quad (?!)$$

This cannot be right since $[OH^-]$ and $[EtNH_2]$ must both be positive.

• *Beyond the Equivalence Point.* In this range, the solution behaves like a simple solution of HCl. Compared to the strong acid HCl, the weakly acidic ethylammonium ion contributes zero to the $H_3O^+(aq)$ concentration. When 40.10 mL of HCl has been added, the first 40.00 mL has gone to produce $EtNH_3^+(aq)$ ion by reacting with all the $EtNH_2(aq)$. The remaining 0.10 mL is free to act as a strong acid. The 0.10 mL of 0.1000 M HCl is of course diluted to 80.10 mL. Every HCl generates one H_3O^+ in aqueous solution: Thus:

$$[H_3O^+] = \frac{0.10}{80.10} \times 0.1000 \text{ M} = 1.25 \times 10^{-4} \text{ M} \qquad \text{pH} = \boxed{3.90}$$

After 50.00 mL of titrant has been added: $[H_3O^+] = (10.00/90.00) \times 0.1000 = 1.111 \times 10^{-2}$ M; $\boxed{\text{pH} = 1.95}$.

10.57 Addition of 46.50 mL of the 0.393 M $NaOH(aq)$ solution must bring the mixture very near to an equivalence point because one more drop of base boosts the pH by more than one entire unit. (At and near the equivalence point in titrations, small additions of titrant cause large changes in pH.) Assume that 46.51 mL of the base brings the titration to the equivalence point. The chemical amount of NaOH added at this point is

$$n_{\text{NaOH}} = 0.04651 \text{ L} \times \left(\frac{0.393 \text{ mol OH}^-}{1 \text{ L}}\right) = 0.01828 \text{ mol}$$

This amount of strong base completes the neutralization of the HCl, but some HCl had previously been neutralized by benzoate ion ($C_6H_5COO^-$, or OBz^-). The benzoate ion, a base, was present in solution from the original sample. Thus:

$$n_{\text{HCl}} = n_{\text{NaOH}} + n_{\text{OBz}^-}$$

The chemical amount of HCl is

$$n_{\text{HCl}} = 0.0500 \text{ L} \times \left(\frac{0.500 \text{ mol HCl}}{1 \text{ L}}\right) = 0.0250 \text{ mol}$$

Substitution gives:

$$0.0250 = 0.01828 + n_{\text{OBz}^-} \qquad \text{hence} \qquad n_{\text{OBz}^-} = 6.7 \times 10^{-3} \text{ mol}$$

The mass of C_6H_5COONa in the sample is

$$m_{\text{NaOBz}} = 6.72 \times 10^{-3} \text{ mol OBz}^- \times \left(\frac{1 \text{ mol NaOBz}}{1 \text{ mol OBz}^-}\right) \times \left(\frac{144.11 \text{ g NaOBz}}{1 \text{ mol NaOBz}}\right) = \boxed{0.97 \text{ g NaOBz}}$$

10.59 Because diethylamine and hydrochloric acid react in a 1-to-1 molar ratio, the chemical amount of HCl to reach the equivalence point equals the chemical amount of diethylamine originally present. It is computed as the volume of the added HCl solution multiplied by the molarity of that solution:

$$n_{\text{HCl}} = (15.90 \text{ mL}) \times \left(\frac{0.0750 \text{ mmol HCl}}{1 \text{ mL}}\right) = 1.1925 \text{ mmol}$$

Thus there was originally 1.1925 mmol of diethylamine. Convert to grams:

$$1.1925 \times 10^{-3} \text{ mol} \times \left(\frac{73.14 \text{ g } (C_2H_5)_2NH}{1 \text{ mol } (C_2H_5)_2NH}\right) = \boxed{0.0872 \text{ g } (C_2H_5)_2NH}$$

Imagine that at the equivalence point, all of the diethylamine is converted to its conjugate acid, the diethylammonium ion $(C_2H_5)_2NH_2^+$. If so, the concentration of diethylammonium ion equals its chemical amount, 1.1925 mmol, divided by the volume of the solution (115.90 mL):

$$[(C_2H_5)_2NH_2^+] = \frac{1.1925 \text{ mmol}}{115.90 \text{ mL}} = 0.0103 \text{ M}$$

In actuality, this concentration is a bit high. Some of the diethylammonium ion reacts away as it donates H^+ ions to increase the H_3O^+ concentration in the solution:

$$(C_2H_5)_2NH_2^+(aq) + H_2O(l) \rightleftharpoons (C_2H_5)_2NH + H_3O^+(aq) \qquad \frac{[H_3O^+][(C_2H_5)_2NH]}{[(C_2H_5)_2NH^+]} = K_a = \frac{K_w}{K_b}$$

where the K_b is the basicity constant of diethylamine. Let x stand for the concentration of H_3O^+, and assume that all H_3O^+ in the solution comes from the reaction of diethylammonium ion as an acid. Then:

$$K_a = \frac{K_w}{K_b} = \frac{1.0 \times 10^{-14}}{3.09 \times 10^{-4}} = 3.236 \times 10^{-11} = \frac{x^2}{0.0103 - x}$$

Solving give $x = 5.77 \times 10^{-7}$. Then $[H_3O^+] = 5.77 \times 10^{-7}$ M for a pH of 6.24.

This concentration of H_3O^+ is only about six times larger than the concentration furnished by autoionization in pure water. How valid then is the assumption that diethylammonium ion furnishes *all* of the H_3O^+? One way to check is to employ the following expression,[7] which takes into account the autoionization of water as a source of H_3O^+ in solutions of weak acids:

$$[H_3O^+]^3 + K_a[H_3O^+]^2 - (K_w + c_a)[H_3O^+] - K_aK_w = 0$$

Inserting $K_w = 1.0 \times 10^{-14}$, $c_a = 0.0103$, and $K_a = 3.24 \times 10^{-11}$ gives the cubic equation:

$$[H_3O^+]^3 + (3.24 \times 10^{-11})[H_3O^+]^2 - (3.433 \times 10^{-13})[H_3O^+] - 3.24 \times 10^{-25} = 0$$

Solving this equation analytically is hard. A better way is to reason that the last term is certainly much smaller than any of the other three because $[H_3O^+]$ can only be larger than 5.77×10^{-7} M. After all, a second source of H_3O^+ ion can only raise the concentration of that ion, never lower it. Omitting the last term on this basis and dividing through by $[H_3O^+]$ gives:

$$[H_3O^+]^2 + (3.24 \times 10^{-11})[H_3O^+] - 3.433 \times 10^{-13} = 0$$

Solution of this quadratic equation is routine (by means of the quadratic formula). The applicable root gives $[H_3O^+] = 5.86 \times 10^{-7}$ M, for a pH of $\boxed{6.23}$. Including the contribution of autoionization lowers the pH only minimally despite the fact that diethylammonium ion is a very weak acid.

Tip. It is a mistake to try to account for the autoionization by adding 1.0×10^{-7} to the answer 5.77×10^{-7} M! Autoionization contributes less H_3O^+ in this solution than in pure water. The reason is that the autoionization equilibrium is shifted to the left by H_3O^+ ion from the diethylammonium ion (LeChâtelier's principle). Of course, this K_a equilibrium is also shifted (slightly) to the left by hydronium ion from the autoionization, which in turn causes an even slighter secondary effect back on the autoionization, which in turn.... The best understanding starts with two points: 1) only one kind of hydronium ion exists in the solution; 2) the equilibrium concentration of H_3O^+ ion comes as a compromise among all the simultaneous competing tendencies to donate or accept it.

A suitable indicator for the titration is $\boxed{\text{bromothymol blue}}$, which changes color in the pH range that includes pH 6.24.[8]

10.61 This buffer solution contains N-ethylmorpholine $C_6H_{13}NO$ (call it "M") $C_6H_{13}NOH^+$ (MH^+), its conjugate acid, which forms from the reaction of the N-ethylmorpholine with HCl. The two species are in chemical equilibrium:

$$M(aq) + H_2O(l) \rightleftharpoons MH^+(aq) + OH^-(aq) \qquad K_b = \frac{[OH^-][MH^+]}{[M]}$$

[7] From text page 352.

[8] See Figure 10.9, text page 330.

The mass-action expression can be used to compute K_b if equilibrium values of all of the concentrations can be determined. The concentration of OH^- is easy because the pH of the solution is given: $[OH^-] = 1.0\times10^{-7}$. There was 10.00 mmol of M in the solution before the addition of the HCl, and the added HCl amounts to 8.00 mmol. If the neutralization reaction goes to completion, it forms 8.00 mmol of MH^+ and leaves 2.00 mmol of M unreacted (in excess). The volume of the solution is deliberately brought to 100.0 mL by the addition of water. The equilibrium concentrations of M and MH^+ therefore are:

$$[\text{M}] = \frac{2.00\text{ mmol}}{100.0\text{ mL}} - 1.0\times10^{-7}\text{ M} \qquad [\text{MH}^+] = \frac{8.00\text{ mmol}}{100.0\text{ mL}} + 1.0\times10^{-7}\text{ M}$$

The subtraction and addition of the 1.0×10^{-7} accounts for the slight amount of conversion of M to MH^+ by the action of the equilibrium. Substitution into the K_b expression gives K_b:

$$K_b = \frac{[\text{OH}^-][\text{MH}^+]}{[\text{M}]} = \frac{(1.0\times10^{-7})(0.0800 + 1.0\times10^{-7})}{(0.0200 - 1.0\times10^{-7})} = \boxed{4\times10^{-7}}$$

Tip. The 1.0×10^{-7} is so small compared to 0.0200 or 0.0800 that actually subtracting or adding it is not worth the trouble.

10.63 Aqueous arsenic acid donates H^+ ions in three steps. Each has a different K_a:

$$\begin{array}{ll} \text{H}_3\text{AsO}_4(aq) + \text{H}_2\text{O}(l) \rightleftharpoons \text{H}_2\text{AsO}_4^-(aq) + \text{H}_3\text{O}^+(aq) & K_{a1} = 5.0\times10^{-3} \\ \text{H}_2\text{AsO}_4^-(aq) + \text{H}_2\text{O}(l) \rightleftharpoons \text{HAsO}_4^{2-}(aq) + \text{H}_3\text{O}^+(aq) & K_{a2} = 9.3\times10^{-8} \\ \text{HAsO}_4^{2-}(aq) + \text{H}_2\text{O}(l) \rightleftharpoons \text{AsO}_4^{3-}(aq) + \text{H}_3\text{O}^+(aq) & K_{a3} = 3.0\times10^{-12} \end{array}$$

K_{a2} is thousands of times smaller than K_{a1}, and K_{a3} is thousands of times smaller yet. This means that the first reaction will predominate in producing H_3O^+ and that the subsequent reactions will be negligible sources of H_3O^+. Compute the hydronium-ion concentration as if the first step occurred separately and use the answer in the equilibrium expressions for the following steps. Ignoring the interaction of the equilibria avoids complicated systems of simultaneous equations.

When the first step is considered separately, the problem is just like **10.29a**. Let x be the equilibrium concentration of H_3O^+, which equals the equilibrium concentration of $H_2AsO_4^-$. The mass-action expression becomes:

$$\frac{[\text{H}_2\text{AsO}_4^-][\text{H}_3\text{O}^+]}{[\text{H}_3\text{AsO}_4]} = K_{a1} = 5.0\times10^{-3} = \frac{x^2}{(0.1000 - x)}$$

Rearrange and substitute into the quadratic formula to obtain:

$$x = \frac{-5.0\times10^{-3} \pm \sqrt{2.50\times10^{-5} + 2.0\times10^{-3}}}{2}$$

The positive root of the equation is 0.0200. Thus:

$$[\text{H}_3\text{AsO}_4] = \boxed{0.080\text{ M}} \qquad [\text{H}_2\text{AsO}_4^-] = \boxed{0.020\text{ M}} \qquad \text{H}_3\text{O}^+] = \boxed{0.020\text{ M}}$$

Now consider the donation of the second hydrogen ion. Let y equal the concentration of $HAsO_4^{2-}$ produced at equilibrium:

	$H_2AsO_4^-(aq)$	$+H_2O(l) \rightleftharpoons$	$HAsO_4^{2-}(aq)$ +	$H_3O^+(aq)$
Init. Conc. (M)	0.0200	–	0	0.020
Change in Conc. (M)	$-y$	–	$+y$	$+y$
Equil. Conc. (M)	$0.020 - y$	–	y	$0.020 + y$

Use of the mass-action expression for K_{a2} gives the equation:

$$\frac{[\text{HAsO}_4^{2-}][\text{H}_3\text{O}^+]}{[\text{H}_2\text{AsO}_4^-]} = K_{a2} = 9.3\times10^{-8} = \frac{y(0.020 + y)}{(0.020 - y)}$$

This equation is easily solved when it is realized that y must be small compared to 0.0200. Then $y = \boxed{9.3 \times 10^{-8}\ \text{M}} = [HAsO_4^{2-}]$. Note that $[HAsO_4^{2-}]$ is equal to K_{a2}.

Finally, consider the third of the three reactions. Let z equal the concentration of AsO_4^{3-} produced at equilibrium:

	$HAsO_4^{2-}(aq)$	$+H_2O(l) \rightleftharpoons$	$AsO_4^{3-}(aq)\ +$	$H_3O^+(aq)$
Init. Conc. (M)	9.3×10^{-8}	–	0	0.0200
Change in Conc. (M)	$-z$	–	$+z$	$+z$
Equil. Conc. (M)	$9.8 \times 10^{-8} - z$	–	z	$0.0200 + z$

Use of the equilibrium expression for K_{a3} gives the equation:

$$\frac{[AsO_4^{3-}][H_3O^+]}{[HAsO_4^{2-}]} = K_{a2} = 3.0 \times 10^{-12} = \frac{z(0.020 + z)}{(9.8 \times 10^{-8} - z)}$$

Solving gives $[AsO_4^{3-}] = \boxed{1.4 \times 10^{-17}\ \text{M}}$. This is a very small concentration. One liter of the arsenic acid solution contains fewer than ten million AsO_4^{3-} ions!

10.65 The phosphate ion accepts hydrogen ions from water in three stages:

$$PO_4^{3-}(aq) + H_2O(l) \rightleftharpoons HPO_4^{2-}(aq) + OH^-(aq) \qquad K_{b1} = K_w/K_{a3} = 4.55 \times 10^{-2}$$
$$HPO_4^{2-}(aq) + H_2O(l) \rightleftharpoons H_2PO_4^-(aq) + OH^-(aq) \qquad K_{b2} = K_w/K_{a2} = 1.61 \times 10^{-7}$$
$$H_2PO_4^-(aq) + H_2O(l) \rightleftharpoons H_3PO_4(aq) + OH^-(aq) \qquad K_{b3} = K_w/K_{a1} = 1.33 \times 10^{-12}$$

Treat the successive equilibria independently. Set up a three-line table for the reaction between PO_4^{3-} ion and water in the usual way:

	$PO_4^{3-}(aq)$	$+H_2O(l) \rightleftharpoons$	$HPO_4^{2-}(aq)\ +$	$OH^-(aq)$
Init. Conc. (M)	0.050	–	0	small
Change in Conc. (M)	$-x$	–	$+x$	$+x$
Equil. Conc. (M)	$0.050 - x$	–	x	x

Writing the mass-action expression then gives:

$$\frac{[HPO_4^{2-}][OH^-]}{[PO_4^{3-}]} = K_{b1} = 4.55 \times 10^{-2} = \frac{x^2}{(0.050 - x)}$$

Rearrange and substitute into the quadratic formula to obtain:

$$x^2 + (4.55 \times 10^{-2})x - 2.27 \times 10^{-3} = 0 \quad \text{which gives} \quad x = 0.0302$$

$$[OH^-] = \boxed{0.030\ \text{M}} \quad [HPO_4^{2-}] = \boxed{0.030\ \text{M}} \quad [PO_4^{3-}] = 0.050 - 0.0302 = \boxed{0.020\ \text{M}}$$

Turn to the second stage. Let y equal the concentration of $H_2PO_4^-$ formed at equilibrium, but use the concentration of OH^- established by the first stage of the reaction in the K_{b2} mass-action expression:

$$\frac{[H_2PO_4^-][OH^-]}{[HPO_4^{2-}]} = K_{b2} = 1.61 \times 10^{-7} = \frac{y(0.0302 + y)}{0.0302 - y}$$

This equation is easily solved because y must be small compared to 0.0302; $y = \boxed{1.61 \times 10^{-7}\ \text{M}} = [H_2PO_4{}^-]$.

Finally, consider the third reaction. The mass-action expression gives:

$$\frac{[H_3PO_4][OH^-]}{[H_2PO_4^-]} = K_{b3} = 1.33 \times 10^{-12} = \frac{z(0.0302 + z)}{1.61 \times 10^{-7} - z}$$

where z equals the equilibrium concentration of phosphoric acid. Solving gives $z = \boxed{7.1 \times 10^{-18}\ \text{M}} = [H_3PO_4]$.

10.67 The major natural contributor to the acidity of rainwater is dissolved CO_2, which reacts to form carbonic acid: $CO_2(g) + H_2O(l) \rightleftharpoons H_2CO_3(aq)$. In recent times, $SO_3(g)$ and $NO_2(g)$, which are air pollutants, have joined $CO_2(g)$ as contributors to the acidity of rain. Carbonic acid donates two hydrogen ions:

$$H_2CO_3(aq) + H_2O(l) \rightleftharpoons HCO_3^-(aq) + H_3O^+(aq) \qquad K_{a1} = 4.3 \times 10^{-7}$$
$$HCO_3^-(aq) + H_2O(l) \rightleftharpoons CO_3^{2-}(aq) + H_3O^+(aq) \qquad K_{a2} = 4.8 \times 10^{-11}$$

At equilibrium, the following equations relate the concentrations:

$$K_{a1} = \frac{[H_3O^+][HCO_3^-]}{[H_2CO_3]} \qquad K_{a2} = \frac{[H_3O^+][CO_3^{2-}]}{[HCO_3^-]}$$

The pH of the raindrop is 5.60. It follows that $[H_3O^+] = 2.51 \times 10^{-6}$ M. Substituting this value of $[H_3O^+]$ and the two K_a's into the preceding gives:

$$0.171 = \frac{[HCO_3^-]}{[H_2CO_3]} \qquad 1.91 \times 10^{-5} = \frac{[CO_3^{2-}]}{[HCO_3^-]}$$

It is convenient to recast these equations so that the concentration of the same species, say HCO_3^-, is in the denominator in both. Take the reciprocal of the first and copy the second:

$$5.84 = \frac{[H_2CO_3]}{[HCO_3^-]} \qquad 1.91 \times 10^{-5} = \frac{[CO_3^{2-}]}{[HCO_3^-]}$$

The fraction f of any of the three species present equals its concentration divided by the sum of the concentrations of all three. If the species is H_2CO_3:

$$f_{H_2CO_3} = \frac{[H_2CO_3]}{[H_2CO_3] + [HCO_3^-] + [CO_3^{2-}]}$$

This expression can be simplified by dividing numerator and denominator by $[HCO_3^-]$ and inserting the ratios just calculated:

$$f_{H_2CO_3} = \frac{[H_2CO_3]/[HCO_3^-]}{[H_2CO_3]/[HCO_3^-] + 1 + [CO_3^{2-}]/[HCO_3^-]}$$

$$f_{H_2CO_3} = \frac{5.84}{5.84 + 1 + (1.91 \times 10^{-5})} = \frac{5.84}{6.84} = 0.854$$

Expressions are obtained to compute the fractions of the other three species by changing the numerator as required. The resulting fractions are 0.146 for HCO_3^- and 2.79×10^{-6} for CO_3^{2-}. The total concentration of all three forms of the carbon-containing species is 1.0×10^{-5} M. The answers equal the respective fractions times this total:

$$[H_2CO_3] = \boxed{8.5 \times 10^{-6}\ \text{M}} \quad [HCO_3^-] = \boxed{1.5 \times 10^{-6}\ \text{M}} \quad [CO_3^{2-}] = \boxed{2.8 \times 10^{-11}\ \text{M}}$$

10.69 The molar mass of thiamine hydrochloride is 337.27 g mol^{-1}, according to the molecular formula given in the problem. 3.0×10^{-5} g of this substance in 1.00 L of water makes a solution that is 8.89×10^{-8} M in $thiH^+$ ion[9] and of course 8.89×10^{-8} M in Cl^- ion. The $thiH^+(aq)$ cation is a weak acid:

$$thiH^+(aq) + H_2O(l) \rightleftharpoons thi(aq) + H_3O^+(aq) \qquad K_a = 3.4 \times 10^{-7}$$

This equilibrium produces only small amounts of $H_3O^+(aq)$ because K_a is small and the original concentration of $thiH^+(aq)$ is quite small. The simultaneous autoionization of water:

$$2\,H_2O(l) \rightleftharpoons H_3O^+(aq) + OH^-(aq)$$

must be reckoned with as a source of $H_3O^+(aq)$.
The following four mathematical relationships always hold in this solution:

$$3.4 \times 10^{-7} = K_a = \frac{[thi][H_3O^+]}{[thiH^+]} \qquad 1.0 \times 10^{-14} = K_w = [H_3O^+][OH^-]$$

$$8.89 \times 10^{-8} = c_a = [thi] + [thiH^+] \qquad [H_3O^+] + [thiH^+] = [OH^-] + [Cl^-]$$

The last equation follows from the principle of electrical neutrality: for every positive charge in the solution there must be a negative charge. The second-to-last equation represents a material balance. Whatever the distribution between its two forms, the *total* concentration of thiamine-material is known. The first two equations are the usual mass-action expressions. The $[Cl^-]$ equals 8.89×10^{-8} M, as stated above, because $Cl^-(aq)$ does not react to any extent with other species. The four simultaneous equations therefore involve four unknowns. It is "merely" a question of algebra to solve for $[H_3O^+]$. The details of the algebra are given in the text for a similar case.[10] The result is a cubic equation in $[H_3O^+]$:

$$[H_3O^+]^3 + K_a[H_3O^+]^2 - (K_w + c_aK_a)[H_3O^+] - K_aK_w = 0$$

Substitute the numbers specific to this case:

$$[H_3O^+]^3 + (3.4 \times 10^{-7})[H_3O^+]^2 - (4.03 \times 10^{-14})[H_3O^+] - 3.4 \times 10^{-21} = 0$$

The best route to a real root is to guess a value of $[H_3O^+]$ near 10^{-7} and make successive approximations. The answer is $[H_3O^+] = 1.367 \times 10^{-7}$ M for a pH of $\boxed{6.86}$.

Tip. If the autoionization of water is (mistakenly) neglected, the result is the quadratic equation:

$$[H_3O^+]^2 + (3.4 \times 10^{-7})[H_3O^+] - 3.02 \times 10^{-14} = 0$$

Solving gives $[H_3O^+] = 7.31 \times 10^{-8}$ M for a pH of 7.14. But this pH is on the basic side of 7, which is impossible when an acid is dissolved in water.

10.71 Maleic acid is a diprotic acid for which K_{a1} and K_{a2} differ by about four orders of magnitude. Consider the course of the titration region by region.

- *Before Addition of Base.* Before any 0.1000 M NaOH is added, the predominant source of $H_3O^+(aq)$ in the solution is the equilibrium:

$$H_2mal(aq) + H_2O(l) \rightleftharpoons Hmal^-(aq) + H_3O^+(aq)$$

Let y equal $[H_3O^+]$. Then:

$$K_{a1} = 1.42 \times 10^{-2} = \frac{[Hmal^-][H_3O^+]}{[H_2mal]} = \frac{y^2}{0.1000 - y}$$

[9] We let "thi" stand for thiamine $C_{12}H_{17}ON_4SCl$. Then $thiH^+$ stands for $(HC_{12}H_{17}ON_4SCl)^+$. This is the "thiammonium" cation, the conjugate acid of thiamine.

[10] Text page 352.

Solving for y using the quadratic formula gives 0.0313. If $[H_3O^+]$ is 0.0313 mol L^{-1}, the pH is $\boxed{1.51}$.

• *After Addition of Base, But Before the Equivalence Point.* The first 5.00 mL of 0.1000 M NaOH reacts with some of the maleic acid (H_2mal). 5.00 mL of this solution contains only 5.00×10^{-4} mol of NaOH, which is less than the 50.00×10^{-4} mol of H_2mal that is present. The acid is in excess, and the reaction ends when the base runs out. Assuming complete reaction and that no other reactions take place, the yield of $Hmal^-(aq)$ is 5.00×10^{-4} mol, and 45.00×10^{-4} mol of $H_2mal(aq)$ remains. Adding 5.00 mL of dilute aqueous solution raises the volume of the solution to 55.00 mL so:

$$[\text{Hmal}^-] = \frac{5.00 \times 10^{-4}\text{ mol}}{0.05500\text{ L}} = 0.009091\text{ M} \quad [\text{H}_2\text{mal}] = \frac{45.00 \times 10^{-4}\text{ mol}}{0.05500\text{ L}} = 0.08182\text{ M}$$

The K_{a1} equilibrium now acts to alter these concentrations slightly. It generates hydronium ions. For every $H_3O^+(aq)$ produced, one $H_2mal(aq)$ is consumed and one additional $Hmal^-(aq)$ is generated. Let y equal the concentration of H_3O^+ that is generated. Then:

$$K_{a1} = [\text{H}_3\text{O}^+]\frac{[\text{Hmal}^-]}{[\text{H}_2\text{mal}]} \qquad 1.42 \times 10^{-2} = y\frac{0.009091 + y}{0.08182 - y}$$

Rearranging and solving this quadratic equation gives $[H_3O^+] = 0.0244$ M. The Ka_2 equilibrium is neglected as a source of H_3O^+. It proceeds to a far lesser extent, and the "starting" concentration of $Hmal^-$ is about nine times smaller than that of H_2mal. The pH equals $\boxed{1.61}$.

• *Halfway to the First Equivalence Point.* At this point, 25.00 mL of titrant has been added raising the total to volume 75.00 mL. Repeating the reasoning just used gives:

$$1.42 \times 10^{-2} = y\frac{0.0333 + y}{0.0333 - y}$$

Again, rearrange and solve by use of the quadratic formula. The answer is $[H_3O^+] = 8.45 \times 10^{-3}$ M and pH $= \boxed{2.07}$.

• *At the First Equivalence Point.* 50.00 mL of 0.1000 M NaOH brings the titration to the *first* equivalence point. The solution consists of 100.00 mL of 0.0500 M NaHmal (sodium hydrogen maleate). The $Hmal^-(aq)$ ion is amphoteric. It behaves as an acid:

$$\text{Hmal}^-(aq) + \text{H}_2\text{O}(l) \rightleftharpoons \text{H}_3\text{O}^+(aq) + \text{mal}^{2-}(aq) \qquad K_{a2} = 8.57 \times 10^{-7}$$

And it behaves as a base:

$$\text{Hmal}^-(aq) + \text{H}_2\text{O}(l) \rightleftharpoons \text{OH}^-(aq) + \text{H}_2\text{mal}(aq) \qquad K_{b2} = \frac{K_w}{K_{a1}} = 7.04 \times 10^{-13}$$

$Hmal^-(aq)$ is just like $HCO_3^-(aq)$ in this respect. Copy the analysis presented for $HCO_3^-(aq)$ in text Section 10.8[11] to obtain:

$$[\text{H}_3\text{O}^+] \approx \sqrt{\frac{K_{a1}K_{a2}[\text{Hmal}^-]_0 + K_{a1}K_w}{K_{a1} + [\text{Hmal}^-]_0}}$$

in which $[Hmal^-]_0$ equals 0.0500 M the "original" concentration of $Hmal^-$. Inserting the numbers gives $[H_3O^+] = 9.73 \times 10^{-5}$ M for a pH of $\boxed{4.01}$. Notice that the approximate formula $[H_3O^+] \approx \sqrt{K_{a1}K_{a2}}$ gives a wrong pH of 3.96. The approximate formula fails because K_{a1} of maleic acid is rather large and cannot be neglected compared to $[Hmal^-]_0$.

• *Halfway to the Second Equivalence Point.* After 75.00 mL of 0.1000 M NaOH has been added, the titration is half-way to the *second* equivalence point. In this range, the main source of $H_3O^+(aq)$ is the reaction:

$$\text{Hmal}^-(aq) + \text{H}_2\text{O}(l) \rightleftharpoons \text{mal}^{2-}(aq) + \text{H}_3\text{O}^+(aq) \qquad K_{a2} = 8.57 \times 10^{-7}$$

[11] Text page 350.

The concentration of $H_2mal(aq)$ is very small because so much base has been added, and consequently the K_{a1} equilibrium has only a negligible effect on the pH. The titration can be viewed as the addition of 25.00 mL of 0.1000 M NaOH to 100.00 mL of 0.0500 M NaHmal, making a total volume of 125.00 mL. Assuming complete reaction, this much NaOH converts exactly half of the $Hmal^-(aq)$ to $mal^{2-}(aq)$. Dilution meanwhile reduces the concentrations of both species by the factor 100/125. Thus *after* completion of the acid-base reaction but *before* any equilibrium starts:

$$[\text{Hmal}^-] = 0.025 \times \frac{100}{125} = 0.020 \text{ M} \qquad [\text{mal}^{2-}] = 0.025 \times \frac{100}{125} = 0.020 \text{ M}$$

The K_{a2} equilibrium now changes these concentrations slightly. It adds z to the concentration of $mal^{2-}(aq)$ and removes z from the concentration of $Hmal^-(aq)$, where z is the concentration of hydronium ion that it produces. The mass-action expression is

$$K_{a2} = 8.57 \times 10^{-7} = z\left(\frac{0.020 - z}{0.020 + z}\right)$$

Solving this equation is very easy because z can be neglected compared to 0.020. The answer is $z = 8.57 \times 10^{-7}$ so the pH is $\boxed{6.07}$.

• *Just Short of the Second Equivalence Point.* By similar computations, the pH after the addition of 99.90 mL of 0.1000 M NaOH is $\boxed{8.77}$.

• *At the Second Equivalence Point.* The solution consists of 150.00 mL of 0.0333 M Na_2mal. The *hydrolysis* of $mal^{2-}(aq)$ ion is a major source of OH^- ions:

$$\text{mal}^{2-}(aq) + \text{H}_2\text{O}(l) \rightleftharpoons \text{Hmal}^-(aq) + \text{OH}^-(aq) \qquad K_{b1} = \frac{K_w}{K_{a2}} = \frac{1.0 \times 10^{-14}}{8.57 \times 10^{-7}}$$

Note how the *first* K_b for the mal^{2-} ion is related to the *second* K_a for H_2mal. Let x be the equilibrium concentration of $OH^-(aq)$. Then:

$$K_{b1} = \frac{1.0 \times 10^{-14}}{8.57 \times 10^{-7}} = \frac{[\text{Hmal}^-][\text{OH}^-]}{[\text{mal}^{2-}]} = \frac{x^2}{0.0333 - x}$$

Solving for x gives 1.97×10^{-5} so the pOH is 4.71 and the pH is $\boxed{9.29}$.

• *Past the Second Equivalence Point.* When excess NaOH has been added, the hydrolysis of mal^{2-} is completely overshadowed by NaOH as a source of $OH^-(aq)$. The first 100.00 mL of NaOH was used up neutralizing the H_2mal. The next 5.00 mL of 0.100 M NaOH makes a solution that is $(5.00/155.00) \times 0.100$ or 3.23×10^{-3} M in $OH^-(aq)$. This corresponds to pOH 2.49 or pH $\boxed{11.51}$.

10.73 The equation for the dissociation of HOAc (acetic acid) in water is

$$\text{HOAc}(aq) + \text{H}_2\text{O}(l) \rightleftharpoons \text{OAc}^-(aq) + \text{H}_3\text{O}^+(aq)$$

LeChâtelier's principle states that this equilibrium shifts to the right if the volume of the system increases. This shift increases the degree of dissociation of the HOAC, but *not* the equilibrium constant of the reaction. The point can be understood mathematically. Suppose that some concentration c of acetic acid is dissolved in water and comes to equilibrium as indicated in the preceding equation. Then

$$K = \frac{(cx)(cx)}{c - cx} = \frac{cx^2}{1 - x}$$

where x is the degree of dissociation of the acetic acid. If c is decreased (by adding water to the solution) then x increases to maintain the equality.

10.75 The equilibrium constants are for the reaction

$$ClCH_2COOH(aq) + H_2O(l) \rightleftharpoons ClCH_2COO^-(aq) + H_3O^+(aq)$$

Call the first constant (observed at $T_1 = 273.15$ K) K_1 and the second (observed at $T_2 = 313.15$ K) K_2. The hint in the problem strongly suggests the use of these constants in van't Hoff equation (Section 9.7). Proceed as follows:

$$\ln\frac{K(T_2)}{K(T_1)} = \ln\left(\frac{1.230\times10^{-3}}{1.528\times10^{-3}}\right) = \frac{-\Delta H^\circ}{R}\left(\frac{1}{313.15\text{ K}} - \frac{1}{273.15\text{ K}}\right)$$

Substituting $R = 8.3145$ J K^{-1}mol^{-1} then gives $\Delta H^\circ = -3.86\times10^3$ J mol^{-1}. The ΔH° of the reaction as it is represented above therefore equals $\boxed{-3.86\text{ kJ}}$.

10.77 Use the relations: pOH = 14.00 − pH; $[H_3O^+] = 10^{-pH}$; $[OH^-] = 10^{-pOH}$.

a)	$[H_3O^+] = 1.6\times10^{-3}$ M	pOH = 11.2	$[OH^-] = 6.3\times10^{-12}$ M
b)	$[H_3O^+] = 1.3\times10^{-4}$ M	pOH = 10.1	$[OH^-] = 7.9\times10^{-11}$ M
c)	$[H_3O^+] = 7.9\times10^{-5}$ M	pOH = 9.9	$[OH^-] = 1.3\times10^{-10}$ M
d)	$[H_3O^+] = 3.2\times10^{-9}$ M	pOH = 5.5	$[OH^-] = 3.2\times10^{-6}$ M
e)	$[H_3O^+] = 1.3\times10^{-12}$ M	pOH = 2.1	$[OH^-] = 7.9\times10^{-3}$ M

10.79 The pH should be $\boxed{\text{low}}$. LeChâtelier's principle indicates that increasing $[H_3O^+]$ shifts the equilibrium in the problem to the left, favoring $Cl_2(aq)$ at the expense of $Cl^-(aq)$.

10.81 The structure is $\boxed{H_2PO(OH)}$, in which two of the hydrogen atoms are bound directly to the central P. The acid $HP(OH)_2$, which has two acidic hydrogen atoms, would be orders of magnitude weaker. See text Table 10.3. On this basis, $H_2PO(OH)$ should be $\boxed{\text{monoprotic}}$.

10.83 Urea is such a weak base that its conjugate acid is almost a strong acid.

a) The formula of the conjugate acid of urea is obtained by adding H^+ to the formula of urea. The answer is $\boxed{NH_2CONH_3^+}$. This ion is called the urea acidium ion.

b) Let "ureaH$^+$" stand for the urea acidium ion. It reacts with water:

	ureaH$^+(aq)$	$+\ H_2O(aq) \rightleftharpoons$	urea(aq) +	$H_3O^+(aq)$
Init. Conc. (M)	0.15	–	0	small
Change in Conc. (M)	$-x$	–	$+x$	$+x$
Equil. Conc. (M)	$0.15 - x$	–	x	x

The K_b for urea is $10^{-13.8} = 1.58\times10^{-14}$. Use this value to calculate K_a for ureaH$^+$. Also set up the K_a mass-action expression:

$$K_a = \frac{K_w}{K_b} = \frac{1.0\times10^{-14}}{1.58\times10^{-14}} = \frac{[\text{urea}][H_3O^+]}{[\text{ureaH}^+]} = \frac{x^2}{(0.15-x)}$$

$$0.630 = \frac{x^2}{(0.15-x)}$$

Solving the last equation by means of the quadratic formula gives $x = 0.125$. The equilibrium concentration of the urea is therefore $\boxed{0.125\text{ M}}$.

10.85 Use the mass-action equation for the K_a equilibrium of acetic acid. Let $[H_3O^+]$ at 25°C be y. Then:

$$K_{a,25} = 1.76 \times 10^{-5} = \frac{y^2}{0.10 - y} \quad \text{which gives} \quad y^2 + (1.76 \times 10^{-5})y - 1.76 \times 10^{-6} = 0$$

The applicable root of the quadratic equation is 1.318×10^{-3}, so at 25°C the pH equals 2.88. Repeat the calculation for the 50°C case. The initial molarity of the acetic acid $[HOAc]_0$ is less at 50°C because the solution expands when heated. The increase in volume is computed from the relative densities at the two temperatures:

$$\rho_{50} = 0.9881\,\rho_{25} \qquad \left(\frac{\text{mass}}{V_{50}}\right) = 0.9881\left(\frac{\text{mass}}{V_{25}}\right) \qquad V_{50} = 1.012\,V_{25}$$

Because V is in the denominator in the definition of molarity;

$$[HOAc]_0 = 0.010\text{ M} \times \left(\frac{1}{1.012}\right) = 0.09881\text{ M} \quad \text{at } 50°\text{C}$$

Let x represent the equilibrium concentration of H_3O^+ at 50°C. Then:

$$K_{a,50} = 1.63 \times 10^{-5} = \frac{x^2}{0.0988 - x} \quad \text{which gives} \quad x^2 + (1.63 \times 10^{-5})x - 1.61 \times 10^{-6} = 0$$

The applicable root is 0.00126, making the pH at 50°C equal 2.90. The **pH increases** slightly when the solution is heated from 25 to 50°C because the acid weakens and the solution becomes more dilute.

Tip. The autoionization of water also changes its extent with temperature. It is not considered because it is a negligible source of hydronium ion at both temperatures.

10.87 The compounds are a strong acid (HCl), a salt of a strong acid and a weak base (NH_4Cl), a salt of a weak acid and a strong base (Na_3PO_4), a salt of a weak acid and a strong base ($NaC_2H_3O_2$), and a salt of a strong acid and a strong base (KNO_3). The 0.100 M solutions of HCl and NH_4Cl are acidic. The 0.100 M solutions of Na_3PO_4 and $NaCH_3COO$ are basic. The 0.100 M solution of KNO_3 is neutral.

10.89 The single quantity that measures the strength of an acid in a given solvent is its K_a. The K_a's of NH_4^+ and HCN in water at room temperature are 5.6×10^{-10} and 6.17×10^{-10} respectively. Therefore HCN is only about 10% stronger than NH_4^+ ion.

10.91 The initial concentrations of C_6F_5COOH and $C_6F_5COO^-$ are:

$$[C_6F_5COOH]_0 = \frac{0.050\text{ mol}}{2.00\text{ L}} = 0.025\text{ M} \quad [C_6F_5COO^-]_0 = \frac{0.060\text{ mol}}{2.00\text{ L}} = 0.030\text{ M}$$

These are the concentrations *after* the complete mixing of the two solutions, but *before* any reactions involving the pentafluorobenzoic acid and its conjugate base the pentafluorobenzoate ion have a chance to occur. Now set up the problem as in Example 10.7[12] or **10.45**. Let y equal the equilibrium concentration of hydronium ion. Then:

$$K_a = \frac{[H_3O^+][C_6F_5COO^-]}{[C_6F_5COOH]} = \frac{y(0.030 + y)}{(0.025 - y)} = 0.033$$

If y is neglected compared to 0.025 and 0.030, then the equation is easy to solve, and y equals 0.0275. This is obviously *wrong* because 0.0275 is *larger* than 0.025 rather than being a great deal smaller. When such things happen, start over and neglect nothing. The original equation rearranges to:

$$y^2 + 0.063y - 0.000825 = 0$$

Use of the quadratic formula gives the root $y = 0.01113$. It follows that the pH of the buffer is **1.95**.

---

[12] Text page 337.

10.93 Procedure d) would not make an effective buffer. A good buffer results when substantial amounts of a weak acid and its conjugate base are mixed in solution. Procedure d) yields a solution that is 1.77×10^{-5} M in HCl mixed with some NaCl. The solution would change pH greatly upon addition of either acid or base. All the other solutions are acetate buffers.

10.95 Assume that heating the original sample of $Na_2CO_3 \cdot 10H_2O$ drove off only water (and not, for example, some CO_2). Then the ability of the sample to neutralize acids remained unchanged, despite its loss of mass. It neutralized some of the HCl when the two were mixed; the NaOH neutralized the rest of the HCl. The chemical amounts of the HCl and NaOH were

$$n_{\text{HCl}} = 30.0 \text{ mL} \times \frac{0.100 \text{ mmol HCl}}{\text{mL}} = 3.00 \text{ mmol HCl}$$

$$n_{\text{NaOH}} = 6.4 \text{ mL} \times \frac{0.200 \text{ mmol NaOH}}{\text{mL}} = 1.28 \text{ mmol NaOH}$$

Because HCl and NaOH neutralize each other in a 1 : 1 molar ratio, 3.00 mmol− 1.28 mmol= 1.72 mmol of acid were neutralized by the partially dehydrated sample, which can be formulated $Na_2CO_3 \cdot xH_2O$ (where x between 0 and 10). The equation for the reaction between the sample and the HCl is

$$Na_2CO_3 \cdot xH_2O(s) + 2\ HCl(aq) \rightarrow 2\ NaCl(aq) + CO_2(g) + (1+x)\ H_2O(l)$$

The chemical amount of $Na_2CO_3 \cdot xH_2O$ was then

$$n_{Na_2CO_3 xH_2O} = 1.72 \text{ mmol HCl} \times \frac{1 \text{ mmol } Na_2CO_3}{2 \text{ mmol HCl}} = 0.860 \text{ mmol}$$

The original chemical amount of the decahydrate ($Na_2CO_3 \cdot 10H_2O$) was also 0.860 mmol because the dehydration reaction

$$Na_2CO_3 \cdot 10H_2O(s) \rightarrow Na_2CO_3 \cdot xH_2O(s) + (10-x)H_2O(g)$$

keeps the decahydrate and the partially dehydrated sodium carbonate in a 1 : 1 molar ratio.
The original mass of $Na_2CO_3 \cdot 10H_2O$ was

$$m_{Na_2CO_3} = 0.860 \text{ mmol } Na_2CO_3 \cdot 10H_2O \times \frac{286.14 \text{ mg } Na_2CO_3 \cdot 10H_2O}{1 \text{ mmol } Na_2CO_3 \cdot 10H_2O} = 246.1 \text{ mg}$$

and the chemical amount of water incorporated in the original decahydrate was $10 \times 0.860 = 8.60$ mmol H_2O. Heating the sample reduced its mass from the original 246.1 mg to 200 mg. The fraction of the water that was lost was

$$\text{fraction lost} = \frac{(246.1 - 200) \text{ mg } H_2O}{8.60 \text{ mmol } H_2O(18.015 \text{ mg } H_2O\ /\text{mmol } H_2O)} = \boxed{0.30}$$

10.97 The solutions in the three flasks have the same pH but contain different acids (HNO_3, HCOOH, and $C_6H_5NH_3^+$ ion) in different concentrations.
(a) To determine which flask contains which solution: Take equal volumes of solution (say 10 mL) from flasks A, B, and C and titrate them (separately) with a strong base (NaOH would work) to the same endpoint (the phenolphthalein endpoint would work). The 10 mL of $C_6H_5NH_3Cl$ solution would require the most titrant because it would contain the most acid. The 10 mL of HNO_3 solution would require the least acid because it would contain the least titrant. These three acids all react with NaOH in a 1 : 1 molar ratio. This is important. If one were a diprotic or triprotic acid, its neutralizing power would be doubled or tripled.
(b) The relative strengths of the three acids are

$$\boxed{\text{strongest } HNO_3 < HCOOH < C_6H_5NH_3^+ \text{ weakest}}$$

It requires a larger concentration of a weaker acid to lower the pH to a given value than it does of a stronger acid. A weaker acid donates H^+ ion less effectively.

(c) Nitric acid (HNO_3) is a strong acid. It dissociates essentially completely in water. This means that $[H_3O^+] = 1.0 \times 10^{-3}$ in the HNO_3 solution and in the two other solutions as well because they are stated to have the same pH. Write the equilibrium equations and acidity-constant expressions for the two weak acids. They have similar forms

$$C_6H_5NH_3^+(aq) + H_2O(l) \rightleftharpoons H_3O^+(aq) + C_6H_5NH_2(aq) \quad K_{C_6H_5NH_3^+} = \frac{[H_3O^+][C_6H_5NH_2]}{[C_6H_5NH_3^+]}$$

$$HCOOH(aq) + H_2O(l) \rightleftharpoons H_3O^+(aq) + HCOO^-(aq) \quad K_{HCOOH} = \frac{[H_3O^+][HCOO^-]}{[HCOOH]}$$

The only source of H_3O^+ ion in either solution, apart from a very slight contribution from the autoioniziation of water, is the dissociation of the weak acid. The acid-dissociation reaction reduces the concentration of the weak acid by 1.0×10^{-3} M and increases the concentration of its conjugate base by the same amount:

$$[C_6H_5NH_3^+] = (4 \times 10^{-2} - 1.0 \times 10^{-3}) \text{ M} \quad [C_6H_5NH_2] = (0 + 1.0 \times 10^{-3}) \text{ M}$$

$$[HCOOH] = (6 \times 10^{-3} - 1.0 \times 10^{-3}) \text{ M} \quad [COO^-] = (0 + 1.0 \times 10^{-3}) \text{ M}$$

Substitution into the equilibrium-constant equations gives the two K_a's

$$K_{C_6H_5NH_3^+} = \frac{(1.0 \times 10^{-3})(1.0 \times 10^{-3})}{3.9 \times 10^{-2}} = 2.6 \times 10^{-4}$$

$$K_{HCOOH} = \frac{(1.0 \times 10^{-3})(1.0 \times 10^{-3})}{5 \times 10^{-3}} = \boxed{2 \times 10^{-4}}$$

The K_b for aniline, which is the conjugate base of $C_6H_5NH_3^+$ ion is then computed using the fact that $K_aK_b = K_w$ for an acid-base conjugate pair

$$K_{C_6H_5NH_2} = \frac{1.0 \times 10^{-14}}{2.6 \times 10^{-4}} = \boxed{4 \times 10^{-11}}$$

Tip. Check the answers against tabulated values in reliable sources. Text table 10.2 gives $K_{HCOOH} = 1.77 \times 10^{-4}$, which is in agreement.

10.99 a) The 0.1000 M solution of weak acid HA has a volume of 50.00 mL because 50.00 mL of the 0.1000 M base titrates it to equivalence. The addition of 40.00 mL of the base converts 40.00/50.00 of the acid to its conjugate base and creates a solution with a volume of 90.00 mL. According to the problem, the pH of this 90.00 mL of solution is 4.50. This means:

$$[H_3O^+] = 10^{-4.50} = 3.16 \times 10^{-5} \text{ M}$$

The solution is at equilibrium. The concentration of HA is the amount of unreacted HA divided by the volume of the solution minus the small concentration lost by the donation of H^+ to water:

$$[HA] = \frac{10.00}{90.00}(0.100) - [H_3O^+] = (0.01111 - 3.16 \times 10^{-5}) \text{ M}$$

Similarly, the equilibrium concentration of A^- is the amount of A^- formed divided by the volume of the solution plus the small concentration added by the HA/A^- equilibrium:

$$[A^-] = \frac{40.00}{90.00}(0.100) + [H_3O^+] = (0.04444 + 3.16 \times 10^{-5}) \text{ M}$$

Substitute these values into the K_a expression:

$$K_a = \frac{[H_3O^+][A^-]}{[HA]} = \frac{(3.16 \times 10^{-5})(0.044476)}{0.011079} = \boxed{1.27 \times 10^{-4}}$$

b) The solution at the equivalence point could have been prepared by dissolving 5.000 mmol of NaA in 100.00 mL of water. In such a solution, the initial concentration (before acid-base equilibria) of A^- ion is 0.05000 M. To determine the pH, consider the reaction of A^- ion with water:

$$A^-(aq) + H_2O(l) \rightleftharpoons HA(aq) + OH^-(aq) \qquad \frac{[HA][OH^-]}{[A^-]} = K_b$$

Let x equal the equilibrium concentration of OH^- ion. Then:

$$\frac{x^2}{0.05000 - x} = \frac{K_w}{K_a} = 7.91 \times 10^{-11}$$

Solving for x gives a $[OH^-]$ of 1.99×10^{-6} M. The pOH is accordingly 5.70, and the pH is $\boxed{8.30}$.

10.101 Phosphonocarboxylic acid ("H_3Pho") donates H^+ in three steps:

$$H_3Pho(aq) + H_2O(l) \rightleftharpoons H_2Pho^-(aq) + H_3O^+(aq) \qquad K_{a1} = 1.0 \times 10^{-2}$$
$$H_2Pho^-(aq) + H_2O(l) \rightleftharpoons HPho^{2-}(aq) + H_3O^+(aq) \qquad K_{a2} = 7.8 \times 10^{-6}$$
$$HPho^{2-}(aq) + H_2O(l) \rightleftharpoons Pho^{3-}(aq) + H_3O^+(aq) \qquad K_{a3} = 2.0 \times 10^{-9}$$

The law of mass action gives the following three equations:

$$K_{a1} = \frac{[H_3O^+][H_2Pho^-]}{[H_3Pho]} \quad K_{a2} = \frac{[H_3O^+][HPho^{2-}]}{[H_2Pho^-]} \quad K_{a3} = \frac{[H_3O^+][Pho^{3-}]}{[HPho^{2-}]}$$

The pH of the blood is 7.40, and the buffering action of the blood maintains this pH despite the addition of the drug. It follows that $[H_3O^+] = 3.98 \times 10^{-8}$ M. Substituting the known value of $[H_3O^+]$ and the three K's gives:

$$2.510 \times 10^5 = \frac{[H_2Pho^-]}{[H_3Pho]} \quad 195.927 = \frac{[HPho^{2-}]}{[H_2Pho^-]} \quad 0.05024 = \frac{[Pho^{3-}]}{[HPho^{2-}]}$$

Recast these equations so that the concentration of the same species, say H_2Pho^-, is in the denominator:

$$3.984 \times 10^{-6} = \frac{[H_3Pho]}{[H_2Pho^-]} \quad 195.927 = \frac{[HPho^{2-}]}{[H_2Pho^-]} \quad 9.8430 = \frac{[Pho^{3-}]}{[H_2Pho^-]}$$

The first new equation is the reciprocal of the first of the preceding group. The third comes by multiplying the second and third equations in the preceding group. The fraction f of any of the four Pho-containing species equals its concentration divided by the sum of the concentrations of all four. For example:

$$f_{H_3Pho} = \frac{[H_3Pho]}{[H_3Pho] + [H_2Pho^-] + [HPho^{2-}] + [Pho^{3-}]}$$

This expression can be evaluated by dividing numerator and denominator by $[H_2Pho^-]$ and inserting the ratios just calculated:

$$f_{H_3Pho} = \frac{[H_3Pho]/[H_2Pho^-]}{[H_3Pho]/[H_2Pho^-] + 1 + [HPho^{2-}]/[H_2Pho^-] + [Pho^{3-}]/[H_2Pho^-]}$$

$$f_{H_3Pho} = \frac{3.98 \times 10^{-6}}{3.98 \times 10^{-6} + 1 + 195.927 + 9.8430} = \frac{3.98 \times 10^{-6}}{206.77} = 1.92 \times 10^{-8}$$

The same approach gives the fractions of the other three species. Simply change the numerator as required. The resulting fractions are 0.004836 for H_2Pho^-, 0.94756 for $HPho^{2-}$, and 0.0476 for Pho^{3-}. The total concentration of all four forms of the drug is 1.0×10^{-5} M. The desired concentrations equal this total multiplied by the respective fractions:

$$[H_3Pho] = \boxed{1.9 \times 10^{-13}\ \text{M}} \qquad [H_2Pho^-] = \boxed{4.8 \times 10^{-8}\ \text{M}}$$
$$[HPho^{2-}] = \boxed{9.5 \times 10^{-6}\ \text{M}} \qquad [Pho^{3-}] = \boxed{4.8 \times 10^{-7}\ \text{M}}$$

10.103 As explained in the problem, hyperventilating causes the loss of CO_2 dissolved in the blood. Carbon dioxide is a weak acid in water. Loss of the weak acid causes the blood to $\boxed{\text{rise in pH}}$.

10.105 Represent the amino acid glycine as glyH. Its conjugate acid is then $glyH_2^+$, and its conjugate base is gly^-. Copy the two equilibria given in the problem:

$$\text{glyH}(aq) + H_2O(l) \rightleftharpoons \text{gly}^-(aq) + H_3O^+(aq) \qquad K_a = 1.7 \times 10^{-10}$$
$$\text{glyH}(aq) + H_2O(l) \rightleftharpoons \text{glyH}_2^+(aq) + OH^-(aq) \qquad K_b = 2.2 \times 10^{-12}$$

The following equations convey the *same* chemical relationships:

$$\text{glyH}_2^+(aq) + H_2O(l) \rightleftharpoons \text{glyH}(aq) + H_3O^+(aq) \qquad K_1 = K_w/K_b$$
$$\text{glyH}(aq) + H_2O(l) \rightleftharpoons \text{gly}^-(aq) + H_3O^+(aq) \qquad K_2 = K_a$$

In this pair of equilibria, the second equation quoted in the problem has been *reversed* and *added* to the water autoionization equation. The change puts the emphasis on $glyH_2^+$ ($^+H_3N—CH_2—COOH$) as a diprotic acid rather than on self-neutralization by the glycine. The new equations reveal that solutions of glycine are just like solutions of other amphoteric species—0.10 M aqueous glycine is like 0.10 M $HCO_3^-(aq)$, for example. The similarity is worth spotting because the case of the pH of an aqueous solution of $HCO_3^-(aq)$ is extensively treated in the text.[13] The text develops the approximate formula $[H_3O^+] \approx \sqrt{K_1K_2}$. According to this formula, the $[H_3O^+]$ in the solution is independent of the concentration of the glycine! Substitution in the formula gives:

$$[H_3O^+] = \sqrt{K_1K_2} = \sqrt{\left(\frac{K_w}{K_b}\right)K_a} = \sqrt{\left(\frac{1.0 \times 10^{-14}}{2.2 \times 10^{-12}}\right)(1.7 \times 10^{-10})} = 8.8 \times 10^{-7}\ \text{M}$$

The pH equals 6.06, as it seems. A more exact analysis[14] gives:

$$[H_3O^+] \approx \sqrt{\frac{K_1K_2c_0 + K_1K_w}{K_1 + c_0}}$$

The treatment leading to this formula includes only one approximation: that the equilibrium concentration of glycine is close to c_0, its original concentration. Substitution of $c_0 = 0.10$ M and the three constants gives $[H_3O^+] = 8.6 \times 10^{-7}$ M, and the pH equals $\boxed{6.07}$.

Tip. If c_0 were 0.01 M, one-tenth of the c_0 given in the problem, the pH of the glycine solution would be 6.14. This deviates substantially from 6.06, the first answer. Thus, as c_0 diminishes it becomes *more* important in determining the pH, at least at first. As c_0 becomes exceedingly small the solution approximates pure water (pH 7.0).

10.107 a) $HC_3H_5O_3(aq) + NaHCO_3(aq) \rightarrow NaC_3H_5O_3(aq) + H_2O(l) + CO_2(g)$

[13] Text Section 10.8, text page 352–354.
[14] Text page 354.

b) Compute the chemical amount of sodium bicarbonate that is neutralized:

$$\frac{1}{2}\text{ tsp} \times \left(\frac{236.6\text{ cm}^3}{48\text{ tsp}}\right) \times \left(\frac{1\text{ mL}}{1\text{ cm}^3}\right) \times \left(\frac{2.46\text{ g NaHCO}_3}{1\text{ mL}}\right) \times \left(\frac{1\text{ mol NaHCO}_3}{84.01\text{ g NaHCO}_3}\right) = 0.0633\text{ mol NaHCO}_3$$

Lactic acid and sodium bicarbonate react in a 1-to-1 molar ratio. Hence the one cup of sour milk contains 0.0633 mol of lactic acid. The concentration of lactic acid is 0.0633 mol/0.2366 L = $\boxed{0.268\text{ M}}$.

c) The same chemical amount (0.0633 mol) of $CO_2(g)$ will be produced. Its volume is computed using the ideal-gas law:

$$V = \frac{nRT}{P} = \frac{(0.0633\text{ mol})(0.08206\text{ L atm mol}^{-1}\text{K}^{-1})(177 + 273.15\text{ K})}{1\text{ atm}} = \boxed{2.34\text{ L}}$$

10.109 Label the gaseous monoprotic acid HY. The data on the temperature, pressure, and density of HY provide its molar mass. As shown in the answer to **4.23**, for an ideal gas:

$$\rho = \frac{m}{V} = \frac{P}{RT}\mathcal{M}$$

Solve for $\mathcal{M}$ and insert the numbers for HY in this case:

$$\mathcal{M}_{\text{HY}} = \rho\left(\frac{RT}{P}\right) = \frac{1.05\text{ g}}{\text{L}}\left(\frac{0.08206\text{ L atm mol}^{-1}\text{K}^{-1}(313.15\text{ K})}{1.00\text{ atm}}\right) = \frac{26.98\text{ g}}{\text{mol}}$$

The concentration of HY when 1.85 g of it is dissolved in 450 mL of water is

$$c_{\text{HY}} = \frac{n_{\text{HY}}}{V} = \frac{m_{\text{HY}}}{\mathcal{M}_{\text{HY}}V} = \frac{1.85\text{ g}}{(26.98\text{ g mol}^{-1})0.450\text{ L}} = 0.1524\text{ mol L}^{-1}$$

As the HY reacts with water, it generates H_3O^+. The final concentration of H_3O^+ equals $10^{-5.01} = 9.77 \times 10^{-6}$ M. For HY as an acid:

	$HY(aq)$	$+ H_2O(l) \rightleftharpoons$	$Y^-(aq)\ +$	$H_3O^+(aq)$
Init. Conc. (M)	0.1524	–	0	small
Change in Conc. (M)	-9.77×10^{-6}	–	$+9.77 \times 10^{-6}$	$+9.77 \times 10^{-6}$
Equil. Conc. (M)	0.1524	–	9.77×10^{-6}	9.77×10^{-6}

Now that the equilibrium concentrations of all of the products and reactants in the acid ionization of HY are known, it is easy to compute K_a:

$$K_a = \frac{[H_3O^+][Y^-]}{[HY]} = \frac{(9.77 \times 10^{-6})^2}{0.1524} = 6.27 \times 10^{-10}$$

Inspection of text Table 10.2 shows that HY must be $\boxed{\text{HCN}}$, which has a tabulated K_a of 6.17×10^{-10}. This conclusion is supported by comparing the molar mass of HCN (27.03 g mol^{-1}) to the molar mass of HY from the gas-density data (27.0 g mol^{-1}).

Chapter 11

Solubility and Precipitation Equilibria

11.1 According to the balanced reaction, converting plaster of paris (the half-hydrate of $CaSO_4$) to gypsum (the dihydrate) uses 3/2 mol of water per mole of plaster of paris. Thus:

$$V_{H_2O} = 25.0 \text{ kg } CaSO_4{\cdot}\frac{1}{2}H_2O \times \left(\frac{1 \text{ mol } CaSO_4{\cdot}\frac{1}{2}H_2O}{0.14515 \text{ kg } CaSO_4{\cdot}\frac{1}{2}H_2O}\right) \times \left(\frac{3 \text{ mol } H_2O}{2 \text{ mol } CaSO_4{\cdot}\frac{1}{2}H_2O}\right)$$
$$\times \left(\frac{0.01802 \text{ kg } H_2O}{1 \text{ mol } H_2O}\right) \times \left(\frac{1 \text{ L } H_2O}{1 \text{ kg } H_2O}\right) = \boxed{4.65 \text{ L } H_2O}$$

11.3 On the graph, read across from "80" on the vertical axis until the solubility curve is reached. Then drop down to the horizontal axis and read the temperature. A solubility of 80 g HBr per 100 g H_2O is reached at a temperature of approximately 48°C. The last of the KBr will dissolve at $\boxed{\text{about } 48°\text{C}}$.

11.5 Solubility-product constant expressions[1] follow the general rules for heterogeneous equilibria. Pure solids and the solvent do not appear in these expressions. For the dissolution of iron(III) sulfate in water:

$$\boxed{Fe_2(SO_4)_3(s) \rightleftharpoons 2\,Fe^{3+}(aq) + 3\,SO_4^{2-}(aq)} \qquad \boxed{K_{sp} = [Fe^{3+}]^2[SO_4^{2-}]^3}$$

11.7 The dissolution of thallium(I) iodate is represented:

$$TlIO_3(s) \rightleftharpoons Tl^+(aq) + IO_3^-(aq) \qquad [Tl^+][IO_3^-] = K_{sp} = 3.07 \times 10^{-6}$$

If S mol per liter of $TlIO_3$ dissolves, then S mol per liter of Tl^+ and also S mol per liter of IO_3^- are present at equilibrium, as long as neither ion reacts further in solution. Thus:

$$K_{sp} = 3.07 \times 10^{-6} = [Tl^+][IO_3^-] = S^2 \quad \text{which gives} \quad S = 1.752 \times 10^{-3} \text{ mol L}^{-1}$$

This means that 1.752×10^{-3} mol of thallium(I) iodate saturates a liter of solution at 25°C. This equals the solubility of the thallium(I) iodate in 1000 mL of water because the small amount of solute does not alter the volume of the solution measurably from the volume of the pure solvent. This chemical amount of thallium(I) iodate has a mass of 0.665 g (obtained by multiplying by $\mathcal{M}_{TlIO_3} = 379.3$ g mol^{-1}). The mass of $TlIO_3$ that saturates 100 mL of water is 1/10 as great: $\boxed{0.0665 \text{ g } TlIO_3/100 \text{ mL}}$.

---

[1] Also called solubility product expressions and K_{sp} expressions.

11.9 The equilibrium equation and K_{sp} for the dissolution of potassium perchlorate are:

$$KClO_4(s) \rightleftharpoons K^+(aq) + ClO_4^-(aq) \qquad [K^+][ClO_4^-] = K_{sp} = 1.07 \times 10^{-2}$$

If S mol L^{-1} of $KClO_4$ dissolves, then there must be S mol L^{-1} of K^+ and S mol L^{-1} of ClO_4^- present at equilibrium, as long as neither ion reacts further. Substitute S into the K_{sp} expression:

$$K_{sp} = 1.07 \times 10^{-2} = [K^+][ClO_4^-] = S^2$$

Solving gives $S = 0.103$ mol L^{-1}. Then:

$$\frac{0.103 \text{ mol KClO}_4}{\text{L}} \times \left(\frac{138.55 \text{ g KClO}_4}{1 \text{ mol KClO}_4}\right) = \boxed{\frac{14.3 \text{ g KClO}_4}{\text{L}}} \text{ at } 25°\text{C}$$

11.11 The equilibrium and K_{sp} expressions are:

$$Hg_2I_2(s) \rightleftharpoons Hg_2^{2+}(aq) + 2\,I^-(aq) \qquad [Hg_2^{2+}][I^-]^2 = K_{sp}$$

If S mol L^{-1} of Hg_2I_2 dissolves, then S mol L^{-1} of Hg_2^{2+} and $2S$ mol L^{-1} of I^- are produced. Substituting into the K_{sp} mass-action expression gives:

$$[Hg_2^{2+}][I^-]^2 = S(2S)^2 = 1.2 \times 10^{-28}$$

from which:

$$4S^3 = 1.2 \times 10^{-28} \qquad \text{which gives} \qquad S = 3.1 \times 10^{-10} \text{ mol L}^{-1}$$

$$[Hg_2^{2+}] = S = \boxed{3.1 \times 10^{-10} \text{ mol L}^{-1}} \qquad [I^-] = 2S = \boxed{6.2 \times 10^{-10} \text{ mol L}^{-1}}$$

11.13 As seen in **7.9**, a solubility differs from a solubility-product constant, although there is often a simple relationship between the two. The equilibrium of interest is

$$Ag_2CrO_4(s) \rightleftharpoons 2\,Ag^+(aq) + CrO_4^{2-}(aq) \qquad K_{sp} = [Ag^+]^2[CrO_4^{2-}]$$

The problem states that 0.0129 g of silver chromate dissolves in 500 mL (0.500 L) of water. Assume that neither Ag^+ nor CrO_4^{2-} reacts with other species once in the water. Then the chemical amounts of the two ions in solution at equilibrium are:

$$n_{Ag^+} = 0.0129 \text{ g} \times \left(\frac{1 \text{ mol Ag}_2\text{CrO}_4}{331.7 \text{ g Ag}_2\text{CrO}_4}\right) \times \left(\frac{2 \text{ mol Ag}^+}{1 \text{ mol Ag}_2\text{CrO}_4}\right) = 7.78 \times 10^{-5} \text{ mol}$$

$$n_{CrO_4^{2-}} = \frac{1}{2} n_{Ag^+} = 3.89 \times 10^{-5} \text{ mol}$$

The equilibrium concentrations of the two ions equal these chemical amounts divided by 0.500 L, which is the volume of the solution:

$$[Ag^+] = 15.6 \times 10^{-5} \text{ mol L}^{-1} \qquad [CrO_4^{2-}] = 7.78 \times 10^{-5} \text{ mol L}^{-1}$$

Substitute into the K_{sp} expression to obtain a numerical K_{sp}:

$$K_{sp} = [Ag^+]^2[CrO_4^{2-}] = (15.6 \times 10^{-5})^2(7.78 \times 10^{-5}) = \boxed{1.9 \times 10^{-12}}$$

Tip. This equals the value in text Table 11.2.

11.15 The dissolution reaction and its K_{sp}-expression are:

$$AgCl(s) \rightleftharpoons Ag^+(aq) + Cl^-(aq) \qquad [Ag^+][Cl^-] = K_{sp}$$

At equilibrium in 1.00 L of the solution at 100°C:

$$n_{Ag^+} = 0.018 \text{ g} \times \left(\frac{1 \text{ mol AgCl}}{143.3 \text{ g AgCl}}\right) \times \left(\frac{1 \text{ mol Ag}^+}{1 \text{ mol AgCl}}\right) = 1.26 \times 10^{-4} \text{ mol}$$

Since the volume of the solution is 1.00 L, the concentration of Ag^+ ion is 1.26×10^{-4} M. The concentration of Cl^- ion is the same—one mole per liter of chloride ion is produced in solution for every mole per liter of silver ion. Substitute the concentrations into the mass-action expression:

$$K_{sp} = [Ag^+][Cl^-] = (1.26 \times 10^{-4})(1.26 \times 10^{-4}) = \boxed{1.6 \times 10^{-8}}$$

Tip. This K_{sp} is larger (by a factor of 100) than the K_{sp} in text Table 11.2[2] because the temperature is 100°, not 25°C.

11.17 Get the initial concentrations of Ba^{2+} ion and CrO_4^{2-} ion and use them to calculate the initial reaction quotient Q_0 for the reaction:

$$BaCrO_4(s) \rightleftharpoons Ba^{2+}(aq) + CrO_4^{2-}(aq)$$

"Initial" in this case means after the solution cools to 25°C, but before any reaction occurs. Compare Q_0 with K_{sp}. If Q_0 exceeds K_{sp}, then a precipitate will form as the reaction proceeds from right to left. If Q_0 is less than K_{sp}, then there can be no precipitate. The initial amount of dissolved Ba^{2+} is

$$n_{Ba^{2+}} = 0.0063 \text{ g} \times \left(\frac{1 \text{ mol BaCrO}_4}{253 \text{ g BaCrO}_4}\right) \times \left(\frac{1 \text{ mol Ba}^{2+}}{1 \text{ mol BaCrO}_4}\right) = 2.49 \times 10^{-5} \text{ mol}$$

The initial concentration of Ba^{2+} ion equals 2.49×10^{-5} M, if the volume of the cooled solution is taken as 1.00 L.[3] The initial concentration of the CrO_4^{2-} ion is, by a similar calculation, also equal to 2.49×10^{-5} M. Then:

$$Q_0 = [Ba^{2+}]_0[CrO_4^{2-}]_0 = (2.49 \times 10^{-5})(2.49 \times 10^{-5}) = 6.2 \times 10^{-10}$$

From text Table 11.2, K_{sp} for $BaCrO_4$ equals 2.1×10^{-10}. $\boxed{BaCrO_4 \text{ precipitates}}$ until Q is lowered to equal K_{sp}.

11.19 Calculate the reaction quotient for the reaction:

$$Ce(IO_3)_3(s) \rightleftharpoons Ce^{3+}(aq) + 3\,IO_3^-(aq) \qquad K_{sp} = 1.9 \times 10^{-10}$$

just after the solutions are mixed and compare it to K_{sp}. The desired reaction quotient is $Q = [Ce^{3+}]_0[IO_3^-]_0^3$. where the subscript zero refers to the concentrations prevailing just after mixing. After mixing, the volume of the solution equals 400.0 mL, the sum of the two starting volumes. Mixing dilutes both solutions according to the formula for dilution given on page 158 of the text. Before mixing, the concentration of the Ce^{3+} ion was 0.0020 M. After mixing:

$$[Ce^{3+}]_0 = 0.0020 \text{ M} \times \left(\frac{250.0 \text{ mL}}{400.0 \text{ mL}}\right) = 1.25 \times 10^{-3} \text{ M}$$

Before mixing, the concentration of the IO_3^- ion was 0.010 M. After mixing:

$$[IO_3^-]_0 = 0.010 \text{ M} \times \left(\frac{150.0 \text{ mL}}{400.0 \text{ mL}}\right) = 3.75 \times 10^{-3} \text{ M}$$

---

[2] text page 369.

[3] Doing this ignores the contraction of the water as it cools from 100 to 25°C. It also overlooks the very slight change in volume caused by the dissolution of the barium chromate in hot water in the first place.

$$Q = [Ce^{3+}]_0[IO_3^-]_0^3 = (1.25 \times 10^{-3})(3.75 \times 10^{-3})^3 = 0.66 \times 10^{-10}$$

Q is less than K_{sp}; $\boxed{\text{no precipitate forms}}$.

11.21 The 50.0 mL of 0.0500 M $Pb(NO_3)_2$ dissolves to give 2.50 mmol of $Pb^{2+}(aq)$ ion; the 40.0 mL of 0.200 $NaIO_3$ gives 8.00 mmol of $IO_3^-(aq)$ ion. The two react:

$$Pb^{2+}(aq) + 2\,IO_3^-(aq) \rightleftharpoons Pb(IO_3)_2(s)$$

Assume that this reaction goes to completion. Then zero Pb^{2+} ion remains in solution (it is the limiting reactant), but $8.00 - 2(2.50) = 3.00$ mmol of IO_3^- remains in solution. The concentration of the excess IO_3^- is 3.00 mmol/90.00 mL = 0.0333 M. For a fact, the reaction does not go to completion, but stops short in the equilibrium state. And if it did go to completion, a small amount of the precipitate would soon redissolve anyway:

$$Pb(IO_3^-)_2(s) \rightleftharpoons Pb^{2+}(aq) + 2\,IO_3^-(aq) \qquad K_{sp} = [Pb^{2+}][IO_3^-]^2 = 2.6 \times 10^{-13}$$

The equilibrium state is of course the same regardless of how it is attained. Let S equal the concentration of Pb^{2+} furnished by back-reaction:

	$Pb(IO_3)_2(s) \rightleftharpoons$	$Pb^{2+}(aq) +$	$2\,IO_3^-(aq)$
Init. Conc. (mol L^{-1})	–	0.0	0.0333
Change in Conc. (mol L^{-1})	–	$+S$	$+2S$
Equil. Conc. (mol L^{-1})	–	S	$0.0333 + 2S$

Substitution from the third line of the table into the K_{sp} expression gives:

$$(S)(0.0333 + 2S)^2 = 2.6 \times 10^{-13}$$

This cubic equation is simplified by assuming that $2S << 0.0333$. Then:

$$(0.0333)^2(S) = 2.6 \times 10^{-13} \qquad \text{which gives} \qquad S = 2.3 \times 10^{-10}$$

Hence: $[Pb^{2+}] = \boxed{2.3 \times 10^{-10}\ \text{M}}$ and $[IO_3^-] = \boxed{0.033\ \text{M}}$. The assumption that $2S$ was much smaller than 0.0333 was obviously justified.

11.23 Follow the procedure used in **11.21**. The solution contains 5.00 mmol of $AgNO_3$ and 1.8 mmol of Na_2CrO_4 after mixing but before reaction. Assume that the precipitation reaction:

$$2\,Ag^+(aq) + CrO_4^{2-}(aq) \rightleftharpoons Ag_2CrO_4(s)$$

goes to completion. As it does, it consumes 2 mmol of Ag^+ for every 1 mmol of CrO_4^{2-} ion. Because the chemical amount of Ag^+ ion is more than twice that of CrO_4^{2-} ion, CrO_4^{2-} ion is the limiting reactant. The chemical amount of Ag^+ ion left in excess is $5.00 - 2(1.80) = 1.40$ mmol. The concentration of the Ag^+ ion equals this amount divided by the volume of the solution:

$$[Ag^+] = \frac{1.40\ \text{mmol}}{(50.0 + 30.0)\ \text{mL}} = 0.01750\ \text{M}$$

Now let some of the precipitate redissolve:

$$Ag_2CrO_4(s) \rightleftharpoons 2\,Ag^+(aq) + CrO_4^{2-}(aq) \qquad K_{sp} = 1.9 \times 10^{-12} = [Ag^+]^2[CrO_4^{2-}]$$

Let S equal the concentration of CrO_4^{2-} in solution after this equilibrium is attained. The concentration of Ag^+ ion is $0.1750 + 2S$ and:

$$K_{sp} = (0.01750 + 2S)^2 S$$

Assume that $2S$ is much smaller than 0.0175. Then:

$$(0.01750)^2 S = 1.9 \times 10^{-12} \quad \text{which gives} \quad S = 6.2 \times 10^{-9}$$

The final concentrations of the two ions are:

$$[CrO_4^{2-}] = \boxed{6.2 \times 10^{-9}\ \text{M}} \qquad [Ag^+] = 0.01750 + 2(6.2 \times 10^{-9}) = \boxed{0.018\ \text{M}}$$

11.25 The $F^-(aq)$ ion from the dissolved NaF depresses the solubility of CaF_2. This is the common-ion effect. CaF_2 dissolves according to the equation:

	$CaF_2(s) \rightleftharpoons$	$Ca^{2+}(aq)\ +$	$2\,F^-(aq)$
Init. Conc. (mol L^{-1})	–	0.0	0.040
Change in Conc. (mol L^{-1})	–	$+S$	$+2S$
Equil. Conc. (mol L^{-1})	–	S	$0.040 + 2S$

where S is the solubility of the CaF_2. For this dissolution reaction:

$$K_{sp} = [Ca^{2+}][F^-]^2 = 3.9 \times 10^{-11}$$

Substitute the equilibrium concentrations from the table, assuming that $2S << 0.040$:

$$S(0.040)^2 = 3.9 \times 10^{-11} \quad \text{which gives} \quad S = 2.4 \times 10^{-8}$$

The computed value is S is indeed much smaller than 0.040, so the assumption is justified. The solubility of the CaF_2 is $\boxed{2.4 \times 10^{-8}\ \text{mol L}^{-1}}$.

11.27 a) For every y mol L^{-1} of $Ni(OH)_2$ that is dissolved at equilibrium, y mol L^{-1} of Ni^{2+} and $2y$ mol L^{-1} of OH^- have formed according to the equation:

$$Ni(OH)_2(s) \rightleftharpoons Ni^{2+}(aq) + 2\,OH^-(aq) \qquad [Ni^{2+}][OH^-]^2 = K_{sp} = 1.6 \times 10^{-16}$$

Substituting into the K_{sp} expression gives the equation: $(y)(2y)^2 = 1.6 \times 10^{-16}$. Solving gives $y = 3.4 \times 10^{-6}$. The solubility of $Ni(OH)_2$ is $\boxed{3.4 \times 10^{-6}\ \text{mol L}^{-1}}$.

b) The presence of a common ion (the OH^- ion) reduces the solubility of the nickel(II) hydroxide. Set up the usual three-line table:

	$Ni(OH)_2(s) \rightleftharpoons$	$Ni^{2+}(aq)+$	$2\,OH^-(aq)$
Init. Conc. (mol L^{-1})	–	0	0.100
Change in Conc. (mol L^{-1})	–	$+z$	$+2z$
Equil. Conc. (mol L^{-1})	–	z	$0.100 + 2z$

Substitute the equilibrium concentrations into the K_{sp} expression:

$$K_{sp} = [Ni^{2+}][OH^-]^2 = z((0.100 + 2z)^2 = 1.6 \times 10^{-16}$$

If $2z << 0.100$, then:

$$(0.100)^2(z) = 1.6 \times 10^{-16} \quad \text{so that} \quad z = 1.6 \times 10^{-14}$$

Clearly, $2z$ is very small compared to 0.100; the solubility is $\boxed{1.6 \times 10^{-14}\ \text{mol L}^{-1}}$.

11.29 As long as the solution is in equilibrium with $Mg(OH)_2(s)$, the following holds:

$$K_{sp} = 1.2 \times 10^{-11} = [Mg^{2+}][OH^-]^2$$

Let S represent the solubility of the $Mg(OH)_2$ *before* any NaOH is added. At this stage:

$$[Mg^{2+}] = S \text{ and } [OH^-] = 2S \qquad \text{so that} \qquad 1.2 \times 10^{-11} = [Mg^{2+}][OH^-]^2 = 4\,S^3$$

Solving gives $S = 1.44 \times 10^{-4}$ mol L^{-1}. Sodium hydroxide dissociates completely to $Na^+(aq)$ and $OH^-(aq)$ ions. Thus, the concentration of OH^- goes up with the addition of NaOH, and the concentration of Mg^{2+} must diminish to maintain the mass-action expression at a constant value. Additional magnesium hydroxide precipitates as NaOH is added. This is the common-ion effect in action. The problem states that the solubility of $Mg(OH)_2$ is reduced to 0.0010 of its original value. This means that after the addition:

$$[Mg^{2+}] = 0.0010(1.44 \times 10^{-4}) = 1.44 \times 10^{-7} \text{ M}$$

Then:

$$[OH^-] = \sqrt{\frac{K_{sp}}{[Mg^{2+}]}} = \sqrt{\frac{1.2 \times 10^{-11}}{1.44 \times 10^{-7}}} = \boxed{9.1 \times 10^{-3} \text{ M}}$$

11.31 If y mol L^{-1} of AgOH(s) dissolves, then y mol L^{-1} of Ag^+ and y mol L^{-1} of OH^- ions are produced. Assume that the concentration of OH^- ion from the dissolution greatly exceeds the concentration of OH^- ion from the autoionization of water:

	AgOH(s) ⇌	$Ag^+(aq)$ +	$OH^-(aq)$
Init. Conc. (mol L^{-1})	–	0.0	small
Change in Conc. (mol L^{-1})	–	$+y$	$+y$
Equil. Conc. (mol L^{-1})	–	y	y

At equilibrium:

$$K_{sp} = [Ag^+][OH^-] = y^2 = 1.5 \times 10^{-8} \quad \text{so that} \quad y = 1.2 \times 10^{-4} \text{ M}$$

The molar solubility of AgOH in water equals $\boxed{0.00012 \text{ mol L}^{-1}}$.

If the solution is buffered at pH 7.00, then the pH stays at 7.00 even though the dissociation of AgOH produces OH^-. A pH of 7.00 means $[OH^-] = 1.0 \times 10^{-7}$ M. Put this concentration into the K_{sp}-expression to obtain the equilibrium concentration of $Ag^+(aq)$:

$$[Ag^+] = \frac{K_{sp}}{[OH^-]} = \frac{1.5 \times 10^{-8}}{1.0 \times 10^{-7}} = 0.15 \text{ M}$$

The solubility of the AgOH(s) equals the chemical amount of Ag^+ ion in solution per liter; it is therefore $\boxed{0.15 \text{ mol L}^{-1}}$ in water buffered at pH 7. This solubility is 1250 times larger than the solubility of AgOH in pure water.

11.33 a) The solubility of PbI_2 will remain $\boxed{\text{unchanged}}$ as the pH of its solution is lowered. The anion is an exceedingly weak base; it has little interaction with H_3O^+ even at a high concentration of H_3O^+.

b) The solubility of AgOH will $\boxed{\text{increase}}$ as the pH of its solution is lowered. The additional H_3O^+ drives additional dissolution by removing OH^- ion.

c) The solubility of $Ca_3(PO_4)_2$ will $\boxed{\text{increase}}$ as the pH of its solution is lowered from 7. A higher concentration of H_3O^+ drives the dissolution by removing product PO_4^{3-} ion as HPO_4^{2-} ion.

11.35 **a)** Imagine slowly adding oxalate ion to the mixture containing Mg^{2+} and Pb^{2+} ions. Both oxalate salts will stay in solution until their respective reaction quotients exceed their K_{sp}'s. The equilibria and K_{sp} expressions are:

$$PbC_2O_4(s) \rightleftharpoons Pb^{2+}(aq) + C_2O_4^{2-}(aq) \qquad [Pb^{2+}][C_2O_4^{2-}] = K_{sp} = 2.7 \times 10^{-11}$$
$$MgC_2O_4(s) \rightleftharpoons Mg^{2+}(aq) + C_2O_4^{2-}(aq) \qquad [Mg^{2+}][C_2O_4^{2-}] = K_{sp} = 8.6 \times 10^{-5}$$

The concentration of oxalate ion needed to precipitate magnesium oxalate from the 1.0 M Mg^{2+} solution is

$$[C_2O_4^{2-}] = \frac{K_{sp}}{[Mg^{2+}]} = \frac{8.6 \times 10^{-5}}{0.10} = 8.6 \times 10^{-4}\ \text{M}$$

If the $[C_2O_4^{2-}]$ is kept at or below $\boxed{8.6 \times 10^{-4}\ \text{M}}$, then magnesium oxalate cannot precipitate. Only the lead oxalate can precipitate. The lead salt precipitates first because its solubility is smaller than that of the magnesium salt.

b) If the $[C_2O_4^{2-}]$ is held at 8.6×10^{-4} M, then:

$$[Pb^{2+}] = \frac{K_{sp}}{[C_2O_4^{2-}]} = \frac{2.7 \times 10^{-11}}{8.6 \times 10^{-4}} = 3.1 \times 10^{-8}\ \text{M}$$

$$\text{fraction } Pb^{2+} \text{remaining} = \frac{3.1 \times 10^{-8}\ \text{M}}{0.10\ \text{M}} = \boxed{3.1 \times 10^{-7}}$$

11.37 Calculate the $[I^-]$ that just suffices to bring about precipitation of each metal ion. The dissolution reactions and their K_{sp}'s are:

$$Hg_2I_2(s) \rightleftharpoons Hg_2^{2+}(aq) + 2\,I^-(aq) \qquad K_{sp} = 1.2 \times 10^{-28} = [Hg_2^{2+}][I^-]^2$$
$$PbI_2(s) \rightleftharpoons Pb^{2+}(aq) + 2\,I^-(aq) \qquad K_{sp} = 1.4 \times 10^{-8} = [Pb^{2+}][I^-]^2$$

The required concentration is quite small in the case of $Hg_2I_2(s)$ because K_{sp} is very small. In the case of $PbI_2(s)$ the required concentration is

$$[I^-] = \sqrt{\frac{1.4 \times 10^{-8}}{0.0500}} = 5.3 \times 10^{-4}\ \text{M}$$

The optimum $[I^-]$ would be just below $\boxed{5.3 \times 10^{-4}\ \text{M}}$. If the concentration of I^- is set to this value, then $PbI_2(s)$ cannot precipitate, but almost all of the $Hg_2^{2+}(aq)$ will precipitate as $Hg_2I_2(s)$.

11.39 Metal ions form sulfides of greatly varying but generally low solubility. Careful control of the pH, which strongly affects these solubilities, allows the separation of the metal ions by differential precipitation of the sulfides. The dissolution of zinc sulfide is represented:

$$ZnS(s) + H_2O(l) \rightleftharpoons Zn^{2+}(aq) + HS^-(aq) + OH^-(aq) \qquad [Zn^{2+}][HS^-][OH^-] = K$$

The equilibrium expression is a triple product, but is otherwise not exceptional. Both the OH^- and HS^- concentrations depend strongly on the concentration of H_3O^+ according to the equations:

$$2\,H_2O(l) \rightleftharpoons H_3O^+(aq) + OH^-(aq) \qquad K_w = [H_3O^+][OH^-]$$
$$H_2S(aq) + H_2O(aq) \rightleftharpoons H_3O^+(aq) + HS^-(aq) \qquad K_{a1} = \frac{[HS^-][H_3O^+]}{[H_2S]}$$

Solve the equations for $[OH^-]$ and $[HS^-]$, and substitute into the triple-product K expression:

$$[Zn^{2+}]\left(\frac{K_{a1}[H_2S]}{[H_3O^+]}\right)\left(\frac{K_w}{[H_3O^+]}\right) = K$$

The K_{a1} of H_2S equals 9.1×10^{-8}; K_w equals 1.0×10^{-14}; the concentration of H_2S equals 0.10 M; the concentration of H_3O^+ equals 1.0×10^{-5} M; and K is 2×10^{-25}.[4] Solve for the concentration of Zn^{2+}, and insert the numbers:

$$[Zn^{2+}] = K\left(\frac{[H_3O^+]}{K_{a1}[H_2S]}\right)\left(\frac{[H_3O^+]}{K_w}\right)$$
$$= 2 \times 10^{-25}\left(\frac{1.0 \times 10^{-5}}{(9.1 \times 10^{-8})(0.10)}\right)\left(\frac{1.0 \times 10^{-5}}{1.0 \times 10^{-14}}\right) = \boxed{2 \times 10^{-13}\text{ M}}$$

11.41 Precipitation of FeS(s) can begin only if the pH is high enough to make the reaction quotient Q for the reaction:

$$\text{FeS}(s) + \text{H}_2\text{O}(l) \rightleftharpoons \text{Fe}^{2+}(aq) + \text{HS}^-(aq) + \text{OH}^-(aq) \qquad [\text{Fe}^{2+}][\text{HS}^-][\text{OH}^-] = 5 \times 10^{-19}$$

exceed the K.[5] Compute the $[H_3O^+]$ that barely causes FeS(s) to precipitate. This concentration is reached when the following equation (obtained as in **11.39**) is satisfied:

$$[Fe^{2+}]\left(\frac{K_{a1}[H_2S]}{[H_3O^+]}\right)\left(\frac{K_w}{[H_3O^+]}\right) = 5 \times 10^{-19}$$

Solve for $[H_3O^+]$ and substitute the various numbers. The K_{a1} of H_2S equals 9.1×10^{-8}; K_w equals 1.0×10^{-14}; the concentration of H_2S is 0.10 M; the concentration of Fe^{2+} is 0.10 M:

$$[H_3O^+] = \sqrt{\frac{[Fe^{2+}]K_{a1}[H_2S]K_w}{5 \times 10^{-19}}}$$
$$= \sqrt{\frac{(0.10)(9.1 \times 10^{-8})(0.10)(1.0 \times 10^{-14})}{5 \times 10^{-19}}} = 4.3 \times 10^{-3}\text{ M}$$

This is the minimum concentration of H_3O^+ that keeps FeS in solution. The maximum pH is therefore $\boxed{2.4}$. Higher pH, (implying lower $[H_3O^+]$ and higher $[OH^-]$) shifts the dissolution reaction to the left, causing a precipitate.

The dissolution of PbS(s) is similar to that of FeS(s):

$$\text{PbS}(s) + \text{H}_2\text{O}(l) \rightleftharpoons \text{Pb}^{2+}(aq) + \text{HS}^-(aq) + \text{OH}^-(aq) \qquad [\text{Pb}^{2+}][\text{HS}^-][\text{OH}^-] = 3 \times 10^{-28}$$

and the expression:

$$[Pb^{2+}]\left(\frac{K_{a1}[H_2S]}{[H_3O^+]}\right)\left(\frac{K_w}{[H_3O^+]}\right) = 3 \times 10^{-28}$$

is therefore easily written. Substitution of 0.10 for $[H_2S]$, 4.3×10^{-3} for $[H_3O^+]$, and 9.1×10^{-8} for K_{a1} gives $[Pb^{2+}]$ equal to $\boxed{6 \times 10^{-11}\text{ M}}$, which is very small.

Tip. The point is that at pH 2.4, all the Fe^{2+} but (essentially) none of the Pb^{2+} stays in solution.

---

[4] See text Table 11.4, text page 378.

[5] The K's in this problem come from text Table 11.3.

11.43 The copper(II) nitrate dissolves readily to give $Cu^{2+}(aq)$ and NO_3^- ions. Imagine that the $Cu^{2+}(aq)$ reacts to completion with the $NH_3(aq)$ (which is in excess) to form $Cu(NH_3)_4^{2+}(aq)$:

$$Cu^{2+}(aq) + 4\,NH_3(aq) \rightarrow Cu(NH_3)_4^{2+}(aq)$$

Then:

$$[Cu(NH_3)_4^{2+}] = 0.10 \text{ M} \quad \text{and} \quad [NH_3] = 1.50 - 4(0.10) = 1.10 \text{ M}$$

Now, imagine free Cu^{2+} ion to come from back-reaction (dissociation of $Cu(NH_3)_4^{2+}$). The back-reaction, or dissociation, would proceed in four steps:

$$Cu(NH_3)_4^{2+}(aq) \rightleftharpoons Cu(NH_3)_3^{2+}(aq) + NH_3(aq) \qquad \frac{[Cu(NH_3)_3^{2+}][NH_3]}{[Cu(NH_3)_4^{2+}]} = 1.1 \times 10^{-2}$$

$$Cu(NH_3)_3^{2+}(aq) \rightleftharpoons Cu(NH_3)_2^{2+}(aq) + NH_3(aq) \qquad \frac{[Cu(NH_3)_2^{2+}][NH_3]}{[Cu(NH_3)_3^{2+}]} = 2 \times 10^{-3}$$

$$Cu(NH_3)_2^{2+}(aq) \rightleftharpoons Cu(NH_3)^{2+}(aq) + NH_3(aq) \qquad \frac{[Cu(NH_3)^{2+}][NH_3]}{[Cu(NH_3)_2^{2+}]} = 5 \times 10^{-4}$$

$$Cu(NH_3)^{2+}(aq) \rightleftharpoons Cu^{2+}(aq) + NH_3(aq) \qquad \frac{[Cu^{2+}][NH_3]}{[Cu(NH_3)^{2+}]} = 1.0 \times 10^{-4}$$

where the four constants equal the reciprocals of K_4 through K_1 in text Table 11.4.[6] Label the concentrations of the four Cu-containing products x, y, z, and w respectively, and calculate them in turn. Treat the steps as if they occurred independently. That is, neglect the amount of Cu-containing product reacted away by later steps and assume that NH_3 from later steps adds only negligibly to the 1.10 M NH_3 present when dissociation starts. For the first step:

	$Cu(NH_3)_4^{2+}(aq) \rightleftharpoons$	$Cu(NH_3)_3^{2+}(aq)$	$+\ NH_3(aq)$
Init. Conc. (mol L^{-1})	0.10	0	1.1
Change in Conc. (mol L^{-1})	$-x$	$+x$	$+x$
Equil. Conc. (mol L^{-1})	$0.10 - x$	x	$1.1 + x$

$$\frac{[Cu(NH_3)_3^{2+}][NH_3]}{[Cu(NH_3)_4^{2+}]} = 1.1 \times 10^{-2} = \frac{x(1.1 + x)}{0.10 - x} \quad \text{which gives} \quad x = 9.9 \times 10^{-4}$$

The set-up for the second step is similar. It gives

$$\frac{[Cu(NH_3)_2^{2+}][NH_3]}{[Cu(NH_3)_3^{2+}]} = 2 \times 10^{-3} = \frac{y(1.1 + y)}{9.9 \times 10^{-4} - y} \quad \text{from which:} \quad y = 1.8 \times 10^{-6}$$

For the third step:

$$\frac{[Cu(NH_3)^{2+}][NH_3]}{[Cu(NH_3)_2^{2+}]} = 5 \times 10^{-4} = \frac{z(1.1 + z)}{1.8 \times 10^{-6} - z} \quad \text{which gives} \quad z = 8.2 \times 10^{-10}$$

For the fourth step:

$$\frac{[Cu^{2+}][NH_3]}{[Cu(NH_3)^{2+}]} = 1.0 \times 10^{-4} = \frac{w(1.1 + w)}{8.2 \times 10^{-10} - w} \quad \text{which gives} \quad w = 7.4 \times 10^{-14}$$

---

[6] See text page 380. The product of K_1 through K_4 equals 0.9×10^{12}, but K_f equals 1.1×10^{12} in the table. This inconsistency arises from rounding off the step-wise K's and is unimportant.

This w equals the concentration of free Cu^{2+}. The concentrations of the partially dissociated complexes are low. Indeed, all dissociation reduces the concentration of $Cu(NH_3)_4^{2+}$ by less than 1%. Therefore:

$$[Cu^{2+}] = \boxed{7 \times 10^{-14} \text{ mol L}^{-1}} \qquad [Cu(NH_3)_4^{2+}] = \boxed{0.10 \text{ mol L}^{-1}}$$

11.45 Assume that the reaction between $K^+(aq)$ and "crown" goes 100% to completion and that free K^+ then comes from back-dissociation of $(Kcrown)^+(aq)$. The equation for this dissociation is the reverse of the equation in the problem:

	$(\text{Kcrown})^+(aq) \rightleftharpoons$	$K^+(aq)$ +	$\text{crown}(aq)$
Init. Conc. (mol L^{-1})	0.0080	0	0
Change in Conc. (mol L^{-1})	$-x$	$+x$	$+x$
Equil. Conc. (mol L^{-1})	$0.0080 - x$	x	x

The reaction has the mass-action expression and K:

$$\frac{[K^+][\text{crown}]}{[(\text{Kcrown})^+]} = \frac{1}{111.6} \qquad \text{hence:} \qquad \frac{1}{111.6} = \frac{x^2}{0.080 - x}$$

Rearranging gives the quadratic equation:

$$x^2 + (8.961 \times 10^{-3})x - 7.169 \times 10^{-5} = 0$$

Solving for x gives 0.0051; the equilibrium concentration of $K^+(aq)$ is $\boxed{0.0051 \text{ M}}$. Calculation of the concentration of free Na^+ proceeds similarly. The analogous quadratic equation is

$$y^2 + 0.152y - 0.00122 = 0$$

(where y is the concentration of free Na^+ ion) based on a K of 1/6.6 instead of 1/111.6. Solving the new equation gives an Na^+ ion concentration of $\boxed{0.0076 \text{ M}}$.

11.47 The problem really asks for a calculation of the solubility of AgCl in a solution that is 1.00 M in Cl^- ion. Let S equal this solubility. For every mole per liter of AgCl that dissolves, either an Ag^+ ion or an $AgCl_2^-$ ion[7] forms. In mathematical form:

$$S = [Ag^+] + [AgCl_2^-]$$

Obviously, this assumes that all of the dissolved silver is present as one of two ions. The solubility equilibrium for AgCl assures that:

$$K_{sp} = 1.6 \times 10^{-10} = [Ag^+][Cl^-]$$

as long as solid silver chloride is present. The formation equilibrium for the $AgCl_2^-$ complex ion means:

$$\frac{[AgCl_2^-]}{[Ag^+][Cl^-]^2} = K_f = 1.8 \times 10^5$$

Solve these equations for $[Ag^+]$ and $[AgCl_2^-]$ and substitute the results into the expression for S:

$$S = \frac{1.6 \times 10^{-10}}{[Cl^-]} + (1.8 \times 10^5)(1.6 \times 10^{-10})[Cl^-]$$

---

[7] Dichloroargenate(I) ion.

Assume that the concentration of Cl^- ion is so large at 1.00 M that it is not substantially reduced by reaction with Ag^+ ion. If $[Cl^-] = 1.00$ M, then:

$$S = \frac{1.6 \times 10^{-10}}{1.00} + (1.8 \times 10^5)(1.6 \times 10^{-10})[1.00] = 2.8 \times 10^{-5} \text{ M}$$

The assumption that $[Cl^-]$ is only negligibly reduced from its original value is vindicated by this low solubility—only about 6×10^{-5} M of Cl^- ion is tied up in the complex. The solubility of AgCl in this solution is more than double the solubility of AgCl in pure water, which equals 1.3×10^{-5} M (by a computation like the one in **11.7**). Hence, AgCl(s) is [more soluble] in 1.00 M NaCl than in pure water.

In 0.100 M NaCl, in which $[Cl^-]$ is 0.100 M, the equation for S becomes:

$$S = \frac{1.6 \times 10^{-10}}{0.100} + (1.8 \times 10^5)(1.6 \times 10^{-10})[0.100] = 2.9 \times 10^{-6} \text{ M}$$

AgCl is [less soluble] in dilute NaCl than in pure water.

Tip. The reversal is remarkable. Complexation plays a potent role in determining solubilities.

11.49 $CuSO_4$ dissolves to give $Cu^{2+}(aq)$ and $SO_4^{2-}(aq)$. The aquated Cu^{2+} ion exists as the $Cu(H_2O)_4^{2+}$ complex ion. This ion acts as a Brønsted-Lowry acid according to the equation:

$$\boxed{Cu(H_2O)_4^{2+}(aq) + H_2O(l) \rightleftharpoons H_3O^+(aq) + Cu(H_2O)_3OH^+(aq)}$$

The solution is [acidic] because the K_a for the complex exceeds K_b for the SO_4^{2-} ion. An equivalent answer is the equation:

$$Cu^{2+}(aq) + 2\,H_2O(l) \rightleftharpoons H_3O^+(aq) + (CuOH)^+(aq)$$

11.51 The computation is like other computations of the pH of solutions of weak acids.[8] The coordinated cobalt(II) ion is acidic:

	$Co(H_2O)_6^{2+}$ $+H_2O \rightleftharpoons$	$H_3O^+(aq)$ +	$Co(H_2O)_5OH^+$
Init. Conc. (mol L^{-1})	0.10	small	0
Change in Conc. (mol L^{-1})	$-x$	$+x$	$+x$
Equil. Conc. (mol L^{-1})	$0.10 - x$	x	x

The equilibrium expression is

$$\frac{[H_3O^+][Co(H_2O)_5OH^+]}{[Co(H_2O)_6^{2+}]} = K_a = 3 \times 10^{-10} = \frac{x^2}{0.10 - x}$$

Solve the equation to obtain $x = 5.5 \times 10^{-6}$. The concentration of H_3O^+ is 5.5×10^{-6} M, and the pH is therefore [5.3].

11.53 The reaction: $Pt(NH_3)_4^{2+}(aq) + H_2O(l) \rightleftharpoons H_3O^+(aq) + Pt(NH_3)_3NH_2^+(aq)$ causes the acidity of the solution. The mass-action expression for this reaction is

$$\frac{[Pt(NH_3)_3NH_2^+][H_3O^+]}{[Pt(NH_3)_4^{2+}]} = K_a$$

The concentration of the $Pt(NH_3)_3NH_2^+$ ion equals the concentration of the H_3O^+ ion in solution as long as this reaction is the only source of either ion. The concentration of the $Pt(NH_3)_4^{2+}$ ion equals 0.15 M

[8] Such as problem 10-29a.

minus the concentration of H_3O^+ ion. The H_3O^+ concentration can be calculated from the pH given in the problem:

$$[H_3O^+] = 10^{-4.92} = 1.20 \times 10^{-5} \text{ M}$$

Substitute this and the other concentrations in the K_a-expression:

$$K_a = \frac{(1.20 \times 10^{-5})(1.20 \times 10^{-5})}{0.15 - 1.20 \times 10^{-5}} = \boxed{9.6 \times 10^{-10}}$$

11.55 The problem concerns the fate of $Pb^{2+}(aq)$ in a solution adjusted to pH 13.0 by the addition of NaOH. The precipitation reaction:

$$Pb^{2+}(aq) + 2\,OH^-(aq) \rightleftharpoons Pb(OH)_2(s)$$

tends to reduce the concentration of $Pb^{2+}(aq)$. The K for this reaction is the reciprocal of the K_{sp} of $Pb(OH)_2(s)$. It is quite large (K_{sp} is 4.2×10^{-15} so $1/K_{sp}$ is 2.38×10^{14}). This apparently means that 1.00 M Pb^{2+} ion gives a precipitate of $Pb(OH)_2(s)$ at pH 13.0. But there is a complication. The equilibrium:

$$Pb^{2+}(aq) + 3\,OH^-(aq) \rightleftharpoons Pb(OH)_3^-(aq)$$

ties up Pb^{2+} ion in a *soluble* form, thereby opposing precipitation of $Pb(OH)_2(s)$. The K for this reaction is K_f for $Pb(OH)_3^-(aq)$ and is large (4×10^{14}). Whether $Pb(OH)_2$ precipitates depends how the competition between these reactions plays out.

Suppose $Pb(OH)_2(s)$ *does* precipitate. Then, at pH 13.0, where $[OH^-] = 0.10$ M, the concentration of Pb^{2+} must fulfill the equation:

$$K_{sp} = 4.2 \times 10^{-15} = [Pb^{2+}][OH^-]^2 = [Pb^{2+}](0.10)^2$$

This means $[Pb^{2+}]$ is locked at 4.2×10^{-13} M if solid $Pb(OH)_2$ is present. The mass-action expression for the complexation equilibrium is

$$K_f = 4 \times 10^{14} = \frac{[Pb(OH)_3^-]}{[Pb^{2+}][OH^-]^3}$$

Substitute $[OH^-] = 0.10$ and $[Pb^{2+}] = 4.2 \times 10^{-13}$ M, and solve for $[Pb(OH)_3^-]$. The answer is 0.17 M. Any concentration of Pb^{2+} ion that exceeds this threshold value causes precipitation. Because 1.00 M exceeds 0.17 M, $Pb(OH)_2(s)$ precipitates in the case defined in this problem. At equilibrium, $[Pb^{2+}]$ equals $\boxed{4.2 \times 10^{-13} \text{ M}}$, and the concentration of $Pb(OH)_3^-$ equals $\boxed{0.17 \text{ M}}$.

An initial concentration of 0.050 M Pb^{2+}, is less than the precipitation threshold of 0.17 M. There is no precipitate of $Pb(OH)_2(s)$. The K_{sp} equilibrium is *not* in effect. Essentially all of the Pb^{2+} ion is tied up in the complex, making the concentration of $Pb(OH)_3^-$ equal $\boxed{0.050 \text{ M}}$. Put this value into the K_f mass-action expression:

$$K_f = 4 \times 10^{14} = \frac{[Pb(OH)_3^-]}{[Pb^{2+}][OH^-]^3} = \frac{0.050}{[Pb^{2+}](0.10)^3}$$

Solving gives the concentration of free $Pb^{2+}(aq)$ as $\boxed{1 \times 10^{-13} \text{ M}}$.

11.57 The mercury(I) ion exists as Hg_2^{2+} in aqueous solution, according to text Table 11.2 and **11.11**. The dissolution equilibrium is

$$Hg_2Cl_2(s) \rightleftharpoons Hg_2^{2+}(aq) + 2\,Cl^-(aq) \qquad K_{sp} = [Hg_2^{2+}][Cl^-]^2$$

11.59 The dissolution of barium sulfate is represented:

$$BaSO_4(s) \rightleftharpoons Ba^{2+}(aq) + SO_4^{2-}(aq) \qquad [Ba^{2+}][SO_4^{2-}] = K_{sp} = 1.1 \times 10^{-10}$$

If the equilibrium concentration of Ba^{2+} equals x, then the concentration of SO_4^{2-} is also x, as long as there are no additional sources (or sinks) of either ion. Then $x^2 = 1.1 \times 10^{-10}$ so that $x = [Ba^{2+}] = \boxed{1.1 \times 10^{-5}\ \text{M}}$. This concentration is too low for any bad effects on patients drinking the suspension of $BaSO_4(s)$.

11.61 It takes 860 mL of 0.0050 M NaF to make 1.00 L of solution when mixed with 140 mL of 0.0010 M $Sr(NO_3)_2$. Just after mixing, but before any precipitation reactions occur, the concentrations of Sr^{2+} and F^- ions are:

$$[Sr^{2+}] = \left(\frac{140}{1000}\right) 0.0010 = 1.4 \times 10^{-4}\ \text{M} \qquad [F^-] = \left(\frac{860}{1000}\right) 0.0050 = 4.3 \times 10^{-4}\ \text{M}$$

The mixture will tend to precipitate SrF_2 only if the initial reaction quotient Q_0 exceeds K_{sp} for the reaction:

$$SrF_2(s) \rightleftharpoons Sr^{2+}(aq) + 2\,F^-(aq)$$

The value of Q_0 is computed by substitution of the initial concentrations into the mass-action expression:

$$Q_0 = [Sr^{2+}]_0[F^-]_0^2 = (1.4 \times 10^{-4})(4.3 \times 10^{-4})^2 = 2.6 \times 10^{-9}$$

Because Q_0 is less than K_{sp} (which equals 2.8×10^{-9}), there is $\boxed{\text{no precipitate of } SrF_2}$ at equilibrium.

Tip. The volumes of differing aqueous solutions are not in general additive (that is, 160 mL of solution A mixed with 840 mL of solution B does *not* always give 1000 mL of solution). However, these solutions are so dilute that additivity can be assumed.

11.63 The K_2CO_3 and $Ca(NO_3)_2$ are both strong electrolytes. They dissolve in water by dissociation into ions

$$K_2CO_3(s) \rightarrow 2\ K^+(aq) + CO_3^{2-}(aq)$$
$$Ca(NO_3)_2(s) \rightarrow Ca^{2+}(aq) + 2\ NO_3^-(aq)$$

When the two solutions are mixed, insoluble $CaCO_3(aq)$ precipitates according to the net ionic equation

$$Ca^{2+}(aq) + CO_3^{2-}(aq) \rightarrow CaCO_3(s)$$

Compute the chemical amounts of the four ions in the two solutions before the two are mixed

$$n_{K^+} = 0.150\ \text{L solution} \times \left(\frac{0.200\ \text{mol}\ K_2CO_3}{\text{L solution}}\right) \times \left(\frac{2\ \text{mol}\ K^+}{1\ \text{mol}\ K_2CO_3}\right) = 0.060\ \text{mol}\ K^+$$

$$n_{CO_3^{2-}} = 0.150\ \text{L solution} \times \left(\frac{0.200\ \text{mol}\ K_2CO_3}{\text{L solution}}\right) \times \left(\frac{1\ \text{mol}\ CO_3^{2-}}{1\ \text{mol}\ K_2CO_3}\right) = 0.030\ \text{mol}\ CO_3^{2-}$$

$$n_{Ca^{2+}} = 0.100\ \text{L solution} \times \left(\frac{0.400\ \text{mol}\ Ca(NO_3)_2}{\text{L solution}}\right) \times \left(\frac{1\ \text{mol}\ Ca^{2+}}{1\ \text{mol}\ Ca(NO_3)_2}\right) = 0.040\ \text{mol}\ Ca^{2+}$$

$$n_{NO_3^-} = 0.100\ \text{L solution} \times \left(\frac{0.400\ \text{mol}\ Ca(NO_3)_2}{\text{L solution}}\right) \times \left(\frac{2\ \text{mol}\ NO_3^-}{1\ \text{mol}\ Ca(NO_3)_2}\right) = 0.040\ \text{mol}\ NO_3^-$$

The Ca^{2+} ion reacts with CO_3^{2-} ion in a 1 : 1 molar ratio. If the $CaCO_3$ is completely insoluble, this precipitation reaction continues until the entire 0.030 mol of CO_3^{2-} ion, which is the limiting reactant, is consumed. At that point, the chemical amount of $CaCO_3(s)$ on the bottom of the container equals 0.030 mol. The mass of this $CaCO_3$ is

$$m_{CaCO_3} = 0.030 \text{ mol } CaCO_3 \times \left(\frac{100.1 \text{ g } CaCO_3}{\text{mol } CaCO_3}\right) = \boxed{3.0 \text{ g } CaCO_3}$$

Obtain the concentrations of the four ions in the solution by dividing their chemical amounts by the total volume of the solution

$$c_{K^+} = \frac{0.060 \text{ mol } K^+}{(0.250 + 0.100) \text{ L}} = \boxed{0.240 \text{ mol L}^{-1}}$$

$$c_{CO_3^{2-}} = \frac{(0.030 - 0.030) \text{ mol } CO_3^{2-}}{(0.250 + 0.100) \text{ L}} = \boxed{0.00 \text{ mol L}^{-1}}$$

$$c_{Ca^{2+}} = \frac{(0.040 - 0.030) \text{ mol } Ca^{2+}}{(0.250 + 0.100) \text{ L}} = \boxed{0.040 \text{ mol L}^{-1}}$$

$$c_{NO_3^-} = \frac{0.040 \text{ mol } NO_3^-}{(0.250 + 0.100) \text{ L}} = \boxed{0.160 \text{ mol L}^{-1}}$$

11.65 The problem asks what would happen to the aqueous solubility of $CaCO_3$ if CO_2 were extremely soluble in water but the rest of its chemistry were unchanged. Represent the dissolution of calcium carbonate in an aqueous solution of a strong acid as the sum of these four steps:

$$CaCO_3(s) \rightleftharpoons Ca^{2+}(aq) + CO_3^{2-}(aq) \qquad K_1 = K_{sp}$$

$$CO_3^{2-}(aq) + 2\ H_3O^+ \rightleftharpoons H_2CO_3(aq) + 2\ H_2O(l) \qquad K_2 = \frac{1}{K_{a1}K_{a2}}$$

$$H_2CO_3(aq) \rightleftharpoons CO_2(aq) + H_2O(l) \qquad K_3$$

$$CO_2(aq) \rightleftharpoons CO_2(g) \qquad K_4$$

The question amounts to asking what would happen to the position of the first equilibrium in the preceding if K_4 became very small, but the other three K's stayed the same. Changing K_4 would not affect the way the second equilibrium removes CO_3^{2-} from among the products of the first equilibrium. Therefore calcium carbonate would still dissolve in strong acids.

11.67 Two solubility equilibria are going on simultaneously:

$$AgBr(s) \rightleftharpoons Ag^+(aq) + Br^-(aq) \qquad K_{sp} = [Ag^+][Br^-] = 7.7 \times 10^{-13}$$

$$CuBr(s) \rightleftharpoons Cu^+(aq) + Br^-(aq) \qquad K_{sp} = [Cu^+][Br^-] = 4.2 \times 10^{-8}$$

Divide the K_{sp} expression for the second by the K_{sp} for the first:

$$\frac{[Cu^+][Br^-]}{[Ag^+][Br^-]} = \frac{4.2 \times 10^{-8}}{7.7 \times 10^{-13}} = 5.45 \times 10^4$$

A single solution at equilibrium can have only one concentration of Br^- ion (or any other ion). Hence the $[Br^-]$ in the numerator equals the $[Br^-]$ in the denominator. Cancellation then gives:

$$\frac{[Cu^+]}{[Ag^+]} = \boxed{5.5 \times 10^4}$$

11.69 Only when Q exceeds K_{sp} can precipitation begin. Calculate the concentration of Ag^+ that will just suffice to precipitate each salt by setting $Q = K_{sp}$. The equilibria and K_{sp}-expressions are:

$$AgCl(s) \rightleftharpoons Ag^+(aq) + Cl^-(aq) \qquad [Ag^+][Cl^-] = 1.6 \times 10^{-10}$$
$$Ag_2CrO_4(s) \rightleftharpoons 2\,Ag^+(aq) + CrO_4^{2-}(aq) \qquad [Ag^+]^2[CrO_4^{2-}] = 1.9 \times 10^{-12}$$

Inserting the given concentrations of Cl^- and CrO_4^{2-} ions and solving the concentration of Ag^+ ion reveals that precipitation of AgCl(s) requires 1.6×10^{-9} M Ag^+ and that precipitation of $AgCrO_4(s)$ requires is 2.8×10^{-5} M Ag^+. The second is much larger. Thus, $\boxed{AgCl(s)}$ will precipitate first.

Solid Ag_2CrO_4 just starts to come down when $[Ag^+] = 2.8 \times 10^{-5}$ M. Use the K_{sp} expression to calculate $[Cl^-]$ when $[Ag^+] = 2.8 \times 10^{-5}$ M:

$$[Cl^-] = \frac{K_{sp}}{[Ag^+]} = \frac{1.6 \times 10^{-10}}{2.8 \times 10^{-5}} = 5.7 \times 10^{-6}\ \text{M}$$

The fraction of Cl^- remaining is

$$f_{Cl^-} = \frac{[Ag^+]}{[Ag^+]_0} = \frac{5.7 \times 10^{-6}\ \text{M}}{0.100\ \text{M}} = \boxed{5.7 \times 10^{-5}}$$

11.71 Magnesia dissolves in water and raises the pH by generating $OH^-(aq)$ ion:

$$MgO(s) + H_2O(l) \rightleftharpoons Mg^{2+}(aq) + 2\,OH^-(aq) \quad K = [Mg^{2+}][OH^-]^2$$

The pH of the solution at 25°C is 10.16. At this temperature, the sum of the pH and pOH of an aqueous solution equals 14.00. This means that the pOH of the saturated solution of magnesia equals 3.84. By the definition of pOH: $[OH^-] = 10^{-3.84} = 1.44 \times 10^{-4}$ M. Assume that dissolution of magnesia is the predominant source of OH^- in the solution, far outpacing the autoionization of water. Then:

$$2\,[Mg^{2+}] = [OH^-]$$

Substitute to obtain the value of K:

$$K = [Mg^{2+}][OH^-]^2 = \frac{[OH^-]}{2}[OH^-]^2 = \frac{(1.44 \times 10^{-4})^3}{2} = 1.5 \times 10^{-12}$$

The solubility of the MgO equals the final concentration of $Mg^{2+}(aq)$:

$$[Mg^{2+}] = \frac{[OH^-]}{2} = \boxed{7.2 \times 10^{-5}\ \text{mol L}^{-1}}$$

11.73 Silver ion is complexed strongly by ammonia:

$$Ag^+(aq) + 2\,NH_3(aq) \rightleftharpoons Ag(NH_3)_2^{2+}(aq) \qquad K_f = 1.7 \times 10^7$$

When AgBr(s) is placed in aqueous ammonia, a new dissolution reaction:

$$AgBr(s) + 2\,NH_3(aq) \rightleftharpoons Ag(NH_3)_2^{2+}(aq) + Br^-(aq) \qquad K = K_f K_{sp}$$

replaces the "regular" dissolution reaction. The new dissolution reaction equals the sum of the regular K_{sp} reaction and the complexation reaction. Its K is 1.7×10^7 times larger than the K_{sp}, which explains the increase in solubility of AgBr when ammonia is present.

11.75 a) The aqueous HCl reacts with CdS(s) to give both $CdCl_4^{2-}(aq)$ and $H_2S(aq)$:

$$\boxed{CdS(s) + 2\,H_3O^+(aq) + 4\,Cl^-(aq) \rightleftharpoons CdCl_4^{2-}(aq) + H_2S(aq) + 2\,H_2O(l)}$$

The HCl(aq) acts on the CdS(s) by removing both sulfide ion (as H_2S) and cadmium ion (as the tetrachloro complex). The problem states that some CdS(s) remains, so the above equation is an accurate description of the final equilibrium.

b) The equilibrium in the preceding part can be constructed as the sum of four reactions. The first represents the dissolution of CdS(s) in pure water; the second and third represent the acid-base reactions of the HS^- and OH^- ions (both are bases) with water; the fourth represents the complexation of Cd^{2+} by Cl^- ions:

$$\begin{aligned} CdS(s) + H_2O(l) &\rightleftharpoons Cd^{2+}(aq) + OH^-(aq) + HS^-(aq) && K_1 \\ HS^-(aq) + H_2O(l) &\rightleftharpoons H_2S(aq) + OH^-(aq) && K_2 = K_w/K_{a1} \\ 2\,OH^-(aq) + 2\,H_3O^+(aq) &\rightleftharpoons 4\,H_2O(l) && K_3 = (1/K_w)^2 \\ Cd^{2+}(aq) + 4\,Cl^-(aq) &\rightleftharpoons CdCl_4^{2-}(aq) && K_4 = K_f \end{aligned}$$

where K_{a1} is the K_a for the first stage of the acid ionization of $H_2S(aq)$. The equilibrium constants of the four reactions are numbered for identification. The desired constant is the product of the four constants because the equation of interest is the sum of the four equations:

$$K = K_1K_2K_3K_4 = K_1\left(\frac{K_w}{K_{a1}}\right)\left(\frac{1}{K_w}\right)^2(K_f)$$

The text[9] gives K_1 as 7×10^{-28} and K_{a1} as 9.1×10^{-8}. The problem gives K_f as 800. Insert these numbers and the well-known value of K_w into the preceding:

$$K = (7 \times 10^{-28})\left(\frac{1.0 \times 10^{-14}}{9.1 \times 10^{-8}}\right)\left(\frac{1}{1.0 \times 10^{-14}}\right)^2(8 \times 10^2) = 6.2 \times 10^{-4}$$

Thus, at equilibrium:

$$\frac{[CdCl_4^{2-}][H_2S]}{[H_3O^+]^2[Cl^-]^4} = K = \boxed{6 \times 10^{-4}}$$

c) Let S equal the molar solubility of the CdS(s) in 6 M HCl. Assume that at equilibrium the cadmium in solution is all in the form of $CdCl_4^{2-}(aq)$, and that the sulfur in solution is all in the form of $H_2S(aq)$. Then:

$$S = [CdCl_4^{2-}] = [H_2S]$$

Now, every Cd^{2+} ion that goes into solution consumes 4 Cl^- ions, and every S^{2-} ion that goes into solution consumes 2 H_3O^+ ions. This means that are equilibrium

$$[H_3O^+] = 6 - 2S \qquad \text{and} \qquad [Cl^-] = 6 - 4S$$

The 6 comes from the original concentration of HCl, which was 6 M. Substitution in the mass-action expression derived in the preceding parts gives:

$$\frac{[CdCl_4^{2-}][H_2S]}{[H_3O^+]^2[Cl^-]^4} = \frac{S^2}{(6-2S)^2(6-4S)^4} = 6.2 \times 10^{-4}$$

Assuming that S is negligible compared to 6 M in this equation does not lead to an acceptable solution, as it is easy to confirm. However, S must lie between 0 and 6 mol L^{-1}. Guess that S equals 1.0 mol L^{-1}. Then

[9] In text Table 11.3, text page 377, and in Example 11-7.

the left side equals 3.9×10^{-3}, which exceeds 6.2×10^{-4}. Guess a smaller S, such as 0.6 mol L^{-1}. The left side then equals 9.3×10^{-5}, which is less than 6.2×10^{-4}. Further adjustments in the range between 0.6 and 1.0 give improved fits. The value $S = 0.8$ fits the equation fairly well. The solubility of CdS(s) in 6 M HCl is thus apparently 0.8 mol L^{-1}.

Now check assumptions. It was assumed that all of the sulfur in solution was in the form of $H_2S(aq)$. Therefore, the concentration of $H_2S(aq)$ should equal 0.8 M. But this exceeds the solubility of H_2S at room temperature, which is only 0.1 M.[10] Adding 6 M HCl to CdS(s) therefore forces H_2S out of solution. Gaseous H_2S bubbles out until the concentration of $H_2S(aq)$ falls to 0.1 M. The previous equation is replaced by:

$$\frac{S\,(0.1)}{(6 - 2S)^2(6 - 4S)^4} = 6.2 \times 10^{-4}$$

Solving this new equation (by approximation), gives S, the molar solubility of CdS(s), equal to $\boxed{1 \text{ mol L}^{-1}}$.

11.77 The solution is prepared by mixing 0.020 mol of $CuCl_2$ and 0.100 mol of NaCN in 1.0 L of water. The original concentration of Cu^{2+} ion is therefore 0.020 M, and the original concentration of CN^- is 0.100 M. These concentrations do not last long. The $Cu^{2+}(aq)$ ion and $CN^-(aq)$ soon combine to form a complex ion:

$$Cu^{2+}(aq) + 4\,CN^-(aq) \rightleftharpoons Cu(CN)_4^{2-}(aq) \qquad \frac{[Cu(CN)_4^{2-}]}{[Cu^{2+}][CN^-]^4} = K_f = 2 \times 10^{30}$$

The very large K_f means that nearly all of the Cu^{2+} ion is tied up as complex. At equilibrium then, $[Cu(CN)_4^{2-}] = 0.020$ M. Complexation reduces the concentration of CN^- ion, which is in excess, from its original 0.100 M to $0.100 - 4(0.020) = 0.020$ M because 1 mol of Cu^{2+} accounts for 4 mol of $CN^-(aq)$. The values:

$$[CN^-] = 0.020 \text{ M} \quad \text{and} \quad [Cu(CN)_4^{2-}] = 0.020 \text{ M}$$

might now be substituted into the K_f mass-action expression and used to compute an equilibrium concentration of Cu^{2+} ion. However, $CN^-(aq)$ also hydrolyzes (reacts with H_2O) to give HCN(aq):

$$CN^-(aq) + H_2O(l) \rightleftharpoons HCN(aq) + OH^-(aq) \qquad \frac{[HCN][OH^-]}{[CN^-]} = \frac{K_w}{K_a} = 2.03 \times 10^{-5}$$

This reaction lowers the concentration of $CN^-(aq)$ from 0.020 M. Let x equal the concentration of CN^- that reacts in this way. Then:

$$\frac{[HCN][OH^-]}{[CN^-]} = 2.03 \times 10^{-5} = \frac{x^2}{0.020 - x}$$

Solving gives x equal to 6.27×10^{-4} M. The correct equilibrium concentration of CN^- is therefore $0.020 - 6.27 \times 10^{-4} = 0.0194$ M. Put this value into the K_f expression and solve for $[Cu^{2+}]$:

$$\frac{[Cu(CN)_4^{2-}]}{[Cu^{2+}][CN^-]^4} = 2 \times 10^{30} = \frac{(0.020)}{[Cu^{2+}](0.0194)^4} \qquad [Cu^{2+}] = \boxed{7 \times 10^{-26} \text{ M}}$$

Tip. If the hydrolysis of CN^- ion is ignored, the answer is 6×10^{-26} M—barely a significant difference.

11.79 a) Text Example 11.10[11] gives K_{a1} for $Fe(H_2O)_6^{3+}$ as 7.7×10^{-3}. The problem gives K_{a2} as 2.0×10^{-5}. Because K_{a2} is about 400 times smaller than K_{a1}, the second stage of the acid ionization has essentially $\boxed{\text{no effect}}$ on the pH. The pH of the 0.100 M solution of $Fe(NO_3)_3$ is 1.62, based solely on the first H^+-donation. This corresponds to $[H_3O^+] = 2.4 \times 10^{-2}$ M. Thus, considering only the first stage:

$$[H_3O^+] = [Fe(H_2O)_5(OH)^{2+}] = 2.4 \times 10^{-2} \text{ M}$$

---

[10] Aqueous H_2S is saturated at a concentration of 0.1 M. See text Example 11-7, text page 378.

[11] Text page 382.

The K_a- expression for the *second* stage is

$$K_{a2} = 2.0 \times 10^{-5} = \frac{[H_3O^+][Fe(H_2O)_4(OH)_2^+]}{[Fe(H_2O)_5OH^{2+}]}$$

Substitute the concentrations obtained from the first-stage-only calculation into this expression. Solving the resulting equation shows that the $[Fe(H_2O)_4(OH)_2^+]$ ion has a concentration of only $\boxed{2.0 \times 10^{-5}\ \text{M}}$. This concentration is negligible compared to 0.024 M, the concentration of $Fe(H_2O)_5OH^{2+}(aq)$. The $[H_3O^+]$ that arises in the second stage is likewise negligible compared to 0.024 M.

b) The question refers to the dissociation of the $Fe(OH)_2^+$ complex ion. Dissociation proceeds through steps that are the reverse of the steps for formation:

$$Fe(OH)_2^+(aq) \rightleftharpoons Fe(OH)^{2+}(aq) + OH^-(aq) \qquad \frac{[Fe(OH)^{2+}][OH^-]}{[Fe(OH)_2^+]} = K_{d1}$$

$$Fe(OH)^{2+}(aq) \rightleftharpoons Fe^{3+}(aq) + OH^-(aq) \qquad \frac{[Fe^{3+}][OH^-]}{[Fe(OH)^{2+}]} = K_{d2}$$

These equilibria have constants labeled with d's for dissociation. Divide the first of the two mass-action equations into the equation $K_w = [H_3O^+][OH^-]$. The result is

$$\frac{K_w}{K_{d1}} = \frac{[H_3O^+][Fe(OH)_2^+]}{[Fe(OH)^{2+}]}$$

The right-hand side of this equation is identical to the mass-action expression for K_{a2} in the previous part except that the chemical formulas in the K_{a2} expression show associated H_2O molecules explicitly. That is, $Fe(OH)_2^+$ is the same as $Fe(H_2O)_4(OH)_2^+$, and $Fe(OH)^{2+}$ is the same as $Fe(H_2O)_5OH^{2+}$. Hence, $K_{a2} = K_w/K_{d1}$. Similarly, $K_{a1} = K_w/K_{d2}$. Numerical values for K_{a1} and K_{a2} are given in the problem and in text Example 11-13. Substitution gives:

$$K_{d1} = \frac{K_w}{K_{a2}} = \frac{1.0 \times 10^{-14}}{2.0 \times 10^{-5}} = 5.0 \times 10^{-10} \qquad K_{d2} = \frac{K_w}{K_{a1}} = \frac{1.0 \times 10^{-14}}{7.7 \times 10^{-3}} = 1.3 \times 10^{-12}$$

Because the two-step dissociation of the complex exactly reverses the two-step formation of the complex, K_f of the complex equals the reciprocal of the product of K_{d1} and K_{d2}:

$$K_f = \frac{1}{K_{d1}K_{d2}} = \frac{1}{(5.0 \times 10^{-10})(1.3 \times 10^{-12})} = \boxed{1.5 \times 10^{21}}$$

11.81 The molar mass of codeine ($C_{18}H_{21}NO_3$) equals 299.370 g mol^{-1}. At room temperature, the molal solubility of this substances is

$$\frac{1.00 \text{ codeine}}{120 \text{ mL water}} \times \left(\frac{1 \text{ mL water}}{1 \text{ cm}^3 \text{ water}}\right) \times \left(\frac{1 \text{ cm}^3 \text{ water}}{1.00 \text{ g water}}\right) \times \left(\frac{1000 \text{ g water}}{1 \text{ kg water}}\right) \times \left(\frac{1 \text{ codeine}}{299.37 \text{ g codeine}}\right) = \boxed{0.0278 \text{ mol kg}^{-1}}$$

At 80°, the same mass of codeine dissolves in half the amount of water, so the molal solubility is double what it is at room temperature: $\boxed{0.0557 \text{ mol kg}^{-1}}$. The dissolution reaction is driven to the right (favoring the dissolved codeine) by the increase in temperature. The reaction is therefore $\boxed{\text{endothermic}}$; the "heat term" for the dissolution reaction is on the left.

11.83 The problem combines a calculation on a formic acid/formate buffer (Chapter 10) with a solubility calculation for the slightly soluble salt CaF_2 (Chapter 11). Start by treating the two calculations separately: compute the pH of the buffer and assume that the pH remains unchanged as the CaF_2 dissolves. This method neglects the effect of the F^- ion, a weak base, on the pH. It also assumes that the autoionization of water is negligible. These points will have to be checked.

The addition of 50.0 mL of 0.15 M HNO_3 to 100.0 mL of 0.12 M NaHCOO creates the buffer. The nitric acid converts 0.0075 mol of $HCOO^-$ ion to HCOOH and leaves 0.0045 mol of $HCOO^-$ ion unreacted. The concentrations of these two species immediately after the conversion, but before either interacts further are:

$$[\mathrm{HCOOH}] = \frac{0.0075\ \mathrm{mol}}{0.150\ \mathrm{L}} = 0.050\ \mathrm{M} \qquad [\mathrm{HCOO^-}] = \frac{0.0045\ \mathrm{mol}}{0.150\ \mathrm{L}} = 0.030\ \mathrm{M}$$

Both concentrations change slightly as the formic acid/formate equilibrium takes effect. This equilibrium generates x mol L^{-1} of H_3O^+ as shown in the following:

	$HCOOH(aq)$	$+H_2O(aq) \rightleftharpoons$	$HCOO^-(aq)\ +$	$H_3O^+(aq)$
Init. Conc. (M)	0.50	–	0.030	small
Change in Conc. (M)	$-x$	–	$+x$	$+x$
Equil. Conc. (M)	$0.50 - x$	–	$0.030 + x$	x

Taking K_a from text Table 10.2[12] and substituting in the mass-action expression gives:

$$K_a = 1.77 \times 10^{-4} = \frac{[\mathrm{HCOO^-}][\mathrm{H_3O^+}]}{[\mathrm{HCOOH}]} = \frac{(0.030 + x)x}{(0.050 - x)}$$

Solving for x is routine. The $[H_3O^+]$ equals 2.95×10^{-4} M.

Dissolution of $CaF_2(s)$ generates $F^-(aq)$ ion. Some of this ion reacts with water to give $HF(aq)$:

$$\mathrm{F^-}(aq) + \mathrm{H_2O}(l) \rightleftharpoons \mathrm{HF}(aq) + \mathrm{OH^-}(aq) \qquad \frac{[\mathrm{HF}][\mathrm{OH^-}]}{[\mathrm{F^-}]} = K_b$$

Once equilibrium is established, the K_b equation holds and therefore the following, which is obtained by divided the K_b equation into the usual K_w equation also holds:

$$K_a = \frac{[\mathrm{H_3O^+}][\mathrm{F^-}]}{[\mathrm{HF}]} = 6.6 \times 10^{-4}$$

By previous assumption, the concentration of hydronium ion is fixed at 2.95×10^{-4} M by the formic acid/formate buffer. Therefore:

$$\frac{2.95 \times 10^{-4}[\mathrm{F^-}]}{[\mathrm{HF}]} = 6.6 \times 10^{-4} \qquad \text{which means} \qquad \frac{[\mathrm{F^-}]}{[\mathrm{HF}]} = 2.237$$

Now, CaF_2 dissolves:

$$\mathrm{CaF_2}(s) \rightleftharpoons \mathrm{Ca^{2+}}(aq) + 2\,\mathrm{F^-}(aq) \qquad K_{sp} = [\mathrm{Ca^{2+}}][\mathrm{F^-}]^2 = 3.9 \times 10^{-11}$$

Obviously, the dissolution reaction generates F^- ion and Ca^{2+} ion in a 2 : 1 ratio. But it is *not* true at equilibrium that the concentration of F^- ion equals twice that of Ca^{2+} ion. Some F^- ion reacts with water to give HF. What *is* true is

$$2[\mathrm{Ca^{2+}}] = [\mathrm{F^-}] + [\mathrm{HF}]$$

[12] Text page 328.

Eliminating [HF] between this and the equation for the ratio [F^-]/[HF] gives:

$$[F^-] = 2[Ca^{2+}] - \frac{[F^-]}{2.237} \qquad \text{which rearranges to:} \qquad [F^-] = 1.382[Ca^{2+}]$$

Insertion of the equation for [F^-] in terms of [Ca^{2+}] into the K_{sp} expression gives:

$$[Ca^{2+}](1.382)^2[Ca^{2+}]^2 = 3.9 \times 10^{-11}$$
$$[Ca^{2+}] = 2.73 \times 10^{-4} \text{ M}$$

One mole of Ca^{2+} is present in solution for every one mole of CaF_2 that dissolved. Therefore, the molar solubility of CaF_2 in the buffer equals $\boxed{2.7 \times 10^{-4} \text{ mol L}^{-1}}$.

Now, check on the assumptions. A side calculation gives [F^-] as 3.8×10^{-4} M, and [HF] as 1.7×10^{-4} M. These concentrations are both small compared to the concentrations of $HCOO^-$ and HCOOH. Therefore the HF/F^- equilibrium can affect the pH only negligibly. The water autoionization is similarly drowned out as a source of H_3O^+ by the large concentration of HCOOH.

Tip. It is instructive to set up the equations for an exact treatment[13] to solve this problem. First, list all the species present in the solution. In this case, nine different species exist at equilibrium (in addition to H_2O itself):

Na^+, H_3O^+, Ca^{2+}, NO_3^-, OH^-, F^-, HF, $HCOO^-$, and HCOOH

Next, establish all possible relationships among the concentrations of the species. The electrical neutrality of the solution requires that:

$$[Na^+] + [H_3O^+] + 2[Ca^{2+}] = [NO_3^-] + [OH^-] + [F^-] + [HCOO^-]$$

The Na^+ and NO_3^- ions do not react with other species in the solution, and it is easy to obtain their final concentrations:

$$[Na^+] = 0.080 \text{ M} \qquad [NO_3^-] = 0.050 \text{ M}$$

Four mass-action relationships are satisfied at equilibrium:

$$1.77 \times 10^{-4} = \frac{[HCOO^-][H_3O^+]}{[HCOOH]} \qquad 6.6 \times 10^{-4} = \frac{[F^-][H_3O^+]}{[HF]}$$
$$3.9 \times 10^{-11} = [Ca^{2+}][F^-]^2 \qquad 1.0 \times 10^{-14} = [H_3O^+][OH^-]$$

Finally, two material-balance relationships exist:

$$[HF] + [F^-] = 2[Ca^{2+}] \qquad [HCOOH] + [HCOO^-] = 0.080$$

There are now seven equations in seven unknowns, and the problem becomes "merely" to solve the simultaneous equations. Computer programs can be used for this, but mechanization ignores the chemical insights provided by the non-exact method. Resort to the exact method to check assumptions or when confusion threatens to sink all efforts. In this case it is worthwhile to list all equilibrium concentrations and confirm that they satisfy the preceding set of simultaneous equations.

[13] Text Section 10.8.

Chapter 12

Electrochemistry

12.1 Electrons flow from the left electrode to the right as Cr(II) is oxidized to Cr(III). In the salt bridge, negative ions flow from right to left and positive ions from left to right.

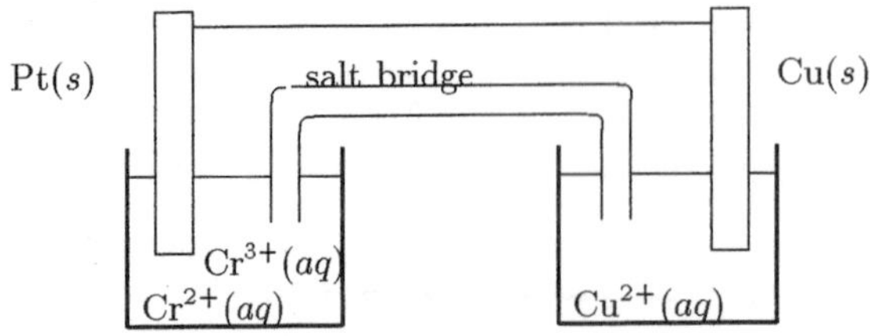

12.3 Formation of 1 mol of $Sn(s)$ from $Sn^{4+}(aq)$ ions requires 4 mol of electrons: $Sn^{4+}(aq) + 4\,e^- \rightarrow Sn(s)$. Hence:

$$N_{Sn} = 6.95 \times 10^4 \text{ C} \times \left(\frac{1 \text{ mol } e^-}{96\,485.3 \text{ C}}\right) \times \left(\frac{1 \text{ mol Sn}}{4 \text{ mol } e^-}\right) = \boxed{0.180 \text{ mol Sn}}$$

Tip. Note the careful use of the word "maximum" in the statement of the problem. No $Sn(s)$ is necessarily formed by the passage of the current because other electrolytic processes could take place to carry the current.

12.5 At the anode, $Zn(s)$ is being oxidized to $Zn^{2+}(aq)$; at the cathode, $Cl_2(g)$ is being reduced to $Cl^-(aq)$.

a) $\boxed{Zn(s) + Cl_2(g) \rightarrow Zn^{2+}(aq) + 2\,Cl^-(aq)}$.

b) An ampere is a coulomb per second. Hence:

$$Q = \left(\frac{0.800 \text{ C}}{1 \text{ s}}\right) \times 25.0 \text{ min} \times \left(\frac{60 \text{ s}}{1 \text{ min}}\right) = \boxed{1.20 \times 10^3 \text{ C}}$$

In moles:

$$n_{e^-} = \left(\frac{0.800 \text{ C}}{1 \text{ s}}\right) \times 25.0 \text{ min} \times \left(\frac{60 \text{ s}}{1 \text{ min}}\right) \times \left(\frac{1 \text{ mol } e^-}{96485 \text{ C}}\right) = \boxed{0.0124 \text{ mol } e^-}$$

c) Two moles of electrons are produced by oxidation of one mole of $Zn(s)$. Passage of 0.0124 mol of electrons therefore means that 0.00622 mol of $Zn(s)$ is oxidized. This is a loss of $\boxed{0.407 \text{ g}}$ (using a molar mass of 65.38 g mol^{-1} for zinc) from the zinc anode.

d) Two moles of electrons is equivalent in this reaction to one mole of $Cl_2(g)$. Passage of 0.0124 mol of electrons accordingly requires reduction of 0.00622 mol of $Cl_2(g)$. Use the ideal-gas law to calculate the volume of this chemical amount of chlorine at 25°C (298 K) and a pressure of 1 atm:

$$V_{\mathrm{Cl_2}} = \frac{n_{\mathrm{Cl_2}}RT}{P} = \frac{(0.00622\ \mathrm{mol})(0.08206\ \mathrm{L\ atm\ mol^{-1}K^{-1}})(298\ \mathrm{K})}{1\ \mathrm{atm}} = \boxed{0.152\ \mathrm{L}}$$

Tip. In fact, it would be very difficult to pass the relatively large current cited in this problem (0.800 A) through any actual salt bridge of a convenient size. The point of the problem however is the computation of the quantities, not the engineering of the cell.

12.7 Calculate the ratio of the chemical amounts of oxygen and copper generated by the operation of the cell. The molar mass of oxygen is 32.0 g mol^{-1}, and the molar mass of copper is 63.54 g mol^{-1}. The cell therefore forms 0.500 mol of O_2 as it forms 1.00 mol of Cu. A balanced half-equation for the oxidation of water to gaseous oxygen is $3\,H_2O(l) \rightarrow 1/2\,O_2(g) + 2\,H_3O^+(aq) + 2\,e^-$. This equation states that the production of 1/2 mol of O_2 releases 2 mol of electrons. Hence:

$$\frac{0.500\ \mathrm{mol\ O_2}}{1.00\ \mathrm{mol\ Cu}} \times \left(\frac{2\ \mathrm{mol}\ e^-}{1/2\ \mathrm{mol\ O_2}}\right) = \frac{2.00\ \mathrm{mol}\ e^-}{1\ \mathrm{mol\ Cu}}$$

The copper starts off in the $\boxed{+2\ \text{oxidation state}}$ and is reduced as follows: $Cu^{2+}(aq) + 2e^- \rightarrow Cu(s)$.

12.9 a) In the electrolysis of molten KCl, the half-reactions are:

$$K^+(l) + e^- \rightarrow K(l) \qquad \text{reduction} \quad \text{cathode}$$

$$Cl^-(l) \rightarrow 1/2\frac{1}{2}\,Cl_2(g) + e^- \qquad \text{oxidation} \quad \text{anode}$$

The sum of these two half-equations represents the overall cell reaction:

$$K^+ + Cl^- \rightarrow K(l) + 1/2\,Cl_2(g)$$

b) A current of 2.00 A is a current of 2.00 C s^{-1}; 500 hours is 1.80×10^4 s. The amount of electricity passing through the cell equals the average current multiplied by the duration of the flow or 3.60×10^4 C. Since 9.6485×10^4 C is a mole of electrons, 0.373 mol of electrons passes through the cell. As one mole of electrons passes through the cell, one mole of K forms, and one half mole of Cl_2 forms. Therefore, 0.373 mol of K and 0.0187 mol of Cl_2 are generated during the 5.00 h electrolysis run. These amounts are $\boxed{13.2\ \mathrm{g}}$ of Cl_2 ($\mathcal{M} = 70.91$ g mol^{-1}) and $\boxed{14.6\ \mathrm{g}}$ of K ($\mathcal{M} = 39.102$ g mol^{-1}).

Tip. A tacit assumption is that the cell has at least 27.8 g of KCl in it.

12.11 Compute the chemical amount of electrons transferred by use of the ratio furnished by the balanced half-equation $Ag^+ + e^- \rightarrow Ag(s)$:

$$n_{e^-} = 1.00\ \mathrm{g\ Ag} \times \left(\frac{1\ \mathrm{mol\ Ag}}{107.9\ \mathrm{g\ Ag}}\right) \times \left(\frac{1\ \mathrm{mol}\ e^-}{1\ \mathrm{mol\ Ag}}\right) = 0.00927\ \mathrm{mol}\ e^-$$

The maximum electrical work *produced* by the cell equals $-w_{\mathrm{elec,max}}$ because positive work is by convention work that is absorbed. This maximum is attained if the cell is operated reversibly.[1] Thus:

$$-w_{\mathrm{elec,max}} = -w_{\mathrm{elec,rev}} = -\Delta G = n\mathcal{F}\Delta\mathcal{E}$$

In this case, all concentrations remain at standard-state values so the equation can be modified:

$$-w_{\mathrm{elec,max}} = -w_{\mathrm{elec,rev}} = -\Delta G^\circ = n\mathcal{F}\Delta\mathcal{E}^\circ$$

[1] Text page 396.

Substitution gives:

$$-w_{\text{elec,max}} = (0.00927 \text{ mol})(96485 \text{ C mol}^{-1})(1.03 \text{ V}) = \boxed{921 \text{ J}}$$

12.13 a) A brief answer to the question is the representation $Co|Co^{2+}||Br_2|Br_2$. The full balanced half-equations and the equation for the overall reaction are:

$$\begin{aligned} &\text{anode:} && Co(s) \rightarrow Co^{2+}(aq) + 2\,e^- \\ &\text{cathode:} && Br_2(l) + 2\,e^- \rightarrow 2\,Br^-(aq) \\ &\text{overall reaction:} && Co(s) + Br_2(l) \rightarrow Co^{2+}(aq) + 2\,Br^-(aq) \end{aligned}$$

b) The $\Delta\mathcal{E}°$ of the cell equals the standard reduction potential at the cathode minus the standard reduction potential at the anode:

$$\Delta\mathcal{E}° = \mathcal{E}°(\text{cathode}) - \mathcal{E}°(\text{anode}) = 1.065 - (-0.28) = \boxed{1.34 \text{ V}}$$

12.15 a) The $In^{3+}|In$ half-reaction must be the reduction because metallic indium plates out when the cell runs. The $Zn^{2+}|Zn$ half-reaction accordingly proceeds as an oxidation:

$$\text{anode:} \quad Zn(s) \rightarrow Zn^{2+}(aq) + 2\,e^- \qquad \text{cathode:} \quad In^{3+}(aq) + 3\,e^- \rightarrow In(s)$$

b) The standard potential difference of the cell is 0.425 V. According to text Appendix E, the standard reduction potential at the zinc anode is −0.763 V. Hence:

$$0.425 \text{ V} = \mathcal{E}°(\text{cathode}) - \mathcal{E}°(\text{anode}) = \mathcal{E}°(\text{cathode}) - (-0.763 \text{ V})$$

Solving gives $\mathcal{E}°$(cathode) equal to $\boxed{-0.338 \text{ V}}$.

12.17 Powdered metallic aluminum should act as a $\boxed{\text{reducing agent}}$. A reducing agent is itself oxidized as it acts. The +3 oxidation state of Al is well-known. It is the obvious product when aluminum gives up electrons. There are no common negative oxidation states of Al; such states would have to result if Al served as an oxidizing agent. Finally, according to text Appendix E the reduction of Al^{3+} to Al(s) has a large negative $\mathcal{E}°$. If Al^{3+} is hard to reduce, then Al(s) is easy to oxidize. Not only is powered aluminum a reducing agent, it is a powerful one.

12.19 The stronger an oxidizing agent is, the easier it is to reduce (see **12.17**). The more powerful oxidizing agent will have the algebraically larger reduction potential. For these two elements, the standard reduction potentials are:

$$\begin{aligned} &Cl_2(g) + 2\,e^- \rightarrow 2\,Cl^-(aq) && \mathcal{E}° = +1.3583 \text{ V} \\ &Br_2(l) + 2\,e^- \rightarrow 2\,Br^-(aq) && \mathcal{E}° = +1.065 \text{ V} \end{aligned}$$

Since the Cl_2—Cl^- couple has a larger $\mathcal{E}°$ than the Br_2—Br^- couple, $\boxed{Cl_2(g)}$ is the stronger oxidizing agent and (probably) the better disinfectant.

12.21 a) The problem is to find the strongest oxidizing agent under standard acidic conditions in this group of six species: Co(s), $Ag^+(aq)$, $Cl^-(aq)$, Cr(s), $BrO_3^-(aq)$ and $I_2(s)$. Compare the ease of reduction of the six by examining their standard reduction potentials. The metals Co(s) and Cr(s) and the $Cl^-(aq)$ ion are *hard* to reduce: negative oxidation states of the metals are rare, and the $Cl^{2-}(aq)$ ion is unknown. These three are immediately eliminated. Text Appendix E gives these reduction half-equations and standard potentials for the other three:

$$Ag^+(aq) + e^- \rightarrow Ag(s) \qquad \mathcal{E}° = 0.7996 \text{ V}$$
$$BrO_3^-(aq) + 6\,H^+(aq) + 5\,e^- \rightarrow 1/2\,Br_2(l) + 3\,H_2O(l) \qquad \mathcal{E}° = 1.52 \text{ V}$$
$$I_2(s) + 2\,e^- \rightarrow I^-(aq) \qquad \mathcal{E}° = 0.535 \text{ V}$$

The strongest oxidizing agent is evidently $\boxed{BrO_3^- \text{ ion}}$.

b) To find the strongest reducing agent, compare the ease of oxidation of the species. These half-equations and standard reduction potentials come from text Appendix E:

$$Co^{2+}(aq) + 2\,e^- \rightarrow Co(s) \qquad \mathcal{E}° = -0.28 \text{ V}$$
$$Cr^{2+}(aq) + 2\,e^- \rightarrow Cr(s) \qquad \mathcal{E}° = -0.557 \text{ V}$$
$$Cr^{3+}(aq) + 3\,e^- \rightarrow Cr(s) \qquad \mathcal{E}° = -0.74 \text{ V}$$
$$Cl_2(g) + 2\,e^- \rightarrow 2\,Cl^-(aq) \qquad \mathcal{E}° = 1.358 \text{ V}$$
$$I_2(s) + 2\,e^- \rightarrow I^-(aq) \qquad \mathcal{E}° = 0.535 \text{ V}$$

The species under comparison are on the *right* sides of these half-equations. $\boxed{Cr(s)}$ is the best reducing agent since it is more easily oxidized than $Co(s)$, $Cl_2(g)$, or $I_2(s)$. Oxidation of the very poor reducing agent $Ag^+(aq)$ would give Ag^{2+}; oxidation of the very poor reducing agent $BrO_3^-(aq)$ would give $BrO_4^-(aq)$. No half-equations involving these species are given in Appendix E.

c) The standard reduction potential of $Co^{2+}(aq)$ ion (−0.28 V) is less than that of $Pb^{2+}(aq)$ ion (−0.1263 V), but higher than that of $Cd^{2+}(aq)$ ion (−0.4026 V). Therefore $\boxed{Co(s)}$ will reduce $Pb^{2+}(aq)$ ion, but not reduce $Cd^{2+}(aq)$ under standard acidic conditions.

12.23 a) The standard potential for the half-reaction: $Mn^{3+}(aq) + 3\,e^- \rightarrow Mn(s)$ is *not* equal to the simple sum of the half-cell potentials of the half-reactions:

$$Mn^{2+}(aq) + 2e^- \rightarrow Mn(s) \qquad \mathcal{E}° = -1.029 \text{ V}$$
$$Mn^{3+}(aq) + e^- \rightarrow Mn^{2+}(aq) \qquad \mathcal{E}° = 1.51 \text{ V}$$

even though the target half-reaction *is* the sum of these two half-reactions. Instead the potential is a *weighted average:*

$$\mathcal{E}_3^\circ = \frac{n_1\mathcal{E}_1^\circ + n_2\mathcal{E}_2^\circ}{n_3}$$

where the three subscripted n's are the numbers of electrons transferred in the two half-reactions being combined and in the half-reaction that results. Substitution gives:

$$\mathcal{E}° = \frac{2(-1.029 \text{ V}) + 1(1.51 \text{ V})}{3} = \boxed{-0.183 \text{ V}}$$

b) The disproportionation: $3\,Mn^{2+}(aq) \rightarrow Mn(s) + 2\,Mn^{3+}(aq)$ combines the reduction of $Mn^{2+}(aq)$ to $Mn(s)$ and the oxidation of $Mn^{2+}(aq)$ to $Mn^{3+}(aq)$. It is represented by the second of the following half-equations subtracted from the first:

$$2\,e^- + Mn^{2+}(aq) \rightarrow Mn(s) \qquad \mathcal{E}° = -1.029 \text{ V}$$
$$2\,Mn^{3+}(aq) + 2\,e^- \rightarrow 2\,Mn^{2+}(aq) \qquad \mathcal{E}° = 1.51 \text{ V}$$

The coefficients in the second half-equation are all twice the coefficients appearing in text Appendix E. Because the final disproportionation reaction is a whole reaction, not a half-reaction, this doubling can be ignored in the computation of $\Delta\mathcal{E}°$:

$$\Delta\mathcal{E}° = \mathcal{E}°(\text{reduction}) - \mathcal{E}°(\text{oxidation}) = -1.029 - 1.51 = -2.539 \text{ V}$$

Solutions of $Mn^{2+}(aq)$ do not disproportionate to $Mn(s)$ and $Mn^{3+}(aq)$; the standard potential difference for the process is negative.

Tip. To confirm why this calculation succeeds, write a weighted-average formula like the one in the preceding part, and use it to compute $\Delta\mathcal{E}°$. Watch what happens when the values of n_1, n_2, and n_3 are substituted:

$$\Delta\mathcal{E}° = \frac{n_1\mathcal{E}_1° - n_2\mathcal{E}_2°}{n_3} = \frac{2(-1.029) - 2(1.51)}{2} = -1.029 - 1.51 = -2.539 \text{ V}$$

In combining half-reactions to give a whole reaction n_1, n_2, and n_3 are *always* equal to each other. This is *never* the case when combining half-reactions to give another half-reaction.

12.25 a) The disproportionation of $Br_2(l)$ in acid is represented:

$$6\,Br_2(l) + 18\,H_2O(l) \rightarrow 2\,BrO_3^-(aq) + 10\,Br^-(aq) + 12\,H_3O^+(aq)$$

for which the standard potential difference is

$$\begin{aligned}\Delta\mathcal{E}° &= \mathcal{E}°(\text{reduction}) - \mathcal{E}°(\text{oxidation})\\ &= \mathcal{E}°(Br_2|Br^-) - \mathcal{E}°(BrO_3^-|Br_2)\\ &= 1.065 - 1.52 = -0.46 \text{ V}\end{aligned}$$

The negative $\Delta\mathcal{E}°$ means Br_2 will not disproportionate to Br^- and BrO_3^- under standard acidic conditions.

b) The reduction giving Br_2 has a larger reduction potential than the one giving Br^- ion. Hence Br^- is more easily oxidized than Br_2 and must be a better reducing agent under standard acidic conditions

---

12.27 The overall reaction in this cell is

$$2\,Cr^{2+}(aq) + Pb^{2+}(aq) \rightarrow Pb(s) + 2\,Cr^{3+}(aq)$$

and the standard potential difference is

$$\begin{aligned}\Delta\mathcal{E}° &= \mathcal{E}°(\text{reduction}) - \mathcal{E}°(\text{oxidation})\\ &= \mathcal{E}°(Pb^{2+}|Pb) - \mathcal{E}°(Cr^{3+}|Cr^{2+})\\ &= -0.1263 - (-0.41) = 0.28 \text{ V}\end{aligned}$$

The standard reduction potentials are correct only if all reactants and products are in standard states. This is rarely the case. In this cell, none of the solute concentrations equals 1 M. The Nernst equation offers the means to correct standard potential differences to account for non-standard concentrations. It turns $\Delta\mathcal{E}°$'s into $\Delta\mathcal{E}$'s:

$$\Delta\mathcal{E} = \Delta\mathcal{E}° - \frac{RT}{n\mathcal{F}}\ln Q \qquad \text{from which} \qquad \Delta\mathcal{E} = \Delta\mathcal{E}° - \frac{0.0592 \text{ V}}{n}\log Q \ \ (\text{at } 25°\text{C})$$

where Q is the reaction quotient. For this particular reaction and initial set of conditions:

$$Q = \frac{[Cr^{3+}]^2}{[Cr^{2+}]^2[Pb^{2+}]} = \frac{(0.0030)^2}{(0.15)(0.20)^2}$$

and n equals 2. Substitution of these values gives:

$$\Delta\mathcal{E} = 0.2837\ \text{V} - \frac{0.0592\ \text{V}}{2}\log\left(\frac{(0.0030)^2}{(0.15)(0.20)^2}\right) = \boxed{0.37\ \text{V}}$$

Tip. Confirm that "0.0592" is correct:

$$\frac{RT}{n\mathcal{F}}\ln Q = \frac{RT}{n\mathcal{F}}2.303\log Q = \frac{(8.3145\ \text{J K}^{-1}\text{mol}^{-1})(298.15\ \text{K})}{n(96485\ \text{C mol}^{-1})}2.303\log Q$$
$$= \frac{(8.3145\ \text{V C K}^{-1}\text{mol}^{-1})(298.15\ \text{K})}{n(96485\ \text{C mol}^{-1})}2.303\log Q = \frac{0.0592\ \text{V}}{n}\log Q$$

12.29 The Nernst equation works for half-reactions as well as for whole reactions. The half-reaction indicated by the cell notation is

$$Cr^{3+}(aq) + e^- \rightarrow Cr^{2+}(aq) \qquad \mathcal{E}^\circ = -0.41\ \text{V}$$

for which:

$$\mathcal{E} = \mathcal{E}^\circ - \frac{RT}{n\mathcal{F}}\ln Q = -0.424\ \text{V} - \left(\frac{0.0592\ \text{V}}{1}\right)\log\left(\frac{0.0019}{0.15}\right) = \boxed{-0.31\ \text{V}}$$

Tip. By using "0.0592 V", one automatically assumes that the temperature is 25°C. Platinum is included in the notation for the half-cell because Pt is an electrode. It conducts electrons in or out but is not changed chemically.

12.31 The I_2/I^- half-reaction is at the cathode, the site of reduction. Hence the H_3O^+—H_2 half-reaction is an oxidation (at the anode). The overall reaction is

$$2\ H_2O(l) + I_2(s) + H_2(g) \rightarrow 2\,H_3O^+(aq) + 2\,I^-(aq)$$

for which $\Delta\mathcal{E}^\circ$ is 0.535 V. This is calculated by combining the standard reduction potentials of the half-reactions:

$$\Delta\mathcal{E}^\circ = \mathcal{E}^\circ(\text{cathode}) - \mathcal{E}^\circ(\text{anode}) = 0.535(I_2|I^-) - (0.000)(H_3O^+|H_2) = 0.535\ \text{V}$$

The measured cell voltage depends on the concentrations and partial pressures of reactants and products according to the Nernst equation:

$$0.841\ \text{V} = 0.535\ \text{V} - \left(\frac{0.0592\ \text{V}}{2}\right)\log\left(\frac{[H_3O^+]^2[I^-]^2}{P_{H_2}}\right)$$

The $[I^-]$ equals 1.00 M; the P_{H_2} equals 1 atm. Substitution gives:

$$0.841 - 0.535 = -\frac{0.0592\ \text{V}}{2}\log\left(\frac{[H_3O^+]^2(1.00)^2}{1.00}\right)$$

Solving for $\log H_3O^+$ gives −5.17. The pH equals $-\log[H_3O^+]$, so it is $\boxed{5.17}$.

12.33 a) In the equation:

$$3\,HClO_2(aq) + 2\,Cr^{3+}(aq) + 12\,H_2O(l) \rightarrow 3\,HClO(aq) + Cr_2O_7^{2-}(aq) + 8\,H_3O^+(aq)$$

Cr^{3+} is oxidized to $Cr_2O_7^{2-}$, and $HClO_2$ is reduced to HClO under standard acidic conditions. Text Appendix E gives these half-equations and reduction potentials:

$$Cr_2O_7^{2-}(aq) + 14\,H_3O^+(aq) + 6\,e^- \rightarrow 2\,Cr^{3+}(aq) + 21\,H_2O(l) \qquad \mathcal{E}^\circ = 1.33\ \text{V}$$
$$3\,HClO_2(aq) + 6\,H_3O^+(aq) + 6\,e^- \rightarrow 3\,HClO(aq) + 9\,H_2O(l) \qquad \mathcal{E}^\circ = 1.64\ \text{V}$$

If the first half-reaction occurs at the anode and the second at the cathode, then the difference between the standard potentials is positive:

$$\Delta\mathcal{E}° = \mathcal{E}°(\text{cathode}) - \mathcal{E}°(\text{anode}) = 1.64 - 1.33 = \boxed{0.31\ \text{V}}$$

b) The concentration of Cr^{3+} ion is related to the measured cell potential by the Nernst equation. For the above overall reaction, the Nernst equation at 25°C becomes:

$$0.15\ \text{V} = 0.31\ \text{V} - \frac{0.0592\ \text{V}}{6}\log\left(\frac{[\text{HClO}]^3[\text{Cr}_2\text{O}_7^{2-}][\text{H}_3\text{O}^+]^8}{[\text{HClO}_2]^3[\text{Cr}^{3+}]^2}\right)$$

Insert the various concentrations, which are given in the problem (recall a pH of 0 means a $[H_3O^+]$ of 1.00 M):

$$0.15\ \text{V} = 0.31\ \text{V} - \frac{0.0592\ \text{V}}{6}\log\left(\frac{(0.20)^3(0.80)(1.00)^8}{(0.15)^3[\text{Cr}^{3+}]^2}\right)$$

Solving for the concentration of Cr^{3+} is straightforward:

$$\frac{6(0.15-0.31)}{0.0592} = -\log\left(\frac{1.896}{[\text{Cr}^{3+}]^2}\right) \qquad \text{hence} \qquad [\text{Cr}^{3+}] = \boxed{1\times10^{-8}\ \text{M}}$$

12.35 The object is to compute the K of this reaction:

$$3\,\text{HClO}_2(aq) + 2\,\text{Cr}^{3+}(aq) + 12\,\text{H}_2\text{O}(l) \rightarrow 3\,\text{HClO}(aq) + \text{Cr}_2\text{O}_7^{2-}(aq) + 8\,\text{H}_3\text{O}^+(aq)$$

It is known that $\Delta\mathcal{E}°$ equals 0.31 V. The K and $\Delta\mathcal{E}°$ are related as follows:

$$\ln K = \frac{n\mathcal{F}\Delta\mathcal{E}°}{RT} = \frac{6(9.6485\times10^4\ \text{C mol}^{-1})(0.31\ \text{V})}{(8.3145\ \text{J K}^{-1}\text{mol}^{-1})(298.15\ \text{K})} = 72.4 \qquad K = \boxed{3\times10^{31}}$$

The equilibrium constant is so very large that the reaction goes to completion for all practical purposes: $HClO_2$ and Cr^{3+} react until one of the other is all used up. The two chromium-containing ions are the only colored species present. To determine the color of the solution, assume complete reaction, and calculate whether Cr^{3+} ion is all consumed or is in excess. There are 2.00 mol of $HClO_2$ and 1.0 mol of Cr^{3+} ion, and the two react in a 3-to-2 ratio. The green Cr^{3+} ion is the limiting reactant. Once all of the green ion is used up, the solution will be $\boxed{\text{orange}}$.

12.37 In a disproportionation reaction, a single species is simultaneously oxidized and reduced. In this instance, In^+ ion is oxidized to In^{3+} ion and also reduced to elemental In. Calculate the $\Delta\mathcal{E}°$ that would be developed if the overall reaction took place in an electrochemical cell. Then get K from $\Delta\mathcal{E}°$:

cathode:	$2\,\text{In}^+(aq) + 2\,e^- \rightarrow 2\,\text{In}(s)$	$\mathcal{E}° = -0.21$ V
anode:	$\text{In}^{3+}(aq) + 2\,e^- \rightarrow \text{In}^+(aq)$	$\mathcal{E}° = -0.40$ V
cell reaction:	$3\,\text{In}^+(aq) \rightarrow \text{In}^{3+}(aq) + 2\,\text{In}(s)$	$\Delta\mathcal{E}° = 0.19$ V

$$\ln K = \frac{n\mathcal{F}\Delta\mathcal{E}°}{RT} = \frac{2(9.6485\times10^4\ \text{C mol}^{-1})(0.19\ \text{V})}{(8.3145\ \text{J K}^{-1}\text{mol}^{-1})(298.15\ \text{K})} = 15 \qquad K = e^{15} = \boxed{3\times10^6}$$

12.39 At the anode, H_2 is oxidized to H_3O^+; at the cathode, H_3O^+ to reduced to H_2. The sum of the oxidation and reduction is

$$\text{H}_2(g,\text{anode}) + 2\,\text{H}_3\text{O}^+(aq,\text{cathode}) \rightarrow \text{H}_2(g,\text{cathode}) + 2\,\text{H}_3\text{O}^+(aq,\text{anode})$$

The two sides of this equation are identical, so $\Delta\mathcal{E}^\circ$, the *standard* potential difference, equals zero. The observed non-zero Δ is caused by the unequal concentrations of H_3O^+ on the two sides. Write the Nernst equation for this reaction, which transfers 2 mol of electrons for every 1 mol of H_2:

$$0.150\text{ V} = 0.00\text{ V} - \frac{0.0592\text{ V}}{2}\log\left(\frac{P_{H_2,\text{ cathode}}[H_3O^+]^2_{\text{anode}}}{P_{H_2,\text{ anode}}[H_3O^+]^2_{\text{cathode}}}\right)$$

$$0.150\text{ V} = -\frac{0.0592\text{ V}}{2}\log\left(\frac{(1.00)[H_3O^+]^2_{\text{anode}}}{(1.00)(1.00)^2_{\text{cathode}}}\right)$$

Solve for the H_3O^+ concentration at the anode. The answer is 0.00293 M. The pH at the anode is therefore $\boxed{2.53}$.

Buffer action in the solution surrounding the anode depends on the reaction:

$$HA(aq) + H_2O(l) \rightleftharpoons H_3O^+(aq) + A^-(aq) \qquad K_a = \frac{[H_3O^+][A^-]}{[HA]}$$

According to the problem, the concentrations of A^- and HA at equilibrium in the buffer solution are equal 0.10 M at the same time that the pH is 2.53. Substitution in the K_a expression gives:

$$K_a = \frac{[H_3O^+][A^-]}{[HA]} = \frac{(10^{-2.53})(0.10)}{(0.10)} = \boxed{0.0029}$$

12.41 a) The cell reaction can be broken down into half-reactions:

cathode:	$Br_2(l) + 2\,e^- \rightarrow 2\,Br^-(aq)$	$\mathcal{E}^\circ = 1.065\text{ V}$
anode:	$2\,H_3O^+(aq) + 2\,e^- \rightarrow H_2(g) + 2\,H_2O(l)$	$\mathcal{E}^\circ = 0.000\text{ V}$

The standard potential difference is then:

$$\Delta\mathcal{E}^\circ = \mathcal{E}^\circ(\text{cathode}) - \mathcal{E}^\circ(\text{anode}) = 1.065 - 0.000 = \boxed{1.065\text{ V}}$$

b) The concentration of Br^- in the cell is related to the measured cell potential and other concentrations (and partial pressures) by the Nernst equation. For this cell (at 25°C) the Nernst equation becomes:

$$1.710\text{ V} = 1.065\text{ V} - \left(\frac{0.0592}{2}\right)\log\left(\frac{[Br^{2-}]^2[H_3O^+]^2}{P_{H_2}}\right)$$

At pH 0 the concentration of H_3O^+ is 1.00 M. The partial pressure of H_2 is 1.0 atm. Substitution of these values gives:

$$1.710\text{ V} = 1.065\text{ V} - \left(\frac{0.0592\text{ V}}{2}\right)\log\left(\frac{[Br^-]^2(1.00)^2}{(1.0)}\right)$$

Solve for the concentration of bromide ion. The result, to two significant figures, is $\boxed{1.3 \times 10^{-11}\text{ M}}$.

c) The dissolution of AgBr(s) is governed by a K_{sp} expression:

$$AgBr(s) \rightleftharpoons Ag^+(aq) + Br^-(aq) \qquad K_{sp} = [Ag^+][Br^-]$$

The $Br^-(aq)$ ion in the cell is at equilibrium with AgBr(s) and $Ag^+(aq)$ ion. The concentrations of both ions are known: $[Br^-]$ was computed in the previous part, and $[Ag^+]$ is 0.060 M. Hence:

$$K_{sp} = (0.060)(1.27 \times 10^{-11}) = \boxed{7.6 \times 10^{-13}}$$

12.43 The half-reactions in a lead-acid cell are:

$$\text{cathode:}\quad PbO_2(s) + SO_4^{2-}(aq) + 4\,H_3O^+(aq) + 2\,e^- \rightarrow PbSO_4(s) + 6\,H_2O(l)$$
$$\text{anode:}\quad Pb(s) + SO_4^{2-}(aq) \rightarrow PbSO_4(s) + 2\,e^-$$

The standard reduction potentials are 1.685 V (cathode) and −0.356 V (anode). The potential difference is $1.685 - (-0.356) = \boxed{2.041\text{ V}}$. When electrochemical cells are connected in series, their voltages add. The voltage generated by six lead-acid cells connected in series equals $6(2.041\text{ V}) = \boxed{12.25\text{ V}}$.

Tip. The standard 12-volt battery used in cars consists of six 2-volt lead-acid cells connected in series.

12.45 The "quantity of charge furnished" means the quantity of charge the battery can force through an outside resistance before its voltage falls to zero.

a) Oxidation of 1 mol of spongy lead requires that 2 mol of electrons pass through the circuit: $Pb(s) + SO_4^{2-}(aq) \rightarrow PbSO_4(s) + 2\,e^-$. Hence:

$$Q = 10\text{ kg Pb} \times \frac{10^3\text{ g}}{\text{kg}} \times \left(\frac{1\text{ mol Pb}}{207\text{ g Pb}}\right) \times \left(\frac{2\text{ mol } e^-}{1\text{ mol Pb}}\right) \times \left(\frac{9.65\times10^4\text{ C}}{1\text{ mol } e^-}\right) = \boxed{9.3\times10^6\text{ C}}$$

b) The maximum amount of electrical work that a battery can perform depends on the maximum amount of charge that it pushes through the outside circuit and the voltage difference between its two electrodes. The maximum work by the battery on the surroundings is

$$-w_{\text{elec,max}} = Q\Delta\mathcal{E}$$

Again, the work out of a system has a negative sign. This maximum work is obtained only if the discharge of the battery proceeds reversibly. Assume that the voltage of this lead-acid battery does not change as it is discharged. Writing the Nernst equation for the reaction (which is the sum of the half-reaction in the preceding problem) shows that this is tantamount to assuming that the concentration of sulfuric acid in the battery stays constant. Then:

$$-w_{\text{elec,max}} = (9.3\times10^6\text{ C})(12\text{ V}) = 1.1\times10^8\text{ V C} = \boxed{1.1\times10^8\text{ J}}$$

12.47 The amounts of Pb and PbO_2 in the battery diminish during discharge. Without reactants, the battery cannot function. Therefore, simply replacing the dilute H_2SO_4 with concentrated H_2SO_4 is not enough to recharge the battery. The $PbSO_4$ that accumulates must be removed and fresh PbO and PbO_2 added.

12.49 The maximum amount of electrical work done in an electrochemical reaction at constant T and P equals the change in free energy for that reaction. This quantity is in turn related to the potential difference and the amount of electricity passing the cell:

$$w_{\text{elec,max}} = \Delta G = -Q\Delta\mathcal{E}$$

If all of the gases in this fuel cell are kept at a pressure of 1 atm and the temperature is 298.15 K, then all reactants and products of the cell process are in standard states. The preceding equation becomes:

$$w_{\text{elec,max}} = \Delta G^\circ = -Q\Delta\mathcal{E}^\circ$$

Break the equation for the reaction in the fuel cell down into half-equations and look up their standard reduction potentials in text Appendix E:

$$\text{anode:}\quad H_2(g) + 2\,H_2O(l) \rightarrow 2\,H_3O^+(aq) + 2e^- \qquad \Delta\mathcal{E}^\circ = 0.00\text{ V}$$
$$\text{cathode:}\quad 1/2\,O_2(g) + 2\,H_3O^+(aq) + 2\,e^- \rightarrow 3\,H_2O(l) \qquad \Delta\mathcal{E}^\circ = 0.229\text{ V}$$

The standard potential difference of the cell is clearly 1.229 V. Now for $\mathcal{Q}$. It equals the amount of electricity transferred as the fuel cell generates one gram of water:

$$\mathcal{Q} = 1 \text{ g H}_2\text{O} \times \left(\frac{1 \text{ mol H}_2\text{O}}{18.015 \text{ g H}_2\text{O}}\right) \times \left(\frac{2 \text{ mol } e^-}{1 \text{ mol H}_2\text{O}}\right) \times \left(\frac{9.6485 \times 10^4 \text{ C}}{1 \text{ mol } e^-}\right) = 1.0711 \times 10^4 \text{ C}$$

The maximum electrical work produced in the surroundings per gram of water generated by this reaction equals:

$$-w_{\text{elec,max}} = \mathcal{Q}\mathcal{E}^\circ = (1.0711 \times 10^4 \text{ C})(1.229 \text{ V}) = 1.316 \times 10^4 \text{ J}$$

At 60% efficiency only six-tenths of this maximum work flows. This is $\boxed{+7900 \text{ J g}^{-1}}$.

12.51 Iron is oxidized, and water is reduced:

$$\text{Fe}(s) + 2\,\text{H}_2\text{O}(l) \rightarrow \text{Fe}^{2+}(aq) + 2\,\text{OH}^-(aq) + \text{H}_2(g)$$

The reaction has the standard potential difference:

$$\Delta\mathcal{E}^\circ = \mathcal{E}^\circ(\text{reduction}) - \mathcal{E}^\circ(\text{oxidation}) = -0.8277 - (-0.409) = \boxed{-0.419 \text{ V}}$$

where the $\mathcal{E}^\circ$'s come from text Appendix E. The negative $\Delta\mathcal{E}^\circ$ means the reaction is not spontaneous with the products and reactants in standard states. But recall LeChâtelier's principle. If the pH lowered from 14 to about 7 (lowering the concentration of OH^- by 7 orders of magnitude), the reaction will become spontaneous. Also, a low concentration of Fe^{2+} ion and a low partial pressure of gaseous H_2 favor spontaneity. Since all three products would have far lower than standard concentrations (or pressures) under practical circumstances, corrosion of iron might well tend to occur by this reaction.

Tip. The question of the rate of corrosion is not considered.

12.53 In a remote theoretical sense, metallic sodium could be used as a sacrificial anode—it is far more easily oxidized than iron according to the standard reduction potentials (see text Appendix E). In practice, however, the ocean water would very rapidly oxidize it. Metallic sodium in fact reacts violently with H_2O to form NaOH(aq) and $H_2(g)$. Sodium would be a $\boxed{\text{bad sacrificial anode}}$.

19.55 The half-equations for the Downs process for sodium are:

$$\text{Cl}^- \rightarrow \frac{1}{2}\text{Cl}_2(g) + e^- \quad \text{anode} \qquad\qquad \text{Na}^+ + e^- \rightarrow \text{Na}(l) \quad \text{cathode}$$

19.57 A steady current of 55,000 A for 24 h means that 4.75×10^9 C passes through a single cell. Dividing by the Faraday constant gives the chemical amount of electricity passing through the cell. It is 4.93×10^4 mol. It takes 3 mol of electrons to deposit 1 mol of Al. The theoretical yield of Al is therefore 1.64×10^4 mol, which is 4.43×10^5 g of Al per cell. There are 100 cells, so the total theoretical yield of Al is 100 times larger than for a single cell. It is $\boxed{4.4 \times 10^7 \text{ g}}$.

19.59 The Kroll process uses the reaction:

$$\boxed{\text{TiCl}_4(l) + 2\,\text{Mg}(s) \rightarrow \text{Ti}(s) + 2\,\text{MgCl}_2(s)}$$

The minimum mass of magnesium to produce 100 kg of titanium by this process is

$$m_{\text{Mg}} = 100 \text{ kg Ti} \times \left(\frac{1 \text{ kmol Ti}}{47.88 \text{ kg Ti}}\right) \times \left(\frac{2 \text{ kmol Mg}}{1 \text{ kmol Ti}}\right) \times \left(\frac{24.305 \text{ kg Mg}}{1 \text{ kmol Mg}}\right) = \boxed{102 \text{ kg Mg}}$$

12.61 7.32 g of zinc is to be coated onto the steel garbage can. This is 0.112 mol of Zn. Each mole of Zn requires 2 mol of electrons to plate it out, and a mole of electrons is 96,485 coulombs. The total charge passed through the cell is therefore 2.161×10^4 C. A current of 8.50 A means that 8.50 C passes through the cell every second. The time required to pass the required charge is

$$t = \frac{Q}{I} = \frac{2.161 \times 10^4 \text{ C}}{8.50 \text{ C s}^{-1}} = 2.54 \times 10^3 \text{ s} = \boxed{42.4 \text{ min}}$$

12.63 a) The product at the cathode could be either gaseous hydrogen from the reduction of 1.0×10^{-5} M $H_3O^+(aq)$ or metallic nickel from the reduction of 1.00 M $Ni^{2+}(aq)$. Direct observation of an operating cell would of course settle the issue at a glance.[2] The reduction potential for 1 M $Ni^{2+}(aq)$ to Ni(s) is −0.23 V, as tabulated in text Appendix E. The reduction potential for H_3O^+/H_2O must be adjusted from the tabulated value of 0.00 V because the $[H_3O^+]$ is not 1 M (standard), but equals 1.0×10^{-5} M. Apply the Nernst equation (at 25°C) to do this

$$\mathcal{E} = \mathcal{E}^\circ - \frac{0.0592 \text{ V}}{1} \log\left(\frac{P_{H_2}^{1/2}}{[H_3O^+]}\right) = 0.0 - (0.0592 \text{ V}) \log\left(\frac{1}{10^{-5}}\right) = -0.296 \text{ V}$$

This reduction potential is algebraically less than the −0.23 V for the reduction for $Ni^{2+}(aq)/Ni(s)$. Therefore $\boxed{\text{nickel}}$ forms first.

b) A current of 2.00 amperes for 10 hours is a current of 2.00 C s^{-1} for 36000 s. Therefore 7.20×10^4 C passes through the cell. The mass of Ni deposited is

$$m_{Ni} = 7.20 \times 10^4 \text{ C} \times \left(\frac{1 \text{ mol } e^-}{96\,485 \text{ C}}\right) \times \left(\frac{1 \text{ mol Ni}(s)}{2 \text{ mol } e^-}\right) \times \left(\frac{58.71 \text{ g Ni}}{1 \text{ mol Ni}}\right) = \boxed{21.9 \text{ g Ni}}$$

The volume of the electrolyte has to be so large that removal of 21.9 g of nickel does not lower the concentration of $Ni^{2+}(aq)$ ion to the point that H_3O^+ ion starts to be reduced.

c) If the pH is 1.0, then $[H_3O^+]$ is 0.10 M. The Nernst equation for the reduction of H_3O^+ to $H_2(g)$ at 1 atm and 25°C becomes:

$$\mathcal{E} = 0.00 - 0.0592 \text{ V} \log\left(\frac{1.00}{1 \times 10^{-1}}\right) = -0.0592 \text{ V}$$

At this pH, $\boxed{H_2(g)}$ rather than Ni(s) tends to form at the cathode.

Tip. The results make sense with respect to LeChâtelier's principle. In the first part, the highly dilute $H_3O^+(aq)$ is harder to reduce than the $Ni^{2+}(aq)$. In the second part, the higher concentration of $H_3O^+(aq)$ raises its reduction potential enough that it is easier to reduce than the $Ni^{2+}(aq)$, the concentration of which is not changed.

12.65 When Drano acts, aluminum is oxidized and water is reduced:

$$\boxed{2\,Al(s) + 6\,H_2O(l) + 2\,OH^-(aq) \rightarrow 2\,Al(OH)_4^-(aq) + 3\,H_2(g)}$$

12.67 The desired reaction equals the reverse of the non-spontaneous reaction that is forced to occur by the application of the outside voltage. It is

$$\boxed{NaClO_3(aq) + 3\,H_2(g) \rightarrow NaCl(aq) + 3\,H_2O(l)}$$

---

[2] The candidates for reduction at the *cathode* are both *cations*. In electrolytic cells, positively charged cations migrate toward the negatively charged cathode.

12.69 a) Compute the chemical amounts of zinc and nickel(II) available for the reaction:

$$n_{\mathrm{Zn}} = 32.68\ \mathrm{g\ Zn} \times \left(\frac{1\ \mathrm{mol\ Zn}}{65.39\ \mathrm{g\ Zn}}\right) = 0.4998\ \mathrm{mol\ Zn}$$

$$n_{\mathrm{Ni^{2+}}} = 0.575\ \mathrm{L\ Ni^{2+}\ solution} \times \left(\frac{1.00\ \mathrm{mol\ Ni^{2+}}}{1\ \mathrm{L\ solution}}\right) = 0.575\ \mathrm{mol\ Ni^{2+}}$$

The balanced equation $Zn(s) + Ni^{2+}(aq) \rightarrow Zn^{2+}(aq) + Ni(s)$ has Zn and Ni^{2+} reacting in a 1-to-1 ratio, so $\boxed{\text{zinc}}$ is the limiting reactant.

b) The cell is discharged (stops generating a potential difference) when the zinc is all gone:

$$t = 0.4998\ \mathrm{mol\ Zn} \times \left(\frac{2\ \mathrm{mol}\ e^-}{1\ \mathrm{mol\ Zn}}\right) \times \left(\frac{9.6485 \times 10^4\ \mathrm{C}}{1\ \mathrm{mol}\ e^-}\right) \times \left(\frac{1\ \mathrm{s}}{0.0715\ \mathrm{C}}\right) = \boxed{1.35 \times 10^6\ \mathrm{s}}$$

c) The cell produces 1 mol of $Ni(s)$ for every 1 mol of $Zn(s)$ that it consumes:

$$m_{\mathrm{Ni}} = 0.4998\ \mathrm{mol\ Zn} \times \left(\frac{1\ \mathrm{mol\ Ni}}{1\ \mathrm{mol\ Zn}}\right) \times \left(\frac{58.70\ \mathrm{g\ Ni}}{1\ \mathrm{mol\ Ni}}\right) = \boxed{29.34\ \mathrm{g\ Ni}}$$

d) The reaction has reduced 0.4998 mol of Ni^{2+} ion when it comes to a stop for want of zinc. There remains $0.575 - 0.4998 = 0.075$ mol of $Ni^{2+}(aq)$. This remaining nickel ion is still dissolved in the original 575 mL of solution. Its concentration is 0.075 mol/0.575 L = $\boxed{0.13\ \mathrm{mol\ L^{-1}}}$.

12.71 Set up a string of unit factors:

$$Q = 1.83\ \mathrm{g\ Zn} \times \left(\frac{1\ \mathrm{mol\ Zn}}{65.38\ \mathrm{g\ Zn}}\right) \times \left(\frac{2\ \mathrm{mol}\ e^-}{1\ \mathrm{mol\ Zn}}\right) \times \left(\frac{9.6485 \times 10^4\ \mathrm{C}}{1\ \mathrm{mol}\ e^-}\right) \times \left(\frac{100\ \mathrm{C\ total}}{0.25\ \mathrm{C\ in\ meter}}\right) = \boxed{2.16 \times 10^6\ \mathrm{C\ total}}$$

Tip. The unit-factors from the molar mass of Zn and the stoichiometry of the half-reaction are routine. The factor derived from the Faraday constant is new in Chapter 12, but of the same type as the others. The fourth unit factor is slightly creative in defining total coulombs as different from coulombs passing through the electric meter.

12.73 In the conversion $Al_2O_3 \rightarrow Al$, aluminum passes from the +3 oxidation state to the 0 oxidation state; 3 mol of electrons is transferred for every 1 mol of aluminum formed. The total charge Q transferred for the year's supply of Al is

$$Q = 1.5 \times 10^{10}\ \mathrm{kg} \times \left(\frac{1\ \mathrm{mol\ Al}}{0.02697\ \mathrm{kg}}\right) \times \left(\frac{3\ \mathrm{mol}\ e^-}{1\ \mathrm{mol\ Al}}\right) \times \left(\frac{9.65 \times 10^4\ \mathrm{C}}{1\ \mathrm{mol}\ e^-}\right) = 1.61 \times 10^{17}\ \mathrm{C}$$

The work required to transfer charge through this electrolysis cell depends on the amount of charge and its difference in potential:

$$w_{\mathrm{elec}} = -Q\,\Delta\mathcal{E} = (1.58 \times 10^{17}\ \mathrm{C})(-5.0\ \mathrm{V}) = 8.05 \times 10^{17}\ \mathrm{J}$$

where the negative potential difference reflects the fact that this is an electrolytic cell. Then:

$$\mathrm{cost} = 8.05 \times 10^{17}\ \mathrm{J} \times \left(\frac{1\ \mathrm{kWh}}{3.6 \times 10^6\ \mathrm{J}}\right) \times \left(\frac{\$0.10}{1\ \mathrm{kWh}}\right) = \$1.5 \times 10^{10} = \boxed{\$22\ \text{billion}}$$

12.75 a) The problem describes in detail the identity and state of the reacting species in two half-cells connected by a salt bridge and a wire to make a galvanic cell. Translate the descriptions into balanced reduction half-equations:

$$O_2(g) + 2\,H_3O^+(aq) + 2e^- \rightarrow H_2O_2(aq) + 2\,H_2O(l) \qquad \mathcal{E}° = 0.682\ \text{V}$$
$$MnO_2(s) + 4\,H_3O^+(aq) + 2e^- \rightarrow Mn^{2+}(aq) + 6\,H_2O(l) \qquad \mathcal{E}° = 1.208\ \text{V}$$

All reactants and products in the cell are in standard states. The quoted standard reduction potentials apply without correction to this cell. In a galvanic cell the two half-cells must combine to give a potential difference greater than 0.00 V. This means that reduction occurs in the half-cell with the algebraically larger $\mathcal{E}°$. Hence, the first half-reaction is the oxidation, and the second is the reduction. The overall reaction is the second half-reaction minus the first:

$$H_2O_2(aq) + MnO_2(s) + 2\,H_3O^+(aq) \rightarrow O_2(g) + Mn^{2+}(aq) + 4\,H_2O(l)$$

b) Since all participating species are in standard states:

$$\text{cell voltage} = \Delta\mathcal{E}° = \mathcal{E}°(\text{cathode}) - \mathcal{E}°(\text{anode}) = 1.208 - 0.682 = \boxed{+0.526\ \text{V}}$$

Tip. The schematic representation of this galvanic cell is

$$\text{C}(\textit{graphite})|MnO_2(s)|Mn^{2+}(aq)||H_2O_2(aq), H_3O^+(aq)|O_2(g)|\text{Pt}(s)$$

The gaseous oxygen is bubbled over the platinum electrode in such a way that it keeps in electrical contact with both the electrode and the solution. The solid MnO_2 must have electrical contact with the graphite electrode for the cell to work. Imposing an outside DC voltage exceeding 0.526 V (and having the negative wire attached to the Pt electrode) would in theory cause the cell to operate in reverse, as an electrolytic cell. The schematic representation of the cell would then be:

$$\text{Pt}(s)|O_2(g)|H_2O_2(aq), H_3O^+(aq)||Mn^{2+}(aq)|MnO_2(s)|\text{C}(\textit{graphite})$$

12.77 a) A piece of metallic iron at the bottom of a solution of $Fe^{2+}(aq)$ removes unwanted $Fe^{3+}(aq)$ by reacting with it:

$$\boxed{Fe(s) + 2\,Fe^{3+}(aq) \rightarrow 3\,Fe^{2+}(aq)}$$

This redox reaction is a "comproportionation", that is, the reverse of a disproportionation. It combines the oxidation of $Fe(s)$ to $Fe^{2+}(aq)$ with the reduction of $Fe^{3+}(aq)$ to $Fe^{2+}(aq)$. It is represented by the first of the following half-equations subtracted from the second:

$$2\,e^- + Fe^{2+}(aq) \rightarrow Fe(s) \qquad \mathcal{E}° = -0.409\ \text{V}$$
$$2\,Fe^{3+}(aq) + 2\,e^- \rightarrow 2\,Fe^{2+}(aq) \qquad \mathcal{E}° = 0.770\ \text{V}$$

The standard potential difference is

$$\Delta\mathcal{E}° = \mathcal{E}°(\text{reduction}) - \mathcal{E}°(\text{oxidation}) = 0.770 - (-0.409) = \boxed{1.179\ \text{V}}$$

b) The $\Delta\mathcal{E}°$ for the reaction of $Mn(s)$ with $Mn^{3+}(aq)$ to give $Mn^{2+}(aq)$ is positive. This was established in **12.23** when a negative $\Delta\mathcal{E}°$ for the *reverse* reaction was obtained. Therefore, $\boxed{\text{put Mn}(s)\text{ in}}$ a solution of $Mn^{2+}(aq)$ to minimize the concentration of $Mn^{3+}(aq)$.

12.79 The $Fe^{3+}|Fe^{2+}$ half-reaction has a standard reduction potential of 0.770 V. If we model the insoluble Mn(III) and Mn(IV) compounds by MnO_2, we are dealing with a reduction potential of 1.208 V at pH 0. A reducing agent such as $\boxed{Br^-(aq)}$ would reduce MnO_2 at pH 0 without reducing the Fe^{3+} because the 1.065 V reduction potential for Br_2/Br^- is less than 1.208 V but more than 0.770 V. Deviations from standard conditions of course affect potentials. This fact and the different rates at which reactions might proceed in a restoration operation make the suggestion of Br^- very tentative.

12.81 The cell reaction is $2\,Ag^+(aq) + Zn(s) \rightarrow 2\,Ag(s) + Zn^{2+}(aq)$. The standard potential difference for the reaction is

$$\Delta\mathcal{E}^\circ = \underbrace{(0.7996)}_{Ag^+|Ag} - \underbrace{(-0.7628)}_{Zn^{2+}|Zn} = 1.5624 \text{ V}$$

since Ag^+ is obviously reduced (cathode) and Zn oxidized (anode). The required voltage of 1.50 V is somewhat less than 1.5624 V. Even if 1 M solutions of $Ag^+(aq)$ and $Zn^{2+}(aq)$ were available, using them would not give the required voltage. The concentrations of one or both of the available solutions must be adjusted (by dilution) so that the cell generates 1.50 V. The Nernst equation for this cell relates its actual to its standard potential difference:

$$1.50 = 1.5624 - \frac{0.0592}{2}\log\left(\frac{[Zn^{2+}]}{[Ag^+]^2}\right) \qquad \text{which gives} \qquad \frac{[Zn^{2+}]}{[Ag^+]^2} = 10^{2.108} = 128$$

This equation must be satisfied to generate the required voltage. If $[Ag^+]$ equals 0.010 M, then $[Zn^{2+}]$ must equal 0.0128 M. There are many other combinations of concentrations that give the required potential difference, but this one is probably the simplest to prepare.

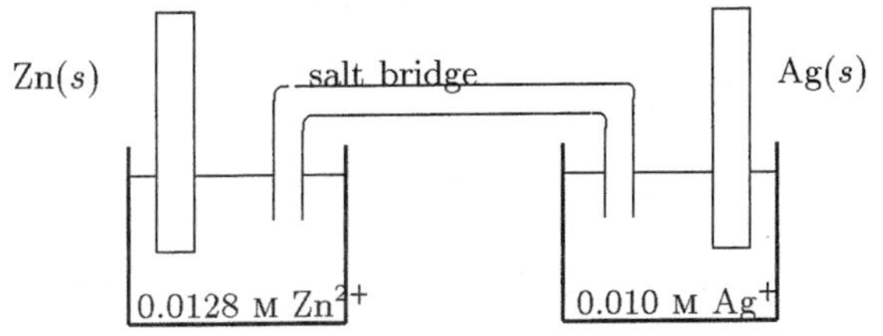

12.83 A gas confined at high pressure expands spontaneously to a lower pressure if a path is available. In a pressure cell, the free-energy decrease accompanying such a spontaneous expansion can appear as electrical work. In this case, the gas is Cl_2. At the cathode, $Cl_2(g)$ is reduced to 1 M $Cl^-(aq)$. At the anode, 1 M $Cl^-(aq)$ is oxidized to $Cl_2(g)$:

$$1/2\,Cl_2(g) + e^- \rightarrow Cl^-(aq) \qquad \text{cathode}$$

$$Cl^-(aq) \rightarrow 1/2\,Cl_2(g) + e^- \qquad \text{anode}$$

The cathode reaction *removes* $Cl_2(g)$ so the reduction must occur in the half-cell held at the *higher* pressure of $Cl_2(g)$, the 0.50 atm half-cell. The overall reaction is

$$Cl_2 \text{ (0.50 atm)} \rightarrow Cl_2 \text{ (0.01 atm)}$$

The $\Delta\mathcal{E}^\circ$, the standard potential difference for this reaction, equals 0.000 V. The Nernst equation at 25°C gives the actual potential difference:

$$\Delta\mathcal{E} = \Delta\mathcal{E}^\circ - \frac{0.0592 \text{ V}}{2}\log\left(\frac{0.010}{0.50}\right) = 0.000 - (-0.050) = \boxed{0.050 \text{ V}}$$

12.85 The reactions in the cell are:

$$Zn(s) \rightarrow Zn^{2+}(aq) + 2\,e^- \qquad \text{anode}$$

$$2\,MnO_2(s) + 2\,NH_4^+(aq) + 2\,e^- \rightarrow Mn_2O_3(s) + 2\,NH_3(aq) + H_2O(l) \qquad \text{cathode}$$

Electrons are released at the anode and taken up at the cathode. Thus, electrons flow from the Zn electrode to the graphite electrode, at which they reduce MnO_2. The stud on the top of a common flashlight battery is positive, and the bottom is negative.

12.87 a) Oxygen is reduced to water at the cathode:

$$O_2(g) + 4\,H_3O^+ + 4\,e^- \rightarrow 6\,H_2O(l)$$

The nickel does not react. This is implied by the H_3O^+ and O_2 in the shorthand representation of the cell.

b) The overall reaction in the cell consumes ethanol and oxygen to give CO_2 and water:

$$C_2H_5OH(l) + 3\,O_2(g) \rightarrow 2\,CO_2(g) + 3\,H_2O(l)$$

This reaction transfers 12 mol of e^- when run as written. Compute its $\Delta G°$ and use it to get $\Delta\mathcal{E}°$. Obtain the necessary $\Delta G_f°$'s from text Appendix D:

$$\Delta G° = 2\,\underbrace{(-394.36)}_{CO_2(g)} + 3\,\underbrace{(-237.18)}_{H_2O(l)} - 1\,\underbrace{(-174.89)}_{C_2H_5OH(l)} = -1325.37\text{ kJ}$$

$$\Delta\mathcal{E}° = \frac{-\Delta G°}{n\mathcal{F}} = \frac{-(-1325.37 \times 10^3\text{ J})}{(12\text{ mol})(96\,485\text{ C mol}^{-1})} = 1.1447\text{ J C}^{-1} = \boxed{1.1447\text{ V}}$$

c) The standard potential difference equals the standard reduction potential at the cathode minus the standard reduction potential at the anode. The $\mathcal{E}°$ at the cathode is for the reduction of gaseous oxygen to water at pH 0. Thus:

$$\Delta\mathcal{E}° = \mathcal{E}°(H_3O^+, O_2|H_2O) - \mathcal{E}°(CO_2, H_3O^+|C_2H_5OH)$$

$$1.1447\text{ V} = 1.229\text{ V} - \mathcal{E}°(CO_2, H_3O^+|C_2H_5OH)$$

$$\mathcal{E}°(CO_2, H_3O^+|C_2H_5OH) = \boxed{+0.084\text{ V}}$$

12.89 a) At the anode of the first cell, water is oxidized: $6\,H_2O(l) \rightarrow O_2(g) + 4\,H_3O^+ + 4\,e^-$. Water is far more easily oxidized than Pt(s), the other possible candidate. In the second cell, metallic nickel is oxidized: $Ni(s) \rightarrow Ni^{2+}(aq) + 2\,e^-$. Nickel is more easily oxidized than water (by comparison of their standard reduction potentials).

b) The charge $\mathcal{Q}$ passing through the cells equals the current times the elapsed time. Compute this in coulombs and use the Faraday constant to convert to moles:

$$n_{e^-} = 0.10\text{ C s}^{-1} \times 10\text{ h} \times \left(\frac{3600\text{ s}}{1\text{ hr}}\right) \times \left(\frac{1\text{ mol}\,e^-}{9.6485 \times 10^4\text{ C}}\right) = 0.0373\text{ mol }e^-$$

Next, set up unit-factors from the half-equations. Treat the electron like any other product or reactant. At the anode in the first cell:

$$m_{O_2} = 0.0373\text{ mol }e^- \times \left(\frac{1\text{ mol }O_2}{4\text{ mol }e^-}\right) \times \left(\frac{32.00\text{ g }O_2}{1\text{ mol }O_2}\right) = \boxed{0.30\text{ g }O_2}$$

In the second cell:

$$m_{Ni^{2+}} = 0.0373\text{ mol }e^- \times \left(\frac{1\text{ mol Ni}}{2\text{ mol }e^-}\right) \times \left(\frac{58.69\text{ g Ni}}{1\text{ mol Ni}}\right) = \boxed{1.1\text{ g Ni}}$$

12.91 a) Text Appendix E gives these standard reduction potentials:

$$Co^{2+}(aq) \rightarrow Co(s) \qquad \mathcal{E}^\circ = -0.28 \text{ V}$$
$$Sn^{2+}(aq) \rightarrow Sn(s) \qquad \mathcal{E}^\circ = -0.1364 \text{ V}$$

$Sn^{2+}(aq)$ is clearly easier to reduce under standard conditions. Both ions have non-standard concentrations, but because their concentrations are equal and both are +2 ions, the effect on the reduction potential is the same for both. Therefore $\boxed{Sn(s) \text{ appears first}}$ if a mixture of 0.10 M $CoCl_2$ and 0.10 M $SnCl_2$ is electrolyzed.

b) The decomposition potential is the minimum $\Delta\mathcal{E}$ that drives a non-spontaneous electrochemical reaction. Start by establishing the overall reaction that takes place when an outside potential is applied. At the cathode, $Sn^{2+}(aq)$ ion is reduced. At the anode, water is oxidized to $O_2(g)$.[3] Hence the overall reaction:

$$Sn^{2+}(aq) + 3\,H_2O(l) \rightarrow Sn(s) + \frac{1}{2}O_2(g) + 2\,H_3O^+(aq)$$

The standard potential difference of this reaction is

$$\Delta\mathcal{E}^\circ = \mathcal{E}^\circ(Sn^{2+}|Sn) - \mathcal{E}^\circ(O_2|H_2O) = -0.1364 - 1.229 = -1.3654 \text{ V}$$

None of the reactants or products (except water) is in a standard state in this cell. Use the Nernst equation to obtain $\Delta\mathcal{E}$ for the concentrations that prevail:

$$\Delta\mathcal{E} = \Delta\mathcal{E}^\circ - \frac{RT}{n\mathcal{F}}\ln Q = -1.3654 \text{ V} - \frac{0.0592 \text{ V}}{2}\log\left(\frac{P_{O_2}^{1/2}[H_3O^+]^2}{[Sn^{2+}]}\right) \quad \text{(at 25° C)}$$

Assume that the $O_2(g)$ is generated at a partial pressure of 1.00 atm and that the concentration of H_3O^+ is 1.0×10^{-7} (pH 7.00). Then:

$$\Delta\mathcal{E} = -1.3654 \text{ V} - \frac{0.0592 \text{ V}}{2}\log\left(\frac{(1.00)^{1/2}[1.0 \times 10^{-7}]^2}{[0.10]}\right) = -0.9806 \text{ V}$$

The decomposition potential is therefore $\boxed{0.981 \text{ V}}$.

c) The balanced equation for the electrolysis that involves Co^{2+} ion is written by simply replacing Sn with Co throughout the previous equation:

$$Co^{2+} + 3\,H_2O(l) \rightarrow Co(s) + 1/2\,O_2(g) + 2\,H_3O^+(aq)$$

The $\Delta\mathcal{E}^\circ$ for this reaction is

$$\Delta\mathcal{E}^\circ = \mathcal{E}^\circ(Co^{2+}|Co) - \mathcal{E}^\circ(O_2|H_2O) = -0.28 - 1.229 = -1.509 \text{ V}$$

The reduction of Co^{2+} cannot start until the potential difference for reduction of Sn^{2+} has risen high enough to make the $\Delta\mathcal{E}$'s of the two reactions equal. Write the Nernst equation for the two reactions and set the $\Delta\mathcal{E}$'s equal:

$$-1.509 \text{ V} - \frac{0.0592 \text{ V}}{2}\log\left(\frac{P_{O_2}^{1/2}[H_3O^+]^2}{[Co^{2+}]}\right) = -1.3654 \text{ V} - \frac{0.0592 \text{ V}}{2}\log\left(\frac{P_{O_2}^{1/2}[H_3O^+]^2}{[Sn^{2+}]}\right)$$

[3] As shown in text Section 12-7, $Cl^-(aq)$ has a lesser tendency to be oxidized than $H_2O(l)$.

Simplify as follows:[4]

$$-0.1436\text{ V} = \frac{0.0592\text{ V}}{2}\log\left(\frac{P_{O_2}^{1/2}[H_3O^+]^2}{[Co^{2+}]}\right) - \frac{0.0592\text{ V}}{2}\log\left(\frac{P_{O_2}^{1/2}[H_3O^+]^2}{[Sn^{2+}]}\right)$$

$$-4.851 = \log\left(\frac{P_{O_2}^{1/2}[H_3O^+]^2}{[Co^{2+}]}\right) - \log\left(\frac{P_{O_2}^{1/2}[H_3O^+]^2}{[Sn^{2+}]}\right)$$

$$-4.851 = \log\left(\frac{[Sn^{2+}]}{[Co^{2+}]}\right) \quad \text{which gives} \quad 1.408 \times 10^{-5} = \frac{[Sn^{2+}]}{[Co^{2+}]}$$

The concentrations of the two metal ions start equal, so only $\boxed{0.000014}$ of the Sn^{2+} remains when the Co^{2+} finally can plate out.

12.93 Compute the volume of zinc to be coated onto the steel, then the mass of the volume of zinc and the chemical amount in that mass. Take the density of zinc from text Appendix F:

$$V_{Zn} = \frac{(0.250 \times 10^{-3}\text{ m})(1.00\text{ m})(100\text{ m})}{1\text{ side}} \times 2\text{ sides} = 0.0500\text{ m}^3$$

$$m_{Zn} = 0.0500\text{ m}^3 \times \left(\frac{10^6\text{ cm}^3}{\text{m}^3}\right) \times \left(\frac{7.133\text{ g Zn}}{\text{cm}^3}\right) = 3.566 \times 10^5\text{ g}$$

$$n_{Zn} = 3.566 \times 10^5\text{ g Zn} \times \left(\frac{1\text{ mol Zn}}{65.38\text{ g Zn}}\right) = 5.454 \times 10^3\text{ mol Zn}$$

Each mole of Zn requires 2 mol of electrons to plate it out, and a mole of electrons is 96485 C. Hence:

$$Q = 5.454 \times 10^3\text{ mol Zn} \times \left(\frac{2\text{ mol }e^-}{1\text{ mol Zn}}\right) \times \left(\frac{96485\text{ C}}{\text{mol }e^-}\right) = 1.053 \times 10^9\text{ C}$$

The energy used in the plating operation is the amount of charge passed multiplied by the voltage that pushes it through the circuit. The voltage is 3.5 V in this case so the energy is 3.68×10^9 V C which is 3.68×10^9 J. Divide this amount of energy by 0.9 because the galvanizing is only 90% efficient. This raises the energy consumption to 4.09×10^9 J, equivalent to 1.14×10^3 kW hr, which costs $\boxed{\$114}$.

Tip. The problem draws on ideas covered in **12.61** and in **12.5**.

12.95 Calculate $\Delta H°$ and $\Delta S°$ for the reaction:

$$Cu(s) + 2\,Ag^+(aq) \rightarrow Cu^{2+}(aq) + 2\,Ag(s)$$

taking the needed $\Delta H_f°$ and $S°$ data from text Appendix D:

$$\Delta H° = \underbrace{(64.77)}_{Cu^{2+}(aq)} + 2\underbrace{(0.00)}_{Ag(s)} - \underbrace{(0.00)}_{Cu(s)} - 2\underbrace{(105.58)}_{Ag^+(aq)} = -146.39\text{ kJ}$$

$$\Delta S° = \underbrace{(-99.6)}_{Cu^{2+}(aq)} + 2\underbrace{(42.55)}_{Ag(s)} - \underbrace{(33.15)}_{Cu(s)} - 2\underbrace{(72.68)}_{Ag^+(aq)} = -193.01\text{ J K}^{-1}$$

Now, eliminate $\Delta G°$ between the two equations:

$$\Delta G° = \Delta H° - T\Delta S° \quad \text{and} \quad -n\mathcal{F}\Delta\mathcal{E}° = \Delta G°$$

Solving the resulting equation for $\Delta\mathcal{E}°$ gives:

$$\Delta\mathcal{E}° = \frac{-\Delta H°}{n\mathcal{F}} + T\frac{\Delta S°}{n\mathcal{F}}$$

[4] Recall that $\log a - \log b = \log(a/b)$.

This equation shows the dependence of the standard potential difference of *any* cell on temperature. If $\Delta S°$ of the cell reaction is positive, then raising the constant temperature T of the system raises the cell voltage; if $\Delta S°$ is negative, then raising T lowers the cell voltage. The $\Delta S°$ of the cell in this problem is negative, so the cell voltage $\boxed{\text{decreases with increasing } T}$.

Tip. It was not necessary to compute $\Delta H°$ to get the answer in this problem. Also, the way the voltage of the cell changes with temperature is of interest. Take the derivative of $\Delta\mathcal{E}°$ with respect to T in the preceding equation, and substitute the various values:

$$\frac{d(\Delta\mathcal{E}°)}{dT} = \frac{\Delta S°}{n\mathcal{F}} = \frac{-193.01 \text{ J K}^{-1}}{2(9.6485 \times 10^4 \text{ C})} = -1.00 \times 10^{-3} \text{ V K}^{-1}$$

The voltage drops by a millivolt for every kelvin that the temperature increases.

12.97 The problem is to estimate the solubility of AgBr in 0.10 M aqueous NaBr. It is possible to look up the K_{sp} of AgBr in text Table 11.2[5] and use the method of **11.7**, but it is more sporting to use the data given in the problem, which include:

$$\text{Ag}^+(aq) + e^- \rightarrow \text{Ag}(s) \qquad \mathcal{E}° = 0.7996 \text{ V}$$
$$\text{AgBr}(s) + e^- \rightarrow \text{Ag}(s) + \text{Br}^-(aq) \qquad \mathcal{E}° = 0.0713 \text{ V}$$

Combine these two half-equations to give the dissolution equation:

$$\text{AgBr}(s) \rightarrow \text{Ag}^+(aq) + \text{Br}^-(aq)$$

Since AgBr must end up on the left side of the dissolution equation, the first half-equation was subtracted from the second. The standard potential difference of this reaction is

$$\Delta\mathcal{E}° = \mathcal{E}°(\text{cathode}) - \mathcal{E}°(\text{anode}) = 0.0713 - 0.7996 = -0.7283 \text{ V}$$

Write the Nernst equation at 25°C for the dissolution:

$$\Delta\mathcal{E} = -0.7283 \text{ V} - \frac{0.0592 \text{ V}}{1} \log\left([\text{Ag}^+][\text{Br}^-]\right)$$

The solubility is measured at equilibrium, so $\Delta\mathcal{E}$ equals zero. Insert 0.10 M, which is a given, as the concentration of Br^- ion. Then:

$$0 = -0.7283 \text{ V} - (0.0592 \text{ V}) \log\left([\text{Ag}^+][0.10]\right) \qquad \text{from which} \qquad [\text{Ag}^+] = 5 \times 10^{-12} \text{ M}$$

The solubility of the AgBr equals the equilibrium concentration of Ag^+ ion because AgBr is the only source of Ag^+ ion and all dissolved silver is in the form of Ag^+ ion. The estimated solubility is therefore $\boxed{5 \times 10^{-12} \text{ mol L}^{-1}}$.

[5] Text page 369.

Chapter 13

Chemical Kinetics

13.1 Text Figure 13.3[1] shows the concentration of NO in a system as a function of time. The instantaneous rate of production of NO equals the slope of the tangent to this line. The slope of the tangent changes constantly. Sketch in the tangent line at t equal to 200 s. Reading from the graph (as shown in the Figure for $t = 150$ s) gives $\boxed{5.3 \times 10^{-5} \text{ mol L}^{-1}\text{s}^{-1}}$ as the instantaneous rate.

13.3 The rate of a reaction is expressed in terms of the rate of disappearance of a reactant, or formation of a product:

$$\text{rate} = \boxed{-\frac{1}{1}\frac{d[N_2]}{dt} = -\frac{1}{3}\frac{d[H_2]}{dt} = +\frac{1}{2}\frac{d[NH_3]}{dt}}$$

13.5 a) The way in which the rate of the reaction is affected by changes in concentration of the two reactants gives the order of the reaction. This reaction is first order in H_2 because the rate varies as to the first power of the concentration of H_2 and second order in NO because the rate varies as to the second power of the concentration of NO. The rate expression is $\boxed{\text{rate} = k[H_2][NO]^2}$. The units of the rate constant k are $\boxed{\text{L}^2 \text{ mol}^{-2} \text{s}^{-1}}$ This can also be written as $\text{M}^{-2}\text{s}^{-1}$. The reaction has an overall order of 3.

b) Multiplying $[H_2]$ by 2 would double the rate, and multiplying [NO] by 3 would increase the rate by a factor of 9. The combined effect would be to increase the rate by a $\boxed{\text{factor of 18}}$.

13.7 a) Compare the second and third data lines in the table, and assume that the difference that is shown is the *only* difference between the two runs. When $[C_5H_5N]$ is held constant and $[CH_3I]$ is doubled, the rate doubles. The reaction is first order in CH_3I. Next, compare the first and second lines in the table. When both concentrations are doubled, the rate is increased by a factor of 4. Half of this is due to the change in the concentration of CH_3I, so the other half is due to the change in the concentration of C_5H_5N. Hence:

$$\boxed{\text{rate} = k[C_5H_5N][CH_3I]}$$

b) Calculate k by substituting the data from any one of the three data points into the rate equation. Using the first line of the table:

$$7.5 \times 10^{-7} \text{ mol L}^{-1}\text{s}^{-1} = k(1.00 \times 10^{-4} \text{ mol L}^{-1})(1.00 \times 10^{-4} \text{ mol L}^{-1})$$

Hence k is $\boxed{75 \text{ L mol}^{-1}\text{s}^{-1}}$.

---

[1] Text page 435.

c) Substitute the known k and the two given concentrations into the rate equation. Remember that "M" stands for mol L^{-1}.

$$\text{rate} = (75\ \text{mol}^{-1}\text{L s}^{-1}))(5.0 \times 10^{-5}\ \text{mol L}^{-1})(2.0 \times 10^{-5}\ \text{mol L}^{-1}) = \boxed{7.5 \times 10^{-8}\ \text{mol L}^{-1}\text{s}^{-1}}$$

13.9 The problem asks for the time it will take for the pressure to fall to half of its initial value. This is exactly the half-life. In a first-order process the half-life depends solely upon the rate constant. In this case:

$$t_{1/2} = \frac{\ln 2}{k} = \frac{0.69315}{2.2 \times 10^{-5}\ \text{s}^{-1}} = \boxed{3.2 \times 10^{4}\ \text{s}}$$

Tip. Recall that partial pressures of gases are directly proportional to their concentrations (assuming ideality). Also, the *total* pressure in this vessel increases during the reaction.

13.11 The decomposition of benzene diazonium chloride is first-order, following the integrated rate law:

$$P_{\text{C}_6\text{H}_5\text{N}_2\text{Cl}} = (P_{\text{C}_6\text{H}_5\text{N}_2\text{Cl}})_0\, e^{-kt}$$

Express the elapsed time in seconds and insert the time, together with the initial partial pressure and the rate constant, into the preceding equation

$$P_{\text{C}_6\text{H}_5\text{N}_2\text{Cl}} = (0.0088\ \text{atm})e^{(-4.3\times10^{-5}\ \text{s}^{-1})(3.60\times10^{4}\ \text{s})} = \boxed{0.0019\ \text{atm}}$$

13.13 This first-order reaction follows the integrated rate law:

$$[\text{C}_2\text{H}_5\text{Cl}] = [\text{C}_2\text{H}_5\text{Cl}]_0 e^{-kt}$$

Divide both sides of this equation by the original concentration of the C_2H_5Cl, and take the natural logarithm of both sides:

$$\ln \frac{[\text{C}_2\text{H}_5\text{Cl}]}{[\text{C}_2\text{H}_5\text{Cl}]_0} = -kt$$

Substitution of two concentrations and the time gives:

$$\ln \frac{0.0016\ \text{M}}{0.0098\ \text{M}} = -k(340\ \text{s})$$

which is easily solved to give k equal to $\boxed{5.3 \times 10^{-3}\ \text{s}^{-1}}$.

13.15 The integrated rate law for this very fast second-order association of iodine atoms is

$$\frac{1}{[\text{I}]} = \frac{1}{[\text{I}]_0} + 2kt$$

Substitute the given concentration, rate constant, and time

$$\frac{1}{[\text{I}]} = \frac{1}{1.00 \times 10^{-4}\ \text{mol L}^{-1}} + 2(8.2 \times 10^{9}\ \text{L mol}^{-1}\ \text{s}^{-1})(2.0 \times 10^{-6}\ \text{s})$$

$$= 1.00 \times 10^{4}\ \text{L mol}^{-1} + 3.28 \times 10^{4}\ \text{L mol}^{-1} = 4.28 \times 10^{4}\ \text{L mol}^{-1}$$

$$[\text{I}] = \boxed{2.34 \times 10^{-5}\ \text{mol L}^{-1}}$$

13.17 The reaction is the neutralization of $OH^-(aq)$ with $NH_4^+(aq)$. Aqueous acid-base reactions are generally fast. This reaction is no exception, as shown by the huge room-temperature rate constant of $k = 3.4 \times 10^{10}$ $M^{-1}\ s^{-1}$. The answer will be a very short time. If 1.00 L of 0.0010 M NaOH and 1.00 L of 0.0010 M NH_4Cl are mixed, then *after* the mixing, but *before* the reaction can start each reactant has a concentration of 5.0×10^{-4} M. The kinetics are second-order overall:

$$\text{rate} = \frac{-d[OH^-]}{dt} = k[OH^-][NH_4^+]$$

Throughout the reaction $[OH^-] = [NH_4^+]$. Let this concentration be represented by c. Then:

$$\frac{-dc}{dt} = kc^2$$

Integrating this equation and inserting the initial condition gives:

$$\frac{1}{c} = \frac{1}{c_0} + kt$$

This equation does not include the factor of 2 that appears in text equation 13.4[2] because the stoichiometry of the reaction lacks that factor. For c_0 equal to 1.0×10^{-5} M and k equal to $3.4 \times 10^{10}\ M^{-1}\,s^{-1}$, the equation becomes:

$$\frac{1}{1.0 \times 10^{-5}\ M} = \frac{1}{5.0 \times 10^{-4}\ M} + (3.4 \times 10^{10}\ M^{-1}\,s^{-1})\,t$$
$$9.8 \times 10^4\ M^{-1} = (3.4 \times 10^{10}\ M^{-1}s^{-1})\,t$$
$$t = \boxed{2.9 \times 10^{-6}\ s}$$

13.19 a) Two particles collide in an elementary reaction. The reaction is therefore bimolecular. Its rate law is: $\boxed{\text{rate} = k[HCO][O_2]}$.

b) Three particles collide in an elementary reaction; the reaction is termolecular: $\boxed{\text{rate} = k[CH_3][O_2][N_2]}$.

c) A single particle decomposes spontaneously in an elementary reaction. The reaction is unimolecular: $\boxed{\text{rate} = k[HO_2NO_2]}$.

13.21 a) The first step is $\boxed{\text{unimolecular}}$; the three subsequent steps are $\boxed{\text{bimolecular}}$. This is determined simply by counting the number of interacting particles on the left sides of the four equations. Molecularity has meaning only in reference to elementary reactions.

b) The overall reaction is the sum of the steps: $\boxed{H_2O_2 + O_3 \rightarrow H_2O + 2\,O_2}$.

c) The intermediates are $\boxed{O,\ ClO,\ CF_2Cl,\ \text{and}\ Cl}$. These species are produced in the course of the reaction and later consumed.

Tip. The CF_2Cl_2 is a catalyst. It reacts in an early stage in the mechanism but is later regenerated. The overall reaction could not proceed according to this mechanism without the presence and participation of CF_2Cl_2, but the compound is neither consumed nor produced.

13.23 The equilibrium constant of this elementary reaction equals the ratio of the rate constant of the forward reaction to the rate constant of the reverse reaction:

$$K = \frac{k_f}{k_r} = 5.0 \times 10^{10} = \frac{1.3 \times 10^{10}\ L\ mol^{-1}s^{-1}}{k_r}$$

[2] Text page 442

Solving for k_r gives 0.26 L mol^{-1}s^{-1}. The reaction in question is in fact just the reverse of the original elementary reaction, so the answer is $\boxed{0.26 \text{ L mol}^{-1}\text{s}^{-1}}$.

13.25 a) The rate-limiting elementary step in a mechanism determines the overall reaction rate. In this case, the slow step is: $C + E \rightarrow F$. A preliminary version of the rate law is:

$$\text{rate} = k_2[C][E]$$

Unfortunately, the expression involves the concentration of C, an intermediate. This is unacceptable. To eliminate [C] in the rate law, consider how C is formed. It arises in the first step of the mechanism, a fast equilibrium. For that first step:

$$k_1[A][B] = k_{-1}[C][D]$$

Solve this equation for the concentration of C and substitute into the preliminary rate law:

$$\boxed{\text{rate} = \frac{k_1 k_2}{k_{-1}} \frac{[A][B][E]}{[D]}}$$

The overall reaction is the sum of the two steps: $\boxed{A + B + E \rightarrow D + F}$.

Tip. In this reaction system, the accumulation of one product (D) slows down the reaction, but the accumulation of the other product (F) does not.

b) The overall reaction in this case is: $\boxed{A + D \rightarrow B + F}$. For the two fast equilibria:

$$k_1[A] = k_{-1}[B][C] \qquad \text{and} \qquad k_2[C][D] = k_{-2}[E]$$

The last, slow step is the rate-determining step:

$$\text{rate} = k_3[E]$$

But E is an intermediate and its concentration may not appear in the final rate expression. To eliminate [E], solve the second of the preceding pair of equations of [E] and substitute:

$$\text{rate} = \frac{k_2 k_3}{k_{-2}}[C][D]$$

This expression *still* contains the concentration of an intermediate (C now). Eliminate [C] by solving the first of the pair for [C] and substituting:

$$\boxed{\text{rate} = \frac{k_1 k_2 k_3}{k_{-1} k_{-2}} \frac{[A][D]}{[B]}} = k_{\text{expt}} \frac{[A][D]}{[B]}$$

where the experimental k is the algebraic composite of the several step-wise rate constants. The reaction is first order in both A and D, is -1 order in B and first order overall.

13.27 The reaction of HCl with propane is first order in propane and third order in HCl. This is an experimental fact. Mechanism (a) proposes the rapid formation of the intermediate H from 2 HCl's followed by slow combination of the H with CH_3CHCH_2. This mechanism thus predicts second-order kinetics in HCl and must be wrong.

Mechanism (b) proposes *two* fast equilibria. The first involves HCl only and the second involves HCl and propane. The slow step is the chemical combination of the two intermediates that these equilibria produce. The rate is accordingly proportional to the concentrations of all the reactants in the two fast equilibria. HCl occurs three times among these reactants and propane occurs once so **mechanism (b) fits** with the observed rate law.

Mechanism (c) involves HCl in the fast production of two different intermediates which then slowly combine to give the product (and to regenerate some HCl). It predicts second-order kinetics in HCl (2 HCl's consumed to furnish reactants for the slow step). It is therefore not consistent with observation.

Tip. A correct mechanism for a reaction must predict the observed rate law; a mechanism that correctly predicts the observed rate law may *still* be wrong. In other words, predicting the rate law is necessary but not sufficient for correctness in a mechanism.

13.29 Write rate expressions for the slow elementary step in each mechanism. Then eliminate from the expressions the concentrations of any intermediates. The results for the three mechanisms (a), (b) and (c) are the three rate laws:

$$\text{rate (a)} = k_1[\text{NO}_2\text{Cl}] \qquad \text{rate (b)} = \frac{k_1 k_2}{k_{-1}}\frac{[\text{NO}_2\text{Cl}]^2}{[\text{Cl}_2]} \qquad \text{rate (c)} = \frac{k_1 k_2 k_3}{k_{-1} k_{-2}}\frac{[\text{NO}_2\text{Cl}]^2}{[\text{NO}_2]}$$

The cluster of constants in the second and third rate expressions can be regarded as a new single rate constant "k_{expt}." Only **mechanism (a)** is consistent with experiment.

Tip. Nothing allows one to conclude that mechanism (a) is the true mechanism.

13.31 The overall reaction is $A + B + E \rightarrow D + F$. It proceeds first by an equilibrium between A and B giving D and the intermediate C, and then by the consumption of C in reaction with E to give F. The rate of appearance of C equals $k_1[A][B]$, and the rate of *disappearance* of C equals $k_{-1}[C][D] + k_2[C][E]$. This latter is a sum because C disappears both by back reaction (with D to give A plus B) and by *further* reaction (with E to give F). If the concentration of intermediate C is constant (the steady state approximation), the rate of disappearance of C must equal its rate of appearance:

$$k_1[A][B] = k_{-1}[C][D] + k_2[C][E]$$

The rate of the reaction can be expressed in terms of the rate of appearance of a product, for example, F:

$$\text{rate} = \frac{d[F]}{dt} = k_2[E][C]$$

Solve the steady-state equation for [C] and substitute the answer in the preceding:

$$\text{rate} = \boxed{\frac{k_1 k_2[A][B][E]}{k_2[E] + k_{-1}[D]}}$$

If $\boxed{k_2[E] \text{ is much smaller than } k_{-1}[D]}$ then this expression becomes:

$$\text{rate} \approx \left(\frac{k_1 k_2}{k_{-1}}\right)\frac{[A][B][E]}{[D]}$$

The second-step rate constant k_2 is much smaller than k_{-1} when the first step of the reaction is a fast equilibrium.

13.33 The reaction is the decomposition of nitryl chloride $2\,NO_2Cl \rightarrow 2\,NO_2 + Cl_2$. The mechanism involves a equilibrium breakdown of the reactant to NO_2 plus Cl followed by reaction of the atomic chlorine with a second molecule of NO_2Cl to generate the products. The change in the concentration of Cl with time is

$$\frac{d[\text{Cl}]}{dt} = k_1[\text{NO}_2\text{Cl}] - k_{-1}[\text{Cl}][\text{NO}_2] - k_2[\text{Cl}][\text{NO}_2\text{Cl}]$$

because the rate of change of the concentration of Cl equals the rate of its production minus the rate of its consumption. The steady-state approximation is that $d[\text{Cl}]/dt = 0$. If so, then:

$$k_1[\text{NO}_2\text{Cl}] - k_{-1}[\text{Cl}][\text{NO}_2] - k_2[\text{Cl}][\text{NO}_2\text{Cl}] = 0$$

and:

$$[\text{Cl}] = \frac{k_1[\text{NO}_2\text{Cl}]}{k_{-1}[\text{NO}_2] + k_2[\text{NO}_2\text{Cl}]}$$

The rate of the overall reaction equals the rate of the final elementary step, which generates the two products:

$$\text{rate} = \frac{d[\text{Cl}_2]}{dt} k_2[\text{NO}_2\text{Cl}][\text{Cl}]$$

Substitute the expression for the concentration of the Cl into this equation:

$$\boxed{\text{rate} = \frac{d[\text{Cl}_2]}{dt} = \frac{k_1 k_2[\text{NO}_2\text{Cl}]^2}{k_{-1}[\text{NO}_2] + k_2[\text{NO}_2\text{Cl}]}}$$

Tip. The answer differs from the rate expression given for the same reaction in **13.29**. It becomes equal to that expression as the second term in the denominator becomes large compared to the first. This happens if k_2 is large compared to k_{-1} or if $[\text{NO}_2]$ is small, as it would be in the initial stages of the reaction.

Tip. Lewis structures for NO_2Cl (nitryl chloride) are given in **3.79**, and the second-order formation of nitryl fluoride is mentioned on text page 435 and used as an example on text page 447.

13.35 a) The rate constant of an elementary reaction depends on the absolute temperature and activation energy E_a according to the Arrhenius equation:

$$k = Ae^{-E_a/RT} \qquad \text{from which} \qquad \ln k = \ln A - \frac{E_a}{RT}$$

This means that a plot of $\ln k$ versus the reciprocal of T should be a straight line with a slope of $-E_a/R$ and an intercept (when $1/T = 0$) of $\ln A$. Two points determine a line. A quick way to estimate E_a is to select any two of the four data points in the problem (such as the first two) and insert the values in the above equation

$$\ln(5.49 \times 10^6) = \ln A - \frac{E_a}{(5000\ K)R} \qquad \text{and} \qquad \ln(9.86 \times 10^6) = \ln A - \frac{E_a}{(1000\ K)R}$$

Then solve for E_a (by eliminating $\ln A$ between the equations). This procedure gives $E_a = 432$ kJ mol^{-1}. Note that E_a has the same units as RT. Selecting *another* pair of points (for example the second two) and doing the same thing gives a somewhat different answer: $E_a = 392$ kJ mol^{-1}. The discrepancy means that the experimental data do not fall exactly on a straight line. The best way to use all data is to perform a *least-squares fit,* mathematically determining the slope of the straight line that comes closest to all four data points. Many electronic calculators are equipped to complete the necessary calculations almost without effort. Based on the minimization of the sum of the squares of the deviations, E_a is $\boxed{425 \text{ kJ mol}^{-1}}$.

b) As $1/T$ goes to zero, $\ln k$ approaches $\ln A$. Recall that using just the first two data points gave $E_a = 432$ kJ mol^{-1}. Substituting this value and the k and T values of the first data point into the Arrhenius equation gives $\ln A$ equal to 25.9. Using an E_a of 392 kJ mol^{-1} and the third or fourth (k, T) pair makes $\ln A$ equal 25.5. The least-squares fitting gives $\ln A = 25.76$ so that $A = \boxed{1.54 \times 10^{11} \text{ L mol}^{-1}\text{s}^{-1}}$. This is the best answer. The units of A are always the same as the units of k.

13.37 **(a)** Calculating $\ln A$ for this reaction using the Arrhenius equation and the values of k and E_a given in the problem. The T is equal to 303.2 K (30.0°C). The (rearranged) Arrhenius equation for this case is

$$\ln A = \ln k + \frac{E_a}{RT} = \ln(1.94 \times 10^{-4}) + \left(\frac{1.61 \times 10^5 \text{ J mol}^{-1}}{(8.3145 \text{ J K}^{-1}\text{mol}^{-1})(303.2 \text{ K})}\right) = 55.31$$

The value of A itself might be calculated at this point, but it is not needed. Simply put $\ln A$ back into the Arrhenius equation with T equal to 313.2 (40.0°C):

$$\ln k = \ln A - \frac{E_a}{RT} = 55.31 - \left(\frac{1.61 \times 10^5 \text{ J mol}^{-1}}{(8.3145 \text{ J K}^{-1}\text{mol}^{-1})(313.2 \text{ K})}\right) = -6.51$$

Taking the antilogarithm of -6.51 gives k equal to $\boxed{1.49 \times 10^{-3} \text{ L mol}^{-1}\text{s}^{-1}}$. A 10 K increase in temperature (fairly small) increases the rate constant of the reaction nearly 8-fold.

b) This reaction is second order, but the following reasoning applies to reactions of any order. The larger the rate constant, the more rapid is the reaction. Faster reactions require less time to reach any designated point in their progress. Increasing the temperature of this reaction from 30.0 to 40.0°C increases k from 1.94×10^{-4} to 14.9×10^{-4} L mol^{-1}s^{-1}, which is a factor of 7.68. The time to reach the half-way mark in the reaction is therefore reduced by a factor of 7.68. The 50% conversion requires only $\boxed{1.30 \times 10^3 \text{ s}}$ at 40.0°C instead of the 10,000 s it requires at 30.0°C.

13.39 **a)** Solve the Arrhenius equation for A and insert the quantities given in the problem:

$$A = \frac{k}{e^{-E_a/RT}} = \frac{0.41 \text{ s}^{-1}}{\exp(-1.61 \times 10^5 \text{ J mol}^{-1}/(8.3145 \text{ J K}^{-1}\text{mol}^{-1})(600 \text{ K}))} = \boxed{4.3 \times 10^{13} \text{ s}^{-1}}$$

b) Assume that neither the activation energy E_a nor the Arrhenius A changes with temperature. Solve the Arrhenius equation for k, set T equal to 1000 K, and insert these values:

$$k = 4.25 \times 10^{13} \text{ s}^{-1} \exp\left(\frac{-1.61 \times 10^5 \text{ J mol}^{-1}}{(8.3145 \text{ J K}^{-1}\text{mol}^{-1})(1000 \text{ K})}\right) = \boxed{1.7 \times 10^5 \text{ s}^{-1}}$$

13.41 The activation energy is the difference in energy between the initial state and the activated complex. The activated complex is 3.5 kJ mol^{-1} higher in energy than the reactants, which are $OH(g)$ plus $HCl(g)$. The products, $H_2O(g)$ plus $Cl(g)$, are themselves 66.8 kJ mol^{-1} lower in energy than the reactants. It follows that the activated complex is 70.3 kJ mol^{-1} higher in energy than the products. To pass from the products to the activated complex requires $\boxed{70.3 \text{ kJ mol}^{-1}}$.

13.43 Equation 13.7,[3] relates the rate constant of a second-order reaction between like molecules to the molecular diameter and molar mass. Rewrite this equation inserting the steric factor P, which accounts for the fact that some collisions with sufficient energy may have the wrong orientation for successful reaction:

$$k = P2d^2 N_0 \sqrt{\frac{\pi RT}{\mathcal{M}}} e^{-E_a/RT}$$

The resulting equation has the form of the Arrhenius equation. Term-by-term comparison with the Arrhenius equation identifies the Arrhenius A as follows:

$$A = P2d^2 N_0 \sqrt{\frac{\pi RT}{\mathcal{M}}}$$

[3] Text page 456.

All of the quantities on the right side of this equation are available. Express them in SI base units, if they are not already in such units. This includes in particular the molar mass of NOCl, which is 0.06546 kg mol^{-1}. Substitute them into the equation and compute A:

$$A = (0.16)(2)(3.0 \times 10^{-10})^2(6.022 \times 10^{23})\sqrt{\frac{(3.1416)(8.3145)(298)}{0.06546}} = 5.98 \times 10^6$$

The units in this computation were omitted. It is wise to repeat the algebra on the units alone:

$$\text{units of } A = \text{m}^2(\text{mol}^{-1})\sqrt{\frac{(\text{ J K}^{-1}\text{mol}^{-1})(\text{K})}{\text{kg mol}^{-1}}} = (\text{m})^2(\text{mol}^{-1})\sqrt{\frac{(\text{kg m}^2\,\text{s}^{-2})}{\text{kg}}}$$
$$= \text{m}^2\ \text{mol}^{-1}(\text{m s}^{-1}) = \text{m}^3\,\text{mol}^{-1}\text{s}^{-1}$$

The answer is therefore 6.0×10^6 $\text{m}^3\,\text{mol}^{-1}\text{s}^{-1}$. The cubic meter is too large for use as a unit of volume in laboratory-scale chemistry. It equals 1000 L. Converting from cubic meters to liters gives a final answer of $\boxed{6.0 \times 10^9 \text{ L mol}^{-1}\text{s}^{-1}}$.

13.45 a) In this reaction, penicillin is S, the substrate, and penicillinase[4] is E, the enzyme. Write the Michaelis-Menten equation and insert the constants K_m and k_2 that are given in the problem:

$$\text{rate} = \frac{k_2[\text{E}]_0[\text{S}]}{[\text{S}] + K_m} = \frac{(2 \times 10^3\ \text{s}^{-1})(6 \times 10^{-7}\ \text{mol L}^{-1})[\text{S}]}{[\text{S}] + 5 \times 10^{-5}\ \text{mol L}^{-1}}$$

The rate of the reaction increases as [S], the concentration of penicillin, increases. The maximum rate will be reached when [S] is large compared to 5×10^{-5} mol L^{-1}. At this point, the denominator of the fraction essentially equals [S] and cancels out the [S] in the numerator:

$$(\text{rate})_{\text{max}} = \frac{(2 \times 10^3\ \text{s}^{-1})(6 \times 10^{-7}\ \text{mol L}^{-1})}{1} = \boxed{1.2 \times 10^{-3}\ \text{mol L}^{-1}\,\text{s}^{-1}}$$

b) Rewrite the Michaelis-Menten equation inserting the desired rate (which equals half the maximum rate), the given concentration of enzyme, and the two constants:

$$\text{rate} = \frac{(\text{rate})_{\text{max}}}{2} = \frac{1.2 \times 10^{-3}\ \text{mol L}^{-1}\,\text{s}^{-1}}{2} = \frac{(2 \times 10^3\ \text{s}^{-1})(6 \times 10^{-7}\ \text{mol L}^{-1})[\text{S}]}{[\text{S}] + 5 \times 10^{-5}\ \text{mol L}^{-1}}$$

Solving for [S] gives the concentration of substrate (penicillin) required. The answer is $\boxed{5.0 \times 10^{-5}\ \text{mol L}^{-1}}$.

13.47 The rate expression for the process is: rate = [hemoglobin][O_2]. Substitute the given data into this expression:

$$\text{rate} = (4 \times 10^7\ \text{L mol}^{-1}\text{s}^{-1})(2 \times 10^{-9}\ \text{mol L}^{-1})(5 \times 10^{-5}\ \text{mol L}^{-1}) = \boxed{4 \times 10^{-6}\ \text{mol L}^{-1}\text{s}^{-1}}$$

Tip. Review the discussion of the equilibria involved in the update and release of O_2 by hemoglobin[5].

13.49 a) For this first-order process, $\ln[\text{In}^+] = -kt + \ln[\text{In}^+]_0$. Prepare a table of the natural logarithm of the concentration of In^+ versus time:

t (s)	0	240	480	720	1000	1200	10000
$\ln[\text{In}^+]$	−4.80	−5.05	−5.30	−5.55	−5.80	−5.80	−5.80

[4]Names ending in "-ase" signify enzymes.
[5]Text pages 284-286

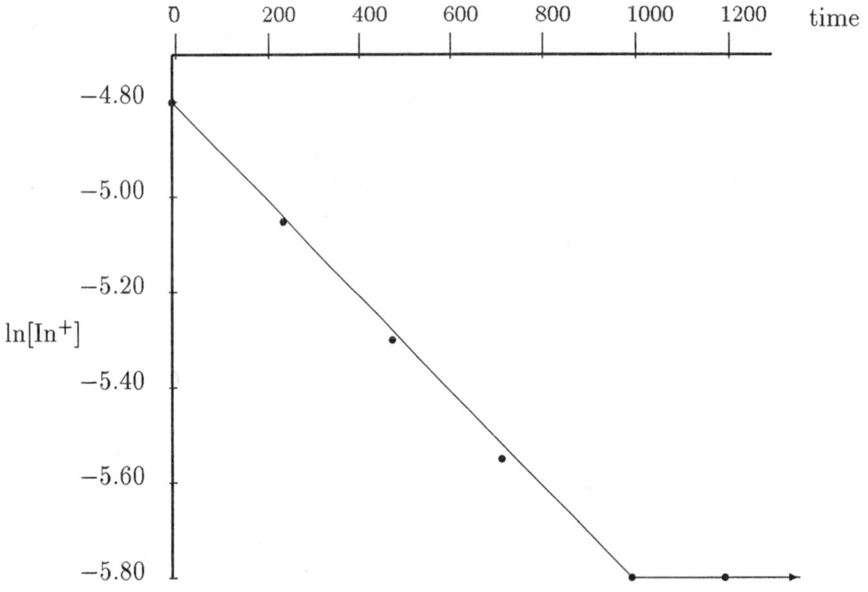

A common error is to make the values on the y axis go up the axis as they become more negative. They should go down the axis as they become more negative. Then the plot consists of a straight line that slopes from northwest to southeast and levels off beyond 1000 s. The initial slope of the line is $-k$ and the intercept is $\ln[\,\mathrm{In}^+]_0$. The slope can be read off the graph, but a least-squares analysis gives a somewhat better value. From such an analysis of the data, the slope is $-1.01 \times 10^{-3}\ \mathrm{s}^{-1}$. The rate constant is therefore $\boxed{1.01 \times 10^{-3}\ \mathrm{s}^{-1}}$.

b) The half-life can be determined from the rate constant,

$$t_{1/2} = \frac{\ln 2}{k} = \frac{0.6931}{1.01 \times 10^{-3}\ \mathrm{s}^{-1}} = \boxed{686\ \mathrm{s}}$$

c) At 10000 seconds, the concentration of In^+ has persisted unchanged for 9000 seconds. The reaction has clearly reached equilibrium. The concentration of In^+ is 3.03×10^{-3} M, and the amount of In^+ in the 1.00 L solution is accordingly 3.03×10^{-3} mol. The equilibrium concentration of In^{3+} is calculated by subtracting this amount from the original amount of In^+, and using the stoichiometric relation between the In^+ and In^{3+} as follows:

$$n_{\mathrm{In}^{3+}} = \frac{8.23 \times 10^{-3} - 3.03 \times 10^{-3}}{3} = 1.73 \times 10^{-3}\ \mathrm{mol}$$

The equilibrium concentration of In^{3+} therefore equals 1.73×10^{-3} M. Substitute in the usual mass-action expression:

$$K = \frac{[\mathrm{In}^{3+}]}{[\mathrm{In}^+]^3} = \frac{1.73 \times 10^{-3}}{(3.03 \times 10^{-3})^3} = \boxed{6.22 \times 10^4}$$

13.51 The reaction is: $\mathrm{OH}^-(aq) + \mathrm{HCN}(aq) \rightarrow \mathrm{H_2O}(l) + \mathrm{CN}^-(aq)$. This reaction is first-order in both OH^- and HCN, second-order overall:

$$\text{rate (forward)} = k_\mathrm{f}[\mathrm{OH}^-][\mathrm{HCN}]$$

At equilibrium the forward rate is exactly equaled by the reverse rate, which, because the concentration of water is constant, depends solely on the concentration of CN^-:

$$\text{rate (reverse)} = k_\mathrm{r}[\mathrm{CN}^-]$$

It follows that:

$$k_f[OH^-][HCN] = k_r[CN^-] \quad \text{from which:} \quad \frac{k_r}{k_f} = \frac{[OH^-][HCN]}{[CN^-]}$$

Note that the units of the quantity on the right-hand side of the second equation are mol L^{-1}. Numerically, the right-hand side of the preceding equation equals the equilibrium constant K_b of the reaction:

$$CN^-(aq) + H_2O(l) \rightleftharpoons HCN(aq) + OH^-(aq)$$

The K_b of CN^- ion is related to K_a of its conjugate acid HCN[6]

$$K_a = \frac{K_w}{K_a} = \frac{1.0 \times 10^{-14}}{4.93 \times 10^{-10}} = 2.03 \times 10^{-5}$$

Therefore:

$$\frac{k_r}{k_f} = 2.03 \times 10^{-5} \text{ mol L}^{-1}$$

Substitution of 3.7×10^{-9} L $\text{mol}^{-1}\text{s}^{-1}$ for k_f gives $k_r = \boxed{7.5 \times 10^4 \text{ s}^{-1}}$.

13.53 Both reactions are third-order, but [M] can be treated as a constant since it is much larger than the original concentrations of the I and Br and is not changed by the progress of the reaction. The integrated rate laws for the two reactions are then:

$$\frac{1}{[I]} - \frac{1}{[I]_0} = 2k_I[M]t \quad \text{and} \quad \frac{1}{[Br]} - \frac{1}{[Br]_0} = 2k_{Br}[M]t$$

After one half-life, $[I] = 1/2\,[I]_0$ and $[Br] = 1/2\,[Br]_0$ so:

$$\frac{1}{[I]_0} = 2k_I[M]t_{1/2,I} \quad \text{and} \quad \frac{1}{[Br]_0} = 2k_{Br}[M]t_{1/2,Br}$$

Dividing the first equation by the second gives:

$$\frac{[Br]_0}{[I]_0} = \left(\frac{k_I}{k_{Br}}\right)\left(\frac{t_{1/2,I}}{t_{1/2,Br}}\right)$$

Substitute $[I]_0 = 2[Br]_0$ and $k_I = 3.0k_{Br}$:

$$\frac{1}{2} = 3.0\left(\frac{t_{1/2,I}}{t_{1/2,Br}}\right) \quad \text{from which} \quad \left(\frac{t_{1/2,I}}{t_{1/2,Br}}\right) = \frac{1}{6.0} = \boxed{0.17}$$

13.55 The two reactions are both reactions of hydrogen with a halogen to form a hydrohalic acid. They must proceed by different mechanisms because their experimental rate laws are different:

$$\text{rate (bromine)} = k[H_2][Br_2]^{1/2} \qquad \text{rate (iodine)} = k[H_2][I_2]$$

The currently accepted mechanisms for both reactions involve a fast equilibrium to split the halogen molecule into its two atoms followed by reaction of one atom with H_2. In the case of Br, this elementary process is rate-limiting, but in the case of I, it is fast. The third steps in the mechanisms differ.

$$H + Br_2 \rightarrow HBr + Br \quad \text{fast} \qquad H_2I + I \rightarrow 2\,HI \quad \text{rate-limiting}$$

Also, in the iodine reaction, the intermediate H_2I is thought to exist, whereas the analogous H_2Br does not appear in the proposed mechanism for the bromine reaction.

---

[6] Taken from text Table 10.2.

13.57 The reaction is the decomposition of ozone by light: $2\,O_3 +$ light $\rightarrow 3\,O_2$. The mechanism involves the production of the intermediate O atom from O_3 (in the first step), and its consumption either to regenerate O_3 (the second step) or to make $2\,O_2$ in an encounter with an O_3 molecule (the third step). The change in the concentration of O with time is

$$\frac{d[\mathrm{O}]}{dt} = k_1[\mathrm{O_3}] - k_2[\mathrm{O}][\mathrm{O_2}][\mathrm{M}] - k_3[\mathrm{O}][\mathrm{O_3}]$$

This equation states that the rate of change of the concentration of O equals its rate of production minus its rate of consumption. The steady-state approximation is that [O] comes to a *steady* value. If [O] is steady it is unchanging, and $d[\mathrm{O}]/dt = 0$. Then:

$$k_1[\mathrm{O_3}] - k_2[\mathrm{O}][\mathrm{O_2}][\mathrm{M}] - k_3[\mathrm{O}][\mathrm{O_3}] = 0$$

so that

$$[\mathrm{O}] = \frac{k_1[\mathrm{O_3}]}{k_2[\mathrm{O_2}][\mathrm{M}] + k_3[\mathrm{O_3}]}$$

All of this concerns the intermediate. The rate of the overall reaction is

$$\text{rate} = \frac{1}{3}\frac{d[\mathrm{O_2}]}{dt} = k_3[\mathrm{O}][\mathrm{O_3}]$$

Insert the expression for the concentration of intermediate O into this rate law:

$$\boxed{\text{rate} = \frac{k_3 k_1[\mathrm{O_3}]^2}{k_2[\mathrm{O_2}][\mathrm{M}] + k_3[\mathrm{O_3}]}}$$

Divide the top and bottom of the fraction by k_3:

$$\text{rate} = \frac{k_1[\mathrm{O_3}]^2}{(k_2/k_3)\,[\mathrm{O_2}][\mathrm{M}] + [\mathrm{O_3}]}$$

Clearly, only the ratio k_2/k_3 affects the rate, not the individual values. This ratio tells how much of the intermediate O cycles back to O_3 relative to how much goes on to give the product.

13.59 The chemical reaction is $A + B + C \rightarrow D + E$. The species F is an intermediate. In the mechanism, F forms rapidly from A and B and then interacts more slowly with C. It interacts in two different ways, forming D in the first way and forming E in the second.
a) Let K_1 equal the equilibrium constant for the first step.

$$K_1 = \frac{k_1}{k_{-1}} = \frac{[\mathrm{F}]}{[\mathrm{A}][\mathrm{B}]}$$

From the second and third steps in the mechanism, the rates of formation of the products D and E are

$$\frac{d[\mathrm{D}]}{dt} = k_2[\mathrm{C}][\mathrm{F}] = k_2K_1[\mathrm{C}][\mathrm{A}][\mathrm{B}]$$
$$\frac{d[\mathrm{E}]}{dt} = k_3[\mathrm{C}][\mathrm{F}] = k_3K_1[\mathrm{C}][\mathrm{A}][\mathrm{B}]$$

The two rates of formation of the two products depend on the same concentrations.
b) Product D forms 10 times faster than product E because a 10 times larger amount of it has formed at the end of the reaction. Therefore $\boxed{k_2 \approx 10k_3}$.
c) The fact that a trace of acid greatly alters the relative amounts of D and E suggests that the acid is a catalyst. Quite possibly, E is thermodynamically favored in comparison to D, and the acid provides a rapid route for the reaction $D \rightarrow E$.

Tip. Reactions that give products other than the thermodynamically most stable products are said to be under kinetic control. The favored product does not form because there is not time for it to form. Changing the conditions (or waiting long enough) then allows expression of the underlying tendency to give the thermodynamically favored product.

13.61 The reaction of interest is an equilibrium

$$NH_3(aq) + H_2O(l) \rightleftharpoons NH_4^+(aq) + OH^-(aq) \qquad K_b = \frac{k_1}{k_{-1}}$$

The problem gives k_1 and K_b. The latter can also be computed from K_a for NH_4^+ in text Table 10.2. Therefore

$$k_{-1} = \frac{k_1}{K_b} = \frac{2 \times 10^5}{1.8 \times 10^{-5}} = \boxed{1 \times 10^{-10} \text{ L mol}^{-1}\text{s}^{-1}}$$

The units of this rate constant are inserted according to the explanation in the footnote on text page 446.

13.63 The initiation step is $CH_3CHO \rightarrow CH_3 + CHO$. The propagation steps involve the intermediates CH_3 (the methyl radical) and CH_2CHO (the acetyl radical). The propagation step is the combination of the second and third elementary reactions in the problem. The CH_3 is consumed in the second reaction and regenerated in the third, which forms the product CO. This chain continues indefinitely to consume all available CH_3CHO except when cut by the termination reaction, which forms the by-product CH_3CH_3 when two methyl radicals encounter each other and react.

13.65 a) Assume that the rate constants of the reactions that occur in cooking vary with the temperature according to the Arrhenius equation. Since the food cooks two times faster at 112°C (385 K) than at 100°C (373 K), the rate constant must be twice as large at 385 K: $k_{385} = 2\,k_{373}$. An Arrhenius equation can be written for each of these k's. Hence:

$$Ae^{-E_a/385R} = 2\,Ae^{-E_a/373R}$$

Cancel out the A's, take the natural logarithm of both sides, and rearrange:

$$\frac{-E_a}{385 \text{ K}} - \frac{-E_a}{373 \text{ K}} = R\ln 2 = (8.3145 \text{ J K}^{-1}\text{mol}^{-1})(0.6931)$$

Solving for E_a gives an activation energy equal to $\boxed{69.0 \text{ kJ mol}^{-1}}$.

b) The rates of the cooking reactions at 94.4°C (367.6 K) depend on the rate constant at that temperature. The following equation involving the rate constant for cooking at 367.6 K comes from dividing the Arrhenius equation at 367.6 K by the Arrhenius equation at 373 K:

$$\frac{k_{367.6}}{k_{373}} = \frac{e^{-E_a/367.6R}}{e^{-E_a/373R}}$$

Taking the natural logarithm of both sides gives

$$\ln\left(\frac{k_{367.6}}{k_{373}}\right) = \frac{-E_a}{367.6R} - \frac{-E_a}{373R} = \frac{-69.0 \times 10^3 \text{ J mol}^{-1}}{8.3145 \text{ J K}^{-1}\text{mol}^{-1}}\left(\frac{1}{367.6} - \frac{1}{373}\right) = -0.339$$

where the value of E_a has been taken from part a). Take the antilogarithm of both sides:

$$\frac{k_{367.6}}{k_{373}} = e^{-0.339} = 0.712$$

Since the rate constant at 94.4°C is smaller by the factor 0.712 times than the rate constant at 100°C, the food takes $1/0.712 = 1.404$ times longer to cook. Instead of 10 minutes, the cooking requires $\boxed{14 \text{ minutes}}$.

13.67 The rate constants of the forward and reverse reactions in the equilibrium between gaseous hydrogen and iodine on the one side and gaseous hydrogen iodide on the other are related to the equilibrium constant by the equation:

$$K = \frac{k_f}{k_r}$$

Write Arrhenius equations for both the forward reaction and the reverse reaction:

$$k_f = Ae^{-E_{a,f}/RT} \qquad \text{and} \qquad k_r = Ae^{-E_{a,r}/RT}$$

Divide the first equation by the second and take the logarithm of both sides:

$$\ln\left(\frac{k_f}{k_r}\right) = \frac{-E_{a,f}}{RT} - \frac{-E_{a,r}}{RT} = \frac{1}{RT}(E_{a,r} - E_{a,f})$$

The left side of this equation equals $\ln K$, the logarithm of the equilibrium constant. But $\ln K$ of the reaction at the temperature T is related to the standard free energy at that temperature by the thermodynamic equation $\Delta G^\circ_T = -RT\ln K$. Substitution gives:

$$-\frac{\Delta G^\circ_T}{RT} = \frac{1}{RT}(E_{a,r} - E_{a,f})$$

Multiply both sides by $-RT$ (at the constant temperature T):

$$\Delta G^\circ_T = (E_{a,f} - E_{a,r})$$

Assuming that ΔH° and ΔS° do not change going from 298 to 1000 K, the standard free energy of this reaction at 1000 K is

$$\Delta G^\circ_{1000} = \Delta H^\circ - 1000\,\Delta S^\circ$$

Use the standard enthalpies of formation of the reactants and products to compute ΔH°:

$$\Delta H^\circ = 2\underbrace{(26.48)}_{HI(g)} - 1\underbrace{(62.44)}_{I_2(g)} - 1\underbrace{(0.00)}_{H_2(g)} = -9.48 \text{ kJ}$$

Do the same with absolute entropies to get ΔS°:

$$\Delta S^\circ = 2\underbrace{(206.48)}_{HI(g)} - 1\underbrace{(260.58)}_{I_2(g)} - 1\underbrace{(130.57)}_{H_2(g)} = 21.81 \text{ J K}^{-1}$$

Combining these values gives ΔG° at 1000 K:

$$\Delta G^\circ_{1000} = -9.48 \times 10^3 \text{ J} - (1000 \text{ K})(21.81 \text{ J K}^{-1}) = -31.29 \times 10^3 \text{ J}$$

Now, two of the three quantities in the relationship $\Delta G^\circ_{1000} = (E_{a,f} - E_{a,r})$ are known. Substitute them:

$$-31.29 \text{ kJ mol}^{-1} = (165 \text{ kJ mol}^{-1} - E_{a,r})$$

Solving gives $\boxed{196 \text{ kJ mol}^{-1}}$ as the activation energy of the reverse reaction.

An easy way to obtain k_r is to calculate the equilibrium constant K_{1000} and use the known k_f in the equation: $K = k_f/k_r$ Thus:

$$\ln K = -\frac{\Delta G^\circ}{RT} = -\frac{-31.29 \times 10^3 \text{ J mol}^{-1}}{8.3145 \text{ J K}^{-1}\text{mol}^{-1}(1000 \text{ K})} = 3.763 \quad \text{so that} \quad K = 43.08$$

$$k_r = \frac{k_f}{K} = \frac{240 \text{ L mol}^{-1}\text{s}^{-1}}{43.08} = \boxed{5.6 \text{ L mol}^{-1}\text{s}^{-1}}$$

13.69 The CF_2Cl_2 enters into the chemical reaction and presumably speeds it up, but is not itself consumed in the reaction. It does not appear in the balanced overall equation representing the reaction because it is consumed in one step of the mechanism but regenerated later. It is a $\boxed{\text{catalyst}}$.

13.71 The mechanism of enzyme catalysis, as modified to allow for the action of an inhibitor, is

$E + S \rightleftharpoons ES$	fast equilibrium	k_1 and k_{-1}
$ES \rightarrow E + P$	slow	k_2
$E + I \rightleftharpoons EI$	fast equilibrium	k_3 and k_{-3}

This is a case of competitive inhibition. The inhibitor (symbolized I) competes with the substrate S in binding to the enzyme E. The generation of product P is thereby slowed because P forms only through the complex ES. Follow the pattern of the derivation in text Section 13.7, but allow for the complication of the inhibitor. Label the total concentration of enzyme $[E]_0$. The enzyme is present in one of three states: free, bound to the inhibitor, or bound to the substrate:

$$[E]_0 = [E] + [EI] + [ES]$$

Write the equilibrium expression for the third step of the mechanism, letting k_3/k_{-3} equal K_3:

$$K_3 = \frac{[EI]}{[E][I]}$$

Solve this expression for [EI], substitute into the first equation, and solve for [E] as follows:

$$[E]_0 = [E] + K_3[E][I] + [ES]$$

$$[E]_0 = [E]\Big(1 + K_3[I]\Big) + [ES]$$

$$[E] = \frac{[E]_0 - [ES]}{1 + K_3[I]}$$

Now, make the steady-state approximation for ES, the intermediate. This approximation is that the ES is generated as fast as it is consumed—its concentration does not change with time. The first step in the mechanism forms it; the reverse of the first step removes it; the second step also removes it:

$$0 = \frac{d[ES]}{dt} = k_1[E][S] - k_{-1}[ES] - k_2[ES]$$

Solve for [ES] and substitute with the previous expression for [E] and simplify. The result is

$$[ES] = \frac{k_1[E]_0[S]}{k_1[S] + \Big(1 + K_3[I]\Big)(k_{-1} + k_2)}$$

The rate of the reaction equals the rate of the slow step, which equals $k_2[ES]$. Therefore:

$$\text{rate} = k_2[ES] = \frac{k_2 k_1[E]_0[S]}{k_1[S] + (1 + K_3[I])(k_{-1} + k_2)} = \frac{k_2[E]_0[S]}{[S] + K_m(1 + K_3[I])}$$

where K_m is defined as $(k_{-1}+k_2)/k_1$. This K_m is called the Michaelis-Menten constant.[7] Any concentration of the inhibitor increases the denominator of this expression and lowers the initial rate of the reaction.

---

[7] See text equation 13.8 on text page 462.

13.73 The reaction is the gas-phase combination of H_2 and I_2 to give HI. The $\Delta H°$ of this change equals -9.48 kJ when two moles of HI are produced. See **13.67**. Obtain the initial rate of the reaction by substituting the rate constant and the initial concentrations of H_2 and I_2 into the rate equation:

$$\text{rate} = k[\text{H}_2][\text{I}_2] = 0.0242\ \text{M}^{-1}\text{s}^{-1}[0.081\ \text{M}][0.036\ \text{M}] = 7.06 \times 10^{-5}\ \text{M}\,\text{s}^{-1}$$

The rate of formation of HI is twice this rate (because HI has a coefficient of 2 in the balanced reaction). The rate of absorption of heat equals the rate at which HI forms times the heat absorbed per mole of HI:

$$\frac{2(7.06 \times 10^{-5}\ \text{mol HI})}{\text{L s}} \times \left(\frac{-9.48\ \text{kJ}}{2\ \text{mol HI}}\right) = \boxed{-6.7 \times 10^{-4}\ \text{kJ L}^{-1}\text{s}^{-1}}$$

13.75 Substitution of the initial concentrations of NO and O_3 into the second-order rate law gives the desired initial rate of the reaction. Use the ideal-gas law to obtain these concentrations from the mole fractions of the two gases:

$$\left(\frac{n}{V}\right)_{\text{NO}} = \frac{P_{\text{NO}}}{RT} = \frac{0.00057(3.26\ \text{atm})}{(0.08206\ \text{L atm mol}^{-1}\text{K}^{-1})(500\ \text{K})} = 4.53 \times 10^{-5}\ \text{mol L}^{-1}$$

$$\left(\frac{n}{V}\right)_{\text{O}_3} = \frac{P_{\text{O}_3}}{RT} = \frac{0.00026(3.26\ \text{atm})}{(0.08206\ \text{L atm mol}^{-1}\text{K}^{-1})(500\ \text{K})} = 2.07 \times 10^{-5}\ \text{mol L}^{-1}$$

Then proceed with the substitution:

$$\text{rate} = k[\text{NO}][\text{O}_3] = (7.6 \times 10^{7}\ \text{L mol}^{-1}\text{s}^{-1})(4.53 \times 10^{-5}\ \text{mol L}^{-1})(2.07 \times 10^{-5}\ \text{mol L}^{-1})$$

$$= \boxed{0.071\ \text{mol L}^{-1}\text{s}^{-1}}$$

Chapter 14

Nuclear Chemistry

14.1 Use these tests for balance in nuclear equations: the sums of the left superscripts on the two sides of the equation must be equal; the sums of the left subscripts on the two sides of the equation must also be equal.

$$\text{a) } 2\,{}^{12}_{6}\text{C} \rightarrow {}^{23}_{12}\text{Mg} + {}^{1}_{0}n \quad \text{b) } {}^{15}_{7}\text{N} + {}^{1}_{1}\text{H} \rightarrow {}^{12}_{6}\text{C} + {}^{4}_{2}\text{He} \quad \text{c) } 2\,{}^{3}_{2}\text{He} \rightarrow {}^{4}_{2}\text{He} + 2\,{}^{1}_{1}\text{H}$$

14.3 a) The total binding energy of the calcium-40 nuclide equals the negative of the energy equivalent of the change in mass that occurs with formation of the nuclide from its component particles:

$$20\,{}^{1}_{1}\text{H} + 20\,{}^{1}_{0}n \rightarrow {}^{40}_{20}\text{Ca}$$

$$\Delta m = m[{}^{40}_{20}\text{Ca}] - 20\,m[{}^{1}_{1}\text{H}] - 20\,m[{}^{1}_{0}n]$$
$$\Delta m = 39.9625912 - 20(1.007825032) - 20(1.0086649158) = -0.3672078 \text{ u}$$

The energy equivalent of 1 u is 931.494 MeV. Therefore:

$$\Delta E = -0.3672078 \text{ u} \times \left(\frac{931.494 \text{ MeV}}{1 \text{ u}}\right) = -342.052 \text{ MeV per atom}$$

The binding energy E_B is the negative of this, $\boxed{342.052 \text{ MeV}}$. To compute ΔE in joules, convert Δm to kilograms and substitute it into the Einstein equation:

$$\begin{aligned}\Delta E &= c^2 \Delta m \\ &= (2.9979246 \times 10^8 \text{ m s}^{-1})^2(-0.3672078 \text{ u}) \times \left(\frac{1.660540 \times 10^{-27} \text{ kg}}{1 \text{ u}}\right) \\ &= -5.480279 \times 10^{-11} \text{ J}\end{aligned}$$

The binding energy of a mole of atoms equals the negative of this answer, which is for a single atom, multiplied by Avogadro's number:

$$E_B = -(-5.480279 \times 10^{-11} \text{ J}) \times (6.022142 \times 10^{23} \text{ mol}^{-1}) = \boxed{3.300301 \times 10^{10} \text{ kJ mol}^{-1}}$$

Since ${}^{40}_{20}\text{Ca}$ has 40 nucleons, the E_B per nucleon is $342.052/40 = \boxed{8.55130 \text{ MeV}}$.

Tip. This is the value graphed in text Figure 14.2.

b) The Δm between the product ${}^{87}_{37}\text{Rb}$ and the reactants $50\,{}^{1}_{0}n$ and $37\,{}^{1}_{1}\text{H}$ equals -0.813589 u. By computations like those in part a), the E_{B} per atom of ${}^{87}_{37}\text{Rb}$ is $\boxed{757.853 \text{ MeV}}$. The binding energy per mole is $\boxed{7.31218 \times 10^{10} \text{ kJ mol}^{-1}}$, and the binding energy per nucleon is E_{B} divided by 87 or $\boxed{8.7110 \text{ MeV}}$.

c) Uranium-238 has 92 protons and 146 neutrons. Compute Δm for the making of the atom by adding up the mass of 92 hydrogen atoms (not protons) and 146 neutrons and subtracting the result from the mass of the U-238 atom. The answer is -1.934198 u. Convert this to a ΔE to obtain E_{B} per atom, which is $\boxed{1801.69 \text{ MeV}}$ or $\boxed{17.3837 \times 10^{10} \text{ kJ mol}^{-1}}$. The binding energy per nucleon is $\boxed{7.57013 \text{ MeV}}$.

Tip. To save time in calculations observe that, according to the Einstein equation

$$\Delta m = 1 \text{ u per atom} \quad \text{implies} \quad \Delta E = 8.98755179 \times 10^{10} \text{ kJ mol}^{-1}$$

14.5 The mass of a single ${}^{8}\text{Be}$ atom equals 8.0053052 u whereas the mass of two ${}^{4}\text{He}$ atoms equals twice 4.0026033 u, which is 8.0052066 u. Because the particles have a larger mass when organized as a ${}^{8}\text{Be}$ atom, the ${}^{8}\text{Be}$ atom is less stable than the pair of ${}^{4}\text{He}$ atoms. In other terms, the Δm for the nuclear reaction: ${}^{8}_{4}\text{Be} \rightarrow 2\,{}^{4}_{2}\text{He}$ is negative. The Δm is $\boxed{-9.86 \times 10^{-5} \text{ u}}$.

14.7 Represent the decay as:

$${}^{8}_{5}\text{B} \rightarrow {}^{8}_{4}\text{Be} + {}^{0}_{1}e^{+} + \nu$$

The difference in mass between the two sides of the reaction appears from this equation to be:

$$\Delta m = \underbrace{8.00530509}_{^{8}\text{Be}} + \underbrace{0.00054858}_{^{0}_{1}e+} - \underbrace{8.024607}_{^{8}\text{B}} = -0.018753 \text{ u ?}$$

using the numbers found in text Table 14.1[1] for the boron atom, beryllium atom, and positron. At this point a trap looms. The tabulated masses include the electrons that surround the nuclei of the atoms. Beryllium has only four electrons, but boron has five. The computation at this stage has wrongly allowed one electron to vanish. This is put right by including another electron mass with the mass of the products. The true change in mass is

$$\Delta m = 8.00530509 + 2(0.00054858) - 8.024607 = -0.018205 \text{ u}$$

This mass change has an energy equivalent of -16.9576 MeV. Therefore $\boxed{16.9576 \text{ MeV}}$ is released by the reaction of 1 atom of ${}^{8}\text{B}$.

Tip. The trap is avoided by balancing the original equation as to charge. The positive charge on the positron cannot appear without compensation. Therefore Be must be a negative ion:

$${}^{8}_{5}\text{B} \rightarrow {}^{8}_{4}\text{Be}^{-} + {}^{0}_{1}e^{+} + \nu$$

14.9 Positron emission (loss of ${}^{0}_{1}e^{+}$) and electron capture by a nucleus always lower the atomic number by one; electron emission (loss of ${}^{0}_{-1}e^{-}$) raises the atomic number by one.

a) ${}^{39}_{17}\text{Cl} \rightarrow {}^{39}_{18}\text{Ar} + {}^{0}_{-1}e^{-} + \bar{\nu}$ **b)** ${}^{22}_{11}\text{Na} \rightarrow {}^{22}_{10}\text{Ne} + {}^{0}_{1}e^{+} + \nu$

c) ${}^{224}_{88}\text{Ra} \rightarrow {}^{220}_{86}\text{Rn} + {}^{4}_{2}\text{He}$ **d)** ${}^{82}_{38}\text{Sr} + {}^{0}_{-1}e \rightarrow {}^{82}_{37}\text{Rb} + \nu$

14.11 The ${}^{19}\text{Ne}$ nucleus is neutron deficient and decays by converting a proton to a neutron. The ${}^{23}\text{Ne}$ nucleus is too rich in neutrons and decays by converting a neutron to a proton. Thus, the decay of ${}^{19}\text{Ne}$ proceeds by $\boxed{\text{positron emission}}$ to give ${}^{19}\text{F}$, and the decay of ${}^{23}\text{Ne}$ proceeds by $\boxed{\text{electron emission (beta decay)}}$ to give ${}^{23}\text{Na}$.

---

[1] Text page 474.

14.13 The electrically neutral neutron decays to a positive proton, a negative electron ($_{-1}^{0}e^{-}$), and an antineutrino. Determine the change in mass and find the equivalent change in energy:

$$\Delta E = (1.007276 + 0.00054858 - 1.008665)\ \text{u} \times \left(\frac{931.494\ \text{MeV}}{1\ \text{u}}\right) = -0.7824\ \text{MeV}$$

The electron has a maximum kinetic energy of $\boxed{0.7824\ \text{MeV}}$.

Tip. This is a maximum because the antineutrino and proton carry off some kinetic energy in most decay events.

14.15 The answer requires the translation of the written description of the process into nuclear equations: $\boxed{{}_{14}^{30}\text{Si} + {}_{0}^{1}n \rightarrow {}_{14}^{31}\text{Si} \rightarrow {}_{15}^{31}\text{P} + {}_{-1}^{0}e^{-} + \bar{\nu}}$.

14.17 ${}_{84}^{210}\text{Po} \rightarrow {}_{82}^{206}\text{C} + {}_{2}^{4}\text{He}$ ${}_{2}^{4}\text{He} + {}_{4}^{9}\text{Be} \rightarrow {}_{6}^{12}\text{C} + {}_{0}^{1}n$

14.19 Compute how many atoms are present in 0.0010 g of ^{209}Po:

$$0.0010\ \text{g} \times \left(\frac{1\ \text{mol Po}}{209\ \text{g Po}}\right) \times \left(\frac{6.02214 \times 10^{23}\ \text{atom Po}}{1\ \text{mol Po}}\right) = 2.88 \times 10^{18}\ \text{atom}\ ^{209}\text{Po}$$

The activity A, which equals the instantaneous rate of disintegration in the polonium, depends on the number of atoms present:

$$A = -\frac{dN}{dt} = kN$$

The k in this equation is a first-order rate constant. It equals $\ln 2/t_{1/2}$ where $t_{1/2}$ is the half-life of the decay. Substituting:

$$A = \left(\frac{\ln 2}{t_{1/2}}\right) N = \left(\frac{0.6931}{103\ \text{yr}}\right) 2.88 \times 10^{18} = 1.94 \times 10^{16}\ \text{yr}^{-1}$$

Convert to a per minute basis as follows:

$$A = 1.94 \times 10^{16}\ \text{yr}^{-1} \times \left(\frac{1\ \text{yr}}{365.2\ \text{day}}\right) \times \left(\frac{1\ \text{day}}{1440\ \text{min}}\right) = 3.7 \times 10^{10}\ \text{min}^{-1}$$

That is, $\boxed{3.7 \times 10^{10}\ \text{atoms}}$ of polonium decay per minute.

14.21 a) At the moment of preparation, the sample has initial activity (rate of decay) A_0. The activity is directly proportional to N_0, the number of atoms of ^{19}O present at the start:

$$A_0 = kN_0$$

The rate constant k is ($\ln 2/29$ s), which equals 0.0239 s^{-1}. Then:

$$N_{^{19}\text{O}} = \frac{A}{k} = \frac{2.5 \times 10^{4}\ \text{s}^{-1}}{0.0239\ \text{s}^{-1}} = 1.046 \times 10^{6}\ \text{atom} = \boxed{1.0 \times 10^{6}\ \text{atom}\ ^{19}\text{O}}$$

b) The number of ^{19}O atoms that remains at any time t is

$$N = N_0 e^{-kt}$$

In this case t is 2.00 min or 120 s. Substitution of k and N_0 gives:

$$N = (1.046 \times 10^{6}) \exp\Big(-(0.0239\ \text{s}^{-1})(120\ \text{s})\Big) = \boxed{5.9 \times 10^{4}\ \text{atom}}$$

14.23 First calculate N, the number of atoms in 44 mg of ^{219}At:

$$N = 44 \times 10^{-3}\text{ g} \times \left(\frac{1\text{ mol}}{219\text{ g}}\right) \times \left(\frac{6.022 \times 10^{23}\text{ atoms}}{1\text{ mol}}\right) = 1.21 \times 10^{20}\text{ atoms}$$

Then compute the activity of this amount of astatine using the half-life as given:

$$A = kN = \left(\frac{\ln 2}{t_{1/2}}\right) N = \left(\frac{0.6931}{54\text{ s}}\right)(1.21 \times 10^{20}) = \boxed{1.6 \times 10^{18}\text{ s}^{-1}}$$

14.25 The activity of ^{14}C decays according to the same law as the number of atoms of ^{14}C:

$$A = A_0 e^{-kt} \quad \text{which gives:} \quad -kt = \ln\left(\frac{A}{A_0}\right)$$

For the papyrus, A is 9.2 disintegrations min^{-1}g^{-1} and A_0 is 15.3 disintegrations min^{-1}g^{-1}. Also, k is $\ln 2/t_{1/2}$ or 1.21×10^{-4} yr^{-1}. Substituting gives:

$$-(1.21 \times 10^{-4}\text{ yr}^{-1})\,t = \ln\left(\frac{9.2\text{ min}^{-1}\text{g}^{-1}}{15.3\text{ min}^{-1}\text{g}^{-1}}\right) \quad \text{so that} \quad t = \boxed{4.2 \times 10^{3}\text{ yr}}$$

Tip. It is assumed that the activity of ^{14}C in the biosphere has not changed since Egyptian times.

14.27 For every atom of U-238 that decays, eight atoms of He are produced. Compute the number of moles of He (using the ideal-gas law) per gram of rock:

$$n_{\text{He}} = \frac{PV}{RT} = \frac{(1\text{ atm})(9.0 \times 10^{-8}\text{ L})}{(0.08206\text{ L atm mol}^{-1}\text{K}^{-1})(273.15\text{ K})} = 4.015 \times 10^{-9}\text{ mol}$$

The number of atoms of U-238 that has decayed is therefore:

$$4.015 \times 10^{-9}\text{ mol He} \times \left(\frac{6.022 \times 10^{23}\text{ atom He}}{1\text{ mol He}}\right) \times \left(\frac{1\text{ atom }^{238}\text{U}}{8\text{ atom He}}\right) = 3.02 \times 10^{14}\text{ atom}$$

The number of atoms of ^{238}U still present per gram of rock is also readily computed:

$$2.0 \times 10^{-7}\text{ g }^{238}\text{U} \times \left(\frac{1\text{ mol}}{238.0\text{ g}}\right) \times \left(\frac{6.022 \times 10^{23}\text{ atom}}{1\text{ mol}}\right) = 5.06 \times 10^{14}\text{ atom}$$

The initial number of atoms of U-238 per gram of rock equals the number decayed plus the number remaining. It is 8.08×10^{14} atoms per gram of rock. The decay process is described by the equation:

$$\ln\left(\frac{N}{N_0}\right) = -kt = -\left(\frac{\ln 2}{t_{1/2}}\right) t$$

Substitution gives:

$$\ln\left(\frac{5.06 \times 10^{14}}{8.08 \times 10^{14}}\right) = -\left(\frac{\ln 2}{4.47 \times 10^{9}\text{ yr}}\right) t$$

Solving for t gives the approximate age of the rock: $\boxed{3.0\text{ billion years}}$.

14.29 First-order kinetics govern the radioactive decay of both ^{235}U and ^{238}U:

$$N(^{235}\text{U}) = N_0(^{235}\text{U})e^{-kt} \qquad \text{and} \qquad N(^{238}\text{U}) = N_0(^{238}\text{U})e^{-kt}$$

In the beginning, the two isotopes were equally abundant. Assume that the current difference in abundance is caused entirely by the faster decay of U-235. (The half-life of ^{235}U is briefer by a factor of about 6.) The current ratio of abundances is 137.7 to 1. In equation form:

$$N_0\left(^{238}\text{U}\right) = N_0\left(^{235}\text{U}\right) \quad \text{and} \quad N\left(^{238}\text{U}\right) = 137.7N\left(^{235}\text{U}\right)$$

This means that:

$$\frac{137.7}{1} = \frac{N_0\left(^{238}\text{U}\right)e^{-k_{238}t}}{N_0\left(^{235}\text{U}\right)e^{-k_{235}t}} = \frac{e^{-k_{238}t}}{e^{-k_{235}t}}$$

where k_{238} is the rate constant for the decay of ^{238}U and k_{235} is the rate constant for the decay of ^{235}U. Take the natural logarithm of both sides of the equation:

$$\ln 137.7 = (-k_{238}t) - (-k_{235}t) = t(k_{235} - k_{238})$$

For each isotope $k = \ln 2/t_{1/2}$ so:

$$\ln 137.7 = t\left(\frac{\ln 2}{t_{1/2,235}} - \frac{\ln 2}{t_{1/2,238}}\right)$$

The half-lives of the isotopes are 7.13×10^8 years and 4.51×10^9 years respectively. Inserting these numbers in the equation and solving for t gives $\boxed{6.0 \times 10^9 \text{ yr}}$. The supposed supernova occurred about 1.5 billion years before the estimated time of the formation of the solar system.

14.31 Positron emission is accompanied by emission of a neutrino:
$^{11}_{6}\text{C} \rightarrow {}^{11}_{5}\text{B} + {}^{0}_{1}e^+ + \nu \qquad {}^{15}_{8}\text{O} \rightarrow {}^{15}_{7}\text{N} + {}^{0}_{1}e^+ + \nu$

14.33 Assume that all of the ^{11}C and ^{15}O atoms decay before any are excreted or else that equal chemical amounts of the two radioactive nuclides are excreted. O-15 deposits 1.74 times more energy per kilogram of body mass than the C-11 because its positrons, which are emitted in equal number, are on the average more energetic by the factor $1.72/0.99 = \boxed{1.74}$.

14.35 a) Determine the number of atoms of I-131 ingested:

$$N_\text{I} = 5.0 \times 10^{-6} \text{ g } ^{131}\text{I}\left(\frac{1 \text{ mol } ^{131}\text{I}}{131 \text{ g } ^{131}\text{I}}\right)\left(\frac{6.022 \times 10^{23} \text{ atoms } ^{131}\text{I}}{1 \text{ mol } ^{131}\text{I}}\right) = 2.3 \times 10^{16} \text{ atoms } ^{131}\text{I}$$

Express the half-life of I-131 in seconds: $8.041 \text{ d} \times 86400 \text{ s d}^{-1} = 6.947 \times 10^5$ s. The ingested activity is then:

$$A = kN = \left(\frac{\ln 2}{t_{1/2}}\right)N = \left(\frac{0.6931}{6.947 \times 10^5 \text{ s}}\right)(2.3 \times 10^{16}) = 2.3 \times 10^{10} \text{ s}^{-1} = \boxed{2.3 \times 10^{10} \text{ Bq}}$$

b) Compute the initial rate at which energy is evolved from the decay of I-131. Use the fact that a becquerel (Bq) is a decay event per second:

$$\left(\frac{2.3 \times 10^{10} \text{ events}}{1 \text{ s}}\right) \times \left(\frac{0.40 \text{ MeV}}{1 \text{ event}}\right) \times \left(\frac{1.602 \times 10^{-13} \text{ J}}{1 \text{ MeV}}\right) = 1.474 \times 10^{-3} \text{ J s}^{-1}$$

This equals 0.147 cJ per second. The victim weighs 60 kg and all of the energy is deposited internally. He or she therefore absorbs 0.00245 cJ per kg of body mass in the first second. A millirad equals 0.0010 cJ per kg of body mass, so the radiation absorbed dose in the first second is $\boxed{2.4 \text{ millirad}}$.

c) The rate of dosage diminishes as the I-131 decays. Assume a constant activity equal to merely half the initial activity (the activity falls to this value after 8.041 d). Even at the artificially low rate of 1.25 millirad per second, the LD_{50} dose of 500 rad is delivered in a frighteningly brief time:

$$500 \text{ rad} \times \left(\frac{1 \text{ s}}{1.25 \times 10^{-3} \text{ rad}}\right) \times \left(\frac{1 \text{ d}}{86400 \text{ s}}\right) = 4.6 \text{ d}$$

The true dose in the first 4.6 d exceeds 500 rad, and dosage continues at a significant rate after the first 4.6 days. The actual dose will therefore $\boxed{\text{surely be lethal}}$.

Tip. Compare closely to **14.36**. The inhaled plutonium in that problem is equal in mass to the radioactive iodine ingested here, but is probably not a lethal dose. Be sure to understand why.

14.37 a) The balanced nuclear reaction is ${}^{90}_{38}\text{Sr} \rightarrow {}^{90}_{40}\text{Zr} + 2\,{}^{\ 0}_{-1}e^- + 2\,\bar{\nu}$. The version ${}^{90}_{38}\text{Sr} \rightarrow {}^{90}_{40}\text{Zr}^{2+} + 2\,{}^{\ 0}_{-1}e^- + 2\,\bar{\nu}$ shows an exact charge balance between the two sides (in the right superscripts), in addition to balance as to Z (left subscripts) and A (left superscripts).

b) The overall nuclear reaction is two consecutive beta decays. The change in mass in beta decay is

$$\Delta m = m\,(\text{daughter atom}) - m\,(\text{parent atom})$$

To get the Δm of the overall reaction, simply subtract the mass of an atom of ^{90}Sr from the mass of an atom of ^{90}Zr. The masses of the beta particles are automatically accounted for when this is done. The required isotopic masses are listed in the problem. The result is a Δm of -0.0030 u. The corresponding energy (taking 1 u as equivalent to 931.494 MeV) is $\boxed{2.8 \text{ MeV}}$.

c) This part is just like **14.19**. Compute the number of atoms in 1.00 g of ^{90}Sr:

$$N_{\text{Sr-90}} = 1.00 \text{ g} \times \left(\frac{1 \text{ mol}}{89.9073 \text{ g}}\right) \times \left(\frac{6.02214 \times 10^{23} \text{ atom}}{1 \text{ mol}}\right) = 6.698 \times 10^{21} \text{ atom } {}^{90}\text{Sr}$$

The activity A, which is the instantaneous rate of disintegration of the Sr-90 depends on the number of Sr-90 atoms present:

$$A = -\frac{dN}{dt} = kN$$

The k in this equation equals $\ln 2/t_{1/2}$ where $t_{1/2}$ is the half-life. Substituting:

$$A = \left(\frac{\ln 2}{t_{1/2}}\right) N = \left(\frac{0.6931}{28.1 \text{ yr}}\right)(6.698 \times 10^{21}) = 1.65 \times 10^{20} \text{ yr}^{-1}$$

This is the number of disintegrations per year at the moment that the ^{90}Sr is released. The problem asks for the activity on a per second basis:

$$A = 1.65 \times 10^{20} \text{ yr}^{-1} \times \left(\frac{1 \text{ yr}}{365.2 \text{ d}}\right) \times \left(\frac{1 \text{ d}}{86400 \text{ s}}\right) = \boxed{5.23 \times 10^{12} \text{ s}^{-1}}$$

d) The activity of the Sr-90 falls off with time as the number of Sr-90 atoms persisting in the 1.00 g sample diminishes. The relationship is

$$A = A_0 e^{-kt} = A_0 \exp\left(-\frac{\ln 2\, t}{t_{1/2}}\right)$$

Substituting the initial activity from part c), the specified time of 100 yr and the half-life of 28.1 yr gives

$$A = (5.23 \times 10^{12} \text{ s}^{-1}) \exp\left(\frac{-0.6931(100 \text{ yr})}{28.1 \text{ yr}}\right) = \boxed{4.44 \times 10^{11} \text{ s}^{-1}}$$

Tip. The activity of the isotope falls off to about 8.5% of its original value in 100 years. The problem could have asked for activities in becquerels (Bq) rather than disintegrations per second (s^{-1}). The conversion from s^{-1} to Bq is particularly simple: the answers are 5.23×10^{12} Bq and 4.44×10^{11} Bq.

14.39 The lighter isotopes of uranium happen to decay faster than the heavier isotopes. The quicker breakdown of the light isotopes leaves heavy isotopes behind, causing the average atomic mass of the uranium to $\boxed{\text{increase}}$ with time. This assumes that none of the lighter isotopes are the products of decay of the heavier isotopes.

14.41 The change in mass when one atom of U-235 gains a neutron and then undergoes fission as specified in the problem is the mass of the products minus the mass of the reactants:

$$\Delta m = 1\underbrace{(93.919)}_{^{94}\text{Kr}} + 1\underbrace{(138.909)}_{^{139}\text{Ba}} + 3\underbrace{(1.0086649)}_{^1_0 n} - 1\underbrace{(235.043925)}_{^{235}\text{U}} - 1\underbrace{(1.0086649)}_{^1_0 n} = -0.1986 \text{ u}$$

Convert to kJ mol^{-1} using the mass-energy equivalence established in **14.3a**. The result is -1.785×10^{10} kJ mol^{-1}. The problem asks for the energy change per gram of ^{235}U:

$$-1.785 \times 10^{10} \text{ kJ mol}^{-1} \times \left(\frac{1 \text{ mol } ^{235}\text{U}}{235.04 \text{ g } ^{235}\text{U}}\right) = -7.59 \times 10^7 \text{ kJ g}^{-1}$$

The energy released is the negative of the energy change of the system: $\boxed{+7.59 \times 10^7 \text{ kJ g}^{-1}}$.

14.43 When a positron and electron meet, they annihilate each other to generate gamma radiation:

$$^0_1e^+ + {}^{\;\,0}_{-1}e^- \rightarrow 2\,\gamma$$

The mass of the electron and positron both equal 0.00054858 u. Therefore, Δm for the annihilation reaction is -0.00109716 u and:

$$\Delta E = -0.00109716 \text{ u} \times \left(\frac{931.494 \text{ MeV}}{1 \text{ u}}\right) = -1.02200 \text{ MeV}$$

Because neither particle had any kinetic energy, only this amount of energy appears in the surroundings, borne by two gamma rays of energy $\boxed{0.51100 \text{ MeV}}$.

14.45 a) The beta decay of ^{64}Cu is

$$^{64}_{29}\text{Cu} \rightarrow {}^{64}_{30}\text{Zn} + {}^{\;\,0}_{-1}e^- + \bar{\nu}$$

For this process:

$$\Delta m = m(^{64}_{30}\text{ Zn}) - m(^{64}_{29}\text{Cu})$$

The ΔE for the process is given as -0.58 MeV. Convert this to atomic mass units and use it in the previous equation:

$$-0.58 \text{ Mev} \times \left(\frac{1 \text{ u}}{931.494 \text{ MeV}}\right) = m(^{64}_{30}\text{Zn}) - m(^{64}_{29}\text{Cu})$$

$$-0.000623 \text{ u} = m(^{64}_{30}\text{Zn}) - 63.92976 \text{ u}$$

Hence the daughter ^{64}Zn weighs $\boxed{63.92914 \text{ u}}$.

b) This nuclear reaction produces ^{64}Ni from ^{64}Cu:

$$^{64}_{29}\text{Cu} \rightarrow {}^{64}_{28}\text{Ni} + {}^0_1e^+ + \nu$$

Its Δm is

$$\Delta m = \left(m(^{64}_{28}\mathrm{Ni}) - m(^{64}_{29}\mathrm{Cu})\right) + 2\left(m(^{0}_{1}e^{+})\right)$$

The last term must be included because a positron is lost from the daughter-parent atom pair and the neutral daughter atom has one fewer electrons than the parent atom. The masses of a positron and an electron are equal. The value of ΔE is given as -0.65 MeV. Convert this energy to atomic mass units and set it equal to Δm in the previous equation:

$$-0.65 \text{ Mev} \times \left(\frac{1 \text{ u}}{931.494 \text{ MeV}}\right) = \left(m(^{64}_{28}\mathrm{Ni}) - m(^{64}_{29}\mathrm{Cu})\right) + 2\,(0.00054858 \text{ u})$$

Solving for the difference in mass between daughter and parent gives -0.00179 u. The parent ^{64}Cu weighs 63.92976 u, so the daughter ^{64}Ni weighs $\boxed{63.92797 \text{ u}}$

14.47 Only an element having Z larger by 2 can decay directly to Ac by alpha emission. Since Ac is element 89, this would be element 91, $\boxed{\text{protactinium}}$. Element 91 is in fact named as the parent of actinium ("proto-actinium"). Only an element with Z less by 1 can decay directly to Ac by beta emission. This would be element 88, which is $\boxed{\text{radium}}$. The fact that compounds of radium contain no actinium tends to rule out beta emission by radium as a significant source of actinium.

14.49 a) The formation of a ^{30}P atom is represented $15\,^{1}_{1}\mathrm{H} + 15\,^{1}_{0}n \rightarrow {}^{30}_{15}\mathrm{P}$. Note that the mass of the electrons is included in the mass of the $^{1}_{1}$H atoms. The mass of the product is 29.9783138 u, and the mass of the reactants is $15(1.00782505 + 1.0086649158)$ or 30.24734949 u. The difference between these masses is -0.2690357 u, which corresponds to a difference in energy of -250.605 MeV. The binding energy equals the negative of this figure; the binding energy per nucleon is then $+250.605/30$ or $\boxed{8.35350 \text{ MeV per nucleon}}$.

b) The equation for position emission by ^{30}P is: $^{30}_{15}\mathrm{P} \rightarrow {}^{30}_{14}\mathrm{Si} + {}^{0}_{1}e^{+} + \nu$. The change in mass in this process is

$$\Delta m = [m(^{30}_{14}\mathrm{Si}) - m(^{30}_{15}\mathrm{P})] + 2\,(0.00054858 \text{ u})$$

$$\Delta m = 29.97377022 - 29.9783138 + 0.00109716 = -0.0034464 \text{ u}$$

The negative sign means that the process is spontaneous. The change in energy of the system is also negative:

$$\Delta E = (-0.0034464 \text{ u}) \times \left(\frac{931.494 \text{ MeV}}{1 \text{ u}}\right) = -3.21032 \text{ MeV}$$

The kinetic energy of the products equals $-\Delta E$ and is distributed among them. The positron has its maximum kinetic energy when the other decay products get none. This maximum is $\boxed{3.21032 \text{ MeV}}$.

c) The quick way to get the fraction of ^{30}P atoms left after 450 s is to recognize that 450 s equals three 150 s half-lives. The fraction is then obviously $(1/2)^3$ or $\boxed{0.125}$. The rate constant is $\ln 2/t_{1/2}$; it is $\boxed{4.62 \times 10^{-3} \text{ s}^{-1}.}$

Tip. The energy equivalent of the mass of the positron and the extra electron in the mass-change equation is 1.02120 MeV. Omitting this term introduces an unacceptable error (about 32%).

14.51 The activity of the gallium-67 has decayed to 5.0% of the initial activity when the number of atoms of Ga-67 reaches 5.0% of the original number of atoms: $N = 0.050N_0$. Insert this relationship into the first-order decay law:

$$\ln\frac{N}{N_0} = -kt \qquad \text{to obtain} \qquad \ln 0.05 = -kt$$

The rate constant k equals $\ln 2$ divided by the half-life, which is given as 77.9 hours. Therefore

$$\ln 0.05 = -\left(\frac{\ln 2}{77.9 \text{ h}}\right) \qquad \text{from which } t = \boxed{337 \text{ h}}$$

14.53 The activity of ^{14}C equals the rate constant for its decay multiplied by the number of ^{14}C atoms present. Consider 1.00 g of carbon from the biosphere. The total number of carbon atoms equals:

$$N_{\text{tot}} = 1.00 \text{ g} \times \left(\frac{1 \text{ mol}}{12.01115 \text{ g}}\right) \times \left(\frac{6.022 \times 10^{23} \text{ atom}}{1 \text{ mol}}\right) = 5.014 \times 10^{22} \text{ atom}$$

The number of atoms of ^{14}C per gram of carbon is given by:

$$N_{\text{C-14}} = \frac{A}{k} = A\left(\frac{t_{1/2}}{\ln 2}\right)$$

where $t_{1/2}$ is the half-life of the ^{14}C and A is its specific activity. Converting $t_{1/2}$ from years to minutes so that the units of A cancel gives:

$$N_{\text{C-14}} = \left(\frac{15.3 \text{ min}^{-1}}{1 \text{ g}}\right) \times \left(\frac{3.014 \times 10^{9} \text{ min}}{\ln 2}\right) = \boxed{6.65 \times 10^{10} \text{ atom}}$$

b) The preceding result means that 1.00 g of ordinary carbon contains 6.65×10^{10} atoms of ^{14}C. The number of atoms of C of all isotopes in 1.00 gram of C is 5.014×10^{22} atoms, which is vastly larger. The required fraction is the first number divided by the second, which is $\boxed{1.32 \times 10^{-12}}$.

14.55 Compute the mass of K-40 that was present in the rock at formation. In the following, the first unit-factor is valid because atoms of K-40 and Ar-40 have essentially the same mass. The second unit-factor deals with the fact that only 10.7%[2] of the original K-40 gives Ar-40:

$$m_{^{40}\text{K}} = 0.42 \text{ mg } ^{40}\text{Ar} \times \left(\frac{1 \text{ mg } ^{40}\text{K by EC}}{1 \text{ mg } ^{40}\text{Ar}}\right) \times \left(\frac{100 \text{ mg}}{10.7 \text{ mg } ^{40}\text{K by EC}}\right) = 3.925 \text{ mg } ^{40}\text{K orig}$$

Since K-40 decays by first-order kinetics we can write:

$$m_{^{40}\text{K}} = (m_{^{40}\text{K}})_{\text{orig}} e^{-kt}$$

where the use of masses instead of number of atoms is valid because the number of atoms of K-40 is directly proportional to its mass. Take the logarithm of both sides and substitute the two masses and the rate constant. The rate constant k equals $\ln 2$ divided by the half-life of ^{40}K, which is available in text Table 14.2:

$$\ln\left(\frac{m_{^{40}\text{K}}}{(m_{^{40}\text{K}})_{\text{orig}}}\right) = -kt = \ln\left(\frac{1.00 \text{ mg}}{3.925 \text{ mg}}\right) = \left(\frac{-\ln 2}{1.28 \times 10^{9} \text{ yr}}\right) t \qquad t = \boxed{2.5 \times 10^{9} \text{ yr}}$$

14.57 The incomplete nuclear equation: $^{10}_{5}\text{B} + ^{1}_{0}n \rightarrow ? + ^{4}_{2}\text{He}$ must be balanced by the insertion of a single symbol for the question mark. The mass number on this symbol must be 7 and the atomic number 3. The element of atomic number 3 is lithium. Hence the other atom that is formed is a $\boxed{^{7}_{3}\text{Li}}$ atom.

14.59 Use unit factors to obtain the TNT that must explode to release the same amount of energy as the small A-bomb:

$$m_{\text{TNT}} = 1.2 \text{ kg U} \times \left(\frac{1 \text{ mol U}}{0.238 \text{ kg U}}\right) \times \left(\frac{2 \times 10^{13} \text{ J}}{1 \text{ mol U}}\right) \times \left(\frac{1 \text{ ton TNT}}{4 \times 10^{9} \text{ J}}\right) = \boxed{2.5 \times 10^{4} \text{ ton TNT}}$$

---

[2] See text Table 14-2. This proportion of K-40 decays by electron capture (EC).

14.61 The Earth orbits the Sun at a radius R of 1.50×10^8 km. Imagine a sphere of this radius surrounding the Sun. The surface area of this immense sphere is $4\pi R^2$. Radiation from the Sun streams out in all directions, cutting through this sphere. Call the 6371 km radius of the Earth r. From the Sun, the Earth appears as a tiny disk of area πr^2. This disk, minuscule in comparison to the area of the big sphere, intercepts a fraction f of the total radiation in proportion to the area of the big sphere that it covers:

$$f = \frac{\pi r^2}{4\pi R^2} = \frac{1}{4}\left(\frac{r}{R}\right)^2 = \frac{1}{4}\left(\frac{6371 \text{ km}}{1.50 \times 10^8 \text{ km}}\right)^2 = 4.5 \times 10^{-10}$$

The surface area of the hemisphere of the Earth that is exposed to the Sun's rays at any time equals $2\pi r^2$. Assume that the radiant flux of 0.135 J s^{-1}cm^{-2} is the *average* value over the Earth's exposed hemisphere. Then the Earth receives the radiant power:

$$P(\text{Earth}) = (0.135 \text{ J s}^{-1}\text{cm}^{-2}) \times 2\pi(6.371 \times 10^8 \text{ cm})^2 = 3.44 \times 10^{17} \text{ J s}^{-1}$$

The total power output of the Sun is P(Earth) divided by the fraction of the Sun's radiant power that hits the Earth:

$$P(\text{Sun}) = \frac{P(\text{Earth})}{f} = \frac{3.44 \times 10^{17} \text{ J s}^{-1}}{4.5 \times 10^{-10}} = 7.6 \times 10^{26} \text{ J s}^{-1}$$

The mass equivalent of energy is given by the equation $\Delta E = c^2 \Delta m$. The Sun emits 7.6×10^{26} J each second, so its ΔE is negative. The equivalent change in mass per second is

$$\Delta m = \frac{\Delta E}{c^2} = \frac{-7.6 \times 10^{26} \text{ J s}^{-1}}{(3.0 \times 10^8 \text{ m s}^{-1})^2} = \boxed{-8.5 \times 10^9 \text{ kg s}^{-1}}$$

Tip. The Sun burns (in the thermonuclear sense) 8.5 million metric tons of matter per second. How long can it keep burning? Its mass equals 1.99×10^{30} kg, so the Sun is good for 2.3×10^{20} s (7.4 trillion years) at the current rate.

14.63 The problem compares aspects of generating one year's energy from three different 500 megawatt power plants. First, calculate the annual energy production. It equals the rated power multiplied by the time of operation

$$E = 500 \text{ MW} \times 1 \text{ yr} \times \left(\frac{10^6 \text{ J s}^{-1}}{\text{MW}}\right) \times \left(\frac{3.156 \times 10^7 \text{ s}}{\text{yr}}\right) = 1.58 \times 10^{16} \text{ J} = 1.58 \times 10^{13} \text{ kJ}$$

(a) Find the mass of coal burned in the coal-fired plant and the mass of ash using unit-factors:

$$m_{\text{coal}} = 1.58 \times 10^{13} \text{ kJ} \times \left(\frac{1 \text{ kg coal theory}}{3.2 \times 10^4 \text{ kJ}}\right) \times \left(\frac{100 \text{ kg coal actual}}{25 \text{ kg coal theory}}\right) = \boxed{2 \times 10^9 \text{ kg}}$$

$$m_{\text{ash}} = 2 \times 10^9 \text{ kg coal} \times \left(\frac{0.10 \text{ kg ash}}{1 \text{ kg coal}}\right) = \boxed{2 \times 10^8 \text{ kg ash}}$$

(b) For the nuclear power plant

$$m_{^{235}\text{U}} = 1.58 \times 10^{13} \text{ kJ} \times \left(\frac{1 \text{ mol } ^{235}\text{U theory}}{1.9 \times 10^{10} \text{ kJ}}\right) \times \left(\frac{100 \text{ mol } ^{235}\text{U actual}}{25 \text{ mol } ^{235}\text{U theory}}\right) \times \left(\frac{0.235 \text{ kg } ^{235}\text{U}}{\text{mol}^{235}\text{U}}\right)$$

$$= \boxed{8 \times 10^2 \text{ kg}}$$

$$m_{\text{fuel}} = 781 \text{ kg } ^{235}\text{U} \times \left(\frac{100 \text{ kg fuel}}{4 \text{ kg } ^{235}\text{U}}\right) = \boxed{2 \times 10^4 \text{ kg fuel}}$$

(c) To figure the area of the "solar farm" power plant, use the required power output

$$A = 500 \text{ MW} \times \left(\frac{1000 \text{ kW}}{\text{MW}}\right) \times \left(\frac{1 \text{ m}^2}{1.5 \text{ kW}}\right) \times \left(\frac{100 \text{ m}^2 \text{ actual}}{25 \text{ m}^2 \text{ theory}}\right) \times \left(\frac{24 \text{ h real}}{6 \text{ h useful}}\right) = \boxed{5 \times 10^6 \text{ m}^2}$$

14.65 a) The $\Delta H°$ of the reaction $N_2H_4(l) + O_2(g) \rightarrow N_2(g) + 2\,H_2O(g)$ is the sum of the $\Delta H_f°$'s of the products less the sum of the $\Delta H_f°$'s of the reactants, according to Hess's law:

$$\Delta H° = 2\underbrace{(-241.82)}_{H_2O(g)} + 1\underbrace{(0.00)}_{N_2(g)} - 1\underbrace{(0.00)}_{O_2(g)} - 1\underbrace{(-50.63)}_{N_2H_4(l)} = \boxed{-534.27 \text{ kJ}}$$

where the numbers come from Appendix D (recall that elements in standard states have $\Delta H_f°$'s of zero).

b) The change in the standard internal energy during the constant-pressure reaction is

$$\Delta E° = \Delta H° - P\Delta V$$

The $P\Delta V$ term equals $\Delta n_g RT$, if it is assumed that the gases in the reaction are ideal and that the volume of the liquid hydrazine is negligible.[3] As a mole of $N_2H_4(l)$ burns in $O_2(g)$ at 298.15 K, Δn_g of the system equals +2 mol, making $\Delta n_g RT$ equal to 4.96 kJ. Hence, for the combustion of one mole of $N_2H_4(l)$:

$$\Delta E° = \Delta H° - P\Delta V = -534.27 - 4.96 = \boxed{-539.23 \text{ kJ}}$$

c) Use $\Delta E°$ of the reaction as ΔE in the Einstein equation:

$$\Delta m = \frac{\Delta E}{c^2} = \frac{-539.23 \times 10^3 \text{ J}}{(2.9979 \times 10^8 \text{ m s}^{-1})^2} = \boxed{-5.9998 \times 10^{-12} \text{ kg}}$$

Tip. The chemical reaction of 32 g of hydrazine and 32 g of oxygen occasions a mass loss by the system of about 6 nanograms. This is too small to detect.

14.67 a) To produce ^{228}Ra, the ^{232}Th must emit an alpha particle in the first step of its decay:

$$^{232}_{90}\text{Th} \rightarrow {}^{228}_{88}\text{Ra} + {}^{4}_{2}\text{He}$$

In the next step, the ^{228}Ra emits a beta particle (an electron) to give ^{228}Ac:

$$^{228}_{88}\text{Ra} \rightarrow {}^{228}_{89}\text{Ac} + {}^{0}_{-1}e^- + \bar{\nu}$$

The decay products over the two steps are an alpha particle, an ^{228}Ac atom, an electron and an anti-neutrino. These products have the same total mass as an ^{228}Ac (228.03117 u) plus a $^{4}_{2}$He atom (4.0026033 u). The sum is 232.03377 u. The mass of the beta particle (electron) is included in the mass tabulated for a neutral actinium atom, and the anti-neutrino is massless. The mass of the reactant is 232.038054 u so Δm for the process is -0.00428 u. This mass has an energy equivalent of -3.98 MeV. Hence, $\boxed{3.98 \text{ MeV}}$ is the energy lost by the system consisting of one Th atom and carried away as kinetic energy by the decay particles.

b) The thorium decays to radium in a first-order process, and the radium goes on to decay to actinium in another first-order process. Let k_1 be the rate constant for the first step and k_2 the rate constant for the second. When the radium is present in a steady-state amount then:

$$\frac{dN_{Ra}}{dt} = 0 = k_1 N_{Th} - k_2 N_{Ra} \qquad \text{from which} \quad N_{Ra} = \frac{k_1}{k_2} N_{Th}$$

For each first-order process, the rate constant is $\ln 2$ divided by the half-file $t_{1/2}$. Applying this fact to the previous equation:

$$N_{Ra} = \left(\frac{t_{1/2,2}}{t_{1/2,1}}\right) N_{Th} = \left(\frac{6.7 \text{ yr}}{1.39 \times 10^{10} \text{ yr}}\right) N_{Th} = (4.8 \times 10^{-10}) N_{Th}$$

The number of ^{228}Ra nuclei equals $\boxed{4.8 \times 10^{-10}}$ of the number of ^{232}Th nuclei.

---

[3] This is the same kind of assumption made in **7.43**.

Chapter 15

Quantum Mechanics and Atomic Structure

15.1 The speed of propagation of a wave equals the product of its frequency and wavelength. A wave-crest hits the beach once every 3.2 s, which means that slightly less than one-third of a wave reaches the beach per second. The frequency of the waves equals the reciprocal of 3.2 s, or 0.3125 s^{-1}. Thus:

$$\text{speed} = \nu\lambda = \frac{1}{3.2\ \text{s}}(2.1\ \text{m}) = \boxed{0.66\ \text{m s}^{-1}}$$

Tip. The interval between recurring identical portions of a wave is called the *period* of the wave. The period equals the reciprocal of the frequency.

15.3 The speed of propagation of electromagnetic radiation through a vacuum is c, a quantity that is very well known. As with all traveling waves, the speed of propagation of the FM radio signal equals the product of its wavelength and frequency: $c = \lambda\nu$. Hence:

$$\lambda = \frac{c}{\nu} = \frac{2.998 \times 10^8\ \text{m s}^{-1}}{9.86 \times 10^7\ \text{s}^{-1}} = \boxed{3.04\ \text{m}}$$

15.5 a) Start with the same relationship as in the preceding, but solve for frequency:

$$\nu = \frac{c}{\lambda} = \frac{2.998 \times 10^8\ \text{m s}^{-1}}{6.00 \times 10^2\ \text{m}} = \boxed{5.00 \times 10^5\ \text{s}^{-1}}$$

b) The time for a wave to travel some distance d equals the distance divided by the speed of the wave. These electromagnetic waves advance at the known speed c. Hence:

$$t = \frac{d}{c} = \frac{8.0 \times 10^{10}\ \text{m}}{3.00 \times 10^8\ \text{m s}^{-1}} \times \left(\frac{1\ \text{min}}{60\ \text{s}}\right) = \boxed{4.4\ \text{min}}$$

15.7 The wavelength of the sound waves can be determined from the frequency and speed of propagation of the waves:

$$\lambda = \frac{\text{speed}}{\nu} = \frac{343.5\ \text{m s}^{-1}}{261.6\ \text{s}^{-1}} = \boxed{1.313\ \text{m}}$$

The time to travel 30.0 m is

$$t = \frac{d}{\text{speed}} = \frac{30.0\ \text{m}}{343.5\ \text{m s}^{-1}} = \boxed{0.0873\ \text{s}}$$

15.9 Blue light has a higher frequency than green light (see text Figure 15.3[1]). The photons of blue light are therefore more energetic than the photons of green light. Since the work function of the surface of the potassium is the same for both colors of light, the $\boxed{\text{electrons ejected by blue light}}$ have higher average kinetic energy.

15.11 Combine the relationships $c = \lambda\nu$ and $E = h\nu$ to obtain an equation for the wavelength of light of specified energy. Then insert the energy needed to eject electrons from a surface of cesium metal:

$$\lambda = \frac{c}{\nu} = \frac{hc}{E} = \frac{(6.626 \times 10^{-34}\ \text{J s})(3.00 \times 10^{8}\ \text{m s}^{-1})}{3.43 \times 10^{-19}\ \text{J}} = 5.80 \times 10^{-7}\ \text{m}$$

This light is yellow (see text Figure 15.3). $\boxed{\text{Yellow light}}$ and light of shorter wavelength (green, blue, violet, ultraviolet, etc.) can eject electrons from cesium in the photoelectric experiment.

For selenium, the work function is bigger (more energy is required to eject electrons):

$$\lambda = \frac{hc}{E} = \frac{(6.626 \times 10^{-34}\ \text{J s})(3.00 \times 10^{8}\ \text{m s}^{-1})}{9.5 \times 10^{-19}\ \text{J}} = 2.1 \times 10^{-7}\ \text{m}$$

This wavelength is well into the $\boxed{\text{ultraviolet}}$.

15.13 a) The maximum kinetic energy of an electron ejected from a chromium surface equals the difference between the energy of the incident photons and the work function of chromium:

$$\begin{aligned} E_{\text{K}}(\text{max}) &= h\nu - \Phi = \frac{hc}{\lambda} - \Phi \\ &= \frac{(6.626 \times 10^{-34}\ \text{J s})(3.00 \times 10^{8}\ \text{m s}^{-1})}{2.50 \times 10^{-7}\ \text{m}} - 7.21 \times 10^{-19}\ \text{J} = \boxed{0.74 \times 10^{-19}\ \text{J}} \end{aligned}$$

b) The kinetic energy of a particle depends on its speed and mass: $E_{\text{K}} = \frac{1}{2}mv^2$. Solve for v, and insert the kinetic energy computed in the previous part and the known mass of the electron:

$$v = \sqrt{\frac{2E_{\text{K}}}{m}} = \sqrt{\frac{2(0.74 \times 10^{-19}\ \text{J})}{9.109 \times 10^{-31}\ \text{kg}}} = \boxed{4.0 \times 10^{5}\ \text{m s}^{-1}}$$

Tip. This speed is less than 0.2% of the speed of light, so relativistic effects (not mentioned in the text) are safely ignored.

15.15 The wavelength 671 nm is 6.71×10^{-7} m. Text Figure 15.3 shows that light of this wavelength is $\boxed{\text{red}}$.

15.17 The frequency corresponding to the transition energy is computed using a rearranged version of the Planck equation $\Delta E = h\nu$:

$$\nu = \frac{\Delta E}{h} = \frac{3.6 \times 10^{-19}\ \text{J}}{6.626 \times 10^{-34}\ \text{J s}} = 5.43 \times 10^{14}\ \text{s}^{-1}$$

[1] Text page 507.

The wavelength equals the speed of propagation divided by the frequency:

$$\lambda = \frac{c}{\nu} = \frac{2.9979 \times 10^{8}\ \text{m s}^{-1}}{5.43 \times 10^{14}\ \text{s}^{-1}} = \boxed{5.5 \times 10^{-7}\ \text{m}}$$

According to text Figure 15.3, this light is $\boxed{\text{green}}$.

15.19 a) The energy change of an atom and the wavelength λ of the radiation it emits are inversely related:

$$-\Delta E = \frac{hc}{\lambda}$$

The λ is 589.3 nm (or 5.893×10^{-7} m). Substitution for λ, h, and c gives:

$$\Delta E = \frac{(6.626 \times 10^{-34}\ \text{J s})(2.998 \times 10^{8}\ \text{m s}^{-1})}{5.893 \times 10^{-7}\ \text{m}} = \boxed{-3.371 \times 10^{-19}\ \text{J}}$$

The negative sign means that the final energy of the sodium atom is less than its original energy.

b) A mole of sodium atoms consists of Avogadro's number of sodium atoms. The energy change per mole is

$$\Delta E = \left(-3.371 \times 10^{-19} \frac{\text{J}}{\text{atom}}\right) \times \left(6.022 \times 10^{23} \frac{\text{atom}}{\text{mol}}\right) = \boxed{-2.030 \times 10^{5}\ \text{J mol}^{-1}}$$

c) The sodium arc light emits 1000 W (watt) of radiant energy; 1000 W equals 1000 J s^{-1}. Assume that all of this energy is carried by photons at the D-line. Then:

$$\frac{1.000 \times 10^{3}\ \text{J emitted}}{1\ \text{s}} \times \left(\frac{1\ \text{mol Na atoms}}{+2.030 \times 10^{5}\ \text{J emitted}}\right) = \boxed{4.926 \times 10^{-3}\ \text{mol s}^{-1}}$$

15.21 a) The observed voltage of the first excitation threshold in the Franck-Hertz experiment on Na atoms equals 2.103 V. This means that an electron accelerated across a potential difference of 2.103 V is just energetic enough to transfer a quantum of energy to an Na atom, which does not accept smaller quanta of energy. The change in the energy of the Na that accepts the quantum of energy equals the product of the charge on the electron and the accelerating voltage:

$$\Delta E = (2.103\ \text{V})(1.602177 \times 10^{-19}\ \text{C}) = 3.3694 \times 10^{-19}\ \text{V C} = 3.3694 \times 10^{-19}\ \text{J}$$

Later, the excited Na atom emits a quantum of light to relax to its original state. Its ΔE during the relaxation equals the negative of its ΔE during the excitation. The wavelength of the light that it emits is

$$\lambda = \frac{hc}{-\Delta E} = \frac{(6.626 \times 10^{-34}\ \text{J s})(2.9979 \times 10^{8}\ \text{m s}^{-1})}{-(-3.3694 \times 10^{-19}\ \text{J})} = \boxed{5.895 \times 10^{-7}\ \text{m}}$$

Tip. The calculated wavelength equals 5895 Å, very close to the two wavelengths (called a doublet) that are quoted for Na atoms in the problem.

15.23 a) The photoelectron spectroscopy experiment measures the kinetic energies of electrons that are ejected from atoms by the absorption of high-frequency photons. The difference between the energy of an incoming photon and the kinetic energy of an outgoing electron equals the binding energy of the electron. Multielectron atoms have many different binding energies.[2]. Some electrons are closer to the nucleus (more

[2] See text Figure 15.39.

tightly bound) and others are farther away. Compute the binding energy of this electron by subtraction, as just discussed:

$$\begin{aligned} BE &= h\nu - E_{\text{K electron}} \\ &= \frac{hc}{\lambda} - E_{\text{K electron}} \\ &= \frac{(6.626 \times 10^{-34}\ \text{J s})(2.9979 \times 10^{8}\ \text{m s}^{-1})}{584.4 \times 10^{-10}\ \text{m}} - (11.7\ \text{eV})\left(\frac{1.602 \times 10^{-19}\ \text{J}}{1\ \text{eV}}\right) \\ &= \boxed{1.52 \times 10^{-18}\ \text{J}} = 9.52\ \text{eV} \end{aligned}$$

15.25 The B^{4+} ion is a hydrogen-like ion. Like H, it has only one electron, but the charge on its nucleus is $5\,e$, not $1\,e$. Answer the questions about it by substitution into these equations:

$$r_n = \frac{n^2}{Z}(5.29 \times 10^{-11}\ \text{m}) \quad \text{and} \quad E_n = -(2.18 \times 10^{-18}\ \text{J})\frac{Z^2}{n^2}$$

The radius for the state $n = 3$ in B^{4+} equals:

$$r_3 = \frac{3^2}{5}(5.29 \times 10^{-11}\ \text{m}) = \boxed{9.52 \times 10^{-11}\ \text{m}}$$

The energy for the same case ($n = 3$ and $Z = 5$) equals:

$$E_3 = -\frac{5^2}{3^2}(2.18 \times 10^{-18}\ \text{J}) = \boxed{-6.06 \times 10^{-18}\ \text{J}}$$

The negative of this answer is the energy needed to strip the electron away from a single B^{4+} ion in the $n = 3$ state. For a mole of B^{4+} ions, this energy must be multiplied by Avogadro's number:

$$E = \frac{-(-6.06 \times 10^{-18}\ \text{J})}{\text{atom}} \times \left(\frac{6.022 \times 10^{23}\ \text{atom}}{\text{mol}}\right) = \boxed{3.65 \times 10^{6}\ \text{J mol}^{-1}}$$

The energy change in a B^{4+} ion undergoing a $3 \rightarrow 2$ transition is the difference between the energies of the two states. The two energies are:

$$\begin{aligned} E_3 &= -\frac{5^2}{3^2}(-2.18 \times 10^{-18}\ \text{J}) = -\frac{25}{9}(-2.18 \times 10^{-18}\ \text{J}) \\ E_2 &= -\frac{5^2}{2^2}(-2.18 \times 10^{-18}\ \text{J}) = -\frac{25}{4}(-2.18 \times 10^{-18}\ \text{J}) \end{aligned}$$

The difference equals the final energy minus the initial:

$$\Delta E = E_2 - E_3 = \left(\frac{-25}{4} - \frac{-25}{9}\right)(2.18 \times 10^{-18}\ \text{J}) = -7.57 \times 10^{-18}\ \text{J}$$

This is the energy change of the ion. The energy gained by the surroundings in the form of a photon equals the negative of this. Dividing this energy by h gives the frequency of the photon:

$$\nu = \frac{-\Delta E}{h} = \frac{-(-7.57 \times 10^{-18}\ \text{J})}{6.626 \times 10^{-34}\ \text{J s}} = \boxed{1.14 \times 10^{16}\ \text{s}^{-1}}$$

The wavelength of the emitted photon is computed as follows:

$$\lambda = \frac{hc}{-\Delta E} = \frac{(6.626 \times 10^{-34}\ \text{J s})(2.9979 \times 10^{8}\ \text{m s}^{-1})}{7.57 \times 10^{-18}\ \text{J}} = \boxed{2.63 \times 10^{-8}\ \text{m}}$$

15.27 The problem could be solved by substitution into the equations of the Bohr model. The fact that the $3 \to 2$ emission in hydrogen occurs at 656.1 nm is then not needed. A quicker solution uses this fact. The allowed energy levels in hydrogen-like atoms are characterized by the factor $-Z^2/n^2$ multiplied by a constant. The $3 \to 2$ transition for the neutral H atom ($Z = 1$) corresponds to an energy jump proportional to $(1^2/2^2 - 1^2/3^2)$, which equals 0.13889. For the Li^{2+} ion, $Z = 3$, and the $3 \to 2$ energy jump is proportional to $3^2/2^2 - 3^2/3^2$, or 1.2500. The energy jump is bigger in the Li^{2+} transition by the factor $(1.2500/0.13889) = 9.000$. Therefore the wavelength of the emitted light in the Li^{2+} transition is 9.000 times *shorter* than 656.1 nm. This is $656.1/9.000 = \boxed{72.90 \text{ nm}}$. Light of this wavelength is in the $\boxed{\text{ultraviolet}}$.

15.29 The wave in a guitar string is a standing wave. Its allowed wavelength satisfies the equation:

$$\frac{n\lambda}{2} = L$$

where L is the length of the string and n is an integer.

a) The first harmonic has $n = 1$: Solving the above equation gives:

$$\lambda_1 = \frac{2L}{1} = \frac{2(50 \text{ cm})}{1} = \boxed{100 \text{ cm}}$$

By substitution of $n = 3$, the wavelength λ_3 of the third harmonic is $\boxed{33 \text{ cm}}$.

b) The number of nodes in a standing wave is always one less than the number of the harmonic. Thus the 1st harmonic has 0 nodes, the 2nd harmonic has 1 node, and the 3rd harmonic has $\boxed{2 \text{ nodes}}$.

15.31 The deBroglie wavelength λ of an object is given by $\lambda = h/p$ where p is the momentum of the object. The momentum of an object equals its mass multiplied by its velocity.

a) For an electron moving at 1.00×10^3 m s^{-1}:

$$\lambda_e = \frac{h}{p} = \frac{h}{m_e v} = \frac{6.626 \times 10^{-34} \text{ J s}}{(9.11 \times 10^{-31} \text{ kg})(1.00 \times 10^3 \text{ m s}^{-1})} = \boxed{7.27 \times 10^{-7} \text{ m}}$$

b) For a proton moving at the same speed:

$$\lambda_p = \frac{h}{m_p v} = \frac{6.626 \times 10^{-34} \text{ J s}}{(1.673 \times 10^{-27} \text{ kg})(1.00 \times 10^3 \text{ m s}^{-1})} = \boxed{3.96 \times 10^{-10} \text{ m}}$$

c) A speed of 75 km hr^{-1} is equivalent to 20.8 m s^{-1} (multiply by 1000 m km^{-1} and then divide by 3600 s h^{-1}). A 145 g baseball has a mass of 0.145 kg. Then:

$$\lambda_{\text{ball}} = \frac{h}{m_{\text{ball}} v} = \frac{6.626 \times 10^{-34} \text{ J s}}{(0.145 \text{ kg})(20.8 \text{ m s}^{-1})} = \boxed{2.2 \times 10^{-34} \text{ m}}$$

15.33 a) According to the Heisenberg uncertainty principle:

$$(\Delta x)(\Delta p) \geq \frac{h}{4\pi} \quad \text{hence} \quad \Delta p_{\text{min}} = \frac{h}{4\pi}\left(\frac{1}{\Delta x}\right)$$

The minimum uncertainty in the momentum of the electron is then:

$$\Delta p_{\text{min}} = \frac{6.626 \times 10^{-34} \text{ J s}}{4\pi(1.0 \times 10^{-9} \text{ m})} = \frac{6.626 \times 10^{-34} \text{ kg m}^2 \text{s}^{-2} \text{ s}}{4\pi(1.0 \times 10^{-9} \text{ m})} = 5.27 \times 10^{-26} \text{ kg m s}^{-1}$$

The minimum uncertainty in the velocity can be computed using the fact that the momentum of the electron is the product of its velocity and mass:

$$\Delta v_{\text{min}} = \frac{\Delta p_{\text{min}}}{m_e} = \frac{(5.27 \times 10^{-26}\text{ kg m s}^{-1})}{9.11 \times 10^{-31}\text{ kg}} = \boxed{5.8 \times 10^4\text{ m s}^{-1}}$$

b) The minimum uncertainty in the momentum is the same as in part a. The computation of the minimum uncertainty of the velocity must use the mass of a helium atom[3]. Conversion from atomic mass units to kilograms gives the m_{He} as 6.647×10^{-27} kg. Substitution then gives:

$$\Delta v_{\text{min}} = \frac{\Delta p_{\text{min}}}{m_{\text{He}}} = \frac{5.27 \times 10^{-26}\text{ kg m s}^{-1}}{6.647 \times 10^{-27}\text{ kg}} = \boxed{7.9\text{ m s}^{-1}}$$

15.35 The allowed energies of a particle in a one-dimensional box are:

$$E_n = n^2\left(\frac{h^2}{8mL^2}\right)$$

This is text equation 15.20.[4] The particle is a particle of known mass (the electron), and the length of the box is 1.34 Å. If all quantities are expressed in SI units:

$$E_n = n^2\left(\frac{(6.626 \times 10^{-34}\text{ J s})^2}{8(9.109 \times 10^{-31}\text{ kg})(1.34 \times 10^{-10}\text{ m})^2}\right) = n^2(3.36 \times 10^{-18}\text{ J})$$

Substitution of $n = 1, 2, 3$ gives:

$$E_1 = \boxed{3.36 \times 10^{-18}\text{ J}} \qquad E_2 = \boxed{13.4 \times 10^{-18}\text{ J}} \qquad E_3 = \boxed{30.2 \times 10^{-18}\text{ J}}$$

To excite an electron from $n = 1$ (the ground state) to $n = 2$ (the first excited state) requires energy equal to the difference between E_1 and E_2. If this energy is supplied by one photon, then the wavelength of the photon must be

$$\lambda = \frac{hc}{E_2 - E_1} = \frac{(6.626 \times 10^{-34}\text{ J s})(2.9979 \times 10^8\text{ m s}^{-1})}{(13.4 \times 10^{-18} - 3.36 \times 10^{-18})\text{ J}} = \boxed{1.97 \times 10^{-8}\text{ m}}$$

This wavelength, 197 Å, occurs in the ultraviolet region of the spectrum.

Tip. In the formula for the allowed energies, the quantum number n appears in combination with a quantity characterizing the universe (Planck's constant h), a quantity characterizing the particle (m), and a quantity characterizing the box (L).

15.37 Combination (a) is not allowed because ℓ must be less than n; it may never equal n; (c) has $m > \ell$, which is not allowed; (d) has $\ell < 0$, which is not allowed. $\boxed{\text{Only combination (b) is allowed}}$.

Tip. The rules are easier to apply when physical significance is attached. $(n-1)$ equals the total number of all nodes of the wave function. The quantum number ℓ tells the number of angular nodes. Since the number of angular nodes cannot exceed the total number of nodes, ℓ may equal $(n-1)$ at most. Its *minimum* is zero because "−1 angular nodes" has no physical meaning. The third quantum number m is related to the orientation of the angular nodes and may be negative.

15.39 **a)** $4p$ **b)** $2s$ **c)** $6f$

---

[3] Text Table 14.1

[4] See text page 534.

15.41 The total number of nodes equals one less than the quantum number n. The number of angular nodes equals the quantum number ℓ, which is obtained by decoding the s, p, d, f notation, as explained on text page 536:
a) $4p$: 2 radial and 1 angular. b) $2s$: 1 radial and 0 angular. c) $6f$: 2 radial and 3 angular.

15.43 The wave function ψ_{2p_z} is the product of a *radial* part R_{2p} and an angular part Y_{p_z}. The two parts of the functions are given in Table 15.2.[5] The total wave function equals:

$$\psi_{2p_z} = \left(\frac{1}{32\pi}\right)^{1/2}\left(\frac{Z}{a_0}\right)^{3/2}\cos\theta\left(\frac{Zr}{a_0}\right)\exp\left(-Zr/2a_0\right)$$

The radial part of the function contributes the exponential dependence on r, and the angular part the $\cos\theta$ dependence. This particular orbital is not a function of the third coordinate ϕ. The probability p of finding an electron in the close vicinity of a point[6] specified by the three coordinates $r, \theta and \phi$ depends on the square of this function:

$$p(r,\theta,\phi) = \left(\psi_{2p_z}\right)^2 = \frac{1}{32\pi}\left(\frac{Z}{a_0}\right)^3\cos^2\theta\left(\frac{Z^2r^2}{a_0^2}\right)\exp\left(-Zr/a_0\right)$$

The question now becomes: what values of r and θ make the quantity on the right equal zero? Clearly, this happens when $r = 0$ (at the nucleus). It also happens when $\theta = \pi/2 = 90°$ (because $\cos^2\pi/2 = 0$), and when $\theta = 3\pi/2 = 270°$ (because $\cos^2 3\pi/2 = 0$). Consult text Figure 15.26[7] to confirm that the coordinate θ is zero along the $+z$ axis and either $\pi/2$ or $3\pi/2$ at right angles to the z axis, in the xy plane. Therefore, the probability equals zero at all points in the xy plane. This plane is a nodal plane.

Writing out and squaring the full wave function is not really necessary since the angular part alone controls the angular nodes of all the functions in text Table 15.2. Thus, the square of the d_{xz} orbital has a $\sin^2\theta\cos^2\theta\cos^2\phi$ angular dependence. This function goes to zero whenever $\theta = \pi/2$ or $\theta = 3\pi/2$ (in the xy plane) and whenever $\phi = \pi/2$ or $\phi = 3\pi/2$ (in the yz plane). The $\boxed{xy \text{ plane}}$ and $\boxed{yz \text{ plane}}$ are the two angular nodes of the d_{xz} orbital.

The square of the $d_{x^2-y^2}$ orbital has a $\sin^4\theta\cos^2 2\phi$ angular dependence. This trigonometric function goes to zero at these values of ϕ:

$$\phi = \pi/4\ (45°) \qquad \phi = 3\pi/4\ (135°) \qquad \phi = 5\pi/4\ (225°) \qquad \phi = 7\pi/4\ (315°)$$

These first and third values of ϕ define a plane containing the z axis and half-way between the x and y axes. The second and fourth values of ϕ define a plane containing the z axis and at right angles to the first plane. These are the nodal planes of the $d_{x^2-y^2}$ orbital. The function also goes to zero at $\theta = 0$. This happens only along the z axis, the line at the intersection of the two nodal planes just identified.

15.45 The ground-state electron configurations are:
a) C $1s^22s^22p^2$ b) Se $1s^22s^22p^63s^23p^63d^{10}4s^24p^4$ c) Fe $1s^22s^22p^63s^23p^63d^64s^2$
The use of the bracketed symbol of a noble gas to represent the electron configuration of that element shortens the notation for most configurations:
a) C [He]$2s^22p^2$ b) Se [Ar]$3d^{10}4s^24p^4$ c) Fe [Ar]$3d^64s^2$

15.47 The ground-state configuration of an ion derives from the ground-state configuration of the atom. In the case of a negative ion, add electrons to available orbitals in order of energy. In the case of positive ions, remove electrons starting with the highest-energy occupied orbitals:

Be^+	$1s^22s^1$	C^-	$1s^22s^22p^3$	Ne^{2+}	$1s^22s^22p^4$	Mg^+	[Ne]$3s^1$
P^{2+}	[Ne]$3s^23p^1$	Cl^-	[Ne]$3s^23p^6$	As^+	[Ar]$3d^{10}4s^24p^2$		
I^-	[Kr]$4d^{10}5s^25p^6$						

[5] Text page 538.
[6] More exactly, in the infinitesimal region surrounding the point.
[7] Text page 535.

All of these electron configurations are ground-state (lowest energy) configurations. Be^+, C^-, Ne^{2+}, Mg^+, P^{2+} and As^+ all have at least one unpaired electron (they have incomplete subshells) and should be paramagnetic. **The Cl^- and I^- ions are diamagnetic; the others are paramagnetic**.

15.49 a) The atom has 49 electrons (36 represented by [Kr]; 13 represented by superscripts). It is **In**.

b) The ion has 18 electrons, and a charge of −2. The atomic number of its nucleus must be 16; it is **S^{2-}**.

c) The ion has 21 electrons, and a charge of +4. Its Z must be 25. it is **Mn^{4+}** ion.

15.51 As a halogen this element has a ground-state electron configuration of the form $\ldots ns^2np^5$. The next p-subshell after the $6p$ (used in the sixth row of the periodic table) is the $7p$. Accordingly, the electron configuration of the element would be $[Rn]\,5f^{14}6d^{10}7s^27p^5$ where [Rn] stands for the configuration of the first 86 electrons. Since the configuration represents 117 electrons, Z equals **117**.

15.53 If only one electron could occupy each orbital in many-electron atoms, then the configurations $1s^1$ and $1s^12s^12p^3$ and $1s^12s^12p^33s^13p^3$ would be closed-shell electron configurations. Atoms with $Z =$ **1, 5, 9** respectively would have these ground-state electron configurations.

15.55 a) A ground-state **K atom** should have a larger radius than a ground-state Na atom. In K atoms the outermost electron occupies a $4s$ orbital, but in Na atoms the outermost electron occupies a closer $3s$ orbital.

b) The **Cs atom** is larger than the Cs^+ ion. As a Cs^+ ion gains an electron to produce a Cs atom, the electron is accommodated in the more distant $n = 6$ shell.

c) The Rb^+ ion and the Kr atom are isoelectronic. The larger species is the one with smaller nuclear charge: **Kr**.

d) A Ca atom has two $4s$ electrons and a K atom has one $4s$ electron. The outermost electrons are in the same shell but Ca has a larger nuclear charge, contracting the electron cloud. Hence **potassium** is larger.

e) The Cl^- ion and the Ar atom are isoelectronic. The larger species is the one with smaller nuclear charge: **Cl^-**.

15.57 a) The **S^{2-}** ion should be larger than the O^- ion. Its outermost electrons occupy the $n = 3$ level whereas in O^- ion the outermost electrons are in the closer $n = 2$ level.

b) The **Ti^{2+}** ion is larger than the Co^{2+} ion because the two have their outermost electrons in the same level, and Ti^{2+} has a smaller nuclear charge.

c) The **Mn^{2+}** ion is larger than the Mn^{4+} ion because outermost electrons (those farthest away) are lost in going from the +2 to +4 ion.

d) The **Sr^{2+}** ion is larger than the Ca^{2+} ion according to the trend to larger size going down the periodic table.

15.59 a) The ionization energy of an element is the minimum energy necessary to remove a single electron from a neutral gaseous atom of the element. The ionization energy of He is particularly high (the largest of any element) because removal of an electron takes place against the attraction of a large effective nuclear charge and from the $1s$ orbital, which has the smallest radius of all orbitals.

b) The element **Li** should have the highest *second* ionization energy. The electron is lost from the Li^+ ion, which has an electron configuration like that of helium, and helium has the largest first ionization energy.

Tip. Review the ionization energies given in Text Table 3.1.

c)

$$\lambda_{\text{max}} = \frac{hc}{\Delta E} = \frac{(6.626 \times 10^{-34}\text{ J s})(2.9979 \times 10^{8}\text{ m s}^{-1})}{2370\text{ kJmol}^{-1}} \times \left(\frac{1\text{ kJ}}{1000\text{ J}}\right) \times \left(\frac{6.022 \times 10^{23}\text{ molecule}}{1\text{ mol}}\right)$$

$$= \boxed{5.047 \times 10^{-8}\text{ m}} = 50.47\text{ nm}$$

15.61 a) The Ca^{2+} ion is smaller than the Ar atom because the two are isoelectronic (18 electrons each) and Ca^{2+} has a larger nuclear charge. The Mg^{2+} ion is smaller than the Ca^{2+} ion because Mg is above Ca in the same column of the periodic table. Compare Ar, the largest species so far, and Br^- by using Cl^- as a bridge. Ar is smaller than Cl^- because the two are isoelectronic and Ar has a larger nuclear charge. But Cl^- is smaller than Br^- ion because it is above it in a column of the periodic table. Hence

$$\boxed{Mg^{2+} < Ca^{2+} < Ar < Br^-}$$

b) Ne and Na^+ have the same electron configuration, but Na^+ has a positive charge, making its ionization energy greater; Ne has a larger ionization energy than O based on the periodic trend in the second period; Na has a lower ionization energy than Li, based on periodic trends, and Li has a lower ionization energy than O. Hence

$$\boxed{Na < O < Ne < Na^+}$$

c) Al is metallic and thus electropositive. The three non-metals should increase in electronegativity according moving to the right in the periodic table. Hence

$$\boxed{Al < H < O < F}$$

15.63 Convert the ionization energy of cesium from kilojoules per mole to joules per atom. This is done by multiplying it by 1000 J kJ^{-1} (to get to joules per mole) and then dividing by 6.022×10^{23} mol^{-1} (Avogadro's number). The answer is 6.239×10^{-19} J. Next, use the relationship $\Delta E = hc/\lambda$ to compute the wavelength that corresponding to this energy:

$$\lambda = \frac{hc}{\Delta E} = \frac{(6.626 \times 10^{-34}\text{ J s})(2.9979 \times 10^{8}\text{ m s}^{-1})}{6.239 \times 10^{-19}\text{ J}} = 3.184 \times 10^{-7}\text{ m} = \boxed{318.4\text{ nm}}$$

This wavelength is in the $\boxed{\text{near ultraviolet}}$ region of the electromagnetic spectrum.

15.65 The wavelength is the speed of the wave divided by its frequency:

$$\lambda = \frac{\text{speed}}{\nu} = \frac{343\text{ m s}^{-1}}{440\text{ s}^{-1}} = \boxed{0.780\text{ m}}$$

Dividing the distance by the speed gives the time. It takes the sound wave $\boxed{0.0292\text{ s}}$ to travel 10.0 m.

15.67 As a blackbody is heated, the wavelength at which the maximum intensity is emitted becomes shorter, which explains the change from red to orange in the perceived color. Also, the intensity of the emitted radiation become larger at all wavelengths. A white-hot object emits strongly across a wide band of visible wavelengths (see the shape of the curve plotted in Figure 15.6.[8] As rising T shifts the wavelength of maximum intensity into the yellow and green, which are near the center of the visible range, the intensities at all other wavelengths are simultaneously great enough that the object appears white.

---

[8] Text page 510.

15.69 The problem gives a formula for the wavelength of the maximum intensity of blackbody radiation as a function of the absolute temperature. Solve the formula for T and substitute the given wavelength, Planck's constant, the speed of light, and the Boltzmann constant. Take care with the units:

$$T = \frac{0.20hc}{k_B \lambda_{\text{max}}} = \frac{0.20(6.626 \times 10^{-34} \text{ J s})(3.00 \times 10^8 \text{ m s}^{-1})}{(1.38 \times 10^{-23} \text{ J K}^{-1})(465.0 \times 10^{-9} \text{ m})} = \boxed{6.2 \times 10^3 \text{ K}}$$

15.71 The energy of the photon is sufficient to overcome the work function of the nickel surface (pry an electron loose) and to impart a kinetic energy as large as 7.04×10^{-19} J to the ejected electron. It is known that:

$$\frac{hc}{\lambda} = \Phi + \tfrac{1}{2}mv^2$$

hence:

$$\Phi = \frac{(6.626 \times 10^{-34}\text{J s})(3.00 \times 10^8 \text{ m s}^{-1})}{131 \times 10^{-9} \text{ m}} - 7.04 \times 10^{-19} \text{ J} = \boxed{8.1 \times 10^{-19} \text{ J}}$$

15.73 The Lyman series is emitted as hydrogen atoms undergo transitions from various excited states to the ground state. The energies of the emitted photons are:

$$E_n(\text{from H}) = Z^2 \left(\frac{1}{n_\text{f}^2} - \frac{1}{n_\text{i}^2}\right) \text{Ry} = (1^2)\left(\frac{1}{1} - \frac{1}{n_\text{i}^2}\right) \text{Ry}$$

where 1 Ry[9] equals 2.18×10^{-18} J, and n_i is the quantum number of the excited state. To be absorbed by a ground-state He^+ ion, the energy of the incoming photon must exactly equal the energy it takes to raise the electron from the $n = 1$ state to the $n = 2, 3, 4 \ldots$ state. These energies are:

$$E_n(\text{from He}^+) = Z^2 \left(\frac{1}{n_\text{i}^2} - \frac{1}{n_\text{f}^2}\right) \text{Ry} = (2^2)\left(\frac{1}{1} - \frac{1}{n_\text{f}^2}\right) \text{Ry}$$

Is there any combination of positive whole numbers for n_i and n_f that makes these two energies equal? To find out, subtract the first from the second and set the difference equal to zero. That is,

$$4\left(1 - \frac{1}{n_\text{f}^2}\right) - \left(1 - \frac{1}{n_\text{i}^2}\right) = 0 \quad \text{from which} \quad 3 + \frac{1}{n_\text{i}^2} = \frac{4}{n_\text{f}^2}$$

The left side of the second expression is always between 3.25 and 3 as n_i takes on its possible values; the right side is always equal to or less than 1 as n_f takes on *its* possible values. Since no combination of allowed n's makes the equation valid, the answer to the question is $\boxed{\text{no}}$.

15.75 The m of the earth and its v and r in its orbit around the sun are all given in SI units. The angular momentum of the earth is the product of the three values. The angular momentum of the earth in its orbit around the sun is quantized in units of $h/2\pi$: $mvr = nh/2\pi$. Thus:

$$mvr = 2.7 \times 10^{40} \text{ kg m}^2 \text{s}^{-1} = n\left(\frac{6.626 \times 10^{-34} \text{ J s}}{2\pi}\right)$$

Solving for n gives the desired answer: $\boxed{2.6 \times 10^{74}}$. Note that one J s is the same as one kg m^2 s^{-1}, so n is unitless. Since n is truly huge, +1 in n has $\boxed{\text{no effect}}$ on the angular momentum.

---

[9] This unit of energy, the rydberg, is introduced on text page 525.

15.77 a) The uncertainty in the kinetic energy of the electron (call it ΔE_{K}) is 0.02×10^{-19} J, the range of the values given in the problem. The uncertainty in the momentum of the electron is related to that of the kinetic energy by:

$$\Delta p = \Delta(mv) = m\Delta v = m\sqrt{\frac{2\,\Delta E_{\text{K}}}{m}}$$

The derivation of this equation employs $E_{\text{K}} = \frac{1}{2}mv^2$, the definition of kinetic energy. Compute Δp:

$$\Delta p = (9.11 \times 10^{-31}\ \text{kg})\sqrt{\frac{2(0.02 \times 10^{-19}\ \text{J})}{9.11 \times 10^{-31}\ \text{kg}}} = 6 \times 10^{-26}\ \text{kg m s}^{-1}$$

From the Heisenberg uncertainty principle:

$$\Delta x \geq \frac{h/4\pi}{\Delta p}$$

it follows that the *minimum* uncertainty in the position of the electron is

$$\Delta x_{\text{min}} = \frac{h/4\pi}{\Delta p} = \frac{(6.626 \times 10^{-34}\ \text{J s})/4\pi}{6 \times 10^{-26}\ \text{kg m s}^{-1}} = \boxed{9 \times 10^{-10}\ \text{m}}$$

b) The mass of a helium atom is 6.647×10^{-27} kg.[10] The uncertainty in the momentum of a helium atom with the same ΔE_{K} as the electron in the previous part is

$$\Delta p = (6.647 \times 10^{-27}\ \text{kg})\sqrt{\frac{2(0.02 \times 10^{-19}\ \text{J})}{6.647 \times 10^{-27}\ \text{kg}}} = 5 \times 10^{-24}\ \text{kg m s}^{-1}$$

Note that the uncertainty is larger for a helium atom than for an electron because of the larger mass of the helium atom. The minimum uncertainty in the position of the helium atom will be proportionately smaller:

$$\Delta x_{\text{min}} = \frac{h/4\pi}{\Delta p} = \frac{6.626 \times 10^{-34}\ \text{J s}/4\pi}{5 \times 10^{-24}\ \text{kg m s}^{-1}} = \boxed{1 \times 10^{-11}\ \text{m}}$$

15.79 Photons have no mass (m), but they do have momentum (p). They therefore exert a force on a object when they hit it, just as the molecules of a gas exert a force on the walls of their container (see Chapter 4). Convert the photonic pressure of 10^{-6} atm to SI units (newtons per square meter)

$$P = 10^{-6}\ \text{atm} \times \left(\frac{1.01325 \times 10^5\ \text{N m}^{-2}}{\text{atm}}\right) = 1.01325 \times 10^{-1}\ \text{N m}^{-2}$$

Imagine that the sail has an area of 1 cm^2. Use the definition of pressure to compute the force that the stream of photons causes on this sail

$$F = PA = (1.01325 \times 10^{-1}\ \text{N m}^{-2})(1\ \text{cm}^2)\left(\frac{1\ \text{m}^2}{10^4\ \text{cm}^2}\right)$$
$$= 1.01325 \times 10^{-5}\ \text{N} = 1.01325 \times 10^{-5}\ \text{kg m s}^{-2}$$

where the last equality uses the definition of a newton in base SI units (text Appendix B). The momentum of a 6000 Å photon is

$$p = \frac{h}{\lambda} = \frac{6.626 \times 10^{-34}\ \text{J s}}{6000 \times 10^{-10}\ \text{m}} \times \left(\frac{1\ \text{kg m}^2\ \text{s}^{-2}}{\text{J}}\right) = 1.104 \times 10^{-27}\ \text{kg m s}^{-1}$$

[10] See text Table 14.1.

If a photon strikes the sail perpendicularly and is not absorbed by the material of the sail, its momentum is reversed in direction but unchanged in magnitude. Because momentum is a vector quantity, the *change* in momentum is

$$\Delta p = p_2 - p_1 = (1.104 \times 10^{-27}) - (-1.104 \times 10^{-27}) \text{ kg m s}^{-1} = 2.208 \times 10^{-27} \text{ kg m s}^{-1}$$

The sail experiences am equal change in momentum in the other direction (momentum is conserved in the collision). According to Newton's second law, the force on an object equals its change in momentum per unit time. Many photons strike the sail per unit time. The force on the sail equals its change in momentum per collision times the rate at which the photons collide.[11]. This rate (call it r) is what the problem asks for. Compute it as follows

$$r = \frac{F}{\Delta p} = \frac{1.01325 \times 10^{-5} \text{ kg m s}^{-2}}{2.208 \times 10^{-27} \text{ kg m s}^{-1}} = \boxed{4.6 \times 10^{21} \text{ s}^{-1}}$$

Tip. See Problem 15-99, which is related.

15.81 The change in the energy of the atom is the same regardless of whether it relaxes from its excited state in two steps or one:

$$\Delta E = \Delta E_1 + \Delta E_2$$

The energy change is inversely proportional to the wavelength of the emitted quantum ($\Delta E = hc/\lambda$) so

$$\frac{hc}{\lambda} = \frac{hc}{\lambda_1} + \frac{hc}{\lambda_2} \qquad \text{which gives} \qquad \boxed{\frac{1}{\lambda} = \frac{1}{\lambda_1} + \frac{1}{\lambda_2}}$$

The change in energy equals $h\nu$. Therefore $\boxed{\nu = \nu_1 + \nu_2}$.

15.83 The wave functions for the particle in a box are sketched in text Figure 15.25b.[12] The $n = 2$ wave function has exactly one node, half-way between $x = 0$ and $x = L$. This node occurs because $\sin(2\pi x/L)$ equals zero when x equals $L/2$. The function has maxima at $x = L/4$ and $3L/4$. The figure clearly reveals the symmetry of the function. The probability of finding the particle at any point x between 0 and L is equal to ψ^2 evaluated at x. A plot of ψ^2 versus x has a zero at $x = L/2$ and symmetrical maxima at $x = L/4$ and $3L/4$ (see Figure 15.25c). Passing from $x = 0$ to $x = L/4$ covers one-fourth of the area under the curve defined by ψ^2, the probability distribution function. Since the particle must be in the box somewhere, the answer is $\boxed{1/4}$.

Tip. The same answer comes from writing out the particle-in-a-box function for $n = 2$, squaring it, and integrating from $x = 0$ to $x = L/4$:

$$\text{probability} = \int_0^{L/4} \left(\sqrt{\frac{2}{L}} \sin \frac{2\pi x}{L} \right)^2 dx$$

In doing this it is helpful to know that:

$$\int \sin^2 y dy = 1/2y - 1/4 \sin 2y$$

---

[11] See text page 109

[12] Text page 533.

15.85 The $3d_{xy}$ orbital in O^{7+} ion has the $\boxed{\text{same shape}}$ as the $3d_{xy}$ orbital in an H atom. Both have two nodal planes at right angles. The $3d_{xy}$ orbital is much smaller in O^{7+} than in H because of the larger nuclear charge in O^{7+}.

Tip. It is instructive to compute the average distance of the electron in these two $3d$ orbitals:

$$\bar{r}_{n,\ell} = \frac{n^2 a_0}{Z}\left[1 + \frac{1}{2}\left(1 - \frac{\ell(\ell+1)}{n^2}\right)\right]$$

$$\bar{r}_{3,2} = \frac{3^2 a_0}{Z}\left[1 + \frac{1}{2}\left(1 - \frac{2(2+1)}{3^2}\right)\right] = \frac{9a_0}{Z}\left[\frac{21}{18}\right] = \frac{10.5a_0}{Z}$$

For H, the average distance is 5.55 Å; for O^{7+}, the average distance is 0.694 Å.

15.87 This atom of sodium is in an $\boxed{\text{excited state}}$. It can lose energy in a variety of ways to end up ultimately in its ground state, which is represented $[Ne]3s^1$.

15.89 In chromium(IV) oxide, the Cr^{4+} ion has the ground-state electron configuration: $\boxed{[Ar]3d^2}$. The neutral Cr atom has lost its $4s$ electron and three of its five $3d$ electrons. The two remaining $3d$ electrons are unpaired (in the ground state) so CrO_2 has $\boxed{\text{two}}$ unpaired spins per Cr atom.

15.91 The smallest by far is the hydrogen-like Co^{25+} ion. The rest of the order follows from periodic trends.

$$\boxed{Co^{25+} < F^+ < F < Br < K < Rb < Rb^-}$$

15.93 The first ionization energy of Li(g) is 520×10^3 J mol^{-1}. Divide this by N_0 to put it on a per atom basis. The result is 8.635×10^{-19} J per atom. It requires this much energy to extract the $2s$ electron from lithium. The energy of an electron in an atom in a Hartree orbital is given by the formula:

$$E_n = -\frac{Z_{\text{eff}}}{n^2}\text{Ry} = (-2.18 \times 10^{-18}\text{ J})\frac{Z_{\text{eff}}^2}{n^2}$$

where Z_{eff} is the effective nuclear charge experienced by the electron and n is its quantum number. For the lithium $2s$ electron:

$$-(-2.18 \times 10^{-18}\text{ J})\frac{Z_{\text{eff}}^2}{2^2} = 8.635 \times 10^{-19}\text{ J} \quad \text{from which} \quad Z_{\text{eff}} = \boxed{1.26}$$

The true Z of lithium is 3. The inner two electrons, which are located mainly between the $2s$ electron and the nucleus, shield the influence of the nucleus considerably, but the screening is imperfect because Z_{eff} exceeds 1.

For Na ($Z = 11$), the $3s$ electron is lost, and the equation becomes:

$$-(-2.18 \times 10^{-18}\text{ J})\frac{Z_{\text{eff}}^2}{3^2} = \frac{496 \times 10^3\text{ J mol}^{-1}}{6.022 \times 10^{23}\text{ mol}^{-1}} \quad \text{from which} \quad Z_{\text{eff}} = \boxed{1.84}$$

For K ($Z = 19$), the $4s$ electron is lost:

$$-(-2.18 \times 10^{-18}\text{ J})\frac{Z_{\text{eff}}^2}{4^2} = \frac{419 \times 10^3\text{ J mol}^{-1}}{6.022 \times 10^{23}\text{ mol}^{-1}} \quad \text{from which} \quad Z_{\text{eff}} = \boxed{2.26}$$

15.95 The $2p \rightarrow 1s$ transition in the Fe atom occurs with emission of X-rays of wavelength 193 nm (which equals 193×10^{-9} m). Compute the energy change

$$\Delta E = \frac{hc}{\lambda} = \frac{(6.626 \times 10^{-34}\text{ J s})(2.9979 \times 10^{10}\text{ m s}^{-1})}{193 \times 10^{-9}\text{ m}} = \boxed{1.03 \times 10^{-15}\text{ J}}$$

This energy exceeds the energy for the similar transition in H by a substantial factor

$$\frac{\Delta E \text{ for Fe}}{\Delta E \text{ for H}} = \frac{1.03 \times 10^{-15}\text{ J}}{16.2 \times 10^{-19}\text{ J}} = 636$$

The much greater energy of the transition in Fe results from the much larger nuclear charge ($Z = 26$ for Fe versus $Z = 1$ for H). The $2p \rightarrow 1s$ transition in the Fe^{25+} ion, which is a one-electron ion, is $(Z_{\text{Fe}}/Z_{\text{H}})^2 = 676$ times more energetic than the same transition in H[13]. The ratio 636 is fairly close to 676. It differs because the outer electrons in Fe slightly shield the inner orbitals from the nucleus.

15.97 The similarity in chemical properties among the alkali metals strongly suggests similar ground-state valence electron configurations. This configuration must be ns^1 because no $(n-1)d$ orbitals exist for Li and Na. Therefore the ns orbital must have lower energy (greater stability) than the $(n-1)d$ orbital in K, Rb, Cs. A similar argument can be made with respect to the alkali-earth elements.

15.99 The fall of photons on a surface exerts a pressure. Use the deBroglie relation, which gives p as a function of λ, to compute the momentum of the photons as they approach the surface:

$$p = \frac{h}{\lambda} = \frac{6.626 \times 10^{-34}\text{ J s}}{550 \times 10^{-9}\text{ m}} = 1.205 \times 10^{-27}\text{ kg m s}^{-1}$$

Each photon bounces away from the wall with momentum of the same magnitude but opposite sign. The change in momentum per collision is

$$\Delta p = p_2 - p_1 = (1.205 \times 10^{-27}) - (-1.205 \times 10^{-27}) = 2.410 \times 10^{-27}\text{ kg m s}^{-1}$$

The number of photons colliding per second equals the given power of the laser (1.0 watt = 1.0 J s^{-1}) divided by the energy delivered per photon. The energy transported by one 550 nm photon is

$$E = \frac{hc}{\lambda} = \frac{(6.626 \times 10^{-34}\text{ J s})(3.00 \times 10^{8}\text{ m s}^{-1})}{550 \times 10^{-9}\text{ m}} = 3.614 \times 10^{-19}\text{ J}$$

Clearly, it requires lots of such photons to transport 1.0 J s^{-1}:

$$\left(\frac{1.0\text{ J}}{1\text{ s}}\right) \times \left(\frac{1\text{ photon}}{3.614 \times 10^{-19}\text{ J}}\right) = \frac{2.77 \times 10^{18}\text{ photons}}{\text{second}}$$

As developed in text Section 4.5, the *total* force equals the change in momentum per collision multiplied by the number of collisions per second:

$$F = (2.410 \times 10^{-27}\text{ kg m s}^{-1}) \times (2.77 \times 10^{18}\text{ s}^{-1}) = 6.67 \times 10^{-9}\text{ kg m s}^{-2}$$

Pressure is defined as force divided by area. The area of the circular wall is πr^2 where r is its radius. Hence:

$$P = \frac{F}{A} = \frac{F}{\pi r^2} = \frac{6.67 \times 10^{-9}\text{ kg m s}^{-2}}{\pi(0.10 \times 10^{-3}\text{ m})^2} = \boxed{0.21\text{ Pa}}$$

Tip. See Problem 15-79, which is related.

---

[13]See text equation 15.11, text page 526

15.101 The problem asks for the lattice energy of KCl(s). This is the ΔE of the reaction:

$$\text{KCl}(s) \rightarrow \text{K}^+(g) + \text{Cl}^-(g) \qquad \Delta E = \text{lattice energy}$$

The best strategy is to discover a series of steps having known ΔE's that add up to the desired overall change. The sum of the ΔE's of the steps then equals the desired ΔE. Obvious steps are the vaporization of the solid KCl to give gaseous atoms of K and Cl:

$$\text{KCl}(s) \rightarrow \text{K}(g) + \text{Cl}(g) \qquad \Delta E = +653 \text{ kJ}$$

and then the transfer of electrons to create ions:

$$\text{K}(g) \rightarrow \text{K}^+(g) + e^- \qquad \Delta E = IE_1 = 418.8 \text{ kJ}$$

$$\text{Cl}(g) + e^- \rightarrow \text{Cl}^-(g) \qquad \Delta E = -EA = -349 \text{ kJ}$$

Since these equations add up to the specified process, simply add their ΔE's:

$$\text{lattice energy} = \Delta E = 418.8 + (-349) + 653 = \boxed{722 \text{ kJ}}$$

Tip. The literature value for the lattice energy of KCl(s) equals 715 kJ mol^{-1}.

Chapter 16

Quantum Mechanics and Molecular Structure

16.1 **a)** Fluorine (F_2) is a homonuclear diatomic molecule with $Z = 9$. It has 14 valence electrons. The F_2^+ ion has only 13 valence electrons. Use the correlation diagram in text Figure 16.11b[1] to get the energetic order of valence molecular orbitals in both species. The MO's are then filled in order of increasing energy with the available valence electrons:

$$\begin{array}{ll} F_2 & (\sigma_{g2s})^2(\sigma^*_{u2s})^2(\sigma_{g2p})^2(\pi_{u2p})^4(\pi^*_{g2p})^4 \\ F_2^+ & (\sigma_{g2s})^2(\sigma^*_{u2s})^2(\sigma_{g2p})^2(\pi_{u2p})^4(\pi^*_{g2p})^3 \end{array}$$

b) The F_2 molecule has two more bonding than antibonding electrons. Its bond order equals $\boxed{1}$; F_2^+ ion has three more bonding than antibonding electrons. Its bond order is $\boxed{3/2}$.

c) The molecule of F_2 has no unpaired electrons; accordingly, F_2 is $\boxed{\text{diamagnetic}}$. The F_2^+ ion has an odd number of electrons. Because a π^*_{2p} electron is unpaired, F_2^+ is $\boxed{\text{paramagnetic}}$.

d) The $\boxed{F_2^+}$ ion has a larger bond order and therefore requires $\boxed{\text{more energy}}$ to dissociate than the F_2 molecule.

16.3 The valence-electron configuration of S_2 should be like that of O_2 except in using $n = 3$ orbitals: $(\sigma_{g3s})^2(\sigma^*_{u3s})^2(\sigma_{u3p})^2(\pi_{u3p})^4(\pi^*_{g3p})^2$. The bond order is $\boxed{2}$, and the molecule should be $\boxed{\text{paramagnetic}}$ (two unpaired electrons).

16.5 In each case, count the valence electrons. This result and the charge on the species identify the column of the periodic table in which the element is located. All the configurations involve MO's from the $n = 2$ shell and therefore involve elements in the second row of the periodic table. The bond order is half the number of bonding electrons minus half the number of antibonding electrons:

a) F_2, bond order 1. **b)** N_2^+, bond order 5/2. **c)** O_2^-, bond order 3/2.

16.7 Check unpaired valence electrons:
a) diamagnetic. **b)** paramagnetic. **c)** paramagnetic.

16.9 Nitrogen is more electronegative than carbon. The energies of its atomic orbitals are *lower* (on the right side in the correlation diagram in text Figure 16.13[2] relative to the energies of the corresponding

[1] Text page 579.
[2] Text page 581.

orbitals of the carbon atom. A CN molecule has 9 valence electrons. The ground-state valence configuration is $(\sigma_{g2s})^2(\sigma^*_{u2s})^2(\pi_{u2p})^4(\sigma_{g2p})^1$. The bond order accordingly is 5/2; the unpaired electron causes paramagnetism.

16.11 The valence-electron configurations are:

$$\text{CF} \quad (\sigma_{g2s})^2(\sigma^*_{u2s})^2(\sigma_{g2p})^2(\pi_{u2p})^4(\pi^*_{g2p})^1 \qquad \text{and} \qquad \text{CF}^+ \quad (\sigma_{g2s})^2(\sigma^*_{u2s})^2(\sigma_{g2p})^2(\pi_{u2p})^4(\pi^*_{g2p})^0$$

Removing an electron from the π^*_{g2p} orbital in the CF molecule gives the CF^+ ion. The loss of an antibonding electron increases the bond order from 5/2 to 3. The bond strengthens.

16.13 The electron configuration for HeH^- would be $(\sigma_{g1s})^2(\sigma^*_{u2s})^2$. The ion has a bond order of zero and should be unstable.

16.15 The central N atom in NH_2^- is surrounded by eight valence electrons (5 from the N, 1 each from the H's and 1 for the overall negative charge). The valence orbitals of the N atom are sp^3 hybridized. Two of the hybrids overlap in σ bonds with $1s$ orbitals on the two H atoms. The other two contain lone pairs. The molecular ion should be bent with an H—N—H angle far less than 180°.

Tip. Experimentally, the angle equals 106.7° (even less than 109.5°).

16.17 In all of these species, the hybridization on the central atom follows from the number of lone pairs plus the number of bonded atoms that surround the central atom (this sum equals the steric number *SN*). The molecular geometry depends on the hybridization, but the shapes of molecules are named only with reference to actual atoms.

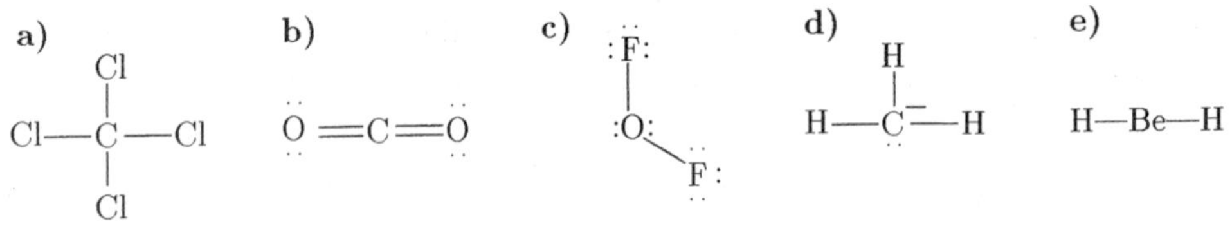

tetrahedral linear bent pyramidal linear

The central C in CCl_4 has *SN* 4. This atom is sp^3 hybridized, and the molecule is tetrahedral. The central C in CO_2 has *SN* 2 and is sp hybridized. The molecule is linear. The central O in OF_2 has *SN* 4 and is sp^3 hybridized. Two of the hybrid orbitals on the O accommodate lone pairs of electrons, and two overlap with orbitals on the fluorine atoms. The molecule is bent. The central C in the CH_3^- ion has *SN* 4 and is sp^3 hybridized. One of the four hybrid orbitals contains a lone pair of electrons. The other three overlap with $1s$ orbitals of the three H atoms. The molecular ion is pyramidal. The central Be in BeH_2 has *SN* 2 and is sp hybridized. The molecule is linear.

16.19 The ClO_3^+ and ClO_2^+ ions have 24 and 18 valence electrons respectively. The central Cl atom in ClO_3^+ has *SN* 3 and therefore three sp^2 hybrid orbitals overlapping with orbitals from the oxygen atoms. It has a trigonal planar geometry. The central Cl atom in ClO_2^+ likewise has a set of three sp^2 hybrid orbitals, but only two overlap with orbitals on oxygen atoms. The third sp^2 orbital contains a lone pair. The ClO_2^+ molecular ion is bent. The central chlorine atoms in the following Lewis structures are shown with expanded octets. Other resonance structures can be drawn; these particular structures minimize formal charges. Compare to **3.77**.

16.21 The central nitrogen atom in the orthonitrate ion can attain an octet by forming four single bonds, one to each of the four oxygen atoms. We expect sp^3 hybridization on the N atom and a tetrahedral geometry.

Tip. The Lewis structure of this ion puts a +3 formal charge on the central nitrogen atom. No wonder the ion is unfamiliar.

16.23 Like the CO_2 molecule, the azide ion N_3^- is linear and has 16 valence electrons. The correlation diagram of text Figure 16.21[3] applies. Two N—N σ bonds result from overlap of sp hybrid orbitals on the central N atom with $2p_z$ orbitals on the two outer N atoms. These bonds use 4 electrons. Lone pairs in each of the $2s$ orbitals of the outer N atoms use another 4 electrons. The π orbitals pictured in text Figure 16.20 accommodate the remaining eight valence electrons. Four of these are in two bonding π orbitals that lie perpendicular to each other. The other four are in the two nonbonding π orbitals. Thus: $(\pi)^4(\pi^{nb})^4$, which means a total of two π bonds. The overall bond order of the molecule is 4: (2 σ bonds plus 2 π bonds). The two N-to-N linkages are identical; each has bond order 2. All of the electrons are paired so the compound is diamagnetic.

The N_3 molecule has 15 valence electrons. It derives from N_3^- by the loss of an electron. The loss comes from the highest energy molecular orbital which is (by consulting text Figure 16.21) a nonbonding MO. N_3 is bound with an overall bond order of 4, just like N_3^-. Unlike N_3^-, N_3 has an unpaired electron and is paramagnetic.

The N_3^+ ion has 14 valence-electrons. It derives from N_3^- by the loss of two nonbonding π electrons. The N_3^+ molecular ion is therefore bound with bond order 4. There are two unpaired electrons in the set of π^{nb} orbitals so N_3^+ is paramagnetic, too.

Tip. The odd electron in N_3 is accommodated in one of the nonbonding orbitals pictured in text Figure 16.20c. Compare the "location" of the odd electron with the location of the odd electron in the Lewis structures of the related compound ONO, which are discussed in **3.81**. Also, compare to these structures while solving **16.24**.

16.25 Draw the Lewis structure for NO_2^- and use VSEPR theory to determine the steric number and structure. The best two Lewis structures are:

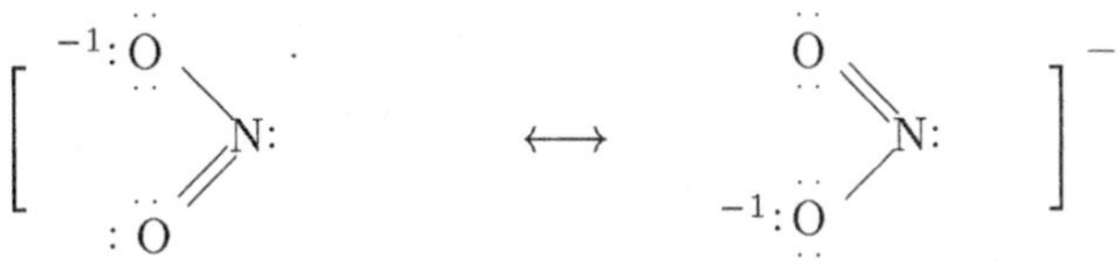

VSEPR theory assigns *SN* 3 to the central N. The O atoms occupy two of the three sites, and the lone pair the third. The molecular ion is therefore bent. The hybridization at the nitrogen atom is sp^2. Two of the three sp^2 hybrid orbitals form the σ bonds to the oxygen atoms, and the third accommodates the lone pair. The unhybridized $2p_z$ atomic orbital on the nitrogen atom is oriented perpendicular to the plane of the molecule. It overlaps with the $2p_z$ atomic orbitals of the two oxygens to form a π system. See text Figure 16.22a. Two electrons occupy the bonding π orbital in this system and two electrons occupy the

[3] Text page 587.

nonbonding (π^{nb}) orbital. The antibonding (π^*) orbital remains empty. Adding the σ MO's to the bonding contributed by the π system gives an overall bond order of 3, which amounts to $\boxed{3/2}$ for each bond. In a localized-orbital scheme, two resonance forms are necessary to represent the bonding in NO_2^-.

Tip. Bonding in the nitrite ion is also the subject of **2.41**.

16.27 The Lewis structure of acetaldehyde is

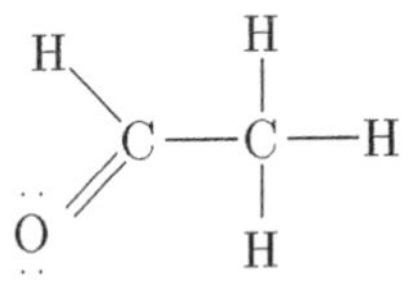

This structure has a total of 18 valence electrons. The *SN*'s (steric numbers) of the carbon atoms are 4 (for the methyl carbon) and 3 (for the carbonyl carbon). The *SN*'s of the other atoms are immaterial because each of them forms only one bond. The *SN* 4 on the methyl C means it has $\boxed{sp^3}$ hybridization; the *SN* 3 on the carbonyl C means it has $\boxed{sp^2}$ hybridization. Constructing the single bond framework of the molecule uses 12 valence electrons. At this point a *p* orbital on the carbonyl C contains a single electron and the three *p* orbitals on the oxygen contain 5 electrons. The *p* orbital on the C and a *p* orbitals on the O overlap to form a π bonding orbital. Two electrons occupy this orbital. The remaining 4 electrons remain as lone pairs on the O. A π^* antibonding orbital is created simultaneously with the π orbital spanning C and O, but it remains empty. The three groups bonded to the carbonyl C lie in a plane with bond angles near $\boxed{120°}$. The geometry at the methyl C atom is approximately tetrahedral, with all six H—C—H and H—C—C angles near $\boxed{109.5°}$.

16.29 The Lewis structures for HCOOH and $HCOO^-$ are

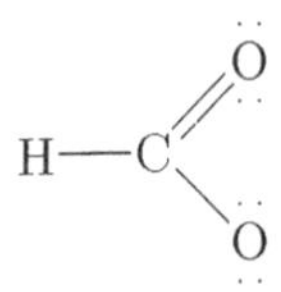

One resonance form is given for HCOOH, but two are given for the formate anion $HCOO^-$. In formic acid, one oxygen atom is doubly bonded to the carbon atom, and the other is singly bonded. In the anion, there is some double-bond character in both C—O bonds. The carbon atom in HCOOH is sp^2 hybridized (*SN* 3), and the OH oxygen atom is sp^3 hybridized (*SN* 4). The immediate surroundings of the carbon atom have trigonal planar geometry, and the C—O—H group is bent. In the $HCOO^-$ ion, the carbon atom and both oxygen atoms are sp^2 hybridized (*SN* 3), possessing a three-center four-electron π system. In HCOOH, π overlap occurs between orbitals on the carbon atom and only one oxygen atom. Both C-to-O bond lengths in the formate ion should lie somewhere between the value for the single bond (1.36 Å) and the value for the double bond (1.23 Å).

16.31 The 60 carbon atoms in fullerene must form 120 bonds in order to satisfy the octet rule for every atom. The reasoning is that each C must have four bonds, but each bond is shared by two C's: $4 \times 60/2 = 120$. The structure of fullerene has 60 vertices (the 60 C atoms), 32 faces (20 hexagonal and 12 pentagonal), and 90 edges. These facts can be obtained by inspection.[4] The 90 edges must consist of 60 single bonds and $\boxed{30}$ double bonds. There is no other way to account for 120 shared pairs of electrons. One simple rule for placing the 30 double bonds is to put them at all $\boxed{\text{edges that join two hexagonal faces}}$.

16.33 a) Refer to text Figure 16.11a to identify the five occupied valence molecular orbitals in the N_2

[4] Inspect a soccer ball. Also, the following formula relates the number of vertices V, edges E and faces F of any polyhedron: $V + F = E + 2$.

molecule:

$$N_2 \quad (\sigma_{g2s})^2(\sigma^*_{u2s})^2(\pi_{u2p_x})^2(\pi_{u2p_y})^2(\sigma_{g2p_z})^2$$

The highest-energy occupied orbital is a σ_{gp_z} MO, derived from $2p_z$-$2p_z$ overlap. Its shape is shown in Figure 16.9a.[5] The next two highest occupied MO's are a pair of π bonding MO's of equal energy and identical shape that differ only in orientation. Their shape is shown in Figure 16.10a.[6] One is from $2p_x$-$2p_x$ overlap, and the other is from $2p_y$-$2p_y$ overlap. Occupation of these two π orbitals by four electrons furnishes a cylindrical muff of electron density surrounding the σ bond between the two N atoms. At lower energy come a σ^* orbital derived from antibonding overlap of the $2s$ orbitals (text Figure 16.9b) and a σ orbital from the bonding overlap of the same orbitals (text Figure 16.9a).

b) Since the highest occupied molecular orbital of N_2 is a bonding orbital, the removal of one electron from N_2 will decrease the bond order, and $\boxed{\text{lengthen}}$ the N-to-N bond.

16.35 The correlation diagram in Figure 16.11a[7] gives the configuration $(\sigma_{g2s})^2(\sigma^*_{u2s})^2(\pi_{u2p_x})^1(\pi_{u2p_y})^1$ for the ground state of B_2, which has six valence electrons. There are two unpaired electrons in this configuration. The diagram in Figure 16.11b on the other hand implies the configuration $(\sigma_{g2s})^2(\sigma^*_{u2s})^2(\sigma_{g2p_z})^2$. There are no unpaired electrons in this configuration. Diagram 16-11b is not consistent with the fact that B_2 is paramagnetic.

16.37 a) Consider the molecular orbital energy-level diagrams for H_2 and O_2 (text Figures 16.6 and 16.11b respectively). The ionization energy equals the energy required to remove the highest energy electron from a gaseous molecule or atom. In the case of H compared to H_2, the $1s$ electron of the atom is higher in energy than a σ_{g1s} electron of the molecule. Therefore, it requires less energy to remove the atomic $1s$ electron than a molecular σ_{g1s} electron. In the case of O versus O_2, the atomic $2p$ electron lies lower in energy than the molecular π^*_{g2p} electron. Consequently, it requires more energy to ionize O than O_2.

b) The highest occupied molecular orbital of F_2 is the π^*_{g2p} orbital (see **16.1** and text Figure 16.11b). It is higher in energy than the atomic $2p$ orbital. Therefore, the F_2 molecule should have a lower ionization energy than the F atom.

16.39 The molecular orbital and the square of the molecular orbital for the ground state of the heteronuclear molecule are:

$$\psi = C_A\psi_A + C_B\psi_B \quad \text{and} \quad \psi^2 = C_A^2\psi_A^2 + 2C_AC_B\psi_A\psi_B + C_B^2\psi_B^2$$

where the C's are constants. The *square* of the wave-function is given because it is the quantity that is related to the probability of finding the electron. Neglecting the overlap of the two orbitals means neglecting the cross-term in the squared wave-function:

$$\psi^2 \approx C_A^2\psi_A^2 + C_B^2\psi_B^2$$

If the electron spends 90 percent of its time in orbital ψ_A, then $C_A^2 = 9C_B^2$. Also, the electron must be either on atom A or atom B so $C_A^2 + C_B^2 = 1$. Solution of the two simultaneous equations gives $C_A = \boxed{0.949}$ and $C_B = \boxed{0.316}$.

16.41 a) Nitramide has 24 valence electrons. It must have one double bond somewhere if the octet rule is obeyed.[8] If the structure is non-planar, this double bond is strongly localized to the —NO_2 portion of the molecule. The two electrons occupy a π orbital derived from $2p_z$ orbitals on the N atom and the two O atoms bonded to it. Inclusion in the π system of orbitals and electrons from the other N atom would require

[5] Text page 577.
[6] Text page 578.
[7] Text page 579.
[8] Confirm this using the procedure on text page 69–70.

coplanarity of the H_2N— and —NO_2 portions of the molecule. If the two portions are not coplanar, then overlap and effective mixing of p orbitals is not possible and the N—N bond order is $\boxed{1}$.

b) If the nitramide molecule were planar, the four $2p_z$ orbitals present on the two nitrogen atoms and two oxygen atoms after completion of the σ bonding could overlap to form one π, two π^{nb}, and one π^* MO's. Four electrons would occupy this π system. Two of the electrons would be in the bonding orbital, and the other two electrons would be in the non-bonding orbitals. The resulting π system would possess a total of two bonding electrons across the four atoms involved. The bond order of the N—N bond would be 1 (from the σ interaction) plus 1/3 (from the π system) or $\boxed{4/3}$.

16.43 The six π molecular orbitals of pyridine arise as a combination of the six p_z orbitals of the nitrogen and five carbons atoms in the ring:

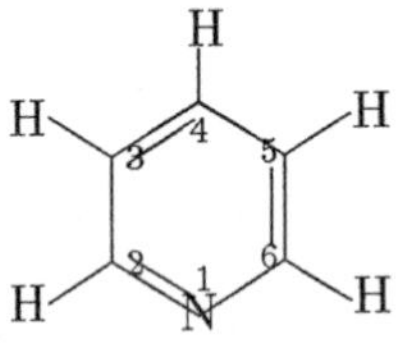

According to the problem, MO's that put electron density onto the N atom will be lower in energy in pyridine than comparable orbitals in benzene. Thus, molecular orbitals that have the p_z(N) orbital among their parents will be lower in energy. Let the N atom occupy position 1 in a numbering scheme that goes clockwise around the ring (see above). Refer to text Figure 16.27,[9] which shows the six lowest energy π MO's of benzene. The strongly bonding and strongly antibonding (the highest and lowest energy MO's among those shown) both have parentage that includes the p_z orbital on atom 1. These two molecular orbitals are therefore *lowered* in energy in pyridine relative to benzene. One of the two weakly bonding molecular orbitals in benzene has p_z(N) parentage, but the other does not. Instead, its parentage includes p_z orbitals from carbon atoms at positions 2, 3, 5, and 6. The first of the two weakly bonding MO's (on the left in Figure 16.27) is therefore lowered in energy in pyridine relative to benzene, but the energy of the second is not affected. Similarly, the two weakly antibonding MO's in benzene are split in energy. The one that has some p_z(N) parentage (on the right in Figure 16.27) is lowered, but the other is unchanged. The result is an energy-level diagram for pyridine with six different π orbital energies, four lower than the corresponding benzene π orbitals, and two unchanged in energy.

16.45 The combustion of fullerene (C_{60}) and its associated enthalpy are represented

$$C_{60}(s) + 60\ O_2(g) \rightarrow 60\ CO_2(g) \qquad \Delta H^\circ = -25,891\ \text{kJ}$$

Using Hess's law and enthalpy of formation data from text Appendix D

$$\begin{aligned} -25,891\ \text{kJ} &= (60\ \text{mol})\Delta H_f^\circ(CO_2(g)) - (1\ \text{mol})\Delta H_f^\circ(C_{60}(s)) - (60\ \text{mol})\Delta H_f^\circ(O_2(g)) \\ &= (60\ \text{mol})(-393.51\ \text{kJ mol}^{-1}) - (1\ \text{mol})(\Delta H_f^\circ(C_{60}(s)) - (60\ \text{mol})(0\ \text{kJ mol}^{-1}) \end{aligned}$$

$$\Delta H_f^\circ(C_{60}) = \boxed{+2280\ \text{kJ mol}^{-1}}$$

Tip. The enthalpy of formation is a large positive number. It takes considerable enthalpy to synthesize fullerene from graphite, about 38 kJ per mole of C atoms that is involved.

[9] Text page 593.

Chapter 17

Interaction of Molecules with Light

17.1 A percent transmittance T of 20.0% means that at this wavelength I_S, the intensity of the light detected through the sample cell is 20.0% of the intensity detected through the reference cell I_R. The absorbance A is defined in terms of these relative intensities

$$A = -\log \frac{I_S}{I_R} = -\log 0.20 = \boxed{0.699}$$

Assume that the Beer-Lambert law applies. Use it to obtain ϵ

$$\epsilon = \frac{A}{c\ell} = \frac{0.699}{(5 \times 10^{-4}\ \text{mol L}^{-1})(1.0\ \text{cm})} = \boxed{1.4 \times 10^3\ \text{L mol}^{-1}\ \text{cm}^{-1}}$$

17.3 Assume that the Beer-Lambert law (Beer's law) applies and that the absorbances due to compounds A and B are additive at both 400 nm and 500 nm. Thus, A and B do not, for example, react with each other. Compute the absorbances of solutions 1, 2, and 3 at 400 and at 500 nm

$$\text{At 400 nm} \begin{cases} A_1 &= -\log(10/100) = 1.000 \\ A_2 &= -\log(80/100) = 0.0969 \\ A_3 &= -\log(40/100) = 0.3979 \end{cases} \qquad \text{At 500 nm} \begin{cases} A_1 &= -\log(60/100) = 0.2218 \\ A_2 &= -\log(20/100) = 0.6990 \\ A_3 &= -\log(50/100) = 0.3010 \end{cases}$$

Solution 1 does not contain compound B. Therefore

$$A_{1,400} = c_A(\epsilon\ell)_{A,400} = (0.001\ \text{mol L}^{-1})(\epsilon\ell)_{A,400} \quad \text{and} \quad A_{1,500} = c_A(\epsilon\ell)_{A,500} = (0.001\ \text{mol L}^{-1})(\epsilon\ell)_{A,500}$$

Solve for $(\epsilon\ell)$ in each equation and insert the A's and c's

$$(\epsilon\ell)_{A,400} = \frac{1.000}{0.001\ \text{L mol}^{-1}} = 1000\ \text{L mol}^{-1} \quad \text{and} \quad (\epsilon\ell)_{A,500} = \frac{0.2218}{0.001\ \text{L mol}^{-1}} = 221.8\ \text{L mol}^{-1}$$

Solution 2 does not contain compound A, so a similar development is possible

$$(\epsilon\ell)_{B,400} = \frac{0.0969}{0.005\ \text{L mol}^{-1}} = 19.38\ \text{L mol}^{-1} \quad \text{and} \quad (\epsilon\ell)_{B,500} = \frac{0.6990}{0.005\ \text{L mol}^{-1}} = 139.8\ \text{L mol}^{-1}$$

The absorbances due to A and B are additive in Solution 3, and the molar extinction coefficients (the ϵ's) of A and B do not change. Therefore, the Beer-Lambert law for Solution 3 gives

$$A_{3,400} = c_A(\epsilon\ell)_{A,400} + c_B(\epsilon\ell)_{B,400} \qquad A_{3,500} = c_A(\epsilon\ell)_{A,500} + c_B(\epsilon\ell)_{B,500}$$

$$0.3979 = c_A(1000\ \text{L mol}^{-1}) + c_B(19.38\ \text{L mol}^{-1}) \qquad 0.3010 = c_A(221.8\ \text{L mol}^{-1}) + c_B(139.8\ \text{L mol}^{-1})$$

where it is also assumed that the ℓ of the sample is the same in all three spectroscopy experiments. Solving the last pair of equations for the unknown concentrations gives

$$c_A = \boxed{3.68 \times 10^{-4} \text{ mol L}^{-1}} \qquad \text{and} \qquad c_B = \boxed{15.7 \times 10^{-4} \text{ mol L}^{-1}}$$

17.5 The rotational energy of diatomic molecules such as NO is given by:

$$E_{\text{rot}} = \left(\frac{h^2}{8\pi^2 I}\right) J(J+1)$$

where I is the moment of inertia of the molecule and J is the rotational quantum number ($J = 0, 1, 2, \ldots$). The rotational energies in the ground state and first excited states of such molecules equal:

$$E_{\text{rot, J=0}} = \left(\frac{h^2}{8\pi^2 I}\right)(0) = 0 \qquad \text{and} \qquad E_{\text{rot, J=1}} = \left(\frac{h^2}{8\pi^2 I}\right)(2)$$

To use these formulas, obtain data on the $^{14}N^{16}O$ molecule[1] to compute the moment of inertia I:

$$\begin{aligned} I = \mu R_e^2 &= \frac{m_N m_O}{m_N + m_O} R_e^2 \\ &= \left(\frac{(14.00307400 \text{ u})(15.9949146 \text{ u})}{(14.00307400 + 15.9949146) \text{ u}}\right)(1.154 \times 10^{-10} \text{ m})^2 \times \left(\frac{1 \text{ kg}}{6.022137 \times 10^{26} \text{ u}}\right) \\ &= 1.651103 \times 10^{-46} \text{ kg m}^2 \end{aligned}$$

Then the desired ΔE is

$$E_{J=1} - E_{J=0} = \frac{h^2}{8\pi^2 I}(2-0) = \frac{(6.626076 \times 10^{-34} \text{ J s})^2}{8\pi^2(1.651103 \times 10^{-46} \text{ kg m}^2)}(2) = \boxed{6.736 \times 10^{-23} \text{ J}} = 40.56 \text{ Jmol}^{-1}$$

17.7 **a)** The spacing of the spectroscopic lines in the pure rotational spectrum of a diatomic species is *uniform* with a frequency separation equal to $h/4\pi^2 I$ where I is the moment of inertia of the species.[2] Average the two differences in frequency to estimate this separation for ^{12}C—^{16}O. It equals 1.155×10^{11} s^{-1}. Then compute the moment of inertia by solving for I as follows:

$$1.155 \times 10^{11} \text{ s}^{-1} = \left(\frac{h}{4\pi^2 I}\right) \qquad I = \left(\frac{6.626 \times 10^{-34} \text{ J s}}{4\pi^2(1.155 \times 10^{11} \text{ s}^{-1})}\right) = \boxed{1.45 \times 10^{-46} \text{ kg m}^2}$$

b) The energy of a rotational state of a linear molecule is given by:

$$E_{\text{rot}} = \left(\frac{h^2}{8\pi^2 I}\right) J(J+1) \quad \text{which is the same as} \qquad E_{\text{rot}} = \frac{h}{2}\left(\frac{h}{4\pi^2 I}\right) J(J+1)$$

For ^{12}C—^{16}O, the factor $h/4\pi^2 I$ equals 1.155×10^{11} s^{-1}. Insert it, $h/2$, and the different J's in the preceding:

$$E_{\text{rot}} = \frac{6.626 \times 10^{-34} \text{ J s}}{2}(1.155 \times 10^{11} \text{ s}^{-1})J(J+1)$$

$$E_{J=1} = \boxed{7.65 \times 10^{-23} \text{ J}} \quad E_{J=2} = \boxed{23.0 \times 10^{-23} \text{ J}} \quad E_{J=3} = \boxed{45.9 \times 10^{-23} \text{ J}}$$

---

[1] The mass data come from text Table 14.1 (text page 474); the bond length comes from text Table 3.3 (text page 64).
[2] See Text page 606.

c) The mass of a ^{12}C atom equals 12.0000 u, and the mass of an ^{16}O atom equals 15.994915 u. Convert these masses to kilograms by dividing by 6.022137×10^{26} u kg^{-1}. The moment of inertia depends on the reduced mass and bond distance:

$$I = \mu Re^2 = \frac{m_O m_C}{m_O + m_C} R_e^2$$

Solve for the bond distance R_e and substitute the masses and moment of inertia:

$$R_e = \sqrt{(1.45 \times 10^{-46}\ \text{kg m}^2)\left(\frac{(2.656 \times 10^{-26}) + (1.993 \times 10^{-26})\ \text{kg}}{(2.656 \times 10^{-26})(1.993 \times 10^{-26})\ \text{kg}^2}\right)}$$
$$= 1.13 \times 10^{-10}\ \text{m} = \boxed{1.13\ \text{Å}}$$

17.9 The thermal population of molecular quantum levels follows the Boltzmann distribution

$$P(E_i) \propto g(E_i)\ \exp(-E_i/k_B T)$$

where $g(E_i)$ is the degeneracy of the i-th quantum state,[3] The energies of the rotational levels in the NaH molecule depend on the moment of inertia of the molecule I and the rotational quantum number J according to

$$E_{\text{rot}} = \frac{h^2}{8\pi^2 I} J(J+1)$$

The degeneracy $g(E_J)$ of a rotational energy level equals $2J+1$. Insert these expressions into the Boltzmann distribution using the quantum number J as a subscript to emphasize the focus on rotation

$$P(E_J) \propto g_J\ \exp(-E_J/k_B T)$$
$$\propto (2J+1)\exp\left(\frac{-h^2\ J(J+1)}{8\pi^2\, I\, k_B T}\right)$$
$$\propto (2J+1)\exp\left(\frac{-(6.626 \times 10^{-34}\ \text{J s})^2\ J(J+1)}{8\pi^2(5.70 \times 10^{-47}\ \text{kg m}^2)\,(1.38 \times 10^{-23}\ \text{J K}^{-1})(298.15\ \text{K})}\right)$$
$$\propto (2J+1)\exp(-\,.0237\, J(J+1))$$

Note how all of the units in the exponential cancel out.

The relative populations of an excited rotational state J of a molecule and the ground state $J = 0$ is the ratio of their Boltzmann populations. For the NaH molecule at 298.15 K,

$$\frac{P(E_J)}{P(E_{J=0})} = \frac{2J+1}{1}\frac{\exp(-\,.0237\, J(J+1))}{\exp(-\,.0237\, 0(0+1))} = (2J+1)\frac{\exp(-\,.0237\, J(J+1))}{1}$$

For the $J = 5$, $J = 15$ and $J = 25$ rotational states the ratios are

a) $$\frac{P(E_{J=5})}{P(E_{J=0})} = (2(5)+1)\frac{\exp(-\,.0237\, 5(5+1))}{1} = \boxed{5.40}$$

b) $$\frac{P(E_{J=15})}{P(E_{J=0})} = (2(15)+1)\frac{\exp(-\,.0237\, 15(15+1))}{1} = \boxed{0.105}$$

c) $$\frac{P(E_{J=25})}{P(E_{J=0})} = (2(25)+1)\frac{\exp(-\,.0237\, 25(25+1))}{1} = \boxed{1.04 \times 10^{-5}}$$

Tip. The point of the problem is that the first dozen or so rotational excited states of this typical small molecule are abundantly populated at room temperature.

---

[3] See text page 605.

17.11 In vibrational spectra, strong absorption is allowed only for transitions between adjacent vibrational states are allowed. Although the transition by Li_2 in this problem is "very weak", assume that the change in the vibrational quantum number $(v_2 - v_1)$ nevertheless equals +1. The change in vibrational energy equals the energy of the final state minus the energy of the initial state:

$$\Delta E_{\text{vib}} = h\left(\frac{1}{2\pi}\right)\sqrt{\frac{k}{\mu}}$$

where k is the desired force constant and μ is the reduced mass of Li_2. The change in vibrational energy is related to the wavelength of the absorbed light λ by $\Delta E_{\text{vib}} = hc/\lambda$. Substitute this relation into the preceding:

$$\frac{hc}{\lambda} = h\left(\frac{1}{2\pi}\right)\sqrt{\frac{k}{\mu}}$$

The wavelength of the absorption line is quoted in the problem as 2.85×10^{-5} m. From text Table 14.1, the mass of ^{7}Li is 7.016004 u; the reduced mass of Li_2 is half of this or 3.508002 u. Converting the reduced mass to kilograms gives 5.8252×10^{-27} kg. Insert this and the other quantities in the preceding equation, solve for k, and complete the arithmetic:

$$k = \left(\frac{2\pi c}{\lambda}\right)^2 \mu = \left(\frac{2\pi(2.9979 \times 10^8 \text{ m s}^{-1})}{2.85 \times 10^{-5} \text{ m}}\right)^2 (5.8252 \times 10^{-27} \text{ kg}) = \boxed{25.4 \text{ kg s}^{-2}}$$

Note that Planck's constant h cancels out of the calculation.

Tip. Confirm that a kg s^{-2} (kilogram per square second) equals a N m^{-1} (newton per meter).

17.13 The frequency of infrared light absorbed by the "signature" C—H stretch is given by $\nu = (1/2\pi)\sqrt{k/\mu}$. Also, $\nu = c/\lambda$. Eliminate ν between these equations and solve for the force constant k:

$$k = \left(\frac{2\pi c}{\lambda}\right)^2 \mu$$

Next, insert the given values of λ and μ. The reduced mass μ is approximated as the mass of the H atom, which equals the molar mass of H divided by Avogadro's number:

$$k = \left(\frac{2\pi(2.9979 \times 10^8 \text{ m s}^{-1})}{3.4 \times 10^{-6} \text{ m}}\right)^2 \frac{0.001008 \text{ kg mol}^{-1}}{6.022 \times 10^{23} \text{ mol}^{-1}} = \boxed{510 \text{ kg s}^{-2}}$$

Tip. The approximation in this problem is equivalent to imagining that the H atom, which has small mass, does all the vibrating, that is, that the rest of the molecule does not move.

17.15 The ratio of the population of two vibrational quantum levels i and j of different energies is given by

$$\frac{P(E_i)}{P(E_j)} = \exp\Big(-(E_i - E_j)/k_{\text{B}}T\Big)$$

The problem asks for this ratio for the vibrational ground state and first excited state in N_2 at 450 K. Let the j-th state be $v = 0$, the ground state, and let the i-th state be $v = 1$, the first excited vibrational state. The difference between the energies of these states is just h times the natural oscillation frequency (vibrational frequency) of the system[4]

$$E_1 - E_0 = h\nu = (6.626 \times 10^{-34} \text{ J s})(7.07 \times 10^{13} \text{ s}^{-1}) = 4.685 \times 10^{-20} \text{ J}$$

[4] See text page 608.

Obtain the desired ratio by substitution in the equation for the distribution:

$$\frac{P(E_1)}{P(E_0)} = \exp\left(\frac{-(4.685 \times 10^{-20}\ \text{J})}{(1.3808 \times 10^{-23}\ \text{J K}^{-1})(450\ \text{K})}\right) = \boxed{0.00053}$$

Tip. At 450 K, which is hot, the lowest excited vibrational level still remains very sparsely populated relative to the ground state.

17.17 The lowest unoccupied molecular orbital of ethylene is a π^* antibonding orbital. The electron that is gained when the $C_2H_4^-$ ion is formed from C_2H_4 goes into this orbital. An additional antibonding electron means that the bond order $\boxed{\text{decreases}}$ in $C_2H_4^-$ relative to C_2H_4.

17.19 The color of a substance is the complement of the color of the light that the substance absorbs. The complementary color of orange is blue. We would therefore expect absorption $\boxed{\text{around 450 nm}}$.

17.21 The benzene molecule contains a cyclic system of three conjugated double bonds; The cyclohexene molecule contains a single double bond. The absorption of UV light in these molecules occurs with excitation of electrons associated with the multiple bonding. Delocalization of the double bonds in benzene should lower the energy for such a transition. Therefore, the absorption occurs at $\boxed{\text{shorter wavelength}}$ in cyclohexene.

17.23 The bond dissociation energy of Cl—F equals 252 kJ mol^{-1}, according to text Table 3.3.[5] Express this energy change in joules per molecule by dividing it by Avogadro's number and calculate the corresponding wavelength:

$$\lambda = \frac{hc}{\Delta E} = \frac{(6.626 \times 10^{-34}\ \text{J s})(2.9979 \times 10^{8}\ \text{m s}^{-1})}{(2.52 \times 10^{5}\ \text{J mol}^{-1})/(6.0221 \times 10^{23}\ \text{mol}^{-1})} = \boxed{4.75 \times 10^{-7}\ \text{m}}$$

Radiation of wavelength equal to or less than 475 nm can dissociate ClF molecules.

17.25 "Low resolution" means that the splitting of nuclear magnetic resonance peaks due to spin-spin coupling is not detected. The three molecules are butane ($CH_3CH_2CH_2CH_3$), dimethyl ether (H_3COCH_3), and dimethylamine (H_3CNHCH_3). All three molecules have two-fold symmetry so that their CH_3 groups (methyl groups) are equivalent. Rapid rotation around the C—C bond axes makes the three protons within these methyl groups chemically equivalent to each other. The protons in the methylene groups (CH_2 groups) in butane differ chemically from those in its methyl groups but are equivalent to each other. Similarly, the N—H proton in dimethylamine differs chemically from its methyl protons. The expected number of peaks and relative peak areas are therefore

Molecule	Number of Peaks	Relative Peak Areas
$CH_3CH_2CH_2CH_3$	2	6 : 4
H_3COCH_3	1	—
H_3CNHCH_3	2	6 : 1

17.27 The binding energy of the electron in each case equals the energy of the photoelectron minus the kinetic energy that the ejected electron carried

$$\begin{aligned}\text{Binding energy} &= h\nu_{\text{photon}} - 1/2 m_e v^2 \\ &= 21.22\ \text{eV} - 5.63\ \text{eV} = \boxed{15.59\ \text{eV}} \\ &= 21.22\ \text{eV} - 4.53\ \text{eV} = \boxed{16.69\ \text{eV}}\end{aligned}$$

[5] See text page 64.

Electrons with the 15.59 eV binding energy are from the $\boxed{\sigma_{g2p_z}}$ molecular orbital, which is the highest occupied molecular orbital in ground-state N_2. See text Figure 17.32 and text Table 16.2. Electrons with the 16.69 eV binding energy come from a $\boxed{\pi_{u2p}}$ molecular orbital (either a π_{u2p_y} or a π_{u2p_x}, the two have the same energy).

17.29 Divide 440 kJ, the energy of a mole of bonds, by Avogadro's number to obtain 7.31×10^{-19} J, the energy change in the dissociation of one bond. Calculate the wavelength corresponding to this energy change as

$$\lambda = \frac{hc}{\Delta E} = \frac{(6.626 \times 10^{-34}\ \text{J s})(2.9979 \times 10^{8}\ \text{m s}^{-1})}{7.31 \times 10^{-19}\ \text{J}} = \boxed{2.72 \times 10^{-7}\ \text{m}}$$

Light of wavelengths shorter than this supplies more than enough energy to break C—F bonds; light of longer wavelengths cannot dissociate these bonds.

Tip. The 272 nm light also suffices to dissociate the C—C bonds and C—Cl bonds in the chlorofluorocarbon because the energies of these bonds are substantially less than the energy of the C—F bond. See text Table 7.3.[6]

17.31 The best Lewis structures are a resonance pair:

The central O atom has a lone pair in both structures. The VSEPR model assigns the central O atom $\boxed{SN\ 3}$ and thereby predicts $\boxed{sp^2}$ hybridization and an angle of (approximately) 120° at the central O atom: the ozone molecule is $\boxed{\text{bent}}$. There are two electrons in a bonding π orbital formed from the three $2p_z$ orbitals perpendicular to the molecular plane. The non-bonding and antibonding orbitals in this π system[7] are unoccupied. The total bond order is 3, which is a bond order of $\boxed{3/2}$ for each O-to-O linkage.

17.33 The moment of inertia of a diatomic molecule is $I = \mu R_e^2$ where R_e is the equilibrium bond distance and μ is the reduced mass. Substitution of the masses[8] of ^{1}H, ^{19}F and ^{81}Br into the formula for the reduced mass gives:

$$\mu_{\text{HF}} = \frac{(1.007825032)(18.9984032)}{1.007825032 + 18.9984032} = 0.957055\ \text{u}$$

$$\mu_{\text{HBr}} = \frac{(1.007825032)(80.916291)}{1.0078250632 + 80.916291} = 0.99543\ \text{u}$$

In kilograms, the two reduced masses are:

$$\mu_{\text{HF}} = \boxed{1.5893 \times 10^{-27}\ \text{kg}} \qquad \text{and} \qquad \mu_{\text{HBr}} = \boxed{1.6529 \times 10^{-27}\ \text{kg}}$$

The equilibrium bond distances equal 0.926×10^{-10} m for HF and 1.424×10^{-10} m for HBr.[9] Using $I = \mu R_e^2$ gives these moments of inertia:

$$I_{\text{HF}} = 1.363 \times 10^{-47}\ \text{kg m}^2 \qquad \text{and} \qquad I_{\text{HBr}} = 3.352 \times 10^{-47}\ \text{kg m}^2$$

---

[6] Text page 217.
[7] The system is diagrammed in text Figure 16.22, text page 588.
[8] From Text Table 14.1.
[9] Text Table 3.3.

The rotational spectra of diatomic molecules consist of lines equally spaced in frequency with the separation between adjacent lines equal to $h/4\pi^2 I$. Therefore:

$$\left(\frac{h}{4\pi^2 I}\right)_{\rm HF} = \frac{6.626\times10^{-34}\ \rm J\ s}{4\pi^2(1.363\times10^{-47}\ \rm kg\ m^2)} = \boxed{12.3\times10^{11}\ \rm s^{-1}}$$
$$\left(\frac{h}{4\pi^2 I}\right)_{\rm HBr} = \frac{6.626\times10^{-34}\ \rm J\ s}{4\pi^2(3.352\times10^{-47}\ \rm kg\ m^2)} = \boxed{5.01\times10^{11}\ \rm s^{-1}}$$

Tip. The large increase in molecular mass from HF and HBr causes only a small increase in the reduced mass of the diatomic molecule. Why? In HF, the center of rotation is already very close to the F atom because F is 19 times heavier than H; the H does most of the moving about the center of rotation. Even a big increase in the mass of the heavy atom (replacement of F by Br) moves the center of mass only fractionally closer to the heavy atom.

17.35 The reduced masses of the three diatomic molecules are:

$$\mu_{\rm NaH} = \frac{(22.9897697)(1.007825032)}{22.989770 + 1.007825032} = \boxed{0.9654995\ \rm u}$$
$$\mu_{\rm NaCl} = \frac{(22.9897697)(34.96885271)}{22.9897697 + 34.96885271} = \boxed{13.870686\ \rm u}$$
$$\mu_{\rm NaI} = \frac{(22.9897697)(126.904468)}{22.9897697 + 126.904468} = \boxed{19.463754\ \rm u}$$

The reduced mass of NaD will also be needed:

$$\mu_{\rm NaD} = \frac{(22.9897697)(2.014101778)}{22.9897697 + 2.014101778} = 1.85186266\ \rm u$$

The force constant of the bond in a diatomic molecule is $k = \mu(2\pi\nu)^2$ where μ is the reduced mass and ν is the vibrational frequency. Therefore:

$$k_{\rm NaH} = \frac{0.9654995\ \rm u}{6.022142\times10^{26}\ \rm u\ kg^{-1}}(4\pi^2)(3.51\times10^{13}\ \rm s)^2 = \boxed{78.0\ \rm kg\ s^{-2}}$$
$$k_{\rm NaCl} = \frac{13.870686\ \rm u}{6.022142\times10^{26}\ \rm u\ kg^{-1}}(4\pi^2)(1.10\times10^{13}\ \rm s)^2 = \boxed{110\ \rm kg\ s^{-2}}$$
$$k_{\rm NaI} = \frac{19.463754\ \rm u}{6.022142\times10^{26}\ \rm u\ kg^{-1}}(4\pi^2)(0.773\times10^{13}\ \rm s)^2 = \boxed{68.6\ \rm kg\ s^{-2}}$$

Insert the reduced mass of NaD and the force constant of NaH into the formula for the vibrational frequency of a diatomic molecule. The reduced mass of NaD is calculated in atomic mass units in the preceding. Converting to kilograms gives 3.0750897×10^{-27} kg. Then:

$$\nu = \frac{1}{2\pi}\sqrt{\frac{k}{\mu}} = \frac{1}{2\pi}\sqrt{\frac{78.0\ \rm kg\ s^{-2}}{3.0750897\times10^{-27}\ \rm kg}} = \boxed{2.53\times10^{13}\ \rm s^{-1}}$$

Tip. The three bond distances were not needed.

17.37 The difference in energy ΔE between the $v=1$ and $v=0$ vibrational states of HgBr(g) equals $h\nu$ where ν is the given vibrational frequency of the molecule. The ratio of the occupation of the two states depends on $e^{-\Delta E/k_{\rm B}T}$ and equals 0.127 at some temperature T. Compute T as follows:

$$\ln\left(\frac{P_1}{P_0}\right) = \frac{-\Delta E}{k_{\rm B}T} \qquad \text{or, after substitution:} \qquad \ln(0.127) = \frac{-h\nu}{k_{\rm B}T}$$

Solve for the temperature and evaluate:

$$T = \frac{-h\nu}{k_B \ln(0.127)} = \frac{-(6.626 \times 10^{-34}\text{ J s})(5.58 \times 10^{12}\text{ s}^{-1})}{(1.3807 \times 10^{-23}\text{ J K}^{-1})(-2.0636)} = \boxed{130\text{ K}}$$

17.39 a) There are five C=C double bonds. The isomer to the left of the arrow has four *trans* C=C double bonds in the chain extending to the right from the six-membered ring. The double bond in the six-membered ring is also *trans* when the relative positions of the two largest groups, one of which is the long side-chain, are considered. Hence, this isomer has [five] *trans* double bonds. The isomer to the right of the arrow is the same except that the second C=C double bond from the right end of the side chain is *cis*. This isomer has [four] *trans* double bonds.

b) The absorption maximum would [shift to shorter wavelength]. Loss of the ring and the —CHO group would reduce the range of delocalization of electrons in a system of alternating single and double bonds because the ring contains a C=C double bond, and the —CHO group contains a C=O double bond.

17.41 a) The carbon atom in formaldehyde is sp^2 hybridized.

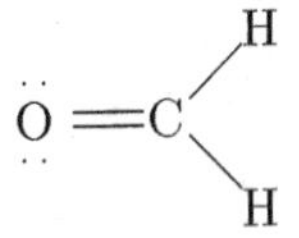

b) Formaldehyde has ten valence orbitals: three σ orbitals formed by overlap of sp^2 orbitals on the C atom with 1*s* orbitals on the two H atoms and the 2*p*-orbital on the O atom that points toward the carbon; three empty σ^* orbitals with the same parents; two lone-pair 2*s* and 2*p* orbitals on the O atom; one occupied π (bonding) orbital derived from the two remaining 2*p* orbitals, which are directed perpendicular to the plane of the molecule; one empty π^* (antibonding) orbital derived from the same parents.

c) The weaker transition at lower frequency is probably due to excitation of an electron from a lone-pair 2*p* orbital on the oxygen atom to the π^* orbital.

17.43 Nitrogen dioxide is a radical. In the stratosphere, NO_2 would photodissociate to give NO which could catalyze the destruction of O_3. Plausible mechanisms are easy to write:

$$NO + O_3 \rightarrow NO_2 + O_2 \qquad NO_2 + O \rightarrow NO + O_2$$

In the troposphere, where the concentration of O_3 is small and the concentration of NO_2 is higher, NO_2 participates in the formation of O_3:

$$NO_2 + h\nu \rightarrow NO + O \qquad O + O_2 + M \rightarrow O_3 + M$$

Ozone is bad in the troposphere because of its high toxicity. Unfortunately, O_3 created in the troposphere is too reactive to diffuse up into the stratosphere, where it might do some good.

17.45 At thermal equilibrium, the rate of excitation from $v = 0 \rightarrow v = 1$ [equals] the rate of the reverse process $v = 1 \rightarrow v = 0$. If this were not so, then the relative populations of the states would change, and the system would not be at equilibrium.

Assume that the rates of excitation and deexcitation depend solely on P_0 and P_1, the populations of the two states. Then:

$$\text{rate}_{0\rightarrow 1} = k_{0\rightarrow 1}P_0 = k_{0\rightarrow 1}\exp(-E_0/k_BT)$$
$$\text{rate}_{1\rightarrow 0} = k_{1\rightarrow 0}P_1 = k_{1\rightarrow 0}\exp(-E_1/k_BT)$$

where the k's are first-order rate constants. The two rates are equal. Set them equal to each other in the two equations and solve for the ratio of the k's:

$$\frac{k_{0\to1}}{k_{1\to0}} = \boxed{\exp\big((E_0 - E_1)/k_\mathrm{B}T\big)}$$

17.47 The problem concerns the hydroxyl radical. This is *not* the species OH^-, which has 8 valence electrons, but is the neutral species OH, which has 7 valence electrons.

a) Convert the concentration of OH radicals to mol L^{-1}:

$$c_\mathrm{OH} = \frac{1\times10^7 \text{ molec.}}{\text{cm}^3} \times \left(\frac{1000 \text{ cm}^3}{\text{L}}\right) \times \left(\frac{1 \text{ mol OH}}{6.022\times10^{23} \text{ molec.}}\right) = 1.66\times10^{-14} \text{ mol L}^{-1}$$

Now use the ideal-gas equation and the definition of mole fraction:

$$P_\mathrm{OH} = \left(\frac{n}{V}\right) RT = \left(\frac{1.66\times10^{-14} \text{ mol}}{\text{L}}\right)(0.08206 \text{ L atm mol}^{-1}\text{K}^{-1})(298 \text{ K}) = \boxed{4\times10^{-12} \text{ atm}}$$

$$X_\mathrm{OH} = \frac{P_\mathrm{OH}}{P_\mathrm{tot}} = \frac{4\times10^{-12} \text{ atm}}{1 \text{ atm}} = \boxed{4\times10^{-12}}$$

b) The OH radical reacts with NO_2 to give nitric acid:

$$\mathrm{OH} + \mathrm{NO_2} \to \mathrm{HNO_3}$$

The oxidation state of N $\boxed{\text{increases}}$ in this reaction. The HNO_3 interacts with atmospheric water and eventually comes to the surface in the form of acid rain.

Chapter 18

Bonding in Transition Metals and Coordination Complexes

18.1 a) The more water-soluble of the two compounds is $\boxed{PtF_4}$. It has Pt in the lower oxidation state and should be more ionic than PtF_6 and therefore more soluble.

b) The more volatile is $\boxed{PtF_6}$, which is the more covalent of the two.

18.3

$$\boxed{V_{10}O_{28}^{6-}(aq) + 16\ H_3O^+(aq) \rightarrow 10\ VO_2^+(aq) + 24\ H_2O}$$

The vanadium is in the $\boxed{+5}$ oxidation state both before and after this acid-base reaction. The oxide of vanadium in which V is in this oxidation state is $\boxed{V_2O_5}$.

18.5 The reduction of titanium(IV) oxide to titanium(III) oxide with hydrogen is represented:

$$\boxed{2\ TiO_4 + 5\ H_2 \rightarrow Ti_2O_3 + 5\ H_2O}$$

The $\boxed{\text{product}}$, titanium(III) oxide, should be more basic. It has Ti in a lower oxidation state.

18.7 Methylamine is a $\boxed{\text{monodentate}}$ ligand that binds to a central metal ion by donating a lone pair of electrons from the $\boxed{\text{N atom}}$. This is the only lone pair in the molecule.

18.9 a) $[V(NH_3)_4Cl_2]$ The V atom is in the $\boxed{+2}$ oxidation state.

b) $[Mo_2Cl_8]^{4-}$ The Mo atom is in the $\boxed{+2}$ oxidation state.

c) $[Co(H_2O)_2(NH_3)Cl_3]^-$ The Co atom is in the $\boxed{+2}$ oxidation state.

d) $[Ni(CO)_4]$ The Ni atom is in the $\boxed{0}$ oxidation state.

18.11 **a)** $Na_2[Zn(OH)_4]$ **b)** $[Co(H_2NCH_2CH_2NH_2)_2Cl_2]NO_3$
c) $[PtBr(H_2O)_3]Cl$ **d)** $[Pt(NH_3)_4(NO_2)_2]Br_2$

18.13 a) Ammonium diamminetetraisothiocyanatochromate(III)
b) Pentacarbonyltechnetium(I) iodide

c) Potassium pentacyanomanganate(IV)
d) Tetraammineaquachlorocobalt(III) bromide

Tip. In part b, the "iso" in the name indicates that the donor atom in the thiocyanate ligand is the N, as in Cr—NCS. If the formula were $NH_4[Cr(NH_3)_2(SCN)_4]$, the linkage would be Cr—SCN and the name would be thiocyanato. Compare to **18.57**. Inorganic chemists are sometimes careless about the order of symbols in ligands.

18.15 If the ligands of a complex ion can be rapidly substituted for by other ligands, the complex ion is labile. A complex that is thermodynamically stable and labile will persist indefinitely as it rapidly exchanges ligands with the surroundings (usually the solvent). The occurrence of exchange can be verified by isotopic labeling experiments.

18.17 The dissociation of the tetraamminecopper(II) ion can be represented:

$$[Cu(NH_3)_4]^{2+}(aq) \rightarrow Cu^{2+}(aq) + 4\,NH_3(aq)$$

Taking data from Appendix D:

$$\Delta G^\circ = 1\,\underbrace{(65.49)}_{Cu^{2+}(aq)} + 4\,\underbrace{(-26.50)}_{NH_3(aq)} - 1\,\underbrace{(-111.07)}_{[Cu(NH_3)_4]^{2+}(aq)} = \boxed{+70.56\text{ kJ}}$$

Because ΔG° exceeds zero, the reaction is not spontaneous as written. The tetraamminecopper(II) ion is thermodynamically $\boxed{\text{stable}}$ with respect to this reaction. Under acidic conditions, the dissociation reaction is

$$[Cu(NH_3)_4]^{2+}(aq) + 4\,H_3O^+(aq) \rightarrow Cu^{2+}(aq) + 4\,NH_4^+(aq) + 4\,H_2O(l)$$

$$\Delta G^\circ = 1\,\underbrace{(65.49)}_{Cu^{2+}(aq)} + 4\,\underbrace{(-79.31)}_{NH_4^+(aq)} + 4\,\underbrace{(-237.18)}_{H_2O(l)} - 1\,\underbrace{(-111.07)}_{[Cu(NH_3)_4]^{2+}(aq)} - 4\,\underbrace{(-237.18)}_{H_3O^+(aq)} = \boxed{-140.68\text{ kJ}}$$

Hence $[Cu(NH_3)_4]^{2+}(aq)$ reacts $\boxed{\text{spontaneously}}$ with water at pH 0.

Tip. LeChâtelier's principle applies. Strong acid (pH 0) favors substitution because the product NH_3 is removed by reaction with H_3O^+ ion.

18.19 The four substances all dissolve in water to make 0.010 M solutions. The more ions per mole of solute then the greater the conductivity of the solution at a given concentration of solute. Hence in order of increasing conductivity:

$[Cu(NH_3)_2Cl_2]$	$< KNO_3$	$< Na_2[PtCl_6]$	$< [Co(NH_3)_6]Cl_3$
0 ions	2 ions	3 ions	4 ions

18.21 a) $[Pt(NH_3)_2BrCl]$ has two isomers, (*cis* and *trans*). Neither is optically active:

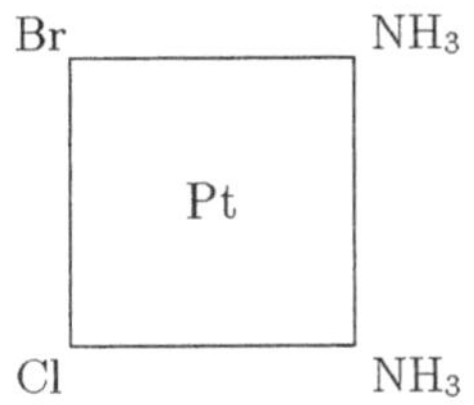

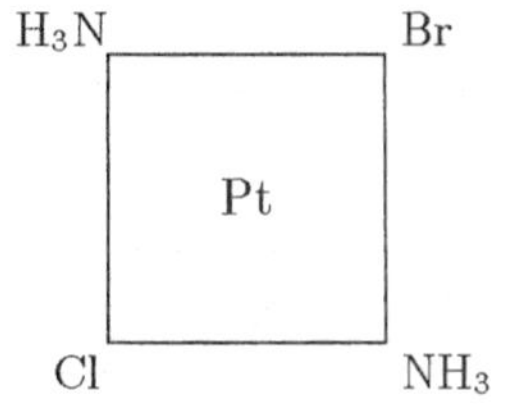

b) The $[Co(CN)_3(H_2O)_2Cl]^-$ ion has three possible isomers. None of the three isomers is optically active.

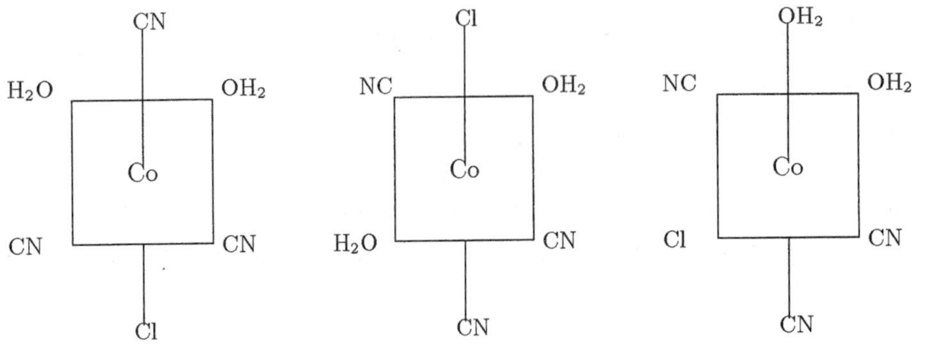

c) $[V(C_2O_4)_3]^{3-}$ ion is enantiomeric with two possible optical isomers. In the following the oxalato ligand (^-OOC—COO^-) is abbreviated as "O—·—·—O":

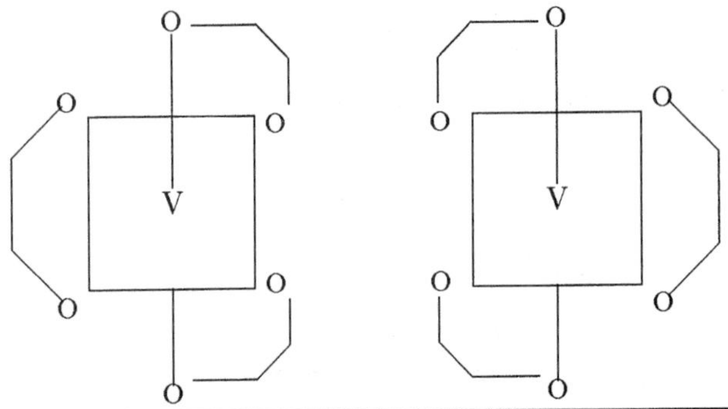

18.23 There are three isomeric $[Fe(en)_2Cl_2]^+$ complexes. They are the *trans*-dichlorobis(ethylenediamine)-iron(III) ion (at the left in the following) and the two mirror-image *cis*-dichlorobis(ethylenediamine)iron(III) ions. All involve octahedral coordination about the Fe atom. The NH_2—CH_2CH_2—NH_2 ligand is abbreviated en. This bidentate ligand ligates through its two —NH_2 groups. It can span an edge of the Fe octahedron but not opposite corners. In the following it is represented "N—·—·—N":

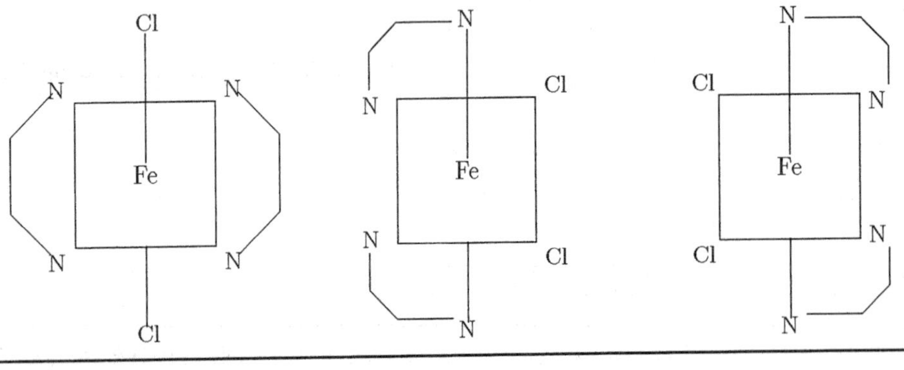

18.25 Strong-field octahedral complexes have a large splitting between the t_{2g} and e_g sets of orbitals; weak-field complexes have a small splitting between the t_{2g} and e_g orbitals. When the splitting energy Δ_o exceeds the pairing energy of the electrons, electrons pair up in the t_{2g} level and fill it completely before occupying the e_g level. Otherwise, electrons remain unpaired as long as possible.

a) The electron configuration of Mn^{2+} is $[Ar]3d^5$. It has $\boxed{5}$ unpaired electrons in a weak field and $\boxed{1}$ unpaired electron in a strong field:

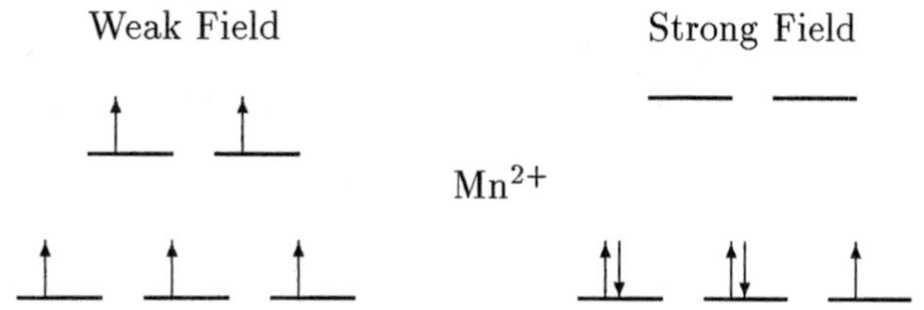

b) Zn^{2+} ion has the electron configuration $[Ar]3d^{10}$. It has zero unpaired electrons in both weak and strong fields:

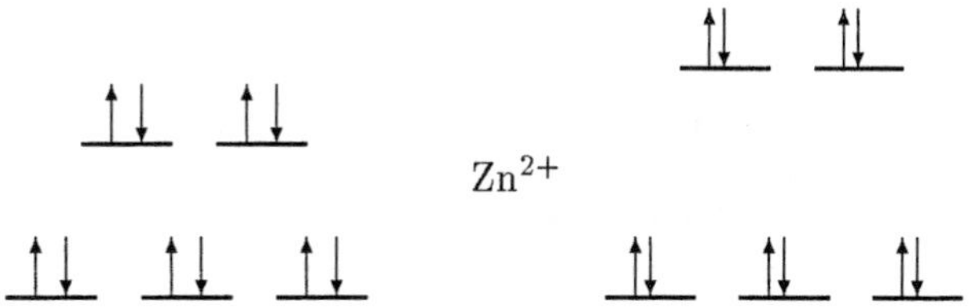

c) Cr^{3+} ion has configuration $[Ar]3d^3$. 3 unpaired electrons in both weak and strong fields:

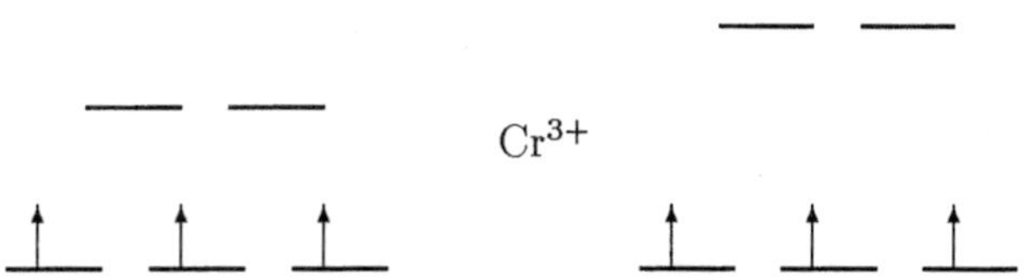

d) Mn^{3+} ion has configuration $[Ar]3d^4$. It has 4 unpaired electrons in weak fields and 2 in strong fields:

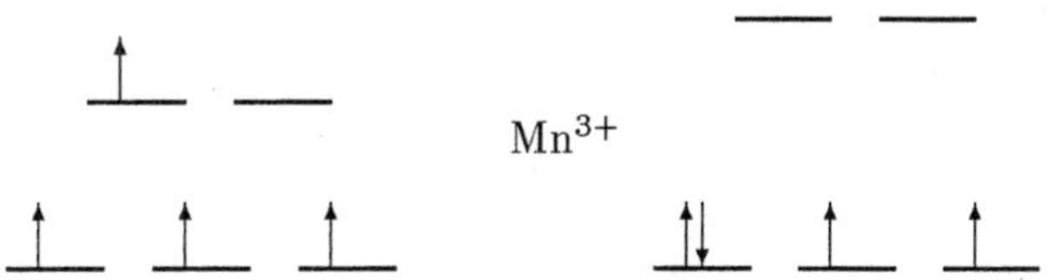

e) Fe^{2+} ion has configuration $[Ar]3d^6$. It has 4 unpaired electrons in weak fields and zero in strong fields:

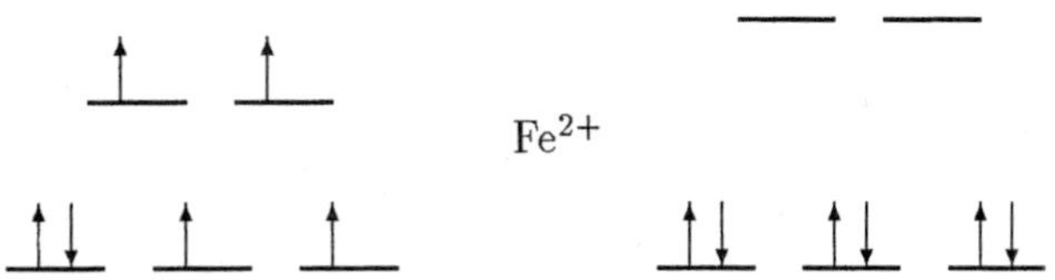

18.27 The ground-state Fe^{3+} ion has 5 d electrons. In the strong octahedral field exerted by six CN^- ligands, the d electron configuration is $(t_{2g})^5(e_g)^0$. All of the d electrons are in the three t_{2g} orbitals; only one electron can be unpaired. In the weak field exerted by six H_2O ligands, the d electron configuration is $(t_{2g})^3(e_g)^2$. All five d electrons remain unpaired.

Each of the five d electrons in t_{2g} levels stabilizes $[Fe(CN)_6]^{3-}$ by $2/5\Delta_o$. The total crystal-field stabilization energy equals $5 \times -2/5\Delta_o$ or $-2\Delta_o$. See text Table 18.4[1].

[1] text page 651

The two e_g electrons in the weak-field $[Fe(H_2O)_6]^{3+}$ complex contribute $+3/5\Delta_o$ each to the CFSE, and the three t_{2g} electrons contribute $-2/5\Delta_0$ each for a total CFSE of $\boxed{\text{zero}}$.

18.29 In an octahedral field, d^3 systems are particularly stable because the t_{2g} set is half filled whether the ligands are strong-field or weak-field. In d^8 octahedral systems, the t_{2g} set is completely filled, and the e_g set is half filled whether the ligand is strong-field or weak-field. This also promotes stability. Octahedral d^5 systems would be expected to be particularly stable in complexes of weak-field ligands. The configuration of the d electron system is then $(t_{2g})^3(e_g)^2$, in which the t_{2g} and e_g sets of orbitals are half filled. Octahedral d^6 systems would be expected to be particularly stable in complexes of strong-field ligands. The configuration of the d electron system is then $(t_{2g})^6(e_g)^0$ in which the t_{2g} orbitals are a filled set.

18.31 The color perceived in a solution is the complement of the color of light absorbed. A colorless ion (such as $[Zn(H_2O)_6]^{2+}$) $\boxed{\text{does not absorb}}$ a significant amount of visible light.

18.33 A solution of $[Fe(CN)_6]^{3-}$ ion transmits red light. Assuming that it absorbs any visible light, the complex ion must absorb light in the green portion of the spectrum. See text Figure 17.12.[2] According to Figure 15.3,[3] green light has a wavelength of about $\boxed{5 \times 10^{-7}\ \text{m}}$. Using the relationship $\Delta E = hc/\lambda$ with Planck's constant and the speed of light in the proper units gives an energy difference of 4×10^{-19} J. This is equivalent to 240 kJ mol^{-1}. Assume that absorption of the light excites a single electron from a low-lying t_{2g} orbital to an e_g level. Then Δ_o equals this energy difference, and is also about $\boxed{240\ \text{kJ mol}^{-1}}$.

18.35 The hexacyanoferrate(III) ion has a d^5 configuration on the central ion that is split by a strong octahedral field. As Table 18.4 shows, the crystal field stabilization energy for the resulting $(t_{2g})^5$ configuration is $-2\Delta_o$. The value of Δ_o is 240 kJ mol^{-1} (see preceding problem) so the CFSE equals $\boxed{-480\ \text{kJ mol}^{-1}}$.

18.37 a) Use the color wheel in text Figure 17.12.[4] The complement of blue-violet is $\boxed{\text{orange-yellow}}$.

b) The absorbed light is orange-yellow with a wavelength λ of maximum absorption near $\boxed{600\ \text{nm}}$. See text Figure 15.3. The experimentally observed transition turns out to be at 575 nm.

c) Cyanide ion is a strong-field ligand, and water is an weak-field ligand. Replacing coordinated water molecules with cyanide ions increases the crystal-field splitting. Increasing the splitting increases the frequency of the light that is absorbed, and causes a $\boxed{\text{decrease}}$ in the wavelength of maximum absorption.

18.39 a) In an aqueous solution of $Fe(NO_3)_3$, the Fe^{3+} ion is coordinated to six water molecules. The weak field of these ligands allows the high-spin electron configuration $(t_{2g})^3(e_g)^2$ on the central Fe^{3+} ion. In the case of $[Fe(CN)_6]^{3-}$, the strong field exerted by the CN^- ligands forces the electron configuration $(t_{2g})^5(e_g)^0$. Replacing the weak-field ligand water with the weak-field ligand fluoride should not change the $(t_{2g})^3(e_g)^2$ configuration. The absorption of light by the fluoride complex ion should therefore resemble that by the aqua complex. The solution of $K_3[FeF_6]$ should be $\boxed{\text{pale}}$.

b) The ground-state electron configuration of Hg^{2+} ion is $[Xe]4f^{14}5d^{10}$. A full subshell of 10 d electrons means that electronic transitions in which electrons are redistributed among d orbitals are not possible. Such transitions are mostly responsible for the colors of coordination complexes. A solution of $K_2[HgI_4]$ should therefore be $\boxed{\text{colorless}}$.

18.41 Common ligands donate a pair of electrons to the central metal atom of a complex except that hydrogen donates only a single electron. The number of valence electrons provided by a metal atom is given by its

---

[2] Text page 612.
[3] Text page 507.
[4] Text page 612.

position in the periodic table.

The compound $[Cr(CO)_4]$ has a total of $\boxed{14}$ valence electrons at the metal, 6 from the Cr atom and 8 from the four CO ligands. The compound $[Os(CO)_5]$ has a total of $\boxed{18}$ valence electrons at the metal: 8 from the Os atom and 10 from the ligands. The compound $[H_2Fe(CO)_4]$ has a total of $\boxed{18}$ valence electrons at the metal: 2 from the H atoms, 8 from the Fe atom, and 8 from the four CO ligands. The compound $K_3[Fe(CN)_5CO]$ contains the $[Fe(CN)_5CO]^{3-}$ ion. The Fe(II) ion contributes 6 valence electrons, and the six ligands contribute 12 for a total of $\boxed{18}$ valence electrons about the Fe(II).

18.43 1.00 mol of vitamin B_{12s} contains 1.00 mol of Co. 1.00 mol of cobalt weighs 58.93 g, but this is only 4.43% of the mass of a mole of the vitamin. The mass of 1.00 mol of the vitamin is therefore larger than that of a mole of cobalt by the factor 100/4.43:

$$\mathcal{M} = \left(\frac{100}{4.43}\right) \times 58.93 \text{ g mol}^{-1} = \boxed{1330 \text{ g mol}^{-1}}$$

18.45 $\boxed{\text{Zinc}}$ has the lowest melting point and lowest boiling point of the fourth-period transition metals. This element has a d^{10} configuration. Bonding in metals, including elemental zinc, arises from the combination of valence atomic orbitals into delocalized bonding and antibonding molecular orbitals. A complete d subshell means that the antibonding orbitals deriving from d orbitals are completely occupied. This makes the bonding in the metal weaker, which implies a lower melting point and boiling point than other metals.

18.47 Electronegativity is a measure of the ability of an atom in a compound to draw electrons to itself. $\boxed{\text{Mo(VI)}}$, the highest oxidation state of Mo has (formally at least) the most positive charge and should therefore have the highest electronegativity.

Tip. The electronegativity values referred to in the problem were computed by the method of Pauling and equal 2.16 for Mo(II), 2.19 for Mo(III), 2.24 for Mo(IV), 2.27 for MO(V), and 2.35 for Mo(VI).[5]

18.49 In $[Ru_2(NH_3)_6Br_3](ClO_4)_2$, all six ammonia ligands are neutral, each bromide ion has a -1 oxidation state and each perchlorate ion has a -1 charge. Because the sum of the oxidation states must equal zero (the overall charge of the complex), the oxidation state of the ruthenium is $\boxed{2.5}$.

Tip. One of the ruthenium atoms may be in the $+2$ oxidation state, and the other in the $+3$ oxidation state.

18.51 Ligands are electron-pair donors. On the basis of simple electrostatics, it is much harder for a positively charged species to donate electron pairs than for a neutral or negatively charged species to do so.

18.53 Water coordinated to the central Cr is more tightly bonded and harder for a dehydrating agent to remove than water held in the solid as water of crystallization. Compound 1 loses two moles of H_2O per mole; it therefore has two waters of crystallization. The other water is in the coordination sphere: $\boxed{[Cr(H_2O)_4Cl_2]Cl\cdot 2H_2O}$. This ion has $\boxed{\text{octahedral}}$ coordination about the central Cr atom. Compound 2 loses only one mole of H_2O per mole so it has only one water of hydration: $\boxed{[Cr(H_2O)_5Cl]Cl_2\cdot H_2O}$. Compound 2 also has an $\boxed{\text{octahedral}}$ structure. Compound 3 loses no water of hydration, so it must have all six water molecules coordinated: $\boxed{[Cr(H_2O)_6]Cl_3}$; compound 3 has an $\boxed{\text{octahedral}}$ structure.

Solutions of silver nitrate precipitate AgCl only with chloride ions that are not in the coordination sphere. Therefore, compound 1 gives one mole of AgCl per mole of complex; compound 2 gives two moles of AgCl

[5] A. L. Allred, *J. Inorg. Nucl. Chem.*, **1961**, *17*, 215.

per mole of complex; compound 3 gives three moles of AgCl per mole of complex. For compound 1:

$$m_{\text{AgCl}} = 100.0\text{ g} \times \left(\frac{1\text{ mol}}{266.44\text{ g}}\right) \times \left(\frac{1\text{ mol AgCl}}{1\text{ mol}}\right) \times \left(\frac{143.32\text{ g AgCl}}{1\text{ mol AgCl}}\right) = \boxed{53.79\text{ g AgCl}}$$

Similar 100.0 g samples of compounds 2 and 3, which have the same molar mass, give respectively twice and three times as much AgCl: $\boxed{107.6\text{ g}}$ and $\boxed{161.4\text{ g}}$.

18.55 Tetrahedral structures do not display *cis-trans* isomerism because each corner of a tetrahedron is the same distance from the other three corners. In this case:

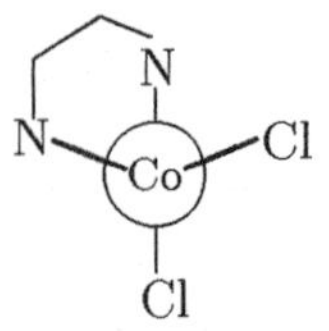

Tetrahedral structures exhibit mirror-image isomerism if they have four different atoms attached to the central atom. Because the complex [$CoCl_2$(en)] has two identical ligands, it does not exhibit mirror-image isomerism. The tetrahedral complex [CoClBr(en)] also lacks *cis-trans* isomers, as explained above. It has no optical isomers because the two ends of the en ligand are equivalent.

18.57 a) In the preferred formulation, the Pt in the $[Pt(en)_2(SCN)_2]^{2+}$ cation is in the +4 oxidation state, while the Pt in the $[PtBr_2(SCN)_2]^{2-}$ anion is in the +2 oxidation state. These complexes form a 1-to-1 ionic compound with the correct empirical formula. The Pt(IV) has 6 *d* electrons, and is surrounded by 6 donors. If all 6 *d* electrons are in the t_{2g} level (strong-field), the ion has no unpaired electrons and is diamagnetic. The Pt(II) has 8 *d* electrons and is surrounded by 4 donors. The anion can therefore also have all of its electrons paired and be diamagnetic. By contrast, if the molecular formula were $[PtBr(en)(SCN)_2]$, then all Pt atoms would be in the +3 oxidation state and have 7 *d* electrons. This compound would be paramagnetic.
b) Bis(ethylenediamine)dithiocyanatoplatinum(IV) dibromodithiocyanatoplatinate(II).

18.59 The cyanide ligand has a −1 charge. This means that in $[Mn(CN)_6]^{5-}$ the oxidation state of the Mn must be $\boxed{+1}$. A +1 added to 6(−1) gives the observed −5 charge on the complex ion. Similarly, the oxidation states of Mn in $[Mn(CN)_6]^{4-}$ and $[Mn(CN)_6]^{3-}$ are $\boxed{+2}$ and $\boxed{+3}$, respectively. The ground-state electron configurations of the manganese ions are:

$$Mn^{+1}\quad [Ar]3d^6 \qquad\qquad Mn^{+2}\quad [Ar]3d^5 \qquad\qquad Mn^{+3}\quad [Ar]3d^4$$

The low-spin (strong-field) *d* orbital occupancy diagrams for each complex are:

Mn(I) Mn(II) Mn(III)

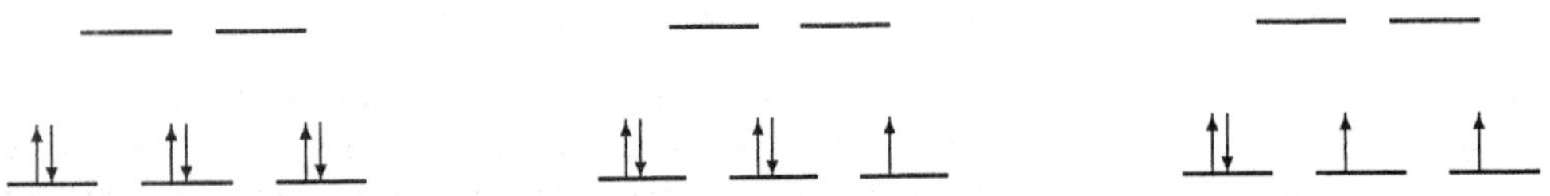

18.61 In the list of the ionic radii, minima occur for the ions with 3 and 8 *d* electrons. These are the V^{2+} and Ni^{2+} ions. Presumably the oxides are high-field, $\boxed{\text{low-spin}}$ complexes in which the 4th and 9th electrons are accommodated in a higher energy orbital, increasing the radius.

18.63 The central cobalt(II) in $[CoCl_4]^{2-}$ ion has a total of $\boxed{7}$ *d* electrons. The Co atom (electron configuration $[Ar]3d^74s^2$) loses the two valence *s*-electrons in becoming the Co(II). The tetrahedral field of the 4 chloride ligands splits the d orbitals of Co(II) into e_g orbitals (at *lower* energy) and t_{2g} orbitals (at *higher* energy). The ground-state electron configuration of the seven electrons is $\boxed{(e_g)^4(t_{2g})^3}$. This configuration results regardless of the strength of the ligand field: only high-spin states are possible for a d^7 species in a tetrahedral field. The tetrahedral complex has crystal-field stabilization energy (CFSE) equal to $-6/5\Delta_t$; this stabilization favors the tetrahedral complex.

18.65 The cesium ions each have a +1 charge, and the fluoride ions each have a −1 charge. Thus, copper is in the $\boxed{+4}$ oxidation state. There are six monodentate ligands attached to the Cu(IV), so the most likely geometry about the central metal atom will be $\boxed{\text{octahedral}}$. The ground-state electron configuration of Cu(IV) is $[Ar]3d^7$. In a weak octahedral field, the d electron configuration would become $\boxed{(t_{2g})^5(e_g)^2}$. This high-spin configuration is far more likely than the low-spin $(t_{2g})^6(e_g)^1$ configuration because the F^- ion is a weak-field ligand.

18.67 The cyclopentadienyl ion ($C_5H_5^-$) has a −1 charge and is a six-electron donor. The neutral C_6H_6 molecule is also a six-electron donor. The other ligands are all two-electron donors.

The Co atom in $[Co(C_5H_5)_2]^{2+}$ has 6 $3d$ electrons and shares 12 more from the two ligands. It sees a total of $\boxed{18}$ valence electrons.

The Fe atom in $[Fe(C_5H_5)(CO)_2Cl]$ also sees a total of $\boxed{18}$ valence electrons: the Fe(II) starts with 6, the $C_5H_5^-$ donates 6, the Cl^- and each CO donate 2.

The Mo in $[Mo(C_5H_5)_2Cl_2]$ sees a total of $\boxed{18}$ valence electrons: the Mo(IV) starts with 2 and each $C_5H_5^-$ contributes 6. The Cl^- ligands donate 2 electrons each.

The Mn in the complex $[Mn(C_5H_5)(C_6H_6)]$ sees a total of $\boxed{18}$ valence electrons: the Mn(I) ion has 6, the $C_5H_5^-$ contributes 6, and the C_6H_6 also contributes 6.

18.69 The rule of 18 holds that special stability is conferred on organometallic compounds having a central metal atom surrounded by 18 electrons. To relate this to ligand-field theory, study the MO diagram in Figure 18.22.[6] The nine molecular orbitals of lowest energy in the diagram are all either bonding or nonbonding. These MO's hold 18 electrons. Any complex that has electrons in just these MO's has zero antibonding electrons. In $Cr(CO)_6$, the ground-state valence electron configuration is

$$\sigma_s^2\sigma_p^6\sigma_d^4(d_{xy}^{\text{nb}})^2(d_{xz}^{\text{nb}})^2(d_{yz}^{\text{nb}})^2$$

with no electrons in antibonding orbitals. Additional electrons would go into antibonding orbitals and decrease the stability of the species.

18.71 Transition metal coordination compounds play a central role in biology. In hemoglobin, for example, iron is essential in binding O_2 for transport to cells and CO_2 for transport from cells. Cobalt is the central metal atom in vitamin B_{12}, a coordination compound that plays a vital role in metabolism.

Some of these biological complexes are colored because of the closely spaced d levels that allow absorption of visible light. Ligand exchange lets these complexes act as catalysts for chemical reactions in living organisms, in analogy to the catalysis developed in synthetic chemistry. Finally, the existence of more than one oxidation state lets some complexes act as oxidizing or reducing agents in biochemical processes.

18.73 Manganese and chlorine appear in the same group ("Gruppe VII") in Mendeleev's early periodic table mainly because of the similarity in their compounds in the +7 oxidation state. Both elements form heptaoxides (Cl_2O_7 and Mn_2O_7) that are liquids are room conditions (indicating covalent bonding) and that

[6] Text page 656.

react with water to give strong acids (perchloric acid $HClO_4$ and permanganic acid $HMnO_4$). Both of these acids are powerful oxidizing agents, and many perchlorate salts resemble permanganate salts closely. Among the lower oxides of manganese, MnO is basic, Mn_2O_3 is weakly basic, MnO_2 is feebly acidic, and MnO_3 is more strongly acidic. A similar trend is found among the oxides of chlorine. Manganic acid (H_2MnO_4) resembles chloric acid $HClO_3$ in that it disproportionates to an acid in a higher oxidation state ($HMnO_4$) and an oxide in a lower oxidation state (MnO_2). However manganates (salts of manganic acid) resemble sulfates and chromates much more than chlorates. Manganese and chlorine both have seven valence electrons, but these include *d* electrons in the case of Mn. The availability of additional low-lying *d* orbitals in Mn leads to metallic bonding in that element and enormous differences between it and Cl.

18.75 The problem concerns these two reactions

$$Cd^{2+}(aq) + 4\ NH_2CH_3 \rightarrow [Cd(NH_2CH_3)_4]^{2+}(aq) \qquad (1)$$
$$Cd^{2+}(aq) + 2\,\text{en} \rightarrow [Cd(\text{en})_2]^{2+}(aq) \qquad (2)$$

where en stands for ethylenediamine $H_2NCH_2CH_2NH_2$. For the two:

$$-RT\ln K_1 = \Delta H_1^\circ - T\Delta S_1^\circ \qquad \text{and} \qquad -RT\ln K_2 = \Delta H_2^\circ - T\Delta S_2^\circ$$

Subtracting the second equation from the first gives:

$$RT\ln K_2 - RT\ln K_1 = \Delta H_1^\circ - \Delta H_2^\circ + T\Delta S_2^\circ - T\Delta S_1^\circ$$

According to the problem, the ΔH°'s of the two reactions are about equal. Therefore:

$$RT\ln K_2 - RT\ln K_1 \approx T\Delta S_2^\circ - T\Delta S_1^\circ$$
$$R\ln\left(\frac{K_2}{K_1}\right) \approx \Delta S_2^\circ - \Delta S_1^\circ$$

Judging from the number of particles present among the reactants, $\boxed{\Delta S_2^\circ}$ is less negative than ΔS_1°. This makes the right-hand side of the preceding equation positive. and means that K_2 exceeds K_1. The second reaction lies farther to the right at equilibrium because of its larger K: the chelate effect stabilizes the $\boxed{[Cd(\text{en})_2]^{2+}}$ complex.

18.77 Let s equal the molar solubility of AgBr. Then

$$s = [Br^-] \quad \text{and} \quad s = [Ag(S_2O_3)_3^{5-}] + [Ag(S_2O_3)_2^{3-}] + [Ag(S_2O_3)^-] + [Ag^+]$$

where the second equation represents material balance for the silver in the solution. The last two terms in this equation are certain to be negligibly small compared to the others when the concentration of $S_2O_3^{2-}$ ion is 0.2 M because K_{2d} and K_{3d} are small compared to K_{1d}. Hence

$$s = [Br^-] = [Ag(S_2O_3)_3^{5-}] + [Ag(S_2O_3)_2^{3-}]$$

Write the equation for the first step in the dissociation of the complex and its associated K

$$Ag(S_2O_3)_3^{5-} \rightleftharpoons Ag(S_2O_3)_2^{3-} + S_2O_3^{2-} \qquad K_{1d} = \frac{[Ag(S_2O_3)_2^{3-}][S_2O_3^{2-}]}{[Ag(S_2O_3)_3^{5-}]} = 0.20$$

The problem states that $[S_2O_3^{2-}]$ is 0.2 M at equilibrium. Inserting that number in the K expression gives

$$[Ag(S_2O_3)_3^{5-}] = [Ag(S_2O_3)_2^{3-}] \qquad \text{from which} \qquad [Ag(S_2O_3)_3^{5-}] = [Ag(S_2O_3)_2^{3-}] = \frac{s}{2}$$

Now, write the equation and the K for the *overall* dissociation of the 3 : 1 complex:

$$Ag(S_2O_3)_3^{5-} \rightleftharpoons Ag^+ + 3\ S_2O_3^{2-} \qquad K_{tot,d} = \frac{[Ag^+][S_2O_3^{2-}]^3}{[Ag(S_2O_3)_2^{5-}]} = 7 \times 10^{-15}$$

Solve for $[Ag^+]$ and insert 0.2 M for $[S_2O_3^{2-}]$

$$[Ag^+] = 7 \times 10^{-15} \frac{[Ag(S_2O_3)_3^{5-}]}{(0.2)^3} = (8.8 \times 10^{-13}) \left(\frac{s}{2}\right)$$

The solubility equilibrium for AgBr also operates in the system. Therefore

$$K_{sp} = [Ag^+][Br^-]$$
$$5.2 \times 10^{-13} = (8.8 \times 10^{-13}) \left(\frac{s}{2}\right)(s)$$
$$s = \sqrt{5.2/4.4} = \boxed{1.1\ M}$$

The initial concentration of thiosulfate ion was enough to provide an average of 2.5 thiosulfate ions for every Ag^+ ion that dissolved and to leave 0.2 M in excess.

$$[(S_2O_3)^{2-}]_{init} = 2.5(1.1) + 0.2 = \boxed{2.95\ M}$$

Chapter 19

Inorganic Chemical Processes

19.1 A batch process is carried out by mixing reactants, letting them react, and then removing products in a series of steps. In a continuous process reactants are continuously added to the reaction vessel and the products are continuously removed. A continuous process requires more than one opening in the reaction vessel; a batch process can operate in a vessel with only one opening.

19.3 **a)** Sulfur occurs in useful amounts in $\boxed{\text{salt domes}}$ under the surface of the earth. The deposits formed when calcium sulfate reacted with natural gas and carbon dioxide. Interestingly, the reaction is catalyzed by enzymes that are secreted by bacteria:

$$CaSO_4(s) + CH_4(g) + CO_2(g) \rightarrow CaCO_3(s) + S(s) + 6\,H_2O(l)$$

b) A useful source of carbon is bituminous $\boxed{\text{coal}}$. Coal is formed from plant matter by bacterial reduction, heat, and pressure.

c) $\boxed{\text{Phosphate rock}}$ is the most useful source of phosphorus, It is $Ca_5(PO_4)_3F$ in a nearly pure condition.

d) A good source of calcium is $\boxed{\text{limestone}}$ or marble, both of which are principally composed of calcium carbonate.

19.5 A good source of small amounts of pure hydrogen is

$$\boxed{Zn(s) + 2\,H_3O^+(aq) \rightarrow H_2(g) + Zn^{2+}(aq) + 2\,H_2O(l)}$$

Zinc is too expensive to use to make large amounts of hydrogen

19.7 The reaction in this problem is the endothermic reforming of methane:

$$CH_4(g) + H_2O(g) \rightarrow CO(g) + 3\,H_2(g)$$

This reaction becomes spontaneous at a high enough temperature. To compute that T, use the relationship $\Delta G = \Delta H^\circ - T\Delta S^\circ$. If ΔG° is equal to zero, then:

$$T = \frac{\Delta H^\circ}{\Delta S^\circ}$$

Text Appendix D supplies the standard entropies and standard enthalpies of formation of the reactants and products. Combine the data to get the ΔH° and ΔS° of the reaction:

$$\Delta H^\circ = 3\underbrace{(0.00)}_{H_2(g)} + 1\underbrace{(-110.52)}_{CO(g)} - 1\underbrace{(-74.81)}_{CH_4(g)} - 1\underbrace{(-241.82)}_{H_2O(g)} = 206.11 \text{ kJ}$$

$$\Delta S^\circ = 3\underbrace{(130.57)}_{H_2(g)} + 1\underbrace{(197.56)}_{CO(g)} - 1\underbrace{(186.15)}_{CH_4(g)} - 1\underbrace{(188.72)}_{H_2O(g)} = +214.40 \text{ J K}^{-1}$$

$$T = \frac{\Delta H^\circ}{\Delta S^\circ} = \frac{206.11 \times 10^3 \text{ J}}{214.40 \text{ J K}^{-1}} = \boxed{960 \text{ K}}$$

19.9 a) The equation is $\boxed{3\,Fe(s) + 4\,H_2O(g) \rightarrow Fe_3O_4(s) + 4\,H_2(g)}$.

b) Use the values of ΔH_f° in Appendix D to calculate ΔH° for the above reaction:

$$\Delta H^\circ = 1\underbrace{(-1118.4)}_{Fe_3O_4(s)} + 4\underbrace{(0)}_{H_2(g)} - 4\underbrace{(-241.82)}_{H_2O(g)} - 3\underbrace{(0)}_{Fe(s)} = \boxed{-151.1 \text{ kJ}}$$

The negative ΔH° means that the reaction is exothermic. Increasing the temperature lowers K and shifts the reaction from right to left. Thus, the yield of the reaction at equilibrium would $\boxed{\text{decrease}}$, although an elevated temperature is needed for the reaction to proceed rapidly.

Tip. This is a standard "catch" in designing industrial processes.

19.11 The balanced equation for the reduction of pyrolusite to manganese by aluminum is

$$MnO_2(s) + \frac{4}{3}\,Al(s) \rightarrow \frac{2}{3}\,Al_2O_3(s) + Mn(s)$$

Combine the standard enthalpies of formation and standard free energies of formation of the two reactants and two products (text Appendix D) to get the standard enthalpy and standard free energy of this reaction at 298.15 K:

$$\Delta H^\circ = 2/3(-1675.7) + 1(0) - 1(-520.03) - 4/3(0) = \boxed{-597.1 \text{ kJ}}$$

$$\Delta G^\circ = 2/3(-1582.3) + 1(0) - 1(-465.17) - 4/3(0) = \boxed{-589.7 \text{ kJ}}$$

Tip. Fractional coefficients are used in the balanced equation so the reaction gives the specified one mole of Mn.

19.13 The balanced equation for the decomposition of mercury(II) oxide to its elements is

$$2\,HgO(s) \rightarrow 2\,Hg(l) + O_2(g)$$

Combine the standard enthalpies of formation and absolute entropies of the reactants and products at 25° (text Appendix D) to get the standard enthalpy and standard entropy of the reaction:

$$\Delta H^\circ = 2(0) + 1(0) - 2(-90.83) = +181.66 \text{ kJ}$$

$$\Delta S^\circ = 1(205.03) + 2(76.02) - 2(70.29) = 216.49 \text{ J K}^{-1}$$

If ΔH° and ΔS° are independent of temperature, ΔG° for this reaction becomes equal to zero at the temperature fulfilling the equation:

$$T = \frac{\Delta H^\circ}{\Delta S^\circ} = \frac{181.66 \times 10^3 \text{ J}}{216.49 \text{ J K}^{-1}} = \boxed{839 \text{ K}}$$

At temperatures exceeding 839 K, ΔG° is negative.

Tip. Mercury(II) oxide, a red solid, indeed does decompose with gentle heating.[1]

19.15 According to its formula, chalcopyrite is 34.62% Cu. Similarly, covellite is 66.46% copper by mass, and bornite is 63.61% copper by mass. The mass of copper per 100 g of this ore is

$$\left(\frac{34.62 \text{ g Cu}}{100 \text{ g chalcopyrite}} \times \frac{1.1 \text{ g chalcopyrite}}{100 \text{ g ore}}\right) + \left(\frac{66.46 \text{ g Cu}}{100 \text{ g covellite}} \times \frac{0.42 \text{ g covellite}}{100 \text{ g ore}}\right) + \left(\frac{63.61 \text{ g Cu}}{100 \text{ g bornite}} \times \frac{0.51 \text{ g bornite}}{100 \text{ g ore}}\right) = \frac{0.984 \text{ g Cu}}{100 \text{ g ore}}$$

A metric ton of ore is 1000 kg of ore. This is 10^4 times more than 100 g of ore. Accordingly there is 0.98×10^4 g of copper per metric ton of ore, or $\boxed{9.8 \text{ kg}}$ of copper per metric ton of ore.

19-17 a) The balanced equations are:

$$\begin{aligned}
&(1)\quad Fe_2O_3(s) + 3\,CO(g) \rightarrow 2\,Fe(s) + 3\,CO_2(g)\\
&(2)\quad Fe_3O_4(s) + 4\,CO(g) \rightarrow 3\,Fe(s) + 4\,CO_2(g)\\
&(3)\quad FeCO_3(s) + CO(g) \rightarrow Fe(s) + 2\,CO_2(g)
\end{aligned}$$

b) The reactions each reduce 1 mol of an iron compound, but the yields are 2, 3, and 1 mol of Fe respectively. For each reaction, ΔG° is the ΔG_f° of the reactants minus the ΔG_f° of the products. Taking free energies of formation from Appendix D:

Equation No.	ΔG°	ΔG° per mol Fe
(1)	−29.4 kJ	−14.7 kJ mol^{-1}
(2)	−13.3	−4.4
(3)	+15.1	+15.1

The first reaction has the most negative ΔG° per mol of Fe: $\boxed{Fe_2O_3}$ is the easiest compound to reduce with CO from the standpoint of thermodynamics. The easiest to reduce in practice depends on factors such as ease of handling and rate of reduction.

19.19 This is a straightforward conversion problem:

$$\frac{2 \times 10^8 \text{ kg N}}{1 \text{ yr}} \times \left(\frac{1000 \text{ g}}{1 \text{ kg}}\right) \times \left(\frac{1 \text{ mol}}{14.0 \text{ g}}\right) \times \left(\frac{6.02 \times 10^{23} \text{ atom}}{1 \text{ mol}}\right) \times \left(\frac{1 \text{ yr}}{3.15 \times 10^7 \text{ s}}\right) = \boxed{\frac{3 \times 10^{26} \text{ atom N}}{\text{s}}}$$

19.21 Higher pressures mean higher thermodynamic yields, but require more expensive equipment. A higher temperature can be used at higher pressure without lowering the yield from what it would have been at the lower pressure. The advantage of the higher temperature is faster reaction.

19.23 The three steps in the Ostwald process are:

$$\begin{aligned}
4\,NH_3(g) + 5\,O_2(g) \rightarrow 4\,NO(g) + 6\,H_2O(g) \quad & \Delta H^\circ = -905.48 \text{ kJ}\\
2\,NO(g) + O_2(g) \rightarrow 2\,NO_2(g) \quad & \Delta H^\circ = -114.14 \text{ kJ}\\
3\,NO_2(g) + H_2O(l) \rightarrow 2\,HNO_3(l) + NO(g) \quad & \Delta H^\circ = -71.66 \text{ kJ}
\end{aligned}$$

All three steps are exothermic. Hence, for all three steps, a high equilibrium yield will be favored by $\boxed{\text{low temperature}}$.

---

[1] See text Figure 1.6, text page 9.

19.25 A good tactic in working out a synthetic route to a target compound is to work backwards. N_2O_4 exists in equilibrium with NO_2. This equilibrium represents the last step in the synthesis

$$2\,NO_2(g) \rightleftharpoons N_2O_4(g)$$

This exothermic reaction can be shifted to the right by cooling. Also, N_2O_4, a gas at room temperature, freezes out at $-11°C$. Gaseous NO_2 is prepared from ammonia as part of the Ostwald process for nitric acid:

$$4\,NH_3(g) + 5\,O_2(g) \rightarrow 4\,NO(g) + 6\,H_2O(g)$$
$$2\,NO(g) + O_2(g) \rightarrow 2\,NO_2(g)$$

Ammonia can be prepared directly from the elements: $N_2(g)+3\,H_2(g) \rightarrow 2\,NH_3(g)$. Thus, the final four-step route to N_2O_4 from the elements:

$$N_2(g) + 3\,H_2(g) \rightarrow 2\,NH_3(g) \qquad 4\,NH_3(g) + 5\,O_2(g) \rightarrow 4\,NO(g) + 6\,H_2O(g)$$
$$2\,NO(g) + O_2(g) \rightarrow 2\,NO_2(g) \qquad 2\,NO_2(g) \rightarrow N_2O_4(s)$$

19.27 Balance the equation by the method discussed in text Section 6.4.[2] Each hydrazine losses 4 electrons as it is oxidized while each nitric acid gains 5 electrons as it is reduced. Note where these numbers appear in the answer:

$$\boxed{5\ N_2H_4(l) + 4\ HNO_3(l) \rightarrow 7\ N_2(g) + 12\ H_2O(l)}$$

Combine ΔH_f°'s according to Hess's law

$$\Delta H^\circ = 12\text{ mol}\left(\frac{-285.83\text{ kJ}}{\text{mol}}\right) + 7\text{ mol}\left(\frac{0\text{ kJ}}{\text{mol}}\right) - 5\left(\frac{50.63\text{ kJ}}{\text{mol}}\right) - 4\left(\text{mol}\frac{-174.10\text{ kJ}}{\text{mol}}\right) = \boxed{-2986.71\text{ kJ}}$$

19.29 The more electronegative the hydrogen-replacing group, the more the nitrogen lone pair is drawn toward it, and the poorer the electron-donating ability of the nitrogen atom. Hydroxylamine should be **less basic** than ammonia because O is more electronegative than H. Experiment bears out this prediction.

19.31 This is the oxidation of phosphorus by sulfuric acid.

$$\boxed{5\ H_2SO_4(aq) + 2\ P(s) \rightarrow 5\ SO_2(g) + 2\ H_3PO_4(aq) + 2\ H_2O(l)}$$

Or: $10\,H_2SO_4(aq) + P_4(s) \rightarrow 10\,SO_2(g) + 4\,H_3PO_4(aq) + 4\,H_2O(l)$.

19.33 If *pairs* of phosphoric acid molecules react and split out water, the reaction must be $2\,H_3PO_4(l) \rightarrow H_4P_2O_7(aq) + H_2O(l)$. The structure of **$H_4P_2O_7$ (diphosphoric acid)** is

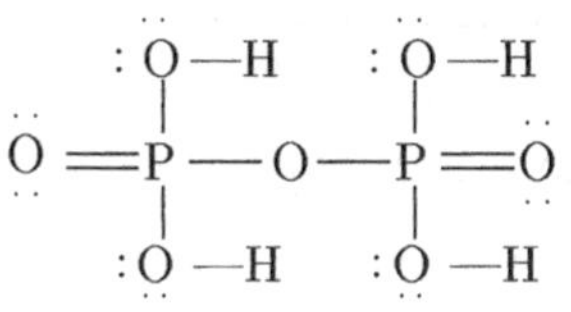

19.35 The reaction is $SO_2(g) + 1/2\,O_2(g) \rightleftharpoons SO_3(g)$. Increasing the pressure would drive this equilibrium to the right. Decreasing the temperature would also favor the products (the reaction is exothermic). Finally, continuous removal of the SO_3 would induce the production of more product to replace it.

---

[2] Text page 163.

19.37 The problem proposes replacing H_2SO_5 in the oxidation of the pollutant SO_2 by H_2O_2:

$$SO_2(g) + H_2O_2(aq) \rightarrow HSO_4^-(aq) + H^+(aq)$$

Taking data from text Appendix D to compute ΔG° gives:

$$\Delta G^\circ = 1\underbrace{(0)}_{H^+(aq)} + 1\underbrace{(-755.91)}_{HSO_4^-(aq)} - 1\underbrace{(-134.03)}_{H_2O_2(aq)} - 1\underbrace{(-300.19)}_{SO_2(g)} = -321.69 \text{ kJ}$$

The reaction is therefore spontaneous and would be thermodynamically $\boxed{\text{feasible}}$.

Tip. The powerful oxidizing agent H_2SO_5 mentioned in the problem can be regarded as containing S in the +8 oxidation state. A better view however is to see it as regular sulfuric acid with one of its O atoms replaced by a peroxide (O_2^{2-}) group. This gives it the formula $H_2SO_3(OO)$, keeps the sulfur in the +6 oxidation state, and explains the name: peroxymonosulfuric acid.

19.39 $ZnS(s) + 2\,O_2(g) + H_2O(l) \rightarrow ZnO(s) + H_2SO_4(l)$. The only additional materials required are oxygen and water. Zinc oxide is a by-product.

19.41 Use ΔG_f° data (text Appendix D) to compute $\Delta G^\circ_{298.15}$ for this reaction. The set-up is

$$\Delta G^\circ_{298.15} = 2\underbrace{(-36.8)}_{OCl^-(aq)} + 1\underbrace{(-237.18)}_{H_2O(l)} - 2\underbrace{(-157.24)}_{OH^-(aq)} - 1\underbrace{(97.9)}_{Cl_2O(g)} = -94.2 \text{ kJ}$$

Use this value to compute K at this temperature:

$$\ln K_{298.15} = \frac{\Delta G^\circ_{298.15}}{-RT} = \frac{-94.2 \times 10^3 \text{ J}}{(8.3145 \text{ J K}^{-1}\text{mol}^{-1})(298.15 \text{ K})} = 38.0 \qquad K_{298.15} = \boxed{3.2 \times 10^{16}}$$

19.43 The overall reaction in the Leblanc process is

$$2\,NaCl(s) + H_2SO_4(l) + 2\,C(s) + CaCO_3(s) \rightarrow Na_2CO_3(s) + 2\,CO_2(g) + CaS(s) + 2\,HCl(g)$$

Combine the enthalpies of formation from text Appendix D in accord with Hess's law to compute the ΔH° of this process:

$$\Delta H^\circ = 1\underbrace{(-1130.68)}_{Na_2CO_3(s)} + 2\underbrace{(-393.51)}_{CO_2(g)} + 1\underbrace{(-482.41)}_{CaS(s)} + 2\underbrace{(-92.31)}_{HCl(g)}$$
$$- 2\underbrace{(-411.15)}_{NaCl(s)} - 1\underbrace{(-813.99)}_{H_2SO_4(l)} - 2\underbrace{(0.00)}_{C(s)} - 1\underbrace{(-1206.92)}_{CaCO_3(s)} = \boxed{+258.48 \text{ kJ}}$$

The LeBlanc process is $\boxed{\text{endothermic}}$.

19.45 The production of Cl_2 is tied to the production of NaOH by the stoichiometry of the reaction: $2\,NaCl + 2\,H_2O \rightarrow Cl_2 + 2\,NaOH + H_2$. According to this equation, 2 mol of NaOH is produced per 1 mol of Cl_2. The mass of 2 mol of NaOH is 80.0 g, and the mass of 1 mol of Cl_2 is 70.9 g. If there were no losses of either material during production, the ratio of their masses would always equal $\boxed{1.13 \text{ to } 1}$. Evidently, more NaOH is lost in practice than Cl_2, reducing this ratio to the 1.05 quoted in the problem.

19.47 The problem reverses the more common task of determining an equilibrium constant from $\Delta G°$ data. It gives an equilibrium constant (in slightly disguised form) and asks for an estimate of $\Delta G°$. The reaction is $Br_2(l) \rightleftharpoons Br_2(aq)$. At 25°C, 33.6 g of bromine dissolves in one liter of water. At saturation, the $l \rightleftharpoons aq$ equilibrium exists. The concentration of $Br_2(aq)$ at saturation is 0.210 M.[3] The mass-action expression for the reaction is $K = [Br_2(aq)]$, so K is 0.210. The equilibrium constant and $\Delta G°$ at this temperature are related:

$$\Delta G° = -RT \ln K = -(8.3145 \text{ J K}^{-1}\text{mol}^{-1})(298.15 \text{ K}) \ln(0.210) = \boxed{3.87 \times 10^3 \text{ J}}$$

for the reaction as written, which is the reaction giving 1 mol of $Br_2(aq)$. The ΔG_f° for one mole of $Br_2(aq)$ is +3.93 kJ, according to text Appendix D.

Tip. Note that some Br_2 does dissolve despite the fact that $\Delta G°$ is positive.

19.49 For the reaction:

$$2\,Br^-(aq) + Cl_2(g) \rightleftharpoons Br_2(g) + 2\,Cl^-(aq)$$

$$\Delta G° = 2\underbrace{(-131.23)}_{Cl^-(aq)} + 1\underbrace{(\ 3.14)}_{Br_2(g)} - 2\underbrace{(-103.96)}_{Br^-(aq)} = -51.40 \text{ kJ}$$

where the numbers come from text Appendix D. Compute the equilibrium constant as follows:

$$\ln K_{298.15} = \frac{-\Delta G^\circ_{298.15}}{RT} = \frac{-(-51.40 \times 10^3 \text{ J})}{(8.3145 \text{ J K}^{-1}\text{mol}^{-1})(298.15 \text{ K})} = 20.7$$

from which K is $\boxed{1.0 \times 10^9}$. The $K_{298.15}$ is large enough to make the extraction of bromine from sea water by oxidation with $Cl_2(g)$ thermodynamically $\boxed{\text{feasible}}$.

Tip. K can also be obtained for the related reaction that gives liquid rather than gaseous bromine:

$$2\,Br^-(aq) + Cl_2(g) \rightleftharpoons Br_2(l) + 2\,Cl^-(aq)$$

Obtain $\Delta\mathcal{E}°$ for this reaction by combining the standard reduction potentials of its two half-reactions (Appendix E). The result is 0.293 V. Substitute this standard potential difference into text equation 12.8:[4]

$$\log K_{298.15} = \frac{n}{0.0592 \text{ V}}\Delta\mathcal{E}° = \frac{2}{0.0592 \text{ V}}(0.293 \text{ V}) = 9.90$$

It follows that $K_{298.15}$ equals 7.9×10^9.

Tip. Thermodynamic feasibility is not enough. If the chlorine is cheap and the reaction is fast, the process might also be economically feasible.

19.51 a) The balanced equation is: $\boxed{Br^-(aq) + H_3PO_4(aq) \rightarrow H_2PO_4^-(aq) + HBr(g)}$. Other equations (ones that involve NaBr as a reactant and give PO_4^{3-} or Na_3PO_4 or other forms of phosphate as product) are possible. This ionic equation is best.

b) The 100 mL of solution contains 0.050 mol L^{-1} × 0.100 L = 0.0050 mol of $Br^-(aq)$. According to the balanced equation, 0.0050 mol of $HBr(g)$ can form. If it does, and if it behaves ideally, its volume is

$$V_{HBr} = \frac{n_{HBr}RT}{P} = \frac{(0.0050 \text{ mol})(0.08206 \text{ L atm mol}^{-1}\text{K}^{-1})(273.15 \text{ K})}{1 \text{ atm}} = \boxed{0.11 \text{ L}}$$

---

[3] Taking the molar mass of Br_2 as 159.82 g mol^{-1}.

[4] Text page 403.

19.53 The standard reduction potential diagram for iodine at pH 14 shows that $I_2(s)$ disproportionates spontaneously to $IO^-(aq)$ and $I^-(aq)$:

$$I_2(s) + 2\,OH^-(aq) \rightarrow I^-(aq) + IO^-(aq) + H_2O(l)$$

This is because 0.535 V, the standard reduction potential for $I_2(s)$ to $I^-(aq)$, exceeds 0.45 V, the potential for $IO^-(aq)$ to $I_2(aq)$. But $IO^-(aq)$ itself disproportionates spontaneously to $IO_3^-(aq)$ and $I^-(aq)$:

$$3\,IO^-(aq) \rightarrow IO_3^-(aq) + 2\,I^-(aq)$$

as shown by a comparison of the IO_3/IO^- and IO^-/I^- standard reduction potentials. The overall balanced equation for the disproportionation is

$$6\,OH^-(aq) + 3\,I_2(aq) \rightarrow IO_3^-(aq) + 5\,I^-(aq) + 3\,H_2O(l) \quad \Delta\mathcal{E}^\circ = 0.49 - 0.14 = 0.35 \text{ V}$$

Because this reaction, which is favored thermodynamically, consumes $IO^-(aq)$, the ultimate products are $\boxed{IO_3^-(aq)}$ and $\boxed{I^-(aq)}$.

b) The half-reaction: $IO_3^-(aq) + 3\,H_2O(l) + 6\,e^- \rightarrow I^-(aq) + 6\,OH^-(aq)$ is the sum of:

$$\begin{array}{ll} IO_3^- + 2\,H_2O + 4\,e^- \rightarrow IO^- + 4\,OH^- & \mathcal{E}^\circ = 0.14 \text{ V} \\ IO^- + H_2O + 2\,e^- \rightarrow I^- + 2\,OH^- & \mathcal{E}^\circ = 0.49 \text{ V} \end{array}$$

The first half-reaction transfers 4 e^-'s, and the second transfers 2 e^-'s for an overall transfer of 6 e^-'s:

$$\mathcal{E}^\circ = \frac{(4 \times 0.14) + (2 \times 0.49)}{6} = \boxed{0.26 \text{ V}}$$

19.55 Calculate the relative number of moles of Na and F. Their ratio is 1 : 3. Enough hydrogen must be present to balance the −1 charges of the extra two fluoride ions. Therefore, the empirical formula is $\boxed{NaF{\cdot}2HF}$.

19.57 The shapes of all of these compounds can be predicted using the valence shell electron pair repulsion (VSEPR) theory (text Chapter 3).

a) OF_2 has a central O atom with a steric number of 4. This includes the two F atoms and two lone pairs of electrons. The molecule is $\boxed{\text{bent}}$. See **16.17c**.

b) BF_3 has a central B atom with *SN* 3. The molecule is $\boxed{\text{trigonal planar}}$.

c) In BrF_3, the central Br has *SN* of 5. The molecule has a $\boxed{\text{distorted T}}$ shape.

d) In BrF_5, the central Br is surrounded by five F atoms and one lone pair for a *SN* of 6. The molecule has a $\boxed{\text{square pyramidal}}$ shape.

e) In IF_7, the central I is surrounded by seven F atoms. The *SN* of the central I is therefore 7. One arrangement that minimizes repulsions among 7 electron pairs distributed about a center is a $\boxed{\text{pentagonal bipyramid}}$. See **3-87b**. This is the structure of IF_7.

f) In SeF_6, the central Se is surrounded by six F atoms and no lone pairs. The *SN* is 6, and the predicted geometry is $\boxed{\text{octahedral}}$. See **3.53c**.

19.59 a) Molecules of thionyl difluoride SOF_2 and selenyl difluoride $SeOF_2$ should have the same geometry because the central atoms of the two have the same number of valence electrons and the same number of bonded atoms. Use the VSEPR model to predict the molecular geometry. The central atoms of the molecules have *SN* 4 with one lone pair and three bonded atoms. The predicted molecular geometry is $\boxed{\text{pyramidal}}$.

b) Recall that Lewis bases are electron-pair donors and Lewis acids are electron-pair acceptors. In the reaction between SOF_2 and BF_3, the SOF_2 molecule donates a lone pair of electrons to the BF_3 molecule, and a coordinate covalent bond results:

$$F_3B + :SOF_2 \rightarrow F_3B\text{—}SOF_2$$

Thus, SOF_2 is acting as a $\boxed{\text{Lewis base}}$.

19.61 Fluorine chemists often think of fluoride-ion donors as bases and fluoride-ion acceptors as acids. The autoionization equilibrium in liquid BrF_3 is

$$\boxed{2\ BrF_3(l) \rightleftharpoons BrF_4^-(solv) + BrF_2^+(solv)}$$

The reaction can be seen as a competition between two Lewis acids, BrF_3 and BrF_2^+, for a Lewis base, F^-. One side of the competition is the acceptance of an electron pair from the Lewis base F^- by the Lewis acid BrF_3 to create a bond:

$$F_3Br + (:\ddot{\underset{..}{F}}:)^- \rightarrow (F_3Br\text{—}\ddot{\underset{..}{F}}:)^-$$

Vying against this is the acceptance of an electron pair from the Lewis base F^- by the Lewis acid BrF_2^+:

$$(F_2Br)^+ + (:\ddot{\underset{..}{F}}:)^- \rightarrow F_2Br\text{—}\ddot{\underset{..}{F}}:$$

Because BrF_2^+ is a much stronger Lewis acid than BrF_3, the first of these reactions lies far to the left at equilibrium and the second lies far to the right. Still, some autoionization occurs, just as in H_2O.

19.63 The molecule with the least ionic character, and weakest intermolecular interactions is expected to have the lowest boiling point. The ranking would therefore be $\boxed{PtF_6 < PtF_4 < CaF_2}$. In fact, PtF_4 decomposes upon melting, and so does not possess a normal boiling point.

19.65 The reaction of interest is: $C_2F_4(g) \rightarrow C(s) + CF_4(g)$. Combine the ΔH_f°'s to obtain ΔH°:

$$\Delta H^\circ = 1\underbrace{(-925)}_{CF_4(g)} + 1\underbrace{(0)}_{C(s)} - 1\underbrace{(-651)}_{CF_4(g)} = -274\text{ kJ}$$

Thus, if one mol of C_2F_2 were to explode, 274 kJ of heat would be released. The molar mass of C_2F_2 is 100 g mol^{-1}. The 1.00 kg of C_2F_4 therefore is 10.0 mol. Its explosion would release about $\boxed{2740\text{ kJ}}$.

19.67 The redox reaction: $XeF_6(g) + 3\,H_2(g) \rightarrow Xe(g) + 6\,HF(g)$ has ΔH° equal to the sum of the ΔH_f°'s of the products minus the sum of the ΔH_f°'s of the reactants:

$$\Delta H^\circ = 1\underbrace{\Delta H_f^\circ}_{Xe(g)} + 6\underbrace{\Delta H_f^\circ}_{HF(g)} - 3\underbrace{\Delta H_f^\circ}_{H_2(g)} - 1\underbrace{\Delta H_f^\circ}_{XeF_6(g)}$$

Inserting data from the problem and text Appendix D gives:

$$-1282\text{ kJ} = 1\underbrace{(0)}_{Xe(g)} + 6\underbrace{(-271.1)}_{HF(g)} - 3\underbrace{(0)}_{H_2(g)} - 1\underbrace{(\Delta H_f^\circ)}_{XeF_6(g)}$$

Solving gives the ΔH_f° for $XeF_6(g)$. It is $\boxed{-345\text{ kJ mol}^{-1}}$.

b) From the preceding part and text Appendix D:

$$XeF_6(g) \rightarrow Xe(g) + 3\,F_2(g) \qquad \Delta H^\circ = 345\text{ kJ}$$

$$\frac{1}{2}F_2(g) \rightarrow F(g) \qquad \Delta H^\circ = 78.99\text{ kJ}$$

Multiplying the second equation by 6 and adding it to the first gives:

$$XeF_6(g) \rightarrow Xe(g) + 6\,F(g) \quad \Delta H^\circ = 818.94 \text{ kJ}$$

The ΔH° here is the enthalpy to atomize 1 mol of $XeF_6(g)$. The average bond enthalpy of the Xe—F bond is 1/6 of this or $\boxed{136 \text{ kJ mol}^{-1}}$.

19.69 Calculate ΔH° for the hydrolysis

$$XeF_6(g) + H_2O(l) \rightarrow XeOF_4(l) + 2\,HF(g)$$

by combining ΔH_f° values according to Hess's law. The first and third in the following are given in the problem; the others are from text Appendix D:

$$\Delta H^\circ = 1\underbrace{(148)}_{XeOF_4(l)} + 2\underbrace{(-271)}_{HF(g)} - 1\underbrace{(-298)}_{XeF_6(g)} - 1\underbrace{(-285.83)}_{H_2O(l)} = 190 \text{ kJ}$$

The standard enthalpy for the hydrolysis of $XeF_6(g)$ is $\boxed{190 \text{ kJ mol}^{-1}}$.

19.71 The balanced half-equations are:

$$Mn^{2+}(aq) + 12\ H_2O(l) \rightarrow MnO_4^-(aq) + 8\ H_3O^+(aq) + 5\,e^-$$
$$XeO_6^{4-}(aq) + 12\ H_3O^+(aq) + 8\,e^- \rightarrow Xe(g) + 18\,H_2O(l)$$

The oxidation of the Mn^{2+} releases 5 e^- per ion, and the reduction of the XeO_6^{4-} consumes 8 e^- per ion. The overall equation is accordingly:

$$\boxed{8\ Mn^{2+}(aq) + 5\ XeO_6^{4-}(aq) + 6\ H_2O(l) \rightarrow 8\ MnO_4^-(aq) + 5\ Xe(g) + 4\,H_3O^+(aq)}$$

19.73 Very reactive chemicals are chemicals of high free energy. A compound of high free energy will tend to react spontaneously with other substances. This is why, for example, there is very little elemental aluminum in the Earth's crust. Any elemental aluminum initially present has long since reacted to form compounds such as Al_2O_3 or $Al_2Si_2O_5{\cdot}(OH)_4$ that have lower free energies.

a) Coal, hydrogen and air do not spontaneously react to form aspirin. This means that ΔG exceeds zero for this reaction. Aspirin has a higher free energy than its constituent carbon (from coal) hydrogen and oxygen (from air).

b) Pure water, sodium chloride and magnesium carbonate react spontaneously to form seawater. Thus, seawater is in a state of lower free-energy.

c) Carbon dioxide and water do not spontaneously react to form vitamin A and oxygen. This means that the vitamin A and oxygen lie in higher free-energy states than carbon dioxide and water.

19.75 Use all of the data in unit factors:

$$m_{CO_2} = 63 \times 10^9 \text{ cans} \times \left(\frac{0.355 \text{ L}}{1 \text{ can}}\right) \times \left(\frac{0.15 \text{ mol } CO_2}{1 \text{ L}}\right) \times \left(\frac{0.0440 \text{ kg } CO_2}{1 \text{ mol } CO_2}\right) = \boxed{1.5 \times 10^8 \text{ kg } CO_2}$$

19.77 The problem requires classification of reactions into three categories: acid-base (see text page 161), redox (see text pages 173), and dissolution-precipitation (see text page 368).

a) This reaction is a $\boxed{\text{redox}}$ reaction. Sulfur is reduced from the +6 oxidation state (in $CaSO_4$) to the 0 oxidation state (in S). Methane is oxidized.

b) The hydrogenation of carbon monoxide is a redox reaction. Hydrogen is oxidized from the 0 oxidation state (in H_2) to the +1 oxidation state (in CH_3OH). The reduction is the conversion of CO (C in the +2 oxidation state) to CH_3OH (C in the −2 oxidation state).

c) This hydrogenation of ethylene is a redox reaction. Hydrogen is oxidized from the 0 oxidation state (in H_2) to the +1 oxidation state (in H_3CCH_3). The reduction is the conversion of $H_2C{=}CH_2$ (C in the −2 oxidation state) to $H_3C{-}CH_3$ (C in the −3 oxidation state).

d) This reaction is a redox reaction. Iron is oxidized from the 0 oxidation state (in Fe) to the +2 oxidation state (in $FeSO_4$). The reduction which accompanies this oxidation involves converting H_2SO_4 (H in the +1 oxidation state) to H_2 (H in the 0 oxidation state).

19-79 The equilibrium $CO_2(g) + C(s) \rightarrow 2\,CO(g)$ is crucial in the reduction of iron ore in a blast furnace. At room temperature it lies far to the left, but at 1875° (2148 K) it is very much shifted to the right. To answer the question, compute $\Delta H°$ and $\Delta S°$ of this reaction from the data in text Appendix D and then use the relationship:

$$-RT\ln K_T = \Delta H° - T\Delta S° \qquad \text{which gives} \qquad \ln K_T = \frac{-\Delta H°}{RT} + \frac{\Delta S°}{R}$$

to solve for K at both of the temperatures. It is found that $\Delta H°$ is 172.47 kJ and $\Delta S°$ is 175.75 J K^{-1}. The answers are $K_{298} = \boxed{9.2 \times 10^{-22}}$ and $K_{2148} = \boxed{9.7 \times 10^{4}}$. The second K is a rough approximation because $\Delta H°$ and $\Delta S°$ do change between 298 and 2148 K.[5]

19-81 Iron ore is Fe_2O_3 mixed with silica, alumina and minor impurities; copper ore is usually a sulfide. Iron ore is reduced with $CO(g)$ in a blast furnace by reaction with coke (carbon) and a limited amount of air. Fluxes like CaO are added to make a fluid slag from the silica and alumina impurities. Blast furnace slag is used as road ballast and in making portland cement. The roasting of copper ores gives off sulfur dioxide, which must not be vented into the atmosphere and is often processed into sulfuric acid. Roasting reduces the copper only partially (to the copper(I) sulfide) and oxidizes impurities. Roasting of copper ores takes place at relatively low temperatures. Removal of impurities goes on at higher temperature (about 1100°C) but still below the 1535°C at which iron is reduced in a blast furnace. The flux in this step of copper recovery is $CaCO_3$, and the slag contains impurity iron. The copper is still combined chemically in Cu_2S. This compound is decomposed into impure metallic copper by heating it in air, which generates more $SO_2(g)$.

19.83 a) $6\,NO_2(g) + 4\,(NH_2)_2CO(aq) \rightarrow 7\,N_2(g) + 4\,CO_2(g) + 8\,H_2O(l)$

b) $6\,NO(g) + 2\,(NH_2)_2CO(aq) \rightarrow 5\,N_2(g) + 2\,CO_2(g) + 4\,H_2O(l)$

19.85 In the Raschig synthesis, hydrazine is produced from aqueous hypochlorite ion and ammonia:

$$2\,NH_3(aq) + OCl^-(aq) \rightarrow N_2H_4(aq) + H_2O(l) + Cl^-(aq)$$

A two-step mechanism that involves NH_2Cl as an intermediate is

$$NH_3(g) + OCl^-(aq) \rightarrow NH_2Cl(aq) + OH^-(aq)$$
$$NH_2Cl(aq) + NH_3(aq) + OH^-(aq) \rightarrow N_2H_4(aq) + H_2O(l) + Cl^-(aq)$$

19.87 a) The molar free energies of formation (in kJ mol^{-1}) of the reactants and products are:

	$6\,Fe_2O_3(s)$	$+\,N_2H_4(aq)$	$\rightarrow 4\,Fe_3O_4(s)$	$+\,N_2(g)$	$+2\,H_2O(l)$
$\Delta G_f°$	−742.2	128.1	−1015.5	0	−237.18

[5]The answer to this problem also appears on text page 680.

Combine these in the usual way to obtain $\Delta G°$ of the reaction:

$$\Delta G° = 4(-1015.5) + 1(0) + 2(-237.18) - 6(-742.2) - 1(128.1) = \boxed{-211.3 \text{ kJ}}$$

b) The proposal is $\boxed{\text{no good}}$. When hydrazine reacts with rust it acts as a reducing agent. Under highly acidic conditions, hydrazine gains H^+ to form the hydrazinium ion $N_2H_5^+$ which is a good oxidizing agent. The suggested improvement would probably aggravate the rusting problem.

19.89 Superphosphate is $(Ca(H_2PO_4)_2{\cdot}H_2O)_3\,(CaSO_4{\cdot}2H_2O)_7$. ($\mathcal{M} = 1961.4$ g mol^{-1}.. The mass percentage of P_2O_5 in superphosphate is

$$\frac{3 \times 141.94 \text{ g mol}^{-1}}{1961.4 \text{ g mol}^{-1}} \times 100\% = \boxed{21.7\%}$$

where 141.94 g mol^{-1} is the molar mass of P_2O_5. This is about one-third of the mass percentage of P_2O_5 in triple superphosphate.

19.91 Compute the standard Gibbs free energies of the two reactions using the $\Delta G_f°$ data in text Appendix D. The $\Delta G°$ of the oxidation of SO_2 by $O_2(g)$ according to the first equation in the problem is −70.89 kJ. The $\Delta G°$ for the oxidation of SO_2 by $NO_2(g)$ according to the second equation in the problem is −35.63 kJ. The $\boxed{\text{oxidation by } O_2}$ has a larger thermodynamic driving force. Oxidation of SO_2 by NO_2 is however $\boxed{\text{faster}}$ at low temperature, which explains the early success of the lead-chamber process for sulfuric acid.

Tip. The $\Delta H°$ and $\Delta S°$ data quoted in the text[6] can be very conveniently used in the equation $\Delta G° = \Delta H° - T\Delta S°$ to obtain $\Delta G°$ for the first reaction. The result equals the result using $\Delta G_f°$'s.

19.93 a) Compute the $\Delta H°$ and $\Delta S°$ of the reaction using data from text Appendix D:

$$\Delta H° = 2\underbrace{(-241.82)}_{H_2O(l)} + 4\underbrace{(-296.83)}_{SO_2(g)} + 1\underbrace{(-393.51)}_{CO_2(g)} - 4\underbrace{(-395.72)}_{SO_3(g)} - 1\underbrace{(-74.81)}_{CH_4(g)} = -406.78 \text{ kJ}$$

$$\Delta S° = 2\underbrace{(188.72)}_{H_2O(l)} + 4\underbrace{(248.11)}_{SO_2(g)} + 1\underbrace{(213.63)}_{CO_2(g)} - 4\underbrace{(256.65)}_{SO_3(g)} - 1\underbrace{(186.15)}_{CH_4(g)} = 370.76 \text{ J K}^{-1}$$

Use these numbers to obtain $\Delta G°_{1000}$ as follows:

$$\Delta G°_{1000} = \Delta H° - T\Delta S° = -406.78 \text{ kJ} - (1000 \text{ K})(0.37076 \text{ kJ K}^{-1}) = \boxed{-780 \text{ kJ}}$$

b) Compute the $\Delta H°$ and $\Delta S°$ for the critic's proposed reaction in the same way:

$$\Delta H° = 1\underbrace{(-241.82)}_{H_2O(l)} + 1\underbrace{(-20.63)}_{H_2S(g)} + 1\underbrace{(-393.51)}_{CO_2(g)} - 1\underbrace{(-395.72)}_{SO_3(g)} - 1\underbrace{(-74.81)}_{CH_4(g)} = -185.43 \text{ kJ}$$

$$\Delta S° = 1\underbrace{(188.72)}_{H_2O(l)}\,1\underbrace{(205.68)}_{H_2S(g)} + 1\underbrace{(213.63)}_{CO_2(g)} - 1\underbrace{(256.65)}_{SO_3(g)} - 1\underbrace{(186.15)}_{CH_4(g)} = 165.23 \text{ J K}^{-1}$$

From which:

$$\Delta G°_{1000} = -185.43 \text{ kJ} - (1000 \text{ K})(0.16523 \text{ kJ K}^{-1}) = \boxed{-351 \text{ kJ}}$$

c) Both reaction are spontaneous at 1000 K. Thermodynamics does not predict which, if either, will occur preferentially. Although the first is more favored than the second, the second could easily predominate if it were faster and if the reaction:

$$H_2S(g) + 3\,SO_3(g) \rightarrow 4\,SO_2(g) + H_2O(g)$$

---

[6] Text page 692.

were slow. Note that this reaction added to the second reaction gives the first. The best way to settle the issue is by experiment.

19.95 Gaseous [chlorine] is a stronger oxidizing agent than $Br_2(l)$ because the reduction potential for Cl_2/Cl^- is more positive than the reduction potential for Br_2/Br^-. The stronger oxidizing agent will be the stronger bleach.

19.97 (a) A current of 100 000 A corresponds to the passage of 100 000 C s^{-1}. There are 86 400 seconds in a day, so 8.64×10^9 C passes through each of the 250 cells daily. This equals 8.95×10^4 mol of electrons per cell (computed using the Faraday constant ($\mathcal{F} = 96485$ C mol^{-1}). For every mole of electrons that passes through a cell, 1/2 mol of Cl_2 is produced, according to the half-reaction $Cl^- \rightarrow Cl_2 + 2\,e^-$. Therefore, 4.48×10^4 mol of Cl_2 is produced by one cell in a day. This is 3.17×10^6 g of Cl_2 per cell. The total production is 7.94×10^8 g of Cl_2 per day for the 250-cell plant. This is [794 metric tons] of Cl_2.

b) The power consumption in watts equals the operating potential in volts multiplied by the current. Each cell uses 3.5 V $\times$ 100 000 A = 350 000 W. The set of 250 cells uses 250 times this: 8.75×10^7 W. Multiplying this power by the 24 hours in a day gives 2.10×10^6 kilowatt-hour as the daily energy consumption of the plant. Since a kWh is 3.600×10^6 J,[7] the daily energy consumption is [7.56×10^{12} J].

c) The electric bill for one day at this plant equals [$105,000].

19.99 a) The trend in acid strength among the hydrogen halides runs:

$$HI > HBr > HCl$$

Therefore HAt should be an even [stronger] acid than HI.

b) The question concerns $\mathcal{E}°$ for the half-reaction:

$$At_2(s) + 2\,e^- \rightarrow 2\,At^-(aq)$$

$At_2(s)$ oxidizes $Zn(s)$ to $Zn^{2+}(aq)$, and $\mathcal{E}°$ for the $Zn^{2+}(aq)/Zn(s)$ half-reaction is -0.763 V. Therefore $\mathcal{E}°$ for the $At_2(s)/At^-(aq)$ reduction exceeds -0.763 V. However, At_2 does not oxidize $Fe^{2+}(aq)$ to Fe^{3+}. Since the standard reduction potential for $Fe^{3+}(aq)$ to $Fe^{2+}(s)$ is 0.770 V, $\mathcal{E}°$ for the reduction of $At_2(s)$ is less than 0.770 V. The range is therefore from [-0.763 to $+0.770$ V]. On the basis of the periodic trends among the halogens, we also expect $\mathcal{E}°$ for At_2/At^- is be less than $\mathcal{E}°$ for I_2/I^-. This would make the range -0.763 to 0.535 V.

c) $Cl_2(g)$ will easily oxidize $At^-(aq)$: [$2At^-(aq) + Cl_2(g) \rightarrow 2Cl^-(g) + At_2(s)$].

d) Solid At_2 should have an even greater tendency to disproportionate in aqueous base than $I_2(s)$. Thus:

$$\boxed{6\,At_2(s) + 12\,OH^-(aq) \rightarrow 2\,AtO_3^-(aq) + 10\,At^-(aq) + 6\,H_2O(l)}$$

19.101 The standard reduction potential $\mathcal{E}°$ for the reduction of $F_2(g)$ to $F^-(aq)$ is 2.87 V. This is much more positive than the 0.815 V potential for the reduction of $O_2(g)$ to 10^{-7} M $OH^-(aq)$ ion. Because 1 M $F^-(aq)$ has a very much smaller tendency to be oxidized than 10^{-7} M $OH^-(aq)$, the product at the anode in the electrolysis of NaF is $O_2(g)$, not $F_2(g)$; $F_2(g)$ is [not obtained.].

19.103 The balanced equation: $4\,HF(aq) + SiO_2(s) \rightarrow SiF_4(g) + 2\,H_2O(l)$ shows that 4 mol of $HF(aq)$ is needed to dissolve 1 mol of quartz rock. The rock contains mere traces of gold (1 part in 10^5 by mass).

[7] See **12.73**.

Suppose enough quartz is dissolved to recover 1 troy ounce (31.3 g) of gold. This is 10^5 times 31.3 g of quartz. The cost of the required HF is

$$\text{cost} = 31.3 \times 10^5 \text{ g quartz} \times \left(\frac{1 \text{ mol quartz}}{60.1 \text{ g}}\right) \times \left(\frac{4 \text{ mol HF}}{1 \text{ mol quartz}}\right) \times \left(\frac{20.0 \text{ g HF}}{1 \text{ mol HF}}\right)$$
$$\times \left(\frac{2 \text{ g HF solution}}{1 \text{ g HF}}\right) \times \left(\frac{1 \text{ L sol'n}}{1170 \text{ g solution}}\right) \times \left(\frac{\$0.25}{1 \text{ L solution}}\right) = \$1780$$

The solvent costs more that the \$350 the troy ounce of gold would bring. The method is a **losing proposition**. It breaks even on materials when the ore is 5.1 times richer in gold (5.1 is the ratio of \$1780 to \$350). For true feasibility the cost of labor and equipment would have to be covered, too.

19.105 Follow the rules in Chapter 3 for writing Lewis dot structures. The fluorine atoms in O_2F_2 are terminal:

$$:\ddot{\underset{\cdot\cdot}{F}}-\ddot{\underset{\cdot\cdot}{O}}-\ddot{\underset{\cdot\cdot}{O}}-\ddot{\underset{\cdot\cdot}{F}}:$$

The bond order of the O—F bond is 1, and the bond order of the O—O bond is 1. Each F—O—O bond angle is roughly 109° reflecting the steric number of four at each O atom. The analogous compound of oxygen and hydrogen is **hydrogen peroxide**.

Tip. The measured O-O-F bond angles in O_2F_2 are both 109°, as predict. The O-O bond distance is 1.217 Å, which is quite short compared to the O-O distance in H_2O_2 These can be rationalized by writing this ionic resonance contributor for O_2F_2:

$$(:\ddot{\underset{\cdot\cdot}{F}}:)^- \quad (\ddot{\underset{\cdot\cdot}{O}}-\ddot{\underset{\cdot\cdot}{O}})^{2+} \quad (:\ddot{\underset{\cdot\cdot}{F}}:)^-$$

The O_2^{2+} ion should have a short O—O distance, based on simple molecular orbital theory (it has lost two antibonding electrons relative to O_2.

19.107 Use the VSEPR model (Chapter 3) to predict the molecular geometry. The Lewis structure of the SF_5^- ion is

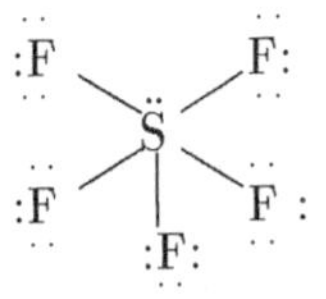

The central S atom in this ion has *SN* 6 with 1 lone pair and 5 bonded atoms; the molecular geometry is **square pyramidal**.

19.109 The reaction of interest is: $Xe(g) + 2\,F_2(g) \rightarrow XeF_4(s)$. The given free energy of formation applies directly to this reaction. Use the relationship $\Delta G^\circ = -RT \ln K$:

$$\ln K = \frac{\Delta G^\circ}{-RT} = \frac{-134 \times 10^3 \text{ J}}{-(8.3145 \text{ J K}^{-1}\text{mol}^{-1})(298.15 \text{ K})} = 54.1 \qquad \text{from which} \qquad K = \boxed{3 \times 10^{23}}$$

Chapter 20

Organic Chemical Processes

20.1 The vapor pressure of pure *n*-hexane exceeds the vapor pressure of pure *n*-octane. The vapor phase should therefore be enriched in *n*-hexane relative to the liquid phase. Use Raoult's law to compute the pressures of the two in the space above the solution. The problem states the vapor pressures of the two pure compounds at the temperature of interest, which is 45°C, and also gives their mole fractions, which are both 0.500. The calculation of the vapor pressures uses these data as follows

$$P_{\text{hexane}} = X_{\text{hexane}} P^{\circ}_{\text{hexane}} = 0.500(0.439 \text{ atm}) = 0.2195 \text{ atm}$$
$$P_{\text{octane}} = X_{\text{octane}} P^{\circ}_{\text{octane}} = 0.500(0.0524 \text{ atm}) = 0.0262 \text{ atm}$$

According to Dalton's law of partial pressures, the mole fraction of a component in a gaseous mixture equals its partial pressure divided by the total pressure of the mixture:

$$X_{\text{hexane}} \text{ in vapor} = \frac{0.2195}{0.2195 + 0.0262} = 0.893 \qquad X_{\text{octane}} \text{ in vapor} = \frac{0.0262}{0.2195 + 0.0262} = 0.107$$

The mole percentages of the two components in the vapor are therefore $\boxed{89.3\%}$ for hexane and $\boxed{10.7\%}$ for octane. $\boxed{\text{Hexane comes off higher}}$ in the distillation column because it is more volatile.

20.3 **a)** The ΔH_f° of gaseous cyclopropane equals the enthalpy change in forming 1 mol of $C_3H_6(g)$ in its standard state from $C(s)$ and $H_2(g)$ in their standard states: $3\,C(s) + 3\,H_2(g) \rightarrow C_3H_6(g)$. Imagine this reaction to proceed by the atomization of 3 mol of $C(s)$ and 3 mol of $H_2(g)$ to $C(g)$ and $H(g)$ followed by the formation of 3 mol of C—C bonds and 6 mol of C—H bonds. The sum of the ΔH°'s of these steps equals the desired ΔH_f°, by Hess's law. Use the bond enthalpies and enthalpies of atomization from Table 7.3[1]

$$\Delta H_f^\circ = 3(716.682) + 6(217.96) + 3(-348) + 6(-413) = \boxed{-64 \text{ kJ mol}^{-1}}$$

b) By Hess's law, the standard enthalpy for the combustion of cyclopropane equals the enthalpy of formation of the products of combustion minus the enthalpy of formation of the reactants:

$$C_3H_6(g) + \tfrac{9}{2}\,O_2(g) \rightarrow 3\,CO_2(g) + 3\,H_2O(g)$$

Thus:

$$\Delta H^\circ = -1959 \text{ kJ} = 3\underbrace{(-393.51)}_{CO_2(g)} + 3\underbrace{(-241.82)}_{H_2O(g)} - \tfrac{9}{2}\underbrace{(0)}_{O_2(g)} - 1\underbrace{(\Delta H_f^\circ)}_{C_3H_6(g)}$$

$$\Delta H_f^\circ = \boxed{53 \text{ kJ mol}^{-1}}$$

[1] Text page 217.

c) The calorimetric ΔH_f° of $C_3H_6(g)$ is considerably higher that the ΔH_f° based on bond enthalpies. It requires more energy to make $C_3H_6(g)$ than would be expected on the basis of the formation of normal single bonds. The extra enthalpy goes to force the formation of C—C—C bond angles of 60°, much smaller than the usual tetrahedral angle, 109.5°. It is the "strain enthalpy" of cyclopropane. It is about $\boxed{117 \text{ kJ mol}^{-1}}$.

20.5 **a)** The catalytic cracking reaction is

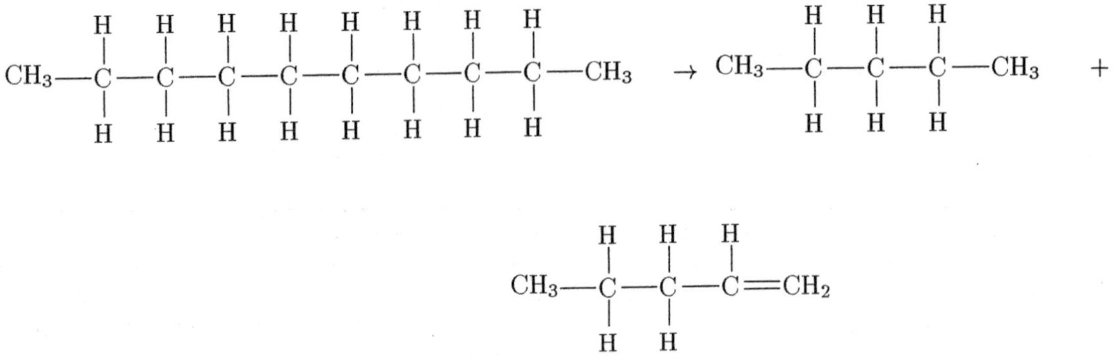

b) Another isomer of the alkene is 2-pentene, in which the double bond lies between the second and third carbon atoms in the chain.

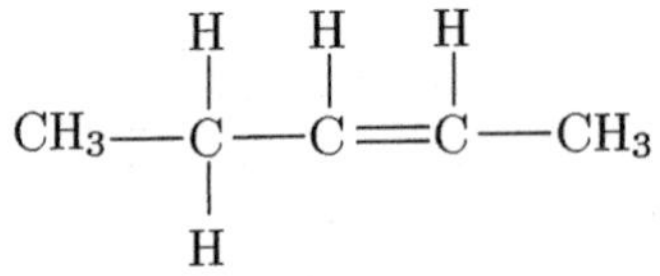

20.7 The structural formulas are:

a) 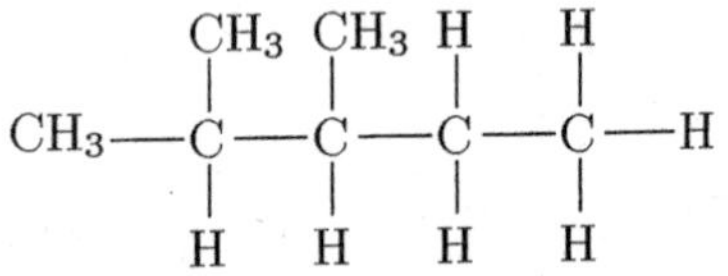

b) 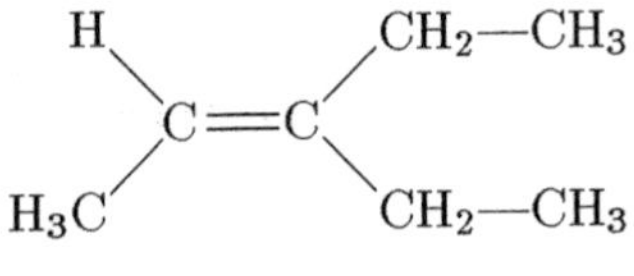

c) 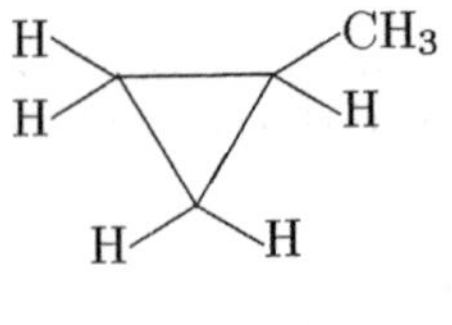

d) 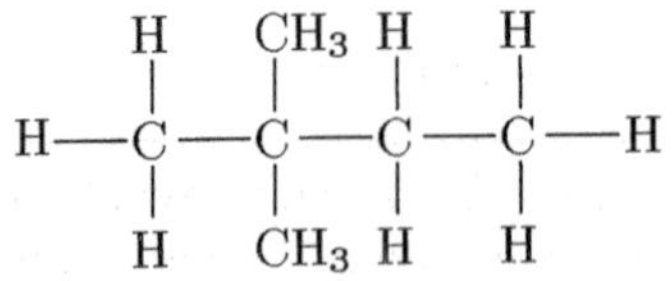

e) 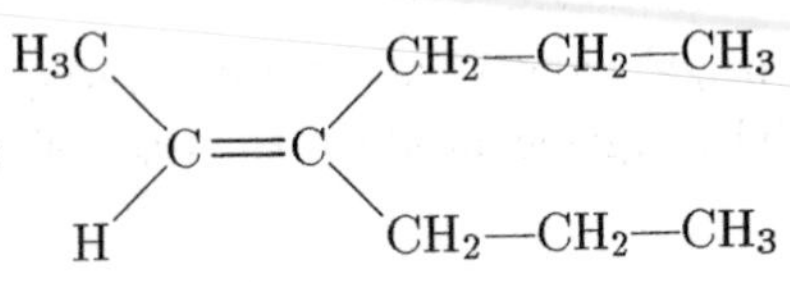

f) 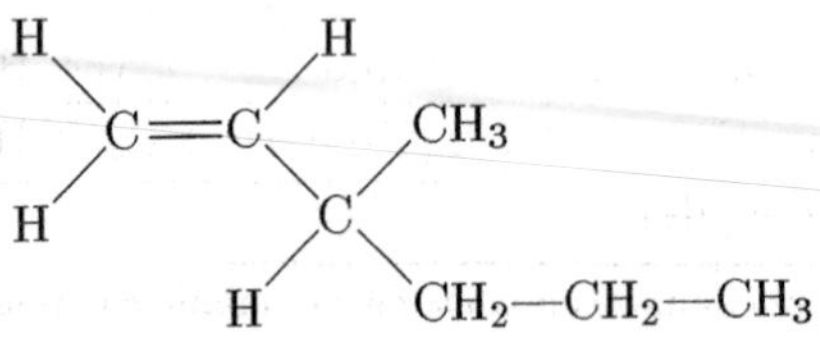

g) 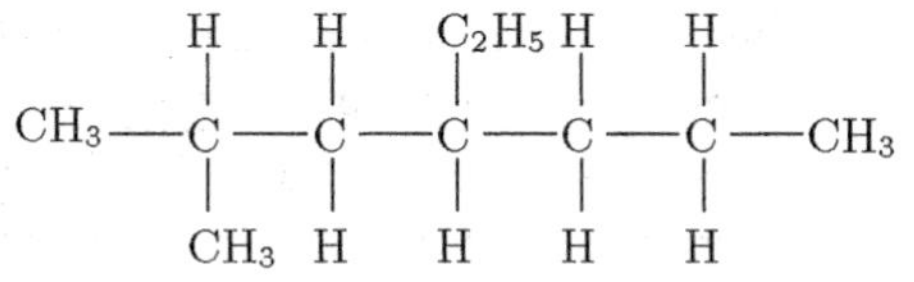 **h)** 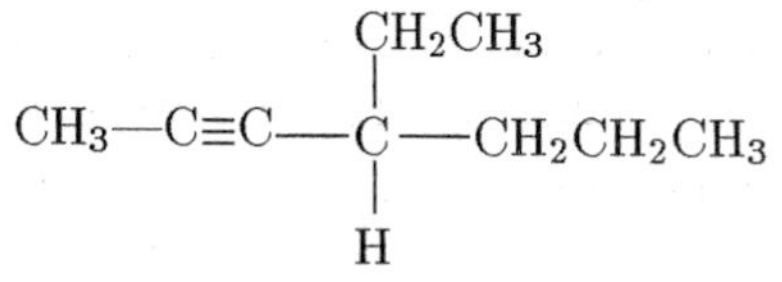

20.9 The *cis* isomers of 3-heptene is at the left and the *trans* is at the right:

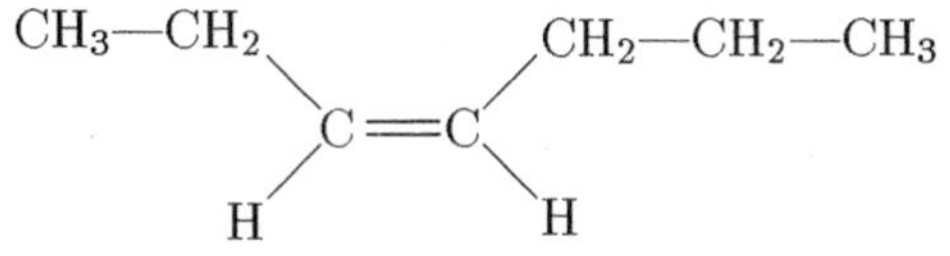 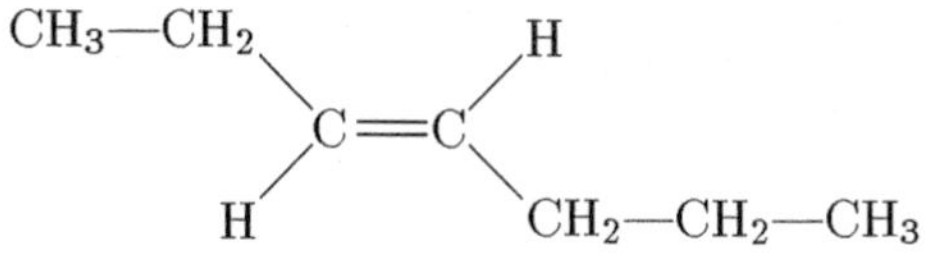

20.11 a) 1,2-hexadiene **b)** 1,3,5-hexatriene **c)** 2-methyl-1-hexene **d)** 3-hexyne

---

20.13 Count the number of atoms linked to the C atom in question, and add the number of lone pairs.[2] The results equals the steric number *SN* of the C in question. If *SN* equals 2, the C is *sp* hybridized; if *SN* equals 3, the C is sp^2 hybridized; if *SN* equals 4, the C is sp^3 hybridized.

a) From left to right in the structure, the hybridization of the C atoms is: $\boxed{sp^2,\ sp,\ sp^2,\ sp^3, \text{ and } sp^3}$.

b) All C atoms are $\boxed{sp^2}$ hybridized.

c) The two C atoms involved in the double bond are $\boxed{sp^2}$ hybridized. The rest are $\boxed{sp^3}$ hybridized.

d) From the left, the hybridization is $\boxed{sp^3,\ sp^3,\ sp,\ sp,\ sp^3, \text{ and } sp^3}$.

20.15 It is clear that the molar ratio of the ethylene to the ethylene dichloride is 1-to-1, based on the formulas of the two compounds. Use this ratio to compute the amount of ethylene required to make the 6.26×10^9 kg of ethylene dichloride. Then:

$$m_{C_2H_4} = 6.26 \times 10^9 \text{ kg } C_2H_4Cl_2 \times \left(\frac{1 \text{ mol } C_2H_4Cl_2}{0.09896 \text{ kg } C_2H_4Cl_2}\right) \times \left(\frac{1 \text{ mol } C_2H_4}{1 \text{ mol } C_2H_4Cl_2}\right)$$
$$\times \left(\frac{0.02805 \text{ kg } C_2H_4}{1 \text{ mol } C_2H_4}\right) = 1.77 \times 10^9 \text{ kg } C_2H_4$$

This is $\boxed{11.2\%}$ of the 15.87×10^9 kg total annual production of ethylene. The mass of the chlorine is $\boxed{4.49 \times 10^9 \text{ kg}}$, by a similar computation.

20.17 a) This is an esterification. It formally resembles an acid-base neutralization with the alcohol playing the part of the base. The organic product is butyl acetate.

$$\boxed{CH_3CH_2CH_2CH_2OH + CH_3COOH \rightarrow CH_3COOCH_2CH_2CH_2CH_3 + H_2O}$$

b) The reaction is a dehydration: $\boxed{H_3C\text{—}COO^-\ NH_4^+ \rightarrow H_3C\text{—}CO\text{—}NH_2 + H_2O}$.

c) The H atom on the O atom and one of the H atoms on the neighboring C atom are removed and combined to give H_2: $\boxed{H_3CCH_2CH_2OH \rightarrow H_3CCH_2CHO + H_2}$. The organic product is propanal (also called propionaldehyde).

[2] Lone pairs are uncommon on C atoms in organic compounds.

d) $\boxed{H_3CCH_2CH_2CH_2CH_2CH_2CH_3 + 11\ O_2 \rightarrow 7\ CO_2 + 8\ H_2O}$.

20.19 a) Brominate ethylene to give 1,2-dibromoethane. Then dehydrobrominate the 1,2-dibromoethane. This means: treat ethylene with bromine so that the bromine molecule adds across the double bond. Then treat the product in such a way that hydrogen bromide is abstracted:

$$CH_2{=}CH_2 + Br_2 \rightarrow CH_2BrCH_2Br \quad \text{then} \quad CH_2BrCH_2Br \rightarrow CH_2{=}CHBr + HBr$$

b) Treat 1-butene with water (in the presence of H_2SO_4)

$$CH_3CH_2CH{=}CH_2 + H_2O \rightarrow CH_3CH_2CH(OH)CH_3$$

c) Treat propene with water to give 2-propanol, and then dehydrogenate over a catalyst (such as metallic copper)

$$CH_3CH{=}CH_2 + H_2O \rightarrow CH_3CH(OH)CH_3 \text{ and } CH_3CH(OH)CH_3 \rightarrow CH_3COCH_3 + H_2$$

20.21

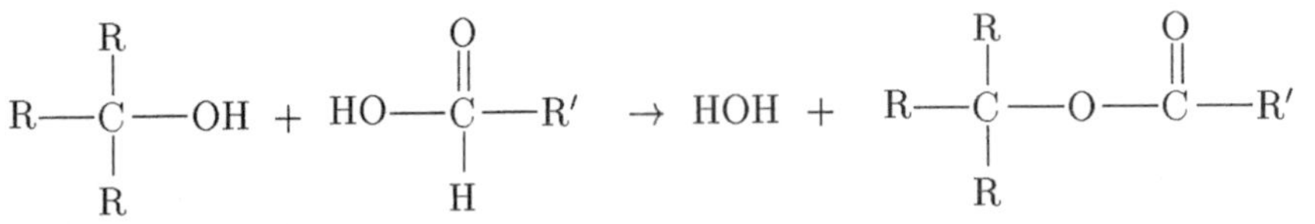

20.23 The balanced chemical equation for the conversion is

$$C_{18}H_{32}O_2 + 2\,H_2(g) \rightarrow C_{18}H_{36}O_2(g)$$

Compute the chemical amount of H_2 needed:

$$n_{H_2} = 500.0\text{ g } C_{18}H_{32}O_2 \times \left(\frac{1\text{ mol}}{280.45\text{ g } C_{18}H_{32}O_2}\right) \times \left(\frac{2\text{ mol } H_2}{1\text{ mol } C_{18}H_{32}O_2}\right) = 3.5657\text{ mol } H_2$$

Then use the ideal-gas equation:

$$V_{H_2} = \frac{n_{H_2}RT}{P} = \frac{(3.5657\text{ mol})(0.082057\text{ L atm mol}^{-1}\text{K}^{-1})(273\text{ K})}{1\text{ atm}} = \boxed{79.9\text{ L}}$$

20.25 Compare the pK_a of methane, which is 49 in text Table 20.4, with that of phenylmethane (41). Following the approach of text Example 20.2 then gives

$$\Delta G^\circ - \Delta G^{\circ\prime} = 2.303RT(\text{p}K_a - \text{p}K_a{}') = 2.303(8.3145\text{ J K}^{-1}\text{mol}^{-1})(298.15\text{ K})(41 - 49)$$
$$= -4.57 \times 10^5\text{ J mol}^{-1} = \boxed{-46\text{ kJ mol}^{-1}}$$

20.27 The pK_{a1} of the diprotic acid succinic acid should be $\boxed{\text{smaller than 4.9}}$, the p$K_a$ of propionic acid, because the additional electronegative atoms on succinic acid offer additional stabilization in the conjugate base of succinic acid (the hydrogen succinate ion). The pK_{a2} should be $\boxed{\text{larger than 4.9}}$ because the hydrogen ion is being removed from a negative ion.

20.29 Neither is a very strong acid, but benzene should be a stronger acid than cyclohexane. In benzene the negative charge left after the loss of a hydrogen ion is delocalized on the benzene ring; in cyclohexane, the negative charge is substantially constrained to reside on a single carbon atom.

20.31 a) Trifluoroacetic acid is stronger than trichloroacetic acid. The high electronegativity of the F's stabilizes the trifluoroacetate ion compared to the trichloroacetate ion.

b) 2-Fluorobutyric acid is stronger than 4-fluorobutyric acid because the F atom is closer to the carboxylic acid group and better able to accommodate some of the negative charge left by the loss of the hydrogen ion on the carboxylic acid group.

c) Benzoic acid is stronger than 2,6-di(*t*-butyl)benzoic acid because the *t*-butyl groups tend to push electron density onto the benzene ring, making it less able to accommodate the negative charge left by the loss of the hydrogen ion on the carboxylic acid group.

20.33

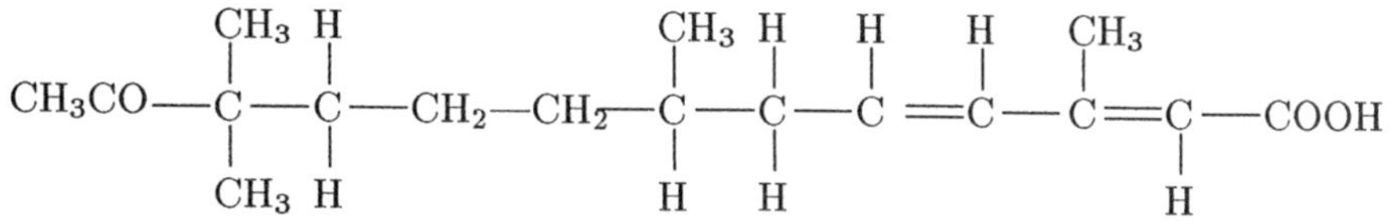

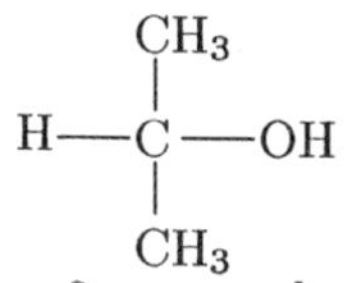

2-propanol

Tip. The name of the carboxylic acid is 11-methoxy-3,7,11-trimethyl-2,4-dodecadienoic acid.

20.35 a) Aspirin has a molecular formula of $C_9H_8O_4$.

b) The molar mass of aspirin is 180.16 g mol^{-1} $n = 0.325 \text{ g} \times (1 \text{ mol}/180.16 \text{ g}) = 1.80 \times 10^{-3} \text{ mol}$.

20.37 The following shows the numbering system that is used to designate the 17 carbons that make up the tetracylic ring system common to all steroids:

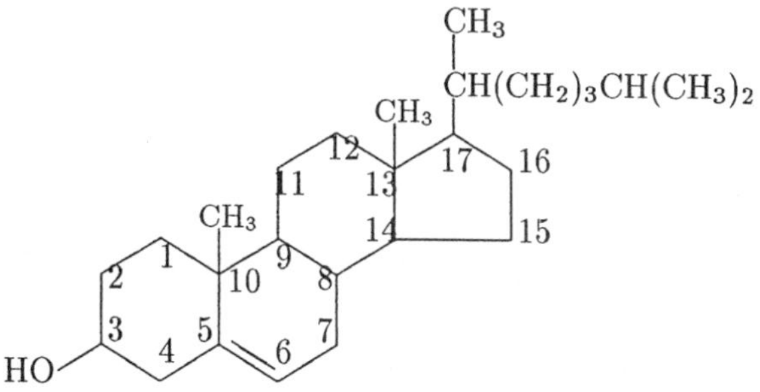

The specific steroid that is shown is cholesterol ($C_{27}H_{46}O$). Cortisone ($C_{21}H_{28}O_5$) derives from cholesterol by: oxidation of the —OH side-group at C-3 to a ketone (loss of one H by the —OH and one H by the C); oxidation of C-11 to a ketone (loss of two H's and gain of one O); relocation of a double bond from C-5/C-6 to C-4/C-5 (loss of one H by C-4 and gain of one H by C-6); replacement of the —H at C-17 by an —OH; replacement of the side-chain at C-17 with the shorter side-chain —$COCH_2OH$.

20.39 Cyclodecene $C_{10}H_{18}$ has 10 carbon atoms bonded in a cycle. One of the 10 connections is a double bond. In the following, only the H's on the double bonded carbon atoms are shown explicitly. In the *cis* isomer these two H's are on the same side of the ring. The figure shows this by representing the bonds to these H's with thicker lines. In the *trans* isomer, these two H's are or opposite sides of the ring. The nearer bond is shown by a thicker line and the more distance bond by a thinner line.

cis 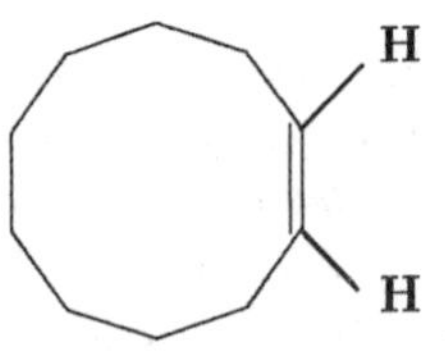 *trans* 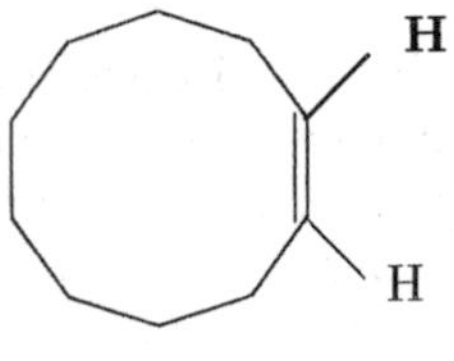

20.41 Rewrite the formula of the compound C_3H_5OH to recognize that it is an alcohol (contains an —OH group). The fragment C_3H_5 does not contain enough H to have a straight-chain alkane; C_3H_7 would be required. Inserting a double bond would reduce the number of H atoms by 2,but double bonds are ruled out. The only other way to reduce the number of H atoms is to allow formation of a ring. The compound is cyclopropanol.

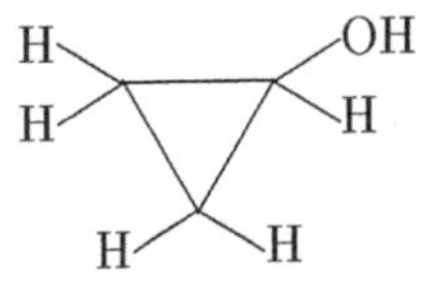

20.43 (a) The statement of the problem makes it clear that the only reactants and products in this acetylation reaction are X, acetyl chloride, Y, and HCl. The equation for the reaction is therefore

$$C_4H_8O_3 + n\ CH_3COCl \rightarrow C_8H_{12}O_5 + n\ HCl$$

The only value of n that balances this equation is 2. Therefore compound X contains two hydroxyl groups.
(b) A possible structure if compound X is an aldehyde is

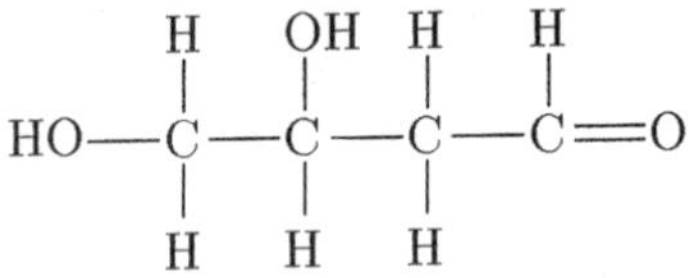

In compound Y, the —OH groups on carbons 3 and 4 are replaced by $—OCOCH_3$ groups.

20.45 The unsaturated hydrocarbon must have a straight-chain skeleton of six carbon atoms because it gives straight-chain hexane when reduced with hydrogen gas. Oxidation at the double bond splits it to a four-carbon acid (butanoic acid) and a two-carbon acid (acetic acid). The double bond is therefore at the 2 position: $CH_3—CH_2—CH_2—CH{=}CH—CH_3$. The compound is 2-hexene. This compound has *cis* and *trans* isomers, but the available data do not allow a decision about which isomer is present. The balanced equations are:

$$C_6H_{12}(l) + H_2(g) \rightarrow C_6H_{14}(l)$$

$$27\,H_3O^+(aq) + 9\,MnO_4^-(aq) + 5\,C_6H_{12}(l) \rightarrow 9\,Mn^{2+}(aq) + 5\,C_4H_8O_2(aq) + 5\,C_2H_3O_2(aq) + 43\,H_2O(l)$$

20.47 The conjugate acid of tertiary amine R_3N has the formula R_3NH^+. The bulk of the R groups in this ion impairs its interaction with the solvent (water) compared to H_3NH^+, which is the conjugate acid of NH_3. On the basis of steric effects, a tertiary amine R_3N should be a weaker base than ammonia.

Tip. Tertiary amines are in fact usually stronger bases than ammonia. For example, $(C_2H_5)_3N$ has a K_b of 9.6×10^{-4}, which is nearly a hundred times larger than the K_b of ammonia (1.8×10^{-5}). Steric effects are *not* the only factors affecting relative acidity and basicity.

20.49 Both pharmaceuticals and pesticides must be biologically active, preferably in as specific a manner as possible. The strategy for delivery of the compound to the target is similar: fooling the organism's own pathways for intake. Hence, mimicking the organism's natural chemicals is important. The use of both classes of compounds requires close attention to possible side-effects. Pharmaceuticals particularly are expected to do one thing in the body and one thing only. A pesticide on the other hand is expected to kill its target by any means. Consequently more modes of action are possible for pesticides. However, ill-effects of a pesticide on non-target organisms can be more adverse, either in the long-term or short-term, than the deprecations of the pest. Numerous pesticides are so toxic to desirable organisms that they may not be used.

20.51 **a)** The combustion reactions are:

$$C_7H_{16}(l) + 11\,O_2(g) \rightarrow 7\,CO_2(g) + 8\,H_2O(g) \quad \text{and} \quad C_8H_{18}(l) + 25/2\,O_2(g) \rightarrow 8\,CO_2(g) + 9\,H_2O(g)$$

The formulas of heptane and isooctane, which are liquids at room conditions, come from the text.[3] Take ΔH_f° data from text Appendix D as needed for the reactants and products other than the two fuels. Combine the ΔH_f°'s to get the ΔH°'s of the two combustions:

$$\Delta H_1^\circ = 8\underbrace{(-241.82)}_{H_2O(g)} + 7\underbrace{(-393.51)}_{CO_2(g)} - 11\underbrace{(0)}_{O_2(g)} - 1\underbrace{(-187.82)}_{\text{heptane}(l)} = \boxed{-4501.31\text{ kJ}}$$

$$\Delta H_2^\circ = 9\underbrace{(-241.82)}_{H_2O(g)} + 8\underbrace{(-393.51)}_{CO_2(g)} - \frac{25}{2}\underbrace{(0)}_{O_2(g)} - 1\underbrace{(-224.13)}_{\text{isooctane}(l)} = \boxed{-5100.33\text{ kJ}}$$

b) The combustion of 1 mol of isooctane clearly produces much more heat (ΔH_2°) than the combustion of 1 mol of heptane (ΔH_1°). The question however concerns the comparison of the ΔH°'s per gallon of the two fuels:

$$\frac{-4501.31\text{ kJ}}{1\text{ mol heptane}} \times \left(\frac{1\text{ mol heptane}}{100.21\text{ g heptane}}\right) \times \left(\frac{453.59\text{ g}}{1\text{ lb}}\right) \times \left(\frac{5.71\text{ lb}}{1\text{ gal}}\right) = \frac{-1.16\times 10^5\text{ kJ}}{1\text{ gal}}$$

$$\frac{-5100.31\text{ kJ}}{1\text{ mol octane}} \times \frac{1\text{ mol octane}}{114.23\text{ g octane}} \times \frac{453.59\text{ g}}{1\text{ lb}} \times \frac{5.77\text{ lb}}{1\text{ gal}} = \frac{-1.17\times 10^5\text{ kJ}}{1\text{ gal}}$$

The $\boxed{\text{isooctane}}$ produces slightly more heat per gallon.

20.53 **a)** The ΔH° of the reaction $6\,C(g) + 6\,H(g) \rightarrow C_6H_6(g)$ equals the ΔH_f°'s of the products minus the ΔH_f°'s of the reactants:

$$\Delta H^\circ = 1\underbrace{(82.93)}_{C_6H_6(g)} - 6\underbrace{(716.682)}_{C(g)} - 6\underbrace{(217.96)}_{H(g)} = \boxed{-5524.92\text{ kJ}}$$

Neither of the ΔH_f°'s of the reactants equals zero because gaseous monatomic H and gaseous C are *not* the standard states of these two elements. The answer is an experimental result; it is based on experimental ΔH_f°'s and Hess's law.

b) The formation of 1 mol of $C_6H_6(g)$ with alternating double and single bonds requires the formation of 6 mol of C—H bonds, 3 mol of C=C bonds, and 3 mol of C—C bonds. The negative of the sum of the bond dissociation enthalpies of these bonds is $\boxed{-5367\text{ kJ}}$.

c) The resonance stabilization in 1 mol of benzene equals the difference between the ΔH° expected and the ΔH° observed: $(-5367) - (-5524.92) = \boxed{158\text{ kJ}}$.

20.55 Conjugation of multiple bonds (π delocalization) tends to increase the wavelength of the absorbed light in electronic transitions. Hence, we expect cyclohexene to absorb at $\boxed{\text{shorter}}$ wavelengths than benzene because the π bonding is localized in cyclohexene and delocalized in benzene.

---

[3] Text Table 20.21, text page 715.

20.57 Ethanol has a high boiling point compared to its isomer dimethyl ether because the intermolecular forces among its molecules are stronger. The structure CH_3CH_2—O—H contains an H bonded to a highly electronegative atom and so allows hydrogen bonds. The structure H_3COCH_3 does not. Similarly, CH_2F_2 molecules are inherently polar, allowing fairly strong interactions between the positive end of one and the negative one of another. CF_4 molecules are non-polar.

Chapter 21

Structure and Bonding in Solids

21.1 a) One side in an isosceles triangle is non-equivalent to the other two; no 3-fold rotation axis exists.

b A 3-fold axis passes through the center of an equilateral triangle.

c) A 3-fold axis passes through the center of each of the four triangular faces in a tetrahedron and out through the opposite vertex.

d) A 3-fold axis passes along each of the four long diagonals of a cube, that is, from each vertex to the most distant opposite vertex.

21.3 The CCl_2F_2 molecule has $\boxed{\text{two mirror planes}}$. The first is defined by the two Cl atoms and the central C atom, and the second is defined by the two F atoms and the central C atom. The intersection of the two mirror planes coincides with a $\boxed{\text{single 2-fold axis}}$ of rotation. This axis passes through the central C atom and bisects the angles defined Cl—C—Cl and F—C—F.

21.5 The Bragg law $n\lambda = 2d \sin\theta$ becomes in this case:

$$2(1.660 \text{ Å}) = 2d \sin\left(\frac{54.70°}{2}\right) \quad \text{from which} \quad d = \frac{1.660 \text{ Å}}{\sin 27.35°} = \boxed{3.613 \text{ Å}}$$

21.7 The Bragg law $n\lambda = 2d \sin\theta$ becomes:

$$4(1.936 \text{ Å}) = 2(4.950 \text{ Å}) \sin\theta$$

where $n = 4$ comes from the specification of fourth-order diffraction and 4.950 Å is the interplanar spacing. Solving gives θ equal to 51.46° and 2θ equal to $\boxed{102.9°}$.

Tip. The angle 128.54° (180 − 51.46°) also fulfills the equation. This gives $2\theta = 257.1°$, which is equivalent to −102.9°. This corresponds to "reflection" from the other side of the layers of atoms.

21.9 Solve the Bragg law for 2θ and substitute the values given for this case of diffraction by crystalline LiCl:

$$2\theta = 2\sin^{-1}\left(\frac{n\lambda}{2d}\right) = 2\sin^{-1}\left(\frac{n\,2.167 \text{ Å}}{2(2.570 \text{ Å})}\right) = 2\sin^{-1}(0.4216n)$$

Inserting integers for n gives 2θ equal to $\boxed{49.87°}$ for $n = 1$ and 2θ equal to $\boxed{115.0°}$ for $n = 2$. Higher values of n lead to arguments of $\sin^{-1}$ that exceed 1.00. The inverse sine function is not defined in such cases. Consequently 2θ has only the four possible values.

21.11 **a)** The cell angles are all 90°, because the crystal is tetragonal. Then:

$$V_{\text{cell}} = abc = (223.5)^2(113.6) = \boxed{5.675 \times 10^6 \text{ Å}^3}$$

b) The volume of the box-shaped crystal is likewise the product of the lengths of the three edges. It equals 3 mm^3—small, but easily visible with the unaided eye. To compare the two volumes divide one by the other and use a suitable unit factor to make sure the units cancel out:

$$\frac{V_{\text{crystal}}}{V_{\text{cell}}} = \frac{3 \text{ mm}^3}{5.675 \times 10^6 \text{ Å}^3} \times \left(\frac{1 \text{ Å}^3}{10^{-21} \text{ mm}^3}\right) = \boxed{5 \times 10^{14}}$$

This ratio equals the number of units cells in the crystal.

21.13 Compute the mass of the contents of the unit cell and divide it by the volume of the cell to obtain the density of the cell. Since the substance consists of many copies of the unit cell side-by-side, this result is the density of the whole crystal. The mass of the contents of the unit cell equals twice the mass of a single formula unit of $Pb_4In_3B_{17}S_{18}$:

$$m_{\text{contents}} = 2 \times 1934.235 = 3868.47 \text{ u}$$

The volume of the cell is

$$V_c = abc\sqrt{1 - \cos^2\alpha - \cos^2\beta - \cos^2\gamma + 2\cos\alpha\cos\beta\cos\gamma} = abc\sqrt{1-\cos^2\beta} = abc\sin\beta$$
$$= (21.021 \text{ Å})(4.014 \text{ Å})(18.989 \text{ Å})\,(0.9924) = 1582.46 \text{ Å}^3$$

The density is then:

$$\rho = \frac{m}{V} = \frac{3868.47 \text{ u}}{1582.46 \text{ Å}^3} \times \left(\frac{10^{24} \text{ Å}^3}{1 \text{ cm}^3}\right) \times \left(\frac{1 \text{ g}}{6.022 \times 10^{23} \text{ u}}\right) = \boxed{4.059 \text{ g cm}^{-3}}$$

The two unit-factors take the answer from an unfamiliar unit of density to a familiar one.

21.15 **a)** The volume of the cubical unit cell in elemental silicon is just the edge of the cell cubed. It equals (5.431 Å)^3, which is 160.19 Å^3. There are 10^8 Å in a centimeter and consequently 10^{24} Å^3 in a cubic centimeter. Hence:

$$\frac{160.19 \text{ Å}^3}{1 \text{ unit cell}} \times \left(\frac{1 \text{ cm}^3}{10^{24} \text{ Å}^3}\right) = \boxed{1.602 \times 10^{-22} \frac{\text{cm}^3}{\text{unit cell}}}$$

b) The mass of the contents of the unit cell of crystalline silicon equals the volume of the unit cell multiplied by its density:

$$\frac{1.602 \times 10^{-22} \text{ cm}^3}{\text{unit cell}} \times \left(\frac{2.328 \text{ g Si}}{1 \text{ cm}^3}\right) = \boxed{\frac{3.729 \times 10^{-22} \text{ g Si}}{\text{unit cell}}}$$

c) The unit cell contains eight atoms of silicon for a total mass of 3.729×10^{-22} g. Consequently, a single atom has a mass of $\boxed{4.662 \times 10^{-23} \text{ g}}$.

d) One mole of silicon contains Avogadro's number of atoms of silicon. The molar mass of silicon is 28.0855 g mol^{-1}. Divide this molar mass by the single-atom mass of silicon to obtain Avogadro's number:

$$\frac{28.0855 \text{ g mol}^{-1}}{4.662 \times 10^{-23} \text{ g}} = \boxed{6.025 \times 10^{23} \text{ mol}^{-1}} = N_0$$

This is only about 0.05% larger than the accepted value.

21.17 The volume V_c of the unit cell in sodium sulfate equals the product of its three cell edges. a, b, and c. This follows because the term under the radical sign in text equation 21.2[1] equals 1. Hence V_c is 708.47 Å^3, which is 7.0847×10^{-22} cm^3. The volume of a mole of unit cells of sodium sulfate is Avogadro's number times the volume of one cell:

$$(7.0847 \times 10^{-22}\ \text{cm}^3) \times (6.022 \times 10^{23}\ \text{mol}^{-1}) = 426.6\ \text{cm}^3\ \text{mol}^{-1}$$

The density of a unit cell equals the density of the substance itself since a crystal consists of many unit cells stacked side by side. Multiplying the volume of a mole of unit cells by the density of the substance gives the mass of a mole of unit cells:

$$\left(\frac{426.6\ \text{cm}^3}{1\ \text{mol}}\right) \times \left(\frac{2.663\ \text{g}}{1\ \text{cm}^3}\right) = 1136.1\ \text{g mol}^{-1}$$

The molar mass of the formula unit Na_2SO_4 is 142.04 g mol^{-1}. This is far less than 1136.1 g mol^{-1}. The unit cell must hold several formula units. Because 142.04 is almost exactly 1/8th of 1136.1, it follows that each unit cell contains $\boxed{8}$ Na_2SO_4 formula units.

Tip. The unit cell contains 56 atoms. Obviously, all of these atoms cannot reside at the corners of the unit cell. They are in fact distributed throughout the volume of the cell.

21.19 In this crystalline compound, rhenium atoms lie at the eight corners of the unit cell, and oxygen atoms lie at the 12 edges. Start by figuring out the number of atoms of Re and O per cell: each cell has 1 rhenium atom ($8 \times 1/8$) and 3 oxygen atoms ($12 \times 1/4$). The 1/8 and 1/4 appear because every corner of a unit cell is shared among a total of eight cells and every edge is shared among four cells. The ratio of these numbers gives the empirical formula because the compound is composed of many repeats of the unit cell. The chemical formula therefore is $\boxed{ReO_3}$.

Tip. Another way to explore the locations of the atoms is with fractional coordinates. The equivalent Re atoms have these coordinates:

$$(0,0,0)\quad(1,0,0)\quad(0,1,0)\quad(0,0,1)\quad(1,1,1)\quad(0,1,1)\quad(1,0,1)\quad(1,1,0)$$

These are the corners of the cube in text Figure 21.13.[2] The O atoms at the centers of the cell edges have these fractional coordinates:

$$\begin{array}{cccc} (\frac{1}{2},0,0) & (0,\frac{1}{2},0) & (\frac{1}{2},1,0) & (1,\frac{1}{2},0) \\ (0,0,\frac{1}{2}) & (1,0,\frac{1}{2}) & (0,1,\frac{1}{2}) & (1,1,\frac{1}{2}) \\ (\frac{1}{2},0,1) & (0,\frac{1}{2},1) & (\frac{1}{2},1,1) & (1,\frac{1}{2},1) \end{array}$$

Only three of these locations are distinct. The nine containing a 1 are translations ("one cell over") of these three.

21.21 a) A body-centered cubic structure means two Fe atoms per unit cell, one in the center of the cell and one at each of the eight corners of the cell (each corner atom is shared by seven neighboring cells). The two atoms have a total mass of 111.694 u and touch along the body diagonal of the cell, but not along the edges. Compute the volume of the unit cell by multiplying its mass by its density:

$$V_c = 111.694\ \text{u Fe} \times \left(\frac{1\ \text{g Fe}}{6.0221 \times 10^{23}\ \text{u Fe}}\right) \times \left(\frac{1\ \text{cm}^3}{7.86\ \text{g Fe}}\right) = 2.36 \times 10^{-23}\ \text{cm}^3$$

The edge a of the cubic unit cell is the cube root of the volume. It is 2.87×10^{-8} cm, which is 2.87 Å. The nearest-neighbor distance is one-half the body diagonal b of the unit cell. The body diagonal is related to the edge as follows:

$$b = \sqrt{3}e = \sqrt{3}(2.87\ \text{Å}) = 4.97\ \text{Å}$$

---

[1] Text page 755.
[2] Text page 755.

Hence nearest neighbors are $\boxed{2.48\ \text{Å}}$ apart.

b) The lattice parameter equals $\boxed{2.87\ \text{Å}}$, the cubic cell's edge. See above.

c) The atomic radius of Fe equals one quarter of the body diagonal of the unit cell because Fe atoms are "in contact" along this diagonal. It is therefore $\boxed{1.24\ \text{Å}}$.[3]

21.23 a) A body-centered cubic lattice has two lattice points per unit cell. In metallic sodium, one Na atom is associated with each lattice point to give $\boxed{\text{two}}$ Na atoms per cell.

b) Let r_{Na} equal the radius of the Na atom. In the crystal, Na atoms touch along the body diagonal b of the cubic cell, which has atoms at its corners and center. This means $4r_{\text{Na}} = b$. But b is $\sqrt{3}$ times the edge of the cell. Hence $4r_{\text{Na}} = \sqrt{3}e$. Cubing this equation gives

$$64r_{\text{Na}}^3 = 3\sqrt{3}e^3$$

The volume of the cell V_c is e^3. The volume of a single Na atom is $4/3\pi(r_{\text{Na}})^3$, and, obviously, two Na atoms have twice this volume:

$$V_c = e^3 \quad \text{and} \quad V_{2\text{Na}} = 2 \times \left(\frac{4\pi(r_{\text{Na}})^3}{3}\right)$$

Solving these equations for e^3 and $(r_{\text{Na}})^3$ respectively and substituting into the equation that precedes them gives:

$$64\left(\frac{3V_{2\text{Na}}}{8\pi}\right) = 3\sqrt{3}V_c \qquad \text{from which} \qquad \left(\frac{V_{2\text{Na}}}{V_c}\right) = \frac{(3\sqrt{3})(8\pi)}{3(64)} = \boxed{0.680}$$

Tip. This is not the most efficient packing of equal spheres. Putting the spheres at the lattice points of a face-centered cubic lattice, gives a more efficient packing (cubic close packing).

21.25 The atoms making up the simple cubic array are the host atoms. These atoms touch along the edges of the cubic unit cell. A guest interstitial atom sits hole at the center of the host unit cell. The body diagonal b of the host unit cell runs between two diagonally opposite host atoms and passes along the diameter of the guest atom. If the guest is as large as it can be without pushing the host atoms out of contact, then:

$$e = 2r_{\text{host}} \qquad b = 2r_{\text{host}} + 2r_{\text{guest}}$$

But the body diagonal of a cube is longer than the edge by a factor of $\sqrt{3}$: Hence:

$$2r_{\text{host}} + 2r_{\text{guest}} = \sqrt{3}\,(2r_{\text{host}}) \qquad \text{so that:} \qquad \frac{r_{\text{guest}}}{r_{\text{host}}} = \sqrt{3} - 1 = \boxed{0.732}$$

21.27 Use electronegativity differences and position in the periodic table.
a) $BaCl_2$–ionic **b)** SiC–covalent **c)** CO–molecular **d)** Co–metallic.

21.29 The network solid SiC should have the highest melting point, and the metallic solid Co should have the second highest. The melting point of the ionic solid $BaCl_2$ should exceed the melting point of the molecular solid CO. The data on the melting points of Co and $BaCl_2$ links these two pairs. Hence $\boxed{\text{CO} < \text{BaCl}_2 < \text{Co} < \text{SiC}}$.

21.31 Consider the various possibilities for the "typical atom" in a crystal. Suppose that it can form zero chemical bonds. Then the only forces available to maintain the crystal are van der Waals forces, which are weaker than chemical bonds. The absence of strong interatomic attractions leads to mechanically weak (soft) crystals of low melting point. If the typical atom forms one bond, then strongly bonded diatomic molecules

[3] This answer equals the value tabulated in Appendix F.

form, but again the crystals are soft and low-melting because the formation of pairs of atoms uses up the atoms' bonding capacity. If the typical atom forms two bonds, then strong linear (thread-like) structures are possible. If the typical atom forms three or more bonds, then it is possible for such threads to cross-link to give two dimensional or three dimensional networks.

21.33 In the simple cubic CsCl lattice, the positive ion has $\boxed{8}$ Cl^- ions as nearest neighbors. The second nearest neighbors are a set of $\boxed{6}$ Cs^+ ions, and the third nearest neighbors are a set of $\boxed{12}$ yet more distant Cs^+ ions.

To obtain this answer, imagine a Cs^+ ion at the center of a home cell that has Cl^- ions on its eight corners. These are the 8 nearest-neighbor Cl^- ions. The home cell has 6 faces and 12 edges. The 6 second-nearest neighbors are the Cs^+ ions at the centers of the 6 face-adjoining unit cells. The 12 third-nearest neighbors are the Cs^+ ions at the centers of the 12 edge-adjoining cells.

Tip. Avoid getting bogged down using messy sketches to count neighbors and decide which neighbors are nearer. A better way uses fractional coordinates. Define an origin $(0,0,0)$ at the Cs^+ ion at the center of the home cell. In fractional coordinates, the edges of the unit cell are used as units of length. This puts a Cl^- ion at coordinates $(\frac{1}{2},\frac{1}{2},\frac{1}{2})$. The cubic symmetry means that the x, y and z coordinates are equivalent and that the plus and minus directions on each coordinate are equivalent, too. Permuting equivalent fractional coordinates and changing the signs of the fractional coordinates therefore generate equivalent locations. For $(\frac{1}{2},\frac{1}{2},\frac{1}{2})$ the following eight sets of coordinates result from these operations:

$$\begin{matrix} (+\frac{1}{2},+\frac{1}{2},+\frac{1}{2}) & (-\frac{1}{2},+\frac{1}{2},+\frac{1}{2}) & (+\frac{1}{2},-\frac{1}{2},+\frac{1}{2}) & (+\frac{1}{2},+\frac{1}{2},-\frac{1}{2}) \\ (-\frac{1}{2},-\frac{1}{2},-\frac{1}{2}) & (+\frac{1}{2},-\frac{1}{2},-\frac{1}{2}) & (-\frac{1}{2},+\frac{1}{2},-\frac{1}{2}) & (-\frac{1}{2},-\frac{1}{2},+\frac{1}{2}) \end{matrix}$$

These are the coordinates of the 8 nearest neighbors of the Cs^+ ion. The 6 second-nearest neighbors have these coordinates:

$$(0,0,1) \quad (0,1,0) \quad (1,0,0) \quad (0,0,-1) \quad (0,-1,0) \quad (-1,0,0)$$

And the 12 third-nearest neighbors have these coordinates:

$$\begin{matrix} (0,1,1) & (0,1,-1) & (0,-1,1) & (0,-1,-1) & (1,0,1) & (1,0,-1) \\ (-1,0,1) & (-1,0,-1) & (1,1,0) & (1,-1,0) & (-1,1,0) & (-1,-1,0) \end{matrix}$$

In this description of CsCl, triples that contain any half-integers locate Cl^- ions, and triples that contain all whole numbers locate Cs^+ ions. Also, fractional coordinates make it easier to compute interatomic distances in a lattice. For a cubic crystal the distance d between two points (x_1,y_1,z_1) and (x_2,y_2,z_2) specified in fractional coordinates equals:

$$d = a\sqrt{(x_2-x_1)^2+(y_2-y_1)^2+(z_2-z_1)^2}$$

where a equals the edge of the cubic cell.

21.35 The problem requests computation of the lattice energy of $RbCl(s)$. The electrostatic (Coulomb) lattice energy of a crystal is given by:

$$\text{Lattice energy} = \frac{N_0 e^2}{4\pi\epsilon_0 R_0} M$$

where M is the Madelung constant and R_0 is the distance between neighboring ions. Substitute the correct values for $RbCl(s)$. The Madelung constant quoted in the problem is for the rock-salt structure, which is the structure of $RbCl(s)$; R_0 equals the sum of the radii of the Rb^+ and Cl^- ions, which is 3.29 Å, or 3.29×10^{-10} m:

$$\text{Lattice energy} = \frac{(6.022\times10^{23}\ \text{mol}^{-1})(1.602\times10^{-19}\ \text{C})^2}{4\pi(8.854\times10^{-12}\ \text{C}^2\,\text{J}^{-1}\text{m}^{-1})(3.29\times10^{-10}\ \text{m})} 1.7476 = 738\times10^3\ \text{J mol}^{-1}$$

Reducing this energy by 10% to account for non-Coulomb effects gives $\boxed{664 \text{ kJ mol}^{-1}}$ for the dissociation energy of RbCl(s). The experimental value is 680 kJ mol^{-1}.

21.37 a) The lattice energy of LiF(s) equals the energy change of the reaction:

$$\text{LiF}(s) \rightarrow \text{Li}^+(g) + \text{F}^-(g) \qquad \text{lattice energy} = \Delta E$$

Direct experimental measurement of this ΔE is not possible. The Born-Haber cycle is a series of lesser steps taking place at 25°C that add up to the above change. The ΔE of each step *can* be measured. The steps are:

1. Decomposition of LiF(s) to give Li(s) and $F_2(g)$;
2. Vaporization of Li(s) to Li(g) and dissociation of $F_2(g)$ to F(g);
3. Transfer of electrons from Li(g) to F(g) to give $F^-(g)$ ions and $Li^+(g)$ ions.

Apply the first law of thermodynamics to this cycle:

$$\Delta E_{\text{cycle}} = \Delta E_1 + \Delta E_2 + \Delta E_3$$

Evaluate ΔE_3 first. It equals the first ionization energy of Li(g) minus the electron affinity of F(g):

$$\Delta E_3 = 520 - 328 = 192 \text{ kJ mol}^{-1}$$

ΔE_2 is the energy change accompanying the vaporization of Li(g) to Li(s) plus the energy change accompanying the dissociation of $F_2(g)$ into atoms. The $\Delta H°$'s for these processes (text Appendix D) equal 159.37 kJ mol^{-1} and 78.99 kJ mol^{-1} respectively. The tabulated $\Delta H°$'s are not the same as the desired ΔE's, but are related as follows:

$$\Delta E = \Delta H° - RT\Delta n_{\text{g}} = \Delta H° - (2.48 \text{ kJ mol}^{-1})\Delta n_{\text{g}} \qquad \text{(at 298 K)}$$

For Li(s) $\rightarrow$ Li(g), Δn_{g} is +1. It follows that:

$$\Delta E_{\text{vap}} = 159.37 - (2.48)(1) = (159.37 - 2.48) \text{ kJ mol}^{-1}$$

For the dissociation $1/2\, F_2(g) \rightarrow F(g)$, Δn_{g} is +1/2. Therefore:

$$\Delta E_{\text{dissoc}} = 78.99 - (2.48)(1/2) = (78.99 - 1.24) \text{ kJ mol}^{-1}$$

Adding the two parts of step 2:

$$\Delta E_2 = (159.37 - 2.48) + (78.99 - 1.24) = 234.64 \text{ kJ mol}^{-1}$$

The first step in the cycle was the decomposition of one mole of LiF(s) to form one mole of Li(s) and one-half mole of $F_2(g)$:

$$\text{LiF}(s) \rightarrow \text{Li}(s) + \frac{1}{2}\text{F}_2(g) \qquad \Delta H° = +615.97 \text{ kJ mol}^{-1}$$

This reaction is the exact "un-formation" of LiF. Its $\Delta H°$ is therefore the negative of the standard enthalpy of formation of LiF(s) from Appendix D. Again, compute the energy change from the energy change and the change in volume:

$$\Delta E_3 = \Delta H_3° - RT\Delta n_{\text{g}} = +615.97 - (2.48)(1/2) = 614.73 \text{ kJ mol}^{-1}$$

Add up the ΔE's for the three steps in the cycle:

$$\Delta E_{\text{cycle}} = 192 + 234.64 + 614.73 = \boxed{1041 \text{ kJ mol}^{-1}}$$

b) The computation of the Coulomb contribution to the lattice energy of LiF(s) follows the pattern of **21.35**:

$$\text{Lattice energy} = \frac{N_0 e^2}{4\pi\epsilon_0 R_0} M$$

where M is the Madelung constant and R_0 is the distance between neighboring positive and negative ions. For lithium fluoride R_0 is 2.014 Å, or 2.014×10^{-10} m.[4] Obtain the M for rock salt from Table 21.5. Then:

$$\text{Lattice energy} = \frac{(6.022 \times 10^{23}\ \text{mol}^{-1})(1.602 \times 10^{-19}\ \text{C})^2}{4\pi(8.854 \times 10^{-12}\ \text{C}^2\,\text{J}^{-1}\text{m}^{-1})(2.014 \times 10^{-10}\ \text{m})} 1.7476 = \boxed{1205 \times 10^3\ \text{J mol}^{-1}}$$

This (theoretical) Coulomb energy is about 15 percent larger than the (experimental) Born-Haber lattice energy. The discrepancy arises because the Coulomb calculation ignores non-Coulomb interactions.

Tip. In part a), if the $\Delta n_g RT$ corrections in step 2 and 3 are omitted, the answer comes out 1046 kJ mol^{-1}. The difference is less than 1%. In view of the experimental uncertainty of many ΔE values, taking ΔE to equal ΔH is often defensible. Also, the cycle is performed at 298.15 K, but the lattice energy is defined at 0 K.

21.39 The presence of Frenkel defects will $\boxed{\text{not change}}$ the density of a crystal by a significant amount, because the vacancies at lattice sites are compensated for by interstitial atoms. Frenkel defects in large numbers might cause a small bulging of the crystal and a consequential decrease in its density.

21.41 a) A sample of 100 g of this iron(II) oxide contains 76.55 g of Fe and 23.45 g of O. This corresponds to 1.3707 mol of Fe and 1.4657 mol of O. Dividing one by the other gives the formulas $FeO_{1.0693}$ or $\boxed{Fe_{0.9352}O}$. It is improper to round off to the stoichiometric formula FeO. The experimental analysis is precise to four significant figures, and the chemical formula should have the same precision.

b) Let a equal the fraction of sites occupied by Fe^{3+} ions and b equal the fraction of sites occupied by Fe^{2+} ions. The Fe^{3+} ions that occur in Fe^{2+} sites compensate with their extra charge for missing Fe^{2+} ions elsewhere and make the compound as a whole electrically neutral. The average positive charge per site must be 2. Also the sum of a and b is 0.9352, as shown by the empirical formula. In equation form this means:

$$3a + 2b = 2 \quad \text{and} \quad a + b = 0.9352$$

Solution of these simultaneous equations gives $a = 0.1296$. This equals the fraction of sites occupied by Fe^{3+} ions. The fraction of the iron in the +3 state is the fraction of sites having +3 iron divided by the fraction having iron of either kind: $0.1296/0.9352 = \boxed{0.1386}$.

21.43 The entropy of the $\boxed{\text{isotropic phase}}$ (the liquid phase) exceeds the entropy in the smectic liquid crystal phase of a substance. Compare the degrees of order apparent in text Figure 21.31a and 21.31b. The enthalpy of the $\boxed{\text{isotropic phase}}$ exceeds that of the smectic phase because heating the smectic phase converts it to the isotropic phase.

21.45 A micelle should form, one containing the hydrocarbon in the interior and water on the outside.

21.47 The Bragg law $n\lambda = 2d \sin\theta$ becomes, in this case of first-order diffraction of water waves:

$$1(3.00\ \text{m}) = 2(5.00\ \text{m}) \sin\theta$$

Solving for θ gives 17.46° so 2θ is $\boxed{35°}$.

---

[4] The ionic radii of Li^+ and F^- ions are 0.68 and 1.33 (text Appendix F). The ratio of these radii is 0.51, which confirms that LiF(s) adopts the rock-salt structure.

21.49 **a)** The unit-cell volume V_c of NaCl is the cell edge cubed or $\boxed{179.43 \text{ Å}^3}$.

b) The volume V_p of the primitive unit cell of NaCl equals one-fourth of the volume of the conventional unit cell or $\boxed{44.856 \text{ Å}^3}$.

c) For relatively long wavelength (2.2896 Å) x-rays:

$$N_{\text{beams}} = \frac{4}{3}\pi\left(\frac{2}{\lambda}\right)^3 V_p = \frac{4}{3}\pi\left(\frac{2}{2.2896 \text{ Å}}\right)^3 (44.856 \text{ Å}^3) = \boxed{125}$$

d) For short wavelength (0.7093 Å) x-rays, there are far more diffracted beams.

$$N_{\text{beams}} = \frac{4}{3}\pi\left(\frac{2}{\lambda}\right)^3 V_p = \frac{4}{3}\pi\left(\frac{2}{0.7093 \text{ Å}}\right)^3 (44.856 \text{ Å}^3) = \boxed{4212}$$

21.51 In diamond the C—C bond distance equals the distance between any two nearest-neighbor atoms. Reviewing the list of coordinates given in the problem shows one such pair of atoms is the C at $(0, 0, 0)$ and the C at $(\frac{1}{4}, \frac{1}{4}, \frac{1}{4})$. This is also clear in Figure 21.23 in the text. Other pairs of carbons are equally close but none is closer. These carbons are separated by one-fourth of the body diagonal of the unit cell. The body diagonal is $\sqrt{3}$ times the edge of the cell or $3.57\sqrt{3}$ Å. The bond distance is 1/4 of this or $\boxed{1.55 \text{ Å}}$.

21.53 **a)** The cell is monoclinic so two of the three cell angles automatically equal 90°.

b) The volume of the cell is

$$V_c = abc\sqrt{1 - \cos^2\alpha - \cos^2\beta - \cos^2\gamma + 2\cos\alpha\cos\beta\cos\gamma}$$

Because both α and γ are 90°, this becomes (with the use of the trigonometric identity $\sin^2\beta + \cos^2\beta = 1$):

$$V_c = abc\sqrt{1 - \cos^2\beta} = abc\sin\beta = (11.04)(10.98)(10.92)\sin 96.73° = 1314.6 \text{ Å}^3$$

The volume equals 1.3146×10^{-21} cm³. The density is then computed as follows:

$$\rho = \frac{n_{\text{S atoms}}\mathcal{M}_{\text{S}}}{N_0 V_c} = \frac{48(32.066 \text{ g mol}^{-1})}{(6.022 \times 10^{23})(1.3146 \times 10^{-21} \text{ cm}^3)} = \boxed{1.944 \text{ g cm}^{-3}}$$

21.55 Any tetrahedral interstitial site can be viewed as occupying the center of a cube that has every other one of its eight corners occupied by spherical atoms of radius r_1. Let the edge of such a cube have length 1. Then the face diagonal f has length $\sqrt{2}$ and the body diagonal b has length $\sqrt{3}$. The four atoms at the alternate corners surround the center and touch each other along the face diagonals of the cube. Therefore:

$$2r_1 = \sqrt{2}$$

Let r_2 be the radius of a spherical atom placed at the interstitial site, the center of the cube. The largest such atom will just touch all four atoms at the corners. The body diagonal in that case equals the sum of the diameters of the two atoms:

$$2r_1 + 2r_2 = b = \sqrt{3}$$

Dividing the second equation by the first gives:

$$\frac{(r_1 + r_2)}{r_1} = \frac{\sqrt{3}}{\sqrt{2}} \quad \text{hence} \quad 1 + \frac{r_2}{r_1} = 1.225$$

Since r_2/r_1 is 0.225, the largest possible value for r_2 is $\boxed{0.225 r_1}$.

21.57 Non-metals like sulfur and the halogens (fluorine, chlorine, bromine, iodine) form molecular crystals in the their solid states; metals like the transition metals (iron, nickel, etc.) and the alkali metals (lithium, sodium, potassium, rubidium, cesium) form metallic crystals. Elements at the center of the periodic table (in Group IV) such as carbon and silicon form covalent crystals.

21.59 a) According to the equations developed in the text[5], the potential energy and intermolecular distance in a face-centered-cubic molecular crystal depend on the Lennard-Jones parameters for the molecules comprising the crystal as follows:

$$R_0 \approx 1.09\sigma \qquad \text{and} \qquad V_{\text{tot}} \approx -8.61\epsilon N_0$$

where σ is the first Lennard-Jones parameter, R_0 is the equilibrium spacing (at 0 K), V_{tot} is the total potential energy of the lattice, and ϵ is the other Lennard-Jones parameter. For N_2, σ is 3.70 Å.[6] Therefore, R_0 is about $\boxed{4.03 \text{ Å}}$.
For N_2, ϵN_0 is 0.790 kJ mol^{-1}. The potential energy of the lattice is accordingly -6.80 kJ mol^{-1}. This makes $\boxed{+6.80 \text{ kJ mol}^{-1}}$ a reasonable estimate of the lattice energy.

b) The density of a crystal is related to the volume of its unit cell by:

$$\rho = \frac{n_c\mathcal{M}}{N_0 V_c}$$

For $N_2(s)$, ρ is 1.026 g cm^{-3}. The crystal has four N_2 molecules per unit cell and each molecule has a mass of 28.014 g mol^{-1}. Solve the preceding for V_c and substitute:

$$V_c = \frac{n_c\mathcal{M}}{N_0\rho} = \frac{4(28.014 \text{ g mol}^{-1})}{6.022 \times 10^{23} \text{ mol}^{-1}(1.026 \text{ g cm}^{-3})} = 181.36 \times 10^{-24} \text{ cm}^3$$

The edge of the cubic cell is the cube root of the volume of the cell. It equals $\boxed{5.660 \times 10^{-8} \text{ cm}}$ (5.660 Å). In a face-centered cubic cell, a nitrogen molecule lies at the center of every face of the cell and at every corner. The face diagonal is $5.660\sqrt{2}$ Å or 8.005 Å long. One-half of this is the distance from an N_2 at a face center to an N_2 at a face corner. This, the intermolecular distance, is $\boxed{4.002 \text{ Å}}$. This result is only about 0.7 percent less than the distance computed using the Lennard-Jones parameter. The good agreement tends to confirm the analysis in text Section 21.4.

21.61 Sodium chloride is an ionic solid. If there are Schottky defects, a fraction of the Na^+ sites is vacant. To maintain electrical neutrality an equal fraction of the Cl^- sites must be vacant. The density of defect-free NaCl is 2.165 g cm^{-3}. Introducing 0.0015 mole fraction of Schottky defects reduces the chemical amount of NaCl per cm^3 to 0.9985 of what had been. Therefore, the mass of NaCl per cm^3 is 0.9985 of what it had been, or $\boxed{2.162 \text{ g cm}^{-3}}$.
Frenkel defects involve displacement from a regular lattice site to an interstitial site. No mass is removed from the crystal, so the density stays at $\boxed{2.165 \text{ g cm}^{-3}}$ as long as the volume of the crystal is not changed.

21.63 a) The binary compound is 28.31 percent O and 71.69 percent Ti by mass. 100 g of the compound contains 1.4973 mol of Ti and 1.7694 mol of O. The formula is $Ti_{0.8462}O$ where the $\boxed{0.8462}$ equals the ratio of 1.4973 to 1.7694.

b) Only 0.8462 of the stoichiometric quantity of Ti is present; 0.1538 of the total Ti^{2+} sites then must be vacant. Let a equal the fraction of Ti^{2+} sites with a Ti^{3+} occupying them, and b the fraction of sites with a Ti^{2+}. Clearly: $a + b = 0.8462$. The net positive charge per oxygen must be +2. Each Ti^{3+} contributes

[5] Text page 765-766
[6] See text Table 4.4, text page 120.

+3 and each Ti^{2+} contributes +2. Electrical neutrality requires $3a + 2b = 2$. Solution of the simultaneous equations gives b equal to $\boxed{0.5386}$ and a equal to $\boxed{0.3026}$. About 30% of the Ti^{2+} sites contain a Ti^{3+} ion, about 15% are vacant, and about 54% contain a Ti^{2+}.

21.65 a) Use the deBroglie relation to obtain the wavelength of the neutrons:

$$\lambda = \frac{h}{m_n v} = \frac{6.626 \times 10^{-34} \text{ J s}}{(1.6750 \times 10^{-27} \text{ kg})(2.639 \times 10^3 \text{ m s}^{-1})} = \boxed{1.499 \times 10^{-10} \text{ m}}$$

b) The edge length of the unit cell is the interplanar spacing of the planes doing the scattering. Compute it by solving the Bragg law for d and substituting:

$$a = d = \frac{n\lambda}{2\sin\theta} = \frac{2(1.499 \times 10^{-10} \text{ m})}{2\sin(36.26°/2)} = 4.817 \times 10^{-10} \text{ m} = \boxed{4.817 \text{ Å}}$$

c) Sodium hydride adopts the rock-salt structure. Therefore, Na^+ and H^- ions touch along the edges of the unit cell. The Na^+ ions occupy the corners and center of each face of the cell, forming a pattern like the pattern of five dots on the face of die. Four H^- ions also lie in each face; they occupy the edges between Na^+ ions. The distance from the center of an Na^+ ion to the center of the adjoining H^- is therefore one-half of the edge of the unit cell. This equals $\boxed{2.409 \text{ Å}}$.

d) As established in slightly different words in the preceding, the edge e of the unit cell is the sum of two Na^+ radii and two H^- radii:

$$2r_{H^-} + 2r_{Na^+} = 4.817 \text{ Å}$$

Substitution of 0.98 Å for r_{Na^+} gives r_{H^-} equal to $\boxed{1.43 \text{ Å}}$.[7]

21.67 Applying the rule of thumb assigns each water molecule a volume of 18 $Å^3$. The mass of a water molecule is 18.02 u so the density of water would be 18.02 u/18 $Å^3$. Convert this density to g cm^{-3}:

$$\rho = \frac{18.02 \text{ u}}{18 \text{ Å}^3} \times \left(\frac{1 \text{ g}}{6.022 \times 10^{23} \text{ u}}\right) \times \left(\frac{10^{24} \text{ Å}^3}{1 \text{ cm}^3}\right) = \boxed{1.7 \text{ g cm}^{-3}}$$

The density based on the rule of thumb is much higher than the actual density of solid water (0.90 g cm^{-3}). The rule of thumb fails in this case because the hydrogen bonding in ice maintains an abnormally open structure.

[7] Text Appendix F tabulates a radius of 1.46 Å for H^- ion.

Chapter 22

Ceramic Materials

22.1 A Lewis structure for the disilicate ion $Si_2O_7^{6-}$ is

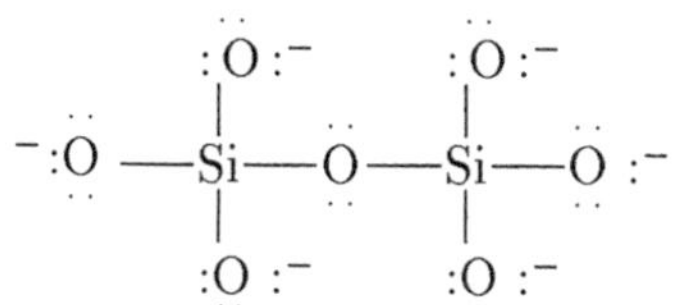

The six O atoms on the perimeter of the structure have three lone pairs and single bonds to an Si atom. All six have a formal charges of -1. The O atom linking the Si atoms has f.c. zero. The Si atoms also have f.c. zero. There are 56 valence electrons in the Lewis structure.

The $P_2O_7^{4-}$ and $S_2O_7^{2-}$ ions are isoelectronic (that is, they also have 56 valence electrons). The Lewis structure drawn above works for $P_2O_7^{4-}$ by simply replacing the Si's with P's. Both P's then have f.c. $+1$. Similarly, the Lewis structure appearing above works for $S_2O_7^{2-}$ ion by simply replacing the Si's with S's. Both S atoms then have f.c. $+2$. The analogous compound of chlorine is Cl_2O_7 (dichlorine heptaoxide). Again, the Si's in the above structure can be replaced, this time with Cl's. The two Cl atoms have f.c. $+3$.

Tip. Many additional resonances structures can be drawn if the octet rule is broken for the Si (or P or S) atoms in these structures. Such structures have one or more double bonds from O atoms to the central atoms. They increase the average bond order and lower the formal charge on the central atoms. See **3.77**.

22.3 In each part, determine the Si : O ratio for the network. Ignore O atoms found in other groups, such as OH^- groups. Then use text Table 22.2.[1]

a) Tetrahedra. Ca, $+2$; Fe, $+3$; Si, $+4$; O, -2.

b) Infinite sheets. Na, $+1$; Zr, $+2$; Si, $+4$; O, -2.

c) Pairs of tetrahedra. Ca, $+2$; Zn, $+2$; Si; $+4$; O, -2.

d) Infinite sheets. Mg, $+2$; Si, $+4$; O, -2; H, $+1$.

22.5 The problem is like the preceding except that Al atoms grouped in the formulas with the Si atoms are counted as Si atoms in determining the Si : O ratio.

a) Infinite network. Li, $+1$; Si, $+4$; Al, $+3$; O, -2.

b) Infinite sheets. K, $+1$; Al, $+3$; Si, $+4$; O, -2; H, $+1$.

c) Closed rings or infinite single chains. Al, $+3$; Mg, $+2$; Si, $+4$; O, -2.

22.7 The standard reduction potential for the half-reaction $Co^{2+}(aq) + 2\,e^- \rightarrow Co(s)$ is -0.28 V at pH 0 at 25°C. As the pH rises the potential remains constant until, after a brief intermediate regime, cobalt(II) hydroxide precipitates, and the half-reaction $Co(OH)_2(s) + 2e^- \rightarrow Co(s) + 2\,OH^-(aq)$ more accurately

[1] Text page 780.

describes matters. The standard potential for this half-reaction is −0.73 V. The Nernst equation for the new half-reaction is

$$\mathcal{E} = \mathcal{E}^\circ - \frac{0.0592\ \text{V}}{2}\log[\text{OH}^-]^2 = -0.73 - 0.0592\ \text{V}\log[\text{OH}^-]$$

The definition of pH and pOH allows us to write

$$-0.0592\log[\text{OH}^-] = +0.0592\,\text{pOH} = 0.0592\,(14 - \text{pH})$$

Therefore:

$$\mathcal{E} = -0.73\ \text{V} + (0.0592\ \text{V})(14 - \text{pH}) = (0.0988 - 0.0592\,\text{pH})\ \text{V}$$

This equation gives the half-cell potential as a function of pH. A plot of $\mathcal{E}$ versus pH is a straight line with a slope of −0.0592 V. If the line is extended back to pH 0, it intercepts the voltage axis at 0.0988 V. This is what the voltage of the cell would be if the $Co(OH)_2$ did not dissolve at low pH. The actual behavior at low pH is governed by the −0.28 V half-reaction.

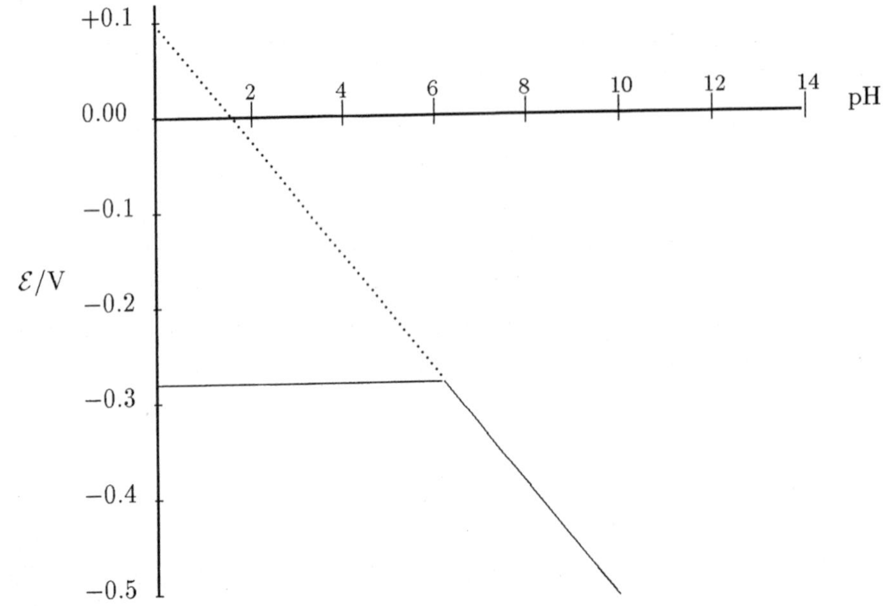

22.9 a) $\boxed{CaCO_3(s) + SiO_2(s) \rightarrow CaSiO_3(s) + CO_2(g)}$.

b)

$$\Delta H^\circ = 1\underbrace{(-1634.94)}_{CaSiO_3(s)} + 1\underbrace{(-393.51)}_{CO_2(g)} - 1\underbrace{(-1206.92)}_{CaCO_3(s)} - 1\underbrace{(-910.94)}_{SiO_2(s)} = \boxed{+89.41\ \text{kJ}}$$

$$\Delta S^\circ = 1\underbrace{(81.92)}_{CaSiO_3(s)} + 1\underbrace{(213.63)}_{CO_2(g)} - 1\underbrace{(92.9)}_{CaCO_3(s)} - 1\underbrace{(41.84)}_{SiO_2(s)} = \boxed{+160.8\ \text{J K}^{-1}}$$

c) Assume that ΔH° and ΔS° are independent of temperature. Then, when ΔG° is zero:

$$T = \frac{\Delta H^\circ}{\Delta S^\circ} = \frac{89.41 \times 10^3\ \text{J}}{160.8\ \text{J K}^{-1}} = \boxed{556\ \text{K}}$$

d) Although the ΔH° of this process is essentially independent of the pressure, the ΔS° *does* depend on pressure. Gaseous CO_2 has less entropy when released at a higher pressure. Hence ΔS for this reaction at

500 atm is less than ΔS°, which is at 1 atm. Compressing 1 mol of $CO_2(g)$ from 1 atm to 500 atm changes the entropy by:

$$\Delta S = -R \ln \frac{P_2}{P_1} = -R \ln(500/1) = -51.67 \text{J K}^{-1}$$

This formula is used in text Example 8.5[2] Therefore, replace 160.8 J K^{-1} with a ΔS of $160.8 + (-51.67)$ or 109.1 J K^{-1}. Write $\Delta G = \Delta H - T\Delta S$ at 500 atm, set ΔG equal to zero, and compute T. It is $\boxed{819 \text{ K}}$.

Tip. At high pressure, it takes a *higher* temperature to make the equilibrium constant of the reaction equal 1. This fits with the sense of LeChâtelier's principle for this reaction: high pressure favors the reactants because their volume is less.

22.11 a) The conversion from calcite to aragonite is

$$1 \text{ mol calcite} \rightarrow 1 \text{ mol aragonite}$$

The ΔH° for this change is the difference between the ΔH_f°'s (text Appendix D) of 1 mol of calcite and 1 mol of aragonite, which is $\boxed{-0.21 \text{ kJ}}$. The ΔS° is the difference in the absolute entropies text (text Appendix D) of the two substances at 298.15 K. It equals $\boxed{-4.2 \text{ J K}^{-1}}$. The $\Delta G^\circ_{298.15}$ of the reaction is $\boxed{+1.04 \text{ kJ}}$, by a similar calculation with ΔG_f°'s, using the same source for data.

b) The $\Delta G^\circ_{298.15}$ for the calcite→aragonite conversion is positive. This means that $\boxed{\text{calcite}}$ in its standard state at 25°C is thermodynamically favored over aragonite in its standard state at 25°C.

c) Assume that ΔH° and ΔS° depend only weakly on T. Then: $\Delta G^\circ_T \approx \Delta H^\circ - T\Delta S^\circ$. When the two forms are equally favored, ΔG° equals zero. Setting ΔG° equal to zero gives $T = 50$ K. Below 50 K, $\boxed{\text{aragonite}}$ is favored. At temperatures above 50 K, calcite is favored (as long as the pressure is 1 atm).

d) Higher pressure favors the more dense form. The molar volume of aragonite is 34.16 cm^3 mol^{-1}. Aragonite is more dense than calcite, which occupies 36.94 cm^3 mol^{-1}. $\boxed{\text{Aragonite}}$ is favored at high pressure.

e) The Clapeyron equation gives the slope of the coexistence line for two phases in a P versus T phase diagram:

$$\frac{dP}{dT} = \frac{\Delta H}{T\Delta V}$$

For the transformation of 1 mol of calcite to 1 mol of aragonite, ΔH° equals -210 J. The ΔV for this transition is $(34.16 - 36.94)$ cm^3 or -2.78 cm^3 which is -2.78×10^{-6} m^3. The coexistence line for the two solids passes through the point defined by the (P, T) combination: ($P = 1$ atm, $T = 50$ K), according to the results of the previous part of this problem. Assume that the ΔH and ΔV values hold correct at this low temperature. Then the slope of the coexistence line at this point is

$$\frac{dP}{dT} = \frac{-210 \text{ J}}{(50 \text{ K})(-2.78 \times 10^{-6} \text{ m}^3)} = 1.5 \times 10^6 \text{ Pa K}^{-1}$$

Text Appendix B confirms that a J m^{-3} equals a pascal (Pa). One atmosphere is 101325 pascal, so an equivalent answer is $\boxed{15 \text{ atm K}^{-1}}$.

Tip. The answer is the rate of change of pressure with temperature at $P = 1$ atm and $T = 50$ K. As long as ΔH and ΔV are both independent of the constant T and the constant P as which the conversion takes place, the coexistence line is straight and has this slope.

22.13 Firing steatite (soapstone) drives out water:

$$\boxed{Mg_3Si_4O_{10}(OH)_2(s) \rightarrow 3\,MgSiO_3(s) + SiO_2(s) + H_2O(g)}$$

---

[2]Text page 247.

22.15 The reaction for the preparation of the glass is

$$Na_2CO_3(s) + CaCO_3(s) + 6\,SiO_2(s) \rightarrow Na_2O{\cdot}CaO{\cdot}(SiO_2)_6(s) + 2\,CO_2(g)$$

The problem is now a routine calculation in stoichiometry. The molar mass of the glass is 479 g mol^{-1}, which equals 0.479 kg mol^{-1}. The chemical amount of CO_2 produced is

$$n_{CO_2} = 2.50 \text{ kg glass} \times \left(\frac{1 \text{ mol glass}}{0.479 \text{ kg glass}}\right) \times \left(\frac{2 \text{ mol } CO_2}{1 \text{ mol glass}}\right) = 10.44 \text{ mol}$$

Use the ideal-gas equation to compute the volume of the CO_2 at 0°C and 1 atm pressure:

$$V_{CO_2} = \frac{n_{CO_2}RT}{P} = \frac{(10.44 \text{ mol})(0.08206 \text{ L atm mol}^{-1}\text{K}^{-1})(273 \text{ K})}{1 \text{ atm}} = \boxed{234 \text{ L } CO_2}$$

22.17 Assume a sample of exactly 100 g of the soda-lime glass and calculate the chemical amount of each element which is present. This requires use of the molar masses of the several binary oxides. The following table summarizes the results:

Mass of Oxide	$\mathcal{M}$(g mol^{-1})	Amounts of Elements	
72.4 g SiO_2	60.08	1.205 mol Si	2.410 mol O
18.1 g Na_2O	61.98	0.5841 mol Na	0.2920 mol O
8.10 g CaO	56.07	0.1444 mol Ca	0.1444 mol O
1.00 g Al_2O_3	101.96	0.01962 mol Al	0.02942 mol O
0.20 g MgO	40.304	0.004962 mol Mg	0.004962 mol O
0.20 g BaO	153.33	0.001304 mol Ba	0.001304 mol O

The total chemical amount of oxygen in the sample equals the sum of all the listings for O in the right-most column. It is 2.882 mol. The chemical amounts of the various elements per mole of oxygen are their amounts in the above table divided by 2.882. After rounding to the correct number of significant digits, they are:

$$\boxed{0.418 \text{ mol Si, } 0.203 \text{ mol Na, } 0.050 \text{ mol Ca, } 0.0068 \text{ mol Al, } 0.002 \text{ mol Mg, } 0.0005 \text{ mol Ba}}$$

Tip. Note how the proportions of the oxides in this glass differ from the nominal proportions in soda-lime glass.

22.19 The reaction for the production of tricalcium silicate is

$$SiO_2(s, quartz) + 3\,CaO(s) \rightarrow (CaO)_3{\cdot}SiO_2(s)$$

The enthalpy of the reaction is the sum of the enthalpies of formation of the products minus the sum of the enthalpies of formation of the reactants. Text Appendix D gives the ΔH_f°'s for $SiO_2(s, quartz)$ and $CaO(s)$. Then:

$$\Delta H^\circ = 1\underbrace{(-2929.2)}_{(CaO)_3SiO_2(s)} - 1\underbrace{(-910.94)}_{SiO_2(s)} - 3\underbrace{(-635.09)}_{CaO(s)} = \boxed{-113.0 \text{ kJ}}$$

22.21 The sum of the oxidations numbers of the atoms in the compound must equal zero. Assign the oxidation numbers −2 to oxygen, +2 to Ba, and +3 to Y. The copper must then have an oxidation number of $\boxed{7/3}$ to bring the sum to zero.

22.23 a) $\boxed{SiO_2(s, quartz) + 3\,C(s, graphite) \rightarrow SiC(s) + 2\,CO(g)}$.

b) Find necessary ΔH_f°'s in Appendix D. Then:

$$\Delta H^\circ = 1\underbrace{(-65.3)}_{SiC(s)} + 2\underbrace{(-110.52)}_{CO(g)} - 1\underbrace{(-910.94)}_{SiO_2(s)} - 3\underbrace{(0)}_{C(s)} = \boxed{624.6 \text{ kJ}}$$

c) Silicon carbide should, like diamond, be hard, high melting, and a poor conductor of electricity.

22.25 The reaction is $SiC(s) + 2\,O_2(g) \rightarrow SiO_2(s, quartz) + CO_2(g)$. Refer to text Appendix D for the necessary values of ΔG_f°:

$$\Delta G^\circ = 1\underbrace{(-394.36)}_{CO_2(g)} + 1\underbrace{(-856.67)}_{SiO_2(s)} - 1\underbrace{(-62.8)}_{SiC(s)} - 2\underbrace{(0)}_{O_2(g)} = \boxed{-1188.2 \text{ kJ}}$$

The ΔG° is less than zero so the reaction is spontaneous. Thus, $SiC(s)$ is thermodynamically unstable in the presence of 1 atm of oxygen at 298.15 K. Reducing the partial pressure of oxygen to 0.2 atm (which is its value in air) makes the ΔG slightly more positive, but the compound is still thermodynamically $\boxed{\text{unstable}}$. Its rate of reaction is however vanishingly slow.

22.27 a) Apophyllite contains infinite sheets of silicate units. The Si and O are in the +4 and −2 oxidation states respectively. The oxidation states are F, −1; K, +1; Ca, +2. The water of hydration in the mineral has H in the +1 and O in the −2 oxidation states.

b) Rhodonite contains infinite single chains of SiO_4 units. The Ca and Mn both have +2 oxidation states.

c) Margarite is an aluminosilicate. It contains infinite sheets of aluminosilicate groups. The Ca and non-infinite-sheet Al are in the +2 and +3 oxidation states, respectively. The Si, Al, and O in the aluminosilicate framework are in the +4, +3 and −2 states; the hydroxide H and O are in the +1 and −2 states respectively.

22.29 Let x equal the oxidation number of the Fe, and write an equation to express the electrical neutrality of the compound:

$$\underbrace{2.36(2)}_{Mg} + \underbrace{0.48(x)}_{Fe} + \underbrace{0.16(3)}_{Al} + \underbrace{2.72(4)}_{Si} + \underbrace{1.28(3)}_{Al} + \underbrace{10(-2)}_{O} + \underbrace{2(-1)}_{OH} + \underbrace{0.32(2)}_{Mg} = 0$$

Solving gives $x = 3$; the oxidation state of the iron is $\boxed{3}$.

22.31 $CaAl_2Si_2O_8(s) + CO_2(aq) + 2\,H_2O(l) \rightarrow CaCO_3(s) + Al_2Si_2O_5(OH)_4(s)$.
Lowering the pH will solubilize the product $CaCO_3$, which dissolves readily in acid (see the following problem). Thus, we predict by LeChâtelier's principle that lower pH $\boxed{\text{increases}}$ the extent of weathering.

22.33 a) The dissolution of $CaCO_3(s)$ in water involves the equilibria:

$$CaCO_3(s) \rightleftharpoons Ca^{2+}(aq) + CO_3^{2-}(aq) \qquad K_{sp} = 7.6 \times 10^{-9}$$
$$CO_3^{2-}(aq) + H_2O(l) \rightleftharpoons HCO_3^-(aq) + OH^-(aq) \qquad K_{b1} = 2.08 \times 10^{-4}$$
$$HCO_3^-(aq) + H_2O(l) \rightleftharpoons H_2CO_3(aq) + OH^-(aq) \qquad K_{b2} = 2.32 \times 10^{-8}$$

The law of mass action for the two acid-base equilibria gives:

$$K_{b1} = \frac{[OH^-][HCO_3^-]}{[CO_3^{2-}]} \quad \text{and} \quad K_{b2} = \frac{[OH^-][H_2CO_3]}{[HCO_3^-]}$$

Note that K_{b1} is K_w divided by the K_{a2} of H_2CO_3 and K_{b2} is K_w divided by K_{a1} of H_2CO_3.[3]

Since the solvent has a pH of 7, $[OH^-]$ is 1.0×10^{-7} M. Substitute this value into the two K_b expressions and rearrange:

$$[HCO_3^-] = (2080)[CO_3^{2-}] \quad \text{and} \quad [H_2CO_3] = (482)[CO_3^{2-}]$$

Let S equal the solubility of the $CaCO_3(s)$. Then S is equal to $[Ca^{2+}]$ and is also equal to the sum of the concentrations of the three carbon-containing species. This statement is a material-balance condition[4] for the carbonate. Expressed mathematically:

$$S = [Ca^{2+}] \qquad \text{and} \qquad S = [CO_3^{2-}] + [HCO_3^-] + [H_2CO_3]$$

Substitute the independent expressions for the bicarbonate and carbonic acid concentrations into the second equation to obtain:

$$S = [CO_3^{2-}]\,(1 + 2080 + 482) = [CO_3^{2-}](2560)$$

Combine this equation with the K_{sp} expression for $CaCO_3(s)$ to calculate S:

$$8.7 \times 10^{-9} = [Ca^{2+}][CO_3^{2-}] = S\frac{S}{2560} \qquad \text{which gives} \qquad S = \boxed{0.0047 \text{ mol L}^{-1}}$$

b) Decreasing the pH will $\boxed{\text{increase}}$ the solubility of $CaCO_3(s)$ in water. More carbonate ion is converted to bicarbonate ion or carbonic acid at lower pH.

c) The river's annual flow is 8.8×10^{12} L. This much water would, at equilibrium, dissolve 4.1×10^{10} mol of $CaCO_3$ ($\mathcal{M} = 100$ g mol^{-1}) which is $\boxed{4.1 \times 10^6 \text{ metric tons}}$.

Tip. Do not thoughtlessly assume that $HCO_3^-(aq)$ is the only carbon-containing species present in significant concentration. This assumption corresponds to leaving out the first and third terms in the parentheses in the equation for S and leads to an S of 0.0042 M, which is 10 percent less than the correct answer. A worse error is to ignore the acid-base interaction of the carbonate ion with the water entirely. This corresponds to omitting the second and third terms within the parentheses and gives an S of 9.3×10^{-5} M, about 50 times too low.

Tip. Compare the approach her to the approach in **18.77**.

22.35 The balanced equation is

$$\boxed{Mg_3Si_4O_{10}(OH)_2(s) + Mg_2SiO_4(s) \rightarrow 5\,MgSiO_3(s) + H_2O(g)}$$

Trial-and-error balancing gives this answer. Another approach is to note that Mg_2SiO_4 loses O^{2-} ions on a per silicon basis, and $Mg_3Si_4O_{10}(OH)_2$ gains O^{2-} ions on the same basis. This approach puts O^{2-} ion in this reaction in the role played by the electron in the standard method of balancing redox reactions. Arranging the gain of O^{2-} to equal the loss of O^{2-} rapidly gives a balanced equation:

$$\begin{array}{ll} O^{2-} \text{ loss} & Mg_2SiO_4(s) \rightarrow MgSiO_3(s) + O^{2-} + Mg^{2+} \\ O^{2-} \text{ gain} & O^{2-} + Mg^{2+} + Mg_3Si_4O_{10}(OH)_2(s) \rightarrow 4\,MgSiO_3(s) + H_2O(g) \end{array}$$

b) Use LeChâtelier's principle. Increasing the total pressure increases the activity of $H_2O(g)$ and shifts the reaction to the left. The products are $\boxed{\text{disfavored}}$.

c) The slope of the coexistence curve is given by the Clapeyron equation:

$$\frac{dP}{dT} = \frac{\Delta H}{T\Delta V} = \frac{\Delta S}{\Delta V}$$

---

[3] These K's and the K_{sp} are from text Table 10.2 (text page 326) and 11.2 (text page 367).

[4] Discussed on text page 350

For this reaction ΔV is clearly positive because the products include 1 mol of gas, which has a large volume, but the reactants include no gas. The ΔS of the reaction is positive, for the same reason. The slope of the curve is accordingly $\boxed{\text{positive}}$.

22.37 To impart a red color to the pot, the oxidation state of the iron must be high. The iron in iron oxides will be in a high oxidation state if bound to many oxide anions. Thus, an air-rich (oxygen-rich) atmosphere should be employed. To impart a black color to the pot, the oxidation state of the iron must be low. A smoky fuel-rich atmosphere has relatively little oxygen in it. In such an atmosphere the iron is not oxidized. $\boxed{\text{For red pot use an air-rich atmosphere; for a black pot use a fuel-rich atmosphere}}$.

22.39 A 100.0 g sample of pure dolomite contains 45.7 g of $MgCO_3$ and 54.3 g of $CaCO_3$. This can be confirmed by dividing the masses of the two compounds by their molar masses (84.31 g mol^{-1} and 100.08 g mol^{-1}). The chemical amounts of the two equal to 0.542 mol. If the compounds are present in equal chemical amount the formula is "$(MgCO_3)_1{\cdot}(CaCO_3)_1$" which is better written $MgCO_3{\cdot}CaCO_3$ or $MgCaC_2O_6$, or $\boxed{MgCa(CO_3)_2}$.

22.41 The equation for the reaction of silicon nitride with hydrofluoric acid is

$$\boxed{Si_3N_4(s) + 12\,HF(aq) \rightarrow 3\,SiF_4(g) + 4\,NH_3(aq)}$$

In this case, no kinetic barrier exists to slow the reaction. Parts fabricated from silicon nitride are rapidly corroded by $HF(aq)$.

Chapter 23

Optical and Electronic Materials

23.1 The conductivity σ is given in text equation 23.3[1]. The cross-sectional area A of a cylinder is πr^2, and Ohm's law applies ($R = V/I$). Substitute these relationships Then

$$\sigma = \frac{\ell}{RA} = \frac{\ell}{\pi r^2}\frac{I}{V} = \frac{(55.0 \times 10^{-3}\ \text{m})(150 \times 10^{-3}\ \text{A})}{\pi(2.5 \times 10^{-3}\ \text{m})^2(17.5\ \text{V})} = 24\ \ \text{A V}^{-1}\ \text{m}^{-1} = \boxed{24\ (\Omega\ \text{m})^{-1}} = 24\ \text{S m}^{-1}$$

Tip. Electrical resistance is measured in ohms (Ω), Electrical conductance, the reciprocal of resistance, is measured in siemens (S). The siemens, which is the reciprocal of the ohm, was formerly called the "mho" (ohm spelled backward).

23.3 Compute the number density of the Na^+ ions in the solution from their concentration

$$n_{\text{Na}^+} = 0.1\ \text{mol L}^{-1} \times \left(\frac{10^3\ \text{L}}{\text{m}^3}\right)\left(\frac{6.022 \times 10^{23}\ \text{ions}}{\text{mol}}\right) = 6.022 \times 10^{25}\ \text{ion m}^{-3}$$

The conductivity σ from the Na^+ ions is the charge density contributed by the ions multiplied by their mobility. The charge density equals the number density multiplied by the charge that each ion carries. The sign of the charge is disregarded, as indicated by the use of absolute magnitude signs in the following

$$\begin{aligned}
\sigma_{\text{Na}^+} &= |z_{\text{Na}^+}|\, e\, n_{\text{Na}^+}\, \mu_{\text{Na}^+} \\
&= (1)\left(\frac{1.602 \times 10^{-19}\ \text{C}}{\text{ion}}\right)\left(\frac{6.022 \times 10^{25}\ \text{ion}}{\text{m}^3}\right)(5.19 \times 10^{-4}\ \text{cm}^2\ \text{V}^{-1}\ \text{s}^{-1})\left(\frac{10^{-4}\ \text{m}^2}{\text{cm}^2}\right) \\
&= 0.5007\ \text{C s}^{-1}\ \text{V}^{-1}\ \text{m}^{-1}
\end{aligned}$$

The Cl^- ions have the same number density as the Na^+ ions because their concentration in the solution is the same. They contribute to the conductivity in a similar way

$$\begin{aligned}
\sigma_{\text{Cl}^-} &= |z_{\text{Cl}^-}|\, e\, n_{\text{Cl}^-}\, \mu_{\text{Cl}^-} \\
&= (1)\left(\frac{1.602 \times 10^{-19}\ \text{C}}{\text{ion}}\right)\left(\frac{6.022 \times 10^{25}\ \text{ion}}{\text{m}^3}\right)(7.91 \times 10^{-4}\ \text{cm}^2\ \text{V}^{-1}\ \text{s}^{-1})\left(\frac{10^{-4}\ \text{m}^2}{\text{cm}^2}\right) \\
&= 0.7631\ \text{C s}^{-1}\ \text{V}^{-1}\ \text{m}^{-1}
\end{aligned}$$

The total conductivity is the sum of the conductivities contributed by the mobile charged species, as shown in text equation 23.8. Therefore

$$\sigma_{\text{tot}} = \sigma_{\text{Na}^+} + \sigma_{\text{Cl}^-} = 0.5007\ \text{C V}^{-1}\ \text{s}^{-1} + 0.7631\ \text{C V}^{-1}\ \text{s}^{-1} = 1.26\ \text{C s}^{-1}\ \text{V}^{-1}\ \text{m}^{-1} = \boxed{1.26\ \text{S m}^{-1}}$$

---

[1] Text page 807

23.5 Use equation 23.9 from text page 809. This equation states the Drude model for the conductivity of a metal. Solve it for n_e, the number density of the electrons in the copper

$$n_e = \frac{\sigma_{Cu}}{e\mu_{in\ Cu}}$$

Substitute the conductivity of Cu from text Table 23.1 and the room-temperature mobility of electrons in Cu, which is given in the problem

$$n_e = \frac{6.0 \times 10^7 \text{ S m}^{-1}}{(1.602 \times 10^{-19} \text{ C (electron)}^{-1})(3.0 \times 10^{-3} \text{ m}^2 \text{ V}^{-1} \text{ s}^{-1})}$$
$$= (1.25 \times 10^{29}) \frac{\text{S m}^{-1}}{\text{A (electron)}^{-1} \text{ m}^2 \text{ V}^{-1}} = 1.25 \times 10^{29} \text{ electron m}^{-3}$$

The cancellation of the units makes use of the fact that an ampere (A) equals a coulomb per second (C s^{-1}) and that a siemens (S), the SI unit of conductivity, equals an ampere per volt (A V^{-1}). Now, compute the number density of Cu atoms in metallic copper from the mass density, which is given in the problem as 8.9 g cm^{-3}

$$n_{Cu} = 8.9 \text{ g cm}^{-3} \times \left(\frac{1 \text{ mol}}{63.55 \text{ g}}\right)\left(\frac{6.022 \times 10^{23} \text{ atoms}}{1 \text{ mol}}\right)\left(\frac{10^6 \text{ cm}^3}{1 \text{ m}^3}\right) = 8.43 \times 10^{28} \text{ atom m}^{-3}$$

The number density of the mobile electrons divided by the number density of the copper atoms equals the number of mobile electrons per atom

$$\frac{1.25 \times 10^{29} \text{ electron m}^{-3}}{8.43 \times 10^{28} \text{ atom m}^{-3}} = \boxed{1.48 \text{ electrons per atom}}$$

23.7 The band-gap energy equals the energy of light of wavelength 920 nm. Use Planck's relation to compute this energy:

$$E_g = h\nu = \frac{hc}{\lambda} = \frac{(6.626 \times 10^{-34} \text{ J s})(2.9979 \times 10^8 \text{ m s}^{-1})}{920 \times 10^{-9} \text{ m}} = \boxed{2.16 \times 10^{-19} \text{ J}}$$

23.9 The problem requires substitution in the formula for the number of electrons excited. The gap energy E_g is 8.7×10^{-19} J, which is equivalent to 5.24×10^5 J mol^{-1}. With T at 300 K and R equal to 8.3145 J $K^{-1}mol^{-1}$ the formula becomes:

$$n_e = (4.8 \times 10^{15} \text{ cm}^{-3}\text{K}^{-3/2})(300 \text{ K})^{3/2} \exp\left(\frac{-5.24 \times 10^5 \text{ J mol}^{-1}}{2(8.3145 \text{ J K}^{-1}\text{mol}^{-1})(300 \text{ K})}\right)$$
$$= 6.1 \times 10^{-27} \text{ cm}^{-3}$$

In a 1.00-cm^3 diamond (pretty big for a diamond) at room temperature, only 6.1×10^{-27} electrons are excited to the conduction band; there are essentially $\boxed{\text{no electrons}}$ in the conduction band.

23.11 a) Phosphorus-doped silicon is an $\boxed{n\text{-type}}$ semiconductor because substitution of a P (five valence electrons) at an Si (four valence electrons) site populates the conduction band. The carriers of electric current are mobile electrons.

b) Zinc-doped indium antimonide is a $\boxed{p\text{-type}}$ semiconductor. Mobile holes are the charge carriers in this material.

23.13 Use the Planck equation to compute the wavelength that corresponds to a difference in energy of 2.9×10^{-19} J:

$$\lambda = \frac{hc}{\Delta E} = \frac{(6.626 \times 10^{-34}\ \text{J s})(2.9979 \times 10^{8}\ \text{m s}^{-1})}{2.9 \times 10^{-19}\ \text{J}} = \boxed{6.8 \times 10^{-7}\ \text{m}}$$

Light of this wavelength is $\boxed{\text{red}}$.

23.15 At room temperature, zinc white does not absorb in the visible region, although it does absorb ultraviolet light. It appears white. When zinc white is heated, the absorption in the UV is shifted into the blue end of the visible region. Yellow is the color complement of blue, so the absorption of blue light makes the substance appear yellow. The shift into the blue from the UV is a shift to lower frequency and indicates a $\boxed{\text{decrease}}$ in band gap.

23.17 First, compute the energy of a single photon of the specified wavelength:

$$E = h\nu = \frac{hc}{\lambda} = \frac{(6.626 \times 10^{-34}\ \text{J s})(2.9979 \times 10^{8}\ \text{m s}^{-1})}{4.30 \times 10^{-7}\ \text{m}} = 4.62 \times 10^{-19}\ \text{J}$$

The energy of 1.00 mol of photons equals this value multiplied by Avogadro's number. It comes out to 278 kJ. The conversion ADP$\rightarrow$ATP has ΔG° equal to +34.5 kJ. The 278 kJ from 1.00 mol of photons is 8.06 times larger than 34.5 kJ. Therefore 8.06 mol of ATP could be produced by 1.00 mol of 430 nm photons. This means that at most $\boxed{\text{8 molecules}}$ of ATP are produced by a single 430 nm photon.

Tip. The value of ΔG° given in the problem is for "biochemical standard conditions." This kind of ΔG°'s is often distinguished by adding a prime to the symbol: $\Delta G^{\circ\prime}$. No $\Delta G^{\circ\prime}$'s appear in text Appendix D. Under biochemical standard conditions the activity of H_3O^+ is defined as 1 at pH 7 (rather than at pH 0). Biochemical standard conditions provide a reference state for thermodynamic values that is closer to the conditions prevailing in living cells. The ΔG of the ADP $\rightarrow$ ATP reaction, like that of most biochemical reactions, is highly dependent on pH.

23.19 The hybridization of silicon atoms in Si(s) is sp^3, giving rise to a 3-dimensional network of tetrahedral silicon atoms that is just like the diamond structure of carbon. Graphite consists of parallel sheets of hexagonally arrayed σ bonded carbon atoms. Less directional bonds join the sheets. Graphite is an excellent electrical conductor in a direction parallel to the sheets as a result of extensive electron delocalization in the out-of-plane π system. If silicon were to adopt the graphite structure, we would expect $\boxed{\text{high}}$ electrical conductivity.

23.21 The empty seat will appear to move to the right at a rate of one seat position per five minutes. The analogy with hole motion in p-type semiconductors is this: each seat is a lattice site, the empty seat is the hole, and the people are the electrons,

---

23.23 The steps in bacterial photosynthesis are:

1. The bacteria gather radiant energy using different "antenna molecules" that are excited to high-energy electronic states but quickly transfer the energy to neighboring molecules and on to the photosynthetic reaction center.
2. The reaction center contains four bacteriochlorophyll molecules: the "special pair" (symbolized $(BChl)_2$) and two others. It also contains two bacteriopheophytin molecules, two ubiquinone molecules (UQ), and an iron(II) ion. These species are arranged in a symmetrical fashion with the ubiquinone molecules, which include long conjugated chains of 50 carbon atoms, forming two branches (the A branch and B branch). The bacteriochlorophyll molecules in the special pair are pushed up into electronic excited states as they briefly trap the input energy. They then transfer an electron (and are themselves oxidized) to a bacteriopheophytin molecule.
3. The electron moves from the bacteriopheophytin to the ubiquinone molecule in the A branch.

4. The electron zips down the ubiquinone molecule and across to the ubiquinone molecule in the B branch. This UQ molecule is reduced to UQ^-.
5. The oxidized special pair is reduced to its original state by picking up an electron from a cytochrome protein (Cyt). The special pair is re-excited (with energy from another photon) and transfer a second electron to the same ubiquinone molecule in the B branch, forming UQ^{2-}, which, being a base, picks up hydrogen ions to form UQH_2.
6. The doubly reduced ubiquinone UQH_2 undocks from the reaction center as a fresh ubiquinone molecule comes in.
7. The UQH_2 reduces Cyt^+ protein back to Cyt. The location of the Cyt^- allows the by-product H^+ ion to be generated outside the cell wall.

The net effect is harness the energy of the light to pump hydrogen ion from inside the cell to outside against the concentration gradient.

Chapter 24

Polymeric Materials

24.1 The addition polymerization is $n\,Cl_2C{=}CH_2 \rightarrow \!\!+\!\!(CCl_2{-}CH_2)\!\!+_n$.

24.3 Addition polymerization does not split out any small molecules. From the formula of the polymer then, the starting monomer must be $\boxed{\text{formaldehyde}}$ ($H_2C{=}O$).

24.5 **a)** As glycine (NH_2CH_2COOH) polymerizes to the polypeptide, one molecule of $\boxed{\text{water}}$ is lost in the formation of each peptide bond.

b) The repeating structure in the polypeptide is

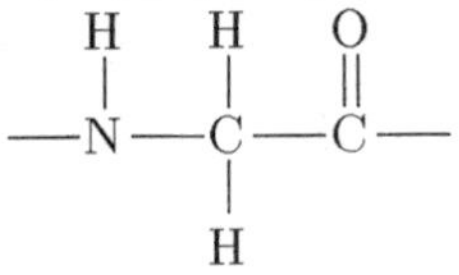

24.7 The repeating unit in the polyamide has the formula $C_{12}H_{22}N_2O_2$. This formula is the sum of the molecular formulas of adipic acid and hexamethylenediamine minus twice the formula of water, a relationship that derives from the fact that the diacid and diamine polymerize by condensation with loss of one molecule of water for each unit added to the chain. The molar mass of the repeating unit is 226.32 g mol^{-1}. Then the chemical amount of the repeating unit that is needed is

$$1.00 \times 10^6 \text{ g polymer} \times \left(\frac{1 \text{ mol of units}}{226.32 \text{ g polymer}}\right) = 4419 \text{ mol}$$

This means that the synthesis needs 4419 mol of adipic acid (which has a molar mass of 146.1 g mol^{-1}) and 4419 mol of hexamethylenediamine (molar mass 116.2 g mol^{-1}). These chemical amounts convert to $\boxed{646 \text{ kg}}$ of adipic acid and $\boxed{513 \text{ kg}}$ of hexamethylenediamine.

24.9 Polyethylene is formed by addition polymerization. This means that the mass of the monomer used to make the polymer equals the mass of the polymer that is formed. No mass is split out in the form of water or other by-product, as in condensation polymerization. Use this fact in a train of unit-conversions and then do an ideal-gas calculation:

$$n_{C_2H_4} = 4.37 \times 10^9 \text{ kg LDPE} \times \left(\frac{1 \text{ kg } C_2H_4}{1 \text{ kg LDPE}}\right) \times \left(\frac{1 \text{ mol } C_2H_4}{0.02805 \text{ kg } C_2H_4}\right) = 1.558 \times 10^{11} \text{ mol } C_2H_4$$

$$V_{C_2H_4} = \frac{n_{C_2H_4}RT}{P} = \frac{(1.558 \times 10^{11} \text{ mol})(0.08206 \text{ L atm mol}^{-1}\text{K}^{-1})(273 \text{ K})}{1.00 \text{ atm}} = \boxed{3.49 \times 10^{12} \text{ L}}$$

Tip. This equals 3.49 km^3 (cubic kilometers!) of gaseous ethylene.

24.11 The compound β-D-galactose has five chiral centers: It is an isomer of β-D-glucose. Note the different chirality at C-4.

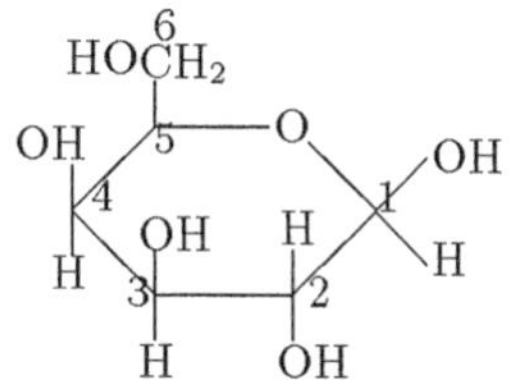

Tip. Structures in the style of the preceding find frequent use in carbohydrate chemistry. Compare the relative positions of the OH's and H's at each carbon to their positions in text Figures 24.11 and 24.9c.

24.13 A tripeptide is a chain of three monomer units and has distinguishable ends. Any of the three kinds of building block can go in the first position, any of the three can go in the second position, and any of the three can go in the third position. There are accordingly $3^3 = 27$ possible tripeptides.

24.15 The pentapeptide is

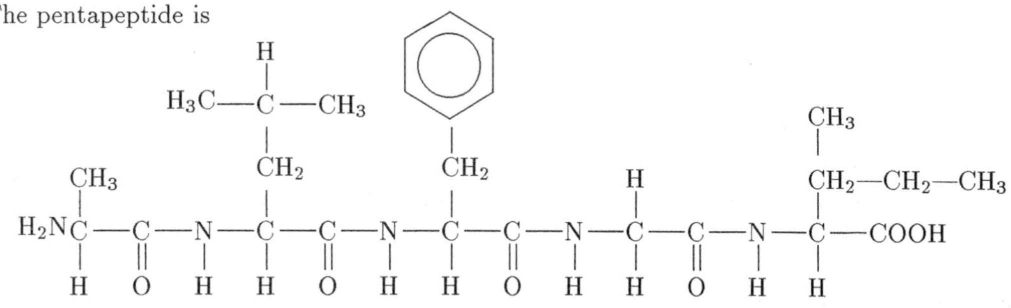

The pentapeptide has all non-polar side-groups. It should be more soluble in octane than in water.

24.17 The line formula of phenylalanine is $C_6H_5CH_2CH(NH_2)COOH$, equivalent to the empirical formula $C_9H_{11}NO_2$. The polypeptide forms with the removal of an H from the amine end of the molecule and an OH from the carboxylic acid end. Except for the two monomer units at the two extreme ends, which are negligible, each phenylalanine loses one HOH as the polymer forms. The empirical formula of the polymer is therefore C_9H_9NO. The molar mass of a C_9H_9NO unit is 147.2 g mol^{-1}. If the molar mass of the polypeptide is 17500 g mol^{-1} it contains $17500/147.2 = 119$ monomer units.

24.19 A catalyst is by definition not consumed in a reaction; it is taken up in one step of a mechanism but regenerated in a subsequent step. In the polymerization of acrylonitrile, the butyl lithium is consumed and the butyl anion is incorporated into the product. Doing this creates an new anion by which chain-building propagates. The butyl lithium is incorporated into the product. It is irrecoverable and hence not a catalyst.

24.21 Polyvinyl chloride is $\text{-(}CH_2\text{—}CHCl\text{)-}_n$. The molar mass of its monomer unit is 65.50 g mol^{-1}. Polyvinyl chloride is formed by polymerization of ethylene dichloride CH_2ClCH_2Cl ($\mathcal{M} = 98.95$ g mol^{-1}) with the loss of one molecule of HCl per monomer unit added to the chain. The theoretical yield from 950 million pounds of monomer is therefore

$$950 \text{ million lb} \times \frac{62.50}{98.95} = 600 \text{ million lb}$$

If the actual yield of polymer is 500 million pounds, then the percent yield is $500/600 \times 100\% = 83\%$. If the actual yield gets as high as 550 million pounds, the percent yield is 92%.

24.23 Hair consists of polymeric chains of amino acid cross-linked by —S—S— bridges. To curl hair, treat the hair with a reducing agent, which breaks some of the cross-links. Then arrange the strands of hair in the desired curls, and treat the hair with an oxidizing agent. The disulfide bridges then reform, but in different locations. The new cross-links maintain the curls.

24.25 Two kinds of amino acid can appear at each of the 22 positions in the polypeptide chain. The two ends of the chain are distinguishable. Therefore, there are $\boxed{2^{22}}$ or 4.194 million possible isomeric molecules.

24.27 The acid form of alanine can donate two hydrogen ions:

$$^{+}H_3NCH(CH_3)COOH(aq) + H_2O(aq) \rightleftharpoons {}^{+}H_3NCH(CH_3)COO^{-}(aq) + H_3O^{+}(aq)$$
$$^{+}H_3NCH(CH_3)COOH(aq) + H_2O(aq) \rightleftharpoons H_2NCH(CH_3)COOH(aq) + H_3O^{+}(aq)$$

The two K's are $K_1 = 10^{-2.3} = 5.0 \times 10^{-3}$ and $K_2 = 10^{-9.7} = 2.0 \times 10^{-10}$. Notice that both K's are K_a's, but that the reactions are concurrent, not consecutive. The notation K_{a1} and K_{a2} is therefore avoided. Abbreviate the formulas of the three forms of alanine:

$$A \Rightarrow {}^{+}H_3NCH(CH_3)COOH \quad Z \Rightarrow {}^{+}H_3NCH(CH_3)COO^{-} \quad B \Rightarrow H_2NCH(CH_3)COOH$$

This makes it easier to write out the mass-action expressions for the above equilibria:

$$\frac{[H_3O^+][Z]}{[A]} = K_1 \quad \text{and} \quad \frac{[H_3O^+][B]}{[A]} = K_2$$

At pH 7 $[H_3O^+]$ equals 1.0×10^{-7} M, and the two expressions become:

$$\frac{(1.0 \times 10^{-7})[Z]}{[A]} = 5.0 \times 10^{-3} \quad \text{and} \quad \frac{(1.0 \times 10^{-7})[B]}{[A]} = 2.0 \times 10^{-10}$$

$$\frac{[Z]}{[A]} = 5.0 \times 10^{4} \quad \text{and} \quad \frac{[B]}{[A]} = 2.0 \times 10^{-3}$$

a) The fraction[1] of the alanine in the Z-form equals the concentration of Z divided by the sum of the concentrations of all three forms:

$$f_Z = \frac{[Z]}{[A]+[Z]+[B]} = \frac{5.0 \times 10^4[A]}{[A] + (5.0 \times 10^4)[A] + (2.0 \times 10^{-3})[A]} = \boxed{0.99998}$$

Essentially $\boxed{\text{all}}$ of the molecules are in the zwitterion-form at pH 7.

b) The fraction of alanine in the B-form is the concentration of that form divided by the sum of the concentrations of all three forms:

$$f_B = \frac{[B]}{[A]+[Z]+[B]} = \frac{2.0 \times 10^{-3}[A]}{[A] + (5.0 \times 10^4)[A] + (2.0 \times 10^{-3})[A]} = \boxed{4.0 \times 10^{-8}}$$

24.29 Diesters of phosphoric acid have the general formula $O{=}P(OH)(OR)_2$. The H in this formula is an acidic hydrogen. The compounds are therefore acids as well is esters.

24.31 Set up a series of unit-factors to compute the length of the DNA molecule

$$l = 2.8 \times 10^9 \text{ g mol}^{-1} \times \left(\frac{1 \text{ base pair}}{650 \text{ g mol}^{-1}}\right) \times \left(\frac{3.4 \text{ Å}}{\text{base pair}}\right) \times \left(\frac{10^{-10} \text{ m}}{\text{Å}}\right) = \boxed{1.5 \times 10^{-3} \text{ m}}$$

The number of base pairs in this DNA is

$$N = 2.8 \times 10^9 \text{ g mol}^{-1} \times \left(\frac{1 \text{ base pair}}{650 \text{ g mol}^{-1}}\right) = \boxed{4.3 \times 10^6 \text{ base pair}}$$

---

[1] Compare to **10.101**.

Appendix A

A.1 The trailing zeros in d) and e) must not be omitted when the number is put into scientific notation. **a)** 5.82×10^{-5} **b)** 1.402×10^{3} **c)** 7.93 **d)** -6.59300×10^{3} **e)** 2.530×10^{-3} **f)** 1.47

A.3 **a)** 0.000537 **b)** 9,390,000 **c)** −0.00247 **d)** 0.006020 **e)** 20,000

A.5 The number is 746 million kilograms or 746,000,000 kg.

A.7 **a)** Statistical methods for deciding when to omit a outlier are not developed in the Appendix. Instead the appeal is to use good judgment. The value 135.6 g is grossly out of line with the others. **b)** The mean is 111.34 g **c)** The standard deviation is 0.22 g and the 98% confidence limit is

$$\text{confidence limit} = \pm\frac{t\sigma}{\sqrt{N}} = \pm\frac{2.57(0.22\text{ g})}{\sqrt{6}} = \pm 0.23\text{ g}$$

where t comes from Table A.2, text page A.4.

A.9 The measurement of mass in problem A.7 is more precise.

A.11 **a)** five **b)** three **c)** ambiguous (two or three significant figures) **d)** three **e)** four.

A.13 **a)** 14 L **b)** −0.0034°C **c)** 3.4×10^{2} lb **d)** 3.4×10^{2} miles **e)** 6.2×10^{-27} J

A.15 2 997 215.55

A.17 **a)** −167.25 **b)** 76 **c)** 3.1693×10^{15} **d)** -7.59×10^{-25}

A.19 **a)** −8.40 **b)** 0.147 **c)** 3.24×10^{-12} **d)** 4.5×10^{13}

A.21 The area of the triangle is 337 cm^2. Three significant figures appear in the answer reflecting the three significant figures in "16.0 cm", a measured quantity. The "1/2" in the formula has an infinite number of significant figures.

Appendix B

B.1 **a)** 6.52×10^{-11} kg **b)** 8.8×10^{-11} s **c)** 5.4×10^{12} kg m^2 s^{-3} **d)** 1.7×10^{4} kg $m^2 s^{-3} A^{-1}$
Note that the unit kilogram has a prefix yet nevertheless is a base unit.

B.3 **a)** 4983°C, but it is very hard to measure such a high temperature to ±1°C. **b)** 37.0°C **c)** 111°C **d)** −40°C.

B.5 **a)** 5256 K **b)** 310.2 K **c)** 384 K **d)** 233 K.

B.7 **a)** 24.6 m s^{-1} **b)** 1.15×10^{3} kg m^{-3} **c)** 1.6×10^{-29}A s m **d)** 1.5×10^{2} mol m^{-3} **e)** 6.7 kg $m^2 s^{-3}$ = 6.7 W.

B.9 One kWh is equal to 3.6×10^{6} J. Hence, 15.3 kWh is 5.51×10^{7} J.

B.11 The engine displacement is 6620 cm^3 or 6.62 L.

Appendix C

C.1 The slope is 50 mi h^{-1}.

C.3 **a)** The equation is in the required form with m (slope) equal to 4 and b (y intercept) equal to −7.
b) The equation is $y = 7/2x - 5/2$. The slope is 7/2, and the y intercept is −5/2.
c) The equation is $y = -2x + 4/3$. The slope is −2 and the y intercept is 4/3.

C.5 The graph of y versus x for the equation $y = 2x^3 - 3x^2 + 6x - 5$ is not linear. The value of y rises from −45 at $x = -2$ and +11 at $x = +2$. The graph cuts the x-axis (has $y = 0$) at $x = 1$.

C.7 **a)** $x = -5/7$ **b)** $x = 3/4$ **c)** $x = 2/3$.

C.9 The answers are given to 4 significant figures. **a)** $x = 0.5447, -2.295$ **b)** $x = -0.6340, -2.366$ **c)** $x = +0.6340, +2.366$.

C.11 a) Assuming that x is small compared to 2.00 gives $x = 6.5 \times 10^{-7}$. There are also two complex roots.

b) The best method of solution is graphical. There are three roots because this is a third-degree equation: $x = 4.07 \times 10^{-2}, 0.399, -1.011$.

c) The only real root is $x = -1.3732$. It can be arrived at graphically. The other two roots are imaginary and so have little interest in chemical applications.

C.13 a) 4.551 (the three significant figures appear in the mantissa) **b)** To help understand the significant figures, divide the exponent in the number by 2.302585093 to re-express it as a power of 10: $10^{-6.814}$. The "6" plays the role of the characteristic when the antilog is taken and the mantissa has three significant figures. Hence the answer has three significant figures: 1.53×10^{-7}. **c)** 2.6×10^{8} **d)** -48.7264

C.15 The answer is 3.015.

C.17 Few calculators accommodate a number with an exponent exceeding 99 in absolute value. To answer this problem, write

$$\log 3.00 \times 10^{121} = \log(3.00) + \log 10^{121} = 121 + 0.477 = 121.477$$

C.19 Simply change the characteristic from 0 to 7 or from 0 to -3 and add it to the same mantissa: $7+0.751 = 7.751$ and $-3 + 0.751 = -2.249$.

C.21 The problem is to find x in the equation $\log \ln x = -x$. One way to proceed is to guess an x, put it into the left side of the equation and see on a calculator if the indicated operations gives back the guess. Adjust the guess and repeat until satisfied. The answer is 1.086.

C.23 a) $8x$ **b)** $3\cos 3x - 8\sin 2x$ **c)** 3 **d)** $1/x$.

C.25 a) 20 **b)** 78125/7 **c)** 0.0675.